ANTHROPOLOGY

Contemporary Perspectives

EIGHTH EDITION

PHILLIP WHITTEN

Allyn and Bacon
Boston   London   Toronto   Sydney   Tokyo   Singapore

Series Editor: Jennifer Jacobson
Executive Marketing Manager: Judeth Hall
Production Editor: Christopher H. Rawlings
Editorial-Production Service: Omegatype Typography, Inc.
Composition and Prepress Buyer: Linda Cox
Manufacturing Buyer: Megan Cochran
Cover Administrator: Linda Knowles
Electronic Composition: Omegatype Typography, Inc.

Copyright © 2001 by Allyn & Bacon
A Pearson Education Company
160 Gould Street
Needham Heights, MA 02494

Internet: www.ablongman.com

Between the time website information is gathered and published, some sites may have closed. Also, the transcription of URLs can result in typographical errors. The publisher would appreciate notification where these occur so that they may be corrected in subsequent editions.

Library of Congress Cataloging-in-Publication Data
Anthropology : contemporary perspectives / [edited by] Phillip Whitten. — 8th ed.
    p. cm.
  Includes bibliographical references.
  ISBN 0-321-04704-4
    1. Anthropology.   I. Whitten, Phillip.

  GN29 .A59 2001
  301—dc21

                                                            00-046895

Printed in the United States of America
10 9 8 7 6 5 4 3 2 1   05 04 03 02 01 00

Credits are found on pages 337–338, which constitute an extension of the copyright page.

BRIEF CONTENTS

CONTENTS

that northern European cultures prohibit touching more than do cultures from southerly regions. This may have important consequences for how people grow up thinking and feeling about themselves and others.

PART V

CULTURAL ANTHROPOLOGY   189

these seemingly strange cultural practices have a firm basis in science.

cultures, we can gain a valuable perspective on our own biases. This, in turn, should help us make more informed medical decisions in our own lives.

knowledge of local plants and their healing properties will also be lost. Ethnobotanists are working with native healers—shamans—to learn how native peoples use plants. Their work may yield great rewards.

PREFACE

Anthropology is an exciting discipline—and why not? It encompasses all of the human experience: from the evolutionary processes that have molded the human race; to civilizations, both ancient and modern; to the ways people communicate with each other; to the kaleidoscopic variety of human culture.

Anthropology is also a fast-changing discipline—enlivened by new discoveries, theories, problems, and debates on issues of fundamental importance to the understanding of human nature, society, and behavior. In this, the eighth edition of *Anthropology: Contemporary Perspectives*, I have attempted to convey the excitement and relevance of contemporary anthropology to today's students.

The needs and interests of these students were foremost in my mind when I selected the articles for this anthology. The selections had to strike a balance between academic quality and level of difficulty. They had to be intrinsically interesting to students, both in subject matter and writing style. They also had to relate to the introductory course in anthropology as it is taught in most North American colleges and universities. The resulting collection thus reflects both the important ongoing work of modern anthropology and the ways introductory anthropology is taught, as well as providing interesting, enjoyable, pertinent reading for college undergraduates.

CONTENT

This eighth edition of *Anthropology: Contemporary Perspectives* is a substantial revision of the book, primarily in terms of subject matter. More than 35 percent of the articles are new to this edition. New articles explore such topics as the changing role of anthropology in understanding modern, industrial societies; the debate over evolution and natural selection; whether apes are conscious and can act with intent; evolutionary psychology; the evolutionary roots of physical attraction; what women look for in a man; human diversity ("race"); the "Garbage Project"; human sacrifice; the new debate over the first Americans; what we've learned from Ice Age cave drawings; where wheat was first domesticated and

how that shaped the development of civilization; the excavation of the world's oldest city; the invention of money; why several Bronze Age civilizations disappeared so suddenly; how, when, and why humans first learned to speak and whether Neanderthals could speak; the effects that differing male and female linguistic styles have in corporate culture; the meaning behind flirting; how ancient, seemingly superstitious rituals are firmly rooted in science; the changing role of women in post-industrial, twenty-first century society; the last remaining tribal peoples untouched by Western civilization; and the uses of anthropology in modern-day consumer culture.

Articles retained from the first seven editions are those judged most successful in a poll of instructors who have adopted the book. As in previous editions, the authors include prominent anthropologists and other scientists including Barry Bogin, Laura Bohannan, Matt Cartmill, Elizabeth Cashdan, Lee Cronk, Jared Diamond, Agnes Estioko-Griffin, Helen Fisher, Stephen Jay Gould, Marvin Harris, William W. Howells, Albert Jacquard, Laurel Kendall, Melvin Konner, Richard Borshay Lee, Alexander Marshack, David Maybury-Lewis, Cherry and Charles Lindholm, Malcolm McFee, Horace Miner, William Rathje, Joann Ellison Rodgers, Ellen Rudolph, Barbara Smuts, Deborah Tannen, Henry T. Wright, and Karen Wright, as well as professional science writers and leading individuals in other social and behavioral sciences.

The articles come from a broad range of sources, including major books and journals and popular magazines such as *American Anthropologist, American Demographics, Archaeology, Discover, Evolutionary Anthropology, Harvard Business Review, Harvard Magazine, Human Nature, McCall's, Mosaic, Natural History, Newsweek, The New York Times Magazine, OMNI, Psychology Today, Science, Science Digest, Science News, Science Times, Smithsonian, The Sciences, UNESCO Courier,* and *U.S. News & World Report.*

Some articles were written specifically for this volume. Many of the articles are very recent: more than half were written since 1990 and almost 30 percent were first published in the last five years. Many of these articles reflect new discoveries and changes in the discipline of anthropology, but also included are a number of the "classic" articles. In particular, these articles address some of the most important and exciting issues with which anthropologists are grappling today:

• The publication of Edward O. Wilson's influential book *Sociobiology* (1975) raised anew—at a more sophisticated level than ever before—the question of the extent to which human behavior is governed, or at least influenced, by genetic inheritance. Are humans, indeed, captives of their own genes—or, to put it more scientifically, is there a human biogram? Are certain behaviors influenced more by our biological than our cultural heritage? These are some of the questions anthropologists have tackled with gusto. A quarter century later, evolutionary psychology (the new name for sociobiology) has become an accepted—and exciting—subdiscipline of anthropology.

• The relationship between human beings and their closest living primate relatives—the chimpanzees, bonobos, and gorillas—also has been brought to the fore in recent years. Molecular biology has demonstrated that humans share almost 99 percent of our genetic endowment with bonobos and chimpanzees. In fact, humans are more closely related to bonobos than horses are to zebras. And long-term studies of apes living in the wild—pioneered in the 1960s by Jane Goodall, Diane Fossey, and others—have shown that these creatures are far more sophisticated than previously imagined. More recently scientists were astonished to discover that West African bonobos—so-called pygmy chimpanzees—have distinct cultures that are passed on from one generation to the next. These bonobo cultures even have a sophisticated division of labor by sex. As one primatologist recently told me: "We're finding out these chimps are more like australopithecines than we thought the australopithecines were!" Finally, teaching apes such as Koko the gorilla and Kanzi the bonobo to communicate using American Sign Language and computers has been remarkably fruitful. These apes can use well over a thousand symbols; can combine them in novel ways; can joke, even lie—in short, they can use language in most of the ways heretofore considered uniquely human. Ironically, just as we finally are learning to understand and appreciate our primate cousins, they teeter on the abyss of extinction in their natural habitats, primarily as a result of human encroachment.

• Gender roles is another topic of intense and heated debate, as it has been these past thirty or more years—a debate to which anthropology can contribute a great deal. Are the gender roles that humans grow up with "natural;" that is, biologically ordained? Or are they cultural conventions, created in the past to solve challenges posed by the environment or current level of civilization and hence subject to modification as the environment and social environment change? If the latter, what are the benefits and costs—both to the individual and to society as a whole—of radically altering a society's traditional gender roles? Because anthropology, far more than any other behavioral science, takes a cross-cultural perspective, it can bring a great deal of research, knowledge, and insight to bear on the discussion of the diversity in human gender roles and other related questions.

ORGANIZATION

After much thought and careful consideration, I have retained the same basic organization of the seventh edition of *Anthropology: Contemporary Perspectives* because of its compatibility with the leading textbooks in both introductory anthropology and cultural anthropology, and because this organization allows it to be used as the only book in either of these courses.

• There are six main parts to the book, with Parts Two through Five corresponding to the major subdisciplines within anthropology: biological anthropology, archaeology, language and communication, and cultural anthropology.

• Within the six parts there are fifteen topics, corresponding to the subject matter common to virtually all texts and courses in introductory anthropology: human evolution; evolutionary psychology; human diversity; archaeology; language, thought, and communication; fieldwork; kinship and marriage; political and economic organization; cultural ecology; gender roles; belief and ritual; the social costs of modernization; and contemporary applications.

In addition, I have significantly expanded both the part and topic introductions, explaining important basic concepts and providing students with a carefully detailed framework that will enhance their understanding and appreciation of the selections that follow.

• I have added several articles to the total number in the book and converted the primate behavior topic in the previous editions to evolutionary psychology. It still includes a consideration of the behavior of nonhuman primates, but focuses on what the exciting new discipline of evolutionary psychology can teach us about human nature.

• I have added several articles to the final topic—Contemporary Applications—to demonstrate the flexibility, utility, and relevance of anthropology in the modern world.

• An extensive glossary contains definitions for more than five hundred important terms used in the book.

ACKNOWLEDGMENTS

I am deeply indebted to the following instructors who not only provided in-depth critiques of the seventh edition and my plans for its revision, but who also provided specific suggestions for new articles, many of which I used: Dr. Alan F. Benjamin, University of North Carolina, Chapel Hill; Dr. Herb Kuehne, Briar Cliff College; Dr. Fran Mascia-Lees, Simon's Rock College of Bard; and Dr. Malcolm C. Webb, University of New Orleans.

I would also like to thank my research assistant at the University of Arizona, Amy Hall, both for her infectious enthusiasm and for the superb job she did in assisting me with this revision.

I am also deeply indebted to my editor at Allyn and Bacon, Sarah Kelbaugh, who provided support, encouragement, and a sense of humor, and evinced a much-appreciated patience as I labored to finish the book.

I am also forever indebted to my wonderful wife, Donna Whitten, for her patience, understanding, support, and assistance.

Finally, I owe an enormous debt of gratitude to the authors whose articles appear in *Anthropology: Contemporary Perspectives*. Without their work, along with their permission (and that of their publishers) to reprint them, this book would not have been possible.

PART I

INTRODUCTION TO ANTHROPOLOGY

The articles in this book introduce you to the field of anthropology. In each part I provide a general introduction to help you understand the significance of the articles selected—that is, how they fit into the overall discipline of anthropology. The introductory notes are especially extensive in Part Two (Biological Anthropology) and Part Three (Archaeology) because these areas are more likely than some of the others covered to lie outside the daily experiences of most students.

Part One of the book consists of only one topic—Topic 1, *The Evolving Study of Anthropology*. Here I sketch the origins and modern subdisciplines of anthropology in order to introduce you to one of the most fascinating of the social sciences and to provide you with an overall framework to organize your reading of the articles collected in this reader.

Whether or not you go on to concentrate your studies in an anthropology major, taking an introductory course in anthropology will enrich your life and broaden your perspectives. It will expose you to distant ancestors, foreign peoples, unexpected customs, new viewpoints, and—again and again—the universals at the heart of the human condition everywhere. I leave it to you to find these universals—to find yourself in the enormous diversities of peoples and cultures, lifestyles, and world views represented in the articles reprinted here.

Given the great amount of attention currently being paid to "multiculturalism"—that is, the rejection of the notion that the ideas and perspectives of Western society and its dominant groups (whites, males) offer universal truths or even just the "best" ways of studying and understanding things—you will find much in anthropology and the articles in this anthology that is pertinent to this issue. Anthropology has, since the early days of the twentieth century, promoted the perspective of "cultural relativism," namely, the idea that each culture—and the norms of behavior it legitimizes—must be understood on its own terms before any meaningful cross-cultural comparisons can be made. However, anthropology is also a living rejection of the currently faddish "politically correct" position that no "outsider" is ever capable of understanding another group and therefore should not be permitted to teach or even speak about its members.

Welcome to the world of controversy! And to the ever-evolving study of anthropology.

THE EVOLVING STUDY OF ANTHROPOLOGY

What is anthropology? For one thing, it is an academic discipline whose history, subdisciplines, and major theories are traced in the article that opens this anthology. But anthropology is more than just an academic discipline—for its scope embraces all of humankind and addresses fundamental issues with which all societies, ethnic groups, families, and individuals must grapple.

In Article 1, "Finding Anthropology," David E. K. Hunter and I trace the historical roots of the discipline, present its modern subdisciplines and key perspectives, and point to some recent theoretical crises that continue to influence the direction of the discipline's evolution.

In these first days of the twenty-first century, anthropology, indeed, finds itself in crisis. One of the questions being raised concerns whether it even makes sense to call anthropology a social *science*, because traditional scientific notions of observer neutrality and objectivity do not lend themselves to understanding the subjective experiences of the people whom one is "studying," and have led to drastic oversimplifications in the analysis of foreign (especially preliterate) cultures. There are no social "facts," these critics argue—just "interpretations of interpretations." Perhaps, therefore, it would be better to place anthropology into the domain of social *studies*. By the end of this course, you, too, may have a strong opinion in this matter.

Finding Anthropology

If you lived in England, you would find your anthropology instructors rubbing elbows with other members of the Humanities faculty—along with teachers of literature, history, and art. In the United States, anthropology is thought of as a social or behavioral science—along with sociology, psychology, and economics.

What is anthropology and where does it belong?

Anthropologists do agree on what they have in common—namely, an interest in studying human beings and their closest primate relatives. The term anthropology suggests this, since it comes from two Greek words: *anthropos,* meaning, "human"; and *logos,* meaning "to reason" (or study). Beyond this, disagreement and controversy rage.

The story of how anthropology evolved as an academic discipline suggests why it is so difficult for scholars to agree on how best to go about studying humankind. What kinds of questions should they ask? What kinds of information are useful data? What descriptions of people and their thoughts, feelings, and behavior are meaningful? A brief review of the historical traditions that gave rise to anthropology will help you understand why these questions are more easily asked than answered.

THE ORIGINS OF ANTHROPOLOGY

The origins of anthropology—as indeed of so much of our civilization—can be traced back to ancient Greece and the civilization of the Middle East. Historians claim as their father a Greek named Herodotus (484?–425? B.C.), and so might anthropologists as well. He traveled widely and recorded the life-styles of some fifty different peoples. He also formulated the idea that all peoples are *ethnocentric*—that is, they consider their own way of life superior to all others, and they judge other lifestyles (for the most part negatively) in terms of the norms and values of their own.

With the fall of Rome in the fifth century A.D., much of the knowledge and thought of the classical civilizations were lost to Europeans for almost a thousand years. Medieval scholars were not so much interested in human beings or even in the na-

ture of the world around them as they were in discovering as much as could be learned about God. Of course, they attempted to learn about God by studying the universe that God had created, and they did make many important discoveries about the world. But their concern to find "divine order" and "divine principles" underlying the manifest world blinded them to many of its most interesting features. It really was not until the Renaissance emerged in the fifteenth century, bringing with it a rediscovery of the treasures of classical learning, that European scholars began to investigate the natural environment as well as human societies with a view to understanding them on their own terms.

Already by medieval times, however, Europeans had been exposed to the existence—on distant shores accessible only to the hardiest of travelers—of many "strange and exotic" peoples. Throughout the Renaissance and Enlightenment periods, as Europe extended its economic interests ever farther abroad, exploration and colonization enabled scholars to visit these faraway places and make records (often fantastically misinformed and distorted) of the peoples they discovered and observed. By the eighteenth century, the vast riches to be made through control of the populations and resources of Africa, Asia, and the Americas induced governments and private enterprises to take more seriously the value of careful study of these so-called primitive peoples. After all, the better one understood them, the more efficiently one could set about exploiting them.

The Church too was quick to grasp the opportunity to extend its influence through missionary activities. Naturally, in order for their activities to be successful, these missionaries required information about the languages and customs of the people they would seek to convert to Christianity.

For many reasons, then, Europeans came to be interested in acquiring information about foreign peoples. Travelers, missionaries, sea captains, colonial administrators, adventurers, traders, and soldiers of fortune ranged across the world recording their impressions of the peoples they encountered. They brought these accounts back with them to European "armchair scholars," who attempted to study them by comparing them to each other—and to European society—in a more or less systematic manner. Inevitably, these efforts tended to "prove" the superiority of European society over all the "primitive" societies thus studied. These eighteenth- and nineteenth-century researches developed into what has come to be called the *comparative method* of social science research. Through the application of this method, a great many schemes of social and cultural evolution were put forward, all of which placed the institutions of European society securely at the top of the evolutionary pyramid.

Until the middle of the eighteenth century, there was no separate discipline that one might call social science. To the extent that society was studied, it was done within the all-purpose framework of history. But by around 1750, the study of society had become sufficiently specialized to deserve the label "social science"—a separate discipline having split off from historical studies and embarked on its own development. For about one hundred years, the study of human nature and society evolved along the lines we have already described, embodying loosely all the different approaches to the building of a science of humankind.

A century later Darwinian evolutionism arrived. The impact of Darwinism on human thought was profound, and its effects on social science were no less dramatic. The two outstanding changes in the study of human nature and society that resulted were (1) the application of evolutionary theory to virtually all aspects of the study of humankind, and (2) the split of such studies into increasingly specialized, separate disciplines.

The Emergence of Evolutionary Thought

The Christian doctrine that Creation had been a single event (pinpointed at 9:00 P.M. on October 23 in 4004 B.C. by Archbishop James Ussher in the early 1600s, who deduced that time from a careful study of Genesis) became more and more troublesome. Already in the sixteenth century Vasco Núñez de Balboa discovered that America was not an extension of Asia but, rather, a separate continent—and the origin of the "Indians" became a source of heated argument. This debate rapidly expanded into controversy about the degree of relatedness—and inherent levels of ability—of all the diverse peoples around the world.

To the *polygenists* the differences between human groups were so vast that they could not accept even a common origin for all people. Rebelling against a narrow acceptance of Genesis, they insisted that scientific inquiry must prevail over the Bible (a courageous position at the time). They argued that God must have created human beings a number of times in different places and that all people were not then descendants of Adam and Eve. Their numbers included many of the period's leading skeptics and intellectuals, such as Voltaire and David Hume. It is hardly surprising that these thinkers, attaching as they did such great significance to human physical variation, should have been racial determinists and indeed racists, ascribing to their own "stock" superior mental abilities. Voltaire, for instance, discussing the state of civilization among Africans, argued:

> If their understanding is not of a different nature from ours, it is at least greatly inferior. They are not capable of any great application or association of ideas, and seemed [sic] formed neither for the advantages nor the abuses of philosophy (quoted in Harris 1968:87).

Monogenicism defended the Scriptures' assertion of a single origin for all humans. Isolated groups, such as the "Indians," were accounted for by the claim that they had come from Atlantis (a mythical continent that was believed to have stretched from Spain to Africa before sinking beneath the waters of the Atlantic Ocean) or that they were the descendants of one of the lost tribes of Israel. Monogenists accounted for "racial" differences in terms of populations adapting to the problems posed by different environments—an idea that would become central to Darwin's principle of natural selection. But they also tended to believe, along with the French biologist Jean Baptiste de Lamarck (1744–1829), that physical characteristics acquired by an individual in the course of his or her lifelong development could be passed on biologically from one generation to the next (an idea rejected by Darwin and the mainstream of subsequent evolutionary thought).

Because monogenists tended to defend the validity of the Biblical version of human origins, they also accepted the very recent dates that Biblical scholars had established for human creation. Thus although they, like the polygenists, divided the human species into "races," they deduced that these "races" must be of very recent origin and that, although people exhibited differences in response to environmental pressures, these differences were of minimal importance with regard to basic human abilities. For instance, Johann Friedrich Blumenbach (1752–1840), a German physician who developed an interest in comparative human anatomy, published a study in 1775 in which he identified five "races": Caucasian, Mongolian, Ethiopian (including all sub-Saharan blacks), Malayan, and American. For this effort he is frequently called the "father" of physical anthropology. However, Blumenbach was far from convinced that these categories were anything more than artificial constructions of convenience in the service of science: "When the matter is thoroughly considered, you see all [human groups] do so run into one another, and that one variety of mankind does so sensibly pass into the other, that you cannot mark out the limits between them." And he adds, with a tone of wryly modern wisdom, "Very arbitrary indeed both in number and definition have been the varieties of mankind accepted by eminent men" (cited in Montagu 1964:41).

(The debate between monogenists and polygenists raged on through the nineteenth century and continues to this day. Although most human biologists since Darwin have aligned themselves in the monogenist camp, the writings of Carleton S. Coon (1904–1981), a contemporary anthropologist, were firmly polygenist. He argued in *The Origin of Races* (1963)—a controversial work—that the human species evolved five different times into the five "races" that he believed constitute the population of the world today.)

Let us return, however, to our account of the emergence of the theory of evolution. By the late eighteenth and early nineteenth centuries, discoveries (especially in biology and geology) were gradually forcing scholars to reassess their acceptance of a date for the creation of the earth derived from scriptural study. More and more geological strata in the earth's crust were coming to light, and it became clear that the thickness of some strata, and the nature of the mineral contents of many, demanded a very long developmental process. In order to account for this process, these scientists faced the need to push back the date of Creation, as we will see shortly. In addition, the fossilized record of extinct life forms accumulated, obliging scientists to produce plausible explanations for the existence and subsequent disappearance of such creatures as the woolly mammoth and the saber-toothed tiger.

In 1833, Sir Charles Lyell (1797–1875) published the third and last volume of his *Principles of Geology*, a work that had a tremendous influence on Darwin. Lyell attacked such schools of thought as *diluvialism*, whose followers claimed that Noah's flood accounted for what was known of the earth's geological structure and history, and *catastrophisim*, whose adherents proposed that localized catastrophes (of which the Biblical flood was merely the most recent) accounted for all the layers and cracks in the earth's crust. He argued that the processes shaping the earth are the same today as they always were—uniform and continuous in character—a position that has come to be called *uniformitarianism*. However, Lyell was unable to free himself entirely from a doctrinaire Christian framework. Although he could envision gradual transformations in the inanimate world of geology, when he discussed living creatures, he continued to believe in the divine creation of each (unchanging) species, and he accounted for the extinction of species in terms of small, localized natural catastrophes.

Some biologists did comprehend the implications of comparative anatomy and the fossil record. For instance, Lamarck advanced his "developmental hypothesis," in which he arranged all known animals into a sequence based on their increasing organic complexity. He clearly implied that human beings were the highest product of a process of organic transformation and had been created through the same processes that had created all other species. However, Lamarck's imagination was also bound by theological constraints, and he did not carry his research through to its logical conclusion. Rather than limiting himself to natural forces as the shapers of organic transformation, Lamarck assumed an underlying, divinely ordered patterning.

Before scholars could fully appreciate the antiquity of the earth and the processes that gave rise to all species—including the human species—they had to free themselves from the constraints of nineteenth-century Christian theology. A revolution of perspective was necessary, a change of viewpoint so convincing that it would overcome people's emotional and intellectual commitment to Christian dogma. The logic of the new position would have to be simple and straightforward and would have to rest on a unified, universally applicable principle.

As we shall see shortly, students of human *society* had been grappling with these issues for almost a century. Herbert Spencer (1820–1903) developed the theory of evolution as applied to societies and based it (in the now immortal phrase) on the "survival of the fittest." His writings and those of Thomas Malthus (1766–1834), the political economist who pessimistically forecast a "struggle for survival" among humankind for dwindling resources, profoundly influenced two naturalists working independently on the problem of the origins of species: Both Alfred Russel Wallace (1823–1913) and Charles Robert Darwin (1809–1882) arrived at the solution at the same time. They hit on the single, unifying (and natural) principle that would account for both the origin and the extinction of species—*natural selection*. In 1858, they presented joint papers on this topic, and the next year Darwin published *On the Origin of Species*, a book that captured scholars' imaginations and became the first influential work that popularized the concept of evolution as applied to the world of living organisms.

What is natural selection? It can be put simply and straightforwardly: *Natural selection is the process through which certain environmentally adaptive features are perpetuated at the expense of less adaptive features.*

Two very important points must be stressed with regard to natural selection: (1) *It is features—not individuals—that are favored,* and (2) *no features are inherently "superior."* Natural selection is entirely dependent on the environment. Change the environment, and the favored adaptive features change as well.

Evolutionism in Social Thought

As we have mentioned, since medieval times, Europeans had been exposed, through the reports of adventurous travelers, to the existence of many "strange" peoples living in "exotic" places on distant shores. Thus, European scholars accumulated a body of information (much of it quite unreliable) about foreign societies, and quite a few set about trying to compare societies in more or less systematic ways. By the late eighteenth century and throughout the nineteenth century, the *comparative method* of social science resulted in the elaboration of theories of social and intellectual progress that developed into full-blown evolutionary theories, frequently referred to as *classical* or *unilineal evolutionism.* The Marquis de Condorcet (1743–1794), for instance, identified ten stages of social evolution marked by the successive acquisition of technological and scientific knowledge: From the limited knowledge needed for hunting and gathering, humanity passes through the development of pastoralism, agriculture, writing, and the differentiation of the sciences, then through a temporary period of darkness and the decline of knowledge in the Middle Ages, leading to the invention of the printing press in 1453, the skeptical rationalism of René Descartes' philosophy, then to the founding of the French Republic of Condorcet's day, and eventually, through the application of scientific knowledge, to a world of peace and equality among the nations and the sexes. His *Outline of the Intellectual Progress of Mankind* (1795) is viewed by many as the outstanding work of social science produced in eighteenth-century Europe, even though its ethnocentric bias is blatant (Harris 1968:35).

Auguste Comte (1798–1857), who is sometimes called one of the "fathers" of social science, followed Condorcet's approach to social evolution. For him, too, the progress of the human intellect moved social evolution forward. However, he identified only three stages of evolution characterized respectively by "theological thought," in which people perceive the universe as animated by a will much like their own (evolving from animism through polytheism to monotheism); "metaphysical thought," in which abstract laws of nature are discovered; and finally "positive thought," represented by the scientific method (of which his own writings were the embodiment in the social sciences). By the way, it is interesting to note that Comte also believed that each person passes through these three stages in the course of his or her individual development.

The writings of Herbert Spencer on social evolution were preeminent during much of the middle and late nineteenth century. As mentioned earlier, it was he who first introduced the term *evolution* into the scientific literature. And in his classic *First Principles,* published in 1862,[1] he provides a definition of the term that has not significantly been improved upon to this day. *Evolution,* Spencer points out, *is not merely change.* It is "change from an indefinite, incoherent homogeneity to a definite, coherent heterogeneity; through continuous differentiations and integrations." In other words, to Spencer *evolution is the progress of life forms and social forms from the simple to the complex.*

Spencer's works is often neglected by contemporary anthropologists, who tend to trace their historical roots to two other major nineteenth-century evolutionists, Sir Edward Burnett Tylor (1832–1917) and Lewis Henry Morgan (1818–1881). Morgan's work in many ways is derived from that of Spencer. Like Spencer, he viewed social evolution as the result of societies adapting to the stresses of their environments. In his classic study, *Ancient Society* (1877), Morgan identified seven stages of social evolution:

I. Lower Status of Savagery
   Marked by simple food gathering
II. Middle Status of Savagery
   Marked by knowledge of fishing and the invention of fire
III. Upper Status of Savagery
   Marked by the invention of the bow and arrow
IV. Lower Status of Barbarism
   Marked by the invention of pottery
V. Middle Status of Barbarism
   Marked by the domestication of plants and animals, irrigation, and stone and brick architecture
VI. Upper Status of Barbarism
   Marked by the invention of iron working
VII. Civilization
   Marked by the invention of the phonetic alphabet

---

[1]The word *evolution* does not appear in Darwin's *On the Origin of Species* until the 1872 edition!

Sir Edward Tylor lacked the concern with social systems of Spencer and Morgan. He was more concerned with *culture* than with society, defining culture all-inclusively as "that complex whole which includes knowledge, belief, art, morals, law, custom, and any other capabilities and habits acquired by man as a member of society" (1958:1: orig. 1871). Tylor attempted to demonstrate that culture had evolved from simple to complex and that it is possible to reconstruct the simple beginnings of culture by the study of its "survivals" in contemporary "primitive" cultures.

In spite of the fact that their individual evolutionary schemes differed from one another in important ways, these classical evolutionists shared one overriding conviction: Society had evolved from simple to complex through identifiable stages. Although it could not be claimed that every single society had passed through each of the stages they described, nevertheless they believed they had found sequences of developmental stages through which a "preponderant number" of societies had passed (Carneiro 1973:91) and that these sequences represented progress. At the turn of the century, this position came under furious assault by Franz Boas and his students and vanished from the American intellectual scene. It reemerged in the 1940s to become one of the major conceptual tools that prehistorians and archaeologists use to reconstruct the human past.

The Emergence of Specialized Disciplines

As we noted earlier, until the mid-eighteenth century, the social sciences had no separate identities—the study of history embodied them all. And it wasn't until the rise of evolutionary theory in the nineteenth century that the social sciences began to differentiate themselves, began to split off from each other through a specialization of interests and research methodologies.

Perhaps the major splitting of the social sciences in the mid-nineteenth century was the emergence of the separate disciplines of sociology and anthropology, which to this day have maintained their distinct and individual identities. Sociologists tended to follow the positivist approach of Auguste Comte, described earlier, and shared with Comte a preoccupying interest in European society. Anthropologists, on the other hand, remained interested in a far broader range of data: archaeological finds, the study of "races" and the distribution of diverse human physical traits, human evolution, the comparative study of cultures and cultural evolution—all more or less unified by evolutionary theory. And whereas sociologists focused on European society,

anthropologists, in their worldwide search for data, tended to concentrate on the "primitive" or preindustrial societies (Voget 1975:114–116).

THE AMERICAN VIEW OF ANTHROPOLOGY

In Europe, academic studies are viewed more holistically than in America. That is, they emphasize the interconnections among all academic disciplines; therefore, scholars in all areas tend to have backgrounds in which knowledge of classical languages, several modern languages, art, world history, and literature is assumed. By contrast, in America academic disciplines tend to emphasize a high degree of specialization with little reference to other studies.

Anthropology is the one American science—if indeed it is a science (a question we raise toward the end of this article)—that has managed to keep an extraordinary breadth of view. Even though anthropologists usually are required to specialize in their research, they also are expected to keep the large questions about human nature and human potentials firmly in mind as they study and teach.

While it is certainly true that in American universities anthropology is thought of as a social science, this was not always the case. Until the beginning of this century American anthropologists followed the European tradition in which anthropology was more or less, as Ruth Benedict once put it, a "happy hunting ground for the romantic lover of primitive things" (Harris 1968:253).

It was Franz Boas (1858–1942)—born and educated in Germany and a trained mathematician, physicist, and geologist—who changed things. In 1899, he became a tenured professor of ethnography (the description and study of human groups and the things they produce) at Columbia University, and he cut to shreds the speculative stages of social and cultural evolution that still were the vogue of European scholarship, showing time and again how they failed to take account of "inconvenient" empirical facts that careful study of particular groups revealed. His students and subsequent generations of American scholars rejected all unsupported speculations and created the social science of anthropology as we now know it. By this we mean that anthropology, in studying human evolution and current functioning, is expected to adhere to the standards of scientific research: to follow logical, systematic methods in posing questions; to consider all kinds of information, regardless of whether findings confirm or disprove cherished notions; to remain skeptical of all findings and to build in tests for assessing the accuracy of data, the logic of analyses, and the reasonableness of conclusions. Science confines itself to the study of what is observable or, in the language of science, to empirical realities—and, in the American tradition, anthropology does so too.

However, science is not the only valid way to study the human condition. Great insights into humankind are offered by the visions found in novels and essays; works of art illuminate the human temper; and theological traditions point to unique qualities of the human spirit. In Europe, anthropology thrives in the company of these pursuits and some of its greatest works, such as Claude Lévi-Strauss's *Tristes Tropiques*, are as much literature and philosophy as anything else.

So although we proceed to describe anthropology as a social science, we hope you will keep in mind that this is a reflection of the American way of viewing, teaching, and doing it. It is admittedly only one approach among several—and as you will see shortly, even in America there is significant disagreement, these days, about whether it is the right approach.

The Four Subfields of Anthropology

As a social science, anthropology addresses such a broad range of interests that it is necessary for members of the discipline to specialize in order to maintain scientific rigor in their research. It is traditional, in America, to divide anthropology into four subfields: biological anthropology, archaeology, linguistics, and cultural anthropology. We describe each of these in turn.

1. *Biological anthropology* is the study of human biology—but not just biology alone. Whether studying the fossil remains of our ancestors, the distribution of diverse genes among the world's contemporary populations, the mechanisms of genetic inheritance, the differing shapes and colors characterizing people in various regions, or even the behavior patterns of humans and their primate relatives, biological anthropologists are concerned with the manner in which all these things are related to the natural and social environments in which the subjects are living. So biological anthropology really is the study of the biological processes of humans and their primate relatives in their nature and social contexts or environments.

2. *Archaeology* is the retrieval and study of human remains. This includes not only their bodily remains (which certainly can tell us a great deal about how they lived and died), but also the remains of the things they built, produced, and made use of. In other words archaeologists attempt to find and study all the traces that human groups have left behind—of themselves and of all their activities—and they seek to understand the ways these remains are related to each other and the environments in which they occur.

3. *Linguistics* is the study and analysis of human communication systems, but most especially of language. Some linguists attempt to reconstruct the earlier language forms from which our present languages have evolved. Others study modern languages in order to learn how they encode the range of human experiences, what grammatical forms they feature, or what separates language from the communication systems of other species. Some linguists are concerned with what language usage can reveal about the different social groups within a society. Others are interested in what can be learned about the nature of the human mind from the study of language. So linguistics is *not* what many people take it to be—the mere learning of a lot of different languages—rather it embodies the use of research into languages in order to better understand the nature of human beings as a species.

4. *Cultural anthropology* is the study of culture and cultures. Culture consists of the shared patterns of behavior and associated meanings that people learn and participate in within the groups to which they belong. Every group, down to each individual family, has its own culture, and each culture is unique. Of course some cultures are quite similar to each other (say, the family cultures of a specific community); others are very different (nomadic Arab culture and Eskimo culture, for example). Some anthropologists study the nature of culture in general as an element of human existence; others are more interested in studying a specific culture (perhaps the culture of a Norwegian fishing village or a *barrio* in Mexico City). Culture, by providing "designs for living," enables humans to be extremely flexible and resourceful in solving problems posed by the natural environment, and our species is unique in that it inhabits virtually every niche that nature has wrought on our planet. The better we understand culture, the closer we shall come to understanding what it means to be a human being.

TROUBLE AT THE TABLE

We have hinted, in the course of this article, that even within American anthropology there are significant disagreements that threaten the cohesive view of the discipline as a social science—the sense that all anthropologists belong to the same family and partake in a shared enterprise. It is fair to say that there is trouble at the table and conversation among anthropologists is strained.

A variety of historical developments and social processes within the field have contributed to this situation.

One kind of difficulty arose as anthropology fell victim to the problem bedeviling all of science: radical splitting. Anthropologists have, over the past four decades, pulled apart into a wild diversity of subspecialites. Cultural anthropology alone has suffered extreme division into cognitive, economic, ecological, religious, political, ethnobotanical, legal, urban, occupational, hermeneutic, symbolic-interactionist, comparative functionalist, semantic analytical, Marxist-critical, and many other studies—and each has developed its own vocabulary and assumptions, to the point where discourse among them is increasingly difficult and the shared vision that united anthropology is being lost.

The most visible victim of this process has been the concept of culture, which until recently was the rich, over-arching concept that united virtually all aspects of anthropology. Referring to all aspects of shared customs and behavior, values and thought, and artifacts produced and used by a given group of people, slowly the encroaching interests of sociology, biology, psychology, and other social and behavioral sciences have chipped away at the concept until there are those who now question whether it should be used at all to characterize the interests of anthropology—and even its utility for explaining the bulk of social facts in human groups.

What is being substituted for culture? Simplism and reductionism. Thus, ecological anthropologists emphasize human responses to environmental pressures; sociobiologists emphasize genetic programming; and so on. Even those scholars who retain their interest in culture diminish its domain to that of "texts" of meaning to be "read."

Faced with a discipline that increasingly is coming to resemble the languages of Babel, many American anthropologists are retreating into an "eclectic" stance that denies any interest in theory. While in some respects this is a refreshing way to cast off the chains of fettered thought, it does threaten the scientific foundation of the field. Data collected without reference to theoretical perspective are impossible to understand; and conclusions that are not held accountable in terms of explicit theoretical formulations are impossible to evaluate.

THE FUTURE OF ANTHROPOLOGY

Perhaps the end of anthropology is not very far off. But we doubt it, for the field has shown an amazing vitality and resilience in the past. We expect that anthropology will be able to rally, to focus its concerns (which, in spite of appearances, have never really disappeared from the profession). Due to the enormous range of interests it encompasses, of all social sciences anthropology is best equipped to explore the fundamental questions of what makes us human and what the study of human beings can contribute to solving the problems of our species and the world we inhabit. If the profession takes this as its charter then it will emerge once again from this period of doubt and self-questioning renewed—as the most vital, relevant, and rewarding of the social sciences.

REFERENCES

Carneiro, Robert. 1973. "The Four Faces of Evolution," in John J. Honigmann (ed.), *Handbook of Social and Cultural Anthropology,* Chicago: Rand McNally, pp. 89–110.

Coon, Carleton S. 1963. *The Origin of Races,* New York: Alfred A. Knopf.

Harris, Marvin. 1968. *The Rise of Anthropological Theory: A History of Culture,* New York: Thomas Y. Crowell.

Montagu, Ashley. 1964. *Man's Most Dangerous Myth: The Fallacy of Race* (4th ed., rev.), New York: Meridian Books.

Tylor, Sir Edward Burnett. 1958. (orig. 1871) *The Origins of Culture,* Part I of *Primitive Culture,* New York: Harper Torchbooks.

Voget, Fred W. 1975. *A History of Ethnology,* New York: Holt, Rinehart and Winston.

PART II

BIOLOGICAL ANTHROPOLOGY

Biological anthropology has broadened a great deal over the last five decades, and it now includes many subjects that overlap with other disciplines. In a loose way, we may define biological anthropology as the study of primate biology in its natural and social environments—with a special emphasis on the study of our own species. Yet it is useful to break apart this large and rather loosely connected branch of anthropology into two major sub-branches: *paleontology*, the study of our extinct ancestors (through their fossilized remains); and *neontology*, the comparative study of living primate groups.

Many scholars trace the origins of modern biological anthropology to the work of Johann Blumenbach (1752–1840), who systematically collected and studied human skulls from many populations around the world. He devised ways of making precise measurements on these skulls and used these measurements to produce an encyclopedic work on what he called the races of the world.

One of Blumenbach's central ideas was that the "races" developed as biological responses to environmental stresses. This notion was elaborated on in the nineteenth century by numerous scholars, such as Anders Retzius (1796–1860), who in 1842 devised a formula for computing long-headedness and narrow-headedness:

$$\frac{\text{head breadth}}{\text{head length}} \times 100 = \text{cephalic index}$$

A low cephalic index indicates a narrow head; a high cephalic index a broad head. Fourteen years later, Retzius published a survey of cranial indexes based on the measurement of skulls from private collections, in which he distinguished a vast number of "races" determined by virtue of their cephalic indexes.

Others followed the lead of Blumenbach and Retzius, and many techniques were developed through which the human body could be measured systematically. Such measuring is called *anthropometry* and remains an important aspect of biological anthropology. Anthropometry contributes to our understanding of fossil remains by providing scholars with precise methods for studying them. It also provides concrete data on variations in body shape among human populations, replacing what previously had been rather impressionistic descriptions. Thus, body measuring became one of the major tools for determining "racial" classifications. However, by the end of the nineteenth century, it was being attacked by scholars who pointed out that anthropometric traits of all ranges were represented among individuals within each of the so-called races.

After the publication of Charles Robert Darwin's *On the Origin of Species* in 1859, natural selection became the core concept of biological anthropology, and evolution its primary concern. Thomas Huxley (1825–1895), a naturalist who enthusiastically took up Darwin's theories, added great impetus to the study of human evolution by showing that the human species was not qualitatively distinct from other primates, but rather only the most complex in an evolutionary continuum ranging from the primitive lower primates to monkeys, the great apes, and finally humankind.

The study of the fossil evidence for human evolution was slow in developing. By 1822, reports had come from Germany about findings of fossilized remains of many extinct animals in limestone caves. These reports impelled William Buckland (1784–1856), reader of geology at Oxford University, to investigate the limestone Paviland Cave on the Welsh coast. There Buckland found the same kinds of extinct animals that had been reported in Germany—as well as flint tools and a human skeleton. This skeleton came to be called the *Red Lady of Paviland*, because it had become stained with red ochre. (Subsequently it was determined that the skeleton was that of a male.) As a Christian minister, Buckland was hard pressed to explain this human presence among extinct creatures. He resorted to the contorted conclusion that the animal remains had probably been swept into the cave by Noah's flood and that the human skeleton had been buried there long after the flood by local inhabitants.

Similar mental gymnastics kept scholars from acknowledging what, in fact, their eyes were seeing: ancient human remains among extinct animals, attesting to a vastly longer human existence than Christian doctrine permitted. Only after the Darwinian revolution could people permit themselves to make accurate interpretations of these fossil materials. In 1860, for example, Edouard Lartet (1801–1873), while investigating a cave near the village of Aurignac in southern France, found human remains associated with the charred bones of such extinct animals as the woolly mammoth, the woolly rhinoceros, the cave bear, and the bison. The evidence he reported finally convinced many people, including the prominent geologist Charles Lyell, of the antiquity of humankind. It is hardly coincidental that these events happened the year after the publication of Darwin's *On the Origin of Species*.

Eight years later, in 1868, Louis Lartet followed his father's lead and excavated an ancient rock shelter that had been exposed in the course of the construction of a railway in the Dordogne region of France. He found five human skeletons: three adult males, one adult female, and one unborn baby. These people were associated with the same kinds of extinct animals and cultural artifacts as those found by his father at Aurignac. They came to be viewed as representatives of the so-called Cro-Magnon population (fully modern humans) that produced the impressive Aurignacian Upper Paleolithic culture.

In 1857, fragments of a human skeleton were found in a limestone cave near Dusseldorf in Germany. The skull cap, however, displayed what at the time seemed to be shockingly apelike features. It was extraordinarily thick, had massive ridges over the eyes, and had little in the way of a forehead. This specimen, which came to be called Neanderthal man (sometimes spelled Neandertal, in keeping with current German spelling), raised for scholars the possibility of finding fossil populations of primitive people who were ancestral to the Cro-Magnon types and, thus, to modern human beings. In 1889, Eugene

Dubois (1859–1940) traveled to Southeast Asia with the deliberate intention of finding fossilized evidence of human evolution. There, during 1891 and 1892, in a site on the banks of the Solo River on the island of Java, he found some molars, a skull cap, and a femur (thigh bone) of such primitive nature that he thought them at first to be the remains of an ancient chimpanzee. By 1892, he revised this assessment and decided that he had indeed found an evolutionary ancestor of the human species, a creature he eventually called *Pithecanthropus erectus* (erect apeman). Naturally, as with all such finds, a great debate about its evolutionary status ensued; but today we agree with Dubois that his Solo River find is, indeed, a human ancestor, one of many that have since been found and are now grouped together under the term *Homo erectus* (erect man).

Although biological anthropology emerged as a fully developed discipline only after the theory of evolution had established itself in the minds of Europe's leading thinkers, in the 1700s scholars were already engaged in the serious study of human population biology—as in the research of Blumenbach and Retzius. However, as indicated in the first article in this book, "Finding Anthropology?" (Hunter and Whitten), eighteenth-century research on human biology was marred by the polarizing effects of the great debate of the day: the bitter feud between the *polygenists* and the *monogenists*. The former saw the biological and behavioral differences between the world's populations as being so substantial in nature that they could not accept a common origins for all the world's peoples. They argued (contrary to the teachings of the Scriptures) that God must have created people a number of different times in a number of different places. Monogenists, on the other hand, argued for a single origin for all peoples. Whereas polygenists perceived "racial" characteristics as permanent and immutable, monogenists insisted that they were changeable and came about as a result of the influence of the natural environment upon local groups.

Blumenbach was a member of the monogenist camp and recognized that the five "races" he posited were as much a matter of classificatory convenience as they were a reflection of the real world. Nevertheless, this debate proved rather fruitless until a means was found to resolve it. That means was the revolutionary theory proposed jointly by Alfred Russel Wallace (1823–1913) and Charles Robert Darwin (1809–1882) in 1858, and popularized by the publication in the following year of Darwin's masterpiece, *On the Origin of Species*.

If there is any one concept that unites the discipline of biological anthropology, it is the theory of evolution. Its assumptions, axioms, hypotheses, and premises are the foundations on which virtually all work in this area rests. It is important that you grasp how pervasive evolutionary thought is—how it has been assimilated into virtually all the social and biological sciences. Many of the readings in this and other sections of this book make explicit and implicit references to evolutionary theory. They speak for themselves, but first I wish to clarify one aspect of evolutionary theory that is widely misunderstood and yet is its central principle—the principle of *natural selection*.

Simply put, natural selection can be defined as *the process through which certain environmentally adaptive features are perpetuated in organisms at the expense of less adaptive features*. That really is it. But its simplicity is deceptive, and the concept frequently (perhaps generally) is misunderstood. Here we shall address two widely held misconceptions about natural selection:

1. There is no such thing as an evolutionary favored individual. *Features* are favored, not individual or-

ganism. (Actually, since the 1980s, most evolutionary biologists have accepted the notion that it is *individual genes* that are the units of selection. In any event, it is not individual organisms.)

2. There is no such thing as an inherently superior feature (let alone an inherently superior organism). What is meant by the term *superior* is the degree to which a feature is adapted to its environment. Change the environment, and a "superior" feature may well become an "inferior" feature.

Natural selection, then, is relative—relative to the environment. And because the environment is always changing, natural selection is an ever-changing process. No group, individual organism, or specific feature will ever reside permanently on top of the evolutionary ladder. Here, as elsewhere, the one constant is change.

In the context of this general introduction, let's explore the articles in this part of the book. They are grouped into three topics: Human Evolution, Evolutionary Psychology, and Human Diversity. Each of these will be discussed separately.

HUMAN EVOLUTION

When the editor of this reader was a college undergraduate (in the 1960s) taking his first anthropology courses, the academic world was still in an uproar over the fossil skull and teeth found by Mary and Louis Leakey in 1959 at Olduvai Gorge in northern Tanzania (East Africa). These fossilized remains, named *Zinjanthropus boisei* by the Leakeys, were dated at 1.75 million years old—almost a million years older than similar fossils that had been found in southern Africa. The possibility that the australopithecines—the direct ancestors of human beings (at least, that is what they were thought to be then)—could be close to 2 million years old was absolutely shocking.

The past four decades have seen the unearthing of previously undreamed of riches in fossil finds. Most of these finds have not been limited to specimens of *Homo erectus* (generally regarded today as our most recent direct ancestor) or of Neanderthals (whose status is still hotly debated, but who are seen by most anthropologists today as an isolated population of European hominids who most likely were our evolutionary cousins). Rather, most of the finds have been of much older hominids and even of their remote ancestors—the earliest primates.

As more fossils, and more ancient fossils, have been unearthed, scholars have not reacted calmly. Almost every significant new find has produced a flurry of heated debate over (1) its taxonomic status (i.e., its place in the evolutionary hierarchy) and (2) its significance (i.e., the degree to which it confirmed or invalidated previous views of human evolution). At first, settling the debates was merely a matter of pushing back the emergence of human ancestors earlier and earlier: The australopithecines became "older" throughout the 1960s, 1970s, 1980s, and 1990s—first one, then two, then three, and now perhaps five million years old. But then, as more fossils were found, the questions became more profound and subtle. For instance, what was the relationship between bipedalism (walking on two legs) and the evolution of the large, complex human brain? Did large brains favor the invention of tools or, the other way around, did

the invention of tools promote the enlarging of the brain? Or, perhaps, was there a "feedback loop" between tool invention and large brains—each one promoting the other?

One of the more recent and, in many ways, the most interesting debate concerns hominid finds from East Africa. There Mary Leakey and her son Richard Leakey, working at Laetoli (thirty miles south of Olduvai Gorge) and at Lake Turkana (in Kenya), respectively, found remarkable hominid specimens. They identified these specimens, some of which are as old as 3.75 million years, as belonging to our own genus, *Homo*. Their main antagonist is Donald Johanson, whose fieldwork has been mainly in the Afar region of Ethiopia. Johanson's finds are the same age or slightly older than the Leakeys', and one of them, a skeleton he named Lucy, is remarkably complete (more than 40 percent of her bones were found). Johanson calls his finds *Australopithecus afarensis*. He claims that the Leakey finds older than 2 million years are members of the same species, and that this species is the earliest example of a true hominid ancestor to human beings.

One of the most puzzling problems that had been confronting students of human evolution was the fact that the interpretations of early hominid fossil remains did not fit in with studies comparing human and ape amino acid molecules. Scientists studying amino acid molecules had, since the 1980s, shown that systematic comparisons of these molecules from related species could be used to compute how far back in the evolutionary past their ancestors had split apart. Using these methods, Allan Wilson and Vincent Sarich of the University of California at Berkeley arrived at a date of 5 or 6 million years ago for the split between the pongids (apes and their ancestors) and the hominids (humans and their ancestors). On the other hand, fossil studies, which counted *Ramapithecus* as the first true hominid, set the date of that split some 9 million years earlier. There seemed to be no way out of this dilemma other than to favor one view or the other (and most anthropologists favored the latter). Some authors argued that the assumption underlying the molecular clock might be wrong—that there was *not* a consistent rate of evolutionary change at the molecular level that could allow us to calculate when species branched off from one another; others even argued that the amino acid time clock might be accurate for the entire animal kingdom except human beings. Two developments contributed to a solution to this puzzle: (1) the reinterpretation of ramapithecine remains and (2) the discovery of Lucy.

David Pilbeam of Harvard University has been one of the world's foremost students of ramapithecines, the small apelike creatures who inhabited Asia and Africa some 8 to 15 million years ago and whose jaws seemed to show true hominid features. In the 1980s, after more complete remains of *Ramapithecus* were discovered (before then only ramapithecine jaws had been found), Pilbeam realized that *Ramapithecus* (and a related form, *Sivapithecus*) was not in the human line at all, but most likely was ancestral to the orangutan. Another possibility is that a later fossil population would be found, one that might qualify as the earliest hominid. This would make possible a meeting of the minds between those who have studied fossils and those who have studied amino acid time clocks. The first fully hominid fossils might, indeed, be only 5 or 6 million years old.

But is there such a fossil population? Richard Leakey thinks he and his associates have found one—a creature he named *Homo habilis* ("handy man"). *Homo habilis*, which dates back more than 2 million years, produced stone tools and had a brain one-third to one-half as large as our own. This population clearly was ancestral to *Homo erectus*, the immediate ancestors of our own species, *Homo sapiens*. But what was the origin of *Homo habilis*?

Leakey believes that *Homo habilis* evolved directly from a much earlier pongid ancestor, possibly the cat-sized pongid, *Aegyptopithecus* (Egyptian ape), whose remains, found near Cairo, date back some 28 million years. Therefore, Leakey considers the other main fossil populations that are similar to, and precede or are contemporary with, *Homo habilis* to be parallel side branches of hominids—that is, evolutionary dead ends.

This is where Johanson's discovery of Lucy becomes important. When discovered, she was the earliest, most complete, fully erect and bipedal hominid fossil ever found. As mentioned earlier, Johanson coined the term *Australopithecus afarensis* for the population of fossils to which Lucy belongs. In 1984, David Pilbeam announced the discovery of some *Australopithecus afarensis* fossils dating back more than 5 million years ago, the earliest hominid remains yet uncovered. Though it walked on two legs, *Australopithecus afarensis* had a smaller brain than *Homo habilis*, and Johanson believes that *Australopithecus afarensis* is the ancestor of the "handy man," the link between *Homo habilis* and the pongid (ape) line. In this view, *Homo habilis* joins *Australopithecus afarensis* and *Australopithecus africanus* (found in southern Africa) as one single, continuous evolutionary line. (In this view, the more rugged, robust line of australopithecines remains an evolutionary cul-de-sac.)

At least one very important issue is at stake in the Leakey–Johanson debate. If Leakey's view is right, it would appear that bipedalism and large brains evolved more or less together and that they were associated with the manufacture and use of tools. If Johanson's view is correct, then our ancestors evolved an upright posture and tool use first, and only afterward did the brain become enlarged.

In the 1990s, a new proposition heated up the field of human evolution: the "Eve Hypothesis." First proposed by Allan C. Wilson and his associate, Rebecca Cann, this theory suggested that, some 200,000 years ago, a single African woman (or a very small group of genetically identical women) was the common ancestor of all human beings. They supported this startling hypothesis through their study of the worldwide distribution of mitochondrial DNA—genetic material outside the nucleus of each cell that is not subject to the mixing together of genes typical of the means through which we inherit our genetic traits. Mitochondrial DNA is inherited exclusively from one's mother; and, allowing for mutation, Wilson and Cann calculated that this genetic material is so uniform worldwide that descendants of only one woman must have migrated across the world and replaced all other hominid populations in the last 200,000 years.

This proposal drew heated response because it flies in the face of most anthropological thought about our origins—specifically, the view that modern human beings, although ultimately of African heritage, evolved more or less where they are found today (or at least where they were before the mass migrations of historical times). Alan G. Thorne and Milford H. Wolpoff refute the "Eve Hypothesis" by noting that the hypothesized evolutionary tree it depends on leaves out the branches of mutational histories of extinct hominid lines, and that the assumption that all changes in mitochondrial DNA are due to mutation alone is simply wrong.

How can scholars debate such essential things within the field of evolutionary study—and yet doubt the fundamental scientific validity of evolution itself? In Article 2, "Darwinism Defined: The Difference between Fact and Theory," Stephen Jay Gould argues that the essence of the scientific method is to search continuously for new facts with which to test and elaborate on our theories; and that all the new facts we have found regarding human origins illuminate and lead to a refinement of our understanding of evolution—but in no manner refute its theoretical foundations.

In Article 3, Jared Diamond describes "The Great Leap Forward" that brought forth modern human beings. In doing so, he answers the titillating question of whether modern humans (Cro-Magnons) ever indulged in sexual escapades with the more "primitive" Neanderthals they replaced rather quickly around 35,000 years ago.

Not that the Neanderthals were all *that* primitive. In Article 4, "The Secret Life of the Neanderthals," Shari Rudavsky portrays Neanderthals as rugged but sophisticated tool users. Indeed, there is also strong evidence that Neanderthals lived in family groups, performed rudimentary surgery, may have engaged in cannibalism, and buried and mourned for their dead.

All of these issues—the emergence of the first hominid, the origin of modern *Homo sapiens*, the mystery of the Neanderthals' sudden disappearance—will be resolved by the middle of the twenty-first century, argues Robert Foley in Article 5, "The Search for Early Man." Scientific progress, particularly in the fields of genetics and molecular biology, he predicts, will finally allow us to fit the pieces of the puzzle of human evolution together.

I end this topic by considering what the study of human evolution has to teach us about our basic nature. In Article 6, "Designed for Another Time: Modern Problems for an Ancient Species," Lee Cronk argues that the social environment of our ancestors created the conditions in which abstract reasoning arose and made us rather unfit for the degree of occupational specialization that is expected of us in industrial society. See if you recognize any of these issues in yourself.

Darwinism Defined: The Difference between Fact and Theory

Charles Darwin, who was, perhaps, the most incisive thinker among the great minds of history, clearly divided his life's work into two claims of different character: establishing the fact of evolution, and proposing a theory (natural selection) for the mechanism of evolutionary change. He also expressed, and with equal clarity, his judgment about their different status: confidence in the facts of transmutation and genealogical connection among all organisms, and appropriate caution about his unproved theory of natural selection. He stated in the *Descent of Man:* "I had two distinct objects in view; firstly, to show that species had not been separately created, and secondly, that natural selection had been the chief agent of change…If I have erred in…having exaggerated its [natural selection's] power…I have at least, as I hope, done good service in aiding to overthrow the dogma of separate creations."

Darwin wrote those words more than a century ago. Evolutionary biologists have honored his fundamental distinction between fact and theory ever since. Facts are the world's data; theories are explanations proposed to interpret and coordinate facts. The fact of evolution is as well established as anything in science (as secure as the revolution of the earth about the sun), though absolute certainty has no place in our lexicon. Theories, or statements about the causes of documented evolutionary change, are now in a period of intense debate—a good mark of science in its healthiest state. Facts don't disappear while scientists debate theories. As I wrote in an early issue of [*Discover*] (May 1981), "Einstein's theory of gravitation replaced Newton's, but apples did not suspend themselves in mid-air pending the outcome."

Since facts and theories are so different, it isn't surprising that these two components of science have had separate histories ever since Darwin. Between 1859 (the year of publication for the *Origin of Species*) and 1882 (the year of Darwin's death), nearly all thinking people came to accept the fact of evolution. Darwin lies beside Newton in Westminster Abbey for this great contribution. His theory of natural selection has experienced a much different, and checkered, history. It attracted some notable followers during his lifetime (Wallace in England, Weismann in Germany), but never enjoyed majority support. It became an orthodoxy among English-speaking evolutionists (but never, to this day, in France or Germany) during the 1930s, and received little cogent criticism until the 1970s. The past fifteen years have witnessed a revival of intense and, this time, highly fruitful debate as scientists discover and consider the implications of phenomena that expand the potential causes of evolution well beyond the unitary focus of strict Darwinism (the struggle for reproductive success among organisms within populations). Darwinian selection will not be overthrown; it will remain a central focus of more inclusive evolutionary theories. But new findings and interpretations at all levels, from molecular change in genes to patterns of overall diversity in geological time, have greatly expanded the scope of important causes—from random, selectively neutral change at the genetic level, to punctuated equilibria and catastrophic mass extinction in geological time.

In this period of vigorous pluralism and intense debate among evolutionary biologists, I am greatly saddened to note that some distinguished commentators among non-scientists, in particular Irving Kristol in a *New York Times* Op Ed piece of Sept. 30, 1986 ("Room for Darwin and the Bible"), so egregiously misunderstand the character of our discipline and continue to confuse this central distinction between secure fact and healthy debate about theory.

I don't speak of the militant fundamentalists who label themselves with the oxymoron "scientific creationists," and try to sneak their Genesis literalism into high school classrooms under the guise of scientific dissent. I'm used to their rhetoric, their dishonest mis- and half-quotations, their constant repetition of "useful" arguments that even they must recognize as nonsense (disproved human footprints on dinosaur trackways in Texas, risible misinterpretation of thermodynamics to argue that life's complexity couldn't increase without a divine boost). Our struggle with these ideologues is political, not intellectual. I speak instead of our allies among people committed to reason and honorable argument.

Kristol, who is no fundamentalist, accuses evolutionary biologists of bringing their troubles with creationists upon themselves by too zealous an insistence upon the truths of Darwin's world. He writes: "...the debate has become a dogmatic crusade on both sides, and our educators, school administrators, and textbook publishers find themselves trapped in the middle." He places the primary blame upon a supposedly anti-religious stance in biological textbooks: "There is no doubt that most of our textbooks are still written as participants in the 'warfare' between science and religion that is our heritage from the 19th century. And there is also little doubt that it is this pseudoscientific dogmatism that has provoked the current religious reaction."

Kristol needs a history lesson if he thinks that current creationism is a product of scientific intransigence. Creationism, as a political movement against evolution, has been a continually powerful force since the days of the Scopes trial. Rather than using evolution to crusade against religion in their texts, scientists have been lucky to get anything at all about evolution into books for high school students ever since Scopes's trial in 1925. My own high school biology text, used in the liberal constituency of New York City in 1956, didn't even mention the word evolution. The laws that were used against Scopes and cowed textbook publishers into submission weren't overturned by the Supreme Court until 1968 (*Epperson* v. *Arkansas*).

But what about Kristol's major charge—anti-religious prejudice and one-dimensional dogmatism about evolution in modern textbooks? Now we come to the heart of what makes me so sad about Kristol's charges and others in a similar vein. I don't deny that some texts have simplified, even distorted, in failing to cover the spectrum of modern debates; this, I fear, is a limitation of the genre itself (and the reason why I, though more of a writer than most scientists, have never chosen to compose a text). But what evidence can Kristol or anyone else provide to demonstrate that evolutionists have been worse than scientists from other fields in glossing over legitimate debate within their textbooks?

Consider the evidence. Two textbooks of evolution now dominate the field. One has as its senior author Theodosius Dobzhansky, the greatest evolu-

tionist of our century, and a lifelong Russian Orthodox; nothing anti-religious could slip past his watchful eye. The second, by Douglas Futuyma, is a fine book by a kind and generous man who could never be dogmatic about anything except intolerance. (His book gives a fair hearing to my own heterodoxies, while dissenting from them.)

When we come to popular writing about evolution, I suppose that my own essays are as well read as any. I don't think that Kristol could include me among Darwinian dogmatists, for most of my essays focus upon my disagreements with the strict version of natural selection. I also doubt that Kristol would judge me anti-religious, since I have campaigned long and hard against the same silly dichotomy of science versus religion that he so rightly ridicules. I have written laudatory essays about several scientists (Burnet, Cuvier, Buckland, and Gosse, among others) branded as theological dogmatists during the nineteenth-century reaction; and, while I'm not a conventional believer, I don't consider myself irreligious.

Kristol's major error lies in his persistent confusion of fact with theory. He accuses us—without giving a single concrete example, by the way—of dogmatism about *theory* and sustains his charge by citing our confidence in the *fact* of transmutation. "It is reasonable to suppose that if evolution were taught more cautiously, as a conglomerate idea consisting of conflicting hypotheses rather than as an unchallengeable certainty, it would be far less controversial."

Well, Mr. Kristol, evolution (as theory) is indeed "a conglomerate idea consisting of conflicting hypotheses," and I and my colleagues teach it as such. But evolution is also a fact of nature, and so do we teach it as well, just as our geological colleagues describe the structure of silicate minerals, and astronomers the elliptical orbits of planets.

Rather than castigate Mr. Kristol any further, I want to discuss the larger issue that underlies both this incident and the popular perception of evolution in general. If you will accept my premise that evolution is as well established as any scientific fact (I shall give the reasons in a moment), then why are we uniquely called upon to justify our chosen profession; and why are we alone subjected to such unwarranted infamy? To this central question of this essay, I suggest the following answer. We haven't received our due for two reasons: (1) a general misunderstanding of the different methods used by all historical sciences (including evolution), for our modes of inference don't match stereotypes of "*the* scientific method"; and (2) a continuing but unjustified fear about the implication both of evolution itself and of Darwin's theory for its mechanism. With these two issues resolved, we can understand both the richness of science (in its pluralistic methods of inquiry) and the absence of any conflict, through lack of common content, between proper science and true religion.

Our confidence in the fact of evolution rests upon copious data that fall, roughly, into three great classes. First, we have the direct evidence of small-scale changes in controlled laboratory experiments of the past hundred years (on bacteria, on almost every measurable property of the fruit fly *Drosophila*), or observed in nature (color changes in moth wings, development of metal tolerance in plants growing near industrial waste heaps), or produced during a few thousand years of human breeding and agriculture. Creationists can scarcely ignore this evidence, so they respond by arguing that God permits limited modification within created types, but that you can never change a cat into a dog (who ever said that you could, or that nature did?).

Second, we have direct evidence for large-scale changes, based upon sequences in the fossil record. The nature of this evidence is often misunderstood by non-professionals who view evolution as a simple ladder of progress, and therefore expect a linear array of "missing links." But evolution is a copiously branching bush, not a ladder. Since our fossil record is so imperfect, we can't hope to find evidence for every tiny twiglet. (Sometimes, in rapidly evolving lineages of abundant organisms restricted to a small area and entombed in sediments with an excellent fossil record, we do discover an entire little bush—but such examples are as rare as they are precious.) In the usual case, we may recover the remains of side branch number 5 from the bush's early history, then bough number 40 a bit later, then the full series of branches 156–161 in a well-preserved sequence of younger rocks, and finally surviving twigs 250 and 287.

In other words, we usually find sequences of structural intermediates, not linear arrays of ancestors and descendants. Such sequences provide superb examples of temporally ordered evolutionary trends. Consider the evidence for human evolution in Africa. What more could you ask from a record of rare creatures living in terrestrial environments that provide poor opportunity for fossilization? We have a temporal sequence displaying clear trends in a suite of features, including threefold increase of brain size and corresponding decrease of jaws and teeth. (We are missing direct evidence for an earlier transition to upright posture, but wide-ranging and unstudied sediments of the right age have been found in East Africa, and we have an excellent chance to fill in this part of our story.) What alternative can we suggest to evolution? Would God—for some inscrutable reason, or merely to test our faith—create five species, one after the other (*Australopithecus afarensis, A. africanus, Homo habilis, H. erectus,* and *H. sapiens*), to mimic a continuous trend of evolutionary change?

Or, consider another example with evidence of structurally intermediate stages—the transition from reptiles to mammals. The lower jaw of mammals contains but a single bone, the dentary. Reptiles build their lower jaws of several bones. In perhaps the most fascinating of those quirky changes in function that mark pathways of evolution, the two bones articulating the upper and lower jaws of reptiles migrate to the middle ear and become the malleus and incus (hammer and anvil) of mammals.

Creationists, ignorant of hard evidence in the fossil record, scoff at this tale. How could jaw bones become ear bones, they ask. What happened in between? An animal can't work with a jaw half disarticulated during the stressful time of transition.

The fossil record provides a direct answer. In an excellent series of temporally ordered structural intermediates, the reptilian dentary gets larger and larger, pushing back as the other bones of a reptile's lower jaw decrease in size. We've even found a transitional form with an elegant solution to the problem of remaking jaw bones into ear bones. This creature has a double articulation—one between the two bones that become the mammalian hammer and anvil (the old reptilian joint), and a second between the squamosal and dentary bones (the modern mammalian condition). With this built-in redundancy, the emerging mammals could abandon one connection by moving two bones into the ear, while retaining the second linkage, which becomes the sole articulation of modern mammals.

Third, and most persuasive in its ubiquity, we have the signs of history preserved within every organism, every ecosystem, and every pattern of biogeographic distribution, by those pervasive quirks, oddities, and imperfections that record pathways of historical descent. These evidences are indirect, since we are viewing modern results, not the processes that caused them, but what else can we make of the pervasive pattern? Why does our body, from the bones of our back to the musculature of our belly, display the vestiges of an arrangement better suited for quadrupedal life if we aren't the descendants of four-footed creatures? Why do the plants and animals of the Galapagos so closely resemble, but differ slightly from, the creatures of Ecuador, the nearest bit of land 600 miles to the east, especially when cool oceanic currents and volcanic substrate make the Galapagos such a different environment from Ecuador (thus removing the potential argument that God makes the best creatures for each place, and small differences only reflect a minimal disparity of environments)? The similarities can only mean the Ecuadorian creatures colonized the Galapagos and then diverged by a natural process of evolution.

This method of searching for oddities as vestiges of the past isn't peculiar to evolution, but a common procedure of all historical science. How, for example, do we know that words have histories, and haven't been decreed by some all-knowing committee in Mr. Orwell's bureau of Newspeak? Doesn't the bucolic etymology of so many words testify to a different life style among our ancestors? In this article, I try to "broadcast" some ideas (a mode of sowing seed) in order to counter the most "egregious" of creationist sophistries (the animal *ex grege,* or outside the flock), for which, given the *quid pro quo* of business, this fine magazine pays me an "amolument" (the fee that millers once received to grind corn).

I don't want to sound like a shrill dogmatist shouting "rally round the flag boys," but biologists have reached a consensus, based on these kinds of data, about the fact of evolution. When honest critics like Irving Kristol misinterpret this agreement, they're either confusing our fruitful consonance about the fact of evolution with our vibrant dissonance about mechanisms of change, or they've misinterpreted part of our admittedly arcane technical literature.

One such misinterpretation has gained sufficient notoriety [recently] that we crave resolution both for its own sake and as an illustration of the frustrating confusion that can arise when scientists aren't clear and when commentators, as a result of hidden agendas, don't listen. Tom Bethell argued in *Harper's* (February 1985) that a group of young taxonomists called pattern cladists have begun to doubt the existence of evolution itself.

This would be truly astounding news, since cladistics is a powerful method dedicated to reforming classification by using only the branching order of lineages on evolutionary trees ("propinquity of descent" in Darwin's lovely phrase) rather than vague notions of overall similarity in form or function. (For example, in the cladistic system, a lungfish is more closely related to a horse than to a salmon because that common ancestor of lungfish and horse is more recent in time than the link point of the lungfish–horse lineage with the branch leading to modern bony fishes (including salmon).

Cladists use only the order of branching to construct their schemes of relationships; it bothers them not a whit that lungfish and salmon look and work so much alike. Cladism, in other words, is the purest of all genealogical systems for classification, since it works only with closeness of common ancestry in time. How preciously ironic then, that this most rig-

idly evolutionary of all taxonomic systems should become the subject of such extraordinary misunderstanding—as devised by Bethell, and perpetuated by Kristol when he writes: "…many younger biologists (the so-called 'cladists') are persuaded that the differences among species—including those that seem to be closely related—are such as to make the very concept of evolution questionable."

This error arose for the following reason. A small splinter group of cladists (not all of them, as Kristol claims)—"transformed" or "pattern" cladists by their own designation—have adopted what is to me an ill-conceived definition of scientific procedure. They've decided, by misreading Karl Popper's philosophy, that patterns of branching can be established unambiguously as a fact of nature, but that processes causing events of branching, since they can't be observed directly, can't be known with certainty. Therefore, they say, we must talk only of pattern and rigidly exclude all discussion of process (hence "pattern cladistics").

This is where Bethell got everything arse-backwards and began the whole confusion. A philosophical choice to abjure all talk about process isn't the same thing as declaring that no reason for patterns of branching exists. Pattern cladists don't doubt that evolution is the cause behind branching; rather, they've decided that our science shouldn't be discussing causes at all.

Now I happen to think that this philosophy is misguided; in unguarded moments I would even deem it absurd. Science, after all, is fundamentally about process; learning why and how things happen is the soul of our discipline. You can't abandon the search for cause in favor of a dry documentation of pattern. You must take risks of uncertainty in order to probe the deeper questions, rather than stopping with sterile security. You see, now I've blown our cover. We scientists do have our passionate debates—and I've just poured forth an example. But as I wrote earlier, this is a debate about the proper approach to causes, not an argument about whether causes exist, or even whether the cause of branching is evolution or something else. No cladist denies that branching patterns arise by evolution.

This incident also raises the troubling issue of how myths become beliefs through adulterated repetition without proper documentation. Bethell began by misunderstanding pattern cladistics, but at least he reports the movement as a small splinter, and tries to reproduce their arguments. Then Kristol picks up the ball and recasts it as a single sentence of supposed fact—and all cladists have now become doubters of evolution by proclamation. Thus a movement, by fiat, is turned into its opposite—as the purest of all methods for establishing genealogical connections becomes a weapon for denying the mechanism that all biologists accept as the cause of branching on life's tree: evolution itself. Our genealogy hasn't been threatened, but my geniality has almost succumbed.

When I ask myself why the evidence for evolution, so clear to all historical scientists, fails to impress intelligent nonscientists, I must believe that more than simple misinformation lies at the root of our difficulty with a man like Irving Kristol. I believe that the main problem centers upon a restrictive stereotype of scientific method accepted by most non-practitioners as the essential definition of all scientific work.

We learn in high school about *the* scientific method—a cut-and-dried procedure of simplification to essential components, experiment in the controlled situation of a laboratory, prediction and replication. But the sciences of history—not just evolution but a suite of fundamental disciplines ranging from geology, to cosmology, to linguistics—can't operate by this stereotype. We are charged with explaining events of extraordinary complexity that occur but once in all their details. We try to understand the past, but don't pretend to predict the future. We can't see past processes directly, but learn to infer their operation from preserved results.

Science is a pluralistic enterprise with a rich panoply of methods appropriate for different kinds of problems. Past events of long duration don't lie outside the realm of science because we cannot make them happen in a month within our laboratory. Direct vision isn't the only, or even the usual, method of inference in science. We don't see electrons, or quarks, or chemical bonds, any more than we see small dinosaurs evolve into birds, or India crash into Asia to raise the Himalayas.

William Whewell, the great English philosopher of science during the early nineteenth century, argued that historical science can reach conclusions, as well confirmed as any derived from experiment and replication in laboratories, by a method he called "consilience" (literally "jumping together") of inductions. Since we can't see the past directly or manipulate its events, we must use the different tactic of meeting history's richness head on. We must gather its wondrously varied results and search for a coordinating cause that can make sense of disparate data otherwise isolated and uncoordinated. We must see if a set of results so diverse that no one had ever considered their potential coordination might jump together as the varied products of a single process. Thus plate tectonics can explain magnetic stripes on the sea floor, the rise and later erosion of the Appalachians, the earthquakes of Lisbon and San Francisco, the eruption of Mount St. Helens, the presence of large flightless ground birds only on continents once united as Gondwanaland, and the discovery of fossil coal in Antarctica.

Darwin, who understood the different rigor of historical science so well, complained bitterly about those critics who denied scientific status to evolution because they couldn't see it directly or reproduce its historical results in a laboratory. He wrote to Hooker in 1861: "Change of species cannot be directly proved...The doctrine must sink or swim according as it groups and explains phenomena. It is really curious how few judge it in this way, which is clearly the right way." And later, in 1868: "This hypothesis may be tested...by trying whether it explains several large and independent classes of facts; such as the geological succession of organic beings, their distribution in past and present times, and their mutual affinities and homologies."

If a misunderstanding of the different methods of historical inquiry has impeded the recognition of evolution as a product of science at its best, then a residual fear for our own estate has continued to foster resentment of the fact that our physical bodies have ancient roots in ape-like primates, waddling reptiles, jawless fishes, worm-like invertebrates, and other creatures deemed even lower or more ignoble. Our ancient hopes for human transcendence have yet to make their peace with Darwin's world.

But what challenge can the facts of nature pose to our own decisions about the moral value of our lives? We are what we are, but we interpret the meaning of our heritage as we choose. Science can no more answer the questions of how we ought to live than religion can decree the age of the earth. Honorable and discerning scientists (most of us, I trust) have always understood that the limits to what science can answer also describe the power of its methods in their proper domain. Darwin himself exclaimed that science couldn't touch the problem of evil and similar moral conundrums: "A dog might as well speculate on the mind of Newton. Let each man hope and believe what he can."

There is no warfare between science and religion, never was except as a historical vestige of shifting taxonomic boundaries among disciplines. Theologians haven't been troubled by the fact of evolution, unless they try to extend their own domain beyond its proper border (hubris and territorial expansionism aren't the sins of scientists alone, despite Mr. Kristol's fears). The Reverend Henry Ward Beecher, our greatest orator during Darwin's century, evoked the most quintessential of American metaphors in dismissing the entire subject of conflict between science and religion with a single epithet: "Design by wholesale is grander than design by retail"—or, general laws rather than creation of each item by fiat will satisfy our notion of divinity.

Similarly, most scientists show no hostility to religion. Why should we, since our subject doesn't intersect the concerns of theology? I strongly dispute Kristol's claim that "the current teaching of evolution in our public schools does indeed have an ideological bias against religious belief." Unless at least half my colleagues are inconsistent dunces, there can be—on the most raw and direct empirical grounds—no conflict between science and religion. I know hundreds of scientists who share a conviction about the fact of evolution, and teach it in much the same way. Among these people I note an entire spectrum of religious attitudes—from devout daily prayer and worship to resolute atheism. Either there's no correlation between religious belief and confidence in evolution—or else half these people are fools.

The common goal of science and religion is our shared struggle for wisdom in all its various guises. I know no better illustration of this great unity than a final story about Charles Darwin. This scourge of fundamentalism had a conventional church burial—in Westminster Abbey no less. J. Frederick Bridge, Abbey organist and Oxford don, composed a funeral anthem especially for the occasion. It may not rank high in the history of music, but it is, as my chorus director opined, a "sweet piece." (I've made what may be the only extant recording of this work, marred only by the voice of yours truly within the bass section.) Bridge selected for his text the finest biblical description of the common aim that will forever motivate both the directors of his building and the inhabitants of the temple of science—wisdom. "Her ways are ways of pleasantness and all her paths are peace" (Proverbs 3:17).

I am only sorry that Dr. Bridge didn't set the very next metaphor about wisdom (Proverbs 3:18), for it describes, with the proper topology of evolution itself, the greatest dream of those who followed the God of Abraham, Isaac, and Jacob: "She is a tree of life to them that lay hold upon her."

The Great Leap Forward

One can hardly blame nineteenth-century creationists for insisting that humans were separately created by God. After all, between us and other animal species lies the seemingly unbridgeable gulf of language, art, religion, writing, and complex machines. Small wonder, then, that to many people Darwin's theory of our evolution from apes appeared absurd.

Since Darwin's time, of course, fossilized bones of hundreds of creatures intermediate between apes and modern humans have been discovered. It is no longer possible for a reasonable person to deny that what once seemed absurd actually happened—somehow. Yet the discoveries of many missing links have only made the problem more fascinating, without fully solving it. When and how did we acquire our uniquely human characteristics?

We know that our lineage arose in Africa, diverging from that of chimpanzees and gorillas sometime between 6 million and 10 million years ago. For most of the time since then we have been little more than glorified baboons. As recently as 35,000 years ago western Europe was still occupied by Neanderthals, primitive beings for whom art and progress scarcely existed. Then there was an abrupt change. Anatomically modern people appeared in Europe, and suddenly so did sculpture, musical instruments, lamps, trade, and innovation. Within a few thousand years the Neanderthals were gone.

Insofar as there was any single moment when we could be said to have become human, it was at the time of this Great Leap Forward 35,000 years ago. Only a few more dozen millennia—a trivial fraction of our 6-to-10-million-year history—were needed for us to domesticate animals, develop agriculture and metallurgy, and invent writing. It was then but a short further step to those monuments of civilization that distinguish us from all other animals—monuments such as the *Mona Lisa* and the Ninth Symphony, the Eiffel Tower and Sputnik, Dachau's ovens and the bombing of Dresden.

What happened at that magic moment in evolution? What made it possible, and why was it so sudden? What held back the Neanderthals, and what was their fate? Did Neanderthals and modern peoples ever meet, and if so, how did they behave toward each other? We still share 98 percent of our genes with chimps; which genes among the other 2 percent had such enormous consequences?

Understanding the Great Leap Forward isn't easy; neither is writing about it. The immediate evidence comes from technical details of preserved bones and stone tools. Archeologists' reports are full of such terms as "transverse occipital torus," "receding zygomatic arches," and "Chatelperronian backed knives." What we really want to understand—the way of life and the humanity of our various ancestors—isn't directly preserved but only inferred from those technical details. Much of the evidence is missing, and archeologists often disagree over the meaning of the evidence that has survived.

I'll emphasize those inferences rather than the technical details, and I'll speculate about the answers to those questions I just listed above. But you can form your own opinions, and they may differ from mine. This is a puzzle whose solution is still unknown.

To set the stage quickly, recall that life originated on Earth several billion years ago, the dinosaurs became extinct around 65 million years ago, and, as I mentioned, our ancestors diverged from the ancestors of chimps and gorillas between 6 and 10 million years ago. They then remained confined to Africa for millions of years.

Initially, our ancestors would have been classified as merely another species of ape, but a sequence of three changes launched them in the direction of modern humans. The first of these changes occurred by around 4 million years ago: the structure of fossilized limb bones shows that by then our ancestors, in contrast to gorillas and chimps, were habitually walking upright. The upright posture freed our forelimbs to do other things, among which toolmaking would eventually prove to be the most important.

The second change occurred around 3 million years ago, when our lineage split in two. As background, remember that members of two animal species living in the same area must fill different ecological roles and do not normally interbreed. For

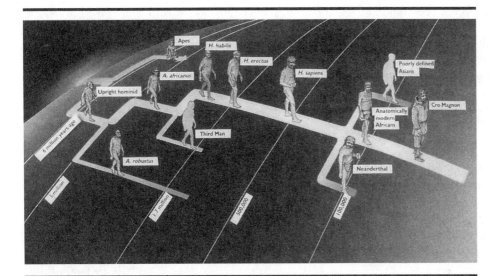

FIGURE 3.1   Some members of our family tree became extinct: the robust australopithecines (and perhaps a "Third Man"), around 1.2 million years ago, and Neanderthals, by 32,000 years ago. What became of Neanderthals' Asian contemporaries is not yet known.

Tom Moore/© 1989. Reprinted with permission of *Discover* Magazine.

example, coyotes and wolves are obviously closely related and, until wolves were exterminated in most of the United States, lived in many of the same areas. However, wolves are larger, they usually hunt big mammals like deer and moose, and they often live in sizable packs, whereas coyotes are smaller, mainly hunt small mammals like rabbits and mice, and normally live in pairs or small groups.

Now, all modern humans unquestionably belong to the same species. Ecological differences among us are entirely a product of childhood education: it is not the case that some of us are born big and habitually hunt deer while others are born small, gather berries, and don't marry the deer hunters. And every human population living today has interbred with every other human population with which it has had extensive contact.

Three million years ago, however, there were hominid species as distinct as wolves and coyotes. On one branch of the family tree was a man-ape with a heavily built skull and very big cheek teeth, who probably ate coarse plant food; he has come to be known as *Australopithecus robustus* (the "robust southern ape"). On the other branch was a man-ape with a more lightly built skull and smaller teeth, who most likely had an omnivorous diet; he is known as *Australopithecus africanus* (the "southern ape of Africa"). Our lineage may have experienced such a radical division at least once more, at the time of the Great Leap

Forward. But the description of that event will have to wait.

There is considerable disagreement over just what occurred in the next million years, but the argument I find most persuasive is that *A. africanus* evolved into the larger-brained form we call *Homo habilis* ("man the handyman"). Complicating the issue is that fossil bones often attributed to *H. habilis* differ so much in skull size and tooth size that they may actually imply another fork in our lineage yielding two distinct *habilis*-like species: *H. habilis* himself and a mysterious "Third Man." Thus, by 2 million years ago there were at least two and possibly three protohuman species.

The third and last of the big changes that began to make our ancestors more human and less apelike was the regular use of stone tools. By around 2.5 million years ago very crude stone tools appear in large numbers in areas of East Africa occupied by the protohumans. Since there were two or three protohuman species, who made the tools? Probably the light-skulled species, since both it and the tools persisted and evolved. (There is, however, the intriguing possibility that at least some of our robust relatives also made tools, as recent anatomical analyses of hand bones from the Sartkrans cave in South Africa suggest.)

With only one human species surviving today but two or three a few million years ago, it's clear that one or two species must have become extinct. Who was our ancestor, which species ended up instead as a discard in the trash heap of evolution, and when did this shakedown occur?

The winner was the light-skulled *H. habilis,* who went on to increase in brain size and body size. By around 1.7 million years ago the differences were sufficient that anthropologists give our lineage the new name *Homo erectus* ("the man who walks upright"—*H. erectus* fossils were discovered before all the earlier ones, so anthropologists didn't realize that *H. erectus* wasn't the first protohuman to walk upright). The robust man-ape disappears somewhat after 1.2 million years ago, and the Third Man (if he ever existed) must have disappeared by then also.

As for why *H. erectus* survived and *A. robustus* didn't, we can only speculate. A plausible guess is that the robust man-ape could no longer compete: *H. erectus* ate both meat and plant food, and his larger brain may have made him more efficient at getting the food on which *A. robustus* depended. It's also possible that *H. erectus* gave his robust brother a direct push into oblivion by killing him for meat.

The shakedown left *H. erectus* as the sole protohuman player on the African stage, a stage to which our closest living relatives (the chimp and gorilla) are still confined. But around one million years ago *H. erectus* began to expand his horizons. His stone tools and bones show that he reached the Near East, then the Far East (where he is represented by the famous fossils known as Peking man and Java man) and Europe. He continued to evolve in our direction by an increase in brain size and in skull roundness. By around 500,000 years ago some of our ancestors looked sufficiently like us, and sufficiently different from earlier *H. erectus,* to be classified as our own species, *Homo sapiens* (the "wise man"), although they still had thicker skulls and brow ridges than we do today.

Was our meteoric ascent to *sapiens* status half a million years ago the brilliant climax of Earth history, when art and sophisticated technology finally burst upon our previously dull planet? Not at all: the appearance of *H. sapiens* was a non-event. The Great Leap Forward, as proclaimed by cave paintings, houses, and bows and arrows, still lay hundreds of thousands of years in the future. Stone tools continued to be the crude ones that *H. erectus* had been making for nearly a million years. The extra brain size of those early *H. sapiens* had no dramatic effect on their way of life. That whole long tenure of *H. erectus* and early *H. sapiens* outside Africa was a period of infinitesimally slow cultural change.

So what was life like during the 1.5 million years that spanned the emergence of *H. erectus* and *H. sapiens*?

The only surviving tools from this period are stone implements that can, charitably, be described as very crude. Early stone tools do vary in size and shape, and archeologists have used those differences to give the tools different names, such as hand-ax, chopper, and cleaver. But these names conceal the fact that none of these early tools had a sufficiently consistent or distinctive shape to suggest any specific function. Wear marks on the tools show that they were variously used to cut meat, bone, hides, wood, and non-woody parts of plants. But any size or shape tool seems to have been used to cut any of these things, and the categories imposed by archeologists may be little more than arbitrary divisions of a continuum of stone forms.

Negative evidence is also significant. All the early stone tools may have been held directly in the hand; they show no signs of being mounted on other materials for increased leverage, as we mount steel ax blades on wooden handles. There were no bone tools, no ropes to make nets, and no fishhooks.

What food did our early ancestors get with those crude tools, and how did they get it? To address this question, anthropology textbooks usually insert a long chapter entitled something like "Man the Hunter." The point they make is that baboons, chimps, and some other primates prey on small vertebrates only occasionally, but recently surviving Stone Age people (like Bushmen) did a lot of big-game hunting. There's no doubt that our early ancestors also ate some meat. The question is, how much meat? Did big-game hunting skills improve gradually over the past 1.5 million years, or was it only since the Great Leap Forward—a mere 35,000 years ago—that they made a large contribution to our diet?

Anthropologists routinely reply that we've long been successful big-game hunters, but in fact there is no good evidence of hunting skills until around 100,000 years ago, and it's clear that even then humans were still very ineffective hunters. So it's reasonable to assume that earlier hunters were even more ineffective.

Yet the mystique of Man the Hunter is now so rooted in us that it's hard to abandon our belief in its long-standing importance. Supposedly, big-game hunting was what induced protohuman males to cooperate with one another, develop language and big brains, join into bands, and share food. Even women were supposedly molded by big-game hunting: they suppressed the external signs of monthly ovulation that are so conspicuous in chimps, so as not to drive men into a frenzy of sexual competition and thereby spoil men's cooperation at hunting.

But studies of modern hunter-gatherers, with far more effective weapons than those of early *H. sapi-*

ens, show that most of a family's calories come from plant food gathered by women. Men catch rats and other small game never mentioned in their heroic campfire stories. Occasionally they get a large animal, which does indeed contribute significantly to protein intake. But it's only in the Arctic, where little plant food is available, that big-game hunting becomes the dominant food source. And humans didn't reach the Arctic until around 30,000 years ago.

So I would guess that big-game hunting contributed little to our food intake until after we had evolved fully modern anatomy and behavior. I doubt the usual view that hunting was the driving force behind our uniquely human brain and societies. For most of our history we were not mighty hunters but rather sophisticated baboons.

To return to our history: *H. sapiens,* you'll recall, took center stage around half a million years ago in Africa, the Near East, the Far East, and Europe. By 100,000 years ago humans had settled into at least three distinct populations occupying different parts of the Old World. These were the last truly primitive people. Let's consider among them those whose anatomy is best known, those who have become a metaphor for brutishness: the Neanderthals.

Where and when did they live? Their name comes from Germany's Neander Valley, where one of the first skeletons was discovered (in German, *thal*—nowadays spelled *tal*—means "valley"). Their geographic range extended from western Europe, through southern European Russia and the Near East, to Uzbekistan in Central Asia, near the border of Afghanistan. As to the time of their origin, that's a matter of definition, since some old skulls have characteristics anticipating later "full-blown" Neanderthals. The earliest full-blown examples date from around 130,000 years ago, and most specimens postdate 74,000 years ago. While their start is thus arbitrary, their end is abrupt: the last Neanderthals died around 32,000 years ago.

During the time that Neanderthals flourished, Europe and Asia were in the grip of the last ice age. Hence Neanderthals must have been a cold-adapted people—but only within limits. They got no farther north than southern Britain, northern Germany, Kiev, and the Caspian Sea.

Neanderthals' head anatomy was so distinctive that, even if a Neanderthal dressed in a business suit or a designer dress were to walk down the street today, all you *H. sapiens* would be staring in shock. Imagine converting a modern face to soft clay, gripping the middle of the face from the bridge of the nose to the jaws, pulling the whole mid-face forward, and letting it harden again. You'll then have some idea of a Neanderthal's appearance. Their eye-brows rested on prominently bulging bony ridges, and their nose and jaws and teeth protruded far forward. Their eyes lay in deep sockets, sunk behind the protruding nose and brow ridges. Their foreheads were low and sloping, unlike our high vertical modern foreheads, and their lower jaws sloped back without a chin. Yet despite these startlingly primitive features, Neanderthal's brain size was nearly 10 percent greater than ours! (This does not mean they were smarter than us; they obviously weren't. Perhaps their larger brains simply weren't "wired" as well.)

A dentist who examined a Neanderthal's teeth would have been in for a further shock. In adult Neanderthals the front teeth were worn down on the outer surface, in a way found in no modern people. Evidently this peculiar wear pattern resulted from their using their teeth as tools, but what exactly did they do? As one possibility, they may have routinely used their teeth like a vise, as my baby sons do when they grip a milk bottle in their teeth and run around with their hands free. Alternatively, Neanderthals may have bitten hides to make leather or wood to make tools.

While a Neanderthal in a business suit or a dress would attract your attention, one in shorts or a bikini would be even more startling. Neanderthals were more heavily muscled, especially in their shoulders and neck, than all but the most avid bodybuilders. Their limb bones, which took the force of those big muscles contracting, had to be considerably thicker than ours to withstand the stress. Their arms and legs would have looked stubby to us, because the lower leg and forearm were relatively shorter than ours. Even their hands were much more powerful than ours; a Neanderthal's handshake would have been bone-crushing. While their average height was only around 5 feet 4 inches, their weight was at least 20 pounds more than that of a modern person of that height, and this excess was mostly in the form of lean muscle.

One other possible anatomical difference is intriguing, although its reality as well as its interpretation are quite uncertain—the fossil evidence so far simply doesn't allow a definitive answer. But a Neanderthal woman's birth canal may have been wider than a modern woman's, permitting her baby to grow inside her to a bigger size before birth. If so, a Neanderthal pregnancy might have lasted one year, instead of nine months.

Besides their bones, our other main source of information about Neanderthals is their stone tools. Like earlier human tools, Neanderthal tools may have been simple hand-held stones not mounted on separate parts such as handles. The tools don't fall into distinct types with unique functions. There were no standardized bone tools, no bows and arrows. Some of the stone tools were undoubtedly used to make wooden tools, which rarely survive. One notable exception is a wooden thrusting spear eight feet long, found in the ribs of a long-extinct species of elephant at an archeological site in Germany. Despite that (lucky?) success, Neanderthals were probably not very good at big-game hunting; even anatomically more modern people living in Africa at the same time as the Neanderthals were undistinguished as hunters.

If you say "Neanderthal" to friends and ask for their first association, you'll probably get back the answer "caveman." While most excavated Neanderthal remains do come from caves, that's surely an artifact of preservation, since open-air sites would be eroded much more quickly. Neanderthals must have constructed some type of shelter against the cold climate in which they lived, but those shelters must have been crude. All that remain are postholes and a few piles of stones.

The list of quintessentially modern human things that Neanderthals lacked is a long one. They left no unequivocal art objects. They must have worn some clothing in their cold environment, but that clothing had to be crude, since they lacked needles and other evidence of sewing. They evidently had no boats, as no Neanderthal remains are known from Mediterranean islands nor even from North Africa, just eight miles across the Strait of Gibraltar from Neanderthal-populated Spain. There was no long-distance overland trade: Neanderthal tools are made of stones available within a few miles of the site.

Today we take cultural differences among people inhabiting different areas for granted. Every modern human population has its characteristic house style, implements, and art. If you were shown chopsticks, a Schlitz beer bottle, and a blowgun and asked to associate one object each with China, Milwaukee, and Borneo, you'd have no trouble giving the right answers. No such cultural variation is apparent for Neanderthals, whose tools look much the same no matter where they come from.

We also take cultural progress with time for granted. It is obvious to us that the wares from a Roman villa, a medieval castle, and a Manhattan apartment circa 1988 should differ. In the 1990s my sons will look with astonishment at the slide rule I used throughout the 1950s. But Neanderthal tools from 100,000 and 40,000 years ago look essentially the same. In short, Neanderthal tools had no variation in time or space to suggest that most human of characteristics, *innovation.*

What we consider old age must also have been rare among Neanderthals. Their skeletons make clear that adults might live to their thirties or early forties but not beyond 45. If we lacked writing and if none of us lived past 45, just think how the ability of our society to accumulate and transmit information would suffer.

But despite all these subhuman qualities, there are three respects in which we can relate to Neanderthals' humanity. They were the first people to leave conclusive evidence of fire's regular, everyday use: nearly all well-preserved Neanderthal caves have small areas of ash and charcoal indicating a simple fireplace. Neanderthals were also the first people who regularly buried their dead, though whether this implies religion is a matter of pure speculation. Finally, they regularly took care of their sick and aged. Most skeletons of older Neanderthals show signs of severe impairment, such as withered arms, healed but incapacitating broken bones, tooth loss, and severe osteoarthritis. Only care by young Neanderthals could have enabled such older folks to stay alive to the point of such incapacitation. After my litany of what Neanderthals lacked, we've finally found something that lets us feel a spark of kindred spirit in these strange creatures of the Ice Age—humans, and yet not really human.

Did Neanderthals belong to the same species as we do? That depends on whether we would have mated and reared a child with a Neanderthal man or woman, given the opportunity. Science fiction novels love to imagine the scenario. You remember the blurb on a pulpy back cover: "A team of explorers stumbles on a steep-walled valley in the center of deepest Africa, a valley that time forgot. In this valley they find a tribe of incredibly primitive people, living in ways that our Stone Age ancestors discarded thousands of years ago. Are they the same species as us?" Naturally, there's only one way to find out, but who among the intrepid explorers—male explorers, of course—can bring himself to make the test? At this point one of the bone-chewing cavewomen is described as beautiful and sexy in a primitively erotic way, so that readers will find the brave explorer's dilemma believable: Does he or doesn't he have sex with her?

Believe it or not, something like that experiment actually took place. It happened repeatedly around 35,000 years ago, around the time of the Great Leap Forward. But you'll have to be patient just a little while longer.

Remember, the Neanderthals of Europe and western Asia were just one of at least three human populations occupying different parts of the Old World around 100,000 years ago. A few fossils from eastern Asia suffice to show that people there differed from Neanderthals as well as from us moderns, but too few have been found to describe these Asians in more detail. The best characterized contemporaries of the Neanderthals are those from Africa, some of whom were almost modern in their skull anatomy. Does this mean that, 100,000 years ago in Africa, we have at last arrived at the Great Leap Forward?

Surprisingly, the answer is still no. The stone tools of these modern-looking Africans were very similar to those of the non-modern-looking Neanderthals, so we refer to them as Middle Stone Age Africans. They still lacked standardized bone tools, bows and arrows, art, and cultural variation. Despite their mostly modern bodies, these Africans were still missing something needed to endow them with modern behavior.

Some South African caves occupied around 100,000 years ago provide us with the first point in human evolution for which we have detailed information about what people were eating. Among the bones found in the caves are many of seals and penguins, as well as shellfish such as limpets; Middle Stone Age Africans are the first people for whom there is even a hint that they exploited the seashore. However, the caves contain very few remains of fish or flying birds, undoubtedly because people still lacked fishhooks and nets.

The mammal bones from the caves include those of quite a few medium-size species, predominant among which are those of the eland, an antelope species. Eland bones in the caves represent animals of all ages, as if people had somehow managed to capture a whole herd and kill every individual. The secret to the hunters' success is most likely that eland are rather tame and easy to drive in herds. Probably the hunters occasionally managed to drive a whole herd over a cliff: that would explain why the distribution of eland ages among the cave kills is like that in a living herd. In contrast more dangerous prey such as Cape buffalo, pigs, elephants, and rhinos yield a very different picture. Buffalo bones in the caves are mostly of very young or very old individuals, while pigs, elephants, and rhinos are virtually unrepresented.

So Middle Stone Age Africans can be considered big-game hunters, but just barely. They either avoided dangerous species entirely or confined themselves to weak old animals or babies. Those choices reflect prudence: their weapons were stiff spears for thrusting rather than bows and arrows, and—along with drinking a strychnine cocktail—poking an adult rhino or Cape buffalo with a spear ranks as one of the most effective means of suicide that I know. As with earlier peoples and modern Stone Age hunters, I suspect that plants and small game made up most of the diet of these not-so-great hunters. They were definitely more effective than baboons, but not up to the skill of modern Bushmen and Pygmies.

Thus, the scene that the human world presented from around 130,000 years ago to somewhat before 50,000 years ago was this: Northern Europe, Siberia, Australia, and the whole New World were still empty of people. In the rest of Europe and western Asia lived the Neanderthals; in Africa, people increasingly like us in anatomy; and in eastern Asia, people unlike either the Neanderthals or Africans but known from only a few bones. All three populations were still primitive in their tools, behavior, and limited innovativeness. The stage was set for the Great Leap Forward. Which among these three contemporary populations would take that leap?

The evidence for an abrupt change—at last!—is clearest in France and Spain, in the late Ice Age around 35,000 years ago. Where there had previously been Neanderthals, anatomically fully modern people (often known as Cro-Magnons, from the French site where their bones were first identified) now appear. Were one of those gentlemen or ladies to stroll down the Champs Elysées in modern attire, he or she would not stand out from the Parisian crowds in any way. Cro-Magnons' tools are as dramatic as their skeletons; they are far more diverse in form and obvious in function than any in the earlier archeological record. They suggest that modern anatomy had at last been joined by modern innovative behavior.

Many of the tools continue to be of stone, but they are now made from thin blades struck off a larger stone, thereby yielding roughly ten times more cutting edge from a given quantity of raw stone. Standardized bone and antler tools appear for the first time. So do unequivocal compound tools of several parts tied or glued together, such as spear points set in shafts or ax heads hafted to handles. Tools fall into many distinct categories whose function is often obvious, such as needles, awls, and mortars and pestles. Rope, used in nets or snares, accounts for the frequent bones of foxes, weasels, and rabbits at Cro-Magnon sites. Rope, fishhooks, and net sinkers explain the bones of fish and flying birds at contemporary South African sites.

Sophisticated weapons for killing dangerous animals at a distance now appear also—weapons such as barbed harpoons, darts, spear-throwers, and bows and arrows. South African caves now yield bones of such vicious prey as adult Cape buffalo and pigs, while European caves are full of bones of bison, elk, reindeer, horse, and ibex.

Several types of evidence testify to the effectiveness of late Ice Age people as big-game hunters. Bagging some of these animals must have required communal hunting methods based on detailed knowledge of each species' behavior. And Cro-Magnon sites are much more numerous than those of earlier Neanderthals or Middle Stone Age Africans, implying more success at obtaining food. Moreover, numerous species of big animals that had survived many previous ice ages became extinct toward the end of the last ice age, suggesting that they were exterminated by human hunters' new skills. Likely victims include Europe's woolly rhino and giant deer, southern Africa's giant buffalo and giant Cape horse, and—once improved technology allowed humans to occupy new environments—the mammoths of North America and Australia's giant kangaroos.

Australia was first reached by humans around 50,000 years ago, which implies the existence of watercraft capable of crossing the 60 miles from eastern Indonesia. The occupation of northern Russia and Siberia by at least 20,000 years ago depended on many advances: tailored clothing, as evidenced by eyed needles, cave paintings of parkas, and grave ornaments marking outlines of shirts and trousers; warm furs, indicated by fox and wolf skeletons minus the paws (removed in skinning and found in a separate pile); elaborate houses (marked by postholes, pavements, and walls of mammoth bones) with elaborate fireplaces; and stone lamps to hold animal fat and light the long Arctic nights. The occupation of Siberia in turn led to the occupation of North America and South America around 11,000 years ago.

Whereas Neanderthals obtained their raw materials within a few miles of home, Cro-Magnons and their contemporaries throughout Europe practiced long-distance trade, not only for raw materials for tools but also for "useless" ornaments. Tools of obsidian, jasper, and flint are found hundreds of miles from where those stones were quarried. Baltic amber reached southeast Europe, while Mediterranean shells were carried to inland parts of France, Spain, and the Ukraine.

The evident aesthetic sense reflected in late Ice Age trade relates to the achievements for which we most admire the Cro-Magnons: their art. Best known are the rock paintings from caves like Lascaux, with stunning polychrome depictions of now-extinct animals. But equally impressive are the bas-reliefs, necklaces and pendants, fired-clay sculptures, Venus figurines of women with enormous breasts and buttocks, and musical instruments ranging from flutes to rattles.

Unlike Neanderthals, few of whom lived past the age of 40, some Cro-Magnons survived to 60. Those additional 20 years probably played a big role in Cro-Magnon success. Accustomed as we are to getting our information from the printed page or television, we find it hard to appreciate how important even just one or two old people are in preliterate society. When I visited Rennell Island in the Solomons in 1976, for example, many islanders told me what wild fruits were good to eat, but only one old man could tell me what other wild fruits could be eaten in an emergency to avoid starvation. He remembered that information from a cyclone that had hit Rennell around 1905, destroying gardens and reducing his people to a state of desperation. One such person can spell the difference between death and survival for the whole society.

I've described the Great Leap Forward as if all those advances in tools and art appeared simultaneously 35,000 years ago. In fact, different innovations appeared at different times: spear-throwers appeared before harpoons, beads and pendants appeared before cave paintings. I've also described the Great Leap Forward as if it was the same everywhere, but it wasn't. Among late Ice Age Africans, Ukrainians, and French, only the Africans made beads out of ostrich eggs, only the Ukrainians built houses out of mammoth bones, and only the French painted woolly rhinos on cave walls.

These variations of culture in time and space are totally unlike the unchanging monolithic Neanderthal culture. They constitute the most important innovation that came with the Great Leap Forward: namely, the capacity for innovation itself. To us innovation is utterly natural. To Neanderthals it was evidently unthinkable.

Despite our instant sympathy with Cro-Magnon art, their tools and hunter-gatherer life make it hard for us to view them as other than primitive. Stone tools evoke cartoons of club-waving cavemen uttering grunts as they drag women off to their cave. But we can form a more accurate impression of Cro-Magnons if we imagine what future archeologists will conclude after excavating a New Guinea village site from as recently as the 1950's. The archeologists will find a few simple types of stone axes. Nearly all other material possessions were made of wood and will have perished. Nothing will remain of the multistory houses, drums and flutes, outrigger canoes, and world-quality painted sculpture. There will be no trace of the village's complex language, songs, social relationships, and knowledge of the natural world.

New Guinea material culture was until recently "primitive" (Stone Age) for historical reasons, but New Guineans are fully modern humans. New Guineans whose fathers lived in the Stone Age now pilot airplanes, operate computers, and govern a modern state. If we could carry ourselves back

35,000 years in a time machine, I expect that we would find Cro-Magnons to be equally modern people, capable of learning to fly a plane. They made stone and bone tools only because that's all they had the opportunity to learn how to make.

It used to be argued that Neanderthals evolved into Cro-Magnons within Europe. That possibility now seems increasingly unlikely. The last Neanderthal skeletons from 35,000 to 32,000 years ago were still full-blown Neanderthals, while the first Cro-Magnons appearing in Europe at the same time were already anatomically fully modern. Since anatomically modern people were already present in Africa and the Near East tens of thousands of years earlier, it seems much more likely that such people invaded Europe rather than evolved there.

What happened when invading Cro-Magnons met the resident Neanderthals? We can be certain only of the result: within a few thousand years, no more Neanderthals. The conclusion seems to me inescapable that Cro-Magnon arrival somehow caused Neanderthal extinction. Yet many anthropologists recoil at this suggestion of genocide and invoke environmental changes instead—most notably, the severe Ice Age climate. In fact, Neanderthals thrived during the Ice Age and suddenly disappeared 42,000 years after its start and 20,000 years before its end.

My guess is that events in Europe at the time of the Great Leap Forward were similar to events that have occurred repeatedly in the modern world, whenever a numerous people with more advanced technology invades the lands of a much less numerous people with less advanced technology. For instance, when European colonists invaded North America, most North American Indians proceeded to die of introduced epidemics; most of the survivors were killed outright or driven off their land; some adopted European technology (horses and guns) and resisted for some time; and many of those remaining were pushed onto lands the invaders did not want, or else intermarried with them. The displacement of aboriginal Australians by European colonists, and of southern African San populations (Bushmen) by invading Iron Age Bantu-speakers, followed a similar course.

By analogy, I suspect that Cro-Magnon diseases, murders, and displacements did in the Neanderthals. It may at first seem paradoxical that Cro-Magnons prevailed over the far more muscular Neanderthals, but weaponry rather than strength would have been decisive. Similarly, humans are now threatening to exterminate gorillas in central Africa, rather than vice versa. People with huge muscles require lots of food, and they thereby gain no advantage if less-muscular people can use tools to do the same work.

Some Neanderthals may have learned Cro-Magnon ways and resisted for a while. This is the only sense I can make of a puzzling culture called the Chatelperronian, which coexisted in western Europe along with a typical Cro-Magnon culture (the so-called Aurignacian culture) for a short time after Cro-Magnons arrived. Chatelperronian stone tools are a mixture of typical Neanderthal and Cro-Magnon tools, but the bone tools and art typical of Cro-Magnons are usually lacking. The identity of the people who produced Chatelperronian culture was debated by archeologists until a skeleton unearthed with Chatelperronian artifacts at Saint-Césaire in France proved to be Neanderthal. Perhaps, then, some Neanderthals managed to master some Cro-Magnon tools and hold out longer than their fellows.

What remains unclear is the outcome of the interbreeding experiment posed in science fiction novels. Did some invading Cro-Magnon men mate with some Neanderthal women? No skeletons that could reasonably be considered Neanderthal–Cro-Magnon hybrids are known. If Neanderthal behavior was as relatively rudimentary and Neanderthal anatomy as distinctive as I suspect, few Cro-Magnons may have wanted to mate with Neanderthals. And if Neanderthal women were geared for a 12-month pregnancy, a hybrid fetus might not have survived. My inclination is to take the negative evidence at face value, to accept that hybridization occurred rarely if ever, and to doubt that any living people carry any Neanderthal genes.

So much for the Great Leap Forward in western Europe. The replacement of Neanderthals by modern people occurred somewhat earlier in eastern Europe, and still earlier in the Near East, where possession of the same area apparently shifted back and forth between Neanderthals and modern people from 90,000 to 60,000 years ago. The slowness of the transition in the Near East, compared with its speed in western Europe, suggests that the anatomically modern people living around the Near East before 60,000 years ago had not yet developed the modern behavior that ultimately let them drive out the Neanderthals.

Thus, we have a tentative picture of anatomically modern people arising in Africa over 100,000 years ago, but initially making the same tools as Neanderthals and having no advantage over them. By perhaps 60,000 years ago, some magic twist of behavior had been added to the modern anatomy. That twist (of which more in a moment) produced innovative, fully modern people who proceeded to spread westward into Europe, quickly supplanting the Neanderthals. Presumably, they also spread east into Asia and Indonesia, supplanting the earlier people there of whom we know little. Some anthropologists think that skull remains of those earlier Asians and Indonesians show traits recognizable in modern Asians and aboriginal Australians. If so, the invading moderns may not have exterminated the original Asians without issue, as they did the Neanderthals, but instead interbred with them.

Two million years ago, several protohuman lineages existed side-by-side until a shakedown left only one. It now appears that a similar shakedown occurred within the last 60,000 years and that all of us today are descended from the winner of that shakedown. What was the Magic Twist that helped our ancestor to win?

The question poses an archeological puzzle without an accepted answer. You can speculate about the answer as well as I can. To help you, let me review the pieces of the puzzle: Some groups of humans who lived in Africa and the Near East over 60,000 years ago were quite modern in their anatomy, as far as can be judged from their skeletons. But they were not modern in their behavior. They continued to make Neanderthal-like tools and to lack innovation. The Magic Twist that produced the Great Leap Forward doesn't show up in fossil skeletons.

There's another way to restate that puzzle. Remember that we share 98 percent of our genes with chimpanzees. The Africans making Neanderthal-like tools just before the Great Leap Forward had covered almost all of the remaining genetic distance from chimps to us, to judge from their skeletons. Perhaps they shared 99.9 percent of their genes with us. Their brains were as large as ours, and Neanderthals' brains were even slightly larger. The Magic Twist may have been a change in only 0.1 percent of our genes. What tiny change in genes could have had such enormous consequences?

Like some others who have pondered this question, I can think of only one plausible answer: the anatomical basis for spoken complex language. Chimpanzees, gorillas, and even monkeys are capable of symbolic communication not dependent on spoken words. Both chimpanzees and gorillas have been taught to communicate by means of sign language, and chimpanzees have learned to communicate via the keys of a large computer-controlled console. Individual apes have thus mastered "vocabularies" of hundreds of symbols. While scientists argue over the extent to which such communication resembles human language, there is little doubt that it constitutes a form of symbolic communication. That is, a particular sign or computer key symbolizes a particular something else.

Primates can use as symbols not just signs and computer keys but also sounds. Wild vervet monkeys,

for example, have a natural form of symbolic communication based on grunts, with slightly different grunts to mean *leopard, eagle,* and *snake.* A month-old chimpanzee named Viki, adopted by a psychologist and his wife and reared virtually as their daughter, learned to "say" approximations of four words: *papa, mama, cup,* and *up.* (The chimp breathed rather than spoke the words.) Given this capability, why have apes not gone on to develop more complex natural languages of their own?

The answer seems to involve the structure of the larynx, tongue, and associated muscles that give us fine control over spoken sounds. Like a Swiss watch, our vocal tract depends on the precise functioning of many parts. Chimps are thought to be physically incapable of producing several of the commonest vowels. If we too were limited to just a few vowels and consonants, our own vocabulary would be greatly reduced. Thus, the Magic Twist may have been some modifications of the protohuman vocal tract to give us finer control and permit formation of a much greater variety of sounds. Such fine modifications of muscles need not be detectable in fossil skulls.

It's easy to appreciate how a tiny change in anatomy resulting in capacity for speech would produce a huge change in behavior. With language, it takes only a few seconds to communicate the message, "Turn sharp right at the fourth tree and drive the male antelope toward the reddish boulder, where I'll hide to spear it." Without language, that message could not be communicated at all. Without language, two protohumans could not brainstorm together about how to devise a better tool, or about what a cave painting might mean. Without language, even one protohuman would have had difficulty thinking out for himself or herself how to devise a better tool.

I don't suggest that the Great Leap Forward began as soon as the mutations for altered tongue and larynx anatomy arose. Given the right anatomy, it must have taken humans thousands of years to perfect the structure of language as we know it—to hit on the concepts of word order and case endings and tenses, and to develop vocabulary. But if the Magic Twist did consist of changes in our vocal tract that permitted fine control of sounds, then the capacity for innovation that constitutes the Great Leap Forward would follow eventually. It was the spoken word that made us free.

This interpretation seems to me to account for the lack of evidence for Neanderthal–Cro-Magnon hybrids. Speech is of overwhelming importance in the relations between men and women and their children. That's not to deny that mute or deaf people learn to function well in our culture, but they do so by learning to find alternatives for an existing spoken language. If Neanderthal language was much simpler than ours or nonexistent, it's not surprising that Cro-Magnons didn't choose to associate with Neanderthals.

I've argued that we were fully modern in anatomy and behavior and language by 35,000 years ago and that a Cro-Magnon could have been taught to fly an airplane. If so, why did it take so long after the Great Leap Forward for us to invent writing and build the Parthenon? The answer may be similar to the explanation why the Romans, great engineers that they were, didn't build atomic bombs. To reach the point of building an A-bomb required 2,000 years of technological advances beyond Roman levels, such as the invention of gunpowder and calculus, the development of atomic theory, and the isolation of uranium. Similarly, writing and the Parthenon depended on tens of thousands of years of cumulative developments after the Great Leap Forward—developments that included, among many others, the domestication of plants and animals.

Until the Great Leap Forward, human culture developed at a snail's pace for millions of years. That pace was dictated by the slowness of genetic change. After the Great Leap Forward, cultural development no longer depended on genetic change. Despite negligible changes in our anatomy, there has been far more cultural evolution in the past 35,000 years than in the millions of years before. Had a visitor from outer space come to Earth before the Great Leap Forward, humans would not have stood out as unique among the world's species. At most, we might have been mentioned along with beavers, bowerbirds, and army ants as examples of species with curious behavior. Who could have foreseen the Magic Twist that would soon make us the first species, in the history of life on Earth, capable of destroying all life?

Shari Rudavsky

The Secret Life of the Neanderthal

The band of Neanderthals stopped outside the cave, and a lone male peered in. Looking around, he noticed that previous occupants, a taller, more graceful group, had left some remnants: smoldering coals, scattered garbage, and a smooth, shell-shaped pendant, purpose unknown. Finding no food, the Neanderthals trekked on, traversing miles of rocky terrain in less than a day. By late afternoon, they'd begun to track a goat. One of the males plunged on top of the animal, wounding it with his crude but heavy spear; the animal thrashed, but the male hung on until the goat died. Uttering a series of meaningful grunts, the Neanderthal band settled down for the night. One of the females built a fire, while another scraped the hide with a sharpened stone. A gray-haired male propped his arthritic leg above a grassy knoll. Devouring the remains of dinner, this Neanderthal family had no way of knowing their future: The rest of their stay on Earth would be arduous and brief.

A time machine and camcorder top the wish list of every scientist hoping to unravel the secret life of the Neanderthals—long viewed as a bumbling people who evolved rapidly (and thankfully) into our direct ancestors. But though today's paleoanthropologists lack the knack of time travel, they have recently acquired access to the next best thing: remarkable new dating technology that is slowly bringing the life and times of early hominids into bold relief. Based on state-of-the-art dating techniques such as thermoluminescence and electron spin resonance, researchers have come up with an increasingly detailed picture of the Neanderthals and how they lived.

No longer viewed as an evolutionary lout, the Neanderthal depicted today is a kinder, gentler, more successful individual with a range of unique cultural characteristics including sophisticated hunting practices and an intimate and elaborate social life.

In addition, paleoanthropologists now believe that Neanderthals coexisted with our direct ancestors, early modern humans, for a longer time span than ever before suspected. This revelation has thrown a monkey wrench into the story of hominid evolution, for if Neanderthals were not our direct ancestors, then who were they?

Scientists have been puzzling over this question since 1856, when quarry workers in the Neander Valley near Dusseldorf, Germany, found pieces of skull in the rock. Considering the way quarry workers go at limestone with picks and shovels (not at all like modern archaeologists, who tiptoe about with scalpels and toothbrushes), it's a wonder that any fossils remained. As University of Chicago anthropologist Richard G. Klein tells the story, the quarry owner thought the bones came from a bear, but he turned them over to Carl Fuhlrott, a local schoolteacher, who pronounced them human, albeit unusual.

Further discoveries over the next 120 years, ensured Neanderthals a place right next to modern humans on the evolutionary continuum. According to early paleoanthropologists, hominid evolution occurred incrementally, with the Neanderthal just one of many forms that led to humans today.

As more Neanderthal remains were unearthed, anthropologists also pieced together startling aspects of Neanderthal life. By the 1950's, researchers could cite definitive fossil evidence of tool use, fire use, and hunting and gathering techniques. And in perhaps the most extraordinary find of that decade, archaeologist Ralph Solecki unearthed a Neanderthal skeleton covered with pollen at the Shanidar site in Iraq. The so-called flower burial sparked a debate still unsettled today. The hard-liners argued that Neanderthals buried their dead only to discourage scavengers and eliminate odor. The flower spores, they held, had drifted into the graves purely by chance. But a new group of researchers, increasingly convinced of Neanderthals' basic *humanity*, cited the pollen as evidence of a ritual Neanderthal burial in which survivors draped flowers over the deceased.

Evidence for the new and improved Neanderthal, one that inhabited the earth for at least 100,000 years and lived side by side with early modern man, has been accumulating since 1980, when archaeologist Eitan Tchernov of Hebrew University in Jerusalem started dating the hominid remains found in three Israeli caves. Since Tchernov could find no dating techniques appropriate to the task at hand, he devised a method of his own. By approximating the dates of rodent bones found in the same layer as human bones, he created a biostratigraphy, an evolutionary time chart based on fossils. Using biostratigraphy, Tchernov and Ofer Bar-Yosef, now a professor of anthropology at Harvard University, set the ages of the *Homo sapiens* found in the Qafzeh and Skhul caves at 80,000 to 100,000 years old, about twice as old as anyone suspected. They dated the Neanderthal-like remains found in the third cave, Kebara, at 50,000 years. According to these figures, Neanderthals were not ancestral to us at all.

Anthropologists immediately protested the accuracy of these dates, saying the biostratigraphy did not provide reliable information. However, in the past few years, two new techniques have confirmed the Israeli results.

One technique, called thermoluminescence (TL), is particularly valuable for dating nonorganic artifacts such as burnt rocks and tools. The TL technique works because objects accumulate electrons over time, yet release electrons whenever they are burned. An accumulation of electrons may be measured by the intensity of light an object emits when it is burned. By heating a previously burnt object—for instance, a flint fired in a Neanderthal hearth a hundred thousand years ago—and then measuring the energy emitted, researchers can estimate the time that has passed since the object was burnt the first time around.

Experienced with TL, French physicist Hélène Valladas of the French National Center for Scientific Research decided to help the Israelis out. Dating prehistoric flints from the three caves with the help of this precise technique, Valladas's findings were clear: Flints used by prehistoric *Homo sapiens* at Qafzeh were about 92,000 years old, while flints used by Neanderthals at Kebara were much younger—50,000 to 60,000 years old, at most.

The dates were also confirmed for organic materials such as tooth enamel, bone, or fossilized pieces of grain, thanks to another high-tech method known as electron spin resonance, or ESR. In ESR dating, paleoanthropologists send a sliver of material to the laboratory, where physicists grind it up and expose it to a strong magnetic field. The magnetic field reacts in direct proportion to the number of trapped electrons that a sample contains. The older the fossil, the more upset the magnetic field becomes.

To Tchernov and Bar-Yosef's delight, ESR dating provided further support for their dates. Their conclusion: Neanderthals did not lead to early modern humans but, rather, were their counterparts.

"Modern-looking hominids were contemporary with the Neanderthals," says Bar-Yosef, "in the same way we are contemporary with people in Paris."

Because Neanderthals and humans are not directly related, it makes sense that their fossils seem distinct, even to the untrained eye. According to Lewis Binford, professor of anthropology at Southern Methodist University, the Neanderthal skeleton looks as though someone took a human skeleton and compacted it into a shorter, broader frame. A skull with a jutting brow topped this stocky body, obviously built to maximize endurance and resist bone damage. "Our anatomy is that of a walker; the Neanderthals' was that of a gymnast," says Binford. "Their whole way of coping with the world was action, not tools." Adds Robert Franciscus, a doctoral student in anthropology at the University of New Mexico, "Neanderthals were really using their bodies. Compared to them, modern humans are basically wimps."

But new theories and research techniques now go beyond the merely obvious, helping researchers flesh out some of the Neanderthals' best-kept physical secrets as well. According to Franciscus, for instance, the robust Neanderthal body may have served as a blanket of warmth against the cold, obviating any need for fitted clothing. Instead, Neanderthals probably relied on animal hides and their truncated limbs and broad noses to protect them from the frigid weather of the Ice Age.

In fact, Franciscus has shown in a recent study that Neanderthals living in colder climates had abbreviated limbs. To reach this conclusion, he measured the brachial indices of their arms—the relative length of the forearm to the rest of the limb—and found that as warmth increased, limb length increased. Interestingly enough, notes Franciscus, legs did not show as much regional disparity as arms. "Perhaps with their legs, the Neanderthals were responding less to climatic stresses than biomechanical ones," Franciscus says.

The Neanderthals' diminutive bodies suggest that they may have suffered not just from climatic stress, but also from nutritional stress, according to Mary Ursula Brennan, an anthropologist at New York University. Originally trained as a nurse, Brennan drew on modern nutritional knowledge to recreate the health of early hominids from their dental remains.

If people do not receive sufficient nutrients in the first seven years of their lives, Brennan explains, their teeth do not develop fully, a condition known as hypoplasia. Aware that this health problem might show up in our prehistoric predecessors, Brennan wound up toting an X-ray machine the size of a bread box throughout France. Her mission: X-raying hominid dental remains in museum storage areas to check for hypoplasia. Of the more than 300 Neanderthals she has tested, 40 percent suffered from hypoplasia, a good indication that resources were scarce. The early moderns showed a hypoplasia rate of only about 30 percent. Further evidence came from a small sample of Neanderthals she studied who were on average about four inches shorter than their successors.

"Neanderthals' short stature may have been an adaptation to low nutrient availability," Brennan concludes. "If they were living in areas where there was not enough food, people who needed fewer calories would survive because they were receiving sufficient nutrition. People born with genes for tallness would require more calories and die. So within a few generations, everyone's shorter."

While resources may have been scarce, bones found near Neanderthal remains indicate that these individuals did manage to find some sustenance. Based on the diets of modern hunter-gatherer societies, paleoanthropologists believe the Neanderthals would have subsisted on plant foods supplemented with meat. Some anthropologists speculate that Neanderthals were "hunter-blunderers" who scavenged the landscape. But according to the latest research, Neanderthals were persistent hunters who downed their prey by brute force. This conclusion comes from University of Michigan anthropologist Loring Brace, who has done a detailed study of skeletal and muscular stress in both Neanderthals and *Homo sapiens* to see which areas would be most likely to break in an encounter. He discovered the Neanderthal skeleton is adapted to resist such injuries as broken bones or dislocated shoulders, which would help them triumph in a battle of strength. Brace concluded that Neanderthals wrestled their prey to death. "The Neanderthals were put together on a heroic scale," Brace says. "For that to have been maintained, there have to have been hunting stresses. They must have literally come to grips with the family dinner."

Other recent studies have attempted to trace the life cycle of Neanderthals, following individuals from birth to death. Erik Trinkaus, professor of anthropology at the University of New Mexico, for instance, has analyzed about 20 complete Neanderthal skeletons as well as fragments from other skeletons. Using a technique known as histomorphic metric analysis, Trinkaus ground up thin slices of Neanderthal bone and placed the resulting powder on slides under a microscope. Trinkaus checked the bone powder for signs of maturity. By comparing the maturity of the Neanderthal bones with that of mammals alive today, Trinkaus estimated the age of each skeleton upon death. A definitive pattern emerged: Neanderthals rarely lived more than 40 years, with both sexes dying at the end of the female's reproductive cycle.

"What you have, then, is no postmenopausal survival," Franciscus says. "Most of all, there would have been no grandparenting." In modern hunter-gatherer societies, grandparents lend a much-needed hand with child rearing. Without grandparents to help care for them, Neanderthal children might have been more precocious than their early modern counterparts, Franciscus suggests.

The absence of grandparents, say other researchers, would have ramifications for the society as a whole. In modern hunter-gatherer societies the elderly are responsible for passing on knowledge of the environment and religious lore, says anthropologist Randall White of New York University. "The idea that you have a Neanderthal group composed of people only to age forty means you have a group of a radically different social fabric. You're missing an entire generation."

But the overriding question when it comes to Neanderthal relationships for many people remains where they should hang on our family tree. Two years ago a group of Berkeley scientists thought they had shown we still had Neanderthal genes. Today anthropologists are not sure. Did the Neanderthals interbreed with the early modern humans who shared their land for at least 10,000 years? Or did Neanderthals have no interaction with modern humans until, ultimately, the humans wiped them out?

Physical distinctions would have been a sufficient obstacle to interbreeding between humans and Neanderthals, says NYU's White. Modern baboon species—which never interbreed—show fewer skeletal differences than Neanderthals and *Homo sapiens*, he points out. This comparison supports the hypothesis that Neanderthals did not become integrated into our gene pool.

Adds Tchernov, "Perhaps early modern humans and Neanderthals were separated by such profound cultural differences they did not interbreed at all."

Even if there was no genetic crossover, no interbreeding, adds Bar-Yosef, we still don't need bloody scenarios to account for the Neanderthals' demise. "Simple inability to compete with modern humans in terms of finding food and shelter and reproducing could have finished Neanderthals off once and for all."

Yet because no clear-cut answers exist, researchers in the field may allow their biases to color their perception. Bar-Yosef charges that some of his colleagues are "Westerncentric," preventing them from accepting that Neanderthals and our ancestors belonged to the same species. "Our image of early *Homo sapiens,* based on the concept of a man painting in a cave, is too limited," he says. "It's only particular to certain parts of Europe. What was happening to the rest of the world?"

Bar-Yosef contends that Western anthropologists may be all too quick to assume that Neanderthals contributed nothing to our gene pool, mostly because they do not want to admit a relationship with somewhat unsavory hominids.

Milford H. Wolpoff of the University of Michigan at Ann Arbor takes an even harder line, vehemently insisting that Neanderthal genes did flow into the evolutionary mainstream. Part of the proof, he says, is as plain as the noses on the faces of Charles de Gaulle, Jimmy Durante, or any number of British knights. "These large noses are Neanderthal features," Wolpoff asserts. "If all modern humans descended from a group of Africans who began migrating northward between one hundred and two hundred thousand years ago, as some anthropologists claim, I am hardpressed to explain the origin of these noses. No African, ancient or modern, has a nose like that."

Perhaps it is the subtle familiarity of the Neanderthal face that continues to enthrall us today. Scientists are not the only ones to let emotions dictate their view of Neanderthals. Erik Trinkaus, who once wrote what he refers to as a "pedestrian" dissertation on the structure of Neanderthal feet, says the general public also reads the evolutionary record selectively.

"People really seem to want to claim the Neanderthals as relatives," Trinkaus says. "Their fossils have been known for almost one hundred fifty years, but our picture of them changes with the times: In the 1930's very few people thought the Neanderthals were cannibals, though there was some evidence for that belief. Then, in the 1940's, in the wake of World War II, without any new fossil evidence, Neanderthals were turned into cannibals to explain the nastiness of the Nuremberg trials. Hollywood in the 1950's perpetuated a brutish caricature of Neanderthals. And during the 1960's and 1970's, Neanderthals became flower children after the Shanidar Cave discovery."

But no matter who the Neanderthals were and where they went, one thing is for sure: Their impact on the environment was minimal. Says White, "They were never milking the environment for more than it would give them. In some ways you can argue they were more successful than their successors in the Upper Paleolithic or ourselves."

The Search for Early Man

EAST AFRICA, JAN. 1, 2050—It was announced today that Dr. Leakey has discovered a new fossil hominid in a remote part of what used to be northern Kenya. Dr. Leakey's find is the oldest and most complete yet unearthed and is likely to lead to a major revision of our current understanding of human evolution....

Not Louis, Mary, or Richard Leakey, of course, but a great (or great great) grandchild. Given the family's tenacity, it is entirely possible that the big news of 2050 will be the latest in a long series of discoveries by the Leakeys, stretching over 100 years, each one more dramatic than the last.

Not every student of human evolution, however, will be setting up camp in East Africa, as the Leakeys have done. Some researchers will be making remarkable discoveries by using computers and related technologies. And still others will be unraveling the story of our species in the genetics laboratory—following the intricate threads of our DNA. In the end, the year 2050 may well see a revolution in evolutionary science that will crown the achievements made by Charles Darwin 200 years before.

In the face of such dazzling prospects, one takes a certain pleasure in the assurance that some things will stay the same. Finding fossils is the heart of palaeoanthropology—the study of human evolution—and progress over the past century can be measured by the discoveries of new fossils: the neanderthals in the late nineteenth century; the pithecanthropines (or *Homo erectus* as they are now known) at the turn of the century; the australopithecines of South Africa in the 1920s; and the wealth of early material discovered in East Africa, starting with *Zinjanthropus* in 1959. Without these discoveries, there would be no development in our understanding, no new synthesis of the pattern of human evolution.

It would not be surprising, therefore, to find developments over the next [50] years firmly based on exciting new finds. Although the fossil record of human evolution is still by no means complete, it is incomparably better than it was just [75] years ago. In 1924 there was only one fossil hominid from the African Plio-Pleistocene; today there are 1,700. If that rate of discovery were to continue, then in another [50] years the gaps in the record should be far fewer, the human tree much more complete.

There remain, however, some important areas of human evolution for which there is virtually no fossil record. We currently think that hominids separated from the great apes of Africa around eight million years ago. But there are no fossils that provide satisfactory evidence about the three million or four million years preceding the separation. The first fossil evidence we have for a hominid lineage is dated at five million years ago. Between that time and three million years ago, there are only a few fragmentary remains, and even the period between three and two million years ago is poorly known. In other words, if hominids have been around for eight million years, only the final quarter of that existence is known in any detail. Consequently there is a desperate need for fossils that flesh out the details—indeed, provide the basic skeleton—of not only the early stages of human evolution but also the entire evolutionary history of African apes.

Even the past two million years are characterized by many significant gaps in the fossil record. Two small areas of Africa—in South and East—have yielded more than 90 percent of the evidence we have. All sorts of vital fossil evidence, about which we know nothing, may lie in other parts of Africa. India, which was probably occupied by hominids about one million years ago, is virtually terra incognita with regard to fossil evidence. Thus, although we have a larger number of fossils from these later periods, they come from only a few areas.

It is simple to predict, therefore, that major developments of the next half century will include the discovery of new fossils. The strategy for the future is quite clear: new techniques must be developed to enhance the efficiency of fossil recovery, and more and more expeditions must be mounted to seek out

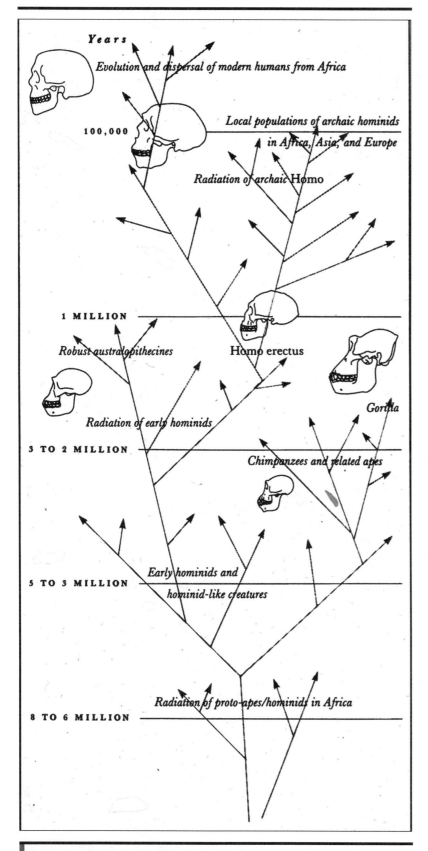

Years

Evolution and dispersal of modern humans from Africa

100,000

Local populations of archaic hominids
in Africa, Asia, and Europe

Radiation of archaic Homo

1 MILLION

Robust australopithecines

Homo erectus

Gorilla

Radiation of early hominids

3 TO 2 MILLION

Chimpanzees and related apes

5 TO 3 MILLION

Early hominids and
hominid-like creatures

Radiation of proto-apes/hominids in Africa

8 TO 6 MILLION

FIGURE 5.1 Radiation of the Hominids

fossils in places that have not been investigated.

But not all the discoveries will be made by expeditions. By the year 2050, there will likely be sophisticated new techniques available for plugging the gaps in the fossil record. Of these, remote sensing may be the most significant. For example, by 2050, the resolution of satellite imagery will probably be sharp enough to determine whether certain ground deposits contain fossils. Perhaps more significantly, subsurface topography will be detectable. Such techniques are already capable of mapping subterranean drainage systems beneath the Sahara Desert. Since fossils are likely to occur in sediments associated with water systems, this will help future palaeoanthropologists locate promising deposits.

Furthermore, the use of coring systems to sample deeply buried sediments—so important in the development of marine geology—is likely to have a major impact on the methods of archaeological and palaeontological excavation. The potential of these techniques may be seen by considering Olduvai Gorge. Although the gorge is just a small gash in the overall landscape of the Serengeti, the deposits that are exposed there must extend underground to either side. Today it is only in this narrow gorge that palaeoanthropologists have access to the deposits, but with remote-sensing and coring techniques the total landscape of the Olduvai hominids may become accessible.

All this suggests a rosy, fossiliferous future. But there is a built-in paradox. With each new fossil find, we are usually less certain about the nature and pattern of human evolution than we were before. As a result, the clear-cut evolutionary trees of the earlier part of this century will have given way to multiple-choice schemes and a myriad of alternative dotted lines linking putative ancestor with putative descendant.

Why do new fossils seem only to complicate matters? The effects of new fossil discoveries are a function of sample size. Only 2,500 pre-Holocene hominid fossils are known to us, but estimates suggest that more than five billion hominids lived between the origin of the group eight million years ago and the end of the Pleistocene 10,000 years ago. Consequently, the chance that the 2,500 hominids known to us represent all the variability of the hominid family is extremely small—after all, we are only finding one in every 200 million of them! Even if we can quadruple the size of the fossil record over the next [50] years, we are not going to alter the situation very much. We are still a long way from a stable understanding of human evolution, and no doubt the fossil record will continue to surprise us (although hopefully to a lesser and lesser extent).

Crucial as they are, however, fossil discoveries alone are not the key to the future. More and more, we can learn about human evolution not from the fossils in isolation but from their comparative context. One kind of context is the geological, palaeontological, and sedimentological context in which a fossil lies. Context can provide information about the environment in which a hominid lived and ultimately died. Distinct from the geological is the anatomical context of each fossil. Through a comparison of the bones and soft tissue of living and extinct animals, we are able to infer evolutionary relationships and functions. For example, Thomas Huxley established in the nineteenth century, through basic comparative primate anatomy, that the apes are our closest relatives. His conclusion was based on observation of gross anatomical features—the broad similarities of the bones, musculature and other soft tissue of apes and humans.

However, a new comparative framework is emerging, based not on gross anatomy but on molecular anatomy. Comparisons between species are now being carried out at the level of the molecule, and the results have been stunning, further eroding the biological pedestal on which humans have placed themselves. The genetic differences between humans and apes, it turns out, are relatively small—certainly far fewer than anatomy and behavior would lead us to expect. Superficial anatomical comparisons can actually be misleading. Anatomically the African apes (chimpanzees and gorillas) appear to be more similar to the great Asian apes (the orangutans) than either group is to modern humans. However, on the molecular and genetic level—which provides us with direct evidence of evolutionary relatedness—we and the African apes share a very close relationship. It is the orang which is the most divergent.

Molecular biology, the direct study of the building blocks of life, is the centerpiece of modern biology. An exciting example of its potential is the recent work on mitochondrial DNA (the genetic material found outside the nucleus) by Allan Wilson and his colleagues at the University of California at Berkeley. Assuming a constant rate of mutation over the millennia, they analyzed the mitochondrial DNA of modern people. Given a constant rate, the number of genetic changes can be used to determine when our own species began; and the amount of mitochondrial DNA variation in modern groups can indicate how closely related their genetic material is to that of the first *Homo sapiens sapiens*. The best explanation of the results obtained by Wilson place the origins of our own species in Africa between 150,000 and 200,000 years ago.

The implication of work on DNA *outside* the nucleus is that the origins of modern humans are relatively recent within hominid history. Complete mapping of the mitochondrial DNA is possible because of its relatively limited size. In comparison, nuclear DNA is a complex, extensive, and complete sequencing of the entire human genome. Mapping of the complete human genome is at an early stage, but major molecular biology laboratories are currently racing to complete this project. The work will probably be completed within the next decade or so, certainly by 2050, and it will release a mass of new

TABLE 5.1	Chronology of Human Evolution

YEARS BEFORE PRESENT

Present
- Extinction of archaic hominids/dispersal of anatomically modern humans/colonization of Australia and the New World
- Evolution of neanderthals in Europe
- Evolution of anatomically modern humans in Africa

1/2 Million
- Archaic hominids widely dispersed
- First hominids out of Africa/colonization of Asia and Africa

1 Million
- Origins of *Homo erectus*

2 Million
- Origins of the genus *Homo*
- Radiation of the australopithecines

5 Million
- First hominids

10 Million
- Evolution of the African hominoid stem that gave rise to hominids

TABLE 5.2	Main Events in Palaeoanthropology
1970	• Period of major discoveries in East Africa
1960	• The Leakeys discover the first early hominid in East Africa
1950	• Piltdown forgery exposed
1940	
1930	• Discoveries of *Home Erectus* in China
1920	• The first australopithecine discovered in South Africa
	• Piltdown man discovered
1910	
1900	• Dubois' discovery of *Homo erectus in Java*
1890	
1880	• Publication of *Descent of Man*
1870	
1860	• Publication of *Origin of Species*
	• Discovery of Neander specimen
1850	• First "neanderthal" discovered at Gibraltar

information about human evolution. One exciting prospect is that it will corroborate or refute the current model of a recent African origin for modern humans suggested by mitochondrial DNA studies. Moreover, complete genetic mapping will yield greater understanding of the function of the genes themselves, and molecular biology will gradually move into the field of behavioral genetics.

Biologists will have the tools to determine how much behavioral patterns in modern humans do—or do not—reflect the genetic basis of individuals and populations. In particular, the genetic basis for the differences between humans and the African apes will be measurable directly, bringing to an end 200 years (as it will be then) of speculation, philosophical debate, and tortuous theology about the chasm separating humans from their animal relatives. The evidence for evolution lies not just in the fossils we unearth, but in the molecules of which we are made.

What, though, will be the consequences of these developments for the way we think human evolution has occurred? The "how and why" questions will be as central in the year 2050 as they are today. At the risk of constraining the future in the straitjacket of the present, I shall concentrate on the issues that are currently at the center of debates and controversies—reassured to some extent by the fact that these debates have been central as long as human evolution has been a subject of study.

Darwin himself first put forward the idea of an African origin, so it is a hypothesis that has survived

more than 100 years of scrutiny—and I suspect it will survive the next hundred. With each new discovery, whether in the field or in the genetics laboratory, the links between humans, the ancient hominids, and the African apes become more solid. We need progress not in finding a new cradle for humanity, but in understanding better *why* Africa is so central; what is it about this continent that generates such evolutionary novelty? The answer to this will come not from studies of humans and hominids in isolation, but only from a better understanding of the mechanisms of evolution and the interactions between coexisting and competing species. The answer to "Why Africa?" in human evolution lies in the animals and plants that evolved with the hominids. I also suspect that [50] years from now, the issue may no longer be "Why Africa?" but why a particular *part* of the continent. For surely the key question is whether the East African Rift Valley is just a repository for excellent fossils or is itself the true cause—for a variety of ecological and geological reasons—of why humans exist at all. This does not relegate the rest of the world to a marginal place in palaeoanthropology—it just means that we should be asking different questions in continents that hominids colonized than in those in which they evolved.

Then, too, what of the scale of human evolution? Human evolution is both African and, under current models, a relatively recent event. Gone is the long line of hominids stretching back into the middle and early Miocene (20 to 25 million years ago), now replaced by a short sequence of Pliocene (about one and a half to five million years ago) apes. Until recently, the emphasis was always on the oldest specimens. The goal of many researchers was to put the human family further and further back in time. The effect of this was also to broaden the gap between humans and other animals, for the more ancient the lineage, the greater the evolutionary distance from other creatures. As a result, humans retained their special status—on a pedestal—in the living world. The shorter time scale with which we now work offers new and exciting possibilities. We no longer envision long sequences of change along a single evolutionary ladder; rather, we think of an array of coexisting, competing hominid species. It is now often more interesting to discover the youngest specimen—the last surviving robust australopithecine or neanderthal, the ones that did not become our ancestors. Evolution is an experimental process, the trial and error of survival. The success of our own species over a very short period should not mislead us into assuming that the evolutionary success of hominids was inevitable. The story of human evolution is as much one of failure as it is of success, with many species surviving for many hundreds of thousands of years but ultimately disappearing, leaving no descendants. A key to understanding our own evolution lies in unraveling the extinctions of all other hominids.

This should be good news for the poor old neanderthals. As the first non-modern fossil hominids to be discovered, they have always been central to discussions about the pattern of human evolution. Their rugged and robust features have generally placed them in a position peripheral to the mainstream of human evolution; it was only for a brief period between 1960 and the 1980s that there has been strong support for neanderthals having a more central, ancestral role relative to modern humans. But the picture I have outlined for the next half century does not augur well for the neanderthals if their only claim to fame lies in their proximity to ourselves. I think that in the future they may be recognized even more firmly as an isolated European population of the last glaciation. (Indeed by 2050, with developments in molecular biology and the ability to retrieve DNA from fossilized material, it may actually be possible to prove this one way or the other.) Interest in them, however, should not stop there, for what makes the neanderthals so interesting from a truly evolutionary perspective is that they are a species of hominid so close to us in time, and yet so different. They underline a major lesson of the Darwinian revolution; there are more ways to be a hominid than by being a modern human. And these extinct hominids may well offer us our best chance within evolutionary biology to study a complex animal—its ecology, behavior, and society—that no longer exists.

Ultimately, though, it is the way we *think* about human evolution that is critical to how we interpret the fossils and their contextual evidence. To the Victorians, the meaning of evolution lay in the ladder it provided, upon each rung of which could be placed the grades of evolutionary complexity—with, of course, modern humans at the top. Early evolution-

ary biology looked at the history of the animal world in terms of progress or development. Only in the past [30] years has evolutionary theory been rejuvenated and the notion of progress within evolution abandoned. The emphasis now centers on adaptation—on evolutionary changes as the product of selection operating at the level of the individual. Evolutionary changes reflect changes in reproductive success—and therefore patterns in the fossil record need to be explained in terms of changing adaptations and reproductive strategies. In this perspective, humans are not an inevitable outcome of evolution but the product of a series of short-term responses to very specific selective conditions. Understanding human evolution, both in the technical sense of sorting out the pattern of fossils and in the more general sense of appreciating our place in nature, depends on relating our unique adaptive features to the conditions in which they evolved.

The approach that can achieve this end is not anthropology or anatomy or geology, but evolutionary, and especially behavioral, ecology. The first half of the twenty-first century will almost certainly see the expansion of this approach—incorporating more and more of human behavior within the overall study of comparative animal behavior. This must be the inevitable conclusion of the Darwinian revolution started in 1859: the full incorporation of hominid evolution within comparative evolutionary biology. In 2050, nearly 200 years after Darwin's *Origin of Species*, the evolution of our species should be understandable in terms of ordinary processes of natural selection—with the human being seen as just another animal, not the pinnacle of evolution. Paradoxically, the achievement of that goal may also mean the end of a discipline, for it will result in the full absorption of palaeoanthropology within evolutionary and biological science. The human species will no longer occupy a pedestal—but will have earned honor enough by coming down from it.

Designed for Another Time: Modern Problems for an Ancient Species

HELP WANTED: Healthy males wanted as semen donors. Help infertile couples.

The advertisement runs in the classified section of *The Battalion,* the student newspaper at Texas A&M University. "Confidentiality ensured. Ages 18 to 35, excellent compensation." But in spite of the blandishments, donors are scarce. Meanwhile, on highways in the surrounding Texas countryside, armadillos routinely kill themselves by springing into the air in front of oncoming cars, in misguided attempts to foil their perceived attackers.

What could two such disparate phenomena possibly have in common? Each of them sheds light on the environment in which a species evolved. In each case some aspect of the original environment has changed, and an old behavior that might once have been adaptive is no longer so. The problem for the armadillos is cars: for most of armadillo evolution there were none, and the armadillo's habit of springing into the air when it is threatened worked well enough to confuse snakes and other predators. Leap two feet high in front of a Buick, though, and you're buzzard bait.

The Texas A&M undergraduates also are disadvantaged—somewhat less drastically, to be sure—by their evolutionary heritage. In a Darwinian sense, an adaptive behavior is one that increases the individual organism's chance of passing on its genes. The adaptive response to the sperm bank's advertisement (which represents a chance to reproduce, free of any cost beyond a few minutes' effort) would be to visit the bank as often as possible. But throughout most of human evolution, reproductive opportunities have involved human females, not test tubes. Focusing on females was adaptive in the past, but here, in the novel environment of a sperm bank, it is a diversion and a handicap. For the few men who do make deposits, the incentive is usually financial, not sexual; an acceptable donor can make more than $100 a week for just a few minutes' work.

The English psychologist John Bowlby, in his treatise *Attachment and Loss,* was the first to point out the importance of understanding the environment in which an adaptation arose—what he called the environment of evolutionary adaptedness. Behavioral and physical adaptations that seem to make no sense in an organism's current environment can be traced to the legacy of an earlier, different environment in which those traits were favored. Human beings, now the major source of environmental change on earth, have altered the environments of many other animals besides the armadillo, and the results have been incongruous and often poignant.

Rabbits dart back and forth in the paths of oncoming cars, attempting to confuse what they perceive as predators intensely bearing down on them at great speed. Toads are undone by their feeding behavior. They snap reflexively at almost any small, moving object—behavior that serves them well in their normal surroundings, where such an object is likely to be a tasty insect. But when cane toads were introduced on the Hawaiian islands in 1932, their environment included a novel element: trees that produce strychnine and deposit the poison in their flowers for protection against insects. As the blossoms fall from the trees and blow along the ground, toads searching for food sometimes snatch them up, with predictable results. In Korea toads faced another novel environment when they were captured by bored American GIs, who amused themselves by rolling shotgun pellets past the toads. The animals would fill up with lead like little amphibious beanbags until they were unable even to hop.

In addition to changing the environments of other species, we humans are building a strange and in many ways novel environment for ourselves. The ability to do so sets us apart from other species. Fortunately, so does the ability to respond flexibly to new conditions of our own making. Any animal is likely to be confused between a new stimulus and a familiar one. Rabbits and armadillos react to moving cars as if they were predators; toads react to blossoms and shotgun pellets as if they were insects. Most people react to sperm banks as if they had nothing to do with reproduction; after all, sperm donation certainly lay outside the behavioral repertoire of our ancestors. But people also have fewer simple behavioral programs, and our intelligence makes it possible for us to shape our behavior to new circumstances. The sperm bank near Texas A&M may not be as popular as the local ice-cream parlor, but the bank still attracts enough donors to stay in business.

Yet there are limits to our flexibility. In some features of our physiology or psychology we seem to be rather like the armadillo and the toad: we carry on in ways that were once adaptive but have become a handicap in our new, artificial environment. Many of those legacies remain obscure. But by conceptually reconstructing the environment of our own evolutionary upbringing and comparing it with our present surroundings, we may be able to locate the roots of certain contemporary medical, behavioral and social problems. We may even find clues about how best to deal with them.

To begin we need a picture of our ancestors' world. That phrase usually conjures images of the African savanna or the caves of Ice Age Europe—in other words, the physical environments in which the human species evolved. Changes in the physical environment surely lie at the root of some of the current difficulties. Certain diseases of advanced age, for example—high blood pressure, heart disease, some cancers—seem to emerge from the clash between a Stone Age physiology and one aspect of the new physical environment: diet. Salt was once scarce, and early humans evolved both a taste for it and some mechanisms for conserving it. Those adaptations no longer serve now that salt is plentiful. By the same token, the human body became adapted, over tens of thousands of years, to a diet low in fat and high in fiber, and the recent departure from that pattern is blamed for many health problems.

But emphasizing the physical aspects of our species' past may be a mistake. Investigators are beginning to explore the possibility that the social environment may have been a source of selective pressure at least as strong as the physical environment during the evolution of humans and other primates. The psychologist Nicholas Humphrey of Kings College at the University of Cambridge draws an analogy between human evolution and the story of Robinson Crusoe. Crusoe certainly faced physical challenges when he was alone on the island—getting enough to eat and drink, avoiding danger and so

on—but, as Humphrey puts it, "it was the arrival of man Friday [that] really made things difficult for Crusoe. If Monday, Tuesday, Wednesday and Thursday had turned up as well then Crusoe would have had every need to keep his wits about him."

Indeed, the anthropologist Sue Taylor Parker of Sonoma State University in Rohnert Park, California, has argued that one defining human characteristic, the capacity for abstract reasoning, evolved in response to the demands of the social world, as well as to the demands of toolmaking and tool use. The traditional human societies in our time all impose on their members an exceedingly complicated social environment, no matter how simple their technology. The Australian aborigines, for example, never developed the bow and arrow, but their social systems are well known among anthropologists for their intricacy. The Tiwi of northern Australia maintain an elaborate system of political bargaining, favors and intrigue, all centered on the rights of men to bestow women on one another. Other aboriginal groups regulate marriage and kinship according to systems of Byzantine complexity. Such social systems, assuming they existed earlier in human evolution, would have strongly favored an ability to generalize rules from experience and apply the rules in new situations.

If the social environment of our ancestors played a major role in shaping human physiology and behavior, current social, economic and political arrangements might be a good hunting ground for conditions that strain our evolutionary heritage. One main difference between the present environment and that of our ancestors is in the nature of work. Traditional societies have simple divisions of labor, based only on age and sex, and consequently their members are generalists. In foraging societies men usually do most of the hunting for meat and women do most of the gathering of plant foods. All grown men take part in such activities as toolmaking, stalking and butchering, and the women likewise share a broad range of activities. Many herding societies go even further in sharing tasks: all members—men, women and children—tend the livestock.

Modern societies, in contrast, subdivide labor in infinite and subtle ways. Some people specialize in deboning chickens or soldering circuit boards; others spend their days taking telephone orders or running office copiers. An office, a hospital or a construction site is a hive of finely divided responsibilities. Although such division of labor has brought enormous increases in productivity and wealth, it has led also to specific physical problems.

Through most of evolution everyone performed a wide range of physical activities. Today specialization has gone so far that some jobs have been reduced to a single pattern of motion, repeated over and over again, day after day. The result, for some workers, is a cumulative trauma disorder. Carpal tunnel syndrome is one of the most common of those ailments: the tissues of the wrist and hand become inflamed and press on the nerves that run through the carpal tunnel, causing pain, numbness and weakness. Butchers, meat packers and assembly line workers have long been subject to carpal tunnel syndrome, but as computer keyboards have proliferated, the ailment has spread to white-collar workers as well. Indeed, carpal tunnel syndrome has now become so common among the new groups that it is sometimes called computeritis or journalist's disease. According to Linda H. Morse, medical director of the Repetitive Motion Institute in San Jose, California, the growth of cumulative trauma disorders is a sign that "the electronic revolution has outstripped our human muscular and skeletal evolution."

Economic changes have not only led to physical activities unanticipated by evolution; they have also disrupted traditional patterns of childbearing and child rearing. Again specialization is to blame, at least in part. Many jobs now require long periods of schooling and apprenticeship. Women are finding increased opportunities in such specialized fields, and as a result they are delaying childbearing, often into their thirties. In response to career pressures, many limit the size of their families and return to work quickly after giving birth. Breast-feeding is also curtailed, since it is rarely accommodated in the workplace. In all, fewer than 10 percent of married American women between the ages of eighteen and thirty-four expect to have more than three babies, and fewer than 20 percent of American women nurse their babies for six months or more.

A strikingly different pattern prevailed for most of human evolution, and it is still evident in traditional societies. There, women usually become pregnant not long after they begin to ovulate, between the ages of fifteen and nineteen. They continue to bear children until menopause, nursing each one for as long as three years. Although both the rights of women and population control make such a pattern unacceptable in modern industrial societies, it may be what human physiology is best equipped for. Consider that tens of thousands of years has settled the body into the strategy of early and abundant childbirth. Only in the past few decades has that pattern changed.

There is increasing evidence that the change may not sit well with our Stone Age reproductive physiology. For example, the change in reproductive behavior may be contributing to the high incidence of breast cancer in industrial society. An epidemiological study by Peter M. Layde and others at the

Centers for Disease Control in Atlanta found that getting pregnant early in life, having several children and breast-feeding them for long periods—in other words, following the reproductive regimen of early humans—all reduced the risk of breast cancer. In some cases the reductions were dramatic. Women who had breast-fed for a total of more than twenty-five months were 33 percent less likely to develop breast cancer than were women who had children but had never breast-fed. And women who had had only one child had more than twice the cancer risk of women with seven or more children.

People have carried a Stone Age physiology into an age of fast food and commuter marriages, but they may also be carrying some aspects of Stone Age psychology—traits evolved over tens of thousands of years of foraging. Are there any signs of an emotional legacy from the past? No one knows how much human behavior comes from the genes and how much is learned; any argument that people are hobbled by a Stone Age psychology is necessarily speculative. But it may prove useful to look at certain modern social problems from the perspective of the early human environment, where aspects of the psyche may have been forged.

Just as the division of labor has fragmented the economy, so it has atomized social life. We move from city to city; we work with colleagues and bosses rather than with kinfolk; we often gain recognition and rewards for our own efforts rather than through family influence. The clans, lineages and extended-family networks that structured life for our ancestors (and for the members of traditional societies today) have disintegrated, and in the West most people now live in nuclear families. The loss of such kin networks may be another factor that has led parents to have fewer children, later in life: many people can no longer call on relatives to share the work of child rearing.

It may also have had disturbing psychological effects. The feelings of alienation so often ascribed to modern urban life may reflect the evolutionary novelty of that environment, in which families and small, often short-lived webs of friendship take the place of widespread kin networks. David P. Barash, a professor of psychology and zoology at the University of Washington in Seattle, has argued that social pathologies such as drug use and crimes against strangers may reflect this uneasy fit between aspects of our psyche, evolved long ago, and the strange social world we now inhabit.

Although traditional societies have drugs, the drugs rarely become the center of a person's life. And crime is less of a problem, because it is difficult to accomplish anonymously. Crimes of passion and impulse concerning adultery, unpaid debts and unreturned favors predominate, whereas premeditated robberies and burglaries barely exist. "A small-town resident doesn't rob the corner grocer; everyone knows nice old Mr. McPherson," Barash writes in his 1986 book *The Hare and the Tortoise.* "But if McPherson is a nameless, familyless, disembodied, and anonymous spirit in a big city, he can be attacked with relative ease."

Even if the novel human environment is perilous to creatures that evolved to meet the demands of the Pleistocene, what can be done about it? After all, the adaptive advantages of the artificial environment far outweigh its drawbacks, as the health and prosperity of many people in the industrial world make clear. Quite apart from its benefits in a Darwinian sense, the modern world created by human effort offers freedoms and pleasures unknown in traditional societies. Alienating as they may be, cities are also exciting and fun. Kinship networks offer psychological support during child rearing, but the obligation to support is reciprocal, and many people prefer their family ties loosely knotted. Delayed reproduction may have medical risks, but careers can bring rewards that breast-feeding cannot.

What is more, it may be possible to relieve some of the problems of the novel contemporary environment without returning to the Stone Age, by mimicking some of its key features. Cumulative trauma disorders such as carpal tunnel syndrome are currently treated with drugs and surgery. But they also improve when the sufferer's job is redesigned to allow a greater range of motion—making it perhaps more like the ancestral activities of root grubbing and spear throwing. The risk of breast cancer may one day be reduced by hormone treatments that mimic the cancer—reducing effects of the traditional reproductive pattern, without its career-reducing effects as well.

Alienation is a more subtle problem, calling for a more imaginative solution. The novelist Kurt Vonnegut offered one in *Slapstick, or Lonesome No More!* The second part of the title is the campaign slogan of Wilbur Daffodil-11 Swain, the last president of the U.S. His sole issue is the loneliness of his compatriots, and his solution is to engage the computers of the federal government in recreating kinship networks like the ones of prehistory.

In Vonnegut's fantasy everyone gets a new middle name, corresponding to something in nature—Chipmunk, Hollyhock, Raspberry, Uranium—and a number. By name and number everyone is instantly linked to 10,000 brothers and sisters and 190,000 cousins, all obligated to help out fellow clan members. That's a lot of kinfolk, but individually the obligations are mild. And, as Swain explains, "We need all the help we can get in a country as big and clumsy as ours."

People may never shed the need for kinship networks, but perhaps some day in the distant future adaptations to the modern environment will begin to appear. As sperm banks account for more and more babies, for instance, men may eventually evolve a propensity to find test tubes downright arousing. By the same token, it is not inconceivable that the division of labor could lead to the development or the atrophy of certain physical characteristics in human beings. But, surely, it will be a long time before laboratory supply catalogs are sold at convenience stores and armadillos stop littering the Texas highways.

EVOLUTIONARY PSYCHOLOGY

Human beings are mammals, members of the order *Primates*. And we are very closely related to some other living primates, most notably bonobos and chimpanzees (with which we share almost 99 percent of our genetic materials), gorillas, and orangutans. As primates, human beings have certain evolutionary traits in common with other primates (and other mammals as well), but our species is also distinctly different from all other animal species. At this moment, scholars are actively debating the degree to which it is possible to understand or explain human behavior in terms of the behavior patterns that seem to be innate in other species, particularly other primates.

In the first article in Topic 3, "What Are Friends For?" Barbara Smuts explores some of the complexities of baboon societies. Baboons are monkeys, and among the most successful of all primates. Like human beings, their ancestors long ago climbed down from the trees to pursue a lifestyle that is largely terrestrial. Smuts has been observing baboons in the wild for almost thirty years. Her observations have enriched our knowledge of these primate relatives of ours and have often shown how humanlike baboons can be. In this article, Smuts describes the world of baboon friendship (often including sexual intimacy) between males and females, and the protective role males often take toward the infants of their female friends. She argues that perhaps for our ancestors, as for baboons today, sex and friendship went hand in hand.

Apes, of course, are even more sophisticated than monkeys. Animals of all kinds use deception to attract mates, bluff competitors, enhance their status, get others to raise their offspring, or bring home a meal. But some evolved an understanding that they are deceiving. This allowed not only for true Machiavellian deception but also for self-reflection. Humans, of course, are the masters of deception; in our species, deception and lying have been developed to an art form. In Article 8, "Games Primates

Play," Marc D. Hauser describes a series of experiments designed to find out whether apes are aware that they are lying.

In 1975, Harvard University's Edward O. Wilson immersed himself in controversy and became a very controversial figure when he published his seminal book, *Sociobiology: The New Synthesis*. In this book he gathered all the information biologists had accumulated about genetically transmitted behavior among the world's animals. But in the book's final chapter, he went one step further: he argued that, contrary to the cherished beliefs strongly held by many anthropologists and psychologists, human behavior also has fundamentally innate patterns. Three years later, in 1978, Wilson developed these views at length in his next book, *On Human Nature*.

Initially, Wilson's arguments stimulated heated and passionate debate which, at times, became ugly and personal. Several of his colleagues at Harvard organized the Sociobiology Study Group of Science, which became a forum for attacking Wilson and his followers. The study group argued that any attempt to account for human behavior genetically will inevitably cater to reactionary politicians seeking to protect the interests of groups with social, economic, and political power in society. In a letter to *The New York Review of Books*, they proclaimed that "Wilson joins the long parade of biological determinists whose work has served to buttress the institutions of their society by exonerating them from responsibility for social problems" (Dec. 11, 1975: 60–61).

A careful reading of Wilson's book reveals, however, that he made no direct, declarative statements tying human behavior to genes. Rather, he used what, to his critics, was a maddening suppositional style: he *supposed* there *might* be genes that would favor certain forms of social behavior, then proceeded to ponder how such genes might be expressed. His critics pointed out, with some justification, that many lay readers were apt to miss this reserve and read Wilson's speculations as definitive. Subsequent work by others did just that, particularly in the area of gender roles, where Wilson, himself, used language decidedly deterministic in flavor. (See Topic 12.)

Over the years, both Wilson and his adversaries toned down their public rhetoric, particularly as more and more research supported Wilson's basic argument. But the debate and its bitterness do show that science is not pursued in a vacuum. Its findings can be, and often are, appropriated for social, economic, and political purposes—regardless of scientists' intentions. Thus, in a society still organized to some degree along "racial" and sexual lines in its distribution of wealth and access to institutions of power, scientific theories and findings that even suggest the possibility that social institutions may, to whatever degree, be rooted in innate biological traits will be used to justify the status quo and undermine pressures for change. For example, if certain research suggests that intelligence is unevenly distributed among the "races" of our society, some pressure groups will use these findings to justify terminating programs, such as Head Start, which are designed to compensate for social inequalities. It was fear of such misuse of Wilson's work that fueled the bitterness of his critics' attacks.

Boyce Rensberger's article, "On Becoming Human," addresses these issues. Rensberger reviews Wilson's work and concludes that human behavior is a result of a complex interplay between our biological heritage and our culture.

Since Wilson first dropped his bombshell in 1975, his ideas have won gradual, if initially grudging, acceptance in growing segments of the academic community. Today, the idea that there are significant biological inputs in human social behavior has become conventional wisdom, and the search is on to find genes that impact a whole host of human behaviors. Interestingly, academia has struggled with what to call this new perspective: sociobiology, biosociology, evolutionary anthropology, psychobiology, and several other monikers have been thrown into the academic ring. Gradually, the term *evolutionary psychology* has won the widest acceptance. Studies in evolutionary psychology in the 1990s and the first years of the new century have illuminated such issues as kin selection, altruism, sexual attraction, mate selection, reproductive success, and wealth.

Perhaps one of the most interesting issues explored by evolutionary psychology is what men and women look for in a mate, and why. Some 70 years ago, the great psychoanalyst Sigmund Freud, as thoroughly confused and clueless as are most men, asked forlornly, "What do women want?" In Article 10, Elizabeth Cashdan utilizes evolutionary psychology to try to answer that question. Cashdan explains what women want in a man and focuses on the ways in which women go about attaining their men, including fighting with other women. She weaves recent studies and contemporary examples with historical and evolutionary data to bolster her argument.

In "Isn't She Lovely?," the final article in this topic, Brad Lemley explores recent experiments in evolutionary psychology to tackle a similar question: What physical characteristics do we find most attractive and sexually appealing? You may think that what you find attractive in another person is strictly a matter of personal taste and cultural bias. Turns out there's more to it than that. Who you find attractive—and why—is largely dictated by evolutionary needs and hardwired into your brain.

Barbara Smuts

What Are Friends For?

Virgil, a burly adult male olive baboon, closely followed Zizi, a middle-aged female easily distinguished by her grizzled coat and square muzzle. On her rump Zizi sported a bright pink swelling, indicating that she was sexually receptive and probably fertile. Virgil's extreme attentiveness to Zizi suggested to me—and all rival males in the troop—that he was her current and exclusive mate.

Zizi, however, apparently had something else in mind. She broke away from Virgil, moved rapidly through the troop, and presented her alluring sexual swelling to one male after another. Before Virgil caught up with her, she had managed to announce her receptive condition to several of his rivals. When Virgil tried to grab her, Zizi screamed and dashed into the bushes with Virgil in hot pursuit. I heard sounds of chasing and fighting coming from the thicket. Moments later Zizi emerged from the bushes with an older male named Cyclops. They remained together for several days, copulating often. In Cyclops's presence, Zizi no longer approached or even glanced at other males.

Primatologists describe Zizi and other olive baboons (*Papio cynocephalus anubis*) as promiscuous, meaning that both males and females usually mate with several members of the opposite sex within a short period of time. Promiscuous mating behavior characterizes many of the larger, more familiar primates, including chimpanzees, rhesus macaques, and gray langurs, as well as olive, yellow, and chacma baboons, the three subspecies of savanna baboon. In colloquial usage, promiscuity often connotes wanton and random sex, and several early studies of primates supported this stereotype. However, after years of laboriously recording thousands of copulations under natural conditions, the Peeping Toms of primate fieldwork have shown that, even in promiscuous species, sexual pairings are far from random.

Some adult males, for example, typically copulate much more often than others. Primatologists have explained these differences in terms of competition: the most dominant males monopolize females and prevent lower-ranking rivals from mating. But

exceptions are frequent. Among baboons, the exceptions often involve scruffy, older males who mate in full view of younger, more dominant rivals.

A clue to the reason for these puzzling exceptions emerged when primatologists began to question an implicit assumption of the dominance hypothesis—that females were merely passive objects of male competition. But what if females were active arbiters in this system? If females preferred some males over others and were able to express these preferences, then models of mating activity based on male dominance alone would be far too simple.

Once researchers recognized the possibility of female choice, evidence for it turned up in species after species. The story of Zizi, Virgil, and Cyclops is one of hundreds of examples of female primates rejecting the sexual advances of particular males and enthusiastically cooperating with others. But what is the basis for female choice? Why might they prefer some males over others?

This question guided my research on the Eburru Cliffs troop of olive baboons, named after one of their favorite sleeping sites, a sheer rocky outcrop rising several hundred feet above the floor of the Great Rift Valley, about 100 miles northwest of Nairobi, Kenya. The 120 members of Eburru Cliffs spent their days wandering through open grassland studded with occasional acacia thorn trees. Each night they retired to one of a dozen sets of cliffs that provided protection from nocturnal predators such as leopards.

Most previous studies of baboon sexuality had focused on females who, like Zizi, were at the peak of sexual receptivity. A female baboon does not mate when she is pregnant or lactating, a period of abstinence lasting about eighteen months. The female then goes into estrus, and for about two weeks out of every thirty-five-day cycle, she mates. Toward the end of this two week period she may ovulate, but usually the female undergoes four or five estrous cycles before she conceives. During pregnancy, she once again resumes a chaste existence. As a result, the typical female baboon is sexually active for less than 10 percent of her adult life. I thought that by focusing on the other 90 percent, I might learn something new. In particular, I suspected that routine, day-to-day relationships between males and pregnant or lactating (nonestrous) females might provide clues to female mating preferences.

Nearly every day for sixteen months, I joined the Eburru Cliffs baboons at their sleeping cliffs at dawn and traveled several miles with them while they foraged for roots, seeds, grass, and occasionally, small prey items, such as baby gazelles or hares (see "Predatory Baboons of Kekopey," *Natural History*, March 1976). Like all savanna baboon troops, Eburru Cliffs functioned as a cohesive unit organized around a core of related females, all of whom were born in the troop. Unlike the females, male savanna baboons leave their natal troop to join another where they may remain for many years, so most of the Eburru Cliffs adult males were immigrants. Since membership in the troop remained relatively constant during the period of my study, I learned to identify each individual. I relied on differences in size, posture, gait, and especially, facial features. To the practiced observer, baboons look as different from one another as human beings do.

As soon as I could recognize individuals, I noticed that particular females tended to turn up near particular males again and again. I came to think of these pairs as friends. Friendship among animals is not a well-documented phenomenon, so to convince skeptical colleagues that baboon friendship was real, I needed to develop objective criteria for distinguishing friendly pairs.

I began by investigating grooming, the amiable simian habit of picking through a companion's fur to remove dead skin and ectoparasites (see "Little Things That Tick Off Baboons," *Natural History*, February 1984). Baboons spend much more time grooming than is necessary for hygiene, and previous research had indicated that it is a good measure of social bonds. Although eighteen adult males lived in the troop, each nonestrous female performed most of her grooming with just one, two, or, occasionally, three males. For example, of Zizi's twenty-four grooming bouts with males, Cyclops accounted for thirteen, and a second male, Sherlock, accounted for all the rest. Different females tended to favor different males as grooming partners.

Another measure of social bonds was simply who was observed near whom. When foraging, traveling, or resting, each pregnant or lactating female spent a lot of time near a few males and associated with the others no more often than expected by chance. When I compared the identities of favorite grooming partners and frequent companions, they overlapped almost completely. This enabled me to develop a formal definition of friendship: any male that scored high on both grooming and proximity measures was considered a friend.

Virtually all baboons made friends; only one female and the three males who had most recently joined the troop lacked such companions. Out of more than 600 possible adult female–adult male pairs in the troop, however, only about one in ten qualified as friends; these really were special relationships.

Several factors seemed to influence which baboons paired up. In most cases, friends were unrelated to each other, since the male had immigrated from another troop. (Four friendships, however, involved a female and an adolescent son who had not yet emigrated. Unlike other friends, these related pairs never mated.) Older females tended to be friends with older males; younger females with younger males. I witnessed occasional May–December romances, usually involving older females and young adult males. Adolescent males and females were strongly rule-bound, and with the exception of mother–son pairs, they formed friendships only with one another.

Regardless of age or dominance rank, most females had just one or two male friends. But among males, the number of female friends varied greatly from none to eight. Although high-ranking males enjoyed priority of access to food and sometimes mates, dominant males did not have more female friends than low-ranking males. Instead it was the older males who had lived in the troop for many years who had the most friends. When a male had several female friends, the females were often closely related to one another. Since female baboons spend a lot of time near their kin, it is probably easier for a male to maintain bonds with several related females at once.

When collecting data, I focused on one nonestrous female at a time and kept track of her every movement toward or away from any male; similarly, I noted every male who moved toward or away from her. Whenever the female and a male moved close enough to exchange intimacies, I wrote down exactly what happened. When foraging together, friends tended to remain a few yards apart. Males more often wandered away from females than the reverse, and females, more often than males, closed the gap. The female behaved as if she wanted to keep the male within calling distance, in case she needed his protection. The male, however, was more likely to make approaches that brought them within actual touching distance. Often, he would plunk himself down right next to his friend and ask her to groom him by holding a pose with exaggerated stillness. The female sometimes responded by groom-

At nine months or so, young baboons often begin seeking out their male friends whenever their mothers are not around. Here a young baboon hitches a ride on the back of his adult male friend.

Photo reprinted by permission from Irven DeVore/Anthro-Photo.

ing, but more often, she exhibited the most reliable sign of true intimacy: she ignored her friend and simply continued whatever she was doing.

In sharp contrast, when a male who was not a friend moved close to a female, she dared not ignore him. She stopped whatever she was doing and held still, often glancing surreptitiously at the intruder. If he did not move away, she sometimes lifted her tail and presented her rump. When a female is not in estrus, this is a gesture of appeasement, not sexual enticement. Immediately after this respectful acknowledgment of his presence, the female would slip away. But such tense interactions with nonfriend males were rare, because females usually moved away before the males came too close.

These observations suggest that females were afraid of most of the males in their troop, which is not surprising: male baboons are twice the size of females, and their canines are longer and sharper than those of a lion. All Eburru Cliffs males directed both mild and severe aggression toward females. Mild aggression, which usually involved threats and chases but no body contact, occurred most often during feeding competition or when the male redirected aggression toward a female after losing a fight with another male. Females and juveniles showed aggression toward other females and juveniles in similar circumstances and occasionally inflicted superficial wounds. Severe aggression by males, which involved body contact and sometimes biting, was less common and also more puzzling, since there was no apparent cause.

An explanation for at least some of these attacks emerged one day when I was watching Pegasus, a young adult male, and his friend Cicily, sitting together in the middle of a small clearing. Cicily moved to the edge of the clearing to feed, and a higher-ranking female, Zora, suddenly attacked her. Pegasus stood up and looked as if he were about to intervene when both females disappeared into the bushes. He sat back down, and I remained with him. A full ten minutes later, Zora appeared at the edge of the clearing; this was the first time she had come into view since her attack on Cicily. Pegasus instantly pounced on Zora, repeatedly grabbed her neck in his mouth and lifted her off the ground, shook her whole body, and then dropped her. Zora screamed continuously and tried to escape. Each time, Pegasus caught her and continued his brutal attack. When he finally released her five minutes later she had a deep canine gash on the palm of her hand that made her limp for several days.

This attack was similar in form and intensity to those I had seen before and labeled "unprovoked."

Certainly, had I come upon the scene after Zora's aggression toward Cicily, I would not have understood why Pegasus attacked Zora. This suggested that some, perhaps many, severe attacks by males actually represented punishment for actions that had occurred some time before.

Whatever the reasons for male attacks on females, they represent a serious threat. Records of fresh injuries indicated that Eburru Cliffs adult females received canine slash wounds from males at the rate of one for every female each year, and during my study, one female died of her injuries. Males probably pose an even greater threat to infants. Although only one infant was killed during my study, observers in Botswana and Tanzania have seen recent male immigrants kill several young infants.

Protection from male aggression, and from the less injurious but more frequent aggression of other females and juveniles, seems to be one of the main advantages of friendship for a female baboon. Seventy times I observed an adult male defend a female or her offspring against aggression by another troop member, not infrequently a high-ranking male. In all but six of these cases, the defender was a friend. Very few of these confrontations involved actual fighting, no male baboon, subordinate or dominant, is anxious to risk injury by the sharp canines of another.

Males are particularly solicitous guardians of their friends' youngest infants. If another male gets too close to an infant or if a juvenile female plays with it too roughly, the friend may intervene. Other troop members soon learn to be cautious when the mother's friend is nearby, and his presence provides the mother with a welcome respite from the annoying pokes and prods of curious females and juveniles obsessed with the new baby. Male baboons at Gombe Park in Tanzania and Amboseli Park in Kenya have also been seen rescuing infants from chimpanzees and lions. These several forms of male protection help to explain why females in Eburru Cliffs stuck closer to their friends in the first few months after giving birth than at any other time.

The male–infant relationship develops out of the male's friendship with the mother, but as the infant matures, this new bond takes on a life of its own. My coworker Nancy Nicolson found that by about nine months of age, infants actively sought out their male friends when the mother was a few yards away, suggesting that the male may function as an alternative caregiver. This seemed to be especially true for infants undergoing unusually early or severe weaning. (Weaning is generally a gradual, prolonged process, but there is tremendous variation among mothers in the timing and intensity of weaning. See "Mother Baboons," *Natural History*, September 1980.)

After being rejected by the mother, the crying infant often approached the male friend and sat huddled against him until its whimpers subsided. Two of the infants in Eburru Cliffs lost their mothers when they were still quite young. In each case, their bond with the mother's friend subsequently intensified, and—perhaps as a result—both infants survived.

A close bond with a male may also improve the infant's nutrition. Larger than all other troop members, adult males monopolize the best feeding sites. In general, the personal space surrounding a feeding male is inviolate, but he usually tolerates intrusions by the infants of his female friends, giving them access to choice feeding spots.

Although infants follow their male friends around rather than the reverse, the males seem genuinely attached to their tiny companions. During feeding, the male and infant express their pleasure in each other's company by sharing spirited, antiphonal grunting duets. If the infant whimpers in distress, the male friend is likely to cease feeding, look at the infant, and grunt softly, as if in sympathy, until the whimpers cease. When the male rests, the infants of his female friends may huddle behind him, one after the other, forming a "train," or, if feeling energetic, they may use his body as a trampoline.

When I returned to Eburru Cliffs four years after my initial study ended, several of the bonds formed between males and the infants of their female friends were still intact (in other cases, either the male or the infant or both had disappeared). When these bonds involved recently matured females, their long-time male associates showed no sexual interest in them, even though the females mated with other adult males. Mothers and sons, and usually maternal siblings, show similar sexual inhibitions in baboons and many other primate species.

The development of an intimate relationship between a male and the infant of his female friend raises an obvious question: Is the male the infant's father? To answer this question definitely we would need to conduct genetic analysis, which was not possible for these baboons. Instead, I estimated paternity probabilities from observations of the temporary (a few hours or days) exclusive mating relationships, or consortships, that estrous females form with a series of different males. These estimates were apt to be fairly accurate, since changes in the female's sexual swelling allow one to pinpoint the timing of conception to within a few days. Most females consorted with only two or three males during this period, and these males were termed likely fathers.

In about half the friendships, the male was indeed likely to be the father of his friend's most recent infant, but in the other half he was not—in fact, he had never been seen mating with the female. Interestingly, males who were friends with the mother but not likely fathers nearly always developed a relationship with her infant, while males who had mated with the female but were not her friend usually did not. Thus friendship with the mother, rather than paternity, seems to mediate the development of male–infant bonds. Recently, a similar pattern was documented for South American capuchin monkeys in a laboratory study in which paternity was determined genetically.

These results fly in the face of a prominent theory that claims males will invest in infants only when they are closely related. If males are not fostering the survival of their own genes by caring for the infant, then why do they do so? I suspected that the key was female choice. If females preferred to mate with males who had already demonstrated friendly behavior, then friendships with mothers and their infants might pay off in the future when the mothers were ready to mate again.

To find out if this was the case, I examined each male's sexual behavior with females he had befriended before they resumed estrus. In most cases, males consorted considerably more often with their friends than with other females. Baboon females typically mate with several different males, including both friends and nonfriends, but prior friendship increased a male's probability of mating with a female above what it would have been otherwise.

This increased probability seemed to reflect female preferences. Females occasionally overtly advertised their disdain for certain males and their desire for others. Zizi's behavior, described [earlier], is a good example. Virgil was not one of her friends, but Cyclops was. Usually, however, females expressed preferences and aversions more subtly. For example, Delphi, a petite adolescent female, found herself pursued by Hector, a middle-aged adult male. She did not run away or refuse to mate with him, but whenever he wasn't watching, she looked around for her friend Homer, an adolescent male. When she succeeded in catching Homer's eye, she narrowed her eyes and flattened her ears against her skull, the friendliest face one baboon can send another. This told Homer she would rather be with him. Females expressed satisfaction with a current consort partner by staying close to him, initiating copulations, and not making advances toward other males. Baboons are very sensitive to such cues, as indicated by an experimental study in which rival hamadryas baboons rarely challenged a male–female pair if the female strongly preferred her current partner. Similarly, in Eburru Cliffs, males were less apt to

challenge consorts involving a pair that shared a long-term friendship.

Even though females usually consorted with their friends, they also mated with other males, so it is not surprising that friendships were most vulnerable during periods of sexual activity. In a few cases, the female consorted with another male more often than with her friend, but the friendship survived nevertheless. One female, however, formed a strong sexual bond with a new male. This bond persisted after conception, replacing her previous friendship. My observations suggest that adolescent and young adult females tend to have shorter, less stable friendships than do older females. Some friendships, however, last a very long time. When I returned to Eburru Cliffs six years after my study began, five couples were still together. It is possible that friendships occasionally last for life (baboons probably live twenty to thirty years in the wild), but it will require longer studies, and some very patient scientists, to find out.

By increasing both the male's chances of mating in the future and the likelihood that a female's infant will survive, friendship contributes to the reproductive success of both partners. This clarifies the evolutionary basis of friendship-forming tendencies in baboons, but what does friendship mean to a baboon? To answer this question we need to view baboons as sentient beings with feelings and goals not unlike our own in similar circumstances. Consider, for example, the friendship between Thalia and Alexander.

The affair began one evening as Alex and Thalia sat about fifteen feet apart on the sleeping cliffs. It was like watching two novices in a singles bar. Alex stared at Thalia until she turned and almost caught him looking at her. He glanced away immediately, and then she stared at him until his head began to turn toward her. She suddenly became engrossed in grooming her toes. But as soon as Alex looked away, her gaze returned to him. They went on like this for more than fifteen minutes, always with split-second timing. Finally, Alex managed to catch Thalia looking at him. He made the friendly eyes-narrowed, ears-back face and smacked his lips together rhythmically. Thalia froze, and for a second she looked into his eyes. Alex approached, and Thalia, still nervous, groomed him. Soon she calmed down, and I found them still together on the cliffs the next morning. Looking back on this event months later, I realized that it marked the beginning of their friendship. Six years later, when I returned to Eburru Cliffs, they were still friends.

If flirtation forms an integral part of baboon friendship, so does jealousy. Overt displays of jealousy, such as chasing a friend away from a potential rival, occur occasionally, but like humans, baboons often express their emotions in more subtle ways. One evening a colleague and I climbed the cliffs and settled down near Sherlock, who was friends with Cybelle, a middle-aged female still foraging on the ground below the cliffs. I observed Cybelle while my colleague watched Sherlock, and we kept up a running commentary. As long as Cybelle was feeding or interacting with females, Sherlock was relaxed, but each time she approached another male, his body would stiffen, and he would stare intently at the scene below. When Cybelle presented politely to a male who had recently tried to befriend her, Sherlock even made threatening sounds under his breath. Cybelle was not in estrus at the time, indicating that male baboon jealousy extends beyond the sexual arena to include affiliative interactions between a female friend and other males.

Because baboon friendships are embedded in a network of friendly and antagonistic relationships, they inevitably lead to repercussions extending beyond the pair, For example, Virgil once provoked his weaker rival Cyclops into a fight by first attacking Cyclops's friend Phoebe. On another occasion, Sherlock chased Circe, Hector's best friend, just after Hector had chased Antigone, Sherlock's friend.

In another incident, the prime adult male Triton challenged Cyclops's possession of meat. Cyclops grew increasingly tense and seemed about to abandon the prey to the younger male. Then Cyclops's friend Phoebe appeared with her infant Phyllis. Phyllis wandered over to Cyclops. He immediately grabbed her, held her close, and threatened Triton away from the prey. Because any challenge to Cyclops now involved a threat to Phyllis as well, Triton risked being mobbed by Phoebe and her relatives and friends. For this reason, he backed down. Males frequently use the infants of their female friends as buffers in this way. Thus, friendship involves costs as well as benefits because it makes the participants vulnerable to social manipulation or redirected aggression by others.

Finally, as with humans, friendship seems to mean something different to each baboon. Several females in Eburru Cliffs had only one friend. They were devoted companions. Louise and Pandora, for example, groomed their friend Virgil and no other male. Then there was Leda, who, with five friends, spread herself more thinly than any other female. These contrasting patterns of friendship were associated with striking personality differences. Louise and Pandora were unobtrusive females who hung around quietly with Virgil and their close relatives. Leda seemed to be everywhere at once, playing with infants, fighting with juveniles, and making friends with males. Similar differences were apparent among the males. Some devoted a great deal of time and energy to cultivating friendships with females, while others focused more on challenging other males. Although we probably will never fully understand the basis of these individual differences, they contribute immeasurably to the richness and complexity of baboon society.

Male–female friendships may be widespread among primates. They have been reported for many other groups of savanna baboons, and they also occur in rhesus and Japanese macaques, capuchin monkeys, and perhaps in bonobos (pygmy chimpanzees). These relationships should give us pause when considering popular scenarios for the evolution of male–female relationships in humans. Most of these scenarios assume that, except for mating, males and females had little to do with one another until the development of a sexual division of labor, when, the story goes, females began to rely on males to provide meat in exchange for gathered food. This, it has been argued, set up new selection pressures favoring the development of long-term bonds between individual males and females, female sexual fidelity, and, as paternity certainty increased, greater male investment in the offspring of these unions. In other words, once women began to gather and men to hunt, presto—we had the nuclear family.

This scenario may have more to do with cultural biases about women's economic dependence on men and idealized views of the nuclear family than with the actual behavior of our hominid ancestors. The nonhuman primate evidence challenges this story in at least three ways.

First, long-term bonds between the sexes can evolve in the absence of a sexual division of labor or food sharing. In our primate relatives, such relationships rest on exchanges of social, not economic, benefits.

Second, primate research shows that highly differentiated, emotionally intense male–female relationships can occur without sexual exclusivity. Ancestral men and women may have experienced intimate friendships long before they invented marriage and norms of sexual fidelity.

Third, among our closest primate relatives, males clearly provide mothers and infants with social benefits even when they are unlikely to be the fathers of those infants. In return, females provide a variety of benefits to the friendly males, including acceptance into the group and, at least in baboons, increased mating opportunities in the future. This suggests that efforts to reconstruct the evolution of hominid societies may have overemphasized what the female must supposedly do (restrict her mating to just one male) in order to obtain male parental investment.

Maybe it is time to pay more attention to what the male must do (provide benefits to females and young) in order to obtain female cooperation. Perhaps among our ancestors, as in baboons today, sex and friendship went hand in hand. As for marriage—well, that's another story.

Games Primates Play

Can apes deceive with intent—can they lie, and know they're lying?
And can you know it, too?

In the movie *Liar Liar,* Jim Carrey plays Fletcher Reede, a man who lives in a world of lies. He lies not only as a lawyer but as a parent, fabricating excuses to his son Max for why he was late or why he broke a promise. Max makes a wish that his father will, just once, spend a day telling the truth. The wish comes true, with calamitous results: Fletcher calls his law partners buffoons, gets in trouble with a police officer who has pulled him over, and ultimately so exasperates his ex-wife that she decides to remarry and leave town with Max.

Fletcher Reede's predicament is funny because we all understand what it is like to distort the truth, and we appreciate how challenging life would be if we simply said whatever we thought. We have the mental tools not only to think about our own beliefs but also to recognize what others are likely to believe, and maneuver in such a way that we can, if we are devious enough, alter the beliefs of our friends and enemies. This capacity derives from our social brain and its exquisite mental circuitry. When that circuitry is damaged, the effects can be devastating psychological problems. Patients with autism, for example, often experience a form of "mindblindness," an inability to read from behavior what others feel, want, and believe.

Are normal human adults unique in their capacity to read others' minds? Are we the only animals that can lie? To be honest, we don't yet know—but given the battle to survive and reproduce, we should not be surprised to discover that through natural selection other animals have evolved strategies to dupe opponents and reap the rewards of competitive struggle. The challenge faced by researchers interested in the question of nonhuman deception is to distinguish between the con artists and the true masters, between those who look as if they are aware of how the process works and those who really do know.

Imagine that you're walking along the beach. All of a sudden you see a plover—a common shorebird—swoop toward you, dive, and spin around on the ground as if her wings were injured. Interested, you approach with caution. As you near, she flies away. She has captured your attention, caused you to stray from your path, and lured you away from the eggs you were inadvertently heading toward. You have been deceived.

The plover is not injured. She faked it. She carries out—and modifies—her charade only when there is an interested audience, someone who looks as if he might poach her eggs. As psychologist Carolyn Ristau of Rockefeller University has documented, if the potential predator approaches but looks away from the nest, the plover will most likely sit still. But if the predator approaches with eyes directed toward the nest, then the injury-feigning display begins in full. The plover appears sensitive to the predator's behavior and has, at her wing tips, a suite of staged moves to pull off the bluff.

Is the plover aware of her deception? Does she understand why the deception works and what might cause it to fail? If so, then she should be able to apply this knowledge to any situation—not just to a threatening predator. Does she understand that the display is relatively ineffective with a predator who has already detected the nest? More generally, does the Plover realize that lying works only when the audience is unaware of her intentions? Unfortunately, we don't have answers to these questions. We lack evidence that plovers use their capacity to deceive in contexts other than predator threat.

If not birds, then, how about our more closely related fellow primates? Over the past decade or so, primatologists have collected many examples of putative deception, cases in which an ape or monkey actively falsifies information or withholds it. And unlike the plover, they do not seem to restrict the practice to a single context. Andrew Whiten and Richard Byrne of the University of St. Andrews in Scotland have written that cases of tactical deception imply that monkeys and apes are Machiavellian, strategizing day and night in the hope of gaining an advantage within their social group. A typical scenario might go like this: one chimp, seeing a second chimp approach, hides some food. The second chimp, apparently taken in, ambles off but then hides behind a tree, only to rush in and snatch the food when the first chimp retrieves his stash. Here's another surprising scenario: a subordinate male chimp, aroused by an off-limits female, shields his erect penis from the view of the dominant male.

If one were to accept these observations at face value, one would be compelled to draw two conclusions: first, that some nonhuman primates actively deceive their colleagues, and second, that they know not only how to deceive but also that they are deceiving. They appear to know about their own beliefs and about what others believe, and they know that if they act just so, they can alter another's beliefs.

Paradoxically, though, experimental evidence doesn't support this inference. Rather it suggests, even more oddly perhaps, that the chimps' Machiavellian moves reflect that while they know how to deceive, they do not know that they are doing so. To understand the problem, it's helpful to explore how we humans acquire a system of beliefs and desires, a system of representation that University of Pennsylvania psychologist David Premack has called a theory of mind.

By the age of three, children look where others are looking and know, to some extent, that where someone is looking is relevant to what that individual knows. They can engage in pretend play and understand some of the relevant differences between living and nonliving objects. But though relatively sophisticated, these children lack an understanding of what others believe and why. Consider the following example: A child watches a puppet show involving two characters, Sally and Anne. After playing with a ball, Sally places it inside a basket and then steps outside. During Sally's absence, Anne takes the ball out of the basket and places it inside a box. Sally returns. When children are asked "Where will Sally search for the ball?" four-year-olds say, "The basket," realizing that Sally holds the (false) belief that the ball is where she left it. In contrast, three-year-olds—and most autistic children—say, "The box." They assume that others know what they know. They ignore a crucial parameter: what another individual sees largely determines what he or she knows. They don't seem to understand the notion of a false belief. Consequently, their lying skills are not quite up to par with an adult's.

Premack was the first to use laboratory experiments to explore the question of whether chimpanzees can deceive by manipulating the beliefs of others. His original experiment, carried out in the mid-1970s in collaboration with the psychologist Guy Woodruff, was designed to assess whether chimpanzees could point out the location of hidden food to a cooperative human trainer who always shared the food, but withhold such information from a mean, uncooperative trainer who simply ate the food once its location was revealed. Following more than 100 training trials, three of the four chimps indicated the food's location to both trainers, thereby obviously failing to "lie" by means of withholding information. The fourth chimp, after more than 25 trials, began indicating the food's location to the cooperative trainer and withholding that information from the uncooperative trainer. A second phase, carried out six months later, elicited slightly higher success: two chimps not only suppressed the knowledge of the food's location but indicated the wrong location. This apparent "lie" emerged only after several hundred trials of pointing out the food stash to the uncooperative trainer.

The third phase included a role reversal; the chimps were to follow the trainer's indication about the food's location. At first, no distinction was made between the cooperative and the uncooperative trainer. After approximately 40 trials, one chimp figured out that the uncooperative trainer provided misleading information. One chimp never worked it out and the other two required approximately 150 trials. When the same test was administered ten months later, all the subjects improved: they either indicated the food's location to, or followed instructions from, the cooperative trainer and misled or withheld information from the uncooperative trainer. Clearly the chimpanzees had learned something. But what?

Premack and Woodruff's experiment followed a classic design in the study of animal learning. It required an initial training phase, in which the chimpanzees learned to indicate food location, followed by a critical transfer test. But there is a problem. Because there are only two choices in the test (indicating the empty or full food container), the probability of a correct hit by pure chance is high. More disconcerting is that a failure on the first trial could readily lead to success on all subsequent trials, but not because the subject understands the problem. It could be that after failing to get food on the first trial—despite indicating its correct location—the subject simply selects the alternative on all subsequent trials. The subject could, for example, point to the empty container instead of the full one after the uncooperative trainer fails to share food on the first trial. Even in the final phase of Premack and Woodruff's experiment, which took place after two years of training, the chimpanzees required several trials before making the appropriate moves. They clearly learned to discriminate between the two trainers, but as Premack has remarked, we lack strong evidence of intentional deception.

Since Premack's landmark work, experimental studies have focused more on the building blocks of a theory of mind rather than on primate deception per se. One of the more active areas concerns the distinction between seeing and knowing. Do monkeys and apes understand that what an individual sees determines a great deal of what it can know? Whiten and Byrne's catalog of primate deception suggests that they do. Experimental work by Daniel Povinelli, an anthropologist at the New Iberia Research Center in Louisiana, suggests that they don't.

Povinelli trained young chimpanzees to reach through a hole in a clear plastic partition and beg for food from a caretaker who faced them. Subsequent test trials involved two caretakers: one who could see the chimp and another who could not, either because his back was turned or because his sight was blocked by a scarf, bag, or screen. Surprisingly, the chimp showed no preference for begging from the caretaker who could see. Monkeys, too, failed when tested under similar circumstances. We can therefore conclude that nonhuman primates do not make the connection between what others see and what they know. They are con artists, knowing how to deceive without knowing that they are deceiving.

Yet understanding point of view and its relevance to false beliefs may depend on how the question is explored. In human experiments, developmental psychologists Wendy Clements and Josef Perner of the University of Sussex discovered an intriguing twist in an experimental design that closely resembled the Sally–Anne test. When asked where Sally will search for the ball, they found, three-year-olds will first look at the basket but then answer, "The box." Somewhere along the path from looking to speaking, there is a computational error. According to Clements and Perner, it may well be that early in development the child generates appropriate expectations but cannot form a judgment about another's behavior from those expectations. In one sense, she is mind blind. It is not until the age of about four that children acquire a more explicit grasp of what others believe and how their own beliefs may differ. Clements and Perner's study demonstrates that some kinds of knowledge can be investigated in the absence of language. We can use patterns of looking as a passport into the minds of young children.

Might the same be true of other primates? Might visual attention reveal a level of understanding that differs from responses such as reaching, pointing, or touching? To explore this question, my students and I have been using a bit of methodological magic, a technique known by those in the trade as the expectancy violation procedure. In short, magic captures our visual attention because it violates our expectations (we don't expect rabbits to pop out of hats). And since expectations are derived from knowledge—from a set of beliefs about the world—we can discover what an individual expects by tracking visual attention. Events that are consistent with the way the world works don't hold our interest. But violations should grab the attention of any organism willing to watch.

We used this procedure on a captive colony of cotton-top tamarins, small New World primates that are native to the rain forests of Colombia. The test, run in collaboration with my graduate student Laurie Santos, is a nonlinguistic version of the Sally–Anne false belief problem. A tamarin watches as a man (call him Joe) enters a room. Joe sits down, eats some apple, hands the tamarin a piece, and then places the remaining apple in one of two opaque boxes on a table. Joe leaves the room while an experimenter removes the apple from box 1 and places it in box 2. If the tamarins understand another's visual perspective, then when Joe returns, they should expect him to search in box 1. Just like Sally, Joe holds a false belief: he thinks the apple is still in the box he put it in. For Joe to search in box 2 is unexpected and should cause the tamarins to look longer.

The tamarins might, of course, look longer simply because Joe is moving toward the apple, something that tamarins are equally interested in. To control for this possibility, we ran a second version, identical to the first except that Joe stayed in the room and watched the experimenter transfer the apple. Here the tamarins should be surprised to see Joe search in box 1 because he witnessed the transfer to box 2.

Consistently, the tamarins looked longer during the unexpected events. They seemed to expect Joe to search for the apple on the basis of his knowledge.

These new findings must be treated cautiously because they have yet to be replicated. Still, they raise several provocative questions. Do the tamarins succeed on this task because they understand false beliefs? If so, might other animals, including newborn human infants and autistic children, pass tests? Might chimpanzees?

We don't know the answers yet. But given the field's scientific infancy, that is more a cause for hope than pessimism. It's possible that the expectancy violation procedure is a more sensitive measure of what an organism knows than other tests. But knowing in what sense? Perhaps the tamarins' understanding of false beliefs—if they indeed have such an understanding—is like that of three-year-old children. Perhaps the tamarins, and other species as well, are able to make predictions about actions without really grasping the reason for such predictions. Perhaps monkeys and apes know how to act given certain pieces of information but don't know that such actions are based on a set of beliefs.

Nature leaves us with a wonderful puzzle. Animals of all kinds deceive. Predatory fireflies lure prey by mimicking their mating signals; molting (and thus defenseless) mantis shrimp bluff intruders with aggressive displays; female plovers feign injury to draw predators away from their young. But during the course of evolution, some organisms acquired an understanding that they are deceiving. This event represented a renaissance in thinking, an awakening of mind. It allowed not only for true Machiavellian deception but also for self-reflection, an understanding of mortality, and an appreciation for how and why belief systems diverge and converge. We humans are unquestionably part of this renaissance. But we have yet to determine when or how it started—or why.

Boyce Rensberger

On Becoming Human

Edward O. Wilson has a theory about what makes people act the way they do. He thinks that broad categories of human behavior—things such as male dominance, incest taboos, and other patterns perpetuated by tradition and cultural practice—are not merely cultural inventions. Instead Wilson believes that social behaviors like these are under a degree of genetic control built into the brain. He thinks these behaviors have been shaped by a special kind of evolution in which genes and culture—the forces of nature *and* nurture—worked together.

But in the two years that Wilson has been promoting his provocative theory, he has learned that many humans find it hard to accept the idea of any genetic control of their behavior. So he likes to explain his theory by taking people on an imaginary trip to another galaxy. There he shows them two species of intelligent beings—the Eidylons and the Xenidrins, who represent extreme examples of the two possible ways of explaining the forces that might govern human behavior.

Eidylons and Xenidrins both look rather human, but they differ in one respect. The Eidylons (Greek for "skilled ones") behave strictly according to genetic control. The Xenidrins (from the Greek for "strangers") act only according to cultural influence.

Eidylons are as intelligent as Earthlings, but they can respond only one way to a given set of circumstances. During embryonic development Eidylon genes build brains that are "hard wired" and thus capable of learning only one set of social behaviors. All Eidylon societies have the same political and economic systems. Details of language, art, and other elements of their cultures may vary, but the basic structures are unchangeable. At Eidylon festivals ritual hymns stir feelings of deep pleasure in the audience, but the music is always the same, note for note. Eidylons teach and learn all that they know, but they are capable of learning only one thing in each category—one language, one creation myth, one courtship ritual. Like the white-crowned sparrows of California, they must hear the song of their species in order to learn it, but it is the only song they can learn.

At the opposite end of the spectrum are the Xenidrins, who are born with minds that are truly blank slates. Their every behavior is shaped by their culture. Like Eidylons, they must be taught in order to learn, but they can learn any form of behavior. In some Xenidrin societies the culture leads men to dominate women, but in as many others the culture leads women to dominate men. Some prohibit incest; others encourage it. Smiles are not the universal language among the Xenidrins; in some Xenidrin cultures the tradition is instead to wrinkle the nose or shake the head.

If Earthlings were guided entirely, or predominantly, by culture, as social scientists often hold, a survey of Earthling societies ought to reveal a species something like the Xenidrins. Or, if human behavior were entirely genetic in control, it ought to resemble that of the Eidylons.

Not even Wilson suggests that humans are genetic automatons like the Eidylons. But he does propose that it is time to move away from the opposite bias, one that had its origin decades ago as a reaction to another, more objectionable brand of genetic determinism. Early in this century many biologists went to extremes in proclaiming that genes governed not only anatomy but behavior. Their views quickly developed into the eugenics movement, which sought to improve humanity by eliminating genetically "inferior" peoples.

Recoiling from this, top anthropologists such as Franz Boas and Alfred Kroeber denied any effect of genes on behavior. For evidence Boas sent his student Margaret Mead to Samoa to find a culture lacking the stressful adolescence that eugenicists said was innate. She found it, and her controversial book, *Coming of Age in Samoa*, was seen as proof of cultural determinism. Between anthropology and biology Kroeber proclaimed an "eternal chasm."

When the eugenics movement faded, partly because of the rise of cultural determinism and partly because extremist eugenics turned into virulent racism, biologists largely withdrew from questions of human behavior. But the issue never quite died within the social sciences. As the influence of Boas and Kroeber began to decline in the 1930s and '40s, some social scientists adopted more moderate stands, sometimes embracing a degree of genetic influence.

Not until Wilson, a shy and mild mannered Harvard professor who specialized in insect societies, took up the question in his epochal 1975 book, *Sociobiology,* did biologists reenter the debate in large numbers. Some did so with vehement opposition, asserting that sociobiology was only the racist ghost of the eugenics movement. In 1978, for example, when Wilson started to address a packed scientific meeting, demonstrators rushed the dais shouting "Nazi!" "Racist!" "Fascist!" and dumped a pitcher of water on the startled man's head. Wilson, hobbled by a broken foot at the time, could do little more than wipe his face, dry his glasses, and, after accepting a standing ovation from the audience, continue his paper.

Beyond invoking a degree of genetic influence over behavior, Wilson's theories have little in common with the eugenics movement. Specifically, Wilson contends that the genes construct a brain organized in such a manner that it processes certain kinds of information and certain kinds of thoughts more readily in one way than another. When an individual is faced with a choice (and is preparing to exercise willful control of behavior), the biological properties of the brain will make it more likely—though not inevitable—for one alternative to be favored.

Wilson can talk for hours about these ideas, citing evidence from this anthropologist's study or that psychologist's findings, conducting the kind of interdisciplinary tour de force that made *Sociobiology* command such respect. That book's last chapter—the only part that dealt with human beings rather than animals—triggered a major furor, monopolizing academic conferences for years in anthropology, psychology, sociology, and other social and behavioral sciences. Although some specialists in each field championed sociobiology as applied to humans, the reaction was largely critical.

Wilson pressed on anyway and, two years ago, published an obtuse, math-laden book, *Genes, Mind, and Culture,* arguing that human social behaviors arose as the result of a special evolutionary process in which genetic evolution—specifically that affecting the brain—is yoked in a feedback loop with cultural evolution. Human genes and human culture, Wilson claimed along with coauthor Charles J. Lumsden, have been irrevocably tied for many thousands of years. They called their hypothesis gene–culture coevolution. It is high time, the pair said, to alloy the social sciences and biology into a new, Darwinized human science.

That was two years ago, and although many social scientists still scoff, more than a few anthropologists and psychologists have rallied to the new view.

A small but growing number consider Wilson a seminal thinker, the catalyst of a paradigm shift that could someday unify the social sciences and the natural sciences. Major centers of sociobiologically oriented social science have grown up not only at Harvard but at the University of Michigan, Northwestern University, and University of Washington.

Now Wilson and Lumsden have a new book, mercifully free of mathematics, and it takes their case even further. They suggest that genetic evolution and cultural evolution became locked onto one another perhaps a couple of million years ago, each fueling the other and igniting a "Promethean fire" (the new book's title) that drove the evolutionary growth of the mind at a pace unprecedented for any other organ. Gene–culture coevolution, they say, is what made the modern human mind and the culture to which it is bound.

If *Promethean Fire* creates as much of a stir as have Wilson's earlier books, it will not be because of the theory; that was already set forth in more scientific trappings two years ago. It will be because Wilson now asserts that a biologically based human science promises to yield new methods by which society can consciously redesign human nature. Wilson does not shrink from advocating what he calls social engineering. In other words, he thinks society may someday decide, for example, that people are too aggressive and that subsequent generations ought to be made less aggressive. It might be done, Wilson feels, by altering the environmental factors with which the child's genes interact to produce an adult with a fully developed human nature.

"One result of a strong human science," Wilson points out in *Promethean Fire,* "might be the creation of a sophisticated form of social engineering, one that touches the deepest levels of human motivation and moral reasoning."

David Barash winced and then rolled his eyes to the ceiling when he heard that quote. "I admire Ed a lot," he allowed. I think he's going to be remembered as one of the most important thinkers in biology, but I wish he wouldn't say things like that." Barash is a University of Washington sociobiologist and one of the top researchers in the field. He is one of Wilson's strongest scientific allies and, in fact, is asked so often to lecture in place of the almost Darwinishly reclusive Wilson that Barash says he's getting tired of being "Ed's West Coast Huxley."

Talk of social engineering, Barash says, is much too premature and, in any case, leads to such negative connotations for most people that they are inclined to reject sociobiology altogether. That, to Wilson, would be unthinkable, given what we now know. "Nobody," he says, "can deny biology any more." He holds that anthropological and psychological studies provide evidence of a deeply seated human nature shared by all peoples.

One of the more obvious, if trivial, examples of a genetic constraint on behavior has to do with the words people use to name colors. Physicists know that the colors of visible light form a continuous spectrum. Yet a study of 20 societies around the world found that practically all perceive a spectrum as composed mainly of discrete color categories. Most recognize four basic ones: red, yellow, green, and blue. "This beautiful illusion," Wilson says, "is genetically programmed into the visual apparatus and brain." It turns out that the eye's retina has nerve endings that are especially sensitive to the wavelengths of light approximating three of these basic colors. Superficially, cultures may have different names for, say, blue, but people everywhere have evolved a nervous system that is particularly sensitive to light with a wavelength of 440 nanometers. The genes, then, *do* influence human color vocabularies, which are a simple kind of behavior.

Facial expressions appear to reflect another form of genetic control. Photographs of Americans acting out anger, surprise, loathing, happiness, and fear were correctly described by New Guinea tribesmen. Pictures of the tribesmen registering the same emotions in their own way were, likewise, immediately recognized by Americans. Support for the idea that the brain is genetically programmed to recognize facial expressions has come from study of a rare brain disorder called prosopagnosia. It is caused by lesions in particular regions of the brain and leaves the victim unable to recognize other people by their faces. Sufferers can still recognize nonracial images but must learn to differentiate people by their voices.

Still another kind of evidence that Wilson cites involves phobias, the unreasoning fears of specific things that, in extreme cases, can incapacitate sufferers with reactions of the autonomic nervous system such as nausea and cold sweat. Wilson observes that phobic reactions are most easily evoked by many of the great dangers that early humans would have faced—heights, thunderstorms, snakes, spiders. If phobias were the result of cultural conditioning, as is often said, why, he asks, are they rarely brought on by modern dangers such as explosives, electric sockets, and automobiles? Wilson suggests that evolution has programmed the brain to regard certain natural phenomena as dangerous and that phobias are extreme examples of this. Evolution has not had time to do the same for dangerous modern inventions.

Perhaps the most important evidence that Wilson cites involves a much more socially complex behavior—the nearly universal practice of incest avoidance. As it happens, incest avoidance has figured prominently in much social science thinking. Anthropologists such as Leslie White and Claude Lévi-Strauss have even held that the origin of an incest prohibition, usually expressed through some cultural device such as a taboo, marked the evolutionary transition of animals to humans. These authorities, like Freud and Bronislaw Malinowski half a century earlier, considered incest avoidance mechanisms to be strictly cultural inventions.

Wilson insists that its origin is genetic. For one thing, many lower animals lacking culture have behavior patterns that avoid incest. For another, inbreeding is known to increase the chances of producing defective offspring. Simple Darwinian natural selection would tend to weed out such individuals and to favor others possessing any inborn mechanism that discouraged inbreeding.

Wilson believes anthropologists have discovered the mechanism in human beings and that it illustrates the process by which genes and culture interact to produce human nature. The best evidence comes from now-classic studies of Israeli kibbutzim, communal living arrangements shared by many families. Typically, the children spend their days in one big day care center. Although the pioneers of the kibbutz movement encouraged children to marry within their own kibbutz, just the opposite has happened. According to one study of 2,769 marriages of children raised in kibbutzim, none were between men and women raised together since birth.

To Wilson this study suggests that some mechanism deeper than culture is at work. After all, the culture encouraged marriage within the kibbutz. Wilson calls the mechanism an epigenetic rule, his name for the genetically determined influence, or bias, that will be triggered by certain cultural conditions. In this case, the epigenetic rule says that children raised closely together during their earliest years will feel little or no sexual attraction toward one another when they grow up. This is the rule, Wilson says, that discourages brothers and sisters from marrying. In kibbutz conditions, where children are raised as closely as if they were siblings, the genes are, in a sense, fooled.

Confirmation of a sort has come from a study of certain Chinese families that adopted brides for their sons when both were young children. Of 19 adoptions in one village, 17 couples refused to consummate the marriage when they reached adulthood. In both consummated marriages the girls were considerably older when adopted, presumably too old to trigger the epigenetic rule.

"Sociobiology has given us the first really cogent explanation for this phenomenon of incest avoidance," says Pierre L. van den Berghe, a University of Washington sociologist. "This is a question that has obsessed lots of sociologists, anthropologists, and psychologists for over a hundred years. For me there is no question any more that we are genetically programmed to avoid inbreeding. And, through sociobiology, we can make a case that holds water scientifically. It's been a long time since any social scientist could do that."

Van den Berghe, in fact, considers sociobiology the salvation of his field. "Sociology today is very much a dead-end discipline. It isn't really a science, and it's not even a good humanity. Wilson is showing us how to get scientific, and I predict that 10 years from now it will be old hat. But right now most sociologists remain blissfully unaware of what has hit them."

When their awareness dawns, there will be work for them to do. The human mind, Wilson believes, contains epigenetic rules guiding many realms of human social behavior. He concedes that most of the rules are unknown but contends that social scientists have not been collecting the kind of data from various cultures to identify them.

Each of the epigenetic rules is presumed to be the product of neural structures. Although the nature of these structures is as yet unknown, they are assumed to have been built in each human mind, like any other brain structure, through the guidance of genes selected over eons of evolution. Wilson does not say—and this is a distinction often overlooked by critics—that the neural structures invariably produce a given behavior in all individuals or even in one individual all the time. Nor does he say that the structures prohibit the development of a culture that contradicts the genetic influence; he does say these should be rare.

Sometimes the behavioral response may be virtually inescapable, as in color naming. More often the genes only bias the choice an individual makes, rendering it more likely that one behavior will be favored over an alternative. In other words, a behavior that is genetically influenced need not be universally displayed. Couples who *wanted* to practice incest, for example, could exercise free will to override any anti-incest genes.

The first book by Lumsden and Wilson, *Genes, Mind, and Culture*, presented lots of elaborate mathematical models to demonstrate what they called the coevolutionary circuit, the central tenet of gene–culture coevolutionary theory. It is a sequence of ideas that runs as follows: The genes dictate the patterns of neural structures (and related hormonal systems). These structures impose the regularities in thinking and behavior that Wilson calls epigenetic rules.

Since the rules are shared by many minds in a society, they readily find expression in the form of cultural institutions or traditions. The coevolutionary circuit is completed when these cultural traditions act the role of the physical environment in ordinary natural selection. Just as a hard freeze favors plants with genes for cold tolerance, human cultural traditions favor individuals with genes for the right epigenetic rules.

Incest avoidance again provides an example. If an epigenetic rule is shared by many minds in a society, it may give rise to a corresponding cultural practice or tradition such as a law, taboo, or ritual. These cultural factors can be as effective in weeding out the wrong genes as would be the biological consequences of inbreeding.

The mathematical models, contributed chiefly by Lumsden, whose background is in math and the physical sciences, indicate that this cyclic feedback mechanism can start with a very small genetic bias— a weak epigenetic rule—and build it into a major cultural institution in only a few thousand years.

Because of typographical errors in the formulas as given in *Genes, Mind, and Culture*, scientists who could follow the math originally said it failed to do what the authors claimed. "Once you correct the misprints, though, there are no conceptual errors in the model," says Montgomery Slatkin, a mathematician turned evolutionary biologist at the University of Washington. "But as far as I'm concerned, you don't need the math at all. It seems to me that the issues Lumsden and Wilson are raising are self-evident."

Gene–culture coevolution, however, is decidedly *not* self-evident to most social scientists.

"Sociobiology is a cultish thing," says Marshall Sahlins, a University of Chicago anthropologist who was a leading critic when Wilson published his 1975 book. "There are so many intellectual concessions one has to make to do sociobiology, but frankly, I don't want to have any more to say about it. Journalistic hype is what keeps it alive."

More vocal in denouncing Wilson's theories is Marvin Harris of the University of Florida, a widely respected anthropologist who has written several books on his own theory of cultural origins. His theory rejects genetic causes. "No respectable anthropologist who knows anything at all about sociocultural evolution could be concerned with gene–culture coevolution," Harris says. "Don't get me wrong. I'm a great enthusiast of sociobiology applied to primates, protohumans, early hominids, and maybe even early human beings up to Neanderthal times. But that's all."

Harris holds that the major steps of human cultural evolution—such as the rise of agriculture, the origins of the state and of modern industrial systems—have all occurred too recently and too quickly for genetic evolution to have played a role. Harris accepts genes as shaping human nature up to the time of humanity's first great economic revolution, the switch from hunting and gathering to agriculture. ("Every anthropologist says there is a human nature. Nobody really has any trouble with that.") What sociobiology fails to explain, Harris says, is the revolutionary cultural changes that have taken place in the last 10,000 or so years.

"There are cultural forces around us that have accounted for these major changes," Harris says, "and gene–culture coevolution can't explain them." Harris holds that his own theory of cultural materialism can. He thinks the major transformations of human culture, as well as regional cultural practices, can be explained as adaptations to ecological and economic conditions. Societies, he says, repeat cycles of exploiting a new technology, overpopulating their land, and intensifying the use of resources to the point of ecological catastrophe, whereupon a new technology or resource is devised to start a new cycle.

Wilson has heard criticisms like this aplenty. His response is to compare the traditional intellectual approaches of natural scientists with those of social scientists.

Natural scientists tend to be reductionist, assuming that complex phenomena can be broken down into simpler components and that one must start by studying these. Only after the simple and the specific are understood does the natural scientist move on to examine the complex. The biologist who hopes to understand the human body starts by trying to figure out how cells work. If even cells are too complex, the reductionist looks to the molecules. Thus was born molecular biology. And thus, Wilson likes to think, will be born a new biologized human science.

Social scientists, on the other hand, usually abhor reductionism. The whole, they say, is often greater than the sum of its parts. Unforeseeable properties emerge when simpler components act in concert. The mind, social scientists have long held, is something more than a collection of brain cells; culture is one of the emergent properties of a collection of human minds.

"If you want to be an influential social scientist," Wilson suggests, "you must present a fully mature theoretical system. In the natural sciences that's easily dismissed, and people tend to look for the most promising seed project. Lumsden and I tried to work within the natural sciences."

"Science is the art of the soluble," he goes on, "and you have to start with simple systems. When the social scientists find somebody taking the natu-

ral science approach, many of them tend to react negatively. They say it's not really going to tell us what we want to know about the origin of political systems or the other major questions of the social sciences. So they often tend to reject the rudimentary approach of the natural sciences. The natural scientists know the value of an embryo."

Still, Wilson does concede ground. "There may be some substance to the objection that some social science questions are too complex, too technically intractable to be solved," he says. He notes that most of the behavioral examples he has studied, such as incest avoidance, involve simple two-choice alternatives. Wilson compares his situation to that of physicists who can easily calculate the forces acting between two bodies of matter but who find "many-body problems" insoluble. No physicist assumes that the forces governing many-body interactions are different from those in two-body interactions. "It could turn out that the gene–culture interactions underlying complex behavioral situations are insoluble. But I'm not ashamed to admit that. It doesn't invalidate the entire approach."

Maybe not. But some of Wilson's closest allies think it *does* mean that it is much too soon to talk about social engineering. Sociologist van den Berghe, for one, says he must part company with Wilson on this point. "Wilson is an amiable optimist. He looks only at the use of knowledge for good ends," says van den Berghe. "I'm a cynical pessimist. I'm not sure we'll ever have the knowledge to do it, but if we do, it'll be used for bad, selfish ends."

Wilson makes no specific engineering proposals beyond suggesting that modern humans carry a burden of outmoded epigenetic rules adapted to the Stone Age. He cites aggression and xenophobia. And he suggests that ways might be found to enhance traits that remain useful, such as the propensity for altruism and cooperation.

Since nobody knows the epigenetic rules for these traits, Wilson uses incest avoidance as a purely hypothetical example of how sociobiological knowledge might permit social engineering. Assume the engineer's goal is to encourage incest. Since the relevant genes cannot be identified, much less engineered, the cultural partner in the gene–culture interaction must be modified. For example, if the epigenetic rule is that people do not become sexually attracted to children with whom they grew up, the social engineer must separate siblings in infancy. Raised apart during the crucial years, a brother and sister would presumably lack an innate revulsion at the idea of incest.

"Close self-examination and planned manipulation of values can be a distasteful exercise," Wilson and Lumsden write in the final chapter of their new book. "But in a world growing steadily more complicated and dangerous, the alternatives are not promising. A society that chooses to ignore the existence of the innate epigenetic rules will nevertheless continue to navigate by them and at each moment of decision yield to their dictates by default." If society continues to live by what it considers "conscience" and "God's will," without challenging "the ancient hereditary oracle dwelling within the epigenetic rules," Wilson and Lumsden suggest, there is little chance of creating a stable and benevolent world.

"On the other hand, the deep scientific study of the epigenetic rules will call the oracle to account and translate its commands into a precise language that can be understood and debated. People who know human nature in this way are more likely to agree on universal goals within the constraints of that nature and recognize absolute ethical truths, if such can be shown to exist. And although societies cannot escape the inborn rules of epigenesis and would lose the very essence of humanness if they even came close to succeeding, they can employ knowledge of the rules to guide individual behavior and cultural evolution to the ends on which their members may someday agree."

Many scientists have pursued their work with epic visions, but few have made so bold as to put them in print in quite such terms. Fewer still have been taken as seriously as the Harvard zoologist whose first love, before he became the standard-bearer of sociobiology, was the flawlessly tuned social structure of ants.

What Do Women Want?

What does a women want? The traditional evolutionist's answer to Freud's famous query is that a woman's extensive investment in each of her children implies that she can maximize her fitness by restricting her sexual activity to one, or at most, a few high-quality males. Because acquiring resources for her offspring is of paramount importance, a woman will try to attract wealthy, high-status men who are willing and able to help her. She must be coy and choosy, limiting her attention to men who are worthy of her and emphasizing her chastity so as not to threaten the paternity confidence of her mate.

The lady has been getting more complicated of late, however. As Sarah Hrdy predicted, we now have evidence that women, like other female primates, are also competitive, randy creatures. Women have been seen competing with their rivals using both physical aggression and more subtle derogation of competitors. While they are still sometimes coy and chaste, women have also been described recently as sexy and sometimes promiscuous creatures, manipulating fatherhood by the timing of orgasm and using their sexuality to garner resources from men.

The real answer to Freud's query, of course, is that a woman wants it all: a man with the resources and inclination to invest, and with genes that make him attractive to other women so that her sons will inherit his success. Her strategies for attaining these somewhat conflicting aims, and her success in doing so, are shaped by her own resources and options and by conflicts of interest with men and other women.

I begin this article by considering women's mating preferences unconstrained by resource limitation or conflicts of interest. The literature has only recently begun to tackle the interesting problem of how women get what they want in spite of other women who want the same thing and men whose preferences differ from theirs. Most of this paper is concerned with the trade-offs engendered by these conflicts of interest.

A caveat is in order before I explore these issues. The preferences and strategies discussed here are assumed to be evolved psychological tendencies. They are not necessarily conscious strategies, nor are they necessarily desirable, except within the limited frame-work of fitness maximization. Here, as elsewhere in evolutionary anthropology, the assumption is that natural selection has favored preferences and behaviors that maximize reproductive success. There is nothing in evolutionary theory to suggest that the route to high fitness is necessarily the route to happiness, or that it forms a useful guide for living.

WHAT TYPE OF MAN DOES A WOMAN WANT?

Good Condition

Women, like men, want healthy mates. We might expect a man in good physical condition to be desirable both because he is likely to be a better provider than others and because the basis for his good health may be heritable, and hence of genetic benefit to offspring. The trouble, here as always, is how to detect an honest signal of good condition. Such a signal must be one that is not easily displayed by cheaters, either because it is sufficiently expensive that it cannot easily be faked or because failure to display it is a natural byproduct of ill health. The most intriguing example of the latter is the recent finding that women prefer males with low fluctuating asymmetry, the deviation from symmetry in bilateral features that are normally symmetrical, which is assumed to result from disruptions in development that might be caused by parasites or environmental toxins. An individual with the genetic constitution to withstand such environmental insults will show less fluctuating asymmetry, and, other things being equal, should be favored as a mate.

Gangestad, Thornhill, and Yeo measured the bilateral asymmetry in seven nonfacial features in their subjects and took photographs of the subjects' faces. Subjects with the lowest fluctuating asymmetry were judged to have the most attractive faces, especially in women's judgements of men. Men with low fluctuating asymmetry also had more sexual partners, on the average, and had their first sexual encounter at an earlier age. Although it is not yet known what facial cues women are using to assess fluctuating asymmetry, it is clear that natural selection has shaped female preferences to be acute evaluative mechanisms for good condition in a mate.

Resources

Females in a wide variety of species (insects, birds, and mammals) prefer males with resources, and the same is true for humans. Buss's cross-cultural questionnaire study of 37 societies showed that women in all of them placed a higher value on the financial prospects of a prospective mate than men did, although the actual values were not as high as might be expected. Women cross-culturally also expressed a preference for mates who had attributes likely to correlate with financial success—maturity, ambition, and industriousness. Closer questioning of an American sample showed that women prefer immediate access to resources when seeking short-term matings but place greater value on cues to future resource acquisition when evaluating long-term mates.

If women act on these stated preferences, we would expect wealthy men to have more mates, and there is ample cross-cultural evidence that they do. The importance of resources to women is apparent even in egalitarian societies such as the Ache and the Sharanahua, in which the best hunters are able to attract the most sexual partners.

The relationship between wealth and male mating success is consistent with female choice for wealthy males. However, this could also indicate differences in competitive ability among men, for a wealthy high-status man is more likely to outcompete his rivals for control over women. It is difficult to disentangle these causes of polygyny, and a discussion of this problem is beyond the scope of this paper. It seems likely, nevertheless, that female choice for wealthy, high-status males (or the choice of her kinsmen on her behalf) is an important factor in many polygynous societies. The best evidence that polygyny is a consequence of women's preferences for wealthy men is Borgerhoff Mulder's field work among the agro-pastoral Kipsigis. In a longitudinal study that followed the marriage histories of pioneers over 17 years, Borgerhoff Mulder showed that women new to the area were more likely to choose as husbands men who could offer them more land (i.e., land available to the prospective wife after division among existing wives). Total wealth (i.e., before division) was unrelated to a man's chances of getting a mate, which indicates that female choice rather than direct male competition is the key to polygamy in this society.

Status

High-status men are wealthy men in a wide range of societies, from subsistence pastoralists and agriculturists to complex stratified states. However, status may hold other attractions as well. The children of high-status men may be treated better by others and may inherit the traits that led their father to high status. A powerful, high-status man may also be more likely to protect a woman from the unwanted attentions of other men.

It is surprising, therefore, that women value indicators of status. Some of these indicators, such as large size, strength, and maturity, have ancient phylogenetic roots. Women cross-culturally prefer men who are taller and older than themselves. In our own society, tall men tend to be wealthier; the politically important "big men" in nonstate societies are sometimes described as being physically big as well. Maturity is also associated with higher status, at least in males, and this apparently translates into attractiveness in the eyes of a women. Keating manipulated various facial features, using the identification materials developed for police agencies, and found that women judge men with more mature facial features (a prominent jaw, bushy eyebrows, small eyes, and thin lips) to be both more dominant and more attractive. The female preference for testosteron associated features such as broad shoulders relative to waist and hip size is probably also related to social dominance.

Chagnon has shown the importance of status, irrespective of its associated material benefits, for the Yanomamo. In this economically egalitarian population, men who have killed enemies have both higher status and more wives. At least some of this appears to be due to the greater attractiveness as mates.

While wealth and status may be attractive to women the world over, societies differ in the ways that wealth and status are attained. The particular traits most desired by women can be expected to vary accordingly. Hill and Hurtado have shown the male hunting success is associated with fertility among forest-living Ache foragers, whereas socio-economic status, but not hunting success, is associated with fertility on the reservation. They infer from this that "Ache women have probably shifted mate choice criteria from favoring good hunters to favoring those who accumulate resources through farming and wage labor."

CONFLICTS OF INTEREST WITH OTHER WOMEN

The ideal man is worth competing for, and women may use a variety of weapons to do so. Some methods are direct, such as hitting their opponents or spreading nasty rumors about them. Others are indirect, such as enticing men with the promise of fidelity, youthful attractiveness, and sometimes dowries. What circumstances favor these different tactics?

Direct Competition

Daly and Wilson have clearly shown that same-sex homicide is overwhelmingly a male affair, as would be expected in a polygynous species in which males compete more strongly for females than vice versa. Nonetheless, women sometimes do resort to violence against other women. In a cross-cultural survey, Burbank found that female–female aggression, when it did occur, usually took place between women who were competing for the attentions of a man. Co-wives in polygynous societies are often reported to be hostile toward each other, particularly in agricultural, as opposed to pastoral, societies. Even in monogamous societies, jealousy among women can erupt into violence.

Accusations of promiscuity or infidelity are a frequent cause of female–female aggression. Campbell, who studied working-class British schoolgirls, found that 73% of her sample had been involved in at least one fight with another girl, usually involving punching, kicking, or slapping. The most frequent cause of fighting among these girls, and among the youngest of the lower-class teenage girls studied by Marsh and Paton, was defense of a girl's integrity and sexual reputation. A reputation for fidelity clearly is important to a woman who wants to secure a long-term mate, because men are often unwilling to invest in a child who is not their own. Paternity issues, such as accusations that a rival's children have been fathered by many men, are a frequent cause of fighting among women on the Venezuelan island of Margarita. Even among American college women, derogation of female competitors usually takes the form of attacking the other woman's sexual reputation.

In her British samples, Campbell found that fighting, especially among older girls and women, was sometimes provoked by jealousy over a particular romantic partner. The same was true for the adult urban Zambian women studied by Schuster, among whom the chief cause of female–female aggression was fighting over a particular man. Schuster reported fierce competition in this society for high-status men and the resources they provide; one woman's attempts to attract another's man frequently resulted in violent aggression and sometimes serious injury.

My readers may be surprised at the level of female aggression reported by these authors, but most of you probably did not come of age in the types of communities these authors studied. What circumstances, then, are likely to make fighting worth the risk? Campbell argues that competitive aggression should be favored where women are able to choose their own mates, where there is a shortage of men, and where there is high variability in male quality. High effective variance in male quality should be exacerbated in stratified societies with socially imposed monogamy; shortage of males should be most acute in the lower classes of such societies, where male homicide rates are high and more males are in prison. Perhaps, then, the large number of same-sex fights among girls in working-class urban communities is not so surprising.

Yet there are unresolved questions about this picture. Why should teenage girls be more concerned with their reputations, whereas adult women are more likely to fight about getting and keeping a particular man? And why the concern with a reputation for fidelity in societies where male investment is low? Paternal investment has been described as being low in both Zambia and Margarita. It is also typically low in poor communities within complex societies, so the same may be true of the British schoolgirls. If so, why should these young women be concerned with a reputation for fidelity? Societies with low paternal investment are generally associated with sexual freedom for women. American women who expect little paternal investment are more likely to flaunt their sexuality than are women who expect to find investing men. Shouldn't the concern with a reputation for fidelity be more acute among the latter, and lower in societies such as Zambia and Margarita, where paternal investment is low? So why are women in societies with investing males less likely to fight? Two things that merit further consideration in answering these questions are how likely women are to form sexual relationships with other women's mates, and how age changes both what a woman wants and how much paternal investment she expects.

Adult women, both in the United States and Zambia, are in competition for material resources and the men who provide them. The Zambian subelite women studied by Schuster were described as being sexually assertive. The matrilineal tradition of most Zambian tribes suggests that paternal confidence would not be high even among more traditional Zambians. The same is likely to be true in the matrifocal communities found toward the bottom of the social ladder in stratified industrial societies. A woman in such a community, therefore, could expect many direct attempts by other women to attract her mate for a short-term relationship. Such attempts would be less of a threat to women in communities where male investment is high and women are less interested in short-term relationships. A larger number of sexually unrestricted competitors, rather than just a shortage of desirable men, may lie behind the greater female–female aggression found in communities with low male parental investment.

Among the young adolescent girls studied by Campbell and by Marsh and Paton, fighting over reputation may stem from age effects on their economic circumstances and their expectations of male investment. They presumably were living at home and perhaps were less in need of resources than they will be later. They may also have been more optimistic about securing the investment of a high-status mate. Schuster described the Zambian women she studied as being optimistic and "starry-eyed" when young, expecting "to find a handsome, wealthy, educated man and marry, then to go on to life in a big house, with the ideal four children...." After a series of disappointing encounters, however, they typically became tough, acquired a number of boyfriends, and became manipulative toward men. In the words of one jaded Zambian woman, "Why put all your eggs in one basket, especially since nearly all of them are rotten anyway?" Concern with a good sexual reputation may have mattered when they were young, but the women faced other problems later. Optimism about finding a desirable mate has also been described among young women in Abidjan, Ivory Coast, for whom "youth is a temporary asset that they utilize to the fullest extent. [Among those who] have been befriended by more successful men...a particular combination of entrepreneurship and delusion often prevails."

A period of mating optimism among young adult women may be a regular feature of female psychology. A women's reproductive value, and hence her chance of marrying upward in the social scale, is at its height when she is young. These odds may favor the type of sexual restraint and concern with sexual reputation that would make finds such a mate more likely. As a woman ages, particularly if she experiences disappointments that suggest she is unlikely to get what she wants, a shift in mating tactics may be expected. Schuster's informants, in other words, may have behaved quite rationally. It would be interesting to know if their experience is widely shared. There was a hint of this shift in Marsh and Paton's teenage girls. These author's reported that the younger girls were ambivalent about their aggressiveness because they were aware that it is not regarded as feminine, whereas the older teens were uninhibited about their aggressiveness and were not concerned about appearing unfeminine.

Indirect Competition

The literature paints a consistent picture of what a man wants in a woman: she should be young (at an age when her reproductive value is highest), beautiful (healthy, fertile, and young), chaste (except with

him), and rich. She should also, though the evidence here is indirect, be careful not to threaten his reputation for dominance with his peers. One way in which women compete for men is to give them more of what they want.

Looking Youthful.   Because youth and health are strong indicators of fertility, it is not surprising that smooth skin, good muscle tone, and other indicators of youth and health are considered attractive by men. Men the world over prefer and mate with women who are younger than they are. Furthermore, women with youthful facial features are judged to be the most attractive. Women who avail themselves of cosmetics and other beauty aids in a quest for "younger-looking skin," therefore, are rationally attempting to manipulate evolved male preferences. A figure with a small waist relative to hip size (low waist–hip ratio) is also judged to be particularly attractive, not only by American males and females, but by those in other ethnic groups as well. Low waist–hip ratio, an estrogen-dependent trait, is a particularly effective marker of good female condition because it is associated with both high fertility and low susceptibility to many degenerative diseases. Fashion, of course, has found many ways to mimic and exaggerate this trait.

Appearing Faithful.   Because men are more willing to invest in offspring when they can be assured of their paternity, women have good reason to reassure them on this score. Mothers—but not fathers!—are more likely to report that their newborn infants look just like Dad. In societies where men invest heavily in their offspring, women are more likely to behave in ways that will ensure greater paternity confidence. Dickemann argued that concern about female chastity reaches a peak in highly stratified polygynous societies, in which "large numbers of beggars, outcasts, floater males, and celibates exist at the bottom while intense polygyny in the form of secondary wives, concubines, and harems occurs at the top. Extreme concern about female chastity is adaptive for husbands in these societies, not only because of high male investment but because of increased competition from a sea of unmated men with little to lose. It is noteworthy that claustration and other forms of sexual control are often enforced by women, not just by men. Clitoridectomy and infibulation, usually viewed as a form of male control over female sexuality are preformed on women by women. Mothers willingly put their daughters through these brutal procedures, presumably because without them their daughters will be unable to secure a desirable mate.

Dowry.   Men worldwide value female beauty and fidelity, and it is reasonable to expect that women worldwide are concerned to advertise these traits, though to variable degrees. Sweetening the pot with economic incentives through dowry, however, is limited to comparatively few societies. Where do we find dowry, and why?

Dowry has been viewed as a form of female–female competition for high quality mates, and Gaulin and Boster predict that it should be found where such competition is most acute. What circumstances give rise to such intense competition? When resources held by males differ widely in quality, polygyny is normally favored; yet polygyny itself acts to mitigate these differences because wealthy males have to share their resources among more wives. The fiercest competition among women for desirable men, therefore, should be in societies that are both highly stratified and strictly monogamous. As predicted, Gaulin and Boster's cross-cultural analysis show that the co-occurrence of stratification with socially imposed monogamy is the best predictor of dowry, although dowry is also found in the upper strata of some extremely stratified polygynous societies. We might wish to add to the criteria of stratification and socially imposed monogamy the additional one of degree of female dependence on male investment. Competition for investing mates should be most intense when the pay-offs of such investment are highest. Hence, greater economic independence of women might be expected to discourage the prevalence of dowry payment, even in monogamous, stratified societies. These arguments suggest that the direction of marriage payments may be a useful proxy for the relative strength of male–male versus female–female mate competition.

CONFLICTS OF INTEREST WITH MEN

Because males and females can best enhance their fitness in different ways, conflicts of interest between women and men are, unfortunately, an intrinsic part of the mating game. A man can enhance his fitness by investing in his children and maximizing his number of mates, but time and resources devoted to one interfere with the other. These trade-offs lead to variation in male strategies, with the polar types, in the words of Draper and Harpending, being "cads" (low-investment males seeking to maximize mating opportunities) and "dads" (high-investment males committed to one sexual partner).

The trade-offs facing men define the choices facing women. Should a woman try to secure an invest-ing mate, who may have lower mate value in other respects, or should she content herself with getting good genes and immediate resources from a noninvesting cad? She will have trouble doing both at the same time, because flaunting her sexuality, the behavior that attracts a cad, will put off a dad, who wants evidence of fidelity, and vice versa.

Having it Both Ways: Mixed Strategies

Recent research suggests that the difficulty of having it both ways is not always insurmountable. Women may try to get investment from one man while mating with another who is desirable in different respects. Baker and Bellis have found that when married women have affairs, matings with the "extra-pair" male occur disproportionately during the woman's fertile period. This finding suggests that one goal of short-term matings for women is to secure "good genes" from another mate, and that women may use deception to play a mixed sexual strategy.

The detailed investigations of Baker and Bellis on human sexual behavior show that this strategy also exists on a more covert level. They have found that "high retention" female orgasms (those that lead to retention of the largest number of sperm) are those occurring between one minute before and forty-five minutes after the male's ejaculation. Questionnaire data from a large sample of women indicate that those who had extra-marital affairs were more likely to have high-retention orgasms with the extra-pair partner than with their regular mate. Baker and Bellis argue, further, that noncopulatory orgasms also affect sperm retention, thereby endowing women with considerable flexibility in attaining their reproductive aims. These data suggest, among other things, that males have good reason to be concerned about the sexual satisfaction of their partners.

The good-genes interpretation of short-term liaisons is supported by the finding that women place a higher value on physical attractiveness in a short-term partner than in a long-term mate. Other reasons that have been suggested for women's short-term matings are the securing of immediate resources, the promotion of sperm competition, the evaluation of men as prospective marriage partners, and enhanced survival of offspring through confusion of paternity.

Making a Choice: Sexual Restrictedness

Proximate Determinants.   Male vigilance limits a woman's ability to play the mixed strategy I have described, and this forces her to make a choice. Should she flaunt her sexuality to win a high-quality cad (with good genes, immediate resources, and perhaps the possibility of changing his mind later) or should she advertise her fidelity and other charms to attract a long-term, investing dad? Gangestad and Simpson have measured how much time and commitment a woman requires before entering a sexual relationship (a variable they call sexual restrictedness), and have explored its genetic underpinnings with twin studies. They have argued that some of the personality traits underlying this behavior are heritable, and that the genetic variation is bimodally distributed. This finding is consistent with the notion that the costs and benefits of sexual restrictedness impose trade-offs, and that a woman may be better off trying to maximize one thing or the other.

There is also evidence supporting the role of early learning in sexual restrictedness, although it is difficult to separate this effect from genetic influence. Hetherington did behavior observation studies of "father-absent" adolescents (those whose mothers had divorced when they were very young) and compared them to adolescents whose fathers were present when they were growing up and to adolescents whose mothers were widowed rather than divorced. The girls who were father-absent due to divorce behaved more seductively toward men than did girls in either of the other two groups. These and related results have been interpreted as evidence of early learning of appropriate mating strategies. If true, the difference between daughters whose mothers were divorced and those whose mothers were widowed suggests that they are learning about men from their mothers, not from their fathers' absence per se. The lesson they are learning is, presumably, "Don't count on male investment—get what resources you can through short-term liaisons with high-status men." The proximate mechanisms leading to differences in sexual restrictedness may, of course, be both genetic and environmental. Evidence for one does not rule out the other.

Adaptive Explanations.   What factors favor these different female strategies? Much probably depends on a woman's other economic options. Much also depends on the likelihood that a woman will be able to secure an investing mate. In a study of undergraduates, I found that women were less likely to flaunt their sexuality and engage in sex with their romantic partners when their expectations of paternal investment were high. High expectations of paternal investment and its associated female mating strategies should be favored in the following circumstances: a) when the ratio of men to women is high, creating from the female perspective a "buyer's market;" b) other women are restricted in their sexuality, so that a man connot obtain sexual access without in-

vestment; c) males are able to provide significant investment; and d) male investment significantly enhances the survival of offspring. There is some evidence in favor of these propositions, which I will discuss in turn.

Can males get what they want without having to invest? Low sex ratios make it more likely, because an excess or marriageable women in the relevant age brackets increases competition for males. The baby boom in the United States between 1946–1957 created such a situation. Women born during this period were seeking mates from the smaller cohort born a few years earlier. Guttentag and Secord have related this phenomenon to the sharp increases in illegitimate births, unmarried couples living together, divorce, and martifocal families—all reflections of weakened commitment—that began in the 1960s. The effects of the marriage squeeze have also been felt by South American (Hiwi and Ache) foragers. Among the Hiwi, a shortage of available women has promoted monogamy and high male investment in spite of relatively low returns from that investment, while the greater availability of women among the Ache has favored males with a low investment strategy. This is true in spite of the fact that fathers have a greater effect on offspring survival among the Ache than the Hiwi. This underscores the fact that a man's investment patterns are shaped as much by his other reproductive options as by the fitness returns on his investment.

Do males have the resources to invest? An inability to provide significant investment resulting from high unemployment has frequently been suggested as a factor promoting matrifocal families in the lower classes of stratified societies in the United States and elsewhere. On the other hand, where there is heterogeneity among the males available to a woman, a man with few material resources may compensate in other ways, such as by providing more direct care of infants and children. This appears to be the case for Ache foragers, among whom hunters who do less holding of infants are more likely than other men to have high status, an influential father, and multiple brothers.

Does paternal investment pay significant returns? This questions is complicated but the fact that when men acquire and distribute resources, and perhaps even when they care directly for children, they may be doing so more to attract additional mates than to enhance the survival of their offspring. This raises the question of whether it is even appropriate to classify such behavior as "paternal investment." Irrespective of the father's motivation, however, the fitness benefits to offspring from a given amount of male effort should be lower when women are able to provide their children with abundant resources without the father's help. Such a woman should also be less willing to make compromises in the interest of securing male investment. For these reasons, we can expect economic self-sufficiency for women to be associated with higher divorce rates and greater female sexual freedom.

Economic independence from men can come from a woman's own efforts, from state aid (as in wealthy socialist countries), or from the help of female kin. Irons has argued that "marriage becomes attenuated when female coalitions are more effective at gaining what is scarce in a particular environment than are either individual men or male coalitions." The clearest example of this is found in matrilocal horticultural societies, where a woman's closest relationships typically are with her female kin, and where the women of the kin group are responsible for most of the food production. Matrilineal, matrilocal societies are famous for the independence of their women and for their comparative lack of concern with female chastity. The same dynamic appears to operate in matrifocal households in lower-class stratified societies. The unreliability of male support in these communities favors investment from maternal kin, particularly a woman's mother. In one poor black community with little male investment, women explicitly favored teen-age child-bearing because it enabled the child's grandmother to be young and healthy enough to take on the main child-rearing role.

The casual nature of the relationship between women's economic independence and low male investment could logically go both ways. Where a woman's economic independence comes from supportive female kin or from her own efforts in the labor market, it may sometimes be a response to low male investment (brought on by low sex ratios or unemployment) rather than a cause of it. The role of women's economic independence in causing lower male investment is perhaps most compelling in wealthy socialist countries such as Sweden, where economic independence is a result of state support. In Sweden "the taxpayers effectively provide what husbands formerly provided, freeing women from their economic dependence on men. Thus, practically no Swedish women are virgins at marriage and hence the value men place on chastity has commensurately declined to a worldwide low."

Making a Choice: Competing against Men

Women may find the combination of economic self-sufficiency and an investing, long-term mate to be desirable but difficult to attain. Men should be less likely to invest when returns on their investment are

small, as they are likely to be if the mother is economically self-sufficient. In addition, maturity, dominance, and successful competition with men, the very traits that favor economic success, may make her less attractive as a mate if they threaten the man's status with his peers.

There is some evidence that mature features in a woman inhibit both sexual interest and investment from men. Women with youthful facial features are, as we have seen, judged to be more attractive. But attractive for what? Cunningham found that a set of neonatal facial features (large eyes, small nose and chin) as well as two mature facial features (narrow cheeks and wide cheekbones) made women more attractive to his American male subjects. The subjects reported that they would also be more likely to hire women with these features for a job. However, only the neonatal features, not the mature ones, made a woman more attractive for sex and more likely to elicit male monetary investment, physical risk, and self-sacrifice. It is not clear whether youthful features have this effect because they signal high reproductive value or because neonatal features elicit caretaking (or both), but the fact that they do suggests that women face a dilemma.

This dilemma is even more clearly seen in the self-deprecating behavior that women often display around males. Women and girls have been found to perform less well when competing against males than when competing in all-female groups. This has been shown for a variety of tasks, both stereotypically masculine and sex-neutral. Women also use more subordinate body postures in mixed-sex than in same-sex group discussions, and girls from coed elementary schools are less likely to overrate their toughness than are girls in all-girls' schools.

I have considered the possibility that this type of behavior advertises a woman's need for investment. Some of my data support this expectation: for example, women who expect little paternal investment are more likely than other women to display their own competence and resources as a way of attracting a mate. However, the hypothesis was not well supported by other data from my study. Another plausible explanation is that a woman who is more successful than her mate threatens his position in the male hierarchy. In other words, economic success may make a woman an attractive mate but, in the process of attaining it, she must be careful not to threaten her man's status, particularly when other men are watching. Either explanation poses a dilemma between the attainment of economic self-sufficiency and the acquisition of a desirable mate. As with the dilemma about sexual restrictiveness (should she flaunt sexuality to attract many short-term mates or advertise fidelity to attract a long-term one?), a woman's best strategy here may depend on her chances of finding an investing mate as well as on her own resources and competitive ability.

CONCLUSION

We have learned a great deal in the last decade about what women want in a mate. It is clear that women value wealthy, high-status men in good physical condition, both for the resources such men can provide and for the genetic quality they can give offspring. Women particularly value high-quality men who are willing as well as able to invest.

Much less research has focused on how women secure such a mate in the face of competition from other women and conflicts of interest with the men they seek. We have known for a long time that one way women compete with other women is by making themselves more attractive. We are now learning that women also compete more directly, and that physical aggression is part of the repertoire. The challenge in both cases is understanding when women choose one competitive "weapon" over another. Thus far, it appears that physical aggression may be favored in populations where there is a shortage of desirable mates and an abundance of women desirous of short-term liaisons with a variety of men.

Women face conflicts of interest with men also, for men are better able to maximize their reproductive success by mating with a variety of women. In search of this aim, men will be attracted to youthful, sexually unrestricted women, but may be unwilling to invest in a woman's offspring unless she can assure him that the children are his. He will be attracted to an economically independent woman but he may be less likely to invest in her, and he will not want his status with his peers to be threatened by her pursuit of economic success. Women sometimes try to get around these trade-offs by playing a mixed sexual strategy, but male vigilance places limits on this ability and imposes choices. Should a woman compete openly with men, which will enhance her economic independence but may make her less desirable as a mate? Should she flaunt her sexuality, which will attract males but at the risk of losing a males's continued investment? Here, too, the challenge is understanding the factors that favor one strategy over the other. In general, it appears that a woman's optimal strategy will be affected by her other economic options and by her expectations of paternal investment. There is evidence that the likelihood of male investment is affected by the sex ratio, the sexual restrictiveness of other women, the economic position of the men she is able to attract, and the payoffs to male investment. We are only just beginning to understand how women's strategies are shaped by these factors. Clarifying this matter remains the primary challenge for future research.

Isn't She Lovely?

If you think that physical appeal is strictly a matter of personal taste and cultural bias, think again. Who you find attractive, say psychobiologists, is largely dictated by evolutionary needs and hardwired into your brain.

She's cute, no question. Symmetrical features, flawless skin, looks to be 22 years old—entering any meat-market bar, a woman lucky enough to have this face would turn enough heads to stir a breeze. But when Victor Johnston points and clicks, the face on his computer screen morphs into what a mesmerized physicist might call a discontinuous state of superheated, crystallized beauty. "You can see it. It's just so extraordinary," says Johnston, a professor of biopsychology at New Mexico State University who sounds a little in love with his creation.

The transformation from pretty woman to knee-weakening babe is all the more amazing because the changes wrought by Johnston's software are, objectively speaking, quite subtle. He created the original face by digitally averaging 16 randomly selected female Caucasian faces. The morphing program then exaggerated the ways in which female faces differ from male faces, creating, in human-beauty-science parlance, a "hyperfemale." The eyes grew a bit larger, the nose narrowed slightly, the lips plumped, and the jaw contracted. These are shifts of just a few millimeters, but experiments in this country and Scotland are suggesting that both males and females find "feminized" versions of averaged faces more beautiful.

Johnston hatched this little movie as part of his ongoing study into why human beings find some people attractive and others homely. He may not have any rock-solid answers yet, but he is far from alone in attempting to apply scientific inquiry to so ambiguous a subject. Around the world, researchers are marching into territory formerly staked out by poets, painters, fashion mavens, and casting directors, aiming to uncover the underpinnings of human attractiveness.

The research results so far are surprising—and humbling. Numerous studies indicate that human beauty may not be simply in the eye of the beholder or an arbitrary cultural artifact. It may be an ancient, hardwired, universal, and potent behavior-driver, on a par with hunger or pain, wrought through eons of evolution that rewarded reproductive winners and killed off losers. If beauty is not truth, it may be health and fertility: Halle Berry's flawless skin may rivet moviegoers because, at some deep level, it persuades us that she is parasite-free and consequently good mating material. Acquired, individual preferences factor in, but research increasingly indicates that their influence is much smaller than many of us would care to know. While romantic writers blather about the transcendence of beauty, Elizabethan poet Edmund Spenser more than 400 years ago pegged the emerging scientific thesis: "Beauty is the bait which with delight allures man to enlarge his kind."

Implications of human-beauty research range from the practical—providing cosmetic surgeons with pretty-people templates—to the political and philosophical. Landmark studies show that attractive males and females not only garner more attention from the opposite sex, they also get more affection from their mothers, more money at work, more votes from the electorate, more leniency from judges, and are generally regarded as more kind, competent, healthy, confident, and intelligent than their big-nosed, weak-chinned counterparts. (Beauty is considered such a valuable trait by some that one entrepreneur recently put up a Web site offering to auction off the unfertilized ova of models.)

Human attractiveness research is a relatively young and certainly contentious field—the allure of hyperfemales, for example, is still hotly debated—but those on its front lines agree on one point: We won't conquer "looks-ism" until we understand its source. As psychologist Nancy Etcoff, author of the 1999 book *Survival of the Prettiest,* puts it: "The idea that beauty is unimportant or a cultural construct is the real beauty myth. We have to understand beauty, or we will always be enslaved by it.''

The modern era of beauty studies got a big push 20 years ago with an awkward question in a small, airless room at Louisiana State University in Baton Rouge. Psychology graduate student Judith Langlois was defending her doctoral dissertation—a study of how preschool children form and keep friendships—when a professor asked whether she had factored the kids' facial attractiveness into her conclusions. "I thought the question was way off the mark," she recalls. "It might matter for college students, but little kids?" After stammering out a noncommittal answer—and passing the examination—she resolved to dig deeper, aiming to determine the age at which human beings could perceive physical attractiveness.

Langlois, who had joined the faculty at the University of Texas at Austin devised a series of experiments. In one, she had adults rate photos of human faces on a spectrum from attractive to unattractive. Then she projected pairs of high- and low-rated faces in front of 6-month-old infants. "The result was straightforward and unambiguous," she declares. "The babies looked longer at the attractive faces, regardless of the gender, race, or age of the face." Studies with babies as young as 2 months old yielded similar results. "At 2 months, these babies hadn't been reading *Vogue* magazine," Langlois observes dryly.

Her search for the source of babies' precocious beauty-detection led her all the way back to nineteenth-century research conducted by Sir Francis Galton, an English dilettante scientist and cousin of Charles Darwin. In the late 1870s, Galton created crude, blurry composite faces by melding mug-shot photographs of various social subgroups, aiming to prove that each group had an archetypal face. While that hypothesis fizzled—the average criminal looked rather like the average vegetarian—Galton was shocked to discover that these averaged faces were better looking than nearly all of the individuals they comprised. Langlois replicated Galton's study, using software to form digitally averaged faces that were later judged by 300 people to be more attractive than most of the faces used to create them.

Human beings may be born "cognitive averagers," theorizes Langlois. "Even very young infants have seen thousands of faces and may have already constructed an average from them that they use for comparison."

Racial preferences bolster the idea, say some scientists. History shows that almost universally, when one race first comes into contact with another, they mutually regard each other as homely, if not freakish. Etcoff relates that a delegation of Japanese samurai visiting the United States in 1860 observed that Western women had "dogs' eyes," which they found "disheartening." Early Western visitors to Japan thought the natives' epicanthic folds made the eyes appear sleepy and small. In each case, Etcoff surmises, the unfamiliar race most likely veered from the internal, averaged ideal.

But why would cognitive averaging have evolved? Evolutionary biology holds that in any given population, extreme characteristics tend to fall away in favor of average ones. Birds with unusually long or short wings die more often in storms. Human babies who are born larger or smaller than average are less likely to survive. The ability to form an average-mate template would have conveyed a singular survival advantage.

Inclination toward the average is called koinophilia from the Greek words *koinos,* meaning "usual," and *philos,* meaning "love." To Langlois, humans are clearly koinophiles. The remaining question is whether our good-mate template is acquired or innate. To help solve the mystery, Langlois's doctoral student Lisa Kalakanis has presented babies who are just 15 minutes old with paired images of attractive and homely faces. "We're just starting to evaluate that data," says Langlois.

But koinophilia isn't the only—or even supreme—criterion for beauty that evolution has promoted, other scientists argue. An innate yearning for symmetry is a major boon, contend biologists Anders Moller and Randy Thornhill, as asymmetry can signal malnutrition, disease, or bad genes. The two have found that asymmetrical animals, ranging from barn swallows to lions, have fewer offspring and shorter lives. Evolution would also logically instill an age preference. Human female fertility peaks in the early 20s, and so do assessments of female attractiveness. Between 1953 and 1990, the average age of *Playboy* centerfold models—who are presumably selected solely for sexual appear—was 21.3 years. Similarly, Johnston has found that the beauty of a Japanese female face is judged to be at its peak when its perceived age is 22.4 years. Because men are fertile throughout most of their adult lives, their attractiveness ratings—while dropping as they age past their late 20s—remain relatively higher as their perceived age increases. As Johnston puts it, "Our feelings of beauty are exceptionally well tuned to the age of maximum fertility."

Still, a species can stagnate without some novelty. When competition for mates is intense, some extreme traits might help to rivet a roving eye. "A male peacock is saying, 'Look at me, I have this big tail. I couldn't grow a tail this big if I had parasites,'" says Johnston. "Even if the trait is detrimental to survival, the benefit in additional offspring brought about by attracting females can more than compensate for the decrease in longevity." The concept seems applicable to humans, too, because it helps to resolve a nagging flaw in average-face studies. In many of them, "there were always a few individual faces in the population that were deemed even prettier than the average," says Etcoff "If average were always best, how could that be?"

Psychologist David Perrett of the University of St. Andrews in Scotland aimed to find out by creating two averaged faces—one from a group of women rated attractive and another from men so judged. He then compared those faces with averaged faces constructed from a larger, random set of images. The composites of the beautiful people were rated more appealing than those made from the larger, random population. More surprising, when Perrett exaggerated the ways in which the prettiest female composite differed from the average female composite, the resulting face was judged to be even more attractive.

"It turned out that the way an attractive female face differs from an average one is related to femininity," says Perrett. "For example, female eyebrows are more arched than males'. Exaggerating that difference from the average increases femininity," and, in tandem, the attractiveness rating. In the traffic-stopping female face created for this experiment, 200 facial reference points all changed in the direction of hyperfemininity: larger eyes, a smaller nose, plumper lips, a narrower jaw, and a smaller chin.

"All faces go through a metamorphosis at puberty," observes Johnston. "In males, testosterone lengthens the jaw. In females, estrogen makes the hips, breasts, and lips swell." So large lips, breasts, and hips combined with a small jaw "are all telling you that I have an abundant supply of estrogen, so I am a fertile female." Like the peacock, whose huge tail is a mating advantage but a practical hindrance, "a small jaw may not, in fact, be as efficient for eating," Johnston says. But it seems attractive because it emphasizes *la différence*; whatever survival disadvantage comes along with a small jaw is more than made up for by the chance to produce more babies, so the trait succeeds.

Along with his morphing program, Johnston approached the hyperfemale hypothesis through another route. Starting with 16 computer-generated random female Caucasian faces, he had visitors to his Web site rate the attractiveness of each face on a scale of one to nine. A second generation of faces was then computed by selecting, crossing, and mu-

tating the first generation in proportion to beauty ratings. After 10,000 people from around the world took part in this merciless business, the empirically derived fairest-of-them-all was born. Facial measurements confirm that she is decidedly hyperfemale. While we might say she is beautiful, Johnston more accurately notes that the face displays "maximum fertility cues."

Johnston's findings have set off a ruckus among beauty scientists. In a paper titled "Attractive Faces Really Are Only Average," Langlois and three other researchers blast the notion that a deviation from the average—what they term "facial extremes"—explains attractiveness better than averageness does. The findings of Perrett and his team, she says, are "artifacts of their methodology," because they used a "forced-choice" scenario that prevented subjects from judging faces as equally attractive. "We did the same kind of test, but gave people a rating scale of one to five," says Langlois. "When you do it that way, there is no significant difference—people would tell us that, basically, the two faces looked like twins." Langlois argues that if extremes create beauty, "then people with micro-jaws or hydrocephalic eyes would be seen as the most beautiful, when, in fact, eyes that are too big for a head make that head unattractive."

But for Etcoff, circumstantial evidence for the allure of some degree of hyperfemininity is substantial. "Female makeup is all about exaggerating the feminine. Eye makeup makes the brow thinner, which makes it look farther from the eye," which, she says, is a classic difference between male and female faces. From high hair (which skews facial proportions in a feminine direction, moving up the center of gravity) to collagen in lips to silicone in breasts, women instinctively exaggerate secondary female sex characteristics to increase their allure. "Langlois is simply wrong," declares Johnston. In one of his studies, published last year in *Psychophysiology*, both male and female subjects rated feminized pictures as more attractive. Further, male subjects attached to electrical-brain-activity monitors showed a greater response in the P_3 component, a measure of emotional intensity. "That is, although both sexes know what is attractive, only the males exhibit an emotional response to the feminized picture," Johnston says.

And what about male attractiveness? It stands to reason that if men salivate for hyperfemales, women should pursue hypermales—that is, men whose features exaggerate the ways in which male faces differ from female ones. Even when adjusted for differing overall body size, the average male face has a more pronounced brow ridge, more sunken eyes, and

NATURE OR NURTURE?　　　　　　　　　　　　Robert Sapolsky

"The 50 Most Beautiful People in the World" Assess the Source of Good Looks

As a scientist doing scads of important research, I am busy, very busy. What with all those midnight experiments in the lab, all that eureka-ing, I hardly have any time to read professional journals. Thus, I only lately got the chance to peruse *People* magazine's most recent compilation of "The 50 Most Beautiful People in the World." It was fabulous. In addition to offering helpful grooming tips, the issue grapples with one of the central conundrums of our time: Which is ultimately more influential, nature or nurture? "About beauty," opine the editors, "the arguments can be endless." No such shilly-shallying for the Chosen Ones themselves: The 50 Most Beautiful and their inner circles appear to harbor militant ideologues in the debate.

Consider first the extreme nurturists, who eschew the notion that anything is biologically fixed. There's Ben Affleck, who in service to stardom has slimmed down, pumped up, and had his teeth capped. Affleck is clearly a disciple of John Watson, famous for the nurture credo: "Give me a child and let me control the total environment in which he is raised, and I will turn him into whatever I wish." It's hardly surprising that Affleck's celebrated affair with Gwyneth Paltrow, clearly of the genetic determinist school (read on), was so short-lived.

A nurture viewpoint is also advanced by TV star Jenna Elfman, who attributes her beauty to drinking 100 ounces of water a day, eating a diet based on her blood type, and using a moisturizer that costs $1,000 a pound. Jaclyn Smith, the erstwhile Charlie's Angel, maintains her beauty has been preserved by not smoking, not drinking, and not doing drugs. However, even a neophyte student of human developmental biology might easily note that no degree of expensive mois-

turizers or virtuous living would get, say, me on *People*'s pulchritudinous list.

Naturally, similarly strong opinions emanate from the opposing, nature faction—the genetic determinists among the Most Beautiful. Perhaps the brashest of this school is Josh Brolin, an actor whose statement could readily serve as a manifesto for his cadre: "I was given my dad's good genes." Similar sentiments emerge from the grandfather of the aforementioned Paltrow, who avows that she was "beautiful from the beginning."

The very epitome of the natalist program, in which genetics forms an imperative trajectory impervious to environmental manipulation, is TV host Meredith Vieira. *People*'s editors cite various disasters that have befallen her—shoddy application of makeup, an impetuous and unfortunate peroxide job on her hair—and yet, it doesn't matter. She is still beautiful because of her "phenomenal genes."

One searches the pages for a middle ground, for the interdisciplinary synthesist who perceives the contribution of both nature and nurture. At last, we espy Monica. The single-name singer, we are told, has an absolutely wondrous skill for applying makeup. This, at first, seems like just more nurture agitprop. But where does she get this cosmetic aptitude?

Her mother supplies the answer. With Monica, Mom says, "It's something that's inborn." One gasps at the insight: There is a genetic influence on how one interacts with the environment. Too bad a few more people can't think this way when figuring out what genes have to do with, say, intelligence, substance abuse, or violence.

---

bushier brows that are set closer to the eyes. The nose and mouth are wider, the lower jaw is wider and longer. Ramp up these features beyond the norm, and you've got a hunk, right?

There's no question that a dose of this classic "maleness" does contribute to what is now called handsome. Actor Brad Pitt, widely regarded as a modern paradigm of male attractiveness, is a wide-jaw guy. Biologically speaking, he subconsciously persuades a female that he could chew more nutrents out of a leafy stalk than the average potential father of her children—a handy trait, in hunter-gatherer days anyway, to pass on to progeny.

But a woman's agenda in seeking a mate is considerably more complex than simply whelping strong-jawed kids. While both men and women desire healthy, fertile mates, a man can—and, to some extent, is biologically driven to—procreate with as

many women as possible. Conversely, a woman, "thinks about the long haul," notes Etcoff. "Much of mate choice is about finding a helpmate to bring up the baby." In several studies, women presented with the hypermale face (the "Neanderthal type" as Etcoff puts it) judged its owner to be uncaring, aggressive, and unlikely to be a good father.

Female preferences in male faces oscillate in tandem with the menstrual cycle, suggests a study conducted by Perrett and Japanese researchers and published [in June 1999] in *Nature*. When a woman is ovulating, she tends to prefer men with more masculine features; at less fertile times in her monthly cycle, she favors male faces with a softer, more feminine look. But amid the hoopla that this widely publicized finding generated, a critical fact was often overlooked. Even the "more masculine" face preferred by the ovulating women was 8 percent feminized from the male average (the less masculine face was 15 to 20 percent feminized). According to Perrett's study, even an averagely masculine face is too male for comfort.

To further complicate the male-appeal picture, research indicates that, across the board in mating species, an ugly guy can make up ground with status and/or wealth. Etcoff notes that female scorpion flies won't even look at a male unless his gift—a tasty bit of insect protein—is at least 16 square millimeters wide. The human situation isn't all that different. Anthropologist John Marshall Townsend showed photos of beautiful and homely people to men and women, and described the people in the photos as being in training for either low-, medium-, or high-paying positions—waiter, teacher, or doctor. "Not surprisingly, women preferred the best-looking man with the most money," Etcoff writes, "but below him, average-looking or even unattractive doctors received the same ratings as very attractive teachers. This was not true when men evaluated women. Unattractive women were not preferred, no matter what their status."

It's all a bit bleak. Talk to enough psychobiologists, and you get the impression that we are all rats—reflexively, unconsciously coupling according to obscure but immutable circuitry. But beauty researchers agree that, along with natural selection and sexual selection, learned behaviors are at least part of the attractiveness radar. In other words, there is room for individuality—perhaps even a smattering of mystery—in this business of attraction between humans.

"Human beauty really has three components," says Johnston. "In order of importance, there's natural selection, which leads to the average face and a limited age range. Then there's sexual selection," which leads men, at least, to be attracted to exaggerated feminine traits like the small lower jaw and the fuller lips. "Finally, there's learning. It's a fine-tuning mechanism that allows you to become even more adapted to your environment and culture. It's why one person can say, 'She's beautiful' and another can say, 'She's not quite right for me.'"

The learned component of beauty detection is perhaps most evident in the give-and-take between races. While, at first meeting, different racial groups typically see each other as unattractive, when one race commands economic or political power, members of other races tend to emulate its characteristics: Witness widespread hair straightening by American blacks earlier in this century. Today, black gains in social equity are mirrored by a growing appreciation for the beauty of such characteristically black features as relatively broader noses and tightly curled hair. "Race is a cultural overlay on beauty, and it's shifting," says Etcoff.

She adds that human appearance is about more than attracting sex partners. "There was a cartoon in the *New Yorker*. A mother and daughter are in a checkout line. The girl is saying to the cashier, 'Oh, no, I *do* look like my mother, with her *first* nose!' As we make ourselves more beautiful, we take away things like family resemblance, and we may realize that's a mistake. Facial uniqueness can be a wonderful emotional tag. Human beings are always looking for kinship as well as beauty."

Midway between goats and gods, human beings can find some accommodation between the notion that beauty is all and that it is nothing. "Perhaps it's best to enjoy the temporary thrill, to enjoy being a mammal for a few moments, and then do a reality check and move on," writes Etcoff. "Our brains cannot help it, but we can."

HUMAN DIVERSITY

Since the beginnings of recorded history, the physical differences characterizing human populations have been of interest both to scholars and lay persons. Neontology, which includes the study of the distribution of modern human biological traits, is a major area of interest to biological anthropologists.

You will recall, from the essay introducing Part Two, that in the eighteenth century Johann Blumenbach developed rigorous standards for measuring physical traits and used clusters of these measurements to identify "races." The concept of race was quickly incorporated into scientific thought, and much of the subsequent research on human diversity has been undertaken using this concept. The term *race* generally is used to refer to a population that is distinguished from all other groups by virtue of displaying a cluster of innate biological traits. Indeed, the concept of race has won general widespread acceptance—so much so that if you were to tell your neighbor today that races do not, in fact, exist, you would likely be dismissed as a fool.

Yet *do* races exist as biological facts of nature? In his now-classic work, *The Mismeasure of Man*, the biologist Stephen Jay Gould argues that all attempts to measure biological differences among human populations have reflected the biases of those groups that had the political power to do the measuring. In painstaking detail he reanalyzes quantitative studies of everything from human head size to IQ and shows that the research conducted by even the most eminent scholars of their time is marred again and again—by such severe distortions as leaving out data (or explaining facts away) that did not fit the popular social preconceptions of the times, by serious statistical malpractice, and even by outright fabrication of "facts." His conclusion is that "claims for a direct biological mapping of human affairs have recorded cultural prejudice and not nature."

Of course it is possible, as Boyce Rensberger observes in the article "Racial Odyssey," which opens

Topic 4, to define human groups using any biological traits one wishes—hair color, facial shape, height, skin color, blood group, and on and on—but there are no known features or clusters of features that neatly divide the human species into clearly defined groups (which is what one would expect if the concept of race had any biological meaning). Therefore, the kind or number of "races" depends on the purpose of the classification system one uses. Rensberger illustrates this by selecting a large number of biological traits and illustrating that no matter what way one wants to organize them, they still wind up cutting across "racial" lines. The conclusion is clear: human diversity is real, but rather than trying to force the mosaic of human biological traits into a predetermined design—as the U.S. Census Bureau so awkwardly tried to do in its 2000 census—we should try to discover what adaptive utility such diversity provides for our species.

In the second article in Topic 4, "'Race': Myths under the Microscope," Albert Jacquard looks at some of the connections between "race" and racism. Racism is something very real indeed: it consists of those beliefs that have been used to justify the subjugation, exploitation, and even extermination of one group by another, when the basis of the distinction between the groups is defined as biological. He points out that there is much greater genetic variation among individuals within any group than there is between the "average" genetic frequencies of groups as wholes. Further, he notes that genetic diversity is a fundamental source of evolutionary robustness, not the threat to "racial purity" over which racist elites raise such alarm.

Anthropology has made two fundamental contributions to the understanding of human diversity: first, by systematically studying the adaptive significance of specific traits in relation to the environments in which they are found most frequently; and second, by demonstrating that the feelings of superiority that are to be found in virtually all human groups (known as *ethnocentrism*) are cultural products, not biological products.

In the final article in this topic, "The Tall *and* the Short of It," Barry Bogin explores the concept of *human plasticity*, and how seeming biological characteristics and proclivities—such as height or predisposition to developing certain diseases—can be affected by our plasticity. The implications are profound and far-reaching.

Racial Odyssey

The human species comes in an artist's palette of colors: sandy yellows, reddish-tans, deep browns, light tans, creamy whites, pale pinks. It is a rare person who is not curious about the skin colors, hair textures, bodily structures and facial features associated with racial background. Why do some Africans have dark brown skin, while that of most Europeans is pale pink? Why do the eyes of most "white" people and "black" people look pretty much alike but differ so from the eyes of Orientals? Did one race evolve before the others? If so, is it more primitive or more advanced as a result? Can it be possible, as modern research suggests, that there is no such thing as a pure race? These are all honest, scientifically worthy questions. And they are central to current research on the evolution of our species on the planet Earth.

Broadly speaking, research on racial differences has led most scientists to three major conclusions. The first is that there are many more differences among people than skin color, hair texture and facial features. Dozens of other variations have been found, ranging from the shapes of bones to the consistency of ear wax to subtle variations in body chemistry.

The second conclusion is that the overwhelming evolutionary success of the human species is largely due to its great genetic variability. When migrating bands of our early ancestors reached a new environment, at least a few already had physical traits that gave them an edge in surviving there. If the coming centuries bring significant environmental changes, as many believe they will, our chances of surviving them will be immeasurably enhanced by our diversity as a species.

There is a third conclusion about race that is often misunderstood. Despite our wealth of variation and despite our constant, everyday references to race, no one has ever discovered a reliable way of distinguishing one race from another. While it is possible to classify a great many people on the basis of certain physical features, there are no known feature or groups of features that will do the job in all cases.

Skin color won't work. Yes, most Africans from south of the Sahara and their descendants around the world have skin that is darker than that of most Europeans. But there are millions of people in India, classified by some anthropologists as members of the Caucasoid, or "white," race who have darker skins than most Americans who call themselves black. And there are many Africans living in sub-Sahara Africa today whose skins are no darker than the skins of many Spaniards, Italians, Greeks or Lebanese.

What about stature as a racial trait? Because they are quite short, on the average, African Pygmies have been considered racially distinct from other dark-skinned Africans. If stature, then, is a racial criterion, would one include in the same race the tall African Watusi and the Scandinavians of similar stature?

The little web of skin that distinguishes Oriental eyes is said to be a particular feature of the Mongoloid race. How, then, can it be argued that the American Indian, who lacks this epicanthic fold, is Mongoloid?

Even more hopeless as racial markers are hair color, eye color, hair form, the shapes of noses and lips or any of the other traits put forth as typical of one race or another.

NO NORMS

Among the tall people of the world there are many black, many white and many in between. Among black people of the world there are many with kinky hair, many with straight or wavy hair, and many in between. Among the broad-nosed, full-lipped people of the world there are many with dark skins, many with light skins and many in between.

How did our modern perceptions of race arise? One of the first to attempt a scientific classification of peoples was Carl von Linne, better known as Linnaeus. In 1735, he published a classification that remains the standard today. As Linnaeus saw it there were four races, classifiable geographically and by skin color. The names Linnaeus gave them were *Homo sapiens Africanus nigrus* (black African human being), *H. sapiens Americanus rubescens* (red American human being), *H. sapiens Asiaticus fuscusens*

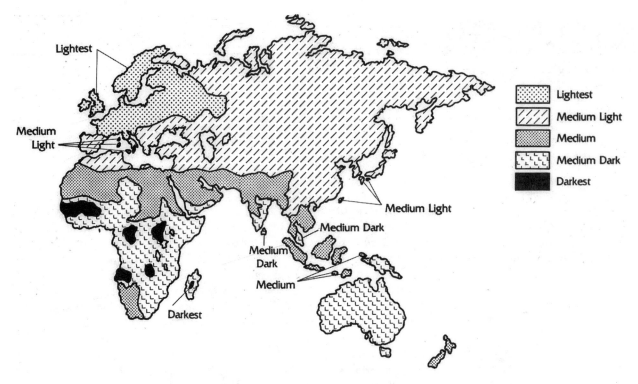

The Distribution of Human Skin Color in 1500 **(North and South America not included)**
The map above suggests the distribution of people in terms of skin color about 1500. In fact, edges between groups have always been blurred, speculative, and difficult to pin down, and since 1500 the picture has been changed drastically and often by massive, worldwide population shifts.

(brownish Asian human being), and *H. sapiens Europeaeus albescens* (white European human being). All, Linnaeus recognized, were members of a single human species.

A species includes all individuals that are biologically capable of interbreeding and producing fertile offspring. Most matings between species are fruitless, and even when they succeed, as when a horse and a donkey interbreed and produce a mule, the progeny are sterile. When a poodle mates with a collie, however, the offspring are fertile, showing that both dogs are members of the same species.

Even though Linnaeus's system of nomenclature survives, his classifications were discarded, especially after voyages of discovery revealed that there were many more kinds of people than could be pigeonholed into four categories. All over the world there are small populations that don't fit. Among the better known are:

- The so-called Bushmen of southern Africa, who look as much Mongoloid as Negroid.
- The Negritos of the South Pacific, who do look Negroid but are very far from Africa and have no known links to that continent.

- The Ainu of Japan, a hairy aboriginal people who look more Caucasoid than anything else.
- The Lapps of Scandinavia, who look as much like Eskimos as like Europeans.
- The aborigines of Australia, who often look Negroid but many of whom have straight or wavy hair and are often blond as children.
- The Polynesians, who seem to be a blend of many races, the proportions differing from island to island.

To accommodate such diversity, many different systems of classification have been proposed. Some set up two or three dozen races. None has ever satisfied all experts.

CLASSIFICATION SYSTEM

Perhaps the most sweeping effort to impose a classification upon all the peoples of the world was made by the American anthropologist Carleton Coon. He concluded there are five basic races, two of which have major subdivisions: Caucasoids; Mongoloids; full-size Australoids (Australian aborigines); dwarf Australoids (Negritos—Andaman Islanders and similar peoples); full-size Congoids (African Negroids); dwarf Congoids (African Pygmies); and Capoids (the so-called Bushmen and Hottentots).

In his 1965 classic, *The Living Races of Man*, Coon hypothesized that before A.D. 1500 there were five *pure* races—five centers of human population that were so isolated that there was almost no mixing.

Each of these races evolved independently, Coon believed, diverging from a pre–*Homo sapiens* stock that was essentially the same everywhere. He speculated that the common ancestor evolved into *Homo sapiens* in five separate regions at five different times, beginning about 35,000 years ago. The populations that have been *Homo sapiens* for the shortest periods of time, Coon said, are the world's "less civilized" races.

The five pure races remained distinct until A.D. 1500; then Europeans started sailing the world, leaving their genes—as sailors always have—in every port and planting distant colonies. At about the same time, thousands of Africans were captured and forcibly settled in many parts of the New World.

That meant the end of the five pure races. But Coon and other experts held that this did not necessarily rule out the idea of distinct races. In this view, there *are* such things as races; people just don't fit into them very well anymore.

The truth is that there is really no hard evidence to suggest that five or any particular number of races evolved independently. The preponderance of evidence today suggests that as traits typical of fully modern people arose in any one place, they spread quickly to all human populations. Advances in intelligence were almost certainly the fastest to spread. Most anthropologists and geneticists now believe that human beings have always been subject to migrating and mixing. In other words, there probably never were any such things as pure races.

Race mixing has not only been a fact of human history but is, in this day of unprecedented global mobility, taking place at a more rapid rate than ever. It is not farfetched to envision the day when, generations hence, the entire "complexion" of major population centers will be different. Meanwhile, we can see such changes taking place before our eyes, for they are a part of everyday reality.

HYBRID VIGOR

Oddly, those who assert scientific validity for their notions of pure and distinct races seem oblivious of a basic genetic principle that plant and animal breeders know well: too much inbreeding can lead to proliferation of inferior traits. Crossbreeding with different strains often produces superior combinations and "hybrid vigor."

The striking differences among people may very well be a result of constant genetic mixing. And as geneticists and ecologists know, in diversity lies strength and resilience.

To understand the origin and proliferation of human differences, one must first know how Darwinian evolution works.

Evolution is a two-step process. Step one is mutation: somehow a gene in the ovary or testes of an individual is altered, changing the molecular configuration that stores instructions for forming a new individual. The children who inherit that gene will be different in some way from their ancestors.

Step two is selection: for a racial difference, or any other evolutionary change, to arise, it must survive and be passed through several generations. If the mutation confers some disadvantage, the individual dies, often during embryonic development. But if the change is beneficial in some way, the individual should have a better chance of thriving than relatives lacking the advantage.

NATURAL SELECTION

If a new trait is beneficial, it will bring reproductive success to its bearer. After several generations of multiplication, bearers of the new trait may begin to outnumber nonbearers. Darwin called this natural selection to distinguish it from the artificial selection exercised by animal breeders.

Skin color is the human racial trait most generally thought to confer an evolutionary advantage of this sort. It has long been obvious in the Old World that the farther south one goes, the darker the skin color. Southern Europeans are usually somewhat darker than northern Europeans. In North Africa, skin colors are darker still, and, as one travels south, coloration reaches its maximum at the Equator. The same progression holds in Asia, with the lightest skins to the north. Again, as one moves south, skin color darkens, reaching in southern India a "blackness" equal to that of equatorial Africans.

This north–south spectrum of skin color derives from varying intensities of the same dark brown pigment called melanin. Skin cells simply have more or less melanin granules to be seen against a background that is pinkish because of the underlying blood vessels. All races can increase their melanin concentration by exposure to the Sun.

What is it about northerly latitudes in the Northern Hemisphere that favors less pigmentation and about southerly latitudes that favors more? Exposure

DISEASE ORIGINS

The gene for sickle cell anemia, a disease found primarily among black people, appears to have evolved because its presence can render its bearer resistant to malaria. Such a trait would have obvious survival value in tropical Africa.

A person who has sickle cell anemia must have inherited genes for the disease from both parents. If a child inherits only one sickle cell gene, he or she will be resistant to malaria but will not have the anemia. Paradoxically, inheriting genes from both parents does not seem to affect resistance to malaria.

In the United States, where malaria is practically nonexistent, the sickle cell gene confers no survival advantage and is disappearing. Today only about 1 out of every 10 American blacks carries the gene.

Many other inherited diseases are found only in people from a particular area. Tay-Sachs disease, which often kills before the age of two, is almost entirely confined to Jews from parts of Eastern Europe and their descendants elsewhere. Paget's disease, a bone disorder, is found most often among those of English descent. Impacted wisdom teeth are a common problem among Asians and Europeans but not among Africans. Children of all races are able to digest milk because their bodies make lactase, the enzyme that breaks down lactose, or milk sugar. But the ability to digest lactose in adulthood is a racially distributed trait.

About 90 percent of Orientals and blacks lose this ability by the time they reach adulthood and become quite sick when they drink milk.

Even African and Asian herders who keep cattle or goats rarely drink fresh milk. Instead, they first treat the milk with fermentation bacteria that break down lactose, in a sense predigesting it. They can then ingest the milk in the form of yogurt or cheese without any problem.

About 90 percent of Europeans and their American descendants, on the other hand, continue to produce the enzyme throughout their lives and can drink milk with no ill effects.

to intense sunlight is not the only reason why people living in southerly latitudes are dark. A person's susceptibility to rickets and skin cancer, his ability to withstand cold and to see in the dark may also be related to skin color.

The best-known explanation says the body can tolerate only a narrow range of intensities of sunlight. Too much causes sunburn and cancer, while too little deprives the body of vitamin D, which is synthesized in the skin under the influence of sunlight. A dark complexion protects the skin from the harmful effects of intense sunlight. Thus, albinos born in equatorial regions have a high rate of skin cancer. On the other hand, dark skin in northerly latitudes screens out sunlight needed for the synthesis of vitamin D. Thus, dark-skinned children living in northern latitudes had high rates of rickets—a bone-deforming disease caused by a lack of vitamin D—before their milk was routinely fortified. In the sunny tropics, dark skin admits enough light to produce the vitamin.

Recently, there has been some evidence that skin colors are linked to differences in the ability to avoid injury from the cold. Army researchers found that during the Korean War blacks were more susceptible to frostbite than were whites. Even among Norwegian soldiers in World War II, brunettes had a slightly higher incidence of frostbite than did blonds.

EYE PIGMENTATION

A third link between color and latitude involves the sensitivity of the eye to various wavelengths of light.

It is known that dark-skinned people have more pigmentation in the iris of the eye and at the back of the eye where the image falls. It has been found that the less pigmented the eye, the more sensitive it is to colors at the red end of the spectrum. In situations illuminated with reddish light, the northern European can see more than a dark African sees.

It has been suggested that Europeans developed lighter eyes to adapt to the longer twilights of the North and their greater reliance on firelight to illuminate caves.

Although the skin cancer–vitamin D hypothesis enjoys wide acceptance, it may well be that resistance to cold, possession of good night vision and other yet unknown factors all played roles in the evolution of skin colors.

Most anthropologists agree that the original human skin color was dark brown, since it is fairly well established that human beings evolved in the tropics of Africa. This does not, however, mean that the first people were Negroids, whose descendants, as they moved north, evolved into light-skinned Caucasoids. It is more likely that the skin color of various populations changed several times from dark to light and back as people moved from one region to another.

Consider, for example, that long before modern people evolved, *Homo erectus* had spread throughout Africa, Europe and Asia. The immediate ancestor of *Homo sapiens*, *Homo erectus*, was living in Africa 1.5 million years ago and in Eurasia 750,000 years ago. The earliest known forms of *Homo sapiens* do not make their appearance until somewhere between

250,000 and 500,000 years ago. Although there is no evidence of the skin color of any hominid fossil, it is probable that the *Homo erectus* population in Africa had dark skin. As subgroups spread into northern latitudes, mutations that reduced pigmentation conferred survival advantages on them and lighter skins came to predominate. In other words, there were probably black *Homo erectus* peoples in Africa and white ones in Europe and Asia.

Did the black *Homo erectus* populations evolve into today's Negroids and the white ones in Europe into today's Caucasoids? By all the best evidence, nothing like this happened. More likely, wherever *Homo sapiens* arose it proved so superior to the *Homo erectus* populations that it eventually replaced them everywhere.

If the first *Homo sapiens* evolved in Africa, they were probably dark skinned; those who migrated northward into Eurasia lost their pigmentation. But it is just as possible that the first *Homo sapiens* appeared in northern climes, descendants of white-skinned *Homo erectus*. These could have migrated southward toward Africa, evolving darker skins. All modern races, incidentally, arose long after the brain had reached its present size in all parts of the world.

North–south variations in pigmentation are quite common among mammals and birds. The tropical races tend to be darker in fur and feather, the desert races tend to be brown, and those near the Arctic Circle are lighter colored.

There are exceptions among humans. The Indians of the Americas, from the Arctic to the southern regions of South America, do not conform to the north–south scheme of coloration. Though most think of Indians as being reddish-brown, most Indians tend to be relatively light skinned, much like their presumed Mongoloid ancestors in Asia. The ruddy complexion that lives in so many stereotypes of Indians is merely what years of heavy tanning can produce in almost any light-skinned person. Anthropologists explain the color consistency as a consequence of the relatively recent entry of people into the Americas— probably between 12,000 and 35,000 years ago. Perhaps they have not yet had time to change.

Only a few external physical differences other than color appear to have adaptive significance. The strongest cases can be made for nose shape and stature.

WHAT'S IN A NOSE

People native to colder or drier climates tend to have longer, more beak-shaped noses than those living in hot and humid regions. The nose's job is to warm and humidify air before it reaches sensitive lung tissues.

The colder or drier the air is, the more surface area is needed inside the nose to get it to the right temperature or humidity. Whites tend to have longer and beakier noses than blacks or Orientals. Nevertheless, there is great variation within races. Africans in the highlands of East Africa have longer noses than Africans from the hot, humid lowlands, for example.

Stature differences are reflected in the tendency for most northern peoples to have shorter arms, legs and torsos and to be stockier than people from the tropics. Again, this is an adaptation to heat or cold. One way of reducing heat loss is to have less body surface, in relation to weight or volume, from which heat can escape. To avoid overheating, the most desirable body is long limbed and lean. As a result, most Africans tend to be leaner than northern Europeans. Arctic peoples are the shortest limbed of all.

Hair forms may also have a practical role to play, but the evidence is weak. It has been suggested that the more tightly curled hair of Africans insulates the top of the head better than does straight or wavy hair. Contrary to expectation, black hair serves better in this role than white hair. Sunlight is absorbed and converted to heat at the outer surface of the hair blanket; it radiates directly into the air. White fur, common on Arctic animals that need to absorb solar heat, is actually transparent and transmits light into the hair blanket, allowing the heat to form within the insulating layer, where it is retained for warmth.

Aside from these examples, there is little evidence that any of the other visible differences among the world's peoples provide any advantage. Nobody knows, for example, why Orientals have epicanthic eye folds or flatter facial profiles. The thin lips of Caucasoids and most Mongoloids have no known advantages over the Negroid's full lips. Why should middle-aged and older Caucasoid men go bald so much more frequently than the men of other races? Why does the skin of Bushmen wrinkle so heavily in the middle and later years? Or why does the skin of Negroids resist wrinkling so well? Why do the Indian men in one part of South America have blue penises? Why do Hottentot women have such unusually large buttocks?

There are possible evolutionary explanations for why such apparently useless differences arise.

One is a phenomenon known as sexual selection. Environmentally adaptive traits arise, Darwin thought, through natural selection—the environment itself chooses who will thrive or decline. In sexual selection, which Darwin also suggested, the choice belongs to the prospective mate.

In simple terms, ugly individuals will be less likely to find mates and reproduce their genes than beautiful specimens will. Take the blue penis as an example. Women might find it unusually attractive or perhaps believe it to be endowed with special powers. If so, a man born with a blue penis will find many more opportunities to reproduce his genes than his ordinary brothers.

Sexual selection can also operate when males compete for females. The moose with the larger antlers or the lion with the more imposing mane will stand a better chance of discouraging less well-endowed males and gaining access to females. It is possible that such a process operated among Caucasoid males, causing them to become markedly hairy, especially around the face.

ATTRACTIVE TRAITS

Anthropologists consider it probable that traits such as the epicanthic fold or the many regional differences in facial features were selected this way.

Yet another method by which a trait can establish itself involves accidental selection. It results from what biologists call genetic drift.

Suppose that in a small nomadic band a person is born with perfectly parallel fingerprints instead of the usual loops, whorls or arches. That person's children would inherit parallel fingerprints, but they would confer no survival advantages. But if our family decides to strike out on its own, it will become the founder of a new band consisting of its own descendants, all with parallel fingerprints.

Events such as this, geneticists and anthropologists believe, must have occurred many times in the past to produce the great variety within the human species. Among the apparently neutral traits that differ among populations are:

Ear Wax.   There are two types of ear wax. One is dry and crumbly and the other is wet and sticky. Both types can be found in every major population, but the frequencies differ. Among northern Chinese, for example, 98 percent have dry ear wax. Among American whites, only 16 percent have dry ear wax. Among American blacks the figure is 7 percent.

Scent Glands.   As any bloodhound knows, every person has his or her own distinctive scent. People vary in the mixture of odoriferous compounds exuded through the skin—most of it coming from specialized glands called apocrine glands. Among whites, these are concentrated in the armpits and near the genitals and anus. Among blacks, they may also be found on the chest and abdomen. Orientals have hardly any apocrine glands at all. In the words of the Oxford biologist John R. Baker, "The Europids

and Negrids are smelly, the Mongolids scarcely or not at all." Smelliest of all are northern European, or so-called Nordic, whites. Body odor is rare in Japan. It was once thought to indicate a European in the ancestry and to be a disease requiring hospitalization.

Blood Groups.   Some populations have a high percentage of members with a particular blood group. American Indians are overwhelmingly group O—100 percent in some regions. Group A is most common among Australian aborigines and the Indians in western Canada. Group B is frequent in northern India, other parts of Asia and western Africa.

Advocates of the pure-race theory once siezed upon blood groups as possibly unique to the original pure races. The proportions of groups found today, they thought, would indicate the degree of mixing. It was subsequently found that chimpanzees, our closest living relatives have the same blood groups as humans.

Taste.   PTC (phenylthiocarbamide) is a synthetic compound that some people can taste and others cannot. The ability to taste it has no known survival value, but it is clearly an inherited trait. The proportion of persons who can taste PTC varies in different populations: 50 to 70 percent of Australian aborigines can taste it, as can 60 to 80 percent of all Europeans. Among East Asians, the percentage is 83 to 100 percent, and among Africans 90 to 97 percent.

Urine.   Another indicator of differences in body chemistry is the excretion of a compound known as BAIB (beta-amino-isobutyric acid) in urine. Europeans seldom excrete large quantities, but high levels of excretion are common among Asians and American Indians. It has been shown that the differences are not due to diet.

No major population has remained isolated long enough to prevent any unique genes from eventually mixing with those of neighboring groups. Indeed, a map showing the distribution of so-called racial traits would have no sharp boundaries, except for coastlines. The intensity of a trait such as skin color, which is controlled by six pairs of genes and can therefore exist in many shades, varies gradually from one population to another. With only a few exceptions, every known genetic possibility possessed by the species can be found to some degree in every sizable population.

EVER-CHANGING SPECIES

One can establish a system of racial classification simply by listing the features of populations at any given moment. Such a concept of race is, however, inappropriate to a highly mobile and ever-changing species such as *Homo sapiens*. In the short view, races may seem distinguishable, but in biology's long haul, races come and go. New ones arise and blend into neighboring groups to create new and racially stable populations. In times, genes from these groups flow into other neighbors, continuing the production of new permutations.

Some anthropologists contend that at the moment American blacks should be considered a race distinct from African blacks. They argue that American blacks are a hybrid of African blacks and European whites. Indeed, the degree of mixture can be calculated on the basis of a blood component known as the Duffy factor.

In West Africa, where most of the New World's slaves came from, the Duffy factor is virtually absent. It is present in 43 percent of American whites. From the number of blacks who are now "Duffy positive" it can be calculated that whites contributed 21 percent of the genes in the American black population. The figure is higher for blacks in northern and western states and lower in the South. By the same token, there are whites who have black ancestors.

The number is smaller because of the tendency to identify a person as black even if only a minor fraction of his ancestors were originally from Africa.

The unwieldiness of race designations is also evident in places such as Mexico where most of the people are, in effect, hybrids of Indians (Mongoloid by some classifications) and Spaniards (Caucasoid). Many South American populations are tri-hybrids—mixtures of Mongoloid, Caucasoid and Negroid. Brazil is a country where the mixture has been around long enough to constitute a racially stable population. Thus, in one sense, new races have been created in the United States, Mexico and Brazil. But in the long run, those races will again change.

Sherwood Washburn, a noted anthropologist, questions the usefulness of racial classification: "Since races are open systems which are intergrading, the number of races will depend on the purpose of the classification. I think we should require people who propose a classification of races to state in the first place why they wish to divide the human species."

The very notion of a pure race, then, makes no sense. But, as evolutionists know full well, a rich genetic diversity within the human species most assuredly *does*.

"Race": Myths under the Microscope

Racism has historical roots. It has not been a universal phenomenon. Many contemporary societies and cultures show little trace of it. It was not evident for long periods in world history. Many forms of racism have arisen out of the conditions of conquest, out of the justification of Negro slavery and its aftermath of racial inequality in the West, and out of the colonial relationship. Among other examples is that of anti-Semitism, which has played a particular role in history, with Jews being the chosen scapegoat to take the blame for problems and crises met by many societies.

Man is a creature endowed with the fabulous power of self-construction, the ability to participate in his own creation; but the price of this capacity is investment with its opposite: that of self-destruction. The latter may take violent forms—even the collective suicide of the species has now become possible, because of the existence of nuclear weapons. But it also manifests itself in mean, shifty, surreptitious types of behaviour, among which racism is surely the most widespread.

Scorn for others because they belong to a different group is by no means a recent phenomenon, but it is one which during the present century has developed along new lines, with the assertion that "recent discoveries of modern science" and "biologically proven models" justify the classification of human populations in hierarchical order.

If scientific progress had indeed led to such conclusions, we would be obliged to take them into account, irrespective of our moral, philosophical or religious opinions. But what science tells us today, notably where the most relevant discipline—genetics—is concerned, is the exact opposite: to claim, on biological grounds, that certain individuals within a given group, or certain groups, naturally constitute an élite is totally to misunderstand the message of biology.

Awareness that scientists should be given the opportunity of stating their views on the subject, unequivocally and before the widest possible audience, led Unesco to organize in Athens, in the spring of 1981, a symposium where representatives of various disciplines could set out their most recent findings, and where racist arguments could be countered in a reasoned, dispassionate manner.

Twenty-two scientists were thus able to spend a week discussing the issues involved in a totally frank and open atmosphere, bringing from a wide spectrum of countries that included Lebanon, Tunisia, Morocco, Israel, Mexico, France, Ivory Coast, Norway, the USA and the USSR, contributions in the fields of anthropology, ethnology, psychology, genetics, sociology, history, mathematics, law and philosophy.

The diversity of cultures and disciplines represented strengthened, rather than weakened, the intensity of the debates; the genuine interdisciplinarity which characterized the exchange of views enabled each participant to understand the ideas communicated by the others and to share with them his own questionings and commentaries.

Racism was successively examined in relation to the following branches of learning: genetics; psychology and neurobiology; sociology; anthropology and ethnology; history and prehistory.

At the conclusion of the symposium, the participating scientists, together with the representatives of Unesco, drew up a joint Appeal, the terms of which were discussed at length and unanimously approved.

GENETICS AND RACISM

Advances in the field of genetics have made it possible to determine with accuracy the content of the biological heritage of human populations; whereas, during the past centuries, attempts at racial definition were based on observable, external features such as skin colour, hair texture and cranial structure, examination of these characteristics has now been replaced by the investigation of the genetic structures which determine them.

The overall frequency with which various genes are encountered in the members of a given group constitutes the genetic structure of that group. The differences between the structures of two populations can be synthesized by establishing a "distance" calculated from frequencies observed in each group. The definition of races thus involves grouping together populations between which genetic distances are small, and attributing to different races populations between which genetic distances are wide.

Where the human species is concerned, however, this procedure proves fruitless. Migratory movements have taken place on such a scale, and the isolation of individual groups has been so short-lived that differentiations between groups have not reached a level which makes it possible to trace boundaries between separate, relatively homogeneous populations. The variability of the human species, which is considerable, is not to be explained in terms of the differences between the average genetic distances between various groups, but in terms of the differences to be found in individual members of the same group. According to findings published by Richard Lewontin in 1974, the average genetic distance between two individuals increases by only 7 or 8 per cent when they belong to two different nations, and by only 15 per cent when they belong to two different "races."

Consequently, the type of grouping described above can only be arbitrary. For the geneticist the concept of race corresponds to no stable or objective reality where humankind is concerned.

Genetics also provides us with an argument to set against the second proposition of racist theory: that races can not only be defined, but can also be classified by order of superiority.

In fact, investigation of mechanisms of selection reveals that their effect is not to retain the "best" and to eliminate what is less satisfactory, but rather to preserve the coexistence of a great variety of characteristics. Wealth, in biological terms, is not synonymous with "good" genes, but with genetic diversity: the "best" group is that which has conserved the widest variety of genes, irrespective of the composition of that variety.

From this point of view, therefore, it is obviously impossible to invoke biological arguments to justify some sort of "natural" hierarchy of individuals or populations.

PSYCHOLOGY, NEUROLOGY, AND RACISM

When psychology became "scientific" in the mid-nineteenth century, it set itself the task of comparing the intellectual performances of individuals and groups. This analysis of differences was quickly replaced by attempts to establish relationships of superiority and inferiority. Techniques of testing were devised whereby human beings were classified in relation to an implicitly accepted norm, the average behaviour of modern Western society. As a general rule, the results of such tests are presented in numerical form, as the Intelligence Quotient, or IQ. This measurement is widely used, but it is rarely interpreted in a way which takes into account the limits of its significance.

The mere fact of expressing the IQ in numerical form creates the illusion that it measures a magnitude with an independent existence. In reality, however, comparisons between individuals of different cultures or between groups which are made using IQ are, by virtue of the definition of IQ itself, devoid of any real meaning.

Misunderstandings about the IQ are particularly dangerous when they are related to the problem of "innate and acquired" characteristics. Abuse of the concept of heritability, devised by geneticists, has led certain psychologists to attribute variations in IQ between individuals or groups to a combination of genetic and environmental factors (the ratio being generally of the order of 80 per cent for the former and 20 per cent for the latter). In fact, none of the conditions necessary to validate the measurements of heritability are here present; the figures advanced are thus not even inaccurate, they are meaningless.

SOCIOLOGY AND RACISM

Racism should not be considered as the inevitable product of a necessary sequence of cause and effect. More particularly, it is false to see racism as a mere consequence of economic phenomena, when it is in fact an interaction in which racial animosity and the quest for a scapegoat combine and focus on a minority the aggressivity engendered by failures and setbacks of all kinds, notably economic.

It is not objective economic situations that encourage racism, but the subjective interpretations of those situations. The manner in which a situation is perceived is of greater consequence than the situation itself. The process is thus one in which political action plays a decisive role, and where the media, by virtue of the notions to which they give currency and the manner in which they present the facts, also play a decisive part. The invocation of a "threshold of tolerance" is a good example of the use of a mechanism presented as natural, in order to justify the rejection of minorities. In fact, such thresholds cannot be measured, and correspond to nothing that can be objectively defined.

The situation of those who are oppressed because of their "race" is not the outcome of an inevitable malediction; it is simply an observable state of affairs which cannot be justified in any way.

The often distorted propagation of certain arguments advanced by sociobiologists can prove extremely dangerous. Sociobiology deals with the causes and circumstances, including those of a genetic nature, which determine the organization of animal societies, ranging from termites to primates. The extrapolation of its findings to humankind is obviously risky and should only be undertaken with the greatest care. For example, the assertion that most human behaviour is genetically conditioned rests on no serious evidence. Little caution is shown by certain journalists who claim that theories which are still the subject of debate are "scientifically proved"; other writers conceal dogmatic attitudes behind what they claim is scientific evidence.

ANTHROPOLOGY, ETHNOLOGY, AND RACISM

Anthropology sets out to make a global study of man, integrating the physical, genetic, cultural and historical points of view. In all these domains, individuals differ from each other, and anthropology endeavoured, over a long period, to take these differences into account in preparing classifications and where possible in tracing the outlines of more or less homogeneous groups, or "races." The latter were thus defined as the product of a division of humanity according to transmissable physical characteristics. But this analysis is of doubtful value because of the importance of the genetic exchanges occurring between groups, the intensity of which has varied in different ages and regions. Such exchanges have increased during the past few centuries, and consequently groups which might have been defined as "races" in the past have disappeared, giving place to other, provisional regroupings.

But the essential contribution of anthropology is to show that the feelings of superiority found in most human groups is related to their culture, and not to their biological heritage; their sentiments are ethnocentric, and not racist. Racism, as a belief in the natural superiority of a given group, is of comparatively recent origin. It developed parallel to the colonial expansion of the European powers, finding scientific justification in a mistaken extrapolation of the theories of Darwin, social Darwinism. Reaching its height during the period of Nazism, it has subsequently declined appreciably, despite the rearguard actions of certain groups (which appear notably in *The Mankind Quarterly*), or individuals, such as the psychologist Arthur Jensen.

Anthropologists have reacted forcefully; for example, an important study by R. Sinha, of India, has shown that "there is no innate difference in intellectual capacities between the different racial groups."

In the last analysis, the problem with which we are confronted is not one of justifying or invalidating racist attitudes, but rather that of understanding why such attitudes persist, despite a total absence of justification.

HISTORY, PREHISTORY, AND RACISM

Over the centuries, racist theories have developed in response to the requirements of dominant groups. Not infrequently, they have embodied contradictory premises. The eighteenth century, for example, saw the simultaneous adoption of the myth of the "noble savage" as opposed to the "wicked sophisticate," and the uninhibited practice of slavery, while, at the present time, when the findings of science are demolishing the very foundations of racism, there are those who consistently invoke science in their attempts to promote its resurgence.

Historical studies enable us to compare the mechanisms which determine the evolution of a racist society (which inevitably drifts into a state of tension between dominant and dominated groups and in which the range of alternatives grows steadily smaller), and those which govern the development of a progressive, pluralist society (open to interchange and to all the different forms of creativity which become possible thanks to a permanent ferment of ideas and action).

The resurgence of racism presents a challenge to which we must respond by a steadfast call for the social diversification which it is in our power to achieve: diversification through science and technology, through culture, through recourse to our origins and through freedom available to all.

Barry Bogin

The Tall *and* the Short of It

Baffled by your future prospects? As a biological anthropologist, I have just one word of advice for you: plasticity. *Plasticity* refers to the ability of many organisms, including humans, to alter themselves—their behavior or even their biology—in response to changes in the environment. We tend to think that our bodies get locked into their final form by our genes, but in fact we alter our bodies as the conditions surrounding us shift, particularly as we grow during childhood. Plasticity is as much a product of evolution's fine-tuning as any particular gene, and it makes just as much evolutionary good sense. Rather than being able to adapt to a single environment, we can, thanks to plasticity, change our bodies to cope with a wide range of environments. Combined with the genes we inherit from our parents, plasticity accounts for what we are and what we can become.

Anthropologists began to think about human plasticity around the turn of the [twentieth] century, but the concept was first clearly defined in 1969 by Gabriel Lasker, a biological anthropologist at Wayne State University in Detroit. At that time scientists tended to consider only those adaptations that were built into the genetic makeup of a person and passed on automatically to the next generation. A classic example of this is the ability of adults in some human societies to drink milk. As children, we all produce an enzyme called lactase, which we need to break down the sugar lactose in our mother's milk. In many of us, however, the lactase gene slows down dramatically as we approach adolescence—probably as the result of another gene that regulates its activity. When that regulating gene turns down the production of lactase, we can no longer digest milk.

Lactose intolerance—which causes intestinal gas and diarrhea—affects between 70 and 90 percent of African Americans, Native Americans, Asians, and people who come from around the Mediterranean. But others, such as people of central and western European descent and the Fulani of West Africa, typically have no problem drinking milk as adults. That's because they are descended from societies with long histories of raising goats and cattle.

Among these people there was a clear benefit to being able to drink milk, so natural selection gradually changed the regulation of their lactase gene, keeping it functioning throughout life.

That kind of adaptation takes many centuries to become established, but Lasker pointed out that there are two other kinds of adaptation in humans that need far less time to kick in. If people have to face a cold winter with little or no heat, for example, their metabolic rates rise over the course of a few weeks and they produce more body heat. When summer returns, the rates sink again.

Lasker's other mode of adaptation concerned the irreversible, lifelong modification of people as they develop—that is, their plasticity. Because we humans take so many years to grow to adulthood, and because we live in so many different environments, from forests to cities and from deserts to the Arctic, we are among the world's most variable species in our physical form and behavior. Indeed, we are one of the most plastic of all species.

One of the most obvious manifestations of human malleability is our great range of height, and it is a subject I've made a special study of for the last 25 years. Consider these statistics: in 1850 Americans were the tallest people in the world, with American men averaging 5' 6". Almost 150 years later, American men now average 5' 8", but we have fallen in the standings and are now only the third tallest people in the world. In first place are the Dutch. Back in 1850 they averaged only 5' 4"—the shortest men in Europe—but today they are a towering 5' 10". (In these two groups, and just about everywhere else, women average about five inches less than men at all times.)

So what happened? Did all the short Dutch sail over to the United States? Did the Dutch back in Europe get an infusion of "tall genes"? Neither. In both America and the Netherlands life got better, but more so for the Dutch, and height increased as a result. We know this is true thanks in part to studies on how height is determined. It's the product of plasticity in our childhood and in our mothers' childhood as well. If a girl is undernourished and suffers poor health, the growth of her body, including her reproductive system, is usually reduced. With a shortage of raw materials, she can't build more cells to construct a bigger body; at the same time, she has to invest what materials she can get into repairing already existing cells and tissues from the damage caused by disease. Her shorter stature as an adult is the result of a compromise her body makes while growing up.

Such a woman can pass on her short stature to her child, but genes have nothing to do with it for either of them. If she becomes pregnant, her small reproductive system probably won't be able to supply a normal level of nutrients and oxygen to her fetus. This harsh environment reprograms the fetus to grow more slowly than it would if the woman was healthier, so she is more likely to give birth to a smaller baby. Low-birthweight babies (weighing less than 5.5 pounds) tend to continue their prenatal program of slow growth through childhood. By the time they are teenagers, they are usually significantly shorter than people of normal birth weight. Some particularly striking evidence of this reprogramming comes from studies on monozygotic twins, which develop from a single fertilized egg cell and are therefore identical genetically. But in certain cases, monozygotic twins end up being nourished by unequal portions of the placenta. The twin with the smaller fraction of the placenta is often born with low birth weight, while the other one is normal. Follow-up studies show that this difference between the twins can last throughout their lives.

As such research suggests, we can use the average height of any group of people as a barometer of the health of their society. After the turn of the century both the United States and the Netherlands began to protect the health of their citizens by purifying drinking water, installing sewer systems, regulating the safety of food, and, most important, providing better health care and diets to children. The children responded to their changed environment by growing taller. But the differences in Dutch and American societies determined their differing heights today. The Dutch decided to provide public health benefits to all the public, including the poor. In the United States, meanwhile, improved health is enjoyed most by those who can afford it. The poor often lack adequate housing, sanitation, and health care. The difference in our two societies can be seen at birth: in 1990 only 4 percent of Dutch babies were born at low birth weight, compared with 7 percent in the United States. For white Americans the rate was 5.7 percent, and for black Americans the rate was a whopping 13.3 percent. The disparity between rich and poor in the United States carries through to adulthood: poor Americans are shorter than the better-off by about one inch. Thus, despite great affluence in the United States, our average height has fallen to third place.

People are often surprised when I tell them the Dutch are the tallest people in the world. Aren't they shrimps compared with the famously tall Tutsi (or "Watusi," as you probably first encountered them) of Central Africa? Actually, the supposed great height of the Tutsi is one of the most durable myths from the age of European exploration. Careful investigation reveals that today's Tutsi men average 5' 7" and that they have maintained that average for more than 100 years. That means that back in the 1800s, when puny European men first met the Tutsi, the Europeans suffered strained necks from looking up all the time. The two-to-three-inch difference in average height back then could easily have turned into fantastic stories of African giants by European adventurers and writers.

The Tutsi could be as tall or taller than the Dutch if equally good health care and diets were available in Rwanda and Burundi, where the Tutsi live. But poverty rules the lives of most African people, punctuated by warfare, which makes the conditions for growth during childhood even worse. And indeed, it turns out that the Tutsi and other Africans who migrate to Western Europe or North America at young ages end up taller than Africans remaining in Africa.

At the other end of the height spectrum, Pygmies tell a similar story. The shortest people in the world today are the Mbuti, the Efe, and other Pygmy peoples of Central Africa. Their average stature is about 4' 9" for adult men and 4' 6" for women. Part of the reason Pygmies are short is indeed genetic: some evidently lack the genes for producing the growth-promoting hormones that course through other people's bodies, while others are genetically incapable of using these hormones to trigger the cascade of reactions that lead to growth. But another important reason for their small size is environmental. Pygmies living as hunter-gatherers in the forests of Central African countries appear to be undernourished, which further limits their growth. Pygmies who live on farms and ranches outside the forest are better fed than their hunter-gatherer relatives and are taller as well. Both genes and nutrition thus account for the size of Pygmies.

Peoples in other parts of the world have also been labeled pygmies, such as some groups in Southeast Asia and the Maya of Guatemala. Well-meaning explorers and scientists have often claimed that they are genetically short, but here we encounter another myth of height. A group of extremely short people in New Guinea, for example, turned out to eat a diet deficient in iodine and other essential nutrients. When they were supplied with cheap mineral and vitamin supplements, their supposedly genetic short stature vanished in their children, who grew to a more normal height.

Another way for these so-called pygmies to stop being pygmies is to immigrate to the United States. In my own research, I study the growth of two groups of Mayan children. One group lives in their homeland of Guatemala, and the other is a group of refugees living in the United States. The Maya in Guatemala live in the village of San Pedro, which has no safe source of drinking water. Most of the water is contaminated with fertilizers and pesticides used on nearby argricultural fields. Until recently, when a deep well was dug, the townspeople depended on an unreliable supply of water from rain-swollen streams. Most homes still lack running water and have only pit toilets. The parents of the Mayan children work mostly at clothing factories and are paid only a few dollars a day.

I began working with the schoolchildren in this village in 1979, and my research shows that most of them eat only 80 percent of the food they need. Other research shows that most of them eat only 80 percent of the food they need. Other research shows that almost 30 percent of the girls and 20 percent of the boys are deficient in iodine, that most of the children suffer from intestinal parasites, and that many have persistent ear and eye infections. As a consequence, their health is poor and their height reflects it: they average about three inches shorter than better-fed Guatemalan children.

The Mayan refugees I work with in the United States live in Los Angeles and in the rural agricultural community of Indiantown in central Florida. Although the adults work mostly in minimum-wage jobs, the children in these communities are generally better off than their counterparts in Guatemala. Most Maya arrived in the 1980s as refugees escaping a civil war as well as a political system that threatened them and their children. In the United States they found security and started new lives, and before long their children began growing faster and bigger. My data show that the average increase in height among the first generation of these immigrants was 2.2 inches, which means that these so-called pygmies have undergone one of the largest single-generation increases in height ever recorded. When people such as my own grandparents migrated from the poverty of rural life in Eastern Europe to the cities of the United States just after World War I, the increase in height of the next generation was only about one inch.

One reason for the rapid increase in stature is that in the United States the Maya have access to treated drinking water and to a reliable supply of food. Especially critical are school breakfast and lunch programs for children from low-income families, as well as public assistance programs such as the federal Women, Infants, and Children (WIC) program and food stamps. That these programs improve health and growth is no secret. What is surprising is how fast they work. Mayan mothers in the United States tell me that even their babies are bigger and healthier than the babies they raised in Guatemala, and hospital statistics bear them out. These women must be enjoying a level of health so improved from that of their lives in Guatemala that their babies are growing faster in the womb. Of course, plasticity means that such changes are dependent on external conditions, and unfortunately the rising height—and health—of the Maya is in danger from political forces that are attempting to cut funding for food stamps and the WIC program. If that funding is cut, the negative impact on the lives of poor Americans, including the Mayan refugees, will be as dramatic as were the former positive effects.

Height is only the most obvious example of plasticity's power; there are others to be found everywhere you look. The Andes-dwelling Quechua people of Peru are well-adapted to their high-altitude homes. Their large, barrel-shaped chests house big lungs that inspire huge amounts of air with each breath, and they manage to survive on the lower pressure of oxygen they breathe with an unusually high level of red blood cells. Yet these secrets of mountain living are not hereditary. Instead the bodies of young Quechua adapt as they grow in their particular environment, just as those of European children do when they live at high altitudes.

Plasticity may also have a hand in determining our risks for developing a number of diseases. For example, scientists have long been searching for a cause for Parkinson's disease. Because Parkinson's tends to run in families, it is natural to think there is a genetic cause. But while a genetic mutation linked to some types of Parkinson's disease was reported in mid-1997, the gene accounts for only a fraction of people with the disease. Many more people with Parkinson's do not have the gene, and not all people with the mutated gene develop the disease.

Ralph Garruto, a medical researcher and biological anthropologist at the National Institutes of Health, is investigating the role of the environment and human plasticity not only in Parkinson's but in Lou Gehrig's disease as well. Garruto and his team traveled to the islands of Guam and New Guinea, where rates of both diseases are 50 to 100 times higher than in the United States. Among the native Chamorro people of Guam these diseases kill one person out of every five over the age of 25. The scientists found that both diseases are linked to a shortage of calcium in the diet.

This shortage sets off a cascade of events that result in the digestive system's absorbing too much of the aluminum present in the diet. The aluminum wreaks havoc on various parts of the body, including the brain, where it destroys neurons and eventually causes paralysis and death.

The most amazing discovery made by Garruto's team is that up to 70 percent of the people they studied in Guam had some brain damage, but only 20 percent progressed all the way to Parkinson's or Lou Gehrig's disease. Genes and plasticity seem to be working hand in hand to produce these lower-than-expected rates of disease. There is a certain amount of genetic variation in the ability that all people have in coping with calcium shortages—some can function better than others. But thanks to plasticity, it's also possible for people's bodies to gradually develop ways to protect themselves against aluminum poi-soning. Some people develop biochemical barriers to the aluminum they eat, while others develop ways to prevent the aluminum from reaching the brain.

An appreciation of plasticity may temper some of our fears about these diseases and even offer some hope. For if Parkinson's and Lou Gehrig's diseases can be prevented among the Chamorro by plasticity, then maybe medical researchers can figure out a way to produce the same sort of plastic changes in you and me. Maybe Lou Gehrig's disease and Parkinson's disease—as well as many other, including some cancers—aren't our genetic doom but a product of our development, just like variations in human height. And maybe their danger will in time prove as illusory as the notion that the Tutsi are giants, or the Maya pygmies—or Americans still the tallest of the tall.

PART III

ARCHAEOLOGY

Archaeology is the systematic retrieval and study of the remains (both of people and their activities) that human beings and their ancestors have left behind on and below the surface of the earth. Like biological anthropology, archaeology gradually emerged as a separate discipline in the course of the nineteenth century. It split off from the generalized study of ancient history as scholars—mostly geologists, initially—began to focus on finding material remains of ancient precivilized populations in Europe.

Actually, it was a geological debate that helped lay the groundwork for the emergence of archaeology. The prevailing view among geologists until well into the nineteenth century was that the various strata that compose the earth's crust were the result of either Noah's flood (diluvialism) or a series of catastrophes of which the flood was the most recent (catastrophism). One of the first geologists to dispute these notions was William Smith (1769–1839). Dubbed "Strata" Smith by his detractors, he assembled a detailed table of all the known strata and their fossil contents and argued a uniformitarian position: that the eternally ongoing processes of erosion, weathering, accumulation, and the movement of the continents accounted for the large number of strata. He was supported by James Hutton (1726–1797) in his influential work, *Theory of the Earth*, published in 1795.

The battle was joined by the greatly respected William Buckland (the discoverer of the "Red Lady of Paviland," which was discussed in the introduction to Part Two), who in 1823 published his work, *Reliquiae Diluvianae*, or *Observations on the Organic Remains Contained in Caves, Fissures and Diluvial Gravel, and on Other Geological Phenomena Attesting to the Action of a Universal Deluge*. Here he vigorously attacked the uniformitarian views that so directly contradicted church dogma. Only the appearance of Sir Charles Lyell's *Principles of Geology* (1830–1833)

managed finally to turn the tide of scholarly sentiment in favor of the uniformitarian view of the earth's history.

Because of the nature of their work, it was for the most part amateur and professional geologists who most frequently encountered fossilized human remains, generally embedded in strata in the floors of limestone caverns. In the roughly six decades following the 1790s, an impressive array of evidence with regard to human antiquity was found in a number of such caves in Europe and England, but the finds were dismissed or their importance unrecognized. As early as 1797, for example, John Frere (1740–1807) found chipped flint tools twelve feet deep in his excavation at Hoxne (northeast of London). These stone tools were associated with the remains of extinct animal species. To Frere, these finds suggested a very ancient human existence, even older than the commonly accepted 6,000-year antiquity of creation. Nobody listened. Forty years later, in 1838, Boucher de Perthes (1788–1868), a customs collector at Abbeville in the northwest of France, disclosed news of some flint "axes" he had found in gravel pit caves on the banks of the Somme River. The world laughed at his assertion that these tools were manufactured by "antediluvial man" (people who existed before Noah's flood), even though they had been found in the immediate vicinity of the bones of extinct cold-adapted animals. In 1846, he published *Antiquités Celtiques et Antediluviènnes*, in which he formally argued his thesis—and was attacked as a heretic by the church.

We have already discussed William Buckland's inability in 1822 to comprehend the significance of his own find, the so-called Red Lady of Paviland. The powerful grip of Christian theology on scholars' minds blinded them from seeing and appreciating the overwhelming pattern that these and numerous other finds presented. As I have emphasized repeatedly, it was the emergence of Darwinism in 1859 that freed people's vision and enabled them to face and reinterpret these materials correctly. The evolutionary perspective, then, was of critical importance for the emergence of archaeology. Without it, there was no way to interpret accurately the significance of the ancient remains that were turning up with increasing frequency.

The excavation of rock shelters revealing human cultural remains of great antiquity was only one of several kinds of archaeological research being undertaken in the nineteenth century. The excavation and description of large prehistoric monuments and burial mounds, begun in the wake of emergent nationalism in the seventeenth and eighteenth centuries, continued. So did the retrieval and preservation of materials accidentally brought to light by road, dam, and building excavations as the industrial revolution changed the face of the earth. By the 1800s, vast quantities of stone and metal implements had been recovered and had found their way into both private and public collections. As the volume of such artifacts mounted, museum curators were faced with the problem of how to organize and display them meaningfully.

In 1836, Christian Jurgensen Thomsen (1788–1865), curator of the Danish National Museum, published a guide to its collections in which he classified all artifacts in terms of the material from which they were made. He argued that the three classes he thus identified represented stages in cultural evolution: a *Stone Age* followed by a *Bronze Age* and then an *Iron Age*. The idea was not new—it had been proposed by Lucretius in ancient Rome—but it was new for its time. Moreover, the *Three-Age System* fit well with the contemporary writings of early nineteenth-century social evolutionists and was of such usefulness that it quickly spread to other countries.

The Three-Age System was clearly evolutionary (and hence radical). It contained a geological perspective in that it proposed clearly defined sequences of cultural stages modeled after geological strata. It was of tremendous value in providing a conceptual framework through which archaeologists could begin systematically to study the artifacts they retrieved from the earth, and in tending to support those scholars arguing for a greatly expanded vision of human antiquity.

Combined with Darwinian evolutionism, the Three-Age System became an even more powerful conceptual tool. In 1865, Sir John Lubbock (1834–1913) published his tremendously influential book, *Prehistoric Times,* in which he vastly extended the Stone Age and divided it in two. He thus proposed that human prehistory be viewed in terms of the following stages: the *Paleolithic* (Old Stone Age, marked by flint tools); the *Neolithic* (New Stone Age, marked by the appearance of pottery); the *Bronze Age;* and the *Iron Age*. Although this system has continued to be refined, it still forms the basis of our understanding of world prehistory, and we continue to make use of its terminology.

At about the same time Lubbock was formulating his broad outline of the stages of cultural evolution, Edouard Lartet (whom we discussed earlier) and his English colleague, Henry Christy, were exploring the now famous rock shelters in the Dordogne region of France. In one cave, called la Madeleine, Christy and Lartet found not only an abundance of spectacular cave art and small engravings of extinct species such as the woolly mammoth, but also a magnificent collection of tools, including intricately carved implements of antler bone and ivory. These became the *type complex* for the identification of the Magdalenian culture, easily the most advanced and spectacular culture of Upper Paleolithic times.

Using the artwork they found in the ten or so caves they explored in this region, Lartet and Christy developed a system to classify the materials they uncovered. Their approach was based on the fact that renderings of different species of animals predominated during different periods. The succession of stages they worked out for the Dordogne region was the following: (1) the Age of the Bison, (2) the Age of the Woolly Mammoth and Rhinoceros, (3) the Age of the Reindeer, and (4) the Age of the Cave Bear.

Gabriel de Mortillet (1821–1898) took the work of Lartet and Christy a step further by developing a chronology of the same region based on the tool industries found at *type sites* (sites used to represent the characteristic features of a culture). The series he ultimately settled on in the 1870s had six stages: Thenaisian, Chellean, Mousterian, Solutrean, Magdalenian, and Robenhausian. Although these materials have been reinterpreted a great deal since that time, prehistoric archaeologists still use Mortillet's approach to naming archaeological cultures and even most of the names he proposed.

The archaeologist of the late nineteenth century who most attracted public attention was probably Heinrich Schliemann (1822–1890). After intensive study of the Homeric epics, Schliemann set out to find the ancient city of Troy. He accomplished this in 1871 at a place called Hissarlik, near the western tip of Anatolia (modern Turkey). He was a romantic figure, and his quest to find the sites of Homeric legend excited public fancy and brought forth private funds to support both his own and other archaeological research. Unfortunately, he was not a very skilled excavator: While digging up the highly stratified site at Hissarlik he focused his attentions on what turned out to be the wrong layer—and virtually destroyed the real Troy in the process.

As the frontiers of knowledge about human origins expanded in Europe with the emergence of increasingly specialized subdisciplines, a parallel development was taking place in the Americas. Wild speculation about the origins of Native Americans gave way to increasingly systematic research by scholars and learned amateurs. Thomas Jefferson (1743–1826) excavated a Native American burial mound in Virginia. Although his digging techniques were crude, he approached his task in a very modern manner. Rather than setting out simply to collect *artifacts*, Jefferson cut into the mound to collect *information*. His cross-section of the mound revealed ancient burial practices similar to those of known historic groups and refuted the popularly held notion that the mound builders had buried their dead in an upright position.

By the 1840s, John Lloyd Stephens and Frederick Catherwood had established new standards for care in the recording of details in their magnificent reports about, and drawings of, the ruins of the Mayan civilization in the Yucatan peninsula, published in works such as Stephens's *Incidents of Travel in Central America: Chiapas and Yucatan* (1842).

The mounds of the southeastern United States attracted a number of excavators, most notably E. G. Squier and E. H. Davis, who described their research in an important monograph published in 1848. By the middle of the century, sufficient work had been done to justify a long synthesis of U.S. archaeology by Samuel Haven, published in 1856.

Archaeology in the New World was always tightly connected to cultural anthropology—much more so than in Europe. This stemmed from the fact that although Europeans engaged in archaeological research as an extension of their researches backward from known historical times to their distant prehistoric past, Americans were investigating foreign societies—whether they were digging in their own backyards or engaging in ethnographic research with their displaced (and decimated) Native American neighbors. To this day that difference persists: In Europe, archaeology is usually thought of as a humanity (an adjunct to history), while in the United States and Canada, archaeology is practiced as a subdiscipline of anthropology and is viewed as a social science.

DOING ARCHAEOLOGY

How do we learn about the past? What kinds of evidence remain behind after ancient societies have vanished? How do we go about retrieving these remains, studying them, interpreting them? These are the concerns of archaeology.

Archaeological remains are the material things left behind by people (or other living creatures being studied) that are found or retrieved by trained specialists. Such remains may be collected from the surface of a site, retrieved from caves or under water, or dug up out of the ground. Amateurs—sometimes called "pot hunters" (see Article 15)—who find remains from prehistoric times and take them home for their private enjoyment or for sale to collectors, destroy archaeological remains by making it impossible to associate these finds with the environment in which they were found and therefore to understand their meaning.

Basically, archaeologists study three kinds of materials: remains of the environment, remains that were created by living creatures (on purpose or inadvertently), and the remains of creatures themselves. Students of archaeological remains have developed sophisticated and highly specialized techniques to retrieve and interpret this evidence from the past. For example, satellite scans of the earth's surface can reveal evidence (such as subtle shifts in vegetation caused by soil changes due to prehistoric activities) of underground prehistoric sites. Handheld radar guns on the ground can reveal buried house floors and even the compacted soil traces of ancient footpaths.

But finding sites (areas containing concentrations of archaeological remains) is only the beginning. After an area has been surveyed for the presence of archaeological remains and sites have been found, a crucial decision then must be made: Should a given site be excavated (and therefore irretrievably destroyed), or should it be preserved for possible excavation in the future when technological advances may vastly enhance what may be learned from it.

In Article 15, "Fingerprints in the Sand," Richard Monastersky discusses the damage done by "pot hunters" and methods that scientists are developing to find and help convict them.

One of the most interesting and ingenious method of gathering archaeological data is by analyzing the garbage people throw out. This has long been a staple in the toolbox of archaeologists studying past civilizations. But William Rathje, an archaeologist at the University of Arizona, uses garbage to learn more about how people live *today*. For more than twenty years, Rathje's Garbage Project has probed the habits of various groups of Americans by sifting through their garbage. Household garbage, it turns out, varies in ways that are quite predictable and reveals secrets, including some that people wouldn't dare admit. It also has many practical uses, from calculating how susceptible people are to different advertisements to use in the national census. In "Garbage Demographics," Rathje and Cullen Murphy describe what your garbage can reveal about you.

Human sacrifice has long been one of archaeology's most contentious issues and unprovable secrets. For the Aztecs, human sacrifice (and cannibalism) was part of their religion. Hernán Cortés and his *conquistadores* reported watching sixty-six of their fellow Spaniards brutally sacrificed in Tenochtitlán (now Mexico City), the Aztec capital, their beating hearts ripped out of their chests.

Strangely, though many groups have been accused of the practice, very little information on the origins and practice of human sacrifice had been collected—until recently. In Article 17, "Temples of Doom," Heather Pringle reports on the research of Canadian archaeologist, Steve Bouchet, who was able to demonstrate precisely how the Moche people of Mexico performed their grisly ritual. Still unanswered, though, is the question: *Why?*

Richard Monastersky

Fingerprints in the Sand

The moon rises heavy over New Mexico's high desert, casting its rays on scattered juniper trees, pinyon pines, and a crime in progress. Two men have just plundered the remnants of an ancient dwelling in the Gila National Forest and are loading up sacks with prehistoric pots and bead jewelry. As their truck swings homeward, they think about the handsome price these relics will fetch from dealers who sell fine antiquities.

That theft in New Mexico last year is but one case in a little-heralded crime wave sweeping the United States. Although the federal government and many states prohibit the unauthorized removal of artifacts from public lands, "pot hunters" illegally raid thousands of archaeological sites each year, ranging from prehistoric burial grounds in Washington state to the graves of Civil War soldiers in Virginia.

"While we tend to think of [archaeological] looting as a phenomenon that occurs outside the United States, the scale of looting inside this country is massive," says James Adovasio, an archaeologist at Mercyhurst College in Erie, Pa., who has investigated several such crimes.

Over the past two decades, the pace of pot hunting has grown steadily, reflecting a burgeoning antiquities market hungry for pretty legacies of the past. Archaeologists and law enforcement agents have responded by stepping up their own efforts. But it's often difficult to put the guilty behind bars, because savvy thieves can claim they collected artifacts legally on private property.

In the last three years, scientists have developed their own "dirty" tactics to circumvent that defense. Using X-rays and electron microscopes, they analyze soil particles recovered from stolen antiquities in an effort to prove the items were illegally removed from protected sites. So far, the high-tech soil tests have contributed to convictions in only a handful of cases. But those who investigate archaeological crimes believe the technique holds great potential in the battle against artifact thieves.

"Soils are probably *the* most important in our arsenal against these people right now, because it's pretty hard to dig in an archaeological site without taking soil away too," says Martin McAllister, an archaeologist and consultant who trains investigators to handle artifact crimes.

The New Mexico case illustrates how a criminal investigation can benefit from some snooping in the soil. The pillaged site once housed members of the Mimbres culture, who lived in the region around 1100 A.D. The looters not only carted off artifacts but also disturbed a Mimbres grave and left human bones strewn about the ancient dwelling, says Linda Kelley, a U.S. Forest Service archaeologist involved in the investigation.

As often happens, authorities did not learn of the crime until long after the thieves had fled. But with the help of informants, federal agents tracked down a pair of suspects and searched the house where they lived. The agents found several bits of evidence there, including a bag of pottery fragments and some reconstructed pots as well as dirt-covered coveralls and excavation tools. The suspects claimed they had collected the artifacts from private property with permission from the landowner.

Because police had not caught the suspects in the act of robbing the Mimbres site, archaeologists had to find circumstantial evidence that would convince a jury the seized material came from national forestland. Focusing on the dirt encrusting the tools, clothing, and pottery found in the suspects' home, Kelley called in a team of soil sleuths who had pioneered a technique for analyzing sediments in cases of archaeological theft.

Adovasio, working with geologist Gary A. Cooke of the R. J. Lee Group, Inc., in Monroeville, Pa., and sedimentologist Jack Donahue from the University of Pittsburgh, examined the recovered dirt and two other soil samples: one collected at the Gila site and another from the private property where the suspects claimed to have found the artifacts. Using a computer-controlled scanning electron microscope, the researchers drew up a list of the minerals and elements in each sample.

Donahue says such analyses provide a distinctive profile of the soil samples. "This is essentially a fingerprint, but you're fingerprinting sediment rather than a person," he explains.

The forensic tests struck pay dirt, revealing that the soil on the seized pottery and tools matched the sediment from the national forest rather than the sediment from the privately owned site.

Kelley found other clues implicating the purported thieves. During excavations at the Gila site she collected more than 8,000 pottery shards left behind by the looters. In scrutinizing the fragments, she found one that matched a pot shard recovered from the suspects' home. The clay bits fit together like adjoining pieces of a jigsaw.

Such a match might seem irrefutable, but this type of evidence hasn't always ensured convictions in the past. For that reason, Kelley says the additional evidence from the soil analysis will prove important when the case goes to trial. "We need this scientific analysis to get rid of the kind of doubt that an attorney could raise," she says.

When Donahue, Adovasio, and Cooke joined the New Mexico investigation, they already had a forensic success record of 2–0, having used soil analyses to provide hard evidence against suspected looters twice before.

The first of those cases involved a man named Earl Shumway, who discovered a spectacular cache of thirteenth-century Anasazi baskets in southeastern Utah, "the likes of which hadn't been collected in over 50 years," says Adovasio. Archaeologists suspected Shumway had looted the baskets from Manti-La Sal National Forest, but he claimed they came from private land.

Although Shumway had cleaned the baskets, Donahue and colleagues managed to collect a small sample of dirt from under the stitching, which enabled them to demonstrate that the baskets had come from the national forest. Prosecutors used this analysis in their case against Shumway, who eventually confessed to the crime.

In the second incident, a man was convicted of stealing a 1,500-year-old mummified infant from a site known as Tin Cave in Arizona's Tonto National Forest. Authorities arrested him in 1988 after he tried to sell the infant's remains for $20,000 to an undercover agent. Through soil analysis, the researchers linked sediment from inside the cave with dirt found with the mummy. Because the man never denied having taken the mummy from the cave, the

soil analysis wasn't critical to his conviction, but the trial provided an important test of the technique's reliability.

In the Utah and Arizona investigations, the scientists analyzed soils using X-ray fluorescence and X-ray diffraction rather than the electron microscopy technique applied to the New Mexico soils. While the X-ray tests can provide an equally accurate portrait of the minerals and elements within soil, the computer-controlled scanning electron microscope technique is faster and easier, says Donahue.

Soil analysis has long played a role in investigations of artifact poaching, notes McAllister, a veteran in the field of archaeological criminology. But until the last five years, he says, authorities have used relatively simple techniques that lack the fingerprint-like accuracy of X-ray and electron microscope analyses.

Investigators have used the high-tech tests in only a few cases so far, primarily because news of the advances has yet to spread and the tests can cost up to $5,000 per case. But Donahue says many universities and research organizations have the necessary equipment to perform this type of analysis.

"I think the soil tests will be used more commonly in the future," McAllister says, noting that it's very difficult to prove that purloined artifacts came from a protected area without such evidence. "Even if you find someone driving, down a road through a national forest with a truckful of pots or other artifacts in their possession, you're not necessarily going to be able to prosecute them," he says.

Paradoxically, the new tests may lose some of their power against criminals as they gain popularity with investigators. That's because looters pay close attention to new legal tactics and adjust their methods to stay ahead of the law.

Several years ago, authorities started using an approach that capitalized on looters' disregard for the environment. Pot hunters often left cigarettes, beer cans, and other garbage at the scene of the crime, and investigators collected the trash as evidence. But the looters soon caught on to that technique. "They're running a much cleaner operation now," says J. Scott Wood, an archaeologist at the Tonto forest who worked on the Tin Cave case.

Investigators have also drawn evidence from distinctive footprints and tire tracks found near excavation sites. Looters have responded by buying boots with common soles and tires with unremarkable treads. Most archaeological thieves are tightly "networked," readily passing on information about new forensic techniques. Already, many have begun fastidiously cleaning off their artifacts and tools, Wood says. As this trend continues, he says, "the success of soil techniques will depend on when we catch them. If we can get them before they clean their stuff off, then we have a chance."

Part of the problem, says Adovasio, is that the techniques work best when soil samples are large enough to allow several tests. "But if worse comes to worse, as was the case with the Shumway business, we can use extremely minuscule portions to do the job—thimble-size or smaller," he says.

Donahue recounts one instance in which the team scraped tiny bits of sediment from within the grooves in an arrowhead and found the sample sufficient for analysis. Thus, he says, "even if [the looters] clean it off very carefully, we still have a chance of finding material that can be analyzed."

Although experts lack detailed statistics showing the extent of archaeological looting in the United States, they say the problem has worsened in recent decades as antiquity prices have reached staggering levels. Most of the plundered material ends up gracing coffee tables of wealthy U.S. collectors, although an increasing proportion reaches Japan, Europe, and Saudi Arabia, says McAllister.

"It's going on everywhere in the United States, anyplace you find an historic or prehistoric artifact that has collector interest. You'll find people stealing from public lands, tribal lands, and even off private property without the permission of the owner," he says.

People outside the archaeological community may wonder whether this looting truly represents a serious problem. After all, the United States has thousands of archaeological sites, and museums have countless artifacts stored away in dusty basements.

Yet that reasoning belies the real impact of pot hunting. There are only a finite number of archaeological sites holding information about prehistoric life; no more will ever exist. The raiding of these sites wipes out our record of past peoples. When looters ransack a site, they not only remove artifacts but also rearrange critical archaeological clues, destroying the contextual information researchers need to understand a particular site, Kelley says.

That information cannot be recovered even if police locate the stolen goods. "A looted artifact has lost 95 percent of its value to tell us what was going

on in the prehistoric or historic period," McAllister says.

He also raises a more subtle concern about the effects of looting. Thieves routinely target the most important archaeological sites, such as ancient villages, because these places are the most likely to contain valuable artifacts, McAllister says. "[Looters] are going to destroy our ability to understand what happened in the prehistoric period because we're losing a whole category of sites," he warns. Imagine, for instance, a future scholar trying to reconstruct U.S. history without access to the information stored in state capitals and Washington, D.C.

In the battle against archaeological crime, investigators continually seek new techniques for outwitting robbers, and they believe soil analysis can play an important role. But forensic tricks alone won't end the raids.

"Most professionals agree that law enforcement isn't the [long-term] solution. Public education is really what we're trying to do," Kelley says.

Archaeologists distinguish between two types of looters: the serious thieves and the "weekend hunters," who often see nothing wrong with their hobby. Through public awareness campaigns and education in schools, federal and state officials hope to reduce casual looting and raise an outcry against commercial raiders. Increased awareness might also translate into stronger antitheft laws and help cut pure vandalism of archaeological remains, a growing problem in many parts of the nation.

This type of outreach program would represent a major shift for archaeological scholars in the United States. "One of the main problems we have with the public is what I call archaeological arrogance," McAllister says. "Archaeologists like to maintain the position that archaeology is for archaeologists only, that it's something the public has no right to have access to. This attitude plays right into the hands of the commercial looters."

Some states have already developed programs to involve lay people in excavations, and the idea seems to be catching on elsewhere. Perhaps such projects can channel the energy of artifact buffs, reducing the temptation to steal pieces of the past.

Garbage Demographics

Analyzing household garbage is an unusual but useful form of demographic research. Household garbage varies in predictable ways, and garbage also reveals what people really do—even if they won't admit it. One research team even devised a way to use garbage to check the 1990 census. They found that plastic is the great garbage equalizer, and they discovered meaning in disarded diapers, toys, and cosmetics.

If you were to identify a hundred households that were home to at least one cat but not to any dogs, here is something that you would learn from garbage from those households: if you collected their garbage for five weeks, you would find that at some point during that period, 30 percent of the households had thrown away a copy of *The National Enquirer.*

If you were to look at garbage from a group of Hispanic households, here in one thing you would discover: the most popular baby-food vegetable by far is squash, which accounts for some 38 percent of the baby-food vegetables that Hispanics consume (squash has been a dietary staple in Mexico and Central America for at least 9,000 years). Among Anglos, in contrast, the most popular baby-food vegetable is peas, accounting for 29 percent of all baby-food vegetables consumed. For Anglos, squash ranks next to last in terms of preference, just above spinach.

If you were to look at household garbage for food waste from fast-food hamburger take-out restaurants and fast-food chicken take-out restaurants, you would learn the following: the wasted food from chicken restaurants (35 percent of all food bought, not counting bones) is considerably greater than the wasted food from hamburger restaurants (only about 7 percent of all food bought).

All of these findings reflect phenomena that are regular and reliable—phenomena that are durable, at least in part, because they involve the behavior, as reflected in garbage, of large numbers of people. As two decades of research by the University of Arizona's Garbage Project have established, the patterns of behavior that link masses of people and masses of garbage are strong and stable. Garbage thus becomes an important tool of demographic research.

WHAT PEOPLE REALLY DO

Garbage can be viewed as part of an ecosystem whose properties depend on the weather, the season of the year, and the rate of growth of the Gross National Product. Perhaps not surprisingly, the solid-waste stream becomes a little thinner during times of recession than it is when the economy is robust and a lot heavier and wetter in the hot months. Summer garbage is also the type most thickly studded with valuable aluminum beer and soda cans.

The properties of garbage vary markedly—but also predictably—from one kind of neighborhood to another. A trash bag containing many nondiet soda cans and relatively little discarded food has a high probability of having originated in a Hispanic household. Garbage with lots of packaging from "status" brand-name foods and drinks is more likely to have come from a middle-income neighborhood than from an affluent one, while an affluent neighborhood is most likely to discard containers that once held diet soft drink or store-brand and generic foods.

Garbage can be a window into specific and private forms of consumer behavior. Let us say that a supermarket chain in a certain city has advertised a special discount price on a specific kind of detergent. Garbage sampling over a period of weeks could reveal: (a) the percentage of households that proved susceptible to the advertisement, (b) the percentage of the households buying the detergent in which it was put to use immediately rather than stockpiled, (c) the percentage of households that bought the detergent and then bought it a second time, and (d) the percentage of households that bought the detergent, didn't like the results, and threw the rest away.

Garbage analysis can also reveal what consumers actually do, even if they won't admit doing it. In 1986, the University of Arizona's Garbage Project was asked by Heinz U.S.A. to undertake a study in Tucson of various aspects of baby-food consumption in the United States. One odd phenomenon was identified accidentally. It was the desire of the Hispanic women surveyed to leave the impression that they prepared all of their baby food from fresh materials. In the course of the study, members of the households whose garbage was going to be analyzed had been asked the following question: "In the past seven days, did your household use any commercially prepared baby food or junior foods?" Not a single Hispanic mother admitted to using even one jar of baby food, but garbage from the Hispanic households had just as many baby-food jars in it as garbage from other households with infants. Forty-five percent of the Hispanic women in the neighborhood were in the labor force. But the Hispanic mothers were still reporting adherence to an idealized form of cultural behavior that may not have been the norm for many years,

GARBAGE TO CHECK THE CENSUS

Also in 1986, the Census Bureau asked the Garbage Project to help solve one of its chronic problems: undercounting. The bureau does a near-perfect job of counting mainstream Americans, but its enumerators have been missing a large share of undocumented aliens, homeless people, residents of urban ghettos (especially men), and others who live in society's nether world. The people missed by the census are often poor, in many cases illiterate, and

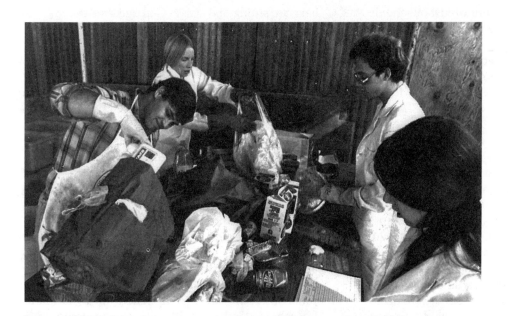

The Tucson Garbage Project

The brainchild of a group of anthropologists at the University of Arizona, the Tucson Garbage Project was launched in 1973 in order to study the material culture of a modern city by ``excavating'' its garbage, considered as evidence of its residents' way of life. In the words of the Project's director, Professor William L. Rathje, ``We believed that assumptions about the way material culture is related to behavior in past civilizations can be tested in a familiar, on-going society. Second, we felt that applying archaeological methods to such a society can produce valuable insights into that society itself.'' Above, Rathje's student workers carefully sort, record, and weigh household garbage for evidence of what contemporary society buys and how it lives. This attempt to take a systematic look at modern society in the United States from the archaeological viewpoint is the prototype of similar studies conducted elsewhere in the United States as well as in Mexico City and Sydney, Australia.

Photo reprinted by permission from W. L. Rathje, Tucson, Arizona.

perhaps fearful of the census if they are aware of it at all.

The Census Bureau came to the Garbage Project to see whether data derived from garbage could reliably be used to check the bureau's enumerations of problematic neighborhoods, particularly neighborhoods where the census was missing large numbers of adult minority men. The Garbage Project's job was to find out if it was possible to roughly reconstruct a community's population by age and sex simply on the basis of what that community threw away. The task was entrusted to a Garbage Project researcher, Masakazv Tani.

To an archaeologist, the idea of using garbage to reconstruct population characteristics is neither bizarre nor uncommon. Archaeologists frequently need to estimate the size of some ancient community without the aid of written records. Indeed, this is one of the classic problems of archaeology, and many techniques for arriving at population size have been tried. But they can be fairly blunt instruments. "Archaeological population estimates," says Jeffrey Reid, an archaeologist at the University of Arizona and the editor of the journal *American Antiquity*, "are just the number of identified dwellings multiplied by some magic number that is a guess at an average number of household residents."

The Garbage Project's Census Bureau study was also a search for a "magic number"—a multiplier that, when applied to certain quantities of certain kinds of garbage, would yield accurate population estimates. But the Garbage Project started out with advantages that other archaeologists could only envy. For one thing, they had a mass of computerized evidence compiled during studies of food consumption and garbage production in 63 demographically distinct households. The data were compiled by actually sorting, counting, weighing, and recording the garbage from these households over a considerable period of time. Thanks to the database (which continues to grow), the patterns of modern American household garbage were already clear.

The project's first task was to come up with a way of making the leap from the quantity of garbage, or the quantity of a particular type of garbage, to an overall population estimate. One could begin, of course, with the knowledge—confirmed by various Garbage Project studies—that in the United States, in general, the larger the household, the more garbage it tends to produce. The idea now was to come up with a magic number. If you multiplied this number by the weight of all the garbage—or that of all of 1 of 16 particular subtypes of garbage—collected from a certain group of households over a specified period of time, you would get the population of those households. It turned out that the categories "total solid waste" and "plastic" had the most accurate predictive power, and it was on the basis of these that the correlation equations were derived.

THE GREAT EQUALIZER

The equation derived from "total solid waste" is, however, less universally reliable than the one for "plastic;" this is because children are responsible for less garbage overall than are adults. Roughly speaking, one adult's total solid waste equals that of 1.45 children. As a result, population counts based on total solid waste would be skewed by data from a neighborhood whose ratio of adults to children was markedly different from that in the 63 original sample households.

Plastic is another story, however. During any given period of time, every man, woman, and child in America seems to generate about the same amount of plastic garbage, usually in the form of many small items. Plastic accounts for about 0.2 pounds of the 2.1 pounds of garbage that is thrown away in a day by the typical household. It is America's great garbage equalizer.

The following equation, which has been stripped of certain technical apparatus, expresses the relationship between plastic and population: household size = 0.2815 × plastic, where the plastic quantity is based on a five-week collection of material and is recorded in pounds.

For a neighborhood of some 100 households, the projected population estimate derived from the Garbage Project equation (or rather, from the average of the "total solid waste" and "plastic" results), applied to one week's worth of garbage, will be accurate to within plus or minus 2.5 percent. That is considerably better than the Census Bureau can do in many places.

Overall population is only one demographic characteristic, however. What about producing estimates by age and sex? This turned out to be a trickier proposition. The easiest subpopulation to discern is infants. Disposable diapers are a convenient marker for this group of people, and infants go through so many of them in a week that infant diapers are an ideal item for establishing correlations: the regularity and the volume of their disposal helps suppress statistical biases. Here's the equation (again, simplified) for estimating the number of babies in any given neighborhood: infant population = 0.01506 × number of diapers, where the number of diapers is based on a five-week collection. Remember that this equation is designed to yield only the number of disposable diapers recorded in household garbage, not the total number of disposable diapers infants use.

Unfortunately, there is not one item of garbage that can help us determine the proportion of men and women in a population, or the proportion of children and elderly people—none, at any rate, with the ease and power that disposable diapers display with respect to infants. It is not that men and women (or children and old people) do not leave traces. But the material correlates for various demographic groups tend to become a little unreliable as one leaves infancy behind.

As a demographic marker, disposable diapers for infants are what is known as an "exclusive:" only infants wear them.* But when it comes to distinguishing between men and women, or middle-aged and elderly adults, there are fewer exclusives and far more "proportionals." These are items that, like disposable razors, may indicate the presence of members of a particular demographic group (in the case of razors, adult men), but don't necessarily do so. Moreover, the exclusives or near-exclusives that do exist for these groups are primarily items that are discarded very infrequently, and thus, for demographic purposes, have little predictive value. In the case of the elderly, for example, a copy of *Modern Maturity* may stay around for six weeks before being discarded.

TOYS, COSMETICS, AND CIGARS

It took a considerable amount of work, but the Garbage Project staff eventually came up with an equation for estimating the proportion of children in a population. The estimate is based on the average rate of discard of toys and toy packages (2.52 per child per week), and the average rate of discard of children's clothes and clothes packaging (0.87 per child per week). It was also possible to derive equa-

tions for estimating the proportion of adult women in a population, based on the number of discarded female-hygiene products (1.58 per woman per week), cosmetics, (0.86 per woman per week), and women's clothing items (0.62 per woman per week).

Finding serviceable material correlates for estimating the proportion of adult men—the Census Bureau's ultimate objective, remember—proved more elusive. Men are not exactly invisible in garbage, but garbage is a more unreliable indicator of their live-in presence than it is for any other demographic group. Women may drink and eat like men. They smoke cigarettes. They sometimes wear men's clothing and men's cologne. Even the presence in garbage of male contraceptive packaging is at best equivocal evidence of a male household resident. The butt-ends of cigars, or packaging from men's underwear, may be indicative of a live-in male. But such diagnostic aids are exceedingly rare.

In the end, the best way to get a figure for the number of adult men in a given neighborhood turns out to be a backdoor procedure. First, find the total neighborhood population. Next, subtract the estimates for infants, children, and adult women from the total population estimate. The result is an estimate of the male population, and it has an accuracy of better than plus or minus 10 percent. Thus, if the actual population of adult males in a neighborhood was 240, the evidence from garbage would yield a range from 216 to 264.

Using garbage for population estimation would not be all that helpful in places like Greenwich or Beverly Hills, where the Census Bureau's data are accurate down to the last scullery maid. But there is not much doubt that estimates derived from garbage could provide a usable snapshot of low-income neighborhoods. As it happened, however, the Garbage Project never got the chance.

In 1988, the director of the Census Bureau's Center for Survey Methods Research decided that, from a public-relations standpoint, "it was risky for the government to hire someone to analyze garbage." A year later, the bureau announced its decision not to adjust the 1990 census to compensate for the expected undercount, a decision to which it has adhered. But the Garbage Project stands ready for the year 2000.

---

*Or so one would like to presume. It is conceivable, of course, that there is an equivalent for disposable diapers of the cloth-diaper fetishist in St. Petersburg, Florida, who posed as a diaper-service driver and stole diapers off people's porches; after the thief's eventual apprehension, in 1987—he was wearing a diaper under his clothes at the time—a search of his home turned up some 370 diapers, all cleaned and neatly folded.

Heather Pringle

Temples of Doom

Human sacrifice has long been one of history's unprovable secrets. Then Steve Bourget began digging at the Pyramid of the Moon in Peru.

Few things so unnerved the Spanish conquerors of the New World as the prospect of death on a sacrificial stone. On one summer afternoon in 1521, while laying siege to the Aztec capital of Tenochtitlán, what is now Mexico City, Hernán Cortés and his army watched in horrified silence as Aztec priests on the opposite lakeshore struggled up the stairs of a temple with 66 Spanish captives. Stretching them one at a time across a narrow stone, the priests carved out their beating hearts then swiftly butchered their bodies so their flesh could be eaten ritually. Four decades later, one of Cortés's lieutenants wrote: "We were not far away from them, yet we could render them no help, and could only pray to God to guard us from such a death."

For the Aztecs, human sacrifices were ironically the stuff of life. Only human blood, they later told Spanish priests, could give the sun strength for its daily climb from the underworld. Other societies shared their belief in the power of the human heart. As Spanish armies ventured into the small Mayan villages of the Guatemalan rain forests and marched over the paved Incan roads of the Andes, they returned with tales of similar terrifying bloodbaths.

But for all the grisly accounts of the early Spanish chroniclers, archeologists have exhumed surprisingly little evidence of these rituals. Even in excavations at Templo Mayor, the most important temple in Tenochtitlán and the place where, according to the Aztecs' own books, some 20,000 war captives were sacrificed in a single ceremony in 1487, archeologists have yet to turn up any mass graves or any of the massive skull racks constructed by Aztec priests from the craniums of their victims. One reason, says John Verano, a physical anthropologist at Tulane University in New Orleans, is that the racks were simply "broken up, burned probably, and thrown out." As a result, scientists have failed to

gather even basic data on the origins and practice of human sacrifice in the Americas.

But now, thanks to a series of stunning archeological discoveries, researchers are gaining a clearer glimpse of these ancient rituals. The picture comes not from the most famous civilizations encountered by the Spanish armies but from a much earlier and lesser known Andean people—the Moche (pronounced MO-chay) of Peru's northern coastal desert. A sophisticated society of farmers and fishers, the Moche flourished from A.D. 100 to 800 in the narrow river valleys that slice down from the Andes to the Pacific near the modern city of Trujillo. The Moche so prospered from their irrigated cornfields and the cold, nutrient-rich waters of the nearby Pacific that they had time to raise ten-story pyramids, rub shoulders in settlements of 50,000 people, and nurture great artists.

For decades, archeologists puzzled over the paintings on Moche pots. Many portrayed knife-wielding gods holding human heads, and owl-headed priests presiding over human sacrifices, but few researchers believed they reflected actual practices. Over the past five years, however, researchers have uncovered startling forensic evidence of human sacrifice—from mass graves of ritually slaughtered and dismembered victims to giant wall murals incorporating butchered human bones. By comparing skeletal remains with painted scenes, they are now assembling what is arguably the most detailed portrait of sacrifice yet to emerge in the ancient world.

The grim finds promise to shed new light on many aspects of Moche culture, from religion to warfare to politics. Although the clearest evidence of human sacrifice had come from a crumbling temple pyramid in what many suggest was the Moche capital, Verano and others have now found tantalizing hints of similar sacrifices at another important

Moche center, suggesting that several ruling houses, perhaps each governing a major river valley, could have held sway over the Moche.

The new discoveries raise a host of questions, not the least of which is why the Moche performed human sacrifices. Experts such as Elizabeth Benson turn for answers to the Andean peoples' religious beliefs and their abiding concern with the fertility of the land. "Blood was like rain; it was like water," says Benson, an independent scholar living in Maryland and the author of several books on the Moche. "It made things grow. It nourished the earth" Other researchers disagree, pointing out that religious beliefs only justified actions taken for other reasons.

The ecology and politics of human sacrifice were a long way from most researchers' minds when a little-known Canadian archeologist, Steve Bourget, began searching five years ago for sites where the Moche performed their slaughter. Bourget, who now teaches at the University of East Anglia in Norwich, England, had just finished his Ph.D. dissertation on Moche art and sacred geography at the University of Montreal. During his studies he had found several depictions of mountaintop rituals in which priests seemed to fling humans to their death down steep slopes. Such scenes, he knew, fit with ancient beliefs in the region: the Incas had regarded mountain peaks as sacred. If the Moche pots showed real events, reasoned Bourget, then the sacrifices could have taken place very near several major Moche temples that stood at the feet of small mountains.

At a sprawling site just a few miles southeast of Trujillo, he spent days clambering up and down the steep, rocky flanks of Cerro Blanco, a small mountain directly above one of the most important Moche temples, called the Pyramid of the Moon. But while Bourget found a likely prominence for sacrifices, he could not find bones or other evidence of such rites. The same disappointment awaited him at a second Moche settlement, Huancaco.

Back home, Bourget began poring over Moche depictions of a different sacrifice ritual, one that had been studied in detail in the 1970s and 1980s by Christopher Donnan, an archeologist at UCLA. The gruesome ritual, which Donnan called the warrior narrative, was a favorite theme of Moche artists, appearing on ancient pots and wall murals. "It starts with Moche warriors going off to combat," says Donnan. "Then there's the combat itself, and some of the warriors are captured. All their weapons, ornaments, and clothing are taken from them. What follows is a stage where the captors make them bleed—very deliberately, I think. They slap their faces and they tear the warriors' nose ornaments out. They put ropes around their necks and parade them. The sacrifice follows." Under the watchful eyes of ritualists—three high priests and a high priestess, each in distinctive ritual finery—attendants slit the captives' throats and catch their blood in ceremonial goblets. Later they dismember the bodies.

Donnan, like other Moche experts, assumed that the warrior narrative owed more to fiction than fact. But in 1987, while excavating a tomb at the site of Sipán, Peruvian archeologist Walter Alva and his colleagues exhumed the body of a great Moche lord, dressed sumptuously for death and dating to approximately A.D. 300. The man wore large circular earspools and an immense gold headdress, a nose ornament, and a back flap, all crescent-shaped like the blade of a sacrificial knife. By his side lay a scepter with a bladelike handle. These were the insignia of the warrior priest. "I never imagined that we would find this stuff," says Donnan. "I didn't even mention it to the (research) team for a few days, because I thought the probabilities were so remote that I must be losing my grip." Further excavations uncovered the tombs of two high priestesses.

But if the sacrifices were actual events, where were all the victims? Back in England, Bourget studied depictions of the warrior narrative for clues. In a few, the ancient artists had painted lines of captured prisoners being led to pyramid-shaped temples. Were they slaughtered there? The more Bourget thought about it, the more likely it seemed. And he even had a hunch about where to look in the rambling temple complexes. At the Pyramid of the Moon, he had noticed a plaza about the size of four tennis courts surrounded by a high adobe wall, built around 500: in one corner of the plaza rose a large outcrop of rock—a mini-mountain. "I extrapolated that if there was a human sacrifice practice in the mountains, and if rocks are a symbolic extension of the mountains themselves, the sacrifices might have been performed in front of these rock altars," he says.

In 1995, Bourget put together a small team of researchers and began excavating the plaza. Peeling back layers of sediment, he was soon surrounded by whitened human skeletons. Splayed and tangled like a truckful of rag dolls tossed into a pit, the dead bore little resemblance to most Moche cadavers, which were laid out neatly on their backs. Near some were fragments of smashed clay figurines of naked men bound about the neck with a rope. Bourget was jubilant. "We'd never found a real sacrificial site before," he says. "We had iconographic representations of sacrificial practices. We had indirect evidence from funerary contexts and some evidence of decapitation. But we never had a real sacrificial site. For the first

WHY DID THE GODS DEMAND BLOOD?

"To the people who say the Moche or the Aztecs did sacrifices because their gods demanded it, I would say, Why did their gods demand it and other peoples' gods did not?" observes Michael Winkelman, an anthropologist at Arizona State University in Tempe. "I think there are good ecological, social, and political reasons people end up in these practices and predicaments."

In the 1980s, Winkelman delved through thousands of pages of published scientific accounts of 45 societies around the world, searching for human sacrifice. He came up with seven sacrifice-performing societies, from the Marquesans of the South Pacific to the Romans. Other research teams had ranked the groups for a multitude of variables, from risk of famine to the adequacy of food-storage systems. By correlating the rankings with human sacrifice, Winkelman detected several traits that distinguished the societies.

While all seven groups were agricultural, only one suffered a high risk of famine and none were notably short of meat protein. But nearly all suffered from relatively high population densities, exceeding 26 people per square mile. And all fought wars over land and scarce resources. "So even if these societies have a very good food availability, the large population creates a lot of pressure because it places them all at risk if something happens to the food supply. So people are sacrificing each other partly to reduce the impact on existing food supplies," says Winkelman.

Moreover, all seven of the sacrificing societies were ruled locally by a leader from a powerful family and regionally by one lord who successfully wooed the support of local leaders. In such a system, treachery and betrayal were constant threats. To intimidate those contemplating betrayal, Winkelman says, leaders naturally gravitated toward human sacrifice.

Although some Moche experts call Winkelman's work thought provoking, few are ready to accept that his analyses apply to the Moche, because not enough is known about their population density or political organization. Still, Verano says of the tortured and executed Pyramid of the Moon warriors: "I could imagine that it would solidify the power of the leaders by terrifying the population. No one really saw what was happening, but they heard screams and the men never came back."

---

time, we could really see how the Moche performed human sacrifice."

Such a rare and complex burial site called for a specialist: a physical anthropologist who had studied the Moche and would approach the tangled bodies with all the fastidiousness of a modern crime investigator. John Verano fit the bill perfectly. An osteologist occasionally called in to assist with present-day forensic cases in the United States, Verano had worked with archeological teams on Peru's north coast since the mid-1980s. He set up an impromptu morgue in the Archeology Museum at the University of Trujillo.

As Bourget trucked in box after box of human remains from the dig over the next two field seasons, Verano and two assistants examined the collections for indicators of age and sex, then pored over each bone, recording all traces of injury, violence, or illness. Nothing could be taken for granted. While some skulls were separated from their bodies, for example, it was entirely possible that gravity had tugged them down a slight slope in the plaza floor as the skeletons decomposed. Only a clear pattern of cut marks could be accepted as evidence of decapitation. "You don't want to accuse anyone of murder if it's an accidental death," says Verano. "And you don't want to accuse someone of mutilating a body if it's just decomposition."

At least 70 corpses had once littered the ground of the temple plaza. All who could be identified belonged to a select demographic group: young, healthy, physically active males. Indeed, the mean age at death was just 23. Many, it turned out, were old hands at combat. One in every four bore healed rib, arm, leg, and skull fractures.

In addition, many of the men had fractures just beginning to knit at the time of death. These confirmed the story. Some of the dead, for example, had broken their arms in a specific spot, the midshaft of the ulna as if from parrying a blow. Others exhibited tiny fractures radiating from their nasal apertures: these corresponded eerily to scenes from the warrior narrative. "In Moche art," Verano says, "the artists often show prisoners being smacked on the nose so their noses will bleed, and that's often done at the time of capture."

Judging from the healing of wounds, the battered men survived for nearly two weeks after their capture, their last weeks mired in misery. Some endured torture in the form of deeply slashed fingers and toes, others suffered worse. "I had someone who had something inserted between the toes up into the arch of his feet and repeatedly pushed back and forth." says Verano, "so it was like a grooved injury."

Death, when it finally arrived, came swiftly. Among the men whose cervical spines were still intact, most bore cut marks that slashed across the front and sides of the neck vertebrae. Someone had slit their throats with a sharp knife. Others had perished from massive skull injuries; it looked as if someone armed with a heavy blunt weapon—perhaps a Moche war club—had bashed in their craniums.

Executioners abandoned most of the corpses to the elements. The soil surrounding the bodies, says Verano, was strewn with the Rice Krispie-like pupa shells of insects that feed on carrion and are incapable of digging for their dinners. This brutal treatment, he suggests, could have been intended to send a message to others. "Proper burial was very important in the Andes for people in the Inca period," says Verano. "One of the worst punishments that you could face was to be denied proper burial."

A few of the victims were set aside for a different fate. In a small enclosure next to the temple plaza, Bourget and his team exhumed the scattered remains of seven men. Cut marks striped their bones, often just where muscles once attached. "People were clearly taking the muscle off the bones for some reason," says Verano. "I think it's as good an argument for cannibalism as you'd find anywhere."

Taken together, Verano's data suggest that the bodies at the Pyramid of the Moon belonged to Moche warriors wounded and captured on the field of battle. It is entirely possible, he says, that the ancient desert dwellers, like the Aztecs, fought at least some battles specifically to capture young males for sacrifice. Little evidence of European-style warfare, which often leaves razed settlements and ruined defensive works in its wake, has ever surfaced in Moche territory. And most war scenes from Moche paintings show pairs of nobles dueling until one warrior is defeated.

What happened after capture is still unclear, but Verano suspects prisoners were marched back to the victors' home villages, where some were tortured, perhaps to prove them worthy of the ritual ahead. Like the Aztecs, notes Verano, the Moche may have considered death on the sacrificial stone an honorable way to go. "And you can see that surviving torture and proving that you were brave throughout the whole episode would have been crucial. You can imagine that it would be critical right up to the point of the sacrifice, because if you are screaming and being dragged up to have your throat slit, you won't look very honorable."

The sacrifice itself was cloaked in high pageantry. Dressed in full regalia, the ritualists watched as the captives were brought forward, naked but for the ropes. As the prisoners perished, the high priestess collected their blood in a goblet and passed it to the warrior priest—with a small addition. In many depictions, Moche artists portrayed a small wineskin-shaped fruit known as the ullucu. Native to the Amazon, the ullucu contains an anticoagulant agent, "which gives you a spooky idea that perhaps its juice was added to keep the blood from coagulating," Verano says.

Just how often the Moche conducted sacrifices and how many lives they took has yet to be determined. Only a small portion of the Pyramid of the Moon has been excavated, and Verano and others now believe that similar sacrifices took place in other Moche settlements. At El Brujo, a Moche community just 40 miles northwest of the Pyramid of the Moon, excavators from the University of Trujillo recently found what appears to be another mass grave. And last summer, Verano discovered something strange about an enormous mural on the site.

The pre-Columbian equivalent of a billboard, the mural was once visible for miles across the valley. Painted in brilliant crimson and electric yellow, it shows a row of Moche nobles dancing hand in hand above the heads of war captives stripped naked and bound with ropes around the necks. While studying the mural, researchers found a fallen chunk of mud plaster from one of the dancer's feet. A piece of bone protruded from one end. Examining it carefully, Verano could see that it was the rounded end of a human femur. It had been chopped from a cadaver, stripped of flesh, and incorporated into the giant mural. "The dancers are stepping on the bones of their enemies," he says, "or they're dancing on the bones of their victims."

While new evidence explains much about how sacrifices were performed, it falls far short of answering why. The dead have little to say on this score, and for clues, most Moche researchers have turned to early Spanish accounts of Incan religion. In the manuscripts of priests living among the Incas, researchers such as Elizabeth Benson have traced an intimate link between the offering of human lives and agricultural fertility. "I think that in the past, people thought they could change the world by ritual," says Benson. "We think we can change it with technology so we've lost a lot of the sense of the importance of ritual. But in the past, people thought that this was how you controlled the world, how you had enough food for your people. And a human being was the most important offering you could make."

For all their importance, the men at the Pyramid of the Moon knew little kindness in their final moments. Only now, a millennium and a half later, concludes Verano, have they received the respect due to the dead. "When I was brushing them off and cleaning the bones and putting them in boxes, I thought, 'The last time anybody touched you, they were cutting your throat or sticking sticks up your feet.' I treated them kindly, but it was a little late."

ISSUES IN ARCHAEOLOGY

In Topic 6 we approach the study of archaeology by focusing on some of the major questions that scholars are attempting to answer today. The first article looks at one of the liveliest debates in American archaeology: the question of when the New World first was populated.

No serious scholars doubt any longer that the Americas were populated by fully evolved human beings in hunting and food-gathering bands. But where did they come from, and when? Until the late 1990s, there was a great deal of agreement: they came about 12,000 years ago, probably migrating in pursuit of big game on the Siberian plains. They crossed over the Bering Strait land bridge connecting Siberia and Alaska sometime during the last glacial period that marked the end of the Ice Age, and found themselves in a paradise rich in wild game and bountiful in plant life.

They thrived and their numbers grew rapidly as they migrated southward and eastward, seeking out the new and incredibly diverse environmental niches that met their needs and fit their fancies. Eventually they developed a spectacular variety of lifestyles that included advanced civilizations in the highlands and jungles of Mesoamerica, vital communities of salmon fishers on the Northwest Coast of North America, adobe cliff dwellers and complex canal builders in the U.S. Southwest, dazzling mound builders in the Midwestern plains, advanced canal-building civilizations high in the Andes Mountains of Peru, and countless bands of seminomadic hunters and food gatherers from the Inuit of Alaska to the bison hunters of the Great Plains to the Yahgan of Tierra del Fuego in Argentina.

It was a wonderful story, but as it turns out, none of it may be true—not the *who*, not the *where*, not the *how*, and certainly not the *when*. In Article 18, Sharon Begley and Andrew Murr describe the search for "The First Americans."

In 1864, one of the most fascinating discoveries in archaeological history was made at La Madeleine, in France. At a riverside rock shelter, excavators dis-covered an incised drawing of a woolly mammoth, the first picture of an extinct species ever discovered. Since that time, dozens of such sites, containing hundreds of hauntingly beautiful paintings, have been discovered in Europe. In "Images of the Ice Age," Alexander Marshack, a researcher with the Peabody Museum of Archaeology and Ethnology at Harvard, explores how the study of these caves has contributed to our understanding of how they were used...and why.

The invention of agriculture was the first in a triple revolution that forever changed the lives of human beings around the world. Where and when was agriculture first invented? Until the 1980s, archaeologists believed the answer was clear. But recent discoveries have challenged many of our notions about the origin of agriculture. People living in widely scattered parts of the world—from southern Europe to western Egypt to the Nile Valley to Kenya, and also in Southeast Asia—may well have domesticated plants and animals as early as 19,000 years ago. That is 8,000 years before the beginnings of the great agricultural civilizations of Mesopotamia (modern Iraq). However, unlike developments in Mesopotamia, early domestication in these places did not lead quickly to the second and third great revolutions in human cultural evolution—the emergence of cities and the rise of civilizations.

In Article 20, "New Clues Show Where People Made the Great Leap to Agriculture," John Noble Wilford describes recent archaeological research that has pinpointed the site (in southeast Turkey) where wheat was first domesticated from a wild species 11,000 years ago. Wheat, it turns out, was much easier to domesticate than maize, which some experts believe was why densely populated agricultural societies arose in the Middle East much earlier than in the New World.

Ever since the 1950s, anthropologists have assumed that newly domesticated cereal grains were first used to bake bread. But even at that time, there was a dissenting view. Jonathan Sauer, a famous botanist, suggested that the domestication of cereals might have been for the purpose of brewing beer. This prompted Robert Braidwood, an eminent anthropologist, to organize a symposium under the title "Did Man Once Live by Beer Alone?" In that symposium, Sauer argued that bread simply was not enough of a payback for the enormous amount of work that farming requires—but that beer might well have been.

Sauer was in a distinct minority; even other botanists disagreed with him. And the debate died …until 1990—when the Anchor Brewing Company in San Francisco revived it as a publicity gimmick. But, interestingly enough, the gimmick produced some exciting research that suggests we should take Sauer's original proposal seriously. In Article 21, "Brewing an Ancient Beer," Solomon H. Katz and Fritz Maytag tell you why.

For whatever reason or reasons it was invented, the emergence of agriculture created the bedrock on which was built the second great reorganization of human existence—the invention of the city.

Most of us take cities for granted, but archaeology reveals how profoundly city dwelling has changed human existence in the last 7,000–8,000 years. Thus, it cannot be denied that some of the most spectacular achievements in philosophy—mathematics, the natural sciences, the arts, and literature—were rooted in the urban way of life. In fact, most refinements of crafts and arts were made by city dwellers. But on the other hand, we must recognize that cities also created the conditions of terrible human filth and poverty by crowding together landless, unskilled, and often unemployed workers and their families. Garbage and waste disposal were (and continue to be) major public health problems for cities, and diseases were bred and spread by urban living conditions. Thus, the city, a hallmark of our own civilization, is a problematic development at best, and archaeology has much to tell us of its origins, development, possibilities, and failures.

In Article 22, Orrin Shane III and Mine Küçük describe "The World's First City." Çatalhöyük, located in central Turkey, was first described in the early 1960s. The site dates to 9,000 years ago, when it boasted a population of several thousand people and stood "at the threshold of civilization." Excavations, using sophisticated new archaeological tools, resumed in 1995, and they have added immensely to our knowledge of the place where human beings first made the transition to urban life.

Money (or is it love?) may make the world go 'round, and we take the concept so much for granted that it's hard to remember that someone first had to come up with the concept of money. When, and where, did humans first use money? "The Cradle of Cash," Article 23, presents some new ideas and archaeological evidence on the use of the first cold hard cash—silver ring money—in Mesopotamia.

The third great revolution in the cumulative sociocultural history of humankind, beginning with the invention of agriculture and marked by the rise of cities, is the emergence of civilization.

Henry T. Wright, in Article 24, "Rise of Civilization: Mesopotamia to Mesoamerica," provides the penultimate article for Topic 6. He reviews the kinds of evidence that have been amassed for the rise of civilization in each of five separate regions. For each geographical region Wright asks: "What kinds of evidence have we got to develop our understanding of events?" and then, "What further kinds of evidence would be helpful?" This is a most useful perspective from which to approach not only archaeology, but all anthropological research also.

Civilizations that rise eventually must fall. Some 4,000 years ago, four of the world's great Bronze Age civilizations, widely scattered, all crumbled and bit the dust at roughly the same time. In "Empires in the Dust," Karen Wright explores the question of why they all disappeared: was it political strife, social unrest, or a change in the climate?

The First Americans

As he sat down to his last meal amid the cattails and sedges on the shore of the ancient lake, the frail man grimaced in agony. A fracture at his left temple was still healing; deep abscesses in his gums shot bolts of pain into his skull. Still, he was a survivor, at forty-something long-lived for his people. But soon after he finished the boiled chub that he had netted from a stream in what is now western Nevada, he felt his strength ebbing like a tide. He lay down. Within hours he was dead, felled by septicemia brought on by the dental abscess. When his people found him, they gently wrapped his body in a rabbit-fur robe and secured his bulrush-lined leather moccasins, his prize possessions; he had patched them twice with antelope hide on the right heel and toe. Surely he would want them where he was going. His people dug a shallow grave in a rock shelter, lined it with reed mats and laid him within. Some 9,400 years

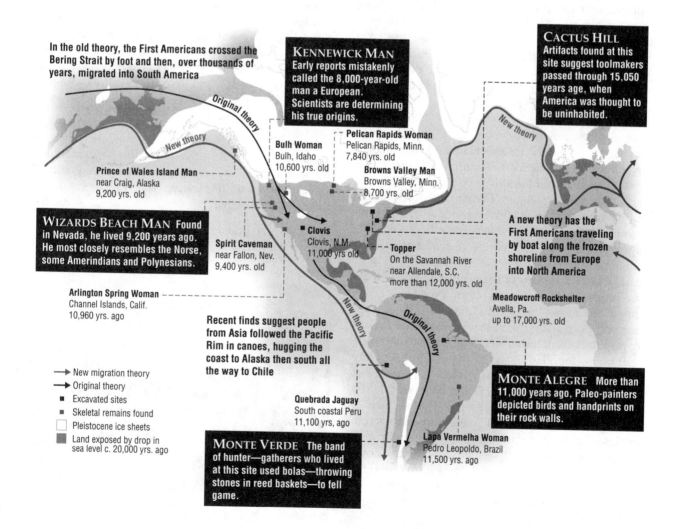

In the old theory, the First Americans crossed the Bering Strait by foot and then, over thousands of years, migrated into South America

KENNEWICK MAN Early reports mistakenly called the 8,000-year-old man a European. Scientists are determining his true origins.

CACTUS HILL Artifacts found at this site suggest toolmakers passed through 15,050 years age, when America was thought to be uninhabited.

Original theory

New theory

New theory

Bulh Woman Bulh, Idaho 10,600 yrs. old

Pelican Rapids Woman Pelican Rapids, Minn. 7,840 yrs. old

Prince of Wales Island Man near Craig, Alaska 9,200 yrs. old

Browns Valley Man Browns Valley, Minn. 8,700 yrs. old

WIZARDS BEACH MAN Found in Nevada, he lived 9,200 years ago. He most closely resembles the Norse, some Amerindians and Polynesians.

Spirit Caveman near Fallon, Nev. 9,400 yrs. old

Clovis Clovis, N.M. 11,000 yrs old

Topper On the Savannah River near Allendale, S.C. more than 12,000 yrs. old

A new theory has the First Americans traveling by boat along the frozen shoreline from Europe into North America

Arlington Spring Woman Channel Islands, Calif. 10,960 yrs. ago

Meadowcroft Rockshelter Avella, Pa. up to 17,000 yrs. old

Recent finds suggest people from Asia followed the Pacific Rim in canoes, hugging the coast to Alaska then south all the way to Chile

New theory

Original theory

→ New migration theory
→ Original theory
■ Excavated sites
■ Skeletal remains found
□ Pleistocene ice sheets
■ Land exposed by drop in sea level c. 20,000 yrs. ago

Quebrada Jaguay South coastal Peru 11,100 yrs, ago

MONTE ALEGRE More than 11,000 years ago, Paleo-painters depicted birds and handprints on their rock walls.

MONTE VERDE The band of hunter—gatherers who lived at this site used bolas—throwing stones in reed baskets—to fell game.

Lapa Vermelha Woman Pedro Leopoldo, Brazil 11,500 yrs. ago later, anthropologists would discover him. They would name him Spirit Caveman.

He wasn't supposed to be there. Spirit Caveman is the wrong guy, in the wrong place, at the wrong time. According to the standard anthropology script, anyone living in America 9,000 years ago should resemble either today's Native Americans or, at the very least, the Asians who were their ancestors and thus, supposedly, the original Americans. But Spirit Caveman does not follow that script—and neither do more than a dozen other skeletons of Stone Age Americans. Together, the misfits have sparked a spirited debate: who were the First Americans?

The emerging answer suggests that they were not Asians of Mongoloid stock who crossed a land bridge into Alaska 11,500 years ago, as the textbooks say, but different ethnic groups, from places very different from what scientists thought even a few years ago. What's more, stone tools, hearths and remains of dwellings unearthed from Peru to South Carolina suggest that Stone Age America was a pretty crowded place for a land that was supposed to be empty until those Asians followed herds of big game from Siberia into Alaska. A far different chronicle of the First Americans is therefore emerging from the clash of theories and discoveries that one anthropologist calls "skull wars." According to the evidence of stones and bones, long before Ellis Island opened its doors America was a veritable Rainbow Coalition of ethnic types, peopled by southern Asians, East Asians—and even, perhaps, Ice Age Europeans, who may have hugged the ice sheets in their animal-skin kayaks to reach America millenniums before it was even a gleam in Leif Ericson's eye. "It's very clear to me," says anthropologist Dennis Stanford of the Smithsonian Institution, "that we are looking at multiple migrations through a very long time period—migrations of many different peoples of many different ethnic origins."

The standard story of the peopling of the Americas holds that wanderers from Northeast Asia fanned out across the Great Plains, into the Southwest and eventually the East to become the founding populations of today's Native Americans. Stone spear points found in Clovis, N.M., in the 1930s were dated at 11,000 years ago and hailed as evidence of the oldest human settlement in the New World. The story was so tidy that any skeletons that seemed to challenge this "Clovis model" were shoved back into the closet by the mandarins of American anthropology; any stone tools that seemed older than Clovis were dismissed as misdated. Clovis had American archeology in a stranglehold; James Adovasio of Mercyhurst College in Pennsylvania calls its defenders the "Clovis mafia."

The small band of hunter-gatherers made its summer camp on the riverbank, at the northern end of the region through which they followed the seasonal game. The location, 45 miles southeast of what is now Richmond, Va., was ideal: winds from the north kept the flying insects down. Some of the band would spend their days striking long slender quartz flakes from stone cores; others made triangular and pentagonal spear points for the hunt. It was 15,050 years ago; the erstwhile "First Americans" would not make the trek across the Bering Strait for 3,500 more years.

Now there are too many skeletons in the closet to ignore. Pushed by a 1990 federal law that requires museums to return Native American remains to their tribes, scientists—called in to figure out who belongs to whom—have amassed a database of "craniometric profiles." Each of the 2,000 or so profiles consists of some 90 skull measurements, such as distance between the eyes, that indicate ancestry. For most skeletons, it has been pretty straightforward to tell a Hopi from a Crow. But some skulls stand out like pale-skinned, redheaded cousins at a family reunion of olive-skinned brunettes. The oldest American found so far, an 11,500-year-old skeleton from central Brazil, resembles southern Asians and Australians, anthropologist Walter Neves of the University of São Paulo reported last year. One skull from Lime Creek, Neb., and two from Minnesota—all 7,840 to 8,900 years old—resemble South Asians or Europeans. Some of the other misfits:

• Buhl Woman, found in 1989, died 10,600 years ago at the age of 19 or so. "She doesn't fit into any modern group," says anthropologist Richard Jantz of the University of Tennessee, "but is most similar to today's Polynesians."

• Spirit Caveman bears less resemblance to American Indians than he does to any other ethnic group

Illustration by Rob Wood—Wood Ronsaville Harlin, Inc.

except African Bushmen. His face is not flattened or wide, his nose is not narrow—all traits of Amerindians. He "does not show affinity to any Amerindian sample [we used]," conclude Jantz and Douglas Owsley of the Smithsonian. Instead, with his long head, wide nose, forward face and strong chin, he resembles the Aboriginal Ainu of Japan or other East Asians.

• Kennewick Man, found on July 28, 1996, by two college students watching a hydroplane race on the Columbia River in Washington, looks almost nothing like a Native American. His face is narrow, with a prominent nose, an upper jaw that juts out slightly and a long, narrow braincase. Although early reports described him as Caucasoid or even European (which led the Asatru Folk Assembly, followers of an ancient Nordic religion, to claim him), in fact the 8,000-year-old man most resembles a cross between the Ainu and the Polynesians.

America, it seems, was a mosaic of peoples and cultures even 11,000 years ago. Based on their study of 11 ancient skulls, conclude Owsley and Jantz in a paper to be published in the *American Journal of Physical Anthropology*, America was home to "at least three distinct groups.... None of the fossils [except for one] shows any particular affinity to modern Native Americans...[Skull measurements] depart from contemporary American Indians, often in the direction of Europeans or South Asians."

One explanation for the lack of a family resemblance between the oldest Americans and today's Amerindians is that the original Americans might simply have changed in appearance over the generations. "You'd expect them to look different," says anthropologist David Hurst Thomas of the American Museum of Natural History. "They're separated by 9,000 years of evolution." A more radical explanation is that the First Americans—perhaps from Polynesia, perhaps from Europe—left no descendants. Whoever got here first, in other words, were not the ancestors of today's Pequot, Shoshone and other tribes. Instead, they were obliterated by later arrivals who made war or made love: killing them or mating with them. Kennewick Man, for instance, had a stone spear point in his hip. Its shape suggests it came from what scientists call the Cascade culture, people who were just moving into the area "It may be a sign of ethnic conflict," says anthropologist James Chatters, who first inspected K Man.

The possibility that today's Native Americans are not the descendants of the original Americans is not going down easily. "If you tell the Native Americans that they weren't first," says Thomas, "you're asking for trouble." That conclusion, even if proved, has no direct legal ramifications for Native Americans' hard-won gains, such as the right to fish ancestral waters and the right to establish casinos. "But it may be just a step before legislation starts being rolled back," Thomas warns. Some Americans resent the newfound wealth of some tribes, and "if the discoveries make today's Native Americans just another Ellis Island group, it makes it hard for them to preserve their sovereignty."

Already, Native Americans are protesting this line of research. The Shoshone-Bannock demanded custody of Buhl Woman and reburied her. The Northern Paiute are asking that Spirit Caveman be reburied, and the Umatilla of Washington want Kennewick Man. "We know that our people have been part of this land since the beginning of time," said Armand Minthorn, a Umatilla religious leader, in a statement. "Scientists believe that because [Kennewick Man's] head measurement does not match ours, he is not Native American. Our elders have told us that Indian people did not always look the way we do today."

The determined band passed up the quartz in the nearby deposits, trekking beyond the Green River in what is now Wyoming and Utah, all the way to the northern Bighorn, 600 miles away. There they found the obsidian and quartz crystal they would fashion into stone points and flakes—and never use. Instead they would bury their caches on a layer of compacted red ocher. Their neighbors had equally strong preferences, but for them the quest was not for exotic materials but for sources imbued with spiritual significance. Rejecting the local quartz, they climbed the peaks to chip out red jasper found at 9,000 feet and flake it into stone tools that they, too, would cache, unused. Stones that lay nearer their gods would make a fitting offering.

For years, no authority would accept any deviation from the party line that the First Americans were the Clovis people of 11,000 years ago. But in 1977, archeologist Tom Dillehay of the University of Kentucky began excavating a site deep in the Chilean hills called Monte Verde. There, some 30 hunter-gatherers lived beside a creek 35 miles inland of the Pacific until a rising peat bog pushed them out—and preserved the site like volcanic ash over Pompeii. The band lived in low, tentlike structures lashed together with cord and covered with bark and mastodon hide to keep out the rain, says Dillehay. Outside were work areas, and fire pits lined with clay. A hut set apart from the others may have served as either a paleohospital or a Stone Age Studio 54: inside, Dillehay found five chewed quid made of boldo leaves, which contain both an analgesic and a mild hallucinogen. Boldo was clearly prized: the nearest supply lay more than 100 miles north, so either someone made a long trek or arranged trades with distant inlanders. Belying the image of the original Americans as full-time big-game hunters, the Monte Verdeans ate a varied diet: freshwater mussels and crawfish, wild potato, fruits and nuts, small game like birds that they brought down with stones and the occasional mastodon that they felled with fire-hardened lances. But the paradigm killer was this: Monte Verde was inhabited 12,500 years ago—1,000 years before the original Americans supposedly flocked across the Bering Strait.

For years archeologists dismissed Dillehay's claim. At scientific conferences, he recalls, "others would be introduced as doctor this and doctor that. I was always 'the guy who is excavating Monte Verde.' Some people wouldn't even shake my hand." Even worse, the Clovis model had such a stranglehold that scientists "would dig until they hit the Clovis level and just stop." Few looked for older bones and tools. Four or five possible pre-Clovis sites in South America were never reported because the scientists feared that doing so would wreck their reputations.

That changed two years ago, when archeology's pooh-bahs finally accepted that Monte Verde was indeed 12,500 years old. The floodgates opened. Sites once dismissed as misdated are being re-examined. At Meadowcroft Rockshelter in Avella, Pa., for instance, where for 26 years Adovasio has been excavating under an overhang that juts out from a rock face 43 feet above the ground, scientists are now reconsidering his claim that the charcoal, stone tools and woven material buried there are at least 14,000 and possibly 17,000 years old. At Saltville, in western Virginia, archeologists are studying what may be a Stone Age mastodon feast. Stone and bone tools (including an ivory-polisher), mastodon bones and fire-cracked rock along an ancient riverbank have been unearthed from a layer that may be 14,000 years old. Saltville has a distinguished pedigree: a friend sent Thomas Jefferson a mastodon tooth from the site in 1782.

Jefferson was curious enough about the prehistory of America that when he dispatched Lewis and Clark to survey the West, he asked them to look for signs of ancient settlements. He might have turned his curiosity closer to home. Archeologists led by Michael Johnson had stopped digging at Cactus Hill in Virginia when they found Clovis material, dated at 10,920 years old, three feet down. But with the theory of the First Americans shifting beneath their feet, they dug deeper—and came upon stone blades and cores (the rock chunks from which flakes are struck) in a layer 15,050 years old. "This looks like a good candidate for a Clovis precursor to me," says the Smithsonian's Stanford. Like Johnson, archeologist Albert Goodyear of the University of South Carolina had never felt much need to dig below the Clovis layer in his Topper site on the Savannah River. But last spring he and colleagues found, beneath the Clovis layer, stone blades and flakes by the score in layers three feet down—a depth that, he estimates, corresponds to more than 12,000 years. "This is pretty substantial evidence," says Goodyear, "that people were here long before we thought."

And they may have come from somewhere no scientists in their right mind would have considered only a few years ago: a French Connection. There are striking similarities between the stone tools attributed to the Clovis culture, in the Americas, and the stone tools attributed to the so-called Solutrean culture of France and the Iberian Peninsula. Both made beveled, crosshatched bone rods, notes archeologist Bruce Bradley. Both made idiosyncratic spear points of mammoth ivory. Both made triangular stone scrapers. Yes, two separate peoples might have invented the same thing, as David Meltzer of Southern Methodist University points out: "These similarities may represent finding the same answer to the same problem" of killing and butchering game. But there's a twist. "The oldest of these tools in America," says Bradley, "are in the East and Southeast, not the Southwest"—where they should be if the Clovis people trickled in from Siberia and then fanned out across the continent. And since glaciers did not retreat from America's midsection until 11,500 years ago, anyone inhabiting the Eastern Seaboard before then must have come from the East rather than the Bering Strait.

How? Crossing the open Atlantic would have posed a perhaps insurmountable challenge, even though people traveled in boats from southern Asia to Australia at least 40,000 years ago. "We don't give early people enough credit," says Stanford. "Yeah, they lived in caves—but they were pretty smart, too." Smart enough, perhaps, to have navigated along the ice sheet and seasonal pack ice that spanned the ocean from England to Nova Scotia. "They could have made it if they worked the glacier for seals and water birds," says Johnson. "They would have seen migratory birds flying west; they would have known there was land in that direction." Similarly, the Asians who reached America from the West may have been seafarers, too.

Deep in the craggy uplands 450 feet above the Amazon, the people of Caverna da Pedra Pintada look nothing like the stereotype of the First Americans as bison-fur-wearing big-game hunters. This band drew sustenance from the river and the forest, dining on turtles, frogs, snakes, fish and freshwater mussels, as well as Brazil nuts and palm nuts. And they did more. The cave floor is splattered with gobs of red and yellow iron-based paint, dripped 11,000 years ago. The Stone Age artists created exuberant scenes of snakes and other animals and even handprints—designs? signatures?—including children's.

"We are rewriting the textbooks on the First Americans," says Stanford. The new edition will show that "the peopling of the Americas was never as simple as simple-minded paradigms said." Instead, it will tell of an America that beckoned to far-flung people long before the Mayflower or the Santa María or the Viking ships, of an unknown continent so alluring that men and women endowed with a technology no more sophisticated than sharp rocks braved Siberian tundra and Atlantic ice packs to get here. It is still the New World. But it is thousands of years older than we thought—home to settlers so diverse that it was, even millenniums ago, the world's melting pot.

Alexander Marshack

Images of the Ice Age

The recent discovery of two major painted and engraved Ice Age caves in southeastern France—Cosquer, whose entrance is 120 feet below the Mediterranean Sea, and Chauvet, on the Ardèche River, a tributary of the Rhône—closes out a century in which more than 200 decorated caves were discovered in one small corner of Europe. What have we learned from these discoveries? How has the study of such caves added to our understanding of how they were used and why they were decorated?

The first body of Ice Age art appeared in the archaeological record of Europe about 35,000 years ago, shortly after anatomically modern humans displaced the Neandertals. There is also evidence for such art, both at this time and in earlier periods, in

Horses, rhinos, and aurochs (wild cattle) dominate this painted rock panel at Chauvet Cave, in the Ardèche Valley of southeastern France.

Ministère de la Culture/Eurelios.

Africa, the Middle East, and Australia, but the so-called great explosion in image-making occurred in Ice Age Europe. Hunters of wooly mammoth and rhinoceros, reindeer, wild horse and cattle, ibex (wild goat), and other species, these early people camped in rock-shelters and on hills overlooking a vast network of rivers flowing west toward the Atlantic, south to the Mediterranean, and, on the Russian plain, south to the Black Sea. These rivers were the highways along which small groups moved with the seasons, and it was at sites overlooking these rivers that they gathered for seasonal rituals and the exchange of flint, tools, skins, personal decorations, and probably mates. Over the millennia a network of rivers had cut through the soft limestone hills of southern France and northwestern Spain, creating narrow valleys with rock-shelters and hills honeycombed with caves. It was here, on rock faces and in the caves, that these people carved, engraved, and painted images of the animals of their day.

In 1864 a ten-inch long section of mammoth ivory was excavated at the riverside rock-shelter of La Madeleine on the Vézère River in southwestern France. On it was incised a woolly mammoth—the first image of an extinct species ever discovered. Five years earlier Charles Darwin had published his *On the Origin of Species*, which postulated a vast stretch of time during which all species, including humans, had evolved. The La Madeleine mammoth engraving was evidence that humans capable of creating art had indeed lived in a distant past when now extinct animals roamed the continent. Since the first discovery, thousands of Ice Age images have been found at riverside sites and shelters across Europe. Why did such art thrive during this period?

One hundred years after the La Madeleine engraving was found, I studied it under a microscope and found that it was far more than mere art or depiction. What I discovered would help me understand many of the images in caves and from excavations throughout Europe that I would later study. The La Madeleine mammoth had three or four extra backs, a second tail standing upright, and a number of extra tusks. It had also been ritually killed by a number of darts engraved in and around the body. The mammoth had apparently served as a symbol to be used in different ways and perhaps at different times. It was ritually killed, by marking it with abstract representations of wounds or weapons, such as darts, and renewed and presumably reused by adding an extra tail and backs.

For 30 years, while at the Peabody Museum of Archaeology and Ethnology at Harvard University, I have conducted research in Palaeolithic archaeology. I have investigated image-making traditions from every period and region of Ice Age Europe, and I pioneered the study of rock art using microscopy, fluorescence, and infrared and ultraviolet light. I have found that many cave depictions resemble the La Madeleine mammoth in their manner of execution and, presumably, in their function as symbolic images.

In the foothills of the Pyrénées in southern France, at the Magdalenian cave of Les Trois Frères, named after three brothers who discovered it, there are hundreds of animal images about as old as the La Madeleine mammoth. One beautifully incised bison has been ritually killed with many darts or spears. It has also been renewed and reused by adding a second, upright tail, much like that on the La Madeleine mammoth. Many animals today, including elephants and rhinos, raise their tails when in danger or under attack. There are many such images in Ice Age caves. At Lascaux a speared and disemboweled bison with upright tail is shown charging a human figure.

The Les Trois Frères bison also has three zigzags engraved on its upper body. I have argued that such markings on certain species indicate the summer moult, when irregular patches of hair fall from the animal's upper body. Painted and engraved images of moulting bison are common in the Magdalenian period and can be seen at Altamira and Lascaux. The Les Trois Frères bison has an upper body without hair, indicating the moult, and scrape-marks on the lower body suggesting remaining hair. I believe the added tail, the three zigzags, and the many spear markings were made with different tools or points at different times, perhaps by different artists, to represent the ritual killing and renewal of bison in spring and early summer. Were bison present in the region in spring or summer? Were they awaited, or had they been killed recently? Many of the species depicted at Les Trois Frères, including bison, horse, reindeer, and ibex, migrated between winter and summer pastures. Images of Atlantic salmon, which would have spawned in the streams of the Pyrenean foothills, are also engraved on bones and stones found in rock-shelters across the region. Clearly the seasonal

There is much evidence at Chauvet Cave of what may be seasonal rituals of renewal. A woolly mammoth was renewed by engraving two schematic mammoths above it. A horse at left bears a serpentine mark representing its summer coat.

Ministère de la Culture/Eurelios.

Painted bison at Lascaux Cave show typical summer moulting, left, and full winter coat, right.

Jean Vertut.

appearance and disappearance of species, which helped delineate a subsistence calendar, were closely observed and recorded.

La Madeleine and other Magdalenian sites date between ca. 15,000 and ca. 10,000 B.C., toward the end of the Ice Age, when warmer temperatures allowed animals to move higher into the river valleys of the Pyrenean foothills, which had been uninhabitable in earlier colder periods. As hunters followed their prey into these valleys, they began to decorate the rock-shelters and caves of the higher slopes. Chauvet Cave, 20 miles west of the lower Rhône Valley, was used ca. 19,000–18,000 B.C., during a colder period of the Ice Age. Because of the cold, the middle reaches of the Pyrénées were uninhabitable except for short seasonal forays. The hunter-gatherers of northern and central Europe and the Russian plain had been forced farther south. Glaciers covered much of the Pyrénées, the Alps, as well as some of the lower mountain ranges. The massive northern ice sheet extended south into what are now England and Germany. The lower Rhône Valley was a refuge: while open to cold northern winds, it was interlaced with tributary rivers and protected valleys and rock-shelters. Its rolling floodplain and adjoining hills offered rich pasturage and an opportunity for seasonal movements of animals and humans. It was here, apparently, that the Solutrean culture evolved to cope with the colder climate.

When the Chauvet images were first published, accompanied by a profusion of nonanalytical first im-

pressions and interpretations, it was at once clear that they documented many of the image-making traditions I had found elsewhere in Europe. Consider the bear with red dots, first thought to be a spotted hyena, in part because the nearby image of a leopard had spots common to that species. Solutrean caves are rich with examples of animals ritually marked with painted spots: a lion at Chauvet; wild aurochs in the nearby cave of Tête du Lion; two horses and a mammoth at Pech-Merle in the Dordogne; and various animals at Cougnac, northwest of Pech-Merle, and La

Serpentine line on Lascaux horse may indicate the summer coat. The animal also has a dart in its rump and is surrounded by various symbols, two of which may represent plants.

Jean Vertut.

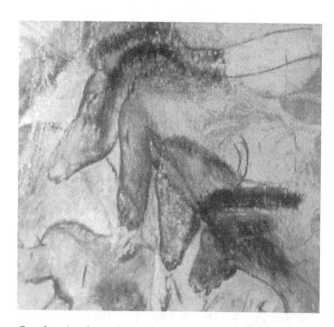

Overlapping horse heads at Chauvet Cave may have been painted at different times in rituals of renewal.

Ministère de la Culture/Eurelios.

Pileta on the southern coast of Spain. Even handprints are frequently surrounded with painted spots. Engraved images of bear-killings have been found in Ice Age caves and rock-shelters. The ritual springtime killing of a bear after it awakened from hibernation was practiced with great ceremony by the Basques, descendants of the Ice Age population, well into the nineteenth century.

At Chauvet the extinct woolly rhinoceros presents a far more powerful image than the bear. A heavy short-legged creature that grazes on grass and bush not far from water, it probably inhabited the floodplain of the Rhône and other rivers. It was probably not a regularly hunted or eaten species, since it does not congregate in herds and is relatively difficult to kill. Early press reports stressed the power and beauty of the rhinoceros images, and one article even suggested that an image of two rhinos facing each other depicted two males in a mating confrontation. Only one of the rhinos, however, appears to be male; horn-to-horn confrontations between males and females are common during rhino courtship.

Many of the Chauvet rhinos are depicted with a black, mid-body, armor-like skin fold common among today's nearly extinct Asian rhinoceros. In Ice Age winters, the woolly rhinoceros would have grown a full coat of hair covering that skin fold. A rhino in full winter coat, for example, is engraved on a stone from the Magdalenian winter camp of Gönnersdorf overlooking the Rhine River in central Germany. The Chauvet rhinos apparently indicate the

species in spring or early summer. A spring or summer rhino was found etched on a pebble at the rock-shelter of La Colombière overlooking the Ain River, a tributary of the Rhône north of the Ardèche. This rhino was ritually killed with three feathered darts in its soft belly and renewed with two or three extra horns. Adult rhinos are difficult to kill with spears and may have been trapped in pitfalls, but a young animal might be brought down by targeting its belly. Points resembling arrowheads found at Solutrean sites suggest that the bow and arrow were invented sometime during this period. The La Colombière image may well represent the ritual killing and renewal of a young moulting rhino in the spring or early summer.

There is much evidence at Chauvet of what may be seasonal rituals of renewal. Several of the rhinos were renewed and reused by scraping and engraving outlines around their bodies. One was renewed by adding six or seven extra horns, three or four extra backs, and one extra rear leg. These images recall the La Madeleine mammoth and the Les Trois Frères bison. Also at Chauvet, four horse heads were painted one above the other. The heads appear to have been made different times, with different degrees of skill, and probably with different mixes of paint. They represent not a herd, but

Rock panel at Chauvet Cave depicts a number of woolly rhinos with black, mid-body skin folds that would not have been visible in winter, when covered with hair. One rhino has been renewed with extra horns, backs, and a hind leg.

Ministère de la Culture/Eurelios.

OUTDOOR CREATIONS OF THE ICE AGE

Paul G. Bahn

Recent discoveries of outdoor Ice Age rock art confirm what has long been suspected—that indoor artistic activity, represented by well-known cave images, is neither representative nor necessarily characteristic of the period. The caves simply owe their predominance in the archaeological record to their preservation. The vast majority of rock art was probably created in the open, on rock faces that over the millennia have weathered smooth. We know of only six sites that have survived intact. That the largest of them, in Portugal's Côa Valley, will soon be drowned by a dam project is an incalculable tragedy (see Archaeology, March/April 1995).

So far, none of the six sites has been accurately dated, though a new method known as microerosion dating, which gauges the age of rock art based on its degree of erosion, may help in the future. For now, virtually all engraved Ice Age images, indoor and outdoor, must be dated by their style. Inevitably, only engravings and peckings have survived outside the caves, though paintings were almost certainly produced as well. By virtue of its location, open-air art appears less mysterious or magical than that in deep caves, but of course location is no sure guide to meaning, about which there is little agreement.

The first open-air rock art discovery—three animal figures, including a fine horse two feet long and one foot three inches high—was made in 1981 on the right bank of the Albaguera, a tributary of the Douro River at Mazouco in northeastern Portugal. The figures, on a rock face at an elevation of 700 feet, had been protected from the elements by their orientation, which sheltered them from the prevailing winds. The animal outlines were made with hammered dots, which were connected by continuous lines scored into the stone. Since its discovery, the horse has been badly damaged by chalking, scoring, and painting. The culprits have been vandals and archaeologists trying to get clearer photographs. Based on style, the horse has been attributed to the early Magdalenian, ca. 15,000 B.C.

In 1981, at Domingo García in Segovia, Spain, a three-foot-long figure of a horse was found hammered into a rocky outcrop at an elevation of 3,150 feet. Since then, a closer examination of this rock and others in the region has revealed at least 115 figures, 82 of them at Domingo García. Stylistically dated to the end of the Solutrean and the beginning of the Magdalenian, ca. 17,000–15,000 B.C., they are dominated by horses, but deer and ibex (wild goats) are also well represented. Wild cattle are comparatively rare.

In 1983 a series of fine incisions was found at Fornols-Haut in the eastern French Pyénées, on a huge block of schist on a mountainside 2,450 feet high. The rock has been greatly weathered, but because its eastern face has been sheltered from the prevailing winds, its engravings, though eroded, are still clearly visible. The rock face is covered with engravings, including some ten small animals—none complete—as well as signs and zigzags. The finest figures are the head of an isard (a Pyrenean chamois) three inches high, and that of an ibex. Stylistically they seem to belong to the Magdalenian.

More recently two additional sites were found in Spain. A deeply incised horse figure was discovered on an inclined block of stone at an elevation of 4,600 feet at Piedras Blancas in the southeastern part of the country; the horse has been dated stylistically to the final Gravettian or the Solutrean, ca. 22,000–17,000 B.C. It is likely that more figures will be found here. About 37 miles south of Mazouco, at Siega Verde on the left bank of the Agueda River, another tributary of the Douro, archaeologists found what they at first thought were a few hammered figures. Further study revealed at least 540 pecked and incised images, most of them within a one-mile stretch, though the majority are concentrated within one-quarter mile. No fewer than half of the identifiable figures are horses, with many bovids (aurochs and bison) and deer also represented. As with other figures in the region, they have been stylistically dated to the final Solutrean or early Magdalenian.

At the Côa Valley site, schist blocks scattered over a distance of eight miles hold at least 150 pecked figures and engravings of horses, wild cattle, and ibex, including two large horses with overlapping heads. When the hydroelectric dam is completed in 1998, all will be irrevocably lost under more than 300 feet of water. A report by a team of specialists from Unesco, who visited the area in early February, has insisted on the world-class importance of the engravings, and urged that work on the dam be halted, at least temporarily, so that an intensive archaeological study can be carried out. It is not yet clear what can or will be done. Abandoning the dam project would be a relatively inexpensive solution, since only a fraction of the funding has so far been used. The Côa Valley engravings need to be studied, not drowned, lest we lose a rare chance to learn more about Ice Age life.

Paul G. Bahn is a *Contributing Editor to Archaeology.*

---

rather the renewal of the horsehead image. What struck me in particular was that these are heads of horses in summer, without the thick hair that would have covered them in winter. During an Ice Age winter, the wild horse would have grown a heavy coat over its entire body, including legs and muzzle, masking many features apparent in the summer. The summer coat is depicted on the famous running horse at Lascaux, which bears a serpentine line indicating the tonal differences between upper and lower body. The same serpentine line often appears on engraved horses, such as those at Les Trois Frères. A crude schematic engraving of a horse at Chauvet has this serpentine summer marking across its body.

Early reports on the Chauvet Cave images expressed surprise at the many depictions of carnivores, primarily lions. Actually, images of the lion occur throughout the Ice Age. The earliest known Ice Age animal images were excavated at the 30,000-year-old Aurignacian cave of Vogelherd, in the hills of south-central Germany. These mammoth-ivory carvings include lions, mammoth, horses, bison, reindeer, and bear. With the exception of woolly rhinoceros, these are the same animals depicted at Chauvet 12,000 years later. Microscopic study of the Vogelherd images indicated that they, too, were at times ritually killed with incised darts and wound marks. One carved lion has a series of spots, perhaps indicating wounds, gouged across its body. An anthropomorphic figure with a lion head, carved from mammoth ivory, was found at the nearby rock-shelter of Hohlenstein-Stadel. Whether it represents a human wearing a lion mask—perhaps a shaman—or a myth-

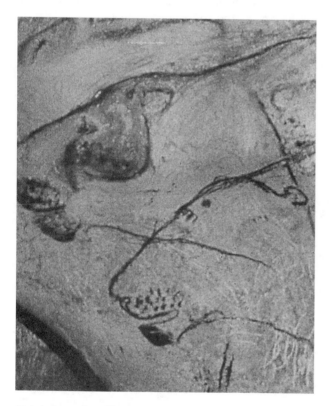

Painted panel at Chauvet Cave depicts two lion heads. The black spots on one lion's muzzle are its whiskers.

Ministère de la Culture/Eurelios.

ical lion spirit in human form, the image seems to represent some aspect of lion power. The Vogelherd lion had been ritually marked, perhaps ritually killed. Could lions have been hunted for their skins or heads?

Almost 18,000 years later, near the end of the Ice Age, a Magdalenian artist engraved the image of a "sorcerer" wearing a beard, lion skin and paws, reindeer antlers and ears, and a horse tail in the cave of Les Trois Frères. There are other lion images in the cave, including one, on a central stone in a small chamber, which has been renewed and reused. At Lascaux there are images of killed lions, one with blood pouring from its nose and mouth. Lion images are also found in the Gravettian culture, ca. 24,000 B.C., at the riverside site of Dolní Věstonice in the Czech Republic. One small lion head was modeled in soft clay, stabbed in both the eye and head, and then fired, perhaps as part of a ritual. The lions at Chauvet, dating to the Solutrean, were painted after the early Ice Age hunters of Germany, Central Europe, and the Russian plain had moved south, taking their traditions and myths with them.

The great cave of Altamira in northern Spain was discovered in 1879. Its painted bison were so realistic and powerful that French archaeologists, who knew of no painted caves in France, declared the images to be fakes. It was not until an engraved and painted cave was discovered at La Mouthe, near La Madeleine and the Vézère River, that the French admitted that Altamira was genuine. The study of Ice Age cave art had begun. After more than a century, however, La Mouthe's most enigmatic image continues to puzzle scholars. Called a "hut" by the Abbé Breuil, one of the leading scholars of Ice Age art in the first half of the twentieth century, the engraving seems to resemble a hut-like structure. But while mammoth-bone huts were built on the Russian plain and tents are known from Gönnersdorf on the Rhine and open-air sites on the Dordogne, there is no evidence that Ice Age hunters in this region of rock-shelters and caves ever built such structures. Variants of this motif, often appearing as a zigzag or a stream, have been found at Lascaux and at other caves in the Dordogne; at Gargas and Les Trois Frères in the Pyrenean region; and at La Pileta in Spain. I have also found variants of this motif at Ice Age settlement sites along rivers in Germany, the Czech Republic, Italy, and on the Russian steppe.

While working at La Mouthe, I happened upon a waterfall of a small tributary of the Vézère. The falls with streams flowing from its sides, was remarkably similar to the La Mouthe image. Could it represent a waterfall and not a hut? During the Ice

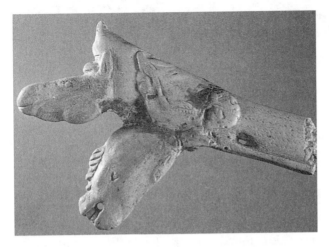

Fragment of a Magdalenian reindeer-antler atlatl (spear thrower) from Le Mas d'Azil cave depicts three horse heads, possibly a colt, a stallion, and a flayed horse head.

Jean Vertut.

Age, rivers, streams, and even waterfalls would have frozen in winter and thawed in spring. The return of salmon to the rivers and migratory animals to the valleys would have accompanied the spring thaw and flooding the Vézère. The thaw would have brought a dramatic renewal of life to these valleys: the dropping of calves, colts, and kids, the return of migratory water-fowl, and the awakening of bears. Indeed, the behavior of the rivers was perhaps as dominant a factor in Ice Age thinking as the movement of animals.

A thorough study of Chauvet will take time. Researchers must date the images by studying remnant charcoal from lamps and fires, organic material in fragments of bone, and paints. The study will require a recreation of the seasonal ecology of the Ardèche River, the high plateau around it, and the Rhône floodplain downriver. They must determine whether it was possible to walk up the gorges of the Ardèche River in the winter, or only after the spring floods had subsided. It will require a study of animal remains at the settlement sites, though this can tell us only about some of the animals that were hunted and killed. They must compare the images at Chau-

vet to others from the Solutrean, as well as from earlier and later periods. The Mediterranean coasts would have provided a warmer climate and a different ecology from the valleys of the middle Rhône and its tributaries. The coastal Mediterranean cave of Cosquer, for example, has paintings of approximately the same date as Chauvet, but there are no depictions of woolly rhino, mammoth, or reindeer. Instead there are paintings of the great auk, a flightless seabird, and engravings of seals.

Can one make inferences from a study of Chauvet about the art and traditions in other caves of this period? Were Solutrean animal images often seasonal markers? The questions and problems are large. Hunting cultures have always created myths and conducted rituals in which the animal species of their time play a part. Different species have been used as clan or tribal symbols, as spirit helpers, as characters in myths of origin, as explanations of human behavior, as guardians of the seasons and nature, and often as creatures to be sacrificed at certain ritual times. It is possible that the animals depicted in the Ice Age were used in similar ways.

What were Ice Age hunter-gatherers thinking as the period came to a close? In the Magdalenian cave site and shelter of Les Mas d'Azil in the foothills of the Pyrénées, the top of a reindeer-antler atlatl, or spear-thrower, was found, bearing three carved horse heads. One is small, perhaps a colt; the second is large, wide-eyed, and open-mouthed, perhaps a stallion; the third represents the flayed head of a dead horse. Life, death, and rebirth—of humans, animals, and the seasons—were by now entrenched Ice Age concepts, part of a ritual mythic lore that had begun 20,000 years earlier with the Vogelherd horse and lion images. At the end of the Ice Age, as the climate changed, the ice melted, and the animals began to disappear, these concepts would have had to accommodate the slow disappearance of species in terms, again, of death and hoped-for rebirth. Later, in entirely different contexts, these concepts of death, rebirth, and sacrifice, would become part of the farming cultures that developed following the end of the Ice Age.

New Clues Show Where People Made the Great Leap to Agriculture

Scientists are figuring out where and how cereal grains were domesticated during agriculture's birth in the Fertile Crescent about 10,000 years ago. Taming meant some changes for the grains like einkorn wheat, perhaps the first to be domesticated, because harvesting methods favored plants that were less able to reproduce on their own. Plants with seeds that stayed attached to sturdy stalks, even after they ripened, were more likely to be gathered and stored for another year's planting.

The greatest thing *before* sliced bread, to reverse the cliché, was bread itself. The first cultivation of wild grains, that is, turned hunter-gatherers into farmers, beginning some 12,000 to 10,000 years ago. In the transition, people gained a more abundant and dependable source of food, including their daily bread, and changed the world forever.

Archeologists and historians agree that the rise of agriculture, along with the domestication of animals for food and labor, produced the most important transformation in human culture since the last ice age—perhaps since the control of fire. Farming and herding led to the growth of large, settled human populations and increasing competition for productive lands, touching off organized warfare. Food surpluses freed people to specialize in crafts like textiles and supported a privileged elite in the first cities, growing numbers of bureaucrats and scribes, soldiers and kings.

Excavations at more than 50 sites over the last half-century have established the Fertile Crescent of the Middle East as the homeland of the first farmers. This arc of land, broadly defined, extends from Israel through Lebanon and Syria, then through the plains and hills of Iraq and southern Turkey and all the way to the head of the Persian Gulf. Among its "founder crops" were wheat, barley, various legumes, grapes, melons, dates, pistachios and almonds. The region also produced the first domesticated sheep, goats, pigs and cattle.

But questions persist: Where in the Fertile Crescent were the first wheat and barley crops pro-duced? What conditions favored this region? Why was the transition from hunting and foraging to farming so swift, occurring in only a few centuries?

New genetic studies suggest possible answers. They pinpoint the Karacadag Mountains, in southeast Turkey at the upper fringes of the Fertile Crescent, as the site where einkorn wheat was first domesticated from a wild species around 11,000 years ago. Moreover, they reveal that cultivated einkorn plants, as botanists had suspected, are remarkably similar genetically and in appearance to their ancestral wild varieties, which seems to explain the relatively rapid transition to farming indicated by archeological evidence.

A team of European scientists, led by Dr. Manfred Heun of the Agricultural University of Norway in As, reported these findings in the current issue of the journal *Science*. The researchers analyzed the DNA from 68 lines of cultivated einkorn wheat, *Triticum monococcum monococcum,* and from 261 wild einkorn lines, *T. m. boeoticum,* still growing in the Middle East and elsewhere.

In the study, the scientists identified a genetically distinct group of 11 varieties that was also most similar to cultivated einkorn. Because that wild group grows today near the Karacadag Mountains, in the vicinity of the modern city of Diyarbakir, and presumably was there in antiquity, the scientists concluded, this is "very probably the site of einkorn domestication."

Knowing the site for the domestication of such a primary crop, the scientists said, did not necessarily imply that the people living there at the time were the first farmers. "Nevertheless," they wrote, "it has been hypothesized that one single human group may have domesticated all primary crops of the region."

Archeologists said that radiocarbon dating was not yet precise enough to establish whether einkorn or emmer wheat or barley was the first cereal to be domesticated. All three domestications occurred in the Fertile Crescent, probably within decades or a few centuries of each other. It was a hybrid of emmer and another species from the Caspian Sea area that produced the first bread wheat.

Dr. Bruce D. Smith, an archeobiologist at the Smithsonian Institution and author of *The Emergence of Agriculture*, published [in 1995] by the Scientific American Library, praised the research as another notable example of new technologies' being applied in trying to solve some of archeology's most challenging problems. The einkorn findings, he said, made sense because they "fit pretty well with archeological evidence."

Not far from the volcanic Karacadag Mountains and also to the south, across the border in northern Syria, archeologists have exposed the ruins of pre-farming settlements and early agricultural villages that appear to have existed only a few centuries apart in time. Sifting the soil turned up seeds of both wild and cultivated einkorn wheat. The ruins of Abu Hureyra, an especially revealing Syrian site on the upper Euphrates River, contained firm evidence of einkorn farming more than 10,000 years ago.

The European research team also pointed to this archeological evidence as supporting its conclusion that the domestication of einkorn wheat began in the Karacadag area.

But some archeologists may not readily accept the new findings. They have their own favorite areas where they think the first steps in plant domestication took place, and these happen to be to the west and south of the Turkish mountains. Mud-brick ruins at the edge of an oasis in the Jordan River valley near Jericho have often been cited as from the world's first known farming village, occupied by an ancient people that archeologists call the Natufians.

Dr. Frank Hole, a Yale University archeologist who specializes in early agriculture, thinks the major center for early plant domestication was more likely in the corridor running north from the Dead Sea to Damascus. Its Mediterranean-type climate, dry summers and mild but wet winters, which prevailed at the time of agricultural origins, would have favored the growth of annual plants like barley and both einkorn and emmer wheat. The Jericho site produced early evidence of barley cultivation.

Commenting on the new research, Dr. Hole said in an interview that "the location of domestication can't be determined by the present distribution of the wild plants." For example, einkorn does not grow wild today around Abu Hureyra, though excavations show that it must have more than 10,000 years ago. So it cannot be assumed, he said, that wild einkorn was growing in southeast Turkey at the time of domestication.

But Dr. Jared Diamond, a specialist in biogeography at the University of California at Los Angeles, disagreed, noting that the Karacadag Mountains supported "stands of wild einkorn so dense and extensive that they were being harvested by hunter-gatherers even before einkorn's domestication."

An experiment more than 25 years ago by Dr. Jack Harlan, an agronomist at the University of Illinois, demonstrated the likely importance of wild einkorn in the diets of post–ice age hunter-gatherers in the region and what might have encouraged them to domesticate it. Harvesting wild einkorn by hand in southeastern Turkey, Dr. Harlan showed that in only three weeks, a small family group could have gathered enough grain to sustain them for a full year.

In reaping the wild grain over a few decades, or at most three centuries, the hunter-gatherers unwittingly caused small but consequential changes in the plants. The new DNA analysis showed that an alteration of only a couple of genes could have transformed the wild einkorn into a cultivated crop.

In the wild, brittle stems hold the einkorn grains to the plant, making it easier for them to scatter naturally and reseed the fields. But natural mutations would have produced some semi-tough stalks that held the seeds more firmly in place. People cutting the plants with sharp stone sickles would have selected the stalks more laden with grain, and these would be stored as next year's seed stock. Birds would be more apt to consume the dispersed grain from brittle stalks, leaving less of it to germinate.

As Dr. Diamond pointed out, repeated cycles of harvesting and reseeding wild einkorn stands "would have selected automatically for those mutations." Those changes included plumper, more nutritious grains in denser clusters that cling to the stem until ripe, instead of scattering before they can be harvested.

"These few, simple changes during einkorn's domestication," Dr. Diamond wrote in a separate article in *Science*, "contrast sharply with the drastic biological reorganization required for the domestication of Native Americans' leading cereal, maize, from its wild ancestor."

This difference alone, he said, "helps explain why densely populated agricultural societies arose so much earlier and developed so much more rapidly in the Crescent than in the New World."

It was several thousand more years before maize, or corn, would become a cultivated crop in central Mexico. There were no native wild wheats and barley in the Americas that might have led to an earlier introduction of agriculture there. Such circumstances based on geographic location have often been critical in the timing and pace of cultural and economic development for diverse societies, as Dr. Diamond argued in *Guns, Germs, and Steel: The Fates of Human Societies*, published [in 1997] by W. W. Norton.

Nothing in the new einkorn research seems to alter current thinking about the timing and climatic circumstances for agriculture's genesis in the Fertile Crescent.

With the end of the ice age 14,000 to 12,000 years ago, retreating glaciers left the world warmer and wetter than before. Greater rainfall in many temperate zones nourished a spread of vegetation, including many grasses like wild wheat and barley. This attracted concentrations of grazing animals. Hunter-gatherers converged on the grasses and animals, in many cases abandoning their nomadic ways and settling down to village life. Such conditions were particularly favorable in the Middle East.

Then followed a brief return of colder, drier weather more than 11,000 years ago and lasting a few centuries. Dr. Ofer Bar-Yosef, an archeologist at Harvard University, thinks the stresses of coping with the Younger Dryas, as the dry spell is called, contributed to the beginning of plant domestication. With the sudden dearth of wild food sources, hunter-gatherers began storing grain for the lean times and learning to cultivate the fields for better yields. In any case, the earliest evidence for agriculture so far comes from the period immediately after the Younger Dryas.

In his book on early agriculture, Dr. Smith of the Smithsonian wrote, "Even in the absence of such an external pressure, gradual growth in their populations and expansion of their villages may have encouraged or necessitated a variety of economic changes, including experimenting with the cultivation of wild grasses."

Whatever the factors behind its origins, Dr. Diamond said, agriculture took a firm hold in the ancient Middle East because of the diversity of plants and animals suitable for domestication. The first farmers, he said in the journal article, quickly assembled "a balanced package of domesticates meeting all of humanity's basic needs: carbohydrate, protein, oil, milk, animal transport and traction, and vegetable and animal fiber for rope and clothing."

Eurasian geography probably favored the rapid spread of agriculture out of the Middle East and throughout much of the two continents. Referring to a thesis developed in his book, Dr. Diamond pointed out that the west–east axis of the Eurasian land mass, as well as of the Fertile Crescent, permitted crops, livestock and people "to expand at the same latitude without having to adapt to new day lengths, climates and diseases."

In contrast, the north–south orientations of the Americas, Africa and the Indian subcontinent probably slowed the diffusion of agricultural innovations. And that, Dr. Diamond contends, could account for the head start some societies had on others in the march of human history.

Solomon H. Katz and Fritz Maytag

Brewing an Ancient Beer

In the 1950s, Robert Braidwood of the University of Chicago published an article in *Scientific American* suggesting a cause–effect relationship between bread-making and the domestication of cereal grains. He cited evidence from his excavations at Jarmo in the Taurus Mountains of modern Iraq. However, Jonathan D. Sauer, a well-known botanist from the University of Wisconsin, responded to Braidwood's article by asking if the earliest utilization of the domesticated cereals may have been for beer rather than bread. This query prompted Braidwood to organize a unique "symposium" for the journal *American Anthropologist* titled "Did Man Once Live by Beer Alone?"

It was not an idle question. We now believe that barley was domesticated about 10,000 years ago in the highland region of the southern Levant. But it seems likely that wild grains were gathered long before then. What prompted the shift from hunting and gathering to agriculture? Many scholars have suggested that overexploitation of wild resources and climate change in the region are behind the transition. But barley can ferment naturally, as we shall explain, and the discovery of beer at an early date may well have been a significant motivating factor in hunter-gatherers settling down and farming the grain.

In his contribution to the symposium, Sauer, with simple elegance, explained that for hunter-gatherers the amount of work involved in cultivating grain would not have been worthwhile if the only reward was a little food. The desire for beer, he felt, might have been sufficient incentive for expending the effort to plant and raise the barley, which he believed to be the earliest crop.

Hans Helbaek, a botanist who had worked with Braidwood at Jarmo, argued that beer was *not* the cause for domestication, but a much later development probably originating with the drying of grain for storage. The argument against Sauer's proposal was best articulated by botanist Paul Manglesdorf, who reasoned that, even though beer was a plausible incentive for the domestication of grain, it was not possible to "live on beer alone." "Did these Neolithic farmers," he asked, "forgo the extraordinary food values of the cereals in favor of alcohol, for which they had no physiological need? Are we to believe that the foundations of western civilization were laid by an ill-fed people living in a perpetual state of partial intoxication?" The majority of the respondents concluded that it was inconceivable that beer came before bread, and the issue was all but forgotten.

Last year the case was reopened. The Anchor Brewing Company of San Francisco, looking for a special event with which to celebrate the tenth anniversary of its new brewhouse, became aware of the Braidwood–Sauer debate after seeing an article on the subject in *Expedition* magazine published by The University Museum, University of Pennsylvania. The authors [Fritz Maytag is president of Anchor Brewing Company; Solomon Katz is a bioanthropologist at The University Museum] were intrigued by the beer–bread question, and conceived the idea of brewing a beer based on an ancient recipe. Such an effort would not only help answer the beer–bread question but might also shed new light on the ancient brewmaster's art.

We focused on the beer-making tradition of Mesopotamia because of its proximity to the region of the earliest cereal domestication. Ancient texts preserved on clay tablets indicate that the earliest beer was Sumerian. From all that we can determine, beer played an important role in Sumerian society, and was consumed by men and women from all social classes. In the Sumerian and Akkadian dictionaries being compiled by scholars today, the word for beer crops up in contexts relating to medicine, ritual, and myth. Beer parlors receive special mention in the laws codified by Hammurabi in the eighteenth century B.C. Apparently stiff penalties were dealt out to owners who overcharged customers (death by drowning) or who failed to notify authorities of the presence of criminals in their establishments (execution). High priestesses who were caught in such places were condemned to death by burning.

In combing the surviving Sumerian literature for a starting point, we examined the "Hymn to Ninkasi." This document, which dates to about 1800 B.C., sings the praises of the Sumerian goddess of brewing. The text, known from tablets found at Nippur, Sippar, and Larsa, had been translated by

Miguel Civil of the Oriental Institute of the University of Chicago in 1964. Coded within the Hymn is an ancient recipe for beer. We would return to the Hymn time and again before attempting to brew the ancient recipe. On several occasions we met with Civil to discuss parts of the text that were vague or ambiguous. In responding to our questions, Civil was led to refine his translation of certain Sumerian words such as honey and wine. His revised translation of the hymn, presented here for the first time (see page 131), allowed us to successfully re-create the Sumerian beer.

We then returned to Braidwood's question: Did beer come before bread? Although Sumerian beer was made several millennia after barley was first domesticated, the process used by the Sumerians is a "time platform" from which we can ask questions about earlier practices. When the "Hymn to Ninkasi" was written, beer was made using bread. But *bappir*, the Sumerian bread, could be kept for long periods of time without spoiling, and so it was a storable resource. We also know, from various annotations on bappir and beer in the Sumerian and Akkadian dictionaries, that bappir was eaten only during food shortages. In essence, making bread was a convenient way to store the raw materials for brewing beer.

Which was more nutritious? Since Braidwood first raised the beer–bread question, we have learned that many traditional food preparation practices involve steps that lower the toxicity and improve the nutritional properties of plants, and become a regular part of traditional cuisine. For example, through fermentation of barley-derived sugars into beer, yeast decreases the levels of tannins, stomach-irritating chemicals, and increases the levels of B vitamins and essential amino acids. But for fermentation to occur, yeast cells need a higher concentration of sugar than is normally present in raw barley. Coincidentally, a unique property of sprouted barley seeds is their production of large amounts of enzymes that can convert starch into sugar. Barley thus has both starch and, in its sprouted form, enzymes that convert starch to sugar. The seeds can be sprouted any time of year, and the final product has excellent nutritional value and can have mildly intoxicating levels of alcohol. Collecting and processing wild barley seeds requires tremendous effort, and at the time of the transition to agriculture, barley was not the only exploitable food resource—in fact, many others were probably more accessible. It is hard to imagine that the effort spent collecting wild seeds would have been for producing loaves of bread. The alcohol content and higher nutritional levels of beer, however, might have been incentive enough.

The front of this lyre from Ur is decorated with a bull's head of gold and lapis lazuli beneath which are inlaid panels showing animals in beer-drinking scenes.

Photo reprinted by permission of the University of Pennsylvania Museum.

Finally, it is worth noting that Nature herself may well have produced the first beer. After harvesting, wild barley seeds might have been placed in a container for storage. If the seeds were exposed to moisture they would sprout. Sprouted barley is sweeter and more tender than unsprouted seeds, and therefore more edible. Sprouted seeds might have been dried for later consumption. Exposed to airborne yeast and more moisture, the barley would have fermented, producing beer. We may never know when some brave soul actually drank the "spoiled" barley. But we do know that someone did.

SECRETS OF THE STANZAS

To make sense of the "Hymn to Ninkasi," we approached it on several levels. First, we had to determine if its sequence was linear. That is, did the ordering of the stanzas reflect the actual sequence of stages in a brewing process. Second, we had to examine the Hymn for metaphors and other literary devices that could give us clues to the meaning of the text. Third, we needed to decipher the specific steps that were suggested in each stage of brewing. Finally, we wanted to determine whether any of the stages of the brewing process had been left out. Our interpretation of the Hymn rested on a combination of the archaeological evidence—Sumerian texts, artistic representations of beer drinking, and artifacts once used in the consumption of beer, such as straws made of gold and lapis lazuli; a thorough knowledge of the stages involved in beer making; and an understanding of the biochemical and nutritional characteristics of barley- and wheat-brewed beers.

We soon learned that the Hymn was, in the broadest sense, a linear description of brewing—the preparation and heating of a mash in which enzymes convert the cereal starch into sugar; the boiling of the processed mash, or wort; the addition of flavoring; and the fermenting of the wort using yeast to convert the sugar into alcohol and improve the nutritional content of the beer. By following the stanza-by-stanza instructions, we could duplicate the process used by the Sumerians.

Stanza I refers to being "borne of flowing water." This conjured up images of the flowing of the Tigris and Euphrates rivers, which are known today for their high salt content. The dissolved mineral content of water can affect the quality of a brew. For example, calcium and bicarbonate have important effects on the acidity of beer. Levels of calcium and magnesium are important in stabilizing enzymes and facilitating the fermentation process. The value and function of dissolved minerals in the waters of the Tigris and Euphrates, however, were probably not understood in antiquity. (Today some of the best breweries are located over wells that flow through lime and dolomite deposits.)

In Stanzas II and III water is referred to again. Perhaps the reference to a sacred lake and great walls calls attention to the use of a lake as a reservoir for the irrigation of crops such as barley from which the beer was made. The sacred lake also attests the importance of religious belief in the production of beer. Stanza III also introduces us to the gods and goddesses who made up Ninkasi's family. A minor goddess in the Sumerian pantheon, Ninkasi's name literally means "you who fill my mouth so full."

Stanza IV addresses the particulars of Mesopotamian beer production. The process begins with *bappir*,

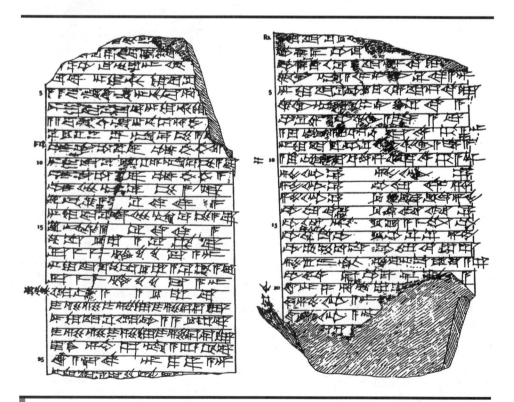

FIGURE 21.1   The Hymn to Ninkasi, inscribed on a nineteenth-century B.C. tablet, contains a recipe for Sumarian beer.

Reprinted by permission of *Archaeology Magazine.*

THE HYMN TO NINKASI

Borne of the flowing water (...),
Tenderly cared for by the Ninhursag,
Borne of the flowing water (...),
Tenderly cared for by the Ninhursag,

Having founded your town by the
sacred lake,
She finished its great walls for you,
Ninkasi, having founded your town by
the sacred lake,
She finished its great walls for you,

Your father is Enki, Lord Nidimmud,
Your mother is Ninti, the queen of the
sacred lake.
Ninkasi, your father is Enki, Lord
Nidimmud,
Your mother is Ninti, the queen of the
sacred lake.

You are the one who handles the dough
[and] with a big shovel,
Mixing in a pit, the bappir with sweet
aromatics,
Ninkasi, you are the one who handles
the dough [and] with a big shovel,
Mixing in a pit, the bappir with
[date]-honey,

You are the one who bakes the bappir in
the big oven,
Puts in order the piles of hulled grains,
Ninkasi, you are the one who bakes the
bappir in the big oven,
Puts in order the piles of hulled grains,

You are the one who waters the malt set
on the ground,
The noble dogs keep away even the
potentates,
Ninkasi, you are the one who waters the
malt set on the ground,

The noble dogs keep away even the
potentates,

You are the one who soaks the malt in
a jar,
The waves rise, the waves fall.
Ninkasi, you are the one who soaks the
malt in a jar,
The waves rise, the waves fall.

You are the one who spreads the cooked
mash on large reed mats,
Coolness overcomes,
Ninkasi, you are the one who spreads the
cooked mash on large reed mats,
Coolness overcomes,

You are the one who holds with both
hands the great sweet wort,
Brewing [it] with honey [and] wine
(You the sweet wort to the vessel)
Ninkasi, (...)
(You the sweet wort to the vessel)

The filtering vat, which makes
a pleasant sound,
You place appropriately on [top of]
a large collector vat.
Ninkasi, the filtering vat, which makes
a pleasant sound,
You place appropriately on [top of]
a large collector vat.

When you pour out the filtered beer of the
collector vat,
It is [like] the onrush of Tigris and
Euphrates.
Ninkasi, you are the one who pours out the
filtered beer of the collector vat,
It is [like] the onrush of Tigris and
Euphrates.

TRANSLATION BY MIGUEL CIVIL

FIGURE 21.2 Translation of the "Hymn to Ninkasi"

a sweet and possibly pungent bread made from barley dough. It is mixed with "sweet aromatics" using a "big shovel...in a pit" and then baked (Stanza V). Bappir seems to have served several purposes. In brewing, it served as a source both of hydrolyzed or gelatinized starch for rapid and efficient sugar production, and of proteins and flavors for the mashing process.

The fermentation process depended on enzymes from malted, i.e. sprouted, barley seeds for the conversion of starches to sugar. It is not surprising that "the noble dogs keep away even the potentates" (Stanza VI), since sprouted barley was a very delicate and valuable resource. Sumerian bappir probably contained little, if any, malt and truly was a barley bread. Flour from malted barley containing the necessary enzymes was probably added later in the process.

Unfortunately, the meaning of "aromatic" has not been sufficiently understood to determine which aromatic was used. However, it is almost certain that dates or date juice provided flavoring. Dates have the aromatic flavor that the Hymn specifies, but we did not know if the flavor would survive the fermentation process. Other candidates for the aromatic were skirret weed, a licorice-flavored plant, and "Assyrian root" or radish, both of which were added to *bouza*, an Egyptian beer made for the past 5,000 years and consumed until a few years ago when stricter laws on sanitation and vending curtailed production.

Stanza VII describes the malt being soaked in a jar in which "the waves rise, the waves fall." Presumably this motion refers to the mashing process during which the malt and the bappir are combined with additional barley (possibly including hulled and crushed seeds that have been toasted or heated to make it easier for the enzymes to convert their starch into sugar). Although it is not mentioned in the text of the Hymn, the mash probably would have been heated if the process was similar to modern brewing methods. How the Sumerians maintained control of the mash temperature remains a bit of a puzzle. The correct temperature and timing probably developed as a result of skill and practice. The production of high quality beer may have become a profession because of the need for such expertise.

In Stanza VIII the "cooked mash" is spread out on mats. This action could have served two purposes. Spreading out the mash would be an ideal way to remove the spent grains from the mixture, and it would also allow the liquid to drain. Cleaning out the spent grains would have been beneficial to Sumerian drinkers who otherwise would have had to rely on straws to bypass the hulls. By the time the

Banquets and beer-drinking were often depicted on seals during the Early Dynastic period (2600–2350 B.C.).

Photo reprinted by permission of the University of Pennsylvania Museum.

Hymn was inscribed, a "filter" had become the symbol of professional brewers. Once filtered, straws were not necessary, and the beer could be consumed directly from cups. The Hymn states that after the "cooked mash" has been laid out, "coolness overcomes." It is, therefore, highly likely that the mash was heated.

After cleaning, the mash, now referred to as "wort," is placed in containers for fermentation. Fermentation proceeds best if the wort is cool, since the high temperature of the mashing step would kill heat-sensitive yeast. Thus, the reference in Stanza VIII to "coolness overcomes" is a crucial step that preceded the addition of yeast for fermentation.

Stanza IX, which describes brewing the "great sweet wort" with honey and wine, was difficult to understand. We were struck by the use of honey. Was it really honey or was it date juice? Thanks to a reinterpretation by Sumeriologist Miguel Civil, we believe that "honey" meant date juice. *Gestin*, translated as "wine," was another matter. In Sumerian gestin means grape, wine, and raisin. At this point in the recipe, yeast needs to be added to start fermentation. Yeast occurs naturally on the skin of grapes and raisins. While it will survive the drying process, yeast on grapes fermented into wine will not remain active. Thus we reasoned that wine could be eliminated as a candidate for gestin, and that the Hymn refers instead to grapes or raisins.

Stanza X mentions the fermentation (collector) vat. Long, narrow-necked vessels would have been preferred over vessels with large, open mouths. The latter form would have allowed too much mixture of the ingredients with air. Exposure to air would have increased the risk of secondary contamination, as well as allowing the acidity to decrease too much, resulting in a lower production of alcohol and stimulation of the growth of yeast.

The "pleasant sound" in Stanza X probably refers to the trickling of the beer through the filter and into the fermentation vat below. Finally, in Stanza XI, the finished beer is poured out of the fermentation vat, through a filter, and into the drinking containers. The pouring of the finished product must have been spectacular; the Hymn describes it as rushing out like the "Tigris and Euphrates." These rivers were the source of life for the ancient Mesopotamians, so the reference to these two great waterways must have been symbolically connected to the Sumerians' appreciation of this fine fermented beverage.

A THRILLING LINK WITH THE PAST

Satisfied with our interpretation of the "Hymn to Ninkasi," we decided to give the recipe a try. From this moment on we began to feel a thrilling link with brewers from ages past. After nearly 4,000 years, Sumerian beer terms such as *bappir* and *gestin* would be spoken in a brewery once again.

To reproduce the recipe in a modern brewery, we made certain assumptions about the ancient method and a few modifications in production to meet the standards of the Anchor Brewing Company in San Francisco, where the beer was to be produced.

First, we used a honey and barley flour mixture to make the bappir. Although in antiquity dates may have been added to sweeten and flavor the bappir before it was baked, we added them only to the final mixture of the bread when it was being put into the mashing vat. (The Federal Government strictly limits such additions, and permission had not been obtained to put in dates.) We decided to use a combination of unmalted, malted, and roasted barley for the flour. However, in baking it we found that it did not dry out and was not storable in baked form. So, we baked it a second time, which made the bread much like the present-day Italian *biscotti* and similar to traditional breads still baked on the island of Crete. Since ancient sources say that bappir was stored, we believe that the bread was twice-baked in antiquity. However, until we have evidence of this technique in the ancient texts, we will avoid further speculation. The bread, which had a consistency like granola, was delicious. However, it should be noted that our bread was not as nutritious as Sumerian bread since ours probably contained less yeast.

We conservatively mixed one-third bappir and two-thirds malt in the mash tank, to insure that all of the starch would convert to sugar. We were initially concerned that the heavy amount of suspended particles from the bappir would foul the modern lautering equipment used to filter the mash, and produce a major plumbing problem in the Anchor brewing vats. Our fears turned out to be unfounded, fortunately, and the lautering process went just fine.

We allowed the wort to cool naturally instead of using modern artificial techniques. The mixture was wonderfully sweet and fragrant, just as the Hymn mentions—the aroma of toasted barley and the scent of dates. We brewed using only a standard brewing yeast in lieu of the gestin mentioned in the Hymn. We wanted to prevent any foreign yeast from infecting the tanks, and to keep the product within controllable standards of purity. In modern beer making, hops are used to provide aromatic flavor and to preserve the beer. Since we could not identify an ancient plant additive that would have served as a hop-like preservative, the beer was flash pasteurized to assure preservation. The final product yielded an alcohol concentration very similar to modern beers of 3.5% by weight. We were ready for the final test. How did it taste?

To celebrate the tenth anniversary of Anchor Brewing Company in its present location, we served the Ninkasi brew to members of the American Association of Micro Brewers, who were having their annual meeting in San Francisco. The beer was consumed in proper Sumerian fashion: sipped from large jugs using long drinking straws fashioned to resemble the gold and lapis-lozuli straws found in the mid-third millennium tomb of Lady Pu-abi at Ur.

Seven months later, a second group, convening at The University Museum to discuss our work, sampled our ancient brew. Not all of the beer had

Photo reprinted by permission of *Archaeology Magazine*.

survived, even with refrigeration. However, those bottles that were still good had aged, much like fine wine—the beer had a dry flavor lacking in bitterness. Aged Ninkasi beer tasted similar to a hard apple cider but retained the fragrance of dates. According to the museum's Patrick McGovern, the beer "had the smoothness and effervescence of champagne and a slight aroma of dates." We had reproduced the beer that made Ninkasi famous! We do not claim to be correct in all of the details, but we have made a sincere effort to bring the art of the modern brewer to bear on the mystery of how ancient beer might have been made four millennia ago.

The World's First City

Scholars are once again working at Çatalhöyük in central Anatolia, seeking the origins of urban life.

Nine thousand years ago, visitors approaching Çatalhöyük from across a vast marshy plain would have seen many hundreds of mud-brick dwellings stacked up on the slopes of an enormous settlement mound. The site's several thousand inhabitants would have been herding sheep or goats; hunting wild cattle (aurochs), horse, and deer; tending crops of peas, lentils, and cereals; or collecting wild plant foods such as tubers from the marshes. Some would have been bringing valuable raw materials to the site, such as obsidian from volcanic peaks to the northeast. In size and complexity, Çatalhöyük was unlike any other site in the world. The American archaeologist Walter Fairservis, Jr., writing in 1975, described it as a community "at the threshold of civilization."

Çatalhöyük was first brought to worldwide attention by James Mellaart, whose excavations from 1961 to 1965 revealed more than 150 dwellings and rooms, many, decorated with murals, plaster reliefs, and sculpture. Some rooms, which Mellaart designated "shrines," contained murals depicting men pulling the tongues and tails of aurochs and stags, or vaulting across the backs of animals while women and men watched. Other scenes seemed to show vultures apparently eating headless bodies and mortuary rituals involving exposure of bodies on scaffolds. Mounted on "shrine" walls, sometimes in two or three tiers, were full-size plaster heads of bulls, sheep, and goats to which real horn cores were attached. Cattle horn cores were mounted on pedestals, and in one room a bizarre plaster bench, long enough for a person to lie on, had six pairs of aurochs' horns mounted along its sides. Painted plaster reliefs of stags, bulls, leopards, and human females also decorated the walls. In one room Mellaart found the world's first known landscape: a view of a twin-peaked volcano erupting over a community of rect-

angular dwellings. The artifacts reported by Mellaart were just as spectacular, including the world's earliest known pottery, polished obsidian mirrors, and bone hook-and-eye closures; preserved basketry, textiles, and carved wooden utensils; and well-fashioned obsidian tools and exquisitely shaped flint daggers with bone handles carved in the forms of animals.

Meaning "fork mound" in Turkish, Çatalhöyük consists of two mounds on either side of an ancient channel of the Çarsamba River on the fertile Konya Plain of central Turkey. The larger mound, Çatalhöyük East, is of Early Neolithic age with occupation levels dated to between 9,600 and 7,500 years ago, and even older undated and unexplored occupation levels at its base. Çatalhöyük West is made up primarily of later Neolithic and Chalcolithic levels 7,500 to 5,000 years old.

Mellaart excavated less than four percent of Çatalhöyük East, but it was enough to indicate the settlement's size and architectural complexity as well as the sophistication of its art. In doing so, he established Çatalhöyük as an important site for studying the origins of settled farming life and the rise of the first cities. Some scholars consider Çatalhöyük to be the world's first city, and its murals are recognized by art historians as unique in world history. Colin Renfrew of the University of Cambridge believes central Anatolia, with Çatalhöyük as its preeminent site, was the wellspring of European settled farming life and perhaps the homeland of the Indo-European language and people.

After 1965, the site lay idle until 1993, when Ian Hodder of the University of Cambridge, a leading archaeological theoretician, launched the Çatalhöyük Research Project. Working in collaboration with the McDonald Institute for Archaeological

Research at Cambridge and the British Institute for Archaeology at Ankara, Hodder has now completed five years of excavation and study as part of a 25-year program. An international and multidisciplinary undertaking, the project has three principal aims: archaeological investigation of the site; conservation of architecture, murals, artifacts, and human remains; and management of the site, including interpretive programs for visitors. A "dig house" to support this work, with research and conservation laboratories, secure storage areas, living quarters for project members, and an interpretive center is under construction north of Çatalhöyük East.

One innovative aspect of the project has been improved communication between field excavators and specialists working in the laboratory. Too often at archaeological sites the two groups work in isolation. Here on-site lab and excavation teams interact daily through site tours and a network that links workstations in the labs and at trenchside with a central computer, making it possible to adjust digging and sampling strategies as work progresses.

We spent three years studying Mellaart's results and conducting noninvasive explorations of Çatalhöyük East, then in 1995 began excavating building 1, a structure in the northern part of the mound. It was cleared in 1997, revealing a complex history of remodeling during at least eight occupation phases. The structure was approximately 29 by 20 feet, with a 20-by-20-foot room and another, smaller chamber divided into two subrooms. The floors were plastered, and platforms were built in the larger room. On the remnants of the larger room's west and north walls were sections of mural with ten painted layers. The fragmentary images appeared to be geometric figures and floral designs. Pieces of horn and antler found set into the plastered west wall or bearing traces of wall plaster indicate that this wall had a plaster relief. Other features of building 1 include traces in the south wall of a ladder to the roof, an oven built into the south wall early in the history of the dwelling and later abandoned and bricked up, and two superimposed ovens in a small room at the building's west end. These ovens, as well as food debris such as lentils and cereal grains found on the floor, indicate the room was used for food preparation.

Buried beneath the platforms and floors of building 1 were the remains of 67 people interred throughout the history of the building. Theya Molleson and Peter Andrews of the Natural History Museum in London lead the team studying the human remains, which include males and females of all ages, from newborns to aged adults, the oldest man well past 60. Tightly flexed bodies were placed in pits, which were then plastered over. The building

was occupied and used while people were being interred, and pits were reopened for later addition of bodies.

Excavation of a large area adjacent to building 1 was begun in 1997 by a team directed by Ruth Tringham of the University of California, Berkeley, revealing a large and elaborate structure (building 3) with thickly plastered walls with red and black paint and the remains of bulls' heads.

An area about 125 feet square within Mellaart's old excavation has been cleared as a first step in excavating to the mound's base, 60 to 70 feet below the summit. Here we hope to reach the earliest settlement levels, which will permit us to study the origins of the mural art and sculpture. Excavations since 1994 have revealed building 2, an elaborate structure, dated to about 9,000 years ago, with remarkably well preserved plaster walls with traces of sculpture and plaster reliefs. There is evidence of paintings, which we will uncover later.

The new research at Çatalhöyük East has already led us to revise some of Mellaart's conclusions about the site. For example, we have found that rooms like those he called shrines—buildings with murals, plaster reliefs, and sculpture—are numerous and occur throughout the mound, demonstrating that there is no evidence of a ritual elite concentrated in a "priestly quarter," as he suggested.

Recently developed techniques unavailable to Mellaart, such as micromorphology, the study of soils and sediments in thin sections under the microscope, are also contributing to our understanding of the site. Directed by Wendy Matthews of the University of Cambridge, this work includes the identification of construction materials such as mud brick and mortar, study of structural details and layering of painted plasters, determination of the contents of hearths and ovens, and identification of activity areas in rooms and open spaces between buildings. Analysis of material trampled in floor plasters may help to determine the function of rooms and to identify activities carried on in them. For example, study of floor trample from an open area between buildings excavated by Mellaart in 1963 and identified by him as a courtyard revealed the presence of animal dung and straw. Comparisons with the floor debris from modern sheep and goat pens suggests a similar function for this area. Such analysis will provide more data for evaluating Mellaart's interpretation of rooms with wall paintings, reliefs, and sculpture as shrines.

Because of the age and fragility of the murals and the plaster finishes to which they are applied, conservation is crucial. The buildings at Çatalhöyük were made of mud-brick walls coated with plaster finishes on which murals were painted or plaster re-liefs built up. Walls, floors, and internal room features such as benches and platforms were also plastered, often with multiple layers applied in thin sequences (less than one millimeter thick) consisting of a base coat and a thinner, overlying finish coat. Surfaces with as many as 40 episodes of replastering are common, and one plaster specimen collected in 1995 had at least 68 pairs of base and finish plasters. Conservation work is being directed by Frank Matero, head of the University of Pennsylvania's Laboratory for Architectural Conservation. Walls and layers of painted plaster will be stabilized in the field, and sections of walls will be lifted and moved to the conservation lab where layers of painted plaster will be separated.

An important part of the project is a regional survey to locate Epipalaeolithic (15,000–10,000 years ago) and Neolithic (10,000–7,000 years ago) sites on the Konya Plain. Headed by Douglas Baird of Liverpool University, the survey has identified several early sites buried by alluvial sediments from the Çarsamba River. At Pinarbaşi, a rocky promontory 20 miles southeast of Çatalhöyük, open-air and rock-shelter sites with deposits contemporary with and older than Çatalhöyük are now under excavation by Trevor Watkins of Edinburgh University and Cengiz Topal of the Karaman Museum in the city of Karaman, 60 miles south of Çatalhöyük. The Konya Plain covers part of the floor of the Konya Basin, which once held a large freshwater lake. Some 18,000 years ago the lake was 100 feet deep at the place where Çatalhöyük later stood. After the Ice Age, it dried up, leaving remnant lakes and wetlands in depressions in the basin's floor. By Early Neolithic times, when people began to live at Çatalhöyük, the site must have been surrounded by marshland and small lakes. By combining the results from excavations at Çatalhöyük and the Pinarbaşi sites with evidence from regional surveys and environmental reconstructions, we may better understand the origins of farming and town life in Anatolia.

Nowadays, few people come to Çatalhöyük, which is 30 miles southeast of the city of Konya and ten miles from the nearest sizable town. The roads to the site are unpaved, poorly marked, and heavily used by tractors and agricultural vehicles. The site's location is not well known and tourists prefer to visit the more spectacular temples, theaters, and monuments of Turkey's rich classical sites. Development of public programming that will attract visitors to the site is an important part of the Çatalhöyük Research Project. The dig house interpretive center, being pre-pared by the Science Museum of Minnesota in collaboration with IDA AJANS, a graphic design agency in Ankara, will house panels explaining the history of the site and current research. On the walls, we plan to re-create a mural from one of the "shrines" excavated by Mellaart and display artifacts from the excavation. A 1:4 scale model of a room with elaborate bulls' heads and benches will also be displayed. For now, temporary exhibits, developed between 1994 and 1996, provide visitors with the site's excavation history and present findings of the Çatalhöyük Research Project. Interpretive panels, maps, and photographic murals describe the surface survey and geophysical prospecting that preceded the start of excavations in 1995, as well as the regional archaeological survey to identify other Early Neolithic sites in the Konya Basin. We also envision a future exhibit—featuring important new findings and artifacts from the project and Mellaart's dig—that will tour Turkey, the United States, and Europe.

One major goal of the project is to reach a global audience through the world wide web. A site at the University of Cambridge…carries information about the project, annually updated summaries and more specialized preliminary reports about the individual excavation areas, the regional survey, micro-morphology, pottery, plant and animal remains, and other topics…. The Science Museum of Minnesota is developing a web site for middle- and high-school teachers and their students. It will present educational themes developed from the first excavations at Çatalhöyük and provide students and teachers access to new discoveries at the site and to archaeologists in Europe and America involved in the project.

As archaeologists and exhibit developers we find working on the Çatalhöyük Research Project both deeply challenging and exciting. Our hope is to convey to the public the sophisticated science and interpretive methods being brought to bear on Çatalhöyük. At the same time it is extremely rewarding to be part of one of the great archaeological projects of the twentieth century. Twenty years from now, at the close of the current investigations, we will be able to view, in a museum setting and on the world wide web, paintings that document the origin and development of the mural art of Çatalhöyük and that illustrate long lost lifeways of the Early Neolithic. More important, we will have plausible and scientifically defensible interpretations concerning the meanings of this art and the cultural context in which it existed. Finally, we will have recovered and presented information that will carry forward our understanding of early urban life.

Heather Pringle

The Cradle of Cash

When money arose in the ancient cities of Mesopotamia, it profoundly and permanently changed civilization.

The scene in the small, stifling room is not hard to imagine: the scribe frowning, shifting in his seat as he tries to concentrate on the words of the woman in front of him. A member of one of the wealthiest families in Sippar, the young priestess has summoned him to her room to record a business matter. When she entered the temple, she explains, her parents gave her a valuable inheritance, a huge piece of silver in the shape of a ring, worth the equivalent of 60 months' wages for an estate worker. She has decided to buy land with this silver. Now she needs someone to take down a few details. Obediently, the scribe smooths a wet clay tablet and gets out his stylus. Finally, his work done, he takes the tablet down to the archive.

For more than 3,700 years, the tablet languished in obscurity, until late-nineteenth-century collectors unearthed it from Sippar's ruins along the Euphrates River in what is now Iraq. Like similar tablets, it hinted at an ancient and mysterious Near Eastern currency, in the form of silver rings, that started circulating two millenia before the world's first coins were struck. By the time that tablet was inscribed, such rings may have been in use for a thousand years.

When did humans first arrive at the concept of money? What conditions spawned it? And how did it affect the ancient societies that created it? Until recently, researchers thought they had the answers. They believed money was born, as coins, along the coasts of the Mediterranean in the seventh or sixth century B.C., a product of the civilization that later gave the world the Parthenon, Plato, and Aristotle. But few see the matter so simply now. With evidence gleaned from such disparate sources as ancient temple paintings, clay tablets, and buried hoards of uncoined metals, researchers have revealed far more ancient money: silver scraps and bits of gold, massive rings, and gleaming ingots. In the process, they

have pushed the origins of cash far beyond the sunny coasts of the Mediterranean, back to the world's oldest cities in Mesopotamia, the fertile plain created by the Tigris and Euphrates rivers. There, they suggest, wealthy citizens were flaunting money at least as early as 2,500 B.C. and perhaps a few hundred years before that. "There's just no way to get around it," says Marvin Powell, a historian at Northern Illinois University in De Kalb. "Silver in Mesopotamia functions like our money today. It's a means of exchange. People use it for a storage of wealth, and they use it for defining value."

Many scholars believe money began even earlier. "My sense is that as far back as the written records go in Mesopotamia and Egypt, some form of money is there," observes Jonathan Williams, curator of Roman and Iron Age coins at the British Museum in London. "That suggests it was probably there beforehand, but we can't tell because we don't have any written records."

Just why researchers have had such difficulties in uncovering these ancient moneys has much to do with the practice of archeology and the nature of money itself. Archeologists, after all, are the ultimate Dumpster divers: they spend their careers sifting through the trash of the past, ingeniously reconstructing vanished lives from broken pots and dented knives. But like us, ancient Mesopotamians and Phoenicians seldom made the error of tossing out cash, and only rarely did they bury their most precious liquid assets in the ground. Even when archeologists have found buried cash, though, they've had trouble recognizing it for what it was. Money doesn't always come in the form of dimes and sawbucks, even today. As a means of payment and a way of storing wealth, it assumes many forms, from debit cards and checks to credit cards and mutual funds. The forms it took in the past have been, to say the least, elusive.

From the beginning, money has shaped human society. It greased the wheels of Mesopotamian commerce, spurred the development of mathematics, and helped officials and kings rake in taxes and impose fines. As it evolved in Bronze Age civilizations along the Mediterranean coast, it fostered sea trade, built lucrative cottage industries, and underlay an accumulation of wealth that might have impressed Donald Trump. "If there were never any money, there would never have been prosperity," says Thomas Wyrick, an economist at Southwest Missouri State University in Springfield, who is studying the origins of money and banking. "Money is making all this stuff happen."

Ancient texts show that almost from its first recorded appearance in the ancient Near East, money preoccupied estate owners and scribes, water carriers, and slaves. In Mesopotamia, as early as 3000 B.C., scribes devised pictographs suitable for recording simple lists of concrete objects, such as grain consignments. Five hundred years later, the pictographs had evolved into a more supple system of writing, a partially syllabic script known as cuneiform that was capable of recording the vernacular: first Sumerian, a language unrelated to any living tongue, and later Akkadian, an ancient Semitic language. Scribes could write down everything from kingly edicts to proverbs, epics to hymns, private family letters to merchants' contracts. In these ancient texts, says Miguel Civil, a lexicographer at the Oriental Institute of the University of Chicago, "they talk about wealth and gold and silver all the time."

In all likelihood, says Wyrick, human beings first began contemplating cash just about the time that Mesopotamians were slathering mortar on mud bricks to build the world's first cities. Until then, people across the Near East had worked primarily on small farms, cultivating barley, dates, and wheat, hunting gazelles and other wild game, and bartering among themselves for the things they could not produce. But around 3500 B.C., work parties started hauling stones across the plains and raising huge flat-topped platforms, known as ziggurats, on which to found their temples. Around their bases, they built street upon twisted street of small mud-brick houses.

To furnish these new temples and to serve temple officials, many farmers became artisans—stonemasons, silversmiths, tanners, weavers, boatbuilders, furniture makers. And within a few centuries, says Wyrick, the cities became much greater than the sum of their parts. Economic life flourished and grew increasingly complex. "Before, you always had people scattered out on the hillsides," says Wyrick, "and whatever they could produce for their families, that

was it. Very little trade occurred because you never had a large concentration of people. But now, in these cities, for the first time ever in one spot, you had lots of different goods, hundreds of goods, and lots of different people trading them."

Just how complex life grew in these early metropolises can be glimpsed in the world's oldest accounting records: 8,162 tiny clay tokens excavated from the floors of village houses and city temples across the Near East and studied in detail by Denise Schmandt-Besserat, an archeologist at the University of Texas at Austin. The tokens served first as counters and perhaps later as promissory notes given to temple tax collectors before the first writing appeared.

By classifying the disparate shapes and markings on the tokens into types and comparing these with the earliest known written symbols, Schmandt-Besserat discovered that each token represented a specified quantity of a particular commodity. And she noticed an intriguing difference between village tokens and city tokens. In the small communities dating from before the rise of cities, Mesopotamians regularly employed just five token types, representing different amounts of three main goods: human labor, grain, and livestock like goats and sheep. But in the cities, they began churning out a multitude of new types, regularly employing 16 in all, with dozens of subcategories representing everything from honey, sheep's milk, and trussed ducks to wool, cloth, rope, garments, mats, beds, perfume, and metals. "It's no longer just farm goods," says Schmandt-Besserat. "There are also finished products, manufactured goods, furniture, bread, and textiles."

Faced with this new profusion, says Wyrick, no one would have had an easy time bartering, even for something as simple as a pair of sandals. "If there were a thousand different goods being traded up and down the street, people could set the price in a thousand different ways, because in a barter economy each good is priced in terms of all other goods. So one pair of sandals equals ten dates, equals one quart of wheat, equals two quarts of bitumen, and so on. Which is the best price? It's so complex that people don't know if they are getting a good deal. For the first time in history, we've got a large number of goods. And for the first time, we have so many prices that it overwhelms the human mind. People needed some standard way of stating value."

In Mesopotamia, silver—a prized ornamental material—became that standard. Supplies didn't vary much from year to year, so its value remained constant, which made it an ideal measuring rod for calculating the value of other things. Mesopotamians were quick to see the advantage, recording the prices of everything from timber to barley in silver by weight in shekels. (One shekel equaled one-third of an ounce, or just a little more than the weight of three pennies.) A slave, for example, cost between 10 and 20 shekels of silver. A month of a freeman's labor was worth 1 shekel. A quart of barley went for three-hundredths of a shekel. Best of all, silver was portable. "You can't carry a shekel of barley on your ass," comments Marvin Powell (referring to the animal). And with a silver standard, kings could attach a price to infractions of the law. In the codes of the city of Eshnunna, which date to around 2000 B.C., a man who bit another man's nose would be fined 60 shekels of silver; one who slapped another in the face paid 10.

How the citizens of Babylon or Ur actually paid their bills, however, depended on who they were. The richest tenth of the population, says Powell, frequently paid in various forms of silver. Some lugged around bags or jars containing bits of the precious metal to be placed one at a time on the pan of a scale until they balanced a small carved stone weight in the other pan. Other members of the upper crust favored a more convenient form of cash: pieces of silver cast in standard weights. These were called *har* in the tablets, translated as "ring" money.

At the Oriental Institute in the early 1970s, Powell studied nearly 100 silver coils—some resembling bedsprings, others slender wire coils—found primarily in the Mesopotamian city of Khafaje. They were not exactly rings, it was true, but they matched other fleeting descriptions of *har*. According to the scribes, ring money ranged from 1 to 60 shekels in weight. Some pieces were cast in special molds. At the Oriental Institute, the nine largest coils all bore a triangular ridge, as if they had been cast and then rolled into spirals while still pliable. The largest coils weighed almost exactly 60 shekels, the smallest from one-twelfth to two and a half shekels. "It's clear that the coils were intended to represent some easily recognizable form of Babylonian stored value," says Powell. "In other words, it's the forerunner of coinage."

The masses in Mesopotamia, however, seldom dealt in such money. It was simply too precious, much as a gold coin would have been for a Kansas dirt farmer in the middle of the Great Depression. To pay their bills, water carriers, estate workers, fishers, and farmers relied on more modest forms of money: copper, tin, lead, and above all, barley. "It's the cheap commodity money," says Powell. "I think barley functions in ancient Mesopotamia like small change in later systems, like the bronze currencies in the Hellenistic period. And essentially that avoids the problem of your being cheated. You measure barley out and it's not as dangerous a thing to try to exchange as

silver, given weighing errors. If you lose a little bit, it's not going to make that much difference."

Measurable commodity money such as silver and barley both simplified and complicated daily life. No longer did temple officials have to sweat over how to collect a one-sixth tax increase on a farmer who had paid one ox the previous year. Compound interest on loans was now a breeze to calculate. Shekels of silver, after all, lent themselves perfectly to intricate mathematical manipulation; one historian has suggested that Mesopotamian scribes first arrived at logarithms and exponential values from their calculations of compound interest.

"People were constantly falling into debt," says Powell. "We find reference to this in letters where people are writing to one another about someone in the household who has been seized for securing a debt." To remedy these disastrous financial affairs, King Hammurabi decreed in the eighteenth century B.C. that none of his subjects could be enslaved for more than three years for failing to repay a debt. Other Mesopotamian rulers, alarmed at the financial chaos in the cities, tried legislating moratoriums on all outstanding bills.

While the cities of Mesopotamia were the first to conceive of money, others in the ancient Near East soon took up the torch. As civilization after civilization rose to glory along the coasts of the eastern Mediterranean, from Egypt to Syria, their citizens begin abandoning the old ways of pure barter. Adopting local standards of value, often silver by weight, they began buying and selling with their own local versions of commodity moneys: linen, perfume, wine, olive oil, wheat, barley, precious metals—things that could be easily divided into smaller portions and that resisted decay.

And as commerce became smoother in the ancient world, people became increasingly selective about what they accepted as money, says Wyrick. "Of all the different media of exchange, one commodity finally broke out of the pack. It began to get more popular than the others, and I think the merchants probably said to themselves, 'Hey, this is great. Half my customers have this form of money. I'm going to start demanding it.' And the customers were happy, too, because there's more than just one merchant coming around, and they didn't know what to hold on to, because each merchant was different. If everyone asked for barley or everyone asked for silver, that would be very convenient. So as one of these media of exchange becomes more popular, everyone just rushes toward that."

What most ancient Near Easterners rushed toward around 1500 B.C. was silver. In the Old Testament, for example, rulers of the Philistines, a seafaring people who settled on the Palestine coast in the twelfth century B.C., each offer Delilah 1,100 pieces of silver for her treachery in betraying the secret of Samson's immense strength. And in a well-known Egyptian tale from the eleventh century B.C., the wandering hero Wen-Amon journeys to Lebanon to buy lumber to build a barge. As payment, he carries jars and sacks of gold and silver, each weighed in the traditional Egyptian measure, the deben. (One deben equals 3 ounces.) Whether these stories are based on history or myth, they reflect the commercial transactions of their time.

To expedite commerce, Mediterranean metalsmiths also devised ways of conveniently packaging money. Coils and rings seem to have caught on in some parts of Egypt: a mural painted during the fourteenth century B.C. in the royal city of Thebes depicts a man weighing a sack of doughnut-size golden rings. Elsewhere, metalsmiths cast cash in other forms. In the Egyptian city of el-Amarna, built and briefly occupied during the fourteenth century B.C., archeologists stumbled upon what they fondly referred to as a crock of gold. Inside, among bits of gold and silver, were several slender rod-shaped ingots of gold and silver. When researchers weighed them, they discovered that some were in multiples or fractions of the Egyptian deben, suggesting different denominations of an ancient currency.

All these developments, says Wyrick, transformed Mediterranean life. Before, in the days of pure barter, people produced a little bit of everything themselves, eking out a subsistence. But with the emergence of money along the eastern Mediterranean, people in remote coastal communities found themselves in a new and enviable position. For the first time, they could trade easily with Phoenician or Syrian merchants stopping at their harbors. They no longer had to be self-sufficient. "They could specialize in producing one thing," says Wyrick. "Someone could just graze cattle. Or they could mine gold or silver. And when you specialize, you become more productive. And then more and more goods start coming your way."

The wealth spun by such specialization and trade became the stuff of legend. It armed the fierce Mycenaean warriors of Greece in bronze cuirasses and chariots and won them victories. It outfitted the tomb of Tutankhamen, sending his soul in grandeur to the next world. And it filled the palace of Solomon with such magnificence that even the Queen of Sheba was left breathless.

But the rings, ingots, and scraps of gold and silver that circulated as money in the eastern Mediterranean were still a far cry from today's money. They lacked a key ingredient of modern cash—a visible guarantee of authenticity. Without such a warranty, many people would never willingly accept them at their face value from a stranger. The lumps of precious metal might be a shade short of a shekel, for example. Or they might not be pure gold or silver at all, but some cheaper alloy. Confidence, suggests Miriam Balmuth, an archeologist at Tufts University in Medford, Massachusetts, could be won only if someone reputable certified that a coin was both the promised weight and composition.

Balmuth has been trying to trace the origins of this certification. In the ancient Near East, she notes, authority figures—perhaps kings or merchants—attempted to certify money by permitting their names or seals to be inscribed on the official carved stone weights used with scales. That way Mesopotamians would know that at least the weights themselves were the genuine article. But such measures were not enough to deter cheats. Indeed, so prevalent was fraud in the ancient world that no fewer than eight passages in the Old Testament forbid the faithful from tampering with scales or substituting heavier stone weights when measuring out money.

Clearly, better antifraud devices were needed. Under the ruins of the old city of Dor along northern Israel's coast, a team of archeologists found one such early attempt. Ephraim Stern of Hebrew University and his colleagues found a clay jug filled with nearly 22 pounds of silver, mainly pieces of scrap, buried in a section of the city dating from roughly 3,000 years ago. But more fascinating than the contents, says Balmuth, who recently studied this hoard, was the way they had been packaged. The scraps were divided into separate piles. Someone had wrapped each pile in fabric and then attached a bulla, a clay tab imprinted with an official seal. "I have since read that these bullae lasted for centuries," says Balmuth, "and were used to mark jars—or in this case things wrapped in fabric—that were sealed. That was a way of signing something."

All that remained was to impress the design of a seal directly on small rounded pieces of metal—which is precisely what happened by around 600 B.C. in an obscure Turkish kingdom by the sea. There traders and perfume makers known as the Lydians struck the world's first coins. They used electrum, a natural alloy of gold and silver panned from local riverbeds. (Coincidentally, Chinese kings minted their first money at roughly the same time: tiny bronze pieces shaped like knives and spades, bearing inscriptions revealing places of origin or weight. Circular coins in China came later.)

First unearthed by archeologists early this century in the ruins of the Temple of Artemis in Ephesus, one of the Seven Wonders of the ancient world, the Lydian coins bore the essential hallmarks of modern coinage. Made of small, precisely measured pieces of precious metal, they were stamped with the figures of lions and other mighty beasts—the seal designs, it seems, of prominent Lydians. And such wealth did they bring one Lydian king, Croesus, that his name became a byword for prosperity.

Struck in denominations as small as .006 ounce of electrum—one-fifteenth the weight of a penny—Lydia's coinage could be used by people in various walks of life. The idea soon caught on in the neighboring Greek city-states. Within a few decades, rulers across Greece began churning out beautiful coins of varied denominations in unalloyed gold and silver, stamped with the faces of their gods and goddesses.

These new Greek coins became fundamental building blocks for European civilization. With such small change jingling in their purses, Greek merchants plied the western Mediterranean, buying all that was rare and beautiful from coastal dwellers, leaving behind Greek colonies from Sicily to Spain and spreading their ideas of art, government, politics, and philosophy. By the fourth century B.C., Alexander the Great was acquiring huge amounts of gold and silver through his conquests and issuing coins bearing his image far and wide, which Wyrick calls "ads for empire building."

Indeed, says Wyrick, the small change in our pockets literally made the Western world what it is today. "I tell my students that if money had never developed, we would all still be bartering. We would have been stuck with that. Money opened the door to trade, which opened the door for specialization. And that made possible a modern society."

Henry T. Wright

Rise of Civilization: Mesopotamia to Mesoamerica

In perhaps as many as six different regions of the world, human societies appear to have evolved—more or less independently—from simple chiefdoms to networks of small states, to empires with fully differentiated social classes and specialized systems of production. Archaeologists early in this century wrote as if these developmental patterns could be documented directly from the archaeological record. Today, we realize that this is impossible. Only the more mundane aspects of the past—a discarded potsherd, a piece of sculptured marble, an ancient text—can be documented with any degree of certainty. Nevertheless, we can use these fragmentary remains to evaluate our interpretations of past events, and even to test general theories that describe and explain the intertwined political, religious, and economic processes behind the rise of the early civilizations. Successive programs of field research and the testing of our theories has led most mid-twentieth-century archaeologists to reject most of the elegant but overly simple explanations. For example, few now seriously believe that irrigation agriculture, population growth, or long-range trade can alone explain the development of any of the early civilizations. We are now increasingly concerned with the complicated interrelationships between these developments and other variables in broader trans-regional contexts.

We are able to ask, and to begin answering, these more complex questions because the twentieth century has been one of profound changes in archaeological methods. We now have not only more precise ways to excavate and recover evidence from sites, we have remote sensing and surface survey techniques that enable us to learn a great deal about ancient regional landscapes with minimal excavation, and we have new methods for dating and artifact analysis, as well as computer facilities to handle the mountains of data that result from all these new methods.

The archaeologists of the future, however, will have a responsibility to go beyond innovation in techniques and forge new ways of thinking about the earliest civilizations. We need a synthesis of current approaches to the material aspects of life developed by anthropological archaeologists with new approaches to social life and communication now being developed by archaeologists in the humanistic traditions, linguists, and cultural anthropologists. Such a synthesis will probably be realized not by a single brilliant scholar but by many, evaluating their ideas in the context of their archaeological studies of specific civilizations. We can gain some idea of the future of such studies by looking at the accomplishments and potential of ongoing research on a selection of five of the early civilizations.

NEAR EAST

The vast nexus of urban societies that centered on the Nile and the Mesopotamian rivers—from Anatolia to Arabia, from Central Asia to the Sudan—formed the world's first great trans-regional civilization, the one that cannot have been influenced by already developed civilizations. Archaeologists working in the heartlands of these regions have the unique opportunity to retrieve some of the "waste paper" of urban economies and state polities from as early as 3400 B.C.—papyrus texts preserved by dessication in sites along the Nile and durable clay documents in Mesopotamia. These are not simply the propaganda of rulers carved in stone; they include information about day-to-day decisions about crops, labor, trade, and conflicts. These texts can be compared with the archaeological remains, the material evidence of the results of these decisions. Some archaeologists argue that decision-making is central to the functioning of culture. If this is true, then Near Eastern specialists have a powerful tool in these texts for examining the development of decision-making hierarchies that seem to characterize all complex societies. The usefulness of these texts is, however, limited by several circumstances. First, early writing was developed in central state and temple institutions and was rarely used in family affairs or even relations among the elite. Second, early administrative texts are often laconic "grocery lists" of goods and items. These texts are difficult to read and their social context is often unclear. Finally, writing developed in the Near East, as elsewhere, long after the first steps toward economic stratification and social hierarchy had been taken. Thus the written records are most informative about the operation of the developed early states, rather than about their predecessors.

The Near East has seen the most comprehensive use of regional survey techniques. By using air photographs, systematic surface studies, and test excavations, archaeologists have been able to map landscapes with settlements, river channels, and canals from as early as 5000 B.C. With better understanding of how recent geological processes have altered the archaeological record of the ancient landscape, and with better remote sensing technologies to record landscapes from satellites or aircraft, such studies will become more and more precise in the twenty-first century. Innovations in coring techniques, now being made in countries such as the Netherlands, may make it possible to extract and study soil samples from deeply buried landscapes such as those under the Nile delta and under the Euphrates alluvium.

What we will see in the Near East in the immediate future is a long overdue integration of the regional archaeological record and the textual record, along with new approaches to excavation. Humanistic archaeologists, with their keen interest in textual records, have devoted decades to the investigation of the great urban centers, understandably focusing on the great institutions where texts are more likely to be found: palaces, temples, and the like. In contrast, the few anthropological archaeologists concerned with the archaeological record of early Near Eastern civilization have spent much time salvaging information about landscapes before the evidence is destroyed by modern agriculture. They have had little chance to use the precise excavation techniques (such as representative excavation sampling, microstratigraphic control, special recovery methods for plant remains, etc.) developed by prehistorians working on the early villages that can shed light on daily activities. Somehow the time and funds must be found to apply the methods developed for early villages to the early urban centers and their subsidiary settlements. We need to recover texts in firm association with the evidence of storehouses, workshops, and homes—not only on major sites but on rural estates, border forts, etc., if we are to have a complete picture of political and economic changes.

Such innovations will require a breaking down of the institutional and disciplinary barriers to research in the Near East. Not only is better communication needed between humanistic and anthropological archaeologists, but there is also a need for better understanding between research archaeologists and the local administrative archaeologists concerned with safeguarding each nation's ancient heritage in the face of modern development. Each group in each country has different ways of recording information from archaeological surveys and excavations, different programs of publication, and different standards for the curation of archaeological remains. Tragically, most archaeological samples in the Near East are discarded after brief study simply because museum space is unavailable. The reanalysis of artifacts, soil samples, etc., as new techniques are devised will rarely be possible until the Egyptian policy of requiring the construction of large storage facilities at the site of each excavation program is generally adopted.

An area of future innovation necessary for any broader use of the Near Eastern archaeological record is that of experimental archaeology. This is because ethnoarchaeology, the study of the material remains of modern peoples, is primarily only useful for the study of questions about rural life in the Near East. The millennia that have elapsed since civilization's formative stages here have seen the destruction of the natural environment, the transformation of technology in classical times, the transformation of social orders by the rise of Islam, not to mention the recent impact of industrial civilization. However, by constructing experimental buildings, farms, and workshops, we may test ideas about both how ancient activities were performed and the processes that turned the debris of ancient activities into the archaeological record that we can excavate today.

If the comprehensive integration of Near Eastern archaeology across disciplinary and national boundaries, envisioned above, can be realized, then by 2050 we should have an unparalleled body of data for evaluating ideas about how urban economics and political hierarchies develop.

SOUTH ASIA

The first civilization on the South Asian subcontinent was centered in the alluvial plain of the Indus River, but societies on the nearby Gangetic plain, on the Afghan Plateau, and even across the Arabian Sea in Oman participated in the broader trans-regional South Asian economic system. Recent research has shown that developed village life flourished in tributary valleys of the Indus by 7000 B.C. and that networks of large settlements surrounded by subsidiary small settlements had emerged before 3000 B.C. So there are no grounds to presume that direct contact with Mesopotamia initiated the formation of complex societies along the Indus. There is, however, increasing evidence of overland and maritime trade between the developed Mesopotamian and Indus heartlands. More extensive application of underwater archaeology in the region will help to document this trade. Though relatively little is known about the early stages of the evolution of Indus civilization, much is known about its great floresence from 2500 to 1800 B.C., in spite of the fact that the rather limited kinds of written texts—apparently mostly brief names and titles carved on stone seals—from the area cannot yet be read. From the beginning of major research along the Indus during the 1920s, archaeologists there have tried to excavate both small and large communities, providing evidence of urban organization as good as that in any other area of the world. Also, researchers along the Indus have been almost unique in paying careful attention to the human biology of these first urban dwellers and their predecessors. For no other early civilization do we have the comparative information on nutrition, disease, and mortality that we have for the occupants of the Indus Valley cities and their predecessors.

What is lacking for most of South Asia is a groundwork of regional archaeological surveys. There have been few modern surveys and none are fully published. Surveys, combined with studies of past environments, will be needed on many samples of the ancient Indus landscape if we are to understand the basic dynamics of agriculture and population in this civilization.

In addition to archaeological surveys and to more precise excavations, there is another form of research important to developing general theories of the evolution of civilizations, one that perhaps can be undertaken in South Asia more fruitfully than anywhere else. In all the other heartlands of early civilization, the rise of the great world religions and the traumas of imperial expansion have sundered the direct ideological links with the earlier stages of civilization. Only in portions of the Indian subcontinent do large communities still flourish in which the social order, the organization of crafts, and many other aspects of life still operate under the guidance of a religious system directly developed from that of the earliest complex societies. Though many aspects of life have changed, South Asia provides unique opportunities for ethnoarchaeological study, both of the archaeological byproducts of religious activities and of the formation of urban archaeological records. This will surely be a major concern for South Asian specialists during the near future.

Given the strengths of the South Asian record—its clear evidence of town organization, crafts, trade, and ritual—and the unfortunately limited extent of its written record, it seems likely that the data from the area will contribute more to an understanding of the operation of urban economies than to that of political hierarchies. Since we yet know little of the earliest stages of the Indus civilization, before 3000 B.C., it seems likely that future research will document completely unexpected aspects of the first steps toward urban life.

EAST ASIA

Ongoing research in China is showing that the formation of the earliest East Asian civilization involved a number of interacting regions, not just the relatively well-known North China plain along the Yellow River. However, work in southern and western China has not yet reached the point at which the larger trans-regional system can be defined, as has been possible in Southwest Asia, South Asia, Mesoamerica, and the Andes. Working in tributaries of the Yellow River, the first Chinese archaeologists were fortunate to uncover extensive areas of a state capital of the Shang, the first major Chinese dynasty. From here they recovered not only evidence of palaces and more modest homes but also a substantial cemetery with tombs ranging from those of kings to those of slaves. They also recovered a range of readable texts written on bone.

Though these are specialized divinatory texts, they contain much information on elite life, politics, and even the weather. Subsequent work has provided evidence of other towns, of areas of craft production, and of earlier centers from the formative stages of North Chinese complex polities, dating as early as 1800 B.C. Because excavations have focused on elite centers and tombs, we know a great deal about the organization of political elites and the material symbols with which they defined their high status. At present, only the Nile Valley has a record of elite art and organization approaching that available for the North China plain.

However, as in the Indus region, even the well-known North China plain lacks published regional archaeological surveys. Much information that could be assembled into a regional overview exists in local files and publications, but neither the task of integrating these data nor the intensive field surveys that will be needed to define networks of smaller settlements has been pursued. This work would be best done soon, since mechanized agriculture has revealed many sites but will soon disperse their surface remains. In the areas of southern China dominated by rice paddies, regional surface surveys will be difficult, but the success of surveys in areas such as the Nara basin, the heartland of state formation in Japan, shows that the recovery of settlement patterns is possible even in such environments.

In the near future, regional surveys, combined with the detailed study of plant and animal use in the area today, will provide an understanding of the systems of agricultural production in early Chinese civilization that we currently lack. Such research will be enhanced by the study of existing traditional Chinese agricultural production systems, many of which have long documentary histories as well. During the coming century, systematic archaeological surveys will doubtless lead to the excavation of sites other than the larger centers. It seems likely that the excavation of waterlogged sites, created by post-glacial sea level rise and by the accumulation of flood sediments in river valleys, will produce ancient economic records written on material such as bamboo (such as have been found in Japan) complementing the known texts which focus on the elite. If so, by the year 2050, Chinese archaeologists will control one of the most comprehensive bodies of data suited for the rigorous evaluation of theories relating to both early economic and early political development.

ANDEAN AMERICA

Early Andeans developed their civilization in what may have been the most diverse environments faced by any early complex society. In spite of these difficult circumstances, the historical information collected after the Spanish conquest destroyed the empire of Tiwantisuyu, the realm of the Inka (the latest phase of native Andean civilization), indicates an extraordinarily successful cultural achievement. There are difficulties facing those who study Andean civilizations, including the virtual erasure of this ancient culture by the Spanish, and the fact that among all the early civilizations, it was only here that writing did not develop. In spite of these problems, a relatively small number of archaeologists have made impressive progress in understanding the systems of terraces and canals, without which Precolumbian agriculture would have produced little, and the networks of interregional exchange that distributed materials throughout the Andes. The layouts of elite centers and cemeteries, and the meaning and use of political and religious symbols in prestate and state systems from as early as 1200 B.C., are increasingly known.

Given the extraordinary progress, and given the fact that Peru was the birthplace of modern regional survey archaeology (just after World War II) it is surprising that only two intensive archaeological surveys in the region have been completed and published. Indeed, it is tragic, because most of the coastal valleys have been leveled by modern agroindustry since 1960, and we have thus lost opportunities to study settlement patterns composed of sites so dessicated that the corncobs, cloth scraps, and even the bodies of the ancient inhabitants were often preserved. Fortunately, much survey work is currently under way, and we can hope for comprehensive publication of regional data in the near future. Perhaps as a result of this lack of work on settlement patterns, there has been only a limited study of community organization. The study of architectural features such as buildings, particularly on the coast, is only beginning, and the excavation of settlements in such a way that one can study the distribution of artifacts in rooms and dumps—and thus the changing organization of human activity—is rare.

There is no question that once such surveys and settlement studies are more advanced, the Andes will become the major testing ground for investigating the relationship between religious ideology and politics, because there is a wealth of retrievable evidence on state-subsidized agriculture works, elite architecture, military architecture, and political and religious art that cannot be matched elsewhere. In spite of centuries of treasure hunting, Peru still has royal cemeteries, which, if excavated with the best of available techniques, will provide a wealth of detail on dynastic politics and ritual in chiefdoms and states. The problem has been and will continue to be that of balancing the costs of conserving and studying this matchless record of an early civilization against the pressing needs of the modern Andean societies. Andean America's small cadre of professional archaeologists is one with a special need for support from colleagues, private foundations, and public agencies in the wealthier nations.

MESOAMERICA

Before the Spanish conquest of Mesoamerica, a single trans-regional sphere of communication united the immense region stretching from the American Southwest almost to the Isthmus of Panama. If the heartland of this nexus was in the central and southern highlands of Mexico, other regions such as the Yucatan Peninsula or parts of Guatemala were no less developed. The ruggedness of Mesoamerica has limited the amount of territory intensively surveyed, but there is no question that some of the completed surveys are among the most thorough ever done. In addition, Mesoamerica has also seen many studies of plant use, without which the results of archaeological surveys cannot be related to agricultural production systems. Finally, Mesoamericanists have, in spite of the erasure of ancient traditions during the Conquest, developed an enviable comprehension of sites as communities, not only of the architecture of elite centers, but also of the architecture of humble villages.

The most exciting current developments are related to our growing comprehension of Mesoamerican writing systems. Many inscriptions can now be shown to have political significance. They are relatively common, at least in certain parts of southern Mesoamerica, and were used in relatively early stages in the development of Mesoamerican civilization, long before the development of urban economies and even before the development of states (before 100 B.C.). Indeed, it seems that Mesoamerican writing may have had a ritual or political origin, rather than the economic origin inferred for the Mesopotamian and other writing systems. If so, this implies an interesting challenge for those attempting to construct general explanations of the development of writing. In any event, the written texts, particularly in the Maya area, provide detailed evidence of the rise and fall of dynasties, knowledge useful in evaluating ideas about the operation of systems of interrelated states.

By the middle of the next century, however, many of the issues of economic and political development may well be resolved, and scholars may be using the Mesoamerican record for very different purposes. In many ways Mesoamerica is the most different of the world's early civilizations. It arose in a land where communication was exceptionally difficult and natural disaster was frequent; its occupants had a wealth of domestic plants but few domestic animals. This meant that not only economics but also the metaphors of daily life, or of religion and politics, were different from those of other civilizations: there could neither be a "bull of heaven" nor a "lamb of god" in ancient Mexico. For all these reasons, Mesoamerica is a critical case for developing and evaluating general ideas about world view as a context for the developing cultural complexity and for the importance of what we term "religion" in the rise of the first hierarchical politics.

The study of the evolution of the early civilizations—of urban economies, of states, and of religions—is a problem that is being successfully approached within the holistic and long-term perspective of archaeology. Even now, however, it is clear that the long-standing focus on a few early civilizations is too narrow. We must diversify the roster of early civilizations. Western Africa contains a yet poorly known nexus of complex societies whose development begins in the first millennium B.C., long before any contact with the Mediterranean world. By the mid-twenty-first century, I have no doubt that Africanists will have a knowledge of such heartlands as the Inner Delta of the Niger rivaling that of Mesopotamia or the

North China plain. Similarly, it is likely that Southeast Asian complex societies developed before direct relations were established with either India or China. There is also much to be gained by contrasting these relatively independent developments with civilizations that developed in varying degrees of interaction with the established early civilizations. Did the Mediterranean, Western Europe, Central Africa, or Japan develop differently from earlier civilizations because of such interaction? The question must be asked.

To answer all the questions we wish to pose will require a range of new methods and the mass application of methods already available. We must be able to trace the sources of clays, stones, and ores if we wish to study the economic systems of these societies. We must routinely date sites and structures to the decade or even the year if we wish to answer questions about political processes. Current techniques for identifying plant tissues or studying the chemistry of human bone are only a beginning. These approaches require not only money but organization. It is a sad fact that the economic circumstances of the 1980s have led to a diminution of our organizational capacities. For example, some of the best of the young ethnobotanists and ethnozoologists trained in the optimistic 1960s and 1970s have left research because there is no stability of employment for them. We and our twenty-first-century successors must develop new organizational mechanisms, perhaps endowed institutes independent of traditional universities and museums, if there is to be more than patchwork progress in understanding the rise of civilization.

Developing useful explanations for long-completed cultural transformations can help us to resolve the global problems of tomorrow. Well-tested models representing long-term relationships between such phenomena as population growth, agricultural intensification, and social conflict will be useful in planning development for the future. However, all our rigorous theoretical explanations and sophisticated computer models will be nothing more than air castles if we lack either an archaeological record on which to test them or the means to undertake such tests. For this reason, a paramount concern must be the conservation of a representative sample of the planet's archaeological resources for future study, and the creation of a worldwide network of support for archaeological researchers. It is only fitting that the industrial nations, whose wealth depends on the accomplishments of the early civilizations, should help the descendants of those early peoples—many of whom live in poverty in environments damaged by civilization's birth-traumas—to safeguard and study what is properly the heritage (and responsibility) of everyone on the planet.

Empires in the Dust

Some 4,000 years ago, a number of mighty Bronze Age cultures crumbled. Were they done in by political strife and societal unrest? Or by a change in the climate?

Mesopotamia: cradle of civilization, the fertile breadbasket of western Asia, a little slice of paradise between the Tigris and Euphrates rivers. Today the swath of land north of the Persian Gulf is still prime real estate. But several millennia ago Mesopotamia was absolutely The Place to Be. There the visionary king Hammurabi ruled, and Babylon's hanging gardens hung. There the written word, metalworking, and bureaucracy were born. From the stately, rational organization of Mesopotamia's urban centers, humanity began its inexorable march toward strip malls and shrink-wrap and video poker bars and standing in line at the DMV. What's more, the emergence of the city-state meant that we no longer had to bow to the whims of nature. We rose above our abject dependence on weather, tide, and tilth; we were safe in the arms of empire. Isn't that what being civilized is all about?

Not if you ask Harvey Weiss. Weiss, professor of Near Eastern archeology at Yale, has challenged one of the cherished notions of his profession: that early civilizations—with their monuments and their grain reserves, their texts and their taxes—were somehow immune to natural disaster. He says he's found evidence of such disaster on a scale so grand it spelled calamity for half a dozen Bronze Age cultures from the Mediterranean to the Indus Valley—including the vaunted vale of Mesopotamia. Historians have long favored political and social explanations for these collapses: disruptions in trade routes, incompetent administrators, barbarian invasions. "Prehistoric societies, simple agriculturists—they can be blown out by natural forces," says Weiss. But the early civilizations of the Old World? "It's not supposed to happen."

Yet happen it did, says Weiss, and unlike his predecessors, he's got some data to back him up. The evidence comes from a merger of his own archeological expertise with the field of paleoclimatology, the

study of climates past. His first case study concerns a series of events that occurred more than 4,000 years ago in a region of northern Mesopotamia called the Habur Plains. There, in the northeast corner of what is present-day Syria, a network of urban centers arose in the middle of the third millennium B.C. Sustained by highly productive organized agriculture, the cities thrived. Then, around 2200 B.C., the region's new urbanites abruptly left their homes and fled south, abandoning the cities for centuries to come.

Weiss believes that the inhabitants fled an onslaught of wind and dust kicked up by a drought that lasted 300 years. He also believes the drought crippled the empire downriver, which had come to count on the agricultural proceeds of the northern plains. Moreover, he contends, the long dry spell wasn't just a local event; it was caused by a rapid, region-wide climate change whose effects were felt by budding civilizations as far west as the Aegean Sea and the Nile and as far east as the Indus Valley. While the Mesopotamians were struggling with their own drought-induced problems, he points out, neighboring societies were collapsing as well: the Old Kingdom in Egypt, early Bronze Age cities in Palestine, and the early Minoan civilization of Crete. And in the Indus Valley, refugees fleeing drought may have overwhelmed the cities of Mohenjo-Daro and Harappa. The troubles of half a dozen Bronze Age societies, says Weiss, can be blamed on a single event—and a natural disaster at that.

Weiss first presented this scenario in 1993, when soil analyses showed that a period of severe dust storms accompanied the mysterious Habur hiatus. "I was thinking you can't have a microregion drought," he recalls, "because that isn't how climate works. It's got to be much bigger. And I said, 'Wait a minute, didn't I read about this in graduate school? Weren't there those who, 30 years ago, had said that drought conditions were probably the agency that accounts for all these collapses that happened in contiguous regions?'" says Weiss. "Back in the late sixties, we had read this stuff and laughed our heads off about it."

In 1966, British archeologist James Mellaart had indeed blamed drought for the downfalls of a whole spectrum of third-millennium civilizations, from the early Bronze Age communities in Palestine to the pyramid builders of Egypt's Old Kingdom. But when Mellaart first put forth this idea, he didn't have much in the way of data to back him up. Weiss, however, can point to new paleoclimate studies for his proof. These studies suggest that an abrupt, widespread change in the climate of western Asia did in fact occur at 2200 B.C. Samples of old ocean sediments from the Gulf of Oman, for example, show signs of extreme drought just when Weiss's alleged exodus took place. A new model of air-mass movement explains how subtle shifts in atmospheric circulation could have scorched Mesopotamia as well as points east, west, and south. And recent analyses of ice cores from Greenland—which offer the most detailed record of global climate change—reveal unusual climatic conditions at 2200 B.C. that could well have brought drought to the region in question.

"I've got some figures I can show you. Figures always help," says paleoclimatologist Peter de-Menocal, swiveling his chair from reporter to computer in his office at Columbia University's Lamont-Doherty Earth Observatory, just north of New York City. On the monitor, deMenocal pulls up a graph derived from the research project known as GISP2 (for Greenland Ice Sheet Project 2). GISP2 scientists, he explains, use chemical signals in ice cores to reconstruct past climates. There are two kinds of naturally occurring oxygen atoms, heavy and light, and they accumulate in ice sheets in predictable ratios that vary with prevailing temperatures. In a cool climate, for example, heavy oxygen isotopes are less easily evaporated out of the ocean and transported as snow or rain to northern landmasses like Greenland. In a warm climate, however, more heavy oxygen isotopes will be evaporated, and more deposited in the Greenland ice sheets.

By tracking oxygen-isotopes ratios within the ice cores, the GISP2 graph reflects temperatures over Greenland for the past 15,000 years. Near the bottom of the graph, a black line squiggles wildly until 11,700 years ago, when the last ice age ended and the current warm era, the Holocene, began. The line then climbs steadily for a few thousand years, wavering only modestly, until 7,000 years before the present. From then until now, global temperatures appear relatively stable—"then until now" comprising, of course, the entire span of human civilization.

"The archeological community—and actually segments of the paleoclimate community—have viewed the Holocene as being climatically stable," says de Menocal. "And so they imagine that the whole drama of civilization's emergence took place on a level playing field in terms of the environment."

Until he met Harvey Weiss, deMenocal wasn't much interested in studying the Holocene; like most of his peers, he was more drawn to the dynamic climate fluctuations that preceded it. In fact, the Holocene had something of a bad rep among climatologists. "It was thought of as kind of a boring time to study," says deMenocal. "Like, why would you possibly want to? All the action is happening 20,000 years earlier."

Then a few years ago he read an account of Weiss's drought theory and had an epiphany of sorts. It occurred to him that even the smallest variations in climate could be interesting if they had influenced the course of history. What if something was going on in the Holocene after all? He looked up the 1993 paper in which Weiss had laid out the evidence for the Habur hiatus and reported the results of the soil analysis.

"I was pretty skeptical," says deMenocal. "I mean, what would you expect if everyone left a town? It would get dusty. Especially in the world's dustiest place. Big surprise."

Weiss, meanwhile, was getting a similar response from many of his peers. But when he and deMenocal met at a conference in 1994, they hit it off right away—largely because Weiss, too, was dismayed at the paucity of his own evidence. "Peter was immediately sensitive to my moaning about how we needed additional data, different kinds of data," says Weiss. "And he immediately understood where such data could be obtained."

DeMenocal told Weiss that if a large-scale drought had in fact occurred, it would have left a mark in the sediments of nearby ocean floors—the floor of the Gulf of Oman, for example. Lying approximately 700 miles southeast of ancient Mesopotamia, the gulf would have caught any windblown dust that swept down from the Tigris and Euphrates valleys. (The Persian Gulf is closer, but because it's so shallow, its sediments get churned up, thereby confusing their chronology.) And deMenocal just happened to know some German scientists who had a sediment core from the Gulf of Oman.

Analysis of the gulf core is ongoing, but deMenocal has already extracted enough information to confirm Weiss's suspicions. To track dry spells in the sediments, he and his colleague Heidi Cullen looked for dolomite, a mineral found in the mountains of Iraq and Turkey and on the Mesopotamian floodplains that could have been transported to the gulf only by wind. Most of the Holocene section of the core consists of calcium carbonate sediments typical of ocean bottoms.

"And then all of a sudden, at exactly 4,200 calendar years, there's this big spike of dolomite," says deMenocal—a fivefold increase that slowly decays over about three centuries. The chemistry of the dolomite dust matches that of the dolomite in the Mesopotamian mountains and plains, verifying the mineral's source. And not only did deMenocal and his colleagues figure out what happened, they may have figured out how. Studies by Gerard Bond at Lamont-Doherty have shown that the timing of the drought coincided with a cooling period in the North Atlantic. According to a survey by Cullen of current meteorological records, such cooling would have dried out the Middle East and western Asia by creating a pressure gradient that drew moisture to the north and away from the Mediterranean.

"The whole disruption, collapse bit, well, I just have to take Harvey at his word," says deMenocal. "What I tried to do is bring some good hard climate data to the problem." Why hasn't anybody seen this signature of calamity before? Simple, says deMenocal. "No one looked for it."

Weiss's first hints of climate-associated calamity came from a survey of his principal excavation site, a buried city in northeastern Syria called Tell Leilan. Tell Leilan (rhymes with "Ceylon") was one of three major cities on the Habur Plains to be taken over by the Akkadian Empire around 2300 B.C. The city covered more than 200 acres topped by a haughty acropolis, and was sustained by a tightly regulated system of rain-fed agriculture that was co-opted and intensified by the imperialists from the south. Weiss had asked Marie-Agnès Courty of the National Center for Scientific Research in France to examine the ancient soils of Tell Leilan to help him understand the agricultural development of the region. She reported that a section dating from 2200 to 1900 B.C. showed evidence of severe drought, including an eight-inch-thick layer of windblown sand and a marked absence of earthworm tunnels.

In his own excavations of the same period, Weiss had already found evidence of desertion: mud-brick walls that had fallen over clay floors and were covered with, essentially, 300 years' worth of compacted dust. And once he made the drought connection at Tell Leilan, he began turning up clues to the catastrophe everywhere he looked. In 1994, for example, Gerry Lemcke, a researcher at the Swiss Technical University in Zurich, presented new analyses of sediment cores taken from the bottom of Lake Van in

Turkey, which lies at the headwaters of the Tigris and the Euphrates. The new results indicated that the volume of water in the lake—which corresponds to the amount of rainfall throughout western Asia—declined abruptly 4,200 fears ago. At the same time, the amount of windblown dust in the lake increased fivefold.

Weiss came to believe that the effects of the drought reached downriver to the heart of Mesopotamia, causing the collapse of the Akkadian Empire. The collapse itself is undisputed: written records describe how, soon after it had consolidated power, Akkad crumbled, giving way to the Ur III dynasty in—when else?—2200 B.C. The cause of this collapse has been the subject of considerable speculation. But Weiss's studies of early civilizations have convinced him that their economies—complex and progressive though they may have been—were still fundamentally dependent on agricultural production. In fact, he notes, one hallmark of any civilization is that it requires a life-support system of farming communities toiling away in the fields and turning over the fruits of their labor to a central authority. The drought on the Habur Plains could have weakened the Akkadian Empire by drastically reducing agricultural revenues from that region. People fleeing the drought moved south, where irrigation-fed agriculture was still sustainable. For want of a raindrop, the kingdom was lost.

"Well, believe it or not, all my colleagues had not figured that out," says Weiss. "They actually believed that somehow this empire was based on bureaucracy, or holding on to trade routes, or getting access to exotic mineral resources in Turkey." But the drought itself is documented, Weiss says, in passages of cuneiform texts. Images from a lengthy composition called the Curse of Akkad, for example, include "large fields" that "produced no grain" and "heavy clouds" that "did not rain." Scholars had decided that these expressions were mere metaphor.

And many still stand by their interpretations. "I don't agree with his literal reading of the Mesopotamian texts, and I think he has exaggerated the extent of abandonment in this time period," says Richard Zettler, curator of the Near East section at the University of Pennsylvania's Museum of Archaeology and Anthropology in Philadelphia. Zettler doesn't question the evidence for drought, but he thinks Weiss has overplayed its implications. Although Tell Leilan may well have been deserted during the putative hiatus, for example, nearby cities on the Habur Plains show signs of continuing occupation, he says. As for the Curse and other Mesopotamian passages describing that period, says Zettler, "there are a lot of questions on how to read these texts—how much of it is just literary license, whatever. Even if there is a core of historical truth, it's hard to determine what the core of truth is."

Instead of backing down in the face of such commentary, Weiss has continued to document his thesis. Echoing Mellaart, he points out that 2200 B.C. saw the nearly simultaneous collapses of half a dozen other city-based civilizations—in Egypt, in Palestine, on Crete and the Greek mainland, and in the Indus Valley. The collapses were caused by the same drought, says Weiss, for the same reasons. But because historians and archeologists look for internal rather than external forces to explain civilizations in crisis, they don't communicate among themselves, he says, and many aren't even aware of what's going on next door, as it were.

"Very few people understand that there was a synchronous collapse and probably drought conditions in both Egypt and Mesopotamia," let alone the rest of the Old World, says Weiss.

It didn't help Weiss's extravagant claims for third-millennium cataclysm that his alleged drought didn't appear in the GISP2 oxygen-isotope record. The graph in deMenocal's office, for example, has no spikes or dips or swerves at 2200 B.C.; just a nice flat plateau. That graph was drawn from an interpretation of the ice-core data. But according to Paul Mayewski of the University of New Hampshire in Durham, who is chief scientist of GISP2, there are plenty of reasons a drought in western Asia might not make it into the oxygen-isotope record in the Greenland glacier. Greenland might be too far away to "feel" the regional event, or the drought may have left a different kind of chemical signature. Only a climatologist like Mayewski could explain these reasons, however. And no one asked him to.

"As a consequence, a lot of people called Harvey Weiss and said, 'Well, the GISP2 record is the most highly resolved record of Holocene climate in the world. And if it's not in there, you're wrong, Harvey,'" says Mayewski. "I didn't realize that poor Harvey was being abused for not existing in our record."

Fortunately Mayewski, like deMenocal, is a curious sort with interests a bit broader than his own specialty. When he happened upon Weiss's 1993 paper, he'd already lent a hand on a few archeological projects, including one on the disappearance of Norse colonies from Greenland in the mid-1300s. But he figured other scientists had already looked for the Mesopotamian drought in the climate record. When he finally met Weiss in 1996, he learned otherwise. Mayewski began reanalyzing his core data

with Weiss's theory in mind, and he uncovered a whole new Holocene.

"We can definitely show from our records that the 2200 B.C. event is unique," says Mayewski. "And what's much more exciting than that, we can show that most of the major turning points in civilization in western Asia also correlate with what we would say would be dry events. We think that we have found a proxy for aridity in western Asia."

Earlier interpretations of the GISP2 data had measured a variety of ions in ice cores that would reveal general information about climate variability. To look for the 2200 B.C. drought in particular, Mayewski used tests based on 2.5-year intervals in the climate record instead of 50- to 100-year intervals. He also collected a broader set of data that allowed him to reconstruct specific patterns of atmospheric circulation—not only over land but over land *and* oceans. When Mayewski focused on the movement of air masses over oceans, he found that air transport from south to north in the Atlantic—so-called meridional circulation—hit a significant winter low some 4,200 years ago. Mayewski and deMenocal are studying how this event relates to drought in western Asia.

"But it seems on the basis of the paleoclimatic data that there is no doubt about the event at 2200 B.C.," says Weiss. "What the qualities of this event were, and what the magnitude of this event was, that is the current research frontier now."

Trouble is, even though the drought may seem like a sure thing, its effects on Mesopotamia are still unproved, as Zettler points out. They will remain controversial, Weiss admits, until archeologists better understand the contributions of politics, agriculture, and climate in the formation of ancient societies. That mission grows more urgent as more archeologists seem ready to grapple with models of "climatic determinism." In the past few years, drought and flooding have been cited in the demise of several New World civilizations, including the Maya of Central America, the Anasazi of the American Southwest, and the Moche and Tiwanaku of Peru and Bolivia.

"Until climatic conditions are quantified, it's going to be very difficult to understand what the effects of climate changes—particularly controversial, abrupt ones—were upon these societies," says Weiss. The precise constellation of forces that led to the collapse of Bronze Age cultures around 2200 B.C. will probably be debated for a very long time. But paleoclimatology has assured Mother Nature a place in that constellation. And the notion that civilizations are immune to natural disaster may soon be ancient history.

PART IV

LANGUAGE AND COMMUNICATION

All animal species have methods of communication, by which I mean the transfer of information from one organism to another. Information is defined as a stimulus that changes or affects the behavior of an organism.

Of all animal species, humankind has developed the most rich, subtle, and versatile of communication systems: *language*. But what is language? Many anthropologists think of language in terms of the thirteen design features proposed by Charles Hockett. In Hockett's terms, language is characterized as follows:

1. *Vocal-auditory channel.* Language is produced through the nose and mouth and received through the ears.

2. *Broadcast transmission and directional fading.* A speaker can be heard in all directions; a listener can hear a speaker no matter what direction the signal is coming from.

3. *Rapid fading.* As soon as they are spoken, words dissipate and subsequently cannot be retrieved.

4. *Interchangeability.* All speakers of a language can both utter and understand the same words.

5. *Total feedback.* A speaker hears everything she or he says, can monitor it, and can correct or account for mistakes.

6. *Specialization.* Speech serves no other purpose than to communicate; as a specialized system, it can be used even when speaker and listener are engaged in other activities.

7. *Semanticity.* There are systematic connections between spoken words and standard, accepted meanings.

8. *Arbitrariness.* These connections between words and their meanings are a matter of convention; hence it is possible both to create new words with new meanings and to change the meanings of old words.

9. *Discreteness.* Human beings can produce an enormous range of sounds, but each language makes use of only a very small subset of these sounds, far from exhausting the human capacity.

10. *Displacement.* Humans can use language to communicate about things and events that are far removed from the immediate context in which they are interacting. These distant events may be separated by time, distance, or both—and may even include things that have never existed and never will (for example, mermaids).

11. *Productivity.* People regularly utter sentences that have never been said before in exactly the same manner, and they can talk about things (such as inventions or discoveries) that have never been observed.

12. *Traditional transmission.* It appears that human beings are genetically programmed to be predisposed to learn a language (or even more than one). However, the specific language that an individual eventually speaks is acquired solely through learning in a social context—it is not inherited genetically.

13. *Duality of patterning.* Language is patterned on at least two separate levels: *phonemes*, the sounds a language recognizes as significant but which by themselves have no meanings; and *morphemes*, the indivisible units of meaning of a language. The word *dog*, for instance, consists of three phonemes ([d], [o], [g]) and one morpheme ([dog]).

One of the earliest recorded instances of interest in language and its significance for human beings appears in the Bible in Genesis. First, Adam names all the creatures of the world—and through this they are placed at his disposal. Later, when through united effort in the land of Shinar, humans attempt to build a tower reaching to the very heavens, God scatters them across the face of the earth and causes them to speak different tongues, thereby forever frustrating attempts at pan-human unity.

Two such themes still preoccupy modern linguists: (1) the ways in which words and the categories they represent affect their speakers' experience of, and approach to, the world around them; and (2) the evolutionary tree of language, or the taxonomic relationships among languages, and the ways and rates of linguistic change.

The first recorded rigorous study of a language was accomplished in the fourth century B.C. by the Indian scholar Panini. He analyzed the structure of ancient (Vedic) Sanskrit and condensed its grammatical rules to algebralike formulas as elegant as any modern grammatical analysis. In doing so, he preserved a language that would otherwise have become extinct, and he set a standard of excellence that still inspires linguistic analysis.

Two thousand years later, another student of Sanskrit, Sir William Jones (1746–1794), systematized means to compare and contrast languages and thereby trace the relationships among them. He is considered by some, therefore, to be the modern father of comparative linguistics.

Contemporary linguistics is divided into several specialized branches and even more schools of thought. *Structural linguists* analyze individual languages, detailing their phonology (sound system), morphology (meaning representation), and syntax (the organization of language units into sequences). *Comparative* (or *historical*) *linguists* compare extant languages, trace their evolution from earlier (proto-) language forms, and attempt to reconstruct the proto-languages from which modern languages evolved. *Sociolinguists* study differences in language uses (or dialectical differences) reflecting socioeconomic groupnings. And *psycholinguists* are interested in the mental apparatuses of speech perception, cognitive processes, and so on.

But human communication is not limited to language. Nonverbally, human beings communicate important messages about many things—including their feelings about (1) themselves, (2) the person they are addressing, and (3) what they are discussing. *Kinesics* is the study of communication through gesturing, and *proxemics* is the study of the meanings of spatial patterns of people and things.

We introduce some of these and also other concerns in Topic 7, Language, Thought, and Communicaiton.

LANGUAGE, THOUGHT, AND COMMUNICATION

There is a story, often told in introductory anthropology courses, that the Greek philosopher Plato one day posed to his students the question, "What sets human beings apart from all other creatures?"

One student came up with what seemed to be an irrefutable reply. "Humans," he said, "are featherless bipeds."

While the student was being congratulated by his peers, Plato is said to have slipped away for a while. Upon returning he announced, "Here is our scholar's human being!"—and threw into the crowd of students a freshly plucked chicken.

The question of what exactly separates human beings as a species from all others has continued to vex philosophers and scientists. Until recently, however, there was at least one thing that most people could agree on: only human beings have language. But was that really saying something meaningful? Does the ability to speak represent fundamental properties of our species, or is it just the epiphenomena of having the curved tongue, short jaw, and minutely controllable lips that facilitate speech? In other words, is the use of language by humans rooted in unique mental properties, or is it something much more superficial?

One of the most perplexing questions in anthropology concerns when our ancestors first began to speak. Did the Neanderthals—whose brains were larger than our own—have the ability to speak? While it's probable that earlier hominids had no or limited language abilities, the jury is still out on the Neanderthals. Some anthropologists believe the structure of their throat allowed only limited verbal communication, though I lean toward the view that argues they probably had language abilities as complex as our own. Unanswered, too, is the question of why our ancestors took the cognitive leap that led to language. In Article 26, "The Gift of Gab," Matt Cartmill explores these fascinating questions.

Some startling studies conducted in the last three decades are suggesting that the ability to use language may not be uniquely human. Various scholars, using plastic chips, hand-sign language (the language used by deaf people), computers, and other means to communicate with ape research subjects seemed to be concluding that, using nonlinguistic communication, apes are capable of the mental operations that underlie language use by humans. First, apes could learn an astonishingly large number of "words." Koko, a female gorilla, has learned well over a thousand. Second, and more important, they could apply rules of grammar to the use of these "words." Finally, there even appeared to be evidence that they could combine two "words" to mean something entirely new, as when the chimpanzee Washoe signed water bird when, for the first time, her trainer showed her a swan. Thus, it appeared that although only humans speak, other animals have the mental facilities for language use in media that they are equipped to manipulate. Language no longer was the defining characteristic of our species.

This view of apes, humans, and language captured the popular imagination. And, for a while, it went relatively unchallenged. The data, after all, were compelling. In the 1980s, however, a general reassessment of these studies cast some doubt on the original findings and dampened some of the enthusiasm with which they were received. This trend was spearheaded by psychologist Herbert Terrace, whose research originally was intended to support the view that apes had language capabilities. However, after reviewing his data, Terrace concluded that serious methodological problems made their interpretation problematic. And when he reviewed the methodologies of other studies, he found similar flaws.

True, some apes did learn large numbers of "words," but it was questionable whether they were using rules of grammar to combine them. For one thing, they may simply have learned sequences of signs just as you learn a telephone number—with no sense that the order *means* anything. Terrace noted that many researchers failed to record sign productions that were out of sequence; some even "corrected" sequences that were "wrong." Further, when camera film showed the humans with whom the apes were communicating, Terrace observed that often the teachers were cueing their ape students unconsciously or leading them through sequences one sign at a time. Thus, the "grammar" of the string of signs produced by the ape was, in fact, created by the human beings interacting with the apes.

Finally, Terrace pointed out that without a full description of the context, it is impossible to assess such episodes as Washoe signing *water bird* when first being shown a swan. For instance, did Washoe first sign *water* and then, when her trainer asked her to sign again, sign *bird*? In other words, did Washoe ever make a mental connection between two "words?" The evidence, at the time, did not allow us to judge.

However, in Article 27, "Koko: 'Fine Animal Gorilla,'" Michael Frisbie by implication asks us to consider whether Terrace's reservations are all that important. Let's accept the notion that some human teachers of apes prompt them and even "read between the lines" in attempting to find meaning in their gestures—that's exactly what human parents do when teaching their own children to talk! Francine Patterson's research methodology with Koko may be flawed from the perspective of scientific rigor, but there are some things that scientific research methods simply cannot capture. The loving relationship within which it is possible for a human being to teach communication to an ape may be one of these things.

Since Terrace first levied his critique, new and much more methodologically rigorous research on teaching language to apes has been conducted, most notably by Sue Savage-Rumbaugh and her colleagues. Savage-Rumbaugh, one of the pioneers in ape language research, has spent almost a quarter century studying and attempting to cultivate the linguistic and cognitive skills of a number of apes. Recently, her work with a bonobo (pygmy chimpanzee) named Kanzi has been acknowledged, even by critics, as having achieved a scientific breakthrough. Kanzi was shown to have acquired linguistic and cognitive skills far beyond those achieved by any nonhuman primate in previous research. In her brilliant book, *Apes, Language and the Human Mind* (1998), Savage-Rumbaugh details how Kanzi has proven himself capable of comprehending spoken English sentences of a complexity surpassing that

mastered by a normal two-and-a-half year-old human child.

It gets even more interesting than that. In the 1990s, it was shown that gray parrots, too, could understand human language and the rules of grammar. Not only that, but they can speak quite clearly. Further experiments showed that they understand conceptual categories such as shape, number, color, and texture.

So where do we stand on the question of nonhuman animals using language? Current research seems to indicate that several species of animals—apes, gray parrots, and possibly dolphins and other mammals—almost certainly have significant linguistic abilities. Still, humans remain the only creatures that use spoken language naturally. Speech, with its infinite possibilities of expression, is the birthright of every human being capable of it. How—and when—this linguistic talent first evolved are matters of continuing speculation. Several theories have been proposed over the past three decades but each, in turn, has been found to be flawed.

One of the most fascinating aspects of human language is the incredible diversity of meanings and relationships it allows us to express, both directly and indirectly. Some languages are structured so that the relative social positions of the speaker and listener(s) are reinforced. Some have no way of expressing past, present, and future tenses, which results in a cultural conception of time quite unlike our own. Others have separate sacred and profane vocabularies, each to be used only in the appropriate situations. Still others have distinct vocabularies for men and women.

Japanese is a language in which men and women have very different ways of speaking: men speak louder, more forcefully, and assertively. Women speak softly, gently, tentatively, and in a higher pitch. In "Women's Talk," Article 28, an insightful account of these differences, Ellen Rudolph describes how modern Japanese women are trying to bridge the linguistic divide.

Though English does not have a separate vocabulary for men and women, we still have problems in communicating across the gender gap. In 1990, Deborah Tannen, a professor of sociolinguistics at Georgetown University, published *You Just Don't Understand*—a book about the complexities of communication between men and women. Tannen concludes that dialogue between the sexes is often fraught with difficulty because we use language in essentially different ways. Consider an incident that recently occurred to me.

A female friend, a recent immigrant from the former Soviet Union, called to say how upset she was.

Her car's brakes had failed and she'd had to drive her daughter to nursery school under dangerous conditions. She was very upset. First, I checked to make sure she was physically okay. She was. Then, thinking she might need assistance in having the car towed or repaired, your intrepid (male) editor volunteered information on how to have the car towed, how to get reimbursed by the insurance company, and where to have the car repaired. It turned out, however, that my friend was not, as I'd imagined, interested in obtaining this information at all. What she wanted was to engage in what Tannen refers to as "trouble talk," an intimate sharing of one's personal woes. In situations like this one, men use language to solve problems. In contrast, for many women, providing solutions to problems is beside the point. What *is* the point is that the dialogue can be continued, with its sharing of concern and sympathy.

In "The Power of Talk," Article 29, Tannen extends her observations on the different linguistic styles typically used by U.S. men and women—this time in a corporate setting. These styles, which grow out of differing linguistic "cultures," often have far-reaching consequence in terms of who gets heard and why; who appears self-assured and competent, and who timid and unsure; who achieves authority; who is credited for work done and ideas generated, and so on.

Of course, as important as speech is to us, we do not communicate through words alone. In fact, if we were limited to speech to communicate, life would be pretty boring. Think for a moment about the many other ways in which human beings communicate—including gestures, facial expressions, distances at which they position themselves, and the special language of the eyes. All of these constitute *nonverbal communication*, which humans use to convey an enormous amount of information to each other. For one thing, nonverbal communication is constantly used to comment on what is being said verbally. In U.S. culture, for example, rolling the eyes upward is a way for a speaker to let a listener know that the speaker means exactly the opposite of what she or he has said. When it comes to expressing feelings, quite likely more information is conveyed quickly and simply through nonverbal means, such as a touch or a smile, than through words (except, perhaps, the words of poets).

One of the important ways we communicate nonverbally is through the use of space. We all have a "bubble" around us that expands and contracts as we mingle with people on the street, in class, in the office, on the elevator, or on a date. The use of space varies by culture, and even within a culture. Edward T. Hall and Mary Reed Hall have noted that most white, middle-class Americans use four main distances in their business and social relations: intimate, personal, social, and public.

Intimate distance, which ranges from direct physical contact to about eighteen inches, is used for our most private activities, such as making love. "At this distance," write the Halls, "you are overwhelmed by sensory inputs from the other person—heat from the body, tactile stimulation from the skin, the fragrance of perfume, even the sound of breathing—all of which literally envelop you." In our society, the public use of intimate distance is discouraged. When overcrowded conditions force us into the intimate distance with strangers, generally we feel very uncomfortable.

Personal distance, which ranges from one-and-one-half to four feet, is generally used by spouses in public and by people who are talking to each other. In contrast, *social distance,* which ranges from four to twelve feet, is used in working relationships, business transactions, and casual social situations. Finally, *public distance,* which ranges from twelve to twenty-five feet and beyond, is used by speakers at public gatherings and by many teachers in the classroom.

An important aspect of nonverbal communication is *touch.* In "Close Encounters," Article 30, Stephen Thayer discusses the power of touch to communicate, and he reports on research efforts that attempt to understand the role that touch plays in our lives. I think you may be surprised at some of these findings.

In another look at nonverbal communication, Joann Ellison Rodgers explores our "Flirting Fascination," in the final article in this topic. Using the perspective of evolutionary psychology, she describes flirting as a vital silent language in which critical information is exchanged about each participant's health and reproductive fitness.

The Gift of Gab

Grooves and holes in fossil skulls may reveal when our ancestors began to speak.
The big question, though, is what drove them to it?

People can talk. Other animals can't. They can all communicate in one way or another—to lure mates, at the very least—but their whinnies and wiggles don't do the jobs that language does. The birds and beasts can use their signals to attract, threaten, or alert each other, but they can't ask questions, strike bargains, tell stories, or lay out a plan of action.

Those skills make *Homo sapiens* a uniquely successful, powerful, and dangerous mammal. Other creatures' signals carry only a few limited kinds of information about what's happening at the moment, but language lets us tell each other in limitless detail about what used to be or will be or might be. Language lets us get vast numbers of big, smart fellow primates all working together on a single task—building the Great Wall of China or fighting World War II or flying to the moon. It lets us construct and communicate the gorgeous fantasies of literature and the profound fables of myth. It lets us cheat death by pouring out our knowledge, dreams, and memories into younger people's minds. And it does powerful things for us inside our own minds because we do a lot of our thinking by talking silently to ourselves. Without language, we would be only a sort of upright chimpanzee with funny feet and clever hands. With it, we are the self-possessed masters of the planet.

How did such a marvelous adaptation get started? And if it's so marvelous, why hasn't any other species come up with anything similar? These may be the most important questions we face in studying human evolution. They are also the least understood. But in the past few years, linguists and anthropologists have been making some breakthroughs, and we are now beginning to have a glimmering of some answers.

We can reasonably assume that by at least 30,000 years ago people were talking—at any rate, they were producing carvings, rock paintings, and jewelry, as well as ceremonial graves containing various goods. These tokens of art and religion are high-level forms of symbolic behavior, and they imply that the everyday symbol-handling machinery of human language must have been in place then as well.

Languages surely goes back further than that, but archeologists don't agree on just how far. Some think that earlier, more basic human behaviors—hunting in groups, tending fires, making tools—also demanded language. Others think these activities are possible without speech. Chimpanzees, after all, hunt communally, and with human guidance they can learn to tend fires and chip flint.

Paleontologists have pored over the fossil bones of our ancient relatives in search of evidence for speech abilities. Because the most crucial organ for language is the brain, they have looked for signs in the impressions left by the brain on the inner surfaces of fossil skulls, particularly impressions made by parts of the brain called speech areas because damage to them can impair a person's ability to talk or understand language. Unfortunately, it turns out that you can't tell whether a fossil hominid was able to talk simply by looking at brain impressions on the inside of its skull. For one thing, the fit between the brain and the bony braincase is loose in people and other large mammals, and so the impressions we derive from fossil skulls are disappointingly fuzzy. Moreover, we now know that language functions are not tightly localized but spread across many parts of the brain.

Faced with these obstacles, researchers have timed from the brain to other organs used in speech, such as the throat and tongue. Some have measured the fossil skulls and jaws of early hominids, tried to reconstruct the shape of their vocal tracts, and then applied the laws of acoustics to them to see whether they might have been capable of producing human speech.

All mammals produce their vocal noises by contracting muscles that compress the rib cage. The air in the lungs is driven out through the windpipe to the larynx, where it flows between the vocal cords. More like flaps than cords, these structures vibrate in the breeze, producing a buzzing sound that becomes the voice. The human difference lies in what happens to the air after it gets past the vocal cords.

In people, the larynx lies well below the back of the tongue, and most of the air goes out through the mouth when we talk. We make only a few sounds by exhaling through the nose—for instance, nasal consonants like *m* or *n*, or the so-called nasal vowels in words like the French *bon* and *vin*. But in most mammals, including apes, the larynx sticks farther up behind the tongue, into the back of the nose, and most of the exhaled air passes out through the nostrils. Nonhuman mammals make mostly nasal sounds as a result.

At some point in human evolution the larynx must have descended from its previous heights, and this change had some serious drawbacks. It put the opening of the windpipe squarely in the path of descending food, making it dangerously easy for us to choke to death if a chunk of meat goes down the wrong way—something that rarely happens to a dog or a cat. Why has evolution exposed us to this danger?

Some scientists think that the benefits outweighed the risks, because lowering the larynx improved the quality of our vowels and made speech easier to understand. The differences between vowels are produced mainly by changing the size and shape of the airway between the tongue and the roof of the mouth. When the front of the tongue almost touches the palate, you get the *ee* sound in *beet;* when the tongue is humped up high in the back (and the lips are rounded), you get the *oo* sound in *boot,* and so on. We are actually born with a somewhat apelike throat, including a flat tongue and a larynx lying high up in the neck, and this arrangement makes a child's vowels sound less clearly separated from each other than an adult's.

Philip Lieberman of Brown University thinks that an apelike throat persisted for some time in our hominid ancestors. His studies of fossil jaws and skulls persuade him that a more modern throat didn't evolve until some 500,000 years ago, and that some evolutionary fines in the genus *Homo* never did acquire modern vocal organs. Lieberman concludes that the Neanderthals, who lived in Europe until perhaps 25,000 years ago, belonged to a dead-end lineage that never developed our range of vow-

els, and that their speech—if they had any at all—would have been harder to understand than ours. Apparently, being easily understood wasn't terribly important to them—not important enough, at any rate, to outweigh the risk of inhaling a chunk of steak into a lowered larynx. This suggests that vocal communication wasn't as central to their lives as it is to ours.

Many paleoanthropologists, especially those who like to see Neanderthals as a separate species, accept this story. Others have their doubts. But the study of other parts of the skeleton in fossil hominids supports some of Lieberman's conclusions. During the 1980s a nearly complete skeleton of a young *Homo* male was recovered from 1.5-million-year-old deposits in northern Kenya. Examining the vertebrae attached to the boy's rib cage, the English anatomist Ann MacLarnon discovered that his spinal cord was proportionately thinner in this region than it is in people today. Since that part of the cord controls most of the muscles that drive air in and out of the lungs, MacLarnon concluded that the youth may not have had the kind of precise neural control over breathing movements that is needed for speech.

This year my colleague Richard Kay, his student Michelle Balow, and I were able to offer some insights from yet another part of the hominid body. The tongue's movements are controlled almost solely by a nerve called the hypoglossal. In its course from the brain to the tongue, this nerve passes through a hole in the skull, and Kay, Balow, and I found that this bony canal is relatively big in modern humans—about twice as big in cross section as that of a like-size chimpanzee. Our larger canal presumably reflects a bigger hypoglossal nerve, giving us the precise control over tongue movements that we need for speech.

We also measured this hole in the skulls of a number of fossil hominids. Australopithecines have small canals like those of apes, suggesting that they couldn't talk. But later *Homo* skulls, beginning with a 400,000-year-old skull from Zambia, all have big, humanlike hypoglossal canals. These are also the skulls that were the first to house brains as big as our own. On these counts our work supports Lieberman's ideas. We disagree only on the matter of Neanderthals. While he claims their throats couldn't have produced human speech, we find that their skulls also had human-size canals for the hypoglossal nerve, suggesting that they could indeed talk.

In short, several lines of evidence suggest that neither the australopithecines nor the early, small-brained species of *Homo* could talk. Only around half a million years ago did the first big-brained *Homo* evolve language. The verdict is still out on the language abilities of Neanderthals. I tend to think that they must have had fully human language. After all, they had brains larger than those of most modern humans, made elegant stone tools, and knew how to use fire. But if Lieberman and his friends are right about those vowels, Neanderthals may have sounded something like the Swedish chef on *The Muppet Show*.

We are beginning to get some idea of when human language originated, but the fossils can't tell us how it got started, or what the intermediate stages between animal calls and human language might have been like. When trying to understand the origin of a trait that doesn't fossilize, it's sometimes useful to look for similar but simpler versions of it in other creatures living today. With luck, you can find a series of forms that suggest how simple primitive makeshifts could have evolved into more complex and elegant versions. This is how Darwin attacked the problem of the evolution of the eye. Earlier biologists had pointed to the human eye as an example of a marvelously perfect organ that must have been specially created all at once in its final form by God. But Darwin pointed out that animal eyes exist in all stages of complexity, from simple skin cells that can detect only the difference between light and darkness, to pits lined with such cells, and so on all the way to the eyes of people and other vertebrates. This series, he argued, shows how the human eye could have evolved from simpler precursors by gradual stages.

Can we look to other animals to find simpler precursors of language? It seems unlikely. Scientists have sought experimental evidence of language in dolphins and chimpanzees, thus far without success. But even if we had no experimental studies, common sense would tell us that the other animals can't have languages like ours. If they had, we would be in big trouble because they would organize against us. They don't. Outside of Gary Larson's *Far Side* cartoons and George Orwell's *Animal Farm*, farmers don't have to watch their backs when they visit the cowshed. There are no conspiracies among cows, or even among dolphins and chimpanzees. Unlike human slaves or prisoners, they never plot rebellions against their oppressors.

Even if language as a whole has no parallels in animal communication, might some of its peculiar properties be foreshadowed among the beasts around us? If so, that might tell us something about how and in what order those properties were acquired. One such property is reference. Most of the units of human languages refer to things—to individuals (like *Fido*), or to types of objects (*dog*), actions (*sit*), or properties (*furry*). Animal signals don't have

this kind of referential meaning. Instead, they have what is called instrumental meaning: that is, they act as stimuli that trigger desired responses from others. A frog's mating croak doesn't *refer* to sex. Its purpose is to get some, not to talk about it. People, too, have signals of this purely animal sort—for example, weeping, laughing, and screaming—but these stand outside language. They have powerful meanings for us but not the kind of meaning that words have.

Some animal signals have a focused meaning that looks a bit like reference. For example, vervet monkeys give different warning calls for different predators. When they hear the "leopard" call, vervets climb trees and anxiously look down; when they hear the "eagle" call, they hide in low bushes or look up. But although the vervets' leopard call is in some sense about leopards, it isn't a word for leopard. Like a frog's croak or human weeping, its meaning is strictly instrumental; it's a stimulus that elicits an automatic response. All a vervet can "say" with it is "*Eeek! A leopard!*"—not "I really hate leopards" or "No leopards here, thank goodness" or "A leopard ate Alice yesterday."

In these English sentences, such referential words as *leopard* work their magic through an accompanying framework of nonreferential, grammatical words, which set up an empty web of meaning that the referential symbols fill in. When Lewis Carroll tells us in "Jabberwocky" that "the slithy toves did gyre and gimble in the wabe," we have no idea what he is talking about, but we do know certain things—for instance, that all this happened in the past and that there was more than one tove but only one wabe. We know these things because of the grammatical structure of the sentence, a structure that linguists call syntax. Again, there's nothing much like it in any animal signals.

But if there aren't any intermediate stages between animal calls and human speech, then how could language evolve? What was there for it to evolve from? Until recently, linguists have shrugged off these questions—or else concluded that language didn't evolve at all, but just sprang into existence by accident, through some glorious random mutation. This theory drives Darwinians crazy, but the linguists have been content with it because it fits neatly into some key ideas in modern linguistics.

Forty years ago most linguists thought that people learn to talk through the same sort of behavior reinforcement used in training an animal to do tricks: when children use a word correctly or produce a grammatical sentence, they are rewarded. This picture was swept away in the late 1950s by the revolutionary ideas of Noam Chomsky. Chomsky argued that the structures of syntax lie in unconscious linguistic patterns—so-called deep structures—that are very different from the surface strings of words that come out of our mouths. Two sentences that look different on the surface (for instance, "A leopard ate Alice" and "Alice was eaten by a leopard") can mean the same thing because they derive from a single deep structure. Conversely, two sentences with different deep structures and different meanings can look exactly the same on the surface (for example, "Fleeing leopards can be dangerous"). Any models of language learning based strictly on the observable behaviors of language, Chomsky insisted, can't account for these deep-lying patterns of meaning.

Chomsky concluded that the deepest structures of language are innate, not learned. We are all born with the same fundamental grammar hard-wired into our brains, and we are preprogrammed to pick up the additional rules of the local language, just as baby ducks are hard-wired to follow the first big animal they see when they hatch. Chomsky could see no evidence of other animals' possessing this innate syntax machinery. He concluded that we can't learn anything about the origins of language by studying other animals and they can't learn language from us. If language learning were just a matter of proper training, Chomsky reasoned, we ought to be able to teach English to lab rats, or at least to apes.

As we have seen, apes aren't built to talk. But they can be trained to use sign language or to point to word-symbols on a keyboard. Starting in the 1960s, several experimenters trained chimpanzees and other great apes to use such signs to ask for things and answer questions to get rewards. Linguists, however, were unimpressed. They said that the apes' signs had a purely instrumental meaning: the animals were just doing tricks to get a treat. And there was no trace of syntax in the random-looking jumble of signs the apes produced; an ape that signed "You give me cookie please" one minute might sign "Me cookie please you cookie eat give" the next.

Duane Rumbaugh and Sue Savage-Rumbaugh set to work with chimpanzees at the Yerkes Regional Primate Research Center in Atlanta to try to answer the linguists' criticisms. After many years of mixed results, Sue made a surprising breakthrough with a young bonobo (or pygmy chimp) named Kanzi. Kanzi had watched his mother, Matata, try to learn signs with little success. When Sue gave up on her and started with Kanzi, she was astonished to discover that he already knew the meaning of 12 of the keyboard symbols. Apparently, he had learned them without any training or rewards. In the years that followed, he learned new symbols quickly and used

them referentially, both to answer questions and to "talk" about things that he intended to do or had already done. Still more amazingly, he had a considerable understanding of spoken English—including its syntax. He grasped such grammatical niceties as case structures ("Can you throw a potato to the turtle?") and if-then implication ('You can have some cereal if you give Austin your monster mask to play with"). Upon hearing such sentences, Kanzi behaved appropriately 72 percent of the time—more than a 30-month-old human child given the same tests.

Kanzi is a primatologist's dream and a linguist's nightmare. His language-learning abilities seem inexplicable. He didn't need any rewards to learn language, as the old behaviorists would have predicted; but he also defies the Chomskyan model, which can't explain why a speechless ape would have an innate tendency to learn English. It looks as though some animals can develop linguistic abilities for reasons unrelated to language itself.

Neuroscientist William Calvin of the University of Washington and linguist Derek Bickerton of the University of Hawaii have a suggestion as to what those reasons might be. In their [2000] book, *Lingua ex Machina*, they argue that the ability to create symbols—signs that refer to things—is potentially present in any animal that can learn to interpret natural signs, such as a trail of footprints. Syntax, meanwhile, emerges from the abstract thought required for a social life. In apes and some other mammals with complex and subtle social relationships, individuals make alliances and act altruistically toward others, with the implicit understanding that their favors will be returned. To succeed in such societies, animals need to choose trustworthy allies and to detect and punish cheaters who take but never give anything in return. This demands fitting a shifting constellation of individuals into an abstract mental model of social roles (debtors, creditors, allies, and so on) connected by social expectations ("If you scratch my back, I'll scratch yours"). Calvin and Bickerton believe that such abstract models of social obligation furnished the basic pattern for the deep structures of syntax.

These foreshadowings of symbols and syntax, they propose, laid the groundwork for language in a lot of social animals but didn't create language itself. That had to wait until our ancestors evolved brains big enough to handle the large-scale operations needed to generate and process complex strings of signs. Calvin and Bickerton suggest that brain enlargement in our ancestry was the result of evolutionary pressures that favored intelligence and motor coordination for making tools and throwing weapons. As a side effect of these selection pressures, which had nothing to do with communication, human evolution crossed a threshold at which language became possible. Big-brained, nonhuman animals like Kanzi remain just on the verge of language.

This story reconciles natural selection with the linguists' insistence that you can't evolve language out of an animal communication system. It is also consistent with what we know about language from the fossil record. The earliest hominids with modern-size brains also seem to be the first ones with modern-size hypoglossal canals. Lieberman thinks that these are also the first hominids with modern vocal tracts. It may be no coincidence that all three of these changes seem to show up together around half a million years ago. If Calvin and Bickerton are right, the enlargement of the brain may have abruptly brought language into being at this time, which would have placed new selection pressures on the evolving throat and tongue.

This account may be wrong in some of its details, but the story in its broad outlines solves so many puzzles and ties up so many loose ends that something like it must surely be correct. It also promises to resolve our conflicting views of the boundary between people and animals. To some people, it seems obvious that human beings are utterly different from any beasts. To others, it's just as obvious that many other animals are essentially like us, only with fewer smarts and more fur. Each party finds the other's view of humanity alien and threatening. The story of language origins sketched above suggests that both parties are right: the human difference is real and profound, but it is rooted in aspects of psychology and biology that we share with our close animal relatives. If the growing consensus on the origins of language can join these disparate truths together, it will be a big step forward in the study of human evolution.

Koko: "Fine Animal Gorilla"

Over breakfast, Penny Patterson's 14-year-old adopted daughter describes last night's dream, in which she bit her mother to get at a pair of much-admired shoes. The two laugh over the half-silly, half-scary image, and Penny gives her daughter an impulsive hug before they turn to the day's activities.

It's not an unusual scene, until you know that Penny's adopted "daughter," Koko, is a 230-pound talking gorilla.

Dr. Francine "Penny" Patterson, 38, is a psychologist who has devoted the past 13 years of her personal and professional life to a remarkable project in interspecies communication. Koko and her 12-year-old companion, Michael, another spirited but gentle lowland gorilla who shares Penny's home, "talk"—to Penny, other humans and each other—through American Sign Language (Ameslan), a system used by many deaf people. Koko regularly uses about 600 signs and has a total vocabulary of about a thousand. Michael has a smaller vocabulary, having joined the project as a three-year-old, after Koko had already been learning to talk for four years.

The gorillas' grasp of language is impressively sophisticated. They understand spoken English (Penny had to stop spelling c-a-n-d-y when Koko was just a toddler) and can fib, tell jokes, hurl insults ("you dirty toilet" is a favorite epithet of Koko's), create metaphors and even rhyme: Koko once surprised Penny by improvising a poem to describe a blossoming plant: "Flower pink, fruit stink. Fruit pink stink." And Koko named her pet kitten All Ball, which is what she thought the tailless Manx looked like. You may have seen Koko on television newscasts last year, tenderly cradling her beloved new pet and signing "Love that." Then came the report that the kitten had been hit by a car and killed.

Koko's reaction to All Ball's death dramatized the gorilla's ability to understand and discuss such abstract concepts as death and love. Told that she would never see All Ball again, Koko mourned for months, signing "Sleep cat" and "Cry, frown, sad."

Project Koko began in 1972 at the San Francisco Zoo, where one-year-old Koko had been separated from her mother as a sickly infant. Penny was a 25-year-old Stanford graduate student, newly arrived from her native Midwest trying to discover whether gorillas had a capacity for language. She'd been inspired by hearing scientists Allan and Beatrice Gardner talk about their success in teaching sign language to a chimpanzee named Washoe, a pioneering project still going on under the direction of psychologist Roger Fouts. Recalls Penny, "Although the Gardners delivered their lecture soberly, I felt that I was hearing about something from the realm of myth or fable: Animals were capable of telling us about themselves if one knew the proper way to ask them." Penny hoped to discover whether gorillas, previously considered too unmanageable and unintelligent for such studies, could learn to talk as well as chimpanzees had.

Penny got permission to work with Koko in the zoo's glass-walled nursery. Curious crowds watched her first attempts to mold Koko's fingers into the sign for "drink" before she gave the tiny gorilla a bottle. At the beginning, Koko was happier grabbing at the bottle or simply spinning with her eyes closed, a favorite gorilla game in the wild. But within a month Koko had signed her first word—food. Her vocabulary soon included drink, more, out, dog, come, gimme, up, toothbrush and that. By the second month she was combining words; by the third she had discovered on her own how to turn a statement into a question by using gestures and facial expressions. She clearly loved talking with Penny and her assistants.

Koko began to acquire signs more rapidly and use them creatively. It is the creative use of symbols that, to Penny, marks the communication of both gorillas as genuine language. Koko frequently coins clever phrases such as "finger bracelet" to describe a ring, "bottle match" for cigarette lighter, "eye hat" for a mask, and "elephant baby" to describe a Pinocchio doll. Michael dubbed peas "bean balls" and poetically calls nectarine yogurt "orange flower sauce."

Some members of the scientific community insist that the apes are simply imitating their teachers without understanding the signs they make. But Dr. Jane Goodall, who has devoted her life to studying chimpanzees in the wild, has enough faith in Koko's language abilities to seek her advice on primate preferences. Eager to confirm her belief that chimps are more comfortable when humans sit, rather than stand, Goodall wrote Penny to ask what Koko preferred, seeking an answer "straight from the horse's mouth, as it were." (Koko replied that she likes people to sit down when they're with her.)

Penny's "child" has developed much like her human counterparts. Between the ages of one and six, Koko scored as slow but not retarded on standard IQ tests for human children, a feat even more remarkable considering the tests' cultural bias against gorillas. For example, Koko was shown pictures of a hat, a spoon, a tree and a house, and asked to point to the one that would provide shelter from the rain. Koko picked the tree and was marked wrong, although the answer made perfect sense to a gorilla.

Penny has seen Koko through the usual childhood stages, from the terrible twos to a defiant adolescence at age seven. "From the beginning of Project Koko I had a dual role," Penny says. "I was a scientist attempting to teach a gorilla human sign language, but I was also a mother to a child with all a child's needs and fears. I discovered the joys and stresses of parenthood. And, like a parent, I was endlessly fascinated by her development and charm." Like most children, Koko faithfully imitated her mother, pretending to talk on the phone, grooming her fingernails when Penny did hers. And, like most children, Koko could throw herself enthusiastically into mischief, dismantling her toilet (she was trained when she was two), setting off the stove timer, pretending to hug Penny while chewing up a tape-recorder microphone pinned to her smock. "But," says Penny, "any irritation was dispelled when she'd kiss her dolls with loud smacks, tickle my ears or make me a part of her bedtime nest by arranging my arms around her, gently pushing my head down and lying down to cuddle."

At first, Penny's goals were relatively modest and short-term. She just wanted to see if a gorilla could learn sign language. She had underestimated both Koko's abilities and the emotional bond that would develop.

"When I started," she recalls, "I thought we'd end it after four years. I hadn't necessarily thought this would be a lifetime commitment." But, when four years had passed and zoo officials began pressuring Penny to give Koko back so she could be sent to the Los Angeles Zoo, she realized that Koko had much more to learn—and that the emotional bond between them was too strong to break. "You can't just say to a mother, 'We're taking the child away,'" she explains. With her life savings and donations from gorilla lovers, Penny bought Koko and a wild-born orphan, Michael.

Since 1979, home for Koko and Michael has been the Gorilla Foundation, seven wooded acres hidden in the foggy foothills south of San Francisco. Its name may conjure up images of elaborate research facilities, but the Gorilla Foundation is in fact charmingly and at time chaotically domestic. Penny lives in the main

Penny Patterson holds Koko's pet kitten "Smoky" as Koko signs "smoke."

Photo reprinted by permission of the The Gorilla Foundation, Box 620530, Woodside, CA 94062.

house with Ronald Cohn, her professional and personal companion, who serves as Project Koko's official photographer and video documentarian. In their living room, computer equipment, stacks of videotapes and piles of files compete for space with a mechanical King Kong bank, Koko's "Christmas plates," on which she's drawn pictures of Santa Claus, and other pieces of gorilla memorabilia.

A few yards from the house, the gorillas live in a trailer with kitchens, bedrooms, playrooms, a bathroom and a yard where they play on warm, sunny days, somewhat rare in the coastal foothills. Their close quarters may help fan the flames of sibling rivalry, which is unfortunate since Penny hopes the pair will someday mate. "It's difficult," she concedes, "for Koko to be attracted to someone she thinks of as her 'rotten stinker' little brother." Koko seems to relish insulting Michael. Penny has recorded this exchange:

Penny: I want to ask you a question.

Koko: Know Mike devil.

Penny: You know that Mike's a devil. That's fine, but that's not what I was going to ask you.

Koko and Michael also tattle on each other. After Penny and a colleague had been discussing whether Michael knew the sign for apple, which he was forming imperfectly, Koko chimed in, "Mike know apple...Mike good fake."

Koko also routinely insults Ron, whom she sees as a dominant male and something of a spoilsport. When asked, "What is funny?," Koko once replied, "Koko love Ron," and kissed him on the cheek. Yet when asked to pick her father from a set of photos—including Bwana, her biological father, Ron and other human males—she will pick Ron. Says Ron, "I think it's touching that, if they are upset or scared by something, they come right to me for protection."

Like many children, Koko and Michael sometimes offer observations that Penny diplomatically avoids translating for visitors. Koko has commented on a visitor's bad breath and nicknamed a potbellied reporter "Stomach"; when guests overstay their welcome, especially at bedtime, she may emphatically sign, "Time you go!"

Penny and Koko have grown close in their years of constant contact; Koko still occasionally cries when Penny leaves her for the night, tucked into her nest of three or four soft rugs laid over a tire. "But Michael is different," says Penny. "First of all, he was three and a half when we got him, and another woman worked with him for his first two and a half years with us. So I didn't get that strong bonding with him. He sees me not as a mother but classified with Koko as part of his

harem. He seems upset if strange males get near me. And," Penny says, laughing and raising her eyebrows, "he sometimes looks at me in that odd way..."

Penny's two children have different personalities. "Koko is outgoing and silly, while Michael is sort of shy and sensitive. He's very artistic; he likes to express himself that way and in fact is very gifted." A painting he titled "Flowers Gorilla More" is a strikingly impressionistic blend of form and color.

Though he's not as creative a conversationalist as Koko, Michael values communication. "With a person he knows well, Michael is more willing than Koko to bare his soul," Penny observes. "Koko changes the subject and won't pursue anything for very long, whereas he will get into it. That quality is really interesting; it's almost as if he needs it, like the time he talked about his parents." In a heart-wrenching conversation with one of his teachers, Michael described the killing of his parents in the wild, recalling an episode of "trouble" that culminated in "red," which is the gorillas' word for violence and blood.

Koko tends to be vainer than Michael, although she sometimes responds to compliments by modestly signing "False." "What's the prettiest thing you've ever seen?" she was asked. "Think hair," she replied. "Whose hair?" "Koko's."

Koko has a strong self-image; when asked if she were human or an animal, Koko replied, "Fine animal gorilla." That doesn't keep her from preening for, and mooning over, human male visitors. "Koko tends to see men as potential candidates for her amorous intentions," says Ron. Though Koko generally ignores television, Penny says, "I once found her on her back watching *Love Boat* upside down. She was mainly interested in the partially undressed bodies of the men, I think."

On a typical day, Koko rises at eight and breakfasts on cereal and fruit as she chats with Penny. Before beginning her morning studies with Penny, she may play with Michael, her pet cats or human companions, favoring "tickle and chase" games, regardless of her playmate's species. After lunch, she studies with another teacher, with frequent breaks for recess, when Koko may play outside, color, play with dolls or adorn herself with makeup, scarves and earrings. After a vegetarian dinner at 4:30, Koko may leaf through her books and play with Michael. At bedtime she brushes her teeth (Penny does the back, she does the front), rubs baby oil on her hands and feet and settles herself into her nest.

Playing stepparent to apes is a full-time job. "We get out once in a while, but we seldom, if ever, get a vacation," says Ron, who has no regrets about giving up his career as a cell biologist to devote himself to Project Koko. "Certainly that creates a lot of tension, but we have to cope with it." The magnitude of Penny's commitment gives her pause only once during a series of lengthy, animated conversations. Asked if she would ever like to travel to Koko and Michael's natural habitat in west Africa, Penny becomes wistful. "If I could ever get away, it would be wonderful, but I don't anticipate having a week or two-week chunk when I could feel comfortable leaving."

What's next for the gorillas? Koko and Michael are beginning yet another astonishing project: They're learning to read. Koko has always enjoyed illustrated books, frequently looking through them and signing to herself, commenting on the stories the pictures represent. Now she's showing a remarkable ability to recognize letters, phonetic groupings and words, an especially amazing achievement when you consider that Koko's primary languages—gorilla gestures and Ameslan—involve no phonetic elements. One difficulty in measuring her progress is distinguishing lack of understanding from lack of interest. "After a session in which Koko learned the written words 'nut,' 'Koko' and 'drink,' I wrote NUP, KOCO and DWINK on cards and asked her what was wrong with those words. She walked away, making no response. A few minutes later, she sauntered past and casually pointed to the C in KOCO. Later still, she strolled past the cards again and pointed to the P in NUP."

While Penny has no plans for human additions to their household, she would like to move to a site that could allow more gorillas into the family. "We're desperately trying to raise enough money to move the project to Hawaii, where Koko and Michael would have a warmer climate—closer to that of their natural habitat—and more room for them and, someday, other gorillas. When we showed Koko a picture of one of the Hawaiian sites, she emphatically signed 'Go!'"

If Penny and company move, they'll take a couple of tiny tagalongs. After the death of All Ball, Koko cried over pictures of cats. Finally she began to ask for another cat—"Tiger, please, tiger"—specifically a tailless Manx.

It took Penny some time to find a Manx kitten; Koko was so frustrated by the delay that she began referring to the promised kitten as "trouble surprise." When Penny proudly presented Koko with a reddish-gold Manx male, the gorilla showed polite interest, looked at the box from which the new pet had emerged and signed "Pick there," remembering that she had been allowed to choose All Ball from a litter. Koko was coolly cordial to the kitten, but stubbornly resisted requests to name it, perversely suggesting "Dog." To complicate matters, Michael began to refer to the kitten as "my cat." Penny solved the problem by letting Koko pick a new cat from a litter—she chose a gray Manx—and giving Michael "his cat." Now Michael and Lips and Koko and Smokey play happily together.

Penny spends as much time attending to Koko and Michael's happiness as she does gathering data for Project Koko. Some critics have suggested that Penny's concern and affection for the gorillas have clouded her perceptions as a scientist. But Roger Fouts of Project Washoe believes that emotional bonds are essential to such work. "When it comes to working with primates, heart—caring—is what it's all about." Penny would no more withhold her warmth from her children than would any other mother. "They aren't things or even laboratory animals," she says. Penny put it simply when asked how she felt about the subject of her groundbreaking experiment. "I guess it's okay to say it," she responded. "I love Koko."

Editor's Note: Michael died unexpectedly and prematurely in April 2000.

Koko's education and care are made possible by grants, and by contributions from members of The Gorilla Foundation, founded by Penny in 1976 to "promote the protection, preservation, and propagation of gorillas and other endangered ape species." If you would like to help support this project, contributions may be sent to The Gorilla Foundation, P.O. Box 620530, Woodside, CA 94062.

Women's Talk

Nobuko Yotsuya struck a blow for feminism in Japan two years ago when she won election as the first female vice chairman of Tokyo's Metropolitan Assembly. But for all the power that was suddenly hers, she was unable to break through a formidable barrier: the linguisitic one. She couldn't bring herself to use a simple three-letter suffix, *-kun.*

In the hitherto all-male assembly, the vice chairman had always called upon members not by using the customary honorific *san,* as in Sato-san, but with *-kun.* This is backslapping, locker-room usage. It isn't so much crude as familiar, and Yotsuya-san wasn't comfortable affecting this sort of macho casualness.

Even Mariko Mitsui, a colleague of Yotsuya-san's and a bold Japanese feminist with a mischievous sense of humor, recalls her trepidation at joining in the traditional catcalls in the legislative chamber. The expressions used are quite rough (read masculine), like *urusai* and *damare,* the Japanese equivalents of "shut up," and "*Nani o itteru ka,*" which means "What the hell are you talking about?" Gentler (that is, feminine) forms of heckling don't exist, or would sound ludicrously polite.

Newspapers and magazines report almost daily on shifting sexual mores in Japan. The Justice Ministry is considering a proposal that would allow married women to retain their maiden names. This spring, a woman won a mayoral election for the first time. A woman has just been named managing editor of the Okinawa *Times,* the first major Japanese newspaper to be run by a woman. But the linguistic divide between the sexes endures, even if it is little acknowledged. In Japan, men and women have different ways of speaking.

One of the first verbal hurdles boys and girls have to overcome is the proper way to end sentences. A boy might say "*Samui yo*" to declare "It's cold, I say!" But a girl would say "*Samui wa,*" expressing what is, in effect, a gentle question: "It's cold, don't you think?" When referring to themselves, boys often use the word *boku* which means

"I." Girls can't; they have to say *watashi,* a pronoun that can be used by either sex but that is more polite.

Parents and teachers are vigilant linguistic police, correcting children who use forms of speech reserved for the other sex. Girls in particular are upbraided with "*Onnanoko na no ni,*" which means "You're a girl, don't forget."

In a country where social interaction turns on an immense number of hierarchical distinctions, women are expected to be verbally correct at all times. All Japanese learn polite usages, but women have to be more polite. Women use the same set of honorifics that are appended to certain nouns and the same special verb forms and sentence constructions used by all Japanese in polite situations. But the frequency with which women employ more formal expressions sets them apart as the humbler sex.

When referring to other people's families, all polite Japanese use the word *go-kazoku* for "family"; when they are talking about their own families, they simply use the word *kazoku.* To be properly deferential, when they are referring to others, the verbs *ikimasu* ("to go"), *kimasu* ("to come") and *imasu* ("to be") are replaced by the more polite *irasshaimasu.* (What this confusing form of humility underscores is not that the Japanese don't know if they are coming or going but the importance of context in conversational Japanese. A listener will know what is meant under the circumstances.) When one humbles oneself to a person in a higher position, *ikimasu* and *kimasu* are replaced by *mairimasu; imasu* by *orimasu.*

In addition to this special vocabulary, women adopt a distinctive tone of voice, carriage and behavior. On a recent afternoon, Suzuko Nishihara, an administrator at the National Language Institute, was telling me how Japanese women generally speak in a higher-pitched voice than men, especially when exceptional politeness is called for. At that moment in our conversation, an older Japanese man appeared at her office door to inform her that a budget meeting was beginning earlier than scheduled. She responded in, of course, a high-pitched voice. "You see?" she said. "That's precisely the sort of thing I was talking about."

Takako Doi, who recently resigned as head of the Socialist Party and is one of the most visible women in Japan, succeeds in breaking many of these rules. Her voice is always low, even when she is passionately pressing a point. She uses honorifics much less often than most women, and she employs the masculine form, *de arimasu*, instead of the more polite, and thus feminine, *de gozaimasu*, meaning "to be." Most noticeable is a bit of unusual body language: she always looks the listener straight in the face when speaking.

There are other signs of change, particularly among younger Japanese. Suzuko Nishihara said that her two college-age daughters use more neutral, less polite and even mildly masculine forms of speech. Instead of ending their sentences with the feminine *wa yo,* they use *da yo* (the masculine form) when they are speaking with their classmates, male or female. Toward their elders, they end their verbs with *-masu* instead of the more polite *gozaimasu.*

But no one knows whether college habits will survive job training, marriage and motherhood. When a Japanese woman marries, she descends to the bottom rung in her husband's family, marked by her having to use the most ingratiating forms of speech. It's not a matter of saying "Excuse me" or "May I?" but of using language to place the husband's family in an honored position.

Thus a married woman would abandon the usual polite suffix *-san* in favor of the very polite form *-sama.* Generally, a newlywed would never call her mother-in-law *okaasan* ("mother") but rather *okaasama.* And she would use decidedly humble forms of speech when referring to herself and her own family.

Furthermore, in Japan's intensely competitive educational system, being linguistically correct is considered so important that many mothers study books on how to speak properly to a child's teachers.

Kumi Sato, a cosmopolitan, American-educated woman who heads a public relations company in Tokyo, casually salts her English with all manner of American colloquialisms. But when she's speaking in Japanese her whole demeanor changes; she becomes unequivocally Japanese.

"In Japan, one's speech shows one's upbringing and education," she says. "Personally, I try not to use male language to state my position. Even when I'm in a commanding position or giving orders, I don't use the suffix *-kun.* I don't believe women have to talk or play a man's game to be successful."

The Power of Talk: Who Gets Heard and Why

We all know what confidence, competence, and authority sound like. Or do we?

The head of a large division of a multinational corporation was running a meeting devoted to performance assessment. Each senior manager stood up, reviewed the individuals in his group, and evaluated them for promotion. Although there were women in every group, not one of them made the cut. One after another, each manager declared, in effect, that every woman in his group didn't have the self-confidence needed to be promoted. The division head began to doubt his ears. How could it be that all the talented women in the division suffered from a lack of self-confidence?

In all likelihood, they didn't. Consider the many women who have left large corporations to start their own businesses, obviously exhibiting enough confidence to succeed on their own. Judgments about confidence can be inferred only from the way people present themselves, and much of that presentation is in the form of talk.

The CEO of a major corporation told me that he often has to make decisions in five minutes about matters on which others may have worked five months. He said he uses this rule: If the person making the proposal seems confident, the CEO approves it. If not, he says no. This might seem like a reasonable approach. But my field of research, sociolinguistics, suggests otherwise. The CEO obviously thinks he knows what a confident person sounds like. But his judgment, which may be dead right for some people, may be dead wrong for others.

Communication isn't as simple as saying what you mean. How you say what you mean is crucial and differs from one person to the next, because using language is learned social behavior: How we talk and listen are deeply influenced by cultural experience. Although we might think that our ways of saying what we mean are natural, we can run into trouble if we interpret and evaluate others as if they

necessarily felt the same way we'd feel if we spoke the way they did.

Since 1974, I have been researching the influence of linguistic style on conversations and human relationships. In the past four years, I have extended that research to the workplace, where I have observed how ways of speaking learned in childhood affect judgments of competence and confidence, as well as who gets heard, who gets credit, and what gets done.

The division head who was dumbfounded to hear that all the talented women in his organization lacked confidence was probably right to be skeptical. The senior managers were judging the women in their groups by their own linguistic norms, but women—like people who have grown up in a different culture—have often learned different styles of speaking than men, which can make them seem less competent and self-assured than they are.

WHAT IS LINGUISTIC STYLE?

Everything that is said must be said in a certain way—in a certain tone of voice, at a certain rate of speed, and with a certain degree of loudness. Whereas often we consciously consider what to say before speaking, we rarely think about how to say it, unless the situation is obviously loaded—for example, a job interview or a tricky performance review. Linguistic style refers to a person's characteristic speaking pattern. It includes such features as directness or indirectness, pacing and pausing, word choice, and the use of such elements as jokes, figures of speech, stories, questions, and apologies. In other words, linguistic style is a set of culturally learned signals by which we not only communicate what we mean but also interpret others' meaning and evaluate one another as people.

Consider turn taking, one element of linguistic style. Conversation is an enterprise in which people take turns: One person speaks, then the other responds. However, this apparently simple exchange requires a subtle negotiation of signals so that you know when the other person is finished and it's your turn to begin. Cultural factors such as country or region of origin and ethnic background influence how long a pause seems natural. When Bob, who is from Detroit, has a conversation with his colleague Joe, from New York City, it's hard for him to get a word in edgewise because he expects a slightly longer pause between turns than Joe does. A pause of that length never comes because, before it has a chance to, Joe senses an uncomfortable silence, which he fills with more talk of his own. Both men fail to realize that differences in conversational style are getting in their way. Bob thinks that Joe is pushy and uninterested in what he has to say, and Joe thinks that Bob doesn't have much to contribute. Similarly, when Sally relocated from Texas to Washington, D.C., she kept searching for the right time to break in during staff meetings—and never found it. Although in Texas she was considered outgoing and confident, in Washington she was perceived as shy and retiring. Her boss even suggested she take an assertiveness training course. Thus slight differences in conversational style—in these cases, a few seconds of pause—can have a surprising impact on who gets heard and on the judgments, including psychological ones, that are made about people and their abilities.

Every utterance functions on two levels. We're all familiar with the first one: Language communicates ideas. The second level is mostly invisible to us, but it plays a powerful role in communication. As a form of social behavior, language also negotiates relationships. Through ways of speaking, we signal—and create—the relative status of speakers and their level of rapport. If you say, "Sit down!" you are signaling that you have higher status than the person you are addressing, that you are so close to each other that you can drop all pleasantries, or that you are angry. If you say, "I would be honored if you would sit down," you are signaling great respect—or great sarcasm, depending on your tone of voice, the situation, and what you both know about how close you really are. If you say, "You must be so tired—why don't you sit down," you are communicating either closeness and concern or condescension. Each of these ways of saying "the same thing"—telling someone to sit down—can have a vastly different meaning.

In every community known to linguists, the patterns that constitute linguistic style are relatively different for men and women. What's "natural" for most men speaking a given language is, in some cases, different from what's "natural" for most women. That is because we learn ways of speaking as children growing up, especially from peers, and children tend to play with other children of the same sex. The research of sociologists, anthropologists, and psychologists observing American children at play has shown that, although both girls and boys find ways of creating rapport and negotiating status, girls tend to learn conversational rituals that focus on the rapport dimension of relationships whereas boys tend to learn rituals that focus on the status dimension.

Girls tend to play with a single best friend or in small groups, and they spend a lot of time talking. They use language to negotiate how close they are; for example, the girl you tell your secrets to becomes your best friend. Girls learn to downplay ways in which one is better than the others and to emphasize ways in which they are all the same. From childhood, most girls learn that sounding too sure of themselves will make them unpopular with their peers—although nobody really takes such modesty literally. A group of girls will ostracize a girl who calls attention to her own superiority and criticize her by saying, "She thinks she's something"; and a girl who tells others what to do is called "bossy." Thus girls learn to talk in ways that balance their own needs with those of others—to save face for one another in the broadest sense of the term.

Boys tend to play very differently. They usually play in larger groups in which more boys can be included, but not everyone is treated as an equal. Boys with high status in their group are expected to emphasize rather than downplay their status, and usually one or several boys will be seen as the leader or leaders. Boys generally don't accuse one another of being bossy, because the leader is expected to tell lower-status boys what to do. Boys learn to use language to negotiate their status in the group by displaying their abilities and knowledge, and by challenging other and resisting challenges. Giving orders is one way of getting and keeping the high-status role. Another is taking center stage by telling stories or jokes.

This is not to say that all boys and girls grow up this way or feel comfortable in these groups or are equally successful at negotiating within these norms. But, for the most part, these childhood play groups are where boys and girls learn their conversational styles. In this sense, they grow up in different worlds. The result is that women and men tend to have different habitual ways of saying what they mean, and conversations between them can be like cross-cultural communication: You can't assume that the other person means what you would mean if you said the same thing in the same way.

My research in companies across the United States shows that the lessons learned in childhood carry over into the workplace. Consider the following example: A focus group was organized at a major multinational company to evaluate a recently implemented flextime policy. The participants sat in a circle and discussed the new system. The group concluded that it was excellent, but they also agreed on ways to improve it. The meeting went well and was deemed a success by all, according to my own observations and everyone's comments to me. But the next day, I was in for a surprise.

I had left the meeting with the impression that Phil had been responsible for most of the suggestions adopted by the group. But as I typed up my notes, I noticed that Cheryl had made almost all those suggestions. I had thought that the key ideas came from Phil because he had picked up Cheryl's points and supported them, speaking at greater length in doing so than she had in raising them.

It would be easy to regard Phil as having stolen Cheryl's ideas—and her thunder. But that would be inaccurate. Phil never claimed Cheryl's ideas as his own. Cheryl herself told me later that she left the meeting confident that she had contributed significantly, and that she appreciated Phil's support. She volunteered, with a laugh, "It was not one of those times when a woman says something and it's ignored, then a man says it and it's picked up." In other words, Cheryl and Phil worked well as a team, the group fulfilled its charge, and the company got what it needed. So what was the problem?

I went back and asked all the participants who they though had been the most influential group member, the one most responsible for the ideas that had been adopted. The pattern of answers was revealing. The two other women in the group named Cheryl. Two of the three men named Phil. Of the men, only Phil named Cheryl. In other words, in this instance, the women evaluated the contribution of another woman more accurately than the men did.

Meetings like this take place daily in companies around the country. Unless managers are unusually good at listening closely to how people say what they mean, the talents of someone like Cheryl may well be undervalued and underutilized.

ONE UP, ONE DOWN

Individual speakers vary in how sensitive they are to the social dynamics of language—in other words, to the subtle nuances of what others say to them. Men tend to be sensitive to the power dynamics of interaction, speaking in ways that position themselves as one up and resisting being put in a one-down posi-

tion by others. Women tend to react more strongly to the rapport dynamic, speaking in ways that save face for others and buffering statements that could be seen as putting others in a one-down position. These linguistic patterns are pervasive; you can hear them in hundreds of exchanges in the workplace every day. And, as in the case of Cheryl and Phil, they affect who gets heard and who gets credit.

Getting Credit

Even so small a linguistic strategy as the choice of pronoun can affect who gets credit. In my research in the workplace, I heard men say "I" in situations where I heard women say "we." For example, one publishing company executive said, "I'm hiring a new manager. I'm going to put him in charge of my marketing division," as if he owned the corporation. In stark contrast, I recorded women saying "we" when referring to work they alone had done. One woman explained that it would sound too self-promoting to claim credit in an obvious way by saying, "I did this." Yet she expected—sometimes vainly—that others would know it was her work and would give her the credit she did not claim for herself.

Managers might leap to the conclusion that women who do not take credit for what they've done should be taught to do so. But that solution is problematic because we associate ways of speaking with moral qualities: The way we speak is who we are and who we want to be.

Veronica, a senior researcher in a high-tech company, had an observant boss. He noticed that many of the ideas coming out of the group were hers but that often someone else trumpeted them around the office and got credit for them. He advised her to "own" her ideas and make sure she got the credit. But Veronica found she simply didn't enjoy her work if she had to approach it as what seemed to her an unattractive and unappealing "grabbing game." It was her dislike of such behavior that had led her to avoid it in the first place.

Whatever the motivation, women are less likely than men to have learned to blow their own horn. And they are more likely than men to believe that if they do so, they won't be liked.

Many have argued that the growing trend of assigning work to teams may be especially congenial to women, but it may also create complications for performance evaluation. When ideas are generated and work is accomplished in the privacy of the team, the outcome of the team's effort may become associated with the person most vocal about reporting results. There are many women and men—but probably relatively more women—who are reluctant to put themselves forward in this way and who consequently risk not getting credit for their contributions.

Confidence and Boasting

The CEO who based his decisions on the confidence level of speakers was articulating a value that is widely shared in U.S. businesses: One way to judge confidence is by an individual's behavior, especially verbal behavior. Here again, many women are at a disadvantage.

Studies show that women are more likely to downplay their certainty and men are more likely to minimize their doubts. Psychologist Laurie Heatherington and her colleagues devised an ingenious experiment, which they reported in the journal *Sex Roles* (Volume 29, 1993). They asked hundreds of incoming college students to predict what grades they would get in their first year. Some subjects were asked to make their predictions privately by writing them down and placing them in an envelope; others were asked to make their predictions publicly, in the presence of a researcher. The results showed that more women than men predicted lower grades for themselves if they made their predictions publicly. If they made their predictions privately, the predictions were the same as those of the men—and the same as their actual grades. This study provides evidence that what comes across as lack of confidence—predicting lower grades for oneself—may reflect not one's actual level of confidence but the desire not to seem boastful.

These habits with regard to appearing humble or confident result from the socialization of boys and girls by their peers in childhood play. As adults, both women and men find these behaviors reinforced by the positive responses they get from friends and relatives who share the same norms. But the norms of behavior in the U.S. business world are based on the style of interaction that is more common among men—at least, among American men.

Asking Questions

Although asking the right questions is one of the hallmarks of a good manager, how and when questions are asked can send unintended signals about competence and power. In a group, if only one person asks questions, he or she risks being seen as the truly ignorant one. Furthermore, we judge others not only by how they speak but also by how they are spoken to. The person who asks questions may end up being lectured to and looking like a novice under a schoolmaster's tutelage. The way boys are socialized makes them more likely to be aware of the underlying power dynamic by which a question asker can be seen in a one-down position.

One practicing physician learned the hard way that any exchange of information can become the basis for judgments—or misjudgments—about competence. During her training, she received a negative evaluation that she thought was unfair, so she asked her supervising physician for an explanation. He said that she knew less than her peers. Amazed at his answer, she asked how he had reached that conclusion. He said, "You ask more questions."

Along with cultural influences and individual personality, gender seems to play a role in whether and when people ask questions. For example, of all the observations I've made in lectures and books, the one that sparks the most enthusiastic flash of recognition is that men are less likely than women to stop and ask for directions when they are lost. I explain that men often resist asking for directions because they are aware that it puts them in a one-down position and because they value the independence that comes with finding their way by themselves. Asking for directions while driving is only one instance—along with many others that researchers have examined—in which men seem less likely than women to ask questions. I believe this is because they are more attuned than women to the potential face-losing aspect of asking questions. And men who believe that asking questions might reflect negatively on them may, in turn, be likely to form a negative opinion of others who ask questions in situations where they would not.

CONVERSATIONAL RITUALS

Conversation is fundamentally ritual in the sense that we speak in ways our culture has conventionalized and expect certain types of responses. Take greetings, for example. I have heard visitors to the United States complain that Americans are hypocritical because they ask how you are but aren't interested in the answer. To Americans, How are you? is obviously a ritualized way to start a conversation rather than a literal request for information. In other parts of the world, including the Philippines, people ask each other, "Where are you going?" when they meet. The question seems intrusive to Americans, who do not realize that it, too, is a ritual query to which the only expected reply is a vague "Over there."

It's easy and entertaining to observe different rituals in foreign countries. But we don't expect differences, and are far less likely to recognize the ritualized nature of our conversations, when we are with our compatriots at work. Our differing rituals can be even more problematic when we think we're all speaking the same language.

Apologies

Consider the simple phrase *I'm sorry.*

CATHERINE: How did that big presentation go?
BOB: Oh, not very well. I got a lot of flak from the VP for finance, and I didn't have the numbers at my fingertips.
CATHERINE: Oh, I'm sorry. I know how hard you worked on that.

In this case, *I'm sorry* probably means "I'm sorry that happened," not "I apologize," unless it was Catherine's responsibility to supply Bob with the numbers for the presentation. Women tend to say *I'm sorry* more frequently than men, and often they intend it in this way—as a ritualized means of expressing concern. It's one of many learned elements of conversational style that girls often use to establish rapport. Ritual apologies—like other conversational rituals—work well when both parties share the same assumptions about their use. But people who utter frequent ritual apologies may end up appearing weaker, less confident, and literally more blameworthy than people who don't.

Apologies tend to be regarded differently by men, who are more likely to focus on the status implications of exchanges. Many men avoid apologies because they see them as putting the speaker in a one-down position. I observed with some amazement an encounter among several lawyers engaged in a negotiation over a speakerphone. At one point, the lawyer in whose office I was sitting accidentally elbowed the telephone and cut off the call. When his secretary got the parties back on again, I expected him to say what I would have said: "Sorry about that. I knocked the phone with my elbow." Instead, he said, "Hey, what happened? One minute you were there, the next minute you were gone!" This lawyer seemed to have an automatic impulse not to admit fault if he didn't have to. For me, it was one of those pivotal moments when you realize that the world you live in is not the one everyone lives in and that the way you assume is the way to talk is really only one of many.

Those who caution managers not to undermine their authority by apologizing are approaching interaction from the perspective of the power dynamic. In many cases, this strategy is effective. On the other hand, when I asked people who frustrated them in their jobs, one frequently voiced complaint was working with or for someone who refuses to apologize or admit fault. In other words, accepting responsibility for errors and admitting mistakes may be an equally effective or superior strategy in some settings.

Feedback

Styles of giving feedback contain a ritual element that often is the cause for misunderstanding. Consider the following exchange: A manager had to tell her marketing director to rewrite a report. She began this potentially awkward task by citing the report's strengths and then moved to the main point: the weaknesses that needed to be remedied. The marketing director seemed to understand and accept his supervisor's comments, but his revision contained only minor changes and failed to address the major weaknesses. When the manager told him of her dissatisfaction, he accused her of misleading him: "You told me it was fine."

The impasse resulted from different linguistic styles. To the manager, it was natural to buffer the criticism by beginning with praise. Telling her subordinate that his report is inadequate and has to be rewritten puts him in a one-down position. Praising him for the parts that are good is a ritualized way of saving face for him. But the marketing director did not share his supervisor's assumption about how feedback should be given. Instead, he assumed that what she mentioned first was the main point and that what she brought up later was an afterthought.

Those who expect feedback to come in the way the manager presented it would appreciate her tact and would regard a more blunt approach as unnecessarily callous. But those who share the marketing director's assumptions would regard the blunt approach as honest and no-nonsense, and the manager's as obfuscating. Because each one's assumptions seemed self-evident, each blamed the other: The manager thought the marketing director was not listening, and he thought she had not communicated clearly or had changed her mind. This is significant because it illustrates that incidents labeled vaguely as "poor communication" may be the result of differing linguistic styles.

Compliments

Exchanging compliments is a common ritual, especially among women. A mismatch in expectations about this ritual left Susan, a manager in the human resources field, in a one-down position. She and her colleague Bill had both given presentations at a national conference. On the airplane home, Susan told Bill, "That was a great talk!" "Thank you," he said. Then she asked, "What did you think of mine?" He responded with a lengthy and detailed critique, as she listened uncomfortably. An unpleasant feeling of having been put down came over her. Somehow she had been positioned as the novice in need of his expert advice. Even worse, she had only herself to blame, since she had, after all, asked Bill what he though of her talk.

But had Susan asked for the response she received? When she asked Bill what he thought about her talk, she expected to hear not a critique but a compliment. In fact, her question had been an attempt to repair a ritual gone awry. Susan's initial compliment to Bill was the kind of automatic recognition she felt was more or less required after a colleague gives a presentation, and she expected Bill to respond with a matching compliment. She was just talking automatically, but he either sincerely misunderstood the ritual or simply took the opportunity to bask in the one-up position of critic. Whatever his motivation, it was Susan's attempt to spark an exchange of compliments that gave him the opening.

Although this exchange could have occurred between two men, it does not seem coincidental that it happened between a man and a woman. Linguist Janet Holmes discovered that women pay more compliments than men (*Anthropological Linguistics*, Volume 28, 1986). And, as I have observed, fewer men are likely to ask, "What did you think of my talk?" precisely because the question might invite an unwanted critique.

In the social structure of the peer groups in which they grow up, boys are indeed looking for opportunities to put others down and take the one-up position for themselves. In contrast, one of the rituals girls learn is taking the one-down position but assuming that the other person will recognize the ritual nature of the self-denigration and pull them back up.

The exchange between Susan and Bill also suggests how women's and men's characteristic styles may put women at a disadvantage in the workplace. If one person is trying to minimize status differences, maintain an appearance that everyone is equal, and save face for the other, while another person is trying to maintain the one-up position and avoid being positioned as one down, the person seeking the one-up position is likely to get it. At the same time, the person who has not been expending any effort to avoid the one-down position is likely to end up in it. Because women are more likely to take (or accept) the role of advice seeker, men are more inclined to interpret a ritual question from a woman as a request for advice.

Ritual Opposition

Apologizing, mitigating criticism with praise, and exchanging compliments are rituals common among women that men often take literally. A ritual common among men that women often take literally is ritual opposition.

A woman in communications told me she watched with distaste and distress as her office mate argued heatedly with another colleague about whose division should suffer budget cuts. She was even more surprised, however, that a short time later they were as friendly as ever. "How can you pretend that fight never happened?" she asked. "Who's pretending it never happened?" he responded, as puzzled by her question as she had been by his behavior. "It happened," he said, "and it's over." What she took as literal fighting to him was a routine part of daily negotiation: a ritual fight.

Many Americans expect the discussion of ideas to be a ritual fight—that is, an exploration through verbal opposition. They present their own ideas in the most certain and absolute form they can, and wait to see if they are challenged. Being forced to defend an idea provides an opportunity to test it. In the same spirit, they may play devil's advocate in challenging their colleagues' ideas—trying to poke holes and find weaknesses—as a way of helping them explore and test their ideas.

This style can work well if everyone shares it, but those unaccustomed to it are likely to miss its ritual nature. They may give up an idea that is challenged, taking the objections as an indication that the idea was a poor one. Worse, they may take the opposition as a personal attack and may find it impossible to do their best in a contentious environment. People unaccustomed to this style may hedge when stating their ideas in order to fend off potential attacks. Ironically, this posture makes their arguments appear weak and is more likely to invite attack from pugnacious colleagues than to fend it off.

Ritual opposition can even play a role in who gets hired. Some consulting firms that recruit graduates from the top business schools use a confrontational interviewing technique. They challenge the candidate to "crack a case" in real time. A partner at one firm told me, "Women tend to do less well in this kind of interaction, and it certainly affects who gets hired. But, in fact, many women who don't 'test well' turn out to be good consultants. They're often smarter than some of the men who looked like analytic powerhouses under pressure."

The level of verbal opposition varies from one company's culture to the next, but I saw instances of it in all the organizations I studied. Anyone who is uncomfortable with this linguistic style—and that includes some men as well as many women—risks appearing insecure about his or her ideas.

NEGOTIATING AUTHORITY

In organizations, formal authority comes from the position one holds. But actual authority has to be negotiated day to day. The effectiveness of individual managers depends in part on their skill in negotiating authority and on whether others reinforce or undercut their efforts. The way linguistic style reflects status plays a subtle role in placing individuals within a hierarchy.

Managing Up and Down

In all the companies I researched, I heard from women who knew they were doing a superior job and knew that their coworkers (and sometimes their immediate bosses) knew it as well, but believed that the higher-ups did not. They frequently told me that something outside themselves was holding them back and found it frustrating because they thought that all that should be necessary for success was to do a great job, that superior performance should be recognized and rewarded. In contrast, men often told me that if women weren't promoted, it was because they simply weren't up to snuff. Looking around, however, I saw evidence that men more often than women behaved in ways likely to get them recognized by those with the power to determine their advancement.

In all the companies I visited, I observed what happened at lunchtime. I saw young men who regularly ate lunch with their boss, and senior men who ate with the big boss. I noticed far fewer women who sought out the highest-level person they could eat with. But one is more likely to get recognition for work done if one talks about it to those higher up, and it is easier to do so if the lines of communication are already open. Furthermore, given the opportunity for a conversation with superiors, men and women are likely to have different ways of talking about their accomplishments because of the different ways in which they were socialized as children. Boys are rewarded by their peers if they talk up their achievements, whereas girls are rewarded if they play theirs down. Linguistic styles common among men may tend to give them some advantages when it comes to managing up.

All speakers are aware of the status of the person they are talking to and adjust accordingly. Everyone speaks differently when talking to a boss than when talking to a subordinate. But, surprisingly, the ways in which they adjust their talk may be different and thus may project different images of themselves.

Communications researchers Karen Tracy and Eric Eisenberg studied how relative status affects the way people give criticism. They devised a business letter that contained some errors and asked 13 male and 11 female college students to role-play delivering criticism under two scenarios. In the first, the speaker was a boss talking to a subordinate; in the second, the speaker was subordinate talking to his or her boss. The researchers measured how hard the speakers tried to avoid hurting the feelings of the person they were criticizing.

One might expect people to be more careful about how they deliver criticism when they are in a subordinate position. Tracy and Eisenberg found that hypothesis to be true for the men in their study but not for the women. As they reported in *Research on Language and Social Interaction* (Volume 24, 1990/1991), the women showed more concern about the other person's feelings when they were playing the role of superior. In other words, the women were more careful to save face for the other person when they were managing down than when they were managing up. This pattern recalls the way girls are socialized: Those who are in some way superior are expected to downplay rather than flaunt their superiority.

In my own recordings of workplace communication, I observed women talking in similar ways. For example, when a manager had to correct a mistake made by her secretary, she did so by acknowledging that there were mitigating circumstances. She said, laughing, "You know, it's hard to do things around here, isn't it, with all these people coming in!" The manager was saving face for her subordinate, just like the female students role-playing in the Tracy and Eisenberg study.

Is this an effective way to communicate? One must ask, effective for what? The manager in question established a positive environment in her group, and the work was done effectively. On the other hand, numerous women in many different fields told me that their bosses say they don't project the proper authority.

Indirectness

Another linguistic signal that varies with power and status is indirectness—the tendency to say what we mean without spelling it out in so many words. Despite the widespread belief in the United States that it's always best to say exactly what we mean, indirectness is a fundamental and pervasive element in human communication. It also is one of the elements that varies most from one culture to another, and it can cause enormous misunderstanding when speakers have different habits and expectations about how it is used. It's often said that American women are more indirect than American men, but in fact everyone tends to be indirect in some situations, and in different ways. Allowing for cultural, ethnic, regional, and individual differences, women are especially likely to be indirect when it comes to telling others what to do, which is not surprising considering girls' readiness to brand other girls as bossy. On the other hand, men are especially likely to be indirect when it comes to admitting fault or weakness, which also is not surprising, considering boys' readiness to push around boys who assume the one-down position.

At first glance, it would seem that only the powerful can get away with bald commands such as, "Have that report on my desk by noon." But power in an organization also can lead to requests so indirect that they don't sound like requests at all. A boss who says, "Do we have the sales data by product line for each region?" would be surprised and frustrated if a subordinate responded, "We probably do" rather than "I'll get it for you."

Examples such as these notwithstanding, many researchers have claimed that those in subordinate positions are more likely to speak indirectly, and that is surely accurate in some situations. For example, linguist Charlotte Linde, in a study published in *Language in Society* (Volume 17, 1988), examined the black-box conversations that took place between pilots and copilots before airplane crashes. In one particularly tragic instance, an Air Florida plane crashed into the Potomac River immediately after attempting takeoff from National Airport in Washington, D.C., killing all but 5 of the 74 people on board. The pilot, it turned out, had little experience flying in icy weather. The copilot had a bit more, and it became heartbreakingly clear on analysis that he had tried to warn the pilot but had done so indirectly. Alerted by Linde's observation, I examined the transcript of the conversations and found evidence of her hypothesis. The copilot repeatedly called attention to the bad weather and to ice buildup on other planes:

COPILOT: Look how the ice is just hanging on his, ah, back, back there, see that? See all those icicles on the back there and everything?

PILOT: Yeah.

[The copilot also expressed concern about the long waiting time since deicing.]

COPILOT: Boy, this is a, this is a losing battle here on trying to deice those things; it [gives] you a false feeling of security, that's all that does.

[Just before they took off, the copilot expressed another concern—about abnormal instrument readings—but again he didn't press the matter when it wasn't picked up by the pilot.]

COPILOT: That don't seem right, does it? [3-second pause] Ah, that's not right. Well—

PILOT: Yes it is, there's 80.

COPILOT: Naw, I don't think that's right. [7-second pause] Ah, maybe it is.

Shortly thereafter, the plane took off, with tragic results. In other instances as well as this one, Linde observed that copilots, who are second in command, are more likely to express themselves indirectly or otherwise mitigate, or soften, their communication when they are suggesting courses of action to the pilot. In an effort to avert similar disasters, some airlines now offer training for copilots to express themselves in more assertive ways.

This solution seems self-evidently appropriate to most Americans. But when I assigned Linde's article in a graduate seminar I taught, a Japanese student pointed out that it would be just as effective to train pilots to pick up on hints. This approach reflects assumptions about communication that typify Japanese culture, which places great value on the ability of people to understand one another without putting everything into words. Either directness or indirectness can be a successful means of communication as long as the linguistic style is understood by the participants.

In the world of work, however, there is more at stake than whether the communication is understood. People in powerful positions are likely to reward styles similar to their own, because we all tend to take as self-evident the logic of our own styles. Accordingly, there is evidence that in the U.S. workplace, where instructions from a superior are expected to be voiced in a relatively direct manner, those who tend to be indirect when telling subordinates what to do may be perceived as lacking in confidence.

Consider the case of the manager at a national magazine who was responsible for giving assignments to reporters. She tended to phrase her assignments as questions. For example, she asked, "How would you like to do the X project with Y?" or said, "I was thinking of putting you on the X project. Is that okay?" This worked extremely well with her staff; they liked working for her, and the work got done in an efficient and orderly manner. But when she had her midyear evaluation with her own boss, he criticized her for not assuming the proper demeanor with her staff.

In any work environment, the higher-ranking person has the power to enforce his or her own view of appropriate demeanor, created in part by linguistic style. In most U.S. contexts, that view is likely to assume that the person in authority has the right to be relatively direct rather than to mitigate orders. There also are cases, however, in which the higher-ranking person assumes a more indirect style. The owner of a retail operation told her subordinate, a store manager, to do something. He said he would do it, but a week later he still hadn't. They were able to trace the difficulty to the following conversation: She had said, "The bookkeeper needs help with the billing. How would you feel about helping her out?" He had said, "Fine." This conversation had seemed to be clear and flawless at the time, but it turned out that they had interpreted this simple exchange in very different ways. She thought he meant, "Fine, I'll help the bookkeeper out." He thought he meant, "Fine, I'll think about how I would feel about helping the bookkeeper out." He did think about it and came to the conclusion that he had more important things to do and couldn't spare the time.

To the owner, "How would you feel about helping the bookkeeper out?" was an obviously appropriate way to give the order "Help the bookkeeper out with the billing." Those who expect orders to be given as bald imperatives may find such locutions annoying or even misleading. But those for whom this style is natural do not think they are being indirect. They believe they are being clear in a polite or respectful way.

What is atypical in this example is that the person with the more indirect style was the boss, so the store manager was motivated to adapt to her style. She still gives orders the same way, but the store manager now understands how she means what she says. It's more common in U.S. business contexts for the highest-ranking people to take a more direct style, with the result that many women in authority risk being judged by their superiors as lacking the appropriate demeanor—and, consequently, lacking in confidence.

WHAT TO DO?

I am often asked, What is the best way to give criticism? or What is the best way to give orders?—in other words, What is the best way to communicate? The answer is that there is no one best way. The results of a given way of speaking will vary depending on the situation, the culture of the company, the relative rank of speakers, their linguistic styles, and how those styles interact with one another. Because of all those influences, any way of speaking could be perfect for communicating with one person in one situation and disastrous with someone else in another. The critical skill for managers is to become aware of

the workings and power of linguistic style, to make sure that people with something valuable to contribute get heard.

It may seem, for example, that running a meeting in an unstructured way gives equal opportunity to all. But awareness of the differences in conversational style makes it easy to see the potential for unequal access. Those who are comfortable speaking up in groups, who need little or no silence before raising their hands, or who speak out easily without waiting to be recognized are far more likely to get heard at meetings. Those who refrain from talking until it's clear that the previous speaker is finished, who wait to be recognized, and who are inclined to link their comments to those of others will do fine at a meeting where everyone else is following the same rules but will have a hard time getting heard in a meeting with people whose styles are more like the first pattern. Given the socialization typical of boys and girls, men are more likely to have learned the first style and women the second, making meetings more congenial for men than for women. It's common to observe women who participate actively in one-on-one discussions or in all-female groups but who are seldom heard in meetings with a large portion of men. On the other hand, there are women who share the style more common among men, and they run a different risk—of being seen as too aggressive.

A manager aware of those dynamics might devise any number of ways of ensuring that everyone's ideas are heard and credited. Although no single solution will fit all contexts, managers who understand the dynamics of linguistic style can develop more adaptive and flexible approaches to running or participating in meetings, mentoring or advancing the careers of others, evaluating performance, and so on. Talk is the lifeblood of managerial work, and understanding that different people have different ways of saying what they mean will make it possible to take advantage of the talents of people with a broad range of linguistic styles. As the workplace becomes more culturally diverse and business becomes more global, managers will need to become even better at reading interactions and more flexible in adjusting their own styles to the people with whom they interact.

Close Encounters

In May 1985, Brigitte Gerney was trapped beneath a 35-ton collapsed construction crane in New York City for six hours. Throughout her ordeal, she held the hand of rescue officer Paul Ragonese, who stayed by her side as heavy machinery moved the tons of twisted steel from her crushed legs. A stranger's touch gave her hope and the will to live.

Other means of communication can take place at a distance, but touch is the language of physical intimacy. And because it is, touch is the most powerful of all the communication channels—and the most carefully guarded and regulated.

From a mother's cradling embrace to a friend's comforting hug, or a lover's caress, touch has the special power to send messages of union and communion. Among strangers, that power is ordinarily held in check. Whether offering a handshake or a guiding arm, the toucher is careful to stay within the culture's narrowly prescribed limits lest the touch be misinterpreted. Touching between people with more personal relationships is also governed by silent cultural rules and restraints.

The rules of touch may be unspoken, but they're visible to anyone who takes the trouble to watch. Psychologist Richard Heslin at Purdue University, for instance, has proposed five categories of touch based on people's roles and relationships. Each category includes a special range of touches, best described by the quality of touch, the body areas touched and whether the touch is reciprocated.

Functional-professional touches are performed while the toucher fulfills a special role, such as that of doctor, barber or tailor. For people in these occupations, touch must be devoid of personal messages.

Social-polite touches are formal, limited to greeting and separating and to expressing appreciation among business associates and among strangers and acquaintances. The typical handshake reflects cordiality more than intimacy.

Friendship-warmth touches occur in the context of personal concern and caring, such as the relationships between extended-family members, friendly neighbors and close work mates. This category straddles the line between warmth and deep affection, a line where friendly touches move over into love touches.

Love-intimacy touches occur between close family members and friends in relationships where there is affection and caring.

Sexual-arousal touches occur in erotic-sexual contexts.

These categories are not hard and fast, since in various cultures and subcultures the rules differ about who can touch whom, in what contexts and what forms the touch may take. In the Northern European "noncontact cultures," overall touch rates are usually quite low. People from these cultures can seem very cold, especially to people from "contact cultures" such as those in the Mediterranean area, where there are much higher rates of touching, even between strangers.

In the United States, a particularly low-touch culture, we rarely see people touch one another in public. Other than in sports and children's play, the most we see of it is when people hold hands in the street, fondle babies or say hello and goodbye. Even on television shows, with the odd exceptions of hitting and kissing, there is little touching.

The cultural differences in contact can be quite dramatic, as researcher Sidney Jourard found in the 1960s when he studied touch between pairs of people in coffee shops around the world. There was more touch in certain cities (180 times an hour between couples in San Juan, Puerto Rico, and 110 times an hour in Paris, France) than in others (2 times an hour between couples in Gainesville, Florida, and 0 times an hour in London, England).

Those cultural contact patterns are embedded early, through child-rearing practices. Psychologist Janice Gibson and her colleagues at the University of Pittsburgh took to the playgrounds and beaches of Greece, the Soviet Union and the United States and compared the frequency and nature of touch between caregivers and children 2 to 5 years old. When it came to retrieving or punishing the children, touching rates were similar in all three countries. But on touches for soothing, holding and play, American children had significantly less contact than those from the other cultures. (Is that why we need bumper stickers to remind us: "Have you hugged your child today?")

Generalizations about different national or ethnic groups can be tricky, however. For example, despite widespread beliefs that Latin Americans are highly contact-oriented, when researcher Robert Shuter at Marquette University compared public contact between couples in Costa Rica, Colombia and Panama, he found that the Costa Ricans both touched and held their partners noticeably more than the couples did in the other two countries.

Within most cultures the rules and meanings of touch are different for men and women, as one recent study in the United States illustrates. Imagine yourself in a hospital bed, about to have major surgery. The nurse comes in to tell you what your operation and after-care will be like. She touches you briefly twice, once on the hand for a few seconds after she introduces herself and again on the arm for a full minute during the instruction period. As she leaves she shakes your hand.

Does this kind of brief reassuring touch add anything to her talk? Does it have any kind of impact on your nervousness or how you respond to the operation? Your reaction is likely to depend upon your gender.

Psychologist Sheryle Whitcher, while working as a graduate student with psychologist Jeffrey Fisher of the University of Connecticut, arranged for a group of surgery patients to be touched in the way described above during their preoperative information session, while other patients got only the information. Women had strikingly positive reactions to being touched; it lowered their blood pressure and anxiety both before surgery and for more than an hour afterwards. But men found the experience upsetting; both their blood pressure and their anxiety rose and stayed elevated in response to being touched.

Why did touch produce such strikingly different responses? Part of the answer may lie in the fact that men in the United States often find it harder to acknowledge dependency and fear than women do; thus, for men, a well-intentioned touch may be a threatening reminder of their vulnerability.

These gender differences are fostered by early experiences, particularly in handling and caretaking. Differences in parents' use of touch with their infant children help to shape and model "male" and "female" touch patterns: Fathers use touch more for play, while mothers use it more for soothing and grooming. The children's gender also affects the kinds of touches they receive. In the United States, for example, girls receive more affectionate touches (kissing, cuddling, holding) than boys do.

By puberty, tactile experiences with parents and peers have already programmed differences in boys' and girls' touching behavior and their use of personal space. Some results of this training are evident when men and women greet people. In one study, psychologists Paul Greenbaum and Howard Rosenfeld of the University of Kansas watched how travelers at the Kansas City International Airport touched people who greeted them. Women greeted women and men more physically, with mutual lip kisses, embraces and more kinds of touch and holding for longer periods of time. In contrast, when men greeted men, most just shook hands and left it at that.

How do you feel about touching and being touched? Are you relaxed and comfortable, or does such contact make you feel awkward and tense? Your comfort with touch may be linked to your personality. Psychologist Knud Larsen and student Jeff LeRoux at Oregon State University looked at how people's personality traits are related to their attitudes toward touching between people of the same sex. The researchers measured touch attitudes through questions such as, "I enjoy persons of my sex who are comfortable with touching," "I sometimes enjoy hugging friends of the same sex" and "Physical expression of affection between persons of the same sex is healthy." Even though men were generally less comfortable about same-sex touching than women were, the more authoritarian and rigid people of both sexes were the least comfortable.

A related study by researchers John Deethardt and Debbie Hines at Texas Tech University in Lubbock, Texas, examined personality and attitudes toward being touched by opposite-sex friends and lovers and by same-sex friends. Touch attitudes were tapped with such questions as, "When I am with my girl-/-boyfriend I really like to touch that person to show affection," "When I tell a same-sex intimate friend that I have just gotten a divorce, I want that person to touch me" and "I enjoy an opposite-sex acquaintance touching me when we greet each other." Regardless of gender, people who were comfortable with touching were also more talkative, cheerful, socially dominant and nonconforming; those discomforted by touch tended to be more emotionally unstable and socially withdrawn.

A recent survey of nearly 4,000 undergraduates by researchers Janis Andersen, Peter Andersen and Myron Lustig of San Diego State University revealed that, regardless of gender, people who were less comfortable about touching were also more apprehensive about communicating and had lower self-esteem.

Several other studies have shown that people who are more comfortable with touch are less afraid and suspicious of other people's motives and intentions and have less anxiety and tension in their everyday lives. Not surprisingly, another study showed they are also likely to be more satisfied with their bodies and physical appearance.

These different personality factors play themselves out most revealingly in the intimacy of love relationships. Couples stay together and break apart for many reasons, including the way each partner expresses and reacts to affection and intimacy. For some, feelings and words are enough; for others, touch and physical intimacy are more critical.

In the film *Annie Hall,* Woody Allen and Diane Keaton are shown split-screen as each talks to an analyst about their sexual relationship. When the analyst asks how often they have sex, he answers, "Hardly ever, maybe three times a week," while she describes it as "constantly, three times a week."

How important is physical intimacy in close relationships? What role does touch play in marital satisfaction? Psychologists Betsy Tolstedt and Joseph Stokes of the University of Illinois at Chicago tried to find out by interviewing and observing couples. They used three measures of intimacy: emotional intimacy (feelings of closeness, support, tolerance); verbal intimacy (disclosure of emotions, feelings, opinions); and physical intimacy (satisfaction with "companionate" and sexual touch). The researchers also measured marital satisfaction and happiness, along with conflicts and actual separations and legal actions.

They found that each form of intimacy made its own contribution to marital satisfaction, but—perhaps surprisingly to some—physical intimacy mattered the least of the three. Conflict and divorce potential were most connected to dissatisfaction with emotional and verbal intimacy.

Touch intimacy may not usually have the power to make or break marriages, but it can sway strangers and even people close to you, often without their knowledge. The expressions "to put the touch on someone" and "that person is an easy touch" refer to the persuasive power of touch. Indeed, research shows that it is harder to say no to someone who makes a request when it is accompanied by a touch.

Politicians know this well. Ignoring security concerns, political candidates plunge into the crowd to kiss babies and "press the flesh." Even a quick handshake leaves a lasting impression—a personal touch—that can pay off later at election time.

A momentary and seemingly incidental touch can establish a positive, temporary bond between strangers, making them more helpful, compliant, generous and positive. In one experiment in a library, a slight hand brush in the course of returning library cards to patrons was enough to influence patrons' positive attitudes toward the library and its staff. In another study, conducted in restaurants, a fleeting touch paid off in hard cash. Waitresses who touched their customers on the hand or shoulder as they returned change received a larger percentage of the bill as their tip. Even though they risked crossing role boundaries by touching customers in such familiar ways, their ingratiating service demeanor offset any threat.

In certain situations, touch can be discomforting because it signals power. Psychologist Nancy Henley of the University of California, Los Angeles, after observing the touch behavior of people as they went about their daily lives, has suggested that higher-status individuals enjoy more touch liberties with their lower-status associates. To Henley, who has noted how touch signals one's place in the status-dominance hierarchy, there is even a sexist "politics of touch." She has found that women generally rank lower than men in the touch hierarchy, very much like the secretary–boss, student–teacher and worker–foreman relationships. In all of these, it is considered unseemly for lower-status individuals to put their hands on superiors. Rank does have its touching privileges.

The rules of the status hierarchy are so powerful that people can infer status differences from watching other people's touch behavior. In one experiment by psychologists Brenda Major and Richard Heslin of Purdue University, observers could see only the silhouettes of pairs of people facing each other, with one touching the other on the shoulder. They judged the toucher to be more assertive and of a higher status than the person touched. Had the touch been reciprocal, status differences would have disappeared.

Psychologist Alvin G. Goldstein and student Judy Jeffords at the University of Missouri have sharpened our understanding of touch and status through their field study of touch among legislators during a Missouri state legislative session. Observers positioned themselves in the gallery and systematically recorded who initiated touch during the many floor conversations. Based on a status formula that included committee leadership and membership, they discovered that among these male peers, the lower-status men were the ones most likely to initiate touch.

When roles are clearly different, so that one individual has control or power over the other, such as a boss and a secretary, then touch usually reflects major dominance or status differences in the relationship. But when roles are more diffuse and overlapping, so that people are almost equal in power—as the legislators were—then lower-status people may try to establish more intimate connections with their more powerful and higher-status colleagues by making physical contact with them.

Touching has a subtle and often ambivalent role in most settings. But there is one special circumstance in which touch is permitted and universally positive: In sports, teammates encourage, applaud and console each other generously through touch. In Western cultures, for men especially, hugs and slaps on the behind are permitted among athletes, even though they are very rarely seen between heterosexual men outside the sports arena. The intense enthusiasm legitimizes tactile expressions of emotion that would otherwise be seen as homosexually threatening.

Graduate student Charles Anderton and psychologist Robert Heckel of the University of South Carolina studied touch in the competitive context of all-male or all-female championship swim meets by recording each instance of touch after success and failure. Regardless of sex, winners were touched similarly, on average six times more than losers, with most of the touches to the hand and some to the back or shoulders; only a small percent were to the head or buttocks.

This swimming study only looked at touch between same-sex teammates, since swim meets have separate races for men and women. Would touch patterns be the same for mixed-gender teams, or would men and women be inhibited about initiating and receiving touches, as they are in settings outside of sports? Psychologists David Smith, Frank Willis and Joseph Gier at the University of Missouri studied touching behavior of men and women in bowling alleys in Kansas City, Missouri, during mixed-league competition. They found almost no differences between men and women in initiating or receiving touches.

Without the social vocabulary of touch, life would be cold, mechanical, distant, rational, verbal. We are created in the intimate union of two bodies and stay connected to the body of one until the cord is cut. Even after birth, we need touch for survival. Healthy human infants deprived of touch and handling for long periods develop a kind of infant depression that leads to withdrawal and apathy and, in extreme cases, wasting away to death.

As people develop, touch assumes symbolic meaning as the primary system for expressing and experiencing affection, inclusion and control. Deprived of those gestures and their meanings, the world might be more egalitarian, but it would also be far more frightening, hostile and chilly. And who would understand why a stranger's touch meant life to Brigitte Gerney?

Flirting Fascination

It's been trivialized, even demonized, but the coquettish behavior indulged in by men and women alike is actually a vital silent language exchanging critical—and startling—information about our general health and reproductive fitness.

"She was," he proclaimed, "so extraordinarily beautiful that I nearly laughed out loud. She...[was] famine, fire, destruction and plague...the only true begetter. Her breasts were apocalyptic, they would topple empires before they withered...her body was a miracle of construction...She was unquestionably gorgeous. She was lavish. She was a dark, unyielding largesse. She was, in short, too bloody much...Those huge violet blue eyes...had an odd glint...Aeons passed, civilizations came and went while these cosmic headlights examined my flawed personality. Every pockmark on my face became a crater of the moon."

So Richard Burton described his first sight of a 19-year-old Elizabeth Taylor. He didn't record what happened next, but a growing cadre of scientists would bet their lab coats and research budgets that sometime after that breath-catching, gut-gripping moment of instant mutual awareness, Liz tossed her hair, swayed her hips, arched her feet, giggled, gazed wide-eyed, flicked her tongue over her lips and extended that apocalyptic chest, and that Dick, for his part, arched his back, stretched his pecs, imperceptibly swayed his pelvis in a tame Elvis performance, swaggered, laughed loudly, tugged his tie and clasped the back of his neck, which had the thoroughly engaging effect of stiffening his stance and puffing his chest.

What eventually got these two strangers from across the fabled crowded room to each other's side was what does it for all of us—in a word, flirtation, the capacity to automatically turn our actions into sexual semaphores signaling interest in the opposite sex as predictably and instinctively as peacocks fan their tails, codfish thrust their pelvic fins or mice twitch their noses and tilt their backs to draw in the object of their attention.

Long trivialized and even demonized, flirtation is gaining new respectability thanks to a spate of provocative studies of animal and human behavior in many parts of the world. The capacity of men and women to flirt and to be receptive to flirting turns out to be a remarkable set of behaviors embedded deep in our psyches. Every come-hither look sent and every sidelong glance received are mutually understood signals of such transcendent history and beguiling sophistication that only now are they beginning to yield clues to the psychological and biological wisdom they encode.

This much is clear so far: flirting is nature's solution to the problem every creature faces in a world full of potential mates—how to choose the right one. We all need a partner who is not merely fertile but genetically different as well as healthy enough to promise viable offspring, provide some kind of help in the hard job of parenting and offer some social compatibility.

Our animal and human ancestors needed a means of quickly and safely judging the value of potential mates without "going all the way" and risking pregnancy with every possible candidate they encountered. Flirting achieved that end, offering a relatively risk-free set of signals with which to sample the field, try out sexual wares and exchange vital information about candidates' general health and reproductive fitness.

"Flirting is a negotiation process that takes place after there has been some initial attraction," observes Steven W. Gangestad, Ph.D., an evolutionary psychologist at the University of New Mexico in Albuquerque who is currently studying how people choose their mates. "Two people have to share with each other the information that they are attracted, and then test each other" on an array of attributes. Simply announcing, 'I'm attracted to you, are you attracted to me?' doesn't work so well. "It works much better to reveal this and have it revealed to you in smaller doses," explains Gangestad. "The flirting then becomes something that enhances the attraction."

It is an axiom of science that traits and behaviors crucial to survival—such as anything to do with attraction and sex—require, and get, a lot of an animal's resources. All mammals and most animals (including birds, fish, even fruit flies) engage in complicated and energy-intensive plots and plans, for attracting others to the business of sex. That is, they flirt.

From nature's standpoint, the goal of life is the survival of our DNA. Sex is the way most animals gain the flexibility to healthfully sort and mix their genes. Getting sex, in turn, is wholly dependent on attracting attention and being attracted. And flirting is the way a person focuses the attention of a specific member of the opposite sex. If our ancestors hadn't done it well enough, we wouldn't be around to discuss it now.

A silent language of elaborate visual and other gestures, flirting is "spoken" by intellect-driven people as well as instinct-driven animals. The very universality of flirting, preserved through evolutionary history from insects to man, suggests that a flirting plan is wired into us, and that it has been embedded in our genes and in our brain's operating system the same way and for the same reasons that every other sexual trait has been—by trial and error, with conservation of what works best.

Like any other language, flirting may be deployed in ways subtle or coarse, adolescent or suave. Nevertheless, it has evolved just like pheasant spurs and lion manes: to advertise ourselves to the opposite sex.

Flirtation first emerged as a subject of serious scrutiny a scant 30 years ago. Irenäus Eibl-Eibesfeldt, now honorary director of the Ludwig-Boltzmann Institute for Urban Ethology in Vienna, was already familiar with the widespread dances and prances of mate-seeking animals. Then he discovered that people in dozens of cultures, from the South Sea Islands to the Far East, Western Europe, Africa and South America, similarly engage in a fairly fixed repertoire of gestures to test sexual availability and interest.

Having devised a special camera that allowed him to point the lens in one direction while actually photographing in another, he "caught" couples on film during their flirtations, and discovered, for one thing, that women, from primitives who have no written language to those who read *Cosmo* and *Marie Claire,* use nonverbal signals that are startlingly alike. On Eibl-Eibesfeldt's screen flickered identical flirtation messages: a female smiling at a male, then arching her brows to make her eyes wide, quickly lowering her lids and, tucking her chin slightly down and coyly to the side, averting her gaze, followed within seconds, almost on cue, by putting her hands on or near her mouth and giggling.

Regardless of language, socioeconomic status or religious upbringing, couples who continued flirting placed a palm up on the table or knees, reassuring the prospective partner of harmlessness. They shrugged their shoulders, signifying helplessness. Women exaggeratedly extended their neck, a sign of vulnerability and submissiveness.

For Eibl-Eibesfeldt, these gestures represented primal behaviors driven by the old parts of our brain's evolutionary memory. A woman presenting her extended neck to a man she wants is not much different, his work suggested, than a gray female wolf's submissiveness to a dominant male she's after.

Since then, researchers have turned up the intensity, looking, for example, at compressed bouts of flirting and courtship in their natural habitat—hotel bars and cocktail lounges. From observations at a Hyatt hotel cocktail lounge, researchers documented a set of signals that whisks a just-met man and woman from barroom to bedroom. Her giggles and soft laughs were followed by hair twirling and head-tossing; he countered with body arching, leaning back in the chair and placing his arms behind head, not unlike a pigeon puffing his chest.

If all went well, a couple would invariably progress from touching themselves to touching each other. The first tentative contacts could be termed "lint-picking." She would lift an imaginary mote from his lapel; he would brush a real or imaginary crumb from her lips. Their heads moved closer, their hands pressed out in front of them on the table, their fingers inches from each other's, playing with salt shakers or utensils. Whoops! An "accidental" finger touch, then perhaps some digital "dirty dancing," more touching and leaning in cheek to cheek. By body language alone, the investigators could predict which pairs would ride up the elevators together.

Social psychologist Timothy Perper, Ph.D., an independent scholar and writer based in Philadelphia, and anthropologist David Givens, Ph.D., spent months in dimly lit lounges documenting these flirtation rituals. Like the ear wiggles, nose flicks and back arches that signal "come hither" in rodents, the women smiled, gazed, swayed, giggled, licked their lips, and aided and abetted by the wearing of high heels, they swayed their backs, forcing their buttocks to tilt out and up and their chests to thrust forward.

The men arched, stretched, swiveled, and made grand gestures of whipping out lighters and lighting up cigarettes. They'd point their chins in the air with a cigarette dangling in their mouth, then loop their arms in a wide arc to put the lighter away. Their swaggers, bursts of laughter and grandiose gestures were an urban pantomime of the prancing and preening indulged in by male baboons and gorillas in the wild. Man or monkey the signals all said, "Look at me, trust me, I'm powerful, but I won't hurt you." And "I don't want anything much…yet."

All the silent swaying, leaning, smiling, bobbing and gazing eventually brought a pair into full frontal alignment. Face to face, they indulged in simultaneous touching of everything from eyeglasses to fingertips to crossed legs. Says Perper, "This kind of sequence—attention, recognition, dancing, synchronization—is fundamental to courtship. From the *Song of Songs* until today, the sequence is the same: look, talk, touch, kiss, do the deed."

The fact that flirting is a largely nonexplicit drama doesn't mean that important information isn't being delivered in those silent signals. By swaying her hips, or emphasizing them in a form-fitting dress, a flirtatious woman is riveting attention on her pelvis, suggesting its ample capacity for bearing a child. By arching her brows and exaggerating her gaze, her eyes appear large in her face, the way a child's eyes do, advertising, along with giggles, her youth and "submissiveness." By drawing her tongue along her lips, she compels attention to what many biologists believe are facial echoes of vaginal lips, transmitting sexual maturity and her interest in sex. By coyly averting her gaze and playing "hard to get," she communicates her unwillingness to give sex to just anyone or to someone who will love her and leave her.

For his part, by extending a strong chin and jaw, expanding and showing off pectoral muscles and a hairy chest, flashing money, laughing loudly or resonantly, smiling, and doing all these things without accosting a woman, a man signals his ability to protect offspring, his resources and the testosterone-driven vitality of his sperm as well as the tamer side of him that is willing to stick around, after the sex, for fatherhood. It's the behavioral equivalent of "I'll respect you in the morning."

"I can't tell you why I was attracted to her the instant she walked into my office," recalls a 32-year-old screenwriter. "It was chemistry. We both flirted and we both knew it would lead nowhere. I'm happily married." The statement is almost stupefyingly commonplace, but also instructive. Each of us "turns on" not to mankind or womankind but to a particular member of the opposite sex. Certain stances, personal styles, gestures, intimations of emotional compatibility, perhaps even odors, automatically arouse our interest because they not only instantly advertise genetic fitness but they match the template of Desired Mate we all carry in our mind's eye.

As with Dick and Liz, or any couple, the rational, thinking part of their brains got them to the place where girl met boy; they had the event on their calendars, planned what they would wear, arranged for transportation. But in that first meeting, their capacity to react with their instinct and hearts, not their heads, overrode their cognitive brains. Otherwise, they might not have had the nerve to look at each other.

The rational brain is always on the lookout for dangers, for complexities, for reasons to act or not act. If every time man and woman met they immediately considered all the possible risks and vulnerabilities they might face if they mated or had children, they'd run screaming from the room.

It's no secret that the brain's emotionally loaded limbic system sometimes operates independently of the more rational neocortex, such as in the face of danger, when the fight-or-flight response is activated. Similarly, when the matter is sex—another situation on which survival depends—we also react without even a neural nod to the neocortex. Instead, the flirtational operating system appears to kick in without conscious consent. If, at the moment they had met, Dick and Liz had stopped to consider all the possible outcomes of a relationship, they both would have been old before they got close enough to speak.

The moment of attraction, in fact, mimics a kind of brain damage. At the University of Iowa, where he is professor and head of neurology, Antonio Damasio, M.D., has found that people with damage to the connection between their limbic structures and the higher brain are smart and rational—but unable to make decisions. They bring commitment phobia to a whole new level. In attraction, we don't stop and think, we react, operating on a "gut" feeling, with butterflies, giddiness, sweaty palms and flushed faces brought on by the reactivity of the emotional brain. We suspend intellect at least long enough to propel us to the next step in the mating game—flirtation.

Somewhere beyond flirtation, as a relationship progresses, courtship gets under way, and with it, intellectual processes resume. Two adults can then evaluate potential mates more rationally, think things over and decide whether to love, honor and cherish. But at the moment of attraction and flirtation, bodies, minds and sense are temporarily hostage to the more ancient parts of the brain, the impulsive parts that humans share with animals.

If flirting is a form of self promotion, nature demands a certain amount of truth in advertising. "For a signaling system to convey something meaningful about a desirable attribute, there has to be some honesty," explains Gangestad, "so that if you don't have the attribute you can't fake it." Just as the extravagant colors of birds that figure so prominently in their flirting rituals proclaim the health of animals so plumed, humans have some signals that can't be faked.

Waist–hip ratio is likely one of them. It's no secret that men snap to attention and even go dry at the mouth at the sight of a shapely woman. Science has now calculated just how curvy a woman has to be to garner such appreciation: the waist must measure no more than 60 to 70% of her hip circumference. It is a visual signal that not only figures powerfully in attraction, but is a moving force in flirtation. And unless steel-boned corsets stage a comeback, it is an attribute that just can't be put into play unless it is real.

In simplest terms, says Gangestad, waist–hip ratio is an honest indicator of health. Studies have shown that hourglass-shaped women are less likely than other women to get diabetes and cardiac disease. They are also most likely to bear children, as hips take their shape at puberty from the feminizing hormone estrogen.

"The literature shows that women with a 0.7 waist–hip ratio have a sex-typical hormone profile in the relationship of estrogen to testosterone, and that women with a straighter torso, meaning a waist–hip ratio closer to 1:1, indeed have lower fertility," Gangestad reports. "It appears that males have evolved to pay attention to this cue that ancestrally was related to fertility."

The virtually visceral responsiveness to physical features in flirtation may also be as good a guarantee as one can get that a potential partner shapes up on a hidden but crucial aspect of health: immunity to disease. Scientists know that the testosterone that gives men jutting jaws, prominent noses and big brows, and, to a lesser extent, the estrogen that gives women soft features and curving hips, also suppresses the ability to fight disease. But looks have their own logic, and bodies and faces that are exemplars of their gender signal that their bearer has biological power to spare; after all, he or she has survived despite the hormonal "handicap."

Take the case of such elaborate male ornamentation as peacock tails and stag antlers. In the 1980s,

evolutionary biologists William Hamilton and Marlena Zuk linked such features to inborn resistance to disease parasites. Antlers and tail feathers are known to be attractive to females of their species and are major machinery of flirtation. But developing and maintaining such extravagant equipment is costly, taking huge nutritional resources and even slowing the animals down, making them more vulnerable to predators.

The only animals that can afford such ornamentation are those with tip-top constitutions. So, like big bones, big horns, big tails and big spurs in animals, jutting jaws are honest markers for a healthy immune system. Scientists point out that such features are in fact respected by other men as well as attractive to women. Studies show that tall, square-jawed men achieve higher ranks in the military than do those with weak chins, and that taller men are over-represented in boardrooms as well as bedrooms.

Whatever specific physical features men and women are primed to respond to, they all have a quality in common—symmetry. That is, attributes deemed attractive have an outward appearance of evenness and right–left balance. Unlike the color and condition of tail feathers, symmetry serves not so much as an honest marker of current health status, but as a signal of a general capacity to be healthy. Symmetry, says Gangestad, is "a footprint left by your whole developmental history." It alone explains why Elizabeth Taylor, Denzel Washington and Queen Nefertiti are universally recognized as beautiful—and full of sex appeal.

"Bilateral symmetry is a hot topic these days," beams Albert Thornhill, a biologist at the University of New Mexico and a pioneer in the study of symmetry in attraction and flirtation. He and Gangestad believe it is a marker of "developmental precision," the extent to which a genetic blueprint is realized in the flesh despite all the environmental and other perturbations that tend to throw development off course.

Recent studies conducted by the two demonstrate not only that women prefer symmetrical men, they prefer them at a very specific time—when they are most fertile. "We found that female preferences change across the menstrual cycle," Gangestad reports. "We think the finding says something about the way female mate preferences are designed. Because the preference for male symmetry is specific to the time of ovulation, when women are most likely to conceive, we think women are choosing a mate who is going to provide better genes for healthy babies. It's an indirect benefit, rather than a direct or material benefit to the female herself."

In their study, 52 women rated the attractiveness of 42 men—by their smell. Each of the men slept in one T-shirt for two nights, after which the women were given a whiff of it. Prior to the smell test, all the men had undergone careful calipered measurement of 10 features, from ear width to finger length. Those whose body features were the most symmetrical were the ones whose smells were most preferred, but only among women who were in the ovulatory phase of their menstrual cycle. At other times in their cycle, women had no preference either for symmetrical or asymmetrical males.

The preference for symmetry is not limited to humans. Thornhill first stumbled upon symmetry two decades ago, during experiments with scorpion flies in Australia, Japan and Europe. He noticed that females chose particular male flies on the basis of the level and quality of "nuptial gifts," nutrients passed to the female during courtship and mating.

"That was the first inkling I had that insects were very sophisticated about their mating strategies," Thornhill recalls. But the more time he spent recording the sexual lives of scorpion flies, the more he realized that the females were selecting partners long before they sampled any gifts, and they were reckoning by the symmetry of the males' wings. "I discovered that males and females with the most symmetrical wings had the most mating success and that by using wing symmetry, I—and presumably the fly—could predict reproductive fitness better than scent or any other factor."

Since then, Thornhill and colleagues around the world have conducted more than 20 separate tests of symmetry of everything from eyes, ears and nostrils to limbs, wrists and fingers. Even if they never speak a word or get closer than a photograph, women view symmetrical men as more dominant, powerful, richer and better sex and marriage material. And symmetrical men view themselves the same way! Men, for their part, rate symmetrical women as more fertile, more attractive, healthier and better sex and marriage material, too—just as such women see themselves as having a competitive edge in the mating sweepstakes.

Flirtation, it turns out, is most successful among the most symmetrical. Men's bodily symmetry matches up with the number of lifetime sex partners they report having. Symmetrical men also engage in more infidelity in their romantic relationships—"extra-pair copulations" in the language of the lab. And they get to sex more quickly after meeting a romantic partner compared to asymmetrical men. They lose their virginity earlier in life, too.

When women flirt with symmetrical men, what their instincts are reading might once have been banned in Boston. Male symmetry is also shorthand for female sexual satisfaction. Gangestad and Thornhill surveyed 86 couples in 1995 and found that symmetrical men "fire off more female copulatory orgasms than asymmetrical men." Women with symmetrical partners were more than twice as likely to climax during intercourse. Thrills are only a short-term payoff, however; female orgasm is really a shill for fertilization, pulling sperm from the vagina into the cervix.

Successful as symmetrical men are at flirtation, it's only their presumably better genes that women really want. Women definitely do not prefer symmetrical men for long-term relationships. There's a definite downside to getting someone with really good DNA. Symmetry, Gangestad explains, affords those men who possess it to take a dastardly mating strategy. His studies show that symmetrical men invest less in any one romantic relationship—less time, less attention, less money. And less fidelity. They're too busy spreading around their symmetry. "They also tend to sexualize other women more," Gangestad reports. "It may be that males who can have the most access without giving a lot of investment take advantage of that."

A guy who will stick around and help out with parenting is on most women's wish list of qualities in a mate, Gangestad concedes. "I wouldn't exclude the possibility that men have been doing some direct parental care for some time, and so a preference for that might also have an evolutionary basis." But also on a woman's wish list from an evolutionary standpoint would be someone who is going to provide good genes for healthy babies. Unfortunately, says the Albuquerque researcher, "what can and does happen in a mating market is that those things don't all come in the same package."

Although the signals and semaphores of flirting are largely devoid of explicit content, the style with which one flirts can be downright revelatory. "*How* a person flirts honestly reveals some important qualities about an individual," says Gangestad. Symmetry isn't everything; there are signals of more subtle skills.

In some species, the females watch the males fight each other and then choose the one who can hold the central territory. But we humans are more differently evolved creatures with more complex lives in which our higher faculties presumably contribute something to success, whether it's surviving in primitive equatorial caves or sophisticated urban ones.

Enter creativity, humor and intelligence. Deployed in flirting, they disclose more about an individual person than all the antlers do about leching animals. "They are likely saying something important about our very viability," says Gangestad. "When we can engage in humor and creativity, they act as an honest signal that we've got a reasonably well put together nervous system. They may indicate there's some developmental integrity underneath our brain." And a certain ability to withstand whatever challenges life throws a person's way.

What's more, our basic social ability to "read" another's facial gestures and emotional expressions acts as a fact-checking system in flirtation. It enables us to glimpse the tone of a prospective mate's inner life and to check for the presence or absence of psychological weakness. And in fact, women are pretty good at doping out information about such important attributes—even when they get very little time to make a judgment.

In a recent set of studies, Gangestad and a colleague extracted one-minute segments from more extensive videotaped interviews with men not in committed relationships. The brief segments were then shown to women who were asked to rate the men on a variety of characteristics, including how attractive they'd be in a pair relationship. The women were able to make judgments about each man's intelligence, ability to be caring and how nice he seemed. They also paid attention to another set of characteristics—how effective a man was likely to be with other males, how socially influential he was.

The men who were rated most attractive for long-term relationships scored high on both sets of characteristics. But what may be most notable about the study was that women's observations, from a mere snippet of videotape, were remarkably accurate. They correlated closely with the men's ratings of their own personality.

After two people share the information that they are attracted, then, through the way they flirt, they may unwittingly let on more about themselves. "It becomes a testing ground as well as an information-revealing process," says Gangestad.

Thus, while we appear to be preprogrammed with an urge to wile or wiggle our way onto another's mental radar screen, we also seem psychologically constituted to pay rapt attention to looks and actions intended to be sexually appealing. Otherwise, neither Liz and Dick nor any two contenders would have a reliable, safe or peaceful means of communicating attraction and getting to the more durable business of courtship, mating and commitment to the offspring that will carry our DNA into the next generation.

PART V

CULTURAL ANTHROPOLOGY

Cultural anthropology has two main areas of study. One, termed *ethnography,* is the intensive study, description, and analysis of a specific group of people and their culture. The other, *ethnology,* is the systematic comparison of materials across cultural boundaries, with the aim of detecting and specifying accurate generalizations (formerly called laws) about human behavior and culture. The concept of *culture* is central to both ethnography and ethnology.

In recent years it has been used more broadly to describe the specific beliefs, interpersonal interactions, patterns of behavior, modes of adaptation, and so on among different subgroups within society—which, more properly, should be described as *subcultures.* Thus, we speak of corporate culture, African American culture, pro-athletic culture, hip-hop culture, academic culture, and so on.

But what, exactly, is *culture?* Surprisingly, although it is the central concept of anthropology, it is difficult to find exact agreement on the meaning of the term among anthropologists. Depending on their interests, scholars emphasize the symbolic nature of culture, its function as a mechanism of adaptation, the ways in which it structures our perception of the world, or the ways it patterns behavior. Nevertheless, it is possible to find agreement among anthropologists with regard to some basic aspects of culture.

1. *Culture is central to human existence.* The biological and cultural sides of humankind evolved together, constantly affecting the other's course. The concept *human being* and the concept *culture* are thus inseparable.

2. *Culture is not inherited through the genes.* Each person acquires his or her culture through interaction with other members of the group(s) into which she or he is born. In other words, culture is learned.

3. *Not only is culture learned, but also everything that is learned is culture.* All human knowledge, activities, beliefs, values, mores, schemes for organizing information about the world, languages, philosophical systems, technologies, art, and major behavioral patterns are learned and hence are aspects of culture.

4. *Culture is a group phenomenon.* The growing infant does not invent a culture for itself; it learns the culture of its society. Left to its own devices, an infant cannot invent culture. Indeed, if a child is deprived of the opportunity to learn a language by the time it is five or six, it is probably unlikely ever to be able to learn one afterward.

5. *Culture is patterned.* All cultures of the world consist of many facets and elements. But these are not randomly thrown together like marbles in a bag or patches on a quilt. There are systematic relationships among the elements of a culture, and change in one area is likely to cause stress or change in other areas.

6. *Culture is symbolic.* This means that all cultural phenomena have meanings beyond their own existence. For example, a cat, in American culture, is not just an animal with the label *cat.* It "has nine lives," is "stealthy," and is "independent." A cat, then, as a part of our culture, represents a set of meanings: in other words, it is a symbol. In other cultures, however, *cat* represents a different set of meanings: In ancient Egypt, cats were considered divine; in some contemporary Asian societies, cats are just another item on the menu—along with rice, beef, snakes, rats, and vegetables. Culture, therefore, provides the backdrop of shared meanings against which all things are experienced.

As you can see, the subject of cultural anthropology is vast. It embodies the study of virtually every aspect of human behavior—from how you nourish yourself to how you feel about yourself and others, from your religion (or lack of one) to how you drive a car.

For convenience, I have organized the articles in this part into seven topics, although I certainly have not come close to covering all areas of cultural anthropology. Nonetheless, I offer you interesting, and, I hope, thought-provoking reading in some of the most important areas.

FIELDWORK

For most anthropologists, fieldwork is one of the most significant experiences of their lives. Few anthropologists return from the field unchanged, and for many, the personal changes are quite deep and enduring. In a distant place among strangers, the fieldworker is cut off from the people and patterns that gave his or her life meaning and in terms of which she or he built a sense of self. In a very real sense, the fieldworker becomes childlike: understanding little, incompetent to perform locally valued tasks, utterly dependent on the good will of others for virtually everything. Like a child, the fieldworker starts to build a social identity; to a great measure, the success of the research will depend on how well she or he succeeds in accomplishing this task. Not the least of fieldwork's challenges is to come to terms with the world view of the hosts and research subjects—which frequently is at significant variance with the fieldworker's own world view.

"Shakespeare in the Bush" (Article 32), by Laura Bohannan, and "Eating Christmas in the Kalahari" (Article 33), by Richard B. Lee, both deal with the problems of cross-cultural (mis)understanding. It is inevitable that the fieldworker will misunderstand—and be misunderstood by—the people she or he is studying. Good researchers, however, use instances of misunderstanding as instruments of investigation into the divergent premises of the culture of their subjects as well as their own culture. The result can be a much deeper understanding of both.

One of the filters through which a fieldworker views and communicates his or her experiences is language. That is the lesson of Horace Miner's classic article, "Body Ritual among the Nacirema," Article 34. Without giving away the whole story, suffice it to say for now that the language used by the researcher in reporting on the behavior of his or her subjects can make them seem much more foreign than they really are.

Sometimes the customs of other people seem strange, based on superstition, dysfunctional, or even just plain crazy. But often, upon scientific investigation, it turns out these strange customs are not crazy at all, but rather, very much based in reality.

For centuries, late each night in June, farmers in the Peruvian and Bolivian Andes have observed the stars in the Pleiades constellation. If the stars appear big and bright, the farmers know to plant their potato crop at the usual time four months later. But if the stars appear dim, the planting is delayed for several weeks.

Or consider the Masai of East Africa, whose high-fat diet appears to be a prescription for a heart attack. It turns out that both these practices—and many others by preliterate peoples around the world—most definitely have a sound basis in science. In Article 35, "Now the Ancient Ways Are Less Mysterious," Henry Fountain explores these and other seemingly curious customs, and spells out their scientific basis.

Laura Bohannan

Shakespeare in the Bush

Just before I left Oxford for the Tiv in West Africa, conversation turned to the season at Stratford. "You Americans," said a friend, "often have difficulty with Shakespeare. He was, after all, a very English poet, and one can easily misinterpret the universal by misunderstanding the particular."

I protested that human nature is pretty much the same the whole world over; at least the general plot and motivation of the greater tragedies would always be clear—everywhere—although some details of custom might have to be explained and difficulties of translation might produce other slight changes. To end an argument we could not conclude, my friend gave me a copy of *Hamlet* to study in the African bush: it would, he hoped, lift my mind above its primitive surroundings, and possibly I might, by prolonged meditation, achieve the grace of correct interpretation.

It was my second field trip to that African tribe, and I thought myself ready to live in one of its remote sections—an area difficult to cross even on foot. I eventually settled on the hillock of a very knowledgeable old man, the head of a homestead of some hundred and forty people, all of whom were either his close relatives or their wives and children. Like the other elders of the vicinity, the old man spent most of his time performing ceremonies seldom seen these days in the more accessible parts of the tribe. I was delighted. Soon there would be three months of enforced isolation and leisure, between the harvest that takes place just before the rising of the swamps and the clearing of new farms when the water goes down. Then, I thought, they would have even more time to perform ceremonies and explain them to me.

I was quite mistaken. Most of the ceremonies demanded the presence of elders from several homesteads. As the swamps rose, the old men found it too difficult to walk from one homestead to the next, and the ceremonies gradually ceased. As the swamps rose even higher, all activities but one came to an end. The women brewed beer from maize and millet. Men, women, and children sat on their hillocks and drank it.

People began to drink at dawn. By midmorning the whole homestead was singing, dancing, and drumming. When it rained, people had to sit inside their huts: there they drank and sang or they drank and told stories. In any case, by noon or before, I either had to join the party or retire to my own hut and my books. "One does not discuss serious matters when there is beer. Come, drink with us." Since I lacked their capacity for the thick native beer, I spent more and more time with *Hamlet.* Before the end of the second month, grace descended on me. I was quite sure that *Hamlet* had only one possible interpretation, and that one universally obvious.

Early every morning, in the hope of having some serious talk before the beer party, I used to call on the old man at his reception hut—a circle of posts supporting a thatched roof above a low mud wall to keep out wind and rain. One day I crawled through the low doorway and found most of the men of the homestead sitting huddled in their ragged cloths on stools, low plank beds, and reclining chairs, warming themselves against the chill of the rain around a smoky fire. In the center were three pots of beer. The party had started.

The old man greeted me cordially. "Sit down and drink." I accepted a large calabash full of beer, poured some into a small drinking gourd, and tossed it down. Then I poured some more into the same gourd for the man second in seniority to my host before I handed my calabash over to a young man for further distribution. Important people shouldn't ladle beer themselves.

"It is better like this," the old man said, looking at me approvingly and plucking at the thatch that had caught in my hair. "You should sit and drink with us more often. Your servants tell me that when you are not with us, you sit inside your hut looking at a paper."

The old man was acquainted with four kinds of "papers": tax receipts, bride price receipts, court fee receipts, and letters. The messenger who brought him letters from the chief used them mainly as a badge of office, for he always knew what was in them and told the old man. Personal letters for the few who had relatives in the government or mission stations were kept until someone went to a large market where there was a letter writer and reader. Since my arrival, letters were brought to me to be read. A few men also brought me bride price receipts, privately, with requests to change the figures to a higher sum. I found moral arguments were of no avail, since in-laws are fair game, and the technical hazards of forgery difficult to explain to an illiterate people. I did not wish them to think me silly enough to look at any such papers for days on end, and I hastily explained that my "paper" was one of the "things of long ago" of my country.

"Ah," said the old man. "Tell us."

I protested that I was not a storyteller. Storytelling is a skilled art among them; their standards are high, and the audiences critical—and vocal in their criticism. I protested in vain. This morning they wanted to hear a story while they drank. They threatened to tell me no more stories until I told them one of mine. Finally, the old man promised that no one would criticize my style "for we know you are struggling with our language." "But," put in one of the elders, "you must explain what we do not understand, as we do when we tell you our stories." Realizing that here was my chance to prove *Hamlet* universally intelligible, I agreed.

The old man handed me some more beer to help me on with my storytelling. Men filled their long wooden pipes and knocked coals from the fire to place in the pipe bowls; then, puffing contentedly, they sat back to listen. I began in the proper style, "Not yesterday, not yesterday, but long ago, a thing occurred. One night three men were keeping watch outside the homestead of the great chief, when suddenly they saw the former chief approach them."

"Why was he no longer their chief?"

"He was dead," I explained. "That is why they were troubled and afraid when they saw him."

"Impossible," began one of the elders, handing his pipe on to his neighbor, who interrupted, "Of course it wasn't the dead chief. It was an omen sent by a witch. Go on."

Slightly shaken, I continued. "One of these three was a man who knew things"—the closest translation for scholar, but unfortunately it also meant witch. The second elder looked triumphantly at the first. "So he spoke to the dead chief saying, 'Tell us what we must do so you may rest in your grave,' but the dead chief did not answer. He vanished, and

they could see him no more. Then the man who knew things—his name was Horatio—said this event was the affair of the dead chief's son, Hamlet."

There was a general shaking of heads round the circle. "Had the dead chief no living brothers? Or was this son the chief"

"No," I replied. "That is, he had one living brother who became the chief when the elder brother died."

The old men muttered: such omens were matters for chiefs and elders, not for youngsters; no good could come of going behind a chief's back; clearly Horatio was not a man who knew things.

"Yes, he was," I insisted, shooing a chicken away from my beer. "In our country the son is next to the father. The dead chief's younger brother had become the great chief. He had also married his elder brother's widow only about a month after the funeral."

"He did well," the old man beamed and announced to the others, "I told you that if we knew more about Europeans, we would find they really were very like us. In our country also," he added to me, "the younger brother marries the elder brother's widow and becomes the father of his children. Now, if your uncle, who married your widowed mother, is your father's full brother, then he will be a real father to you. Did Hamlet's father and uncle have one mother?"

His question barely penetrated my mind; I was too upset and thrown too far off balance by having one of the most important elements of *Hamlet* knocked straight out of the picture. Rather uncertainly I said that I thought they had the same mother, but I wasn't sure—the story didn't say. The old man told me severely that these genealogical details made all the difference and that when I got home I must ask the elders about it. He shouted out the door to one of his younger wives to bring his goatskin bag.

Determined to save what I could of the mother motif, I took a deep breath and began again. "The son Hamlet was very sad because his mother had married again so quickly. There was no need for her to do so, and it is our custom for a widow not to go to her next husband until she has mourned for two years."

"Two years is too long" objected the wife, who had appeared with the old man's battered goatskin bag. "Who will hoe your farms for you while you have no husband?"

"Hamlet," I retorted without thinking, "was old enough to hoe his mother's farms himself. There was no need for her to remarry." No one looked convinced. I gave up. "His mother and the great chief told Hamlet not to be sad, for the great chief himself would be a father to Hamlet. Furthermore, Hamlet would be the next chief: therefore he must stay to learn the things of a chief. Hamlet agreed to remain, and all the rest went off to drink beer."

While I paused, perplexed at how to render Hamlet's disgusted soliloquy to an audience convinced that Claudius and Gertrude had behaved in the best possible manner, one of the young men asked me who had married the other wives of the dead chief.

"He had no other wives," I told him.

"But a chief must have many wives! How else can he brew beer and prepare food for all his guests?"

I said firmly that in our country even chiefs had only one wife, that they had servants to do their work, and that they paid them from tax money.

It was better, they returned, for a chief to have many wives and sons who would help him hoe his farms and feed his people; then everyone loved the chief who gave much and took nothing—taxes were a bad thing.

I agreed with the last comment, but for the rest fell back on their favorite way of fobbing off my questions: "That is the way it is done, so that is how we do it."

I decided to skip the soliloquy. Even if Claudius was here thought quite right to marry his brother's widow, there remained the poison motif, and I knew they would disapprove of fratricide. More hopefully I resumed, "That night Hamlet kept watch with the three who had seen his dead father. The dead chief again appeared, and although the others were afraid, Hamlet followed his dead father off to one side. When they were alone, Hamlet's dead father spoke."

"Omens can't talk!" The old man was emphatic.

"Hamlet's dead father wasn't an omen. Seeing him might have been an omen, but he was not." My audience looked as confused as I sounded. "It *was* Hamlet's dead father. It was a thing we call a 'ghost.'" I had to use the English word, for unlike many of the neighboring tribes, these people didn't believe in the survival after death of any individuating part of the personality.

"What is a 'ghost?' An omen?"

"No, a 'ghost' is someone who is dead but who walks around and can talk, and people can hear him and see him but not touch him."

They objected. "One can touch zombis."

"No, no! It was not a dead body the witches had animated to sacrifice and eat. No one else made Hamlet's dead father walk. He did it himself."

"Dead men can't walk," protested my audience as one man.

I was quite willing to compromise. "A 'ghost' is the dead man's shadow."

But again they objected. "Dead men cast no shadows."

"They do in my country," I snapped.

The old man quelled the babble of disbelief that arose immediately and told me with that insincere, but courteous, agreement one extends to the fancies of the young, ignorant, and superstitious, "No doubt in your country the dead can also walk without being zombis." From the depths of his bag he produced a withered fragment of kola nut, bit off one end to show it wasn't poisoned, and handed me the rest as a peace offering.

"Anyhow," I resumed, "Hamlet's dead father said that his own brother, the one who became chief, had poisoned him. He wanted Hamlet to avenge him. Hamlet believed this in his heart, for he did not like his father's brother." I took another swallow of beer. "In the country of the great chief, living in the same homestead, for it was a very large one, was an important elder who was often with the chief to advise and to help him. His name was Polonius. Hamlet was courting his daughter, but her father and her brother…[I cast hastily about for some tribal analogy] warned her not to let Hamlet visit her when she was alone on her farm, for he would be a great chief and so could not marry her."

"Why not?" asked the wife, who had settled down on the edge of the old man's chair. He frowned at her for asking stupid questions and growled, "They lived in the same homestead."

"That was not the reason," I informed them. "Polonius was a stranger who lived in the homestead because he helped the chief, not because he was a relative."

"Then why couldn't Hamlet marry her?"

"He could have," I explained, "but Polonius didn't think he would. After all, Hamlet was a man of great importance who ought to marry a chief's daughter, for in his country a man could have only one wife. Polonius was afraid that if Hamlet made love to his daughter, then no one else would give a high price for her."

"That might be true" remarked one of the shrewder elders, "but a chief's son would give his mistress's father enough presents and patronage to more than make up the difference. Polonius sounds like a fool to me."

"Many people think he was," I agreed. "Meanwhile Polonius sent his son Laertes off to Paris to learn the things of that country, for it was the homestead of a very great chief indeed. Because he was afraid that Laertes might waste a lot of money on beer and women and gambling, or get into trouble by fighting, he sent one of his servants to Paris secretly, to spy out what Laertes was doing. One day Hamlet came upon Polonius's daughter Ophelia. He behaved so oddly he frightened her. "Indeed,"—I was fumbling for words to express the dubious quality of Hamlet's madness—"the chief and many others had also noticed that when Hamlet talked one could understand the words but not what they meant. Many people thought that he had become mad." My audience suddenly became much more attentive. "The great chief wanted to know what was wrong with Hamlet, so he sent for two of Hamlet's age mates [school friends would have taken a long explanation] to talk to Hamlet and find out what troubled his heart. Hamlet, seeing that they had been bribed by the chief to betray him, told them nothing. Polonius, however, insisted that Hamlet was mad because he had been forbidden to see Ophelia, whom he loved."

"Why," inquired a bewildered voice, "should anyone bewitch Hamlet on that account?"

"Bewitch him?"

"Yes, only witchcraft can make anyone mad, unless of course, one sees the beings that lurk in the forest."

I stopped being a storyteller, took out my notebook and demanded to be told more about these two causes of madness. Even while they spoke and I jotted notes, I tried to calculate the effect of this new factor on the plot. Hamlet had not been exposed to the beings that lurk in the forest. Only his relatives in the male line could bewitch him. Barring relatives not mentioned by Shakespeare, it had to be Claudius who was attempting to harm him. And, of course, it was.

For the moment I staved off questions by saying that the great chief also refused to believe that Hamlet was mad for the love of Ophelia and nothing else. "He was sure that something much more important was troubling Hamlet's heart."

"Now Hamlet's age mates," I continued, "had brought with them a famous storyteller. Hamlet decided to have this man tell the chief and all his homestead a story about a man who had poisoned his brother because he desired his brother's wife and wished to be chief himself. Hamlet was sure the great chief could not hear the story without making a sign if he was indeed guilty, and then he would discover whether his dead father had told him the truth."

The old man interrupted, with deep cunning, "Why should a father lie to his son?" he asked.

I hedged: "Hamlet wasn't sure that it really was his dead father." It was impossible to say anything, in that language, about devil-inspired visions.

"You mean," he said, "it actually was an omen, and he knew witches sometimes send false ones. Hamlet was a fool not to go to one skilled in reading omens and divining the truth in the first place. A man-who-sees-the-truth could have told him how his father died, if he really had been poisoned, and if there was witchcraft in it; then Hamlet could have called the elders to settle the matter."

The shrewd elder ventured to disagree. "Because his father's brother was a great chief, one-who-sees-the-truth might therefore have been afraid to tell it. I think it was for that reason that a friend of Hamlet's father—a witch and an elder—sent an omen so his friend's son would know. Was the omen true?"

"Yes," I said, abandoning ghosts and the devil; a witch-sent omen it would have to be. "It was true, for when the storyteller was telling his tale before all the homestead, the great chief rose in fear. Afraid that Hamlet knew his secret, he planned to have him killed."

The stage set of the next bit presented some difficulties of translation. I began cautiously. "The great chief told Hamlet's mother to find out from her son what he knew. But because a woman's children are always first in her heart, he had the important elder Polonius hide behind a cloth that hung against the wall of Hamlet's mother's sleeping hut. Hamlet started to scold his mother for what she had done."

There was a shocked murmur from everyone. A man should never scold his mother.

"She called out in fear and Polonius moved behind the cloth. Shouting, 'A rat!' Hamlet took his machete and slashed through the cloth." I paused for dramatic effect. "He had killed Polonius!"

The old men looked at each other in supreme disgust. "That Polonius truly was a fool and a man who knew nothing! What child would not know enough to shout, 'It's me!'" With a pang, I remembered that these people are ardent hunters, always armed with bow, arrow, and machete; at the first rustle in the grass an arrow is aimed and ready, and the hunter shouts "Game!" If no human voice answers immediately, the arrow speeds on its way. Like a good hunter Hamlet had shouted, "A rat!"

I rushed in to save Polonius's reputation. "Polonius did speak. Hamlet heard him. But he thought it was the chief and wished to kill him to avenge his father. He had meant to kill him earlier that evening...." I broke down, unable to describe to these pagans, who had no belief in individual afterlife, the difference between dying at one's prayers and dying "unhousell'd, disappointed, unaneled."

This time I had shocked my audience seriously. "For a man to raise his hand against his father's brother and the one who has become his father—that is a terrible thing. The elders ought to let such a man be bewitched."

I nibbled at my kola nut in some perplexity, then pointed out that after all the man had killed Hamlet's father.

"No," pronounced the old man, speaking less to me than to the young men sitting behind the elders. "If your father's brother has killed your father, you must appeal to your father's age mates; *they* may avenge him. No man may use violence against his senior relatives." Another thought struck him. "But if his father's brother had indeed been wicked enough to bewitch Hamlet and make him mad that would be a good story indeed, for it would be his fault that Hamlet, being mad, no longer had any sense and thus was ready to kill his father's brother."

There was a murmur of applause. *Hamlet* was again a good story to them, but it no longer seemed quite the same story to me. As I thought over the coming complications of plot and motive, I lost courage and decided to skim over dangerous ground quickly.

"The great chief," I went on, "was not sorry that Hamlet had killed Polonius. It gave him a reason to send Hamlet away, with his two treacherous age mates, with letters to a chief of a far country, saying that Hamlet should be killed. But Hamlet changed the writing on their papers, so that the chief killed his age mates instead." I encountered a reproachful glare from one of the men whom I had told undetectable forgery was not merely immoral but beyond human skill. I looked the other way.

"Before Hamlet could return, Laertes came back for his father's funeral. The great chief told him Hamlet had killed Polonius. Laertes swore to kill Hamlet because of this, and because his sister Ophelia, hearing her father had been killed by the man she loved, went mad and drowned in the river."

"Have you already forgotten what we told you?" The old man was reproachful. "One cannot take vengeance on a madman; Hamlet killed Polonius in his madness. As for the girl, she not only went mad, she was drowned. Only witches can make people drown. Water itself can't hurt anything. It is merely something one drinks and bathes in."

I began to get cross. "If you don't like the story, I'll stop."

The old man made soothing noises and himself poured me some more beer. "You tell the story well, and we are listening. But is clear that the elders of your country have never told you what the story really means. No, don't interrupt! We believe you when you say your marriage customs are different, or your clothes and weapons. But people are the same everywhere; therefore, there are always witches and it is we, the elders, who know how witches work. We told you it was the great chief who wished to kill Hamlet, and now your own words have proved us right. Who were Ophelia's male relatives?"

"There were only her father and her brother." *Hamlet* was clearly out of my hands.

"There must have been many more; this also you must ask of your elders when you get back to your country. From what you tell us, since Polonius was dead, it must have been Laertes who killed Ophelia, although I do not see the reason for it."

We had emptied one pot of beer, and the old men argued the point with slightly tipsy interest. Finally one of them demanded of me, "What did the servant of Polonius say on his return?"

With difficulty I recollected Reynaldo and his mission. "I don't think he did return before Polonius was killed."

"Listen," said the elder, "and I will tell you how it was and how your story will go, then you may tell me if I am right. Polonius knew his son would get into trouble, and so he did. He had many fines to pay for fighting, and debts from gambling. But he had only two ways of getting money quickly. One was to marry off his sister at once, but it is difficult to find a man who will marry a woman desired by the son of a chief. For if the chief's heir commits adultery with your wife, what do you do? Only a fool calls a case against a man who will someday be his judge. Therefore Laertes had to take the second way: he killed his sister by witchcraft, drowning her so he could secretly sell her body to the witches."

I raised an objection. "They found her body and buried it. Indeed Laertes jumped into the grave to see his sister once more—so, you see, the body was truly there. Hamlet, who had just come back, jumped in after him."

"What did I tell you?" The elder appealed to the others. "Laertes was up to no good with his sister's body. Hamlet prevented him, because the chief's heir, like a chief, does not wish any other man to grow rich and powerful. Laertes would be angry, because he would have killed his sister without benefit to himself. In our country he would try to kill Hamlet for that reason. Is this not what happened?"

"More or less," I admitted. "When the great chief found Hamlet was still alive, he encouraged Laertes to try to kill Hamlet and arranged a fight with machetes between them. In the fight both the young men were wounded to death. Hamlet's mother drank the poisoned beer that the chief meant for Hamlet in case he won the fight. When he saw his mother die of poison, Hamlet, dying, managed to kill his father's brother with his machete."

"You see, I was right!" exclaimed the elder.

"That was a very good story," added the old man, "and you told it with very few mistakes. There was just one more error, at the very end. The poison Hamlet's mother drank was obviously meant for the survivor of the fight, whichever it was. If Laertes had won, the great chief would have poisoned him, for no one would know that he arranged Hamlet's death. Then, too, he need not fear Laertes' witchcraft; it takes a strong heart to kill one's only sister by witchcraft.

"Sometime," concluded the old man, gathering his ragged toga about him, "you must tell us some more stories of your country. We, who are elders, will instruct you in their true meaning, so that when you return to your own land your elders will see that you have not been sitting in the bush, but among those who know things and who have taught you wisdom."

Richard Borshay Lee

Eating Christmas in the Kalahari

The !Kung Bushmen's knowledge of Christmas is thirdhand. The London Missionary Society brought the holiday to the southern Tswana tribes in the early nineteenth century. Later, native catechists spread the idea far and wide among the Bantu-speaking pastoralists, even in the remotest corners of the Kalahari Desert. The Bushmen's idea of the Christmas story, stripped to its essentials, is "praise the birth of white man's god-chief"; what keeps their interest in the holiday high is the Tswana–Herero custom of slaughtering an ox for his Bushmen neighbors as an annual goodwill gesture. Since the 1930's, part of the Bushmen's annual round of activities has included a December congregation at the cattle posts for trading, marriage brokering, and several days of trance-dance feasting at which the local Tswana headman is host.

As a social anthropologist working with !Kung Bushmen, I found that the Christmas ox custom suited my purposes. I had come to the Kalahari to study the hunting and gathering subsistence economy of the !Kung, and to accomplish this it was essential not to provide them with food, share my own food, or interfere in any way with their food-gathering activities. While liberal handouts of tobacco and medical supplies were appreciated, they were scarcely adequate to erase the glaring disparity in wealth between the anthropologist, who maintained a two-month inventory of canned goods, and the Bushmen, who rarely had a day's supply of food on hand. My approach, while paying off in terms of data, left me open to frequent accusations of stinginess and hard-heartedness. By their lights, I was a miser.

The Christmas ox was to be my way of saying thank you for the cooperation of the past year; and since it was to be our last Christmas in the field, I de-termined to slaughter the largest, meatiest ox that money could buy, insuring that the feast and trance dance would be a success.

Through December I kept my eyes open at the wells as the cattle were brought down for watering. Several animals were offered, but none had quite the grossness that I had in mind. Then, ten days before the holiday, a Herero friend led an ox of astonishing size and mass up to our camp. It was solid black, stood five feet high at the shoulder, had a five-foot span of horns, and must have weighed 1,200 pounds on the hoof. Food consumption calculations are my specialty, and I quickly figured that bones and viscera aside, there was enough meat—at least four pounds—for every man, woman, and child of the 150 Bushmen in the vicinity of /ai/ai who were expected at the feast.

Having found the right animal at last, I paid the Herero £20 ($56) and asked him to keep the beast with his herd until Christmas day. The next morning word spread among the people that the big solid black one was the ox chosen by /ontah (my Bushman name; it means, roughly, "whitey") for the Christmas feast. That afternoon I received the first delegation. Ben!a, an outspoken sixty-year-old mother of five, came to the point slowly.

"Where were you planning to eat Christmas?"

"Right here at /ai/ai," I replied.

"Alone or with others?"

"I expect to invite all the people to eat Christmas with me."

"Eat what?"

"I have purchased Yehave's black ox, and I am going to slaughter and cook it."

"That's what we were told at the well but refused to believe it until we heard it from yourself."

"Well, it's the black one," I replied expansively, although wondering what she was driving at.

"Oh, no!" Ben!a groaned, turning to her group. "They were right." Turning back to me she asked, "Do you expect us to eat that bag of bones?"

"Bag of bones! It's the biggest ox at /ai/ai."

"Big, yes, but old. And thin. Everybody knows there's no meat on that old ox. What did you expect us to eat off it, the horns?"

Editor's Note: The !Kung and other Bushmen speak click languages. In the story, three different clicks are used:
1. The dental click (/), as in /ai/ai, /ontah, and /gaugo. The click is sometimes written in English as tsk-tsk.
2. The alveopalatal click (!), as in Ben!a and !Kung.
3. The lateral click (//), as in //gom. Clicks function as consonants; a word may have more than one, as in /n!nu.

Everybody chuckled at Ben!a's one-liner as they walked away, but all I could manage was a weak grin.

That evening it was the turn of the young men. They came to sit at our evening fire. /gaugo, about my age, spoke to me man-to-man.

"/ontah, you have always been square with us," he lied. "What has happened to change your heart? That sack of guts and bones of Yehave's will hardly feed one camp, let alone all the Bushmen around /ai/ai." And he proceeded to enumerate the seven camps in the /ai/ai vicinity, family by family. "Perhaps you have forgotten that we are not few, but many. Or are you too blind to tell the difference between a proper cow and an old wreck? That ox is thin to the point of death."

"Look, you guys," I retorted, "that is a beautiful animal, and I'm sure you will eat it with pleasure at Christmas."

"Of course we will eat it; it's food. But it won't fill us up to the point where we will have enough strength to dance. We will eat and go home to bed with stomachs rumbling.

That night as we turned in, I asked my wife, Nancy: "What did you think of the black ox?"

"It looked enormous to me. Why?

"Well, about eight different people have told me I got gypped; that the ox is nothing but bones."

"What's the angle?" Nancy asked. "Did they have a better one to sell?"

"No, they just said that it was going to be a grim Christmas because there won't be enough meat to go around. Maybe I'll get an independent judge to look at the beast in the morning."

Bright and early, Halingisi, a Tswana cattle owner, appeared at our camp. But before I could ask him to give me his opinion on Yehave's black ox, he gave me the eye signal that indicated a confidential chat. We left the camp and sat down.

"/ontah, I'm surprised at you; you've lived here for three years and still haven't learned anything about cattle."

"But what else can a person do but choose the biggest, strongest animal one can find?" I retorted.

"Look, just because an animal is big doesn't mean that it has plenty of meat on it. The black one was a beauty when it was younger, but now it is thin to the point of death."

"Well I've already bought it. What can I do at this stage ?"

"Bought it already? I thought you were just considering it. Well you'll have to kill it and serve it, I suppose. But don't expect much of a dance to follow."

My spirits dropped rapidly. I could believe that Ben!a and /gaugo just might be putting me on about

the black ox, but Halingisi seemed to be an impartial critic. I went around that day feeling as though I had bought a lemon of a used car.

In the afternoon it was Tomazo's turn. Tomazo is a fine hunter, a top trance performer (see "The Trance Cure of the !Kung Bushmen," *Natural History*, November, 1967), and one of my most reliable informants. He approached the subject of the Christmas cow as part of my continuing Bushmen education.

"My friend, the way it is with us Bushmen," he began, "is that we love meat. And even more than that, we love fat. When we hunt we always search for the fat ones, the ones dripping with layers of white fat: fat that turns into a clear, thick oil in the cooking pot, fat that slides down your gullet, fills your stomach and gives you a roaring diarrhea," he rhapsodized.

"So, feeling as we do," he continued, "it gives us pain to be served such a scrawny thing as Yehave's black ox. It is big, yes, and no doubt its giant bones are good for soup, but fat is what we really crave and so we will eat Christmas this year with a heavy heart."

The prospect of a gloomy Christmas now had me worried, so I asked Tomazo what I could do about it.

"Look for a fat one, a young one…smaller, but fat. Fat enough to make us //gom ('evacuate the bowels'), then we will be happy."

My suspicions were aroused when Tomazo said that he happened to know of a young, fat, barren cow that the owner was willing to part with. Was Toma working on commission, I wondered? But I dispelled this unworthy thought when we approached the Herero owner of the cow in question and found that he had decided not to sell.

The scrawny wreck of a Christmas ox now became the talk of the /ai/ai water hole and was the first news told to the outlying groups as they began to come in from the bush for the feast. What finally convinced me that real trouble might be brewing was the visit from u!au, an old conservative with a reputation for fierceness. His nickname meant spear and referred to an incident thirty years ago in which he had speared a man to death. He had an intense manner; fixing me with his eyes, he said in clipped tones:

"I have only just heard about the black ox today, or else I would have come here earlier. /ontah, do you honestly think you can serve meat like that to people and avoid a fight?" He paused, letting the implications sink in. "I don't mean fight you, /ontah; you are a white man. I mean a fight between Bushmen. There are many fierce ones here, and with such a small quantity of meat to distribute, how can you give everybody a fair share? Someone is sure to accuse another of taking too much or hogging all the choice pieces. Then you will see what happens when some go hungry while others eat."

The possibility of at least a serious argument struck me as all too real. I had witnessed the tension that surrounds the distribution of meat from a kudu or gemsbok kill, and had documented many arguments that sprang up from a real or imagined slight in meat distribution. The owners of a kill may spend up to two hours arranging and rearranging the piles of meat under the gaze of a circle of recipients before handing them out. And I also knew that the Christmas feast at /ai/ai would be bringing together groups that had feuded in the past.

Convinced now of the gravity of the situation, I went in earnest to search for a second cow; but all my inquiries failed to turn one up.

The Christmas feast was evidently going to be a disaster, and the incessant complaints about the meagerness of the ox had already taken the fun out of it for me. Moreover, I was getting bored with the wisecracks, and after losing my temper a few times, I resolved to serve the beast anyway. If the meat fell short, the hell with it. In the Bushmen idiom, I announced to all who would listen:

"I am a poor man and blind. If I have chosen one that is too old and too thin, we will eat it anyway and see if there is enough meat there to quiet the rumbling of our stomachs."

On hearing this speech, Ben!a offered me a rare word of comfort. "It's thin," she said philosophically, "but the bones will make a good soup."

At dawn Christmas morning, instinct told me to turn over the butchering and cooking to a friend and take off with Nancy to spend Christmas alone in the bush. But curiosity kept me from retreating. I wanted to see what such a scrawny ox looked like on butchering, and if there *was* going to be a fight, I wanted to catch every word of it. Anthropologists are incurable that way.

The great beast was driven up to our dancing ground, and a shot in the forehead dropped it in its tracks. Then, freshly cut branches were heaped around the fallen carcass to receive the meat. Ten men volunteered to help with the cutting. I asked /gaugo to make the breast bone cut. This cut, which begins the butchering process for most large game, offers easy access for removal of the viscera. But it also allows the hunter to spot-check the amount of fat on the animal. A fat game animal carries a white layer up to an inch thick on the chest, while in a thin one, the knife will quickly cut to bone. All eyes fixed on his hand as /gaugo, dwarfed by the great carcass, knelt to the breast. The first cut opened a pool of solid white in the black skin. The second and third cut widened and deepened the creamy white. Still no

bone. It was pure fat; it must have been two inches thick.

"Hey /gau," I burst out, "that ox is loaded with fat. What's this about the ox being too thin to bother eating? Are you out of your mind?"

"Fat?" /gau shot back, "You call that fat? This wreck is thin, sick, dead!" And he broke out laughing. So did everyone else. They rolled on the ground, paralyzed with laughter. Everybody laughed except me; I was thinking.

I ran back to the tent and burst in just as Nancy was getting up. "Hey, the black ox. It's fat as hell! They were kidding about it being too thin to eat. It was a joke or something. A put-on. Everyone is really delighted with it!"

"Some joke," my wife replied. "It was so funny that you were ready to pack up and leave /ai/ai."

If it had indeed been a joke, it had been an extraordinarily convincing one, and tinged, I thought, with more than a touch of malice as many jokes are. Nevertheless, that it was a joke lifted my spirits considerably, and I returned to the butchering site where the shape of the ox was rapidly disappearing under the axes and knives of the butchers. The atmosphere had become festive. Grinning broadly, their arms covered with blood well past the elbow, men packed chunks of meat into the big cast-iron cooking pots, fifty pounds to the load, and muttered and chuckled all the while about the thinness and worthlessness of the animal and /ontah's poor judgment.

We danced and ate that ox two days and two nights; we cooked and distributed fourteen potfuls of meat and no one went home hungry and no fights broke out.

But the "joke" stayed in my mind. I had a growing feeling that something important had happened in my relationship with the Bushmen and that the clue lay in the meaning of the joke. Several days later, when most of the people had dispersed back to the bush camps, I raised the question with Hakekgose, a Tswana man who had grown up among the !Kung, married a !Kung girl, and who probably knew their culture better than any other non-Bushman.

"With us whites," I began, "Christmas is supposed to be the day of friendship and brotherly love. What I can't figure out is why the Bushmen went to such lengths to criticize and belittle the ox I had bought for the feast. The animal was perfectly good and their jokes and wisecracks practically ruined the holiday for me."

"So it really did bother you," said Hakekgose. "Well, that's the way they always talk. When I take my rifle and go hunting with them, if I miss, they laugh at me for the rest of the day. But even if I hit and bring one down, it's no better. To them, the kill is always too small or too old or too thin; and as we sit down on the kill site to cook and eat the liver, they keep grumbling, even with their mouths full of meat. They say things like, 'Oh this is awful! What a worthless animal! Whatever made me think that this Tswana rascal could hunt!'"

"Is this the way outsiders are treated?" I asked.

"No, it is their custom; they talk that way to each other too. Go and ask them."

/gaugo had been one of the most enthusiastic in making me feel bad about the merit of the Christmas ox. I sought him out first.

"Why did you tell me the black ox was worthless, when you could see that it was loaded with fat and meat?"

"It is our way," he said smiling. "We always like to fool people about that. Say there is a Bushman who has been hunting. He must not come home and announce like a braggard, 'I have killed a big one in the bush!' He must first sit down in silence until I or someone else comes up to his fire and asks, 'What did you see today?' He replies quietly, 'Ah, I'm no good for hunting. I saw nothing at all [pause] just a little tiny one.' Then I smile to myself," /gaugo continued, "because I know he has killed something big."

"In the morning we make up a party of four or five people to cut up and carry the meat back to the camp. When we arrive at the kill we examine it and cry out, 'You mean to say you have dragged us all the way out here in order to make us cart home your pile of bones? Oh, if I had known it was this thin I wouldn't have come.' Another one pipes up, 'People, to think I gave up a nice day in the shade for this. At home we may be hungry but at least we have nice cool water to drink.' If the horns are big, someone says, 'Did you think that somehow you were going to boil down the horns for soup?'

"To all this you must respond in kind. 'I agree,' you say, 'this one is not worth the effort; let's just cook the liver for strength and leave the rest for the hyenas. It is not too late to hunt today and even a duiker or a steenbok would be better than this mess.'

"Then you set to work nevertheless; butcher the animal, carry the meat back to the camp and everyone eats," /gaugo concluded.

Things were beginning to make sense. Next, I went to Tomazo. He corroborated /gaugo's story of the obligatory insults over a kill and added a few details of his own.

"But," I asked, "why insult a man after he has gone to all that trouble to track and kill an animal and when he is going to share the meat with you so that your children will have something to eat?"

"Arrogance," was his cryptic answer.

"Arrogance?"

"Yes, when a young man kills much meat he comes to think of himself as a chief or a big man, and he thinks of the rest of us as his servants or inferiors. We can't accept this. We refuse one who boasts, for someday his pride will make him kill somebody. So we always speak of his meat as worthless. This way we cool his heart and make him gentle."

"But why didn't you tell me this before?" I asked Tomazo with some heat.

"Because you never asked me," said Tomazo, echoing the refrain that has come to haunt every field ethnographer.

The pieces now fell into place. I had known for a long time that in situations of social conflict with Bushmen I held all the cards. I was the only source of tobacco in a thousand square miles, and I was not incapable of cutting an individual off for noncooperation. Though my boycott never lasted longer than a few days, it was an indication of my strength. People resented my presence at the water hole, yet simultaneously dreaded my leaving. In short I was a perfect target for the charge of arrogance and for the Bushmen tactic of enforcing humility.

I had been taught an object lesson by the Bushmen; it had come from an unexpected corner and had hurt me in a vulnerable area. For the big black ox was to be the one totally generous, unstinting act of my year at /ai/ai, and I was quite unprepared for the reaction I received.

As I read it, their message was this: There are no totally generous acts. All "acts" have an element of calculation. One black ox slaughtered at Christmas does not wipe out a year of careful manipulation of gifts given to serve your own ends. After all, to kill an animal and share the meat with people is really no more than Bushmen do for each other every day and with far less fanfare.

In the end, I had to admire how the Bushmen had played out the farce—collectively straight-faced to the end. Curiously, the episode reminded me of the *Good Soldier Schweik* and his marvelous encounters with authority. Like Schweik, the Bushmen had retained a thoroughgoing skepticism of good intentions. Was it this independence of spirit, I wondered, that had kept them culturally viable in the face of generations of contact with more powerful societies, both black and white? The thought that the Bushmen were alive and well in the Kalahari was strangely comforting. Perhaps, armed with that independence and with their superb knowledge of their environment, they might yet survive the future.

Body Ritual among the Nacirema

The anthropologist has become so familiar with the diversity of ways in which different peoples behave in similar situations that he is not apt to be surprised by even the most exotic customs. In fact, if all of the logically possible combinations of behavior have not been found somewhere in the world, he is apt to suspect that they must be present in some yet undescribed tribe. This point has, in fact, been expressed with respect to clan organization by Murdock (1949:71). In this light, the magical beliefs and practices of the Nacirema present such unusual aspects that it seems desirable to describe them as an example of the extremes to which human behavior can go.

Professor Linton first brought the ritual of the Nacirema to the attention of anthropologists twenty years ago (1936:326), but the culture of this people is still very poorly understood. They are a North American group living in the territory between the Canadian Cree, the Yaqui and Tarahumare of Mexico, and the Carib and Arawak of the Antilles. Little is known of their origin, although tradition states that they came from the east. According to Nacirema mythology, their nation was originated by a culture hero, Notgnihsaw, who is otherwise known for two great feats of strength—the throwing of a piece of wampum across the river Pa-To-Mac and the chopping down of a cherry tree in which the Spirit of Truth resided.

Nacirema culture is characterized by a highly developed market economy which has evolved in a rich natural habitat. While much of the people's time is devoted to economic pursuits, a large part of the fruits of these labors and a considerable portion of the day are spent in ritual activity. The focus of this activity is the human body, the appearance and health of which loom as a dominant concern in the ethos of the people. While such a concern is certainly not unusual, its ceremonial aspects and associated philosophy are unique.

The fundamental belief underlying the whole system appears to be that the human body is ugly and that its natural tendency is to debility and disease. Incarcerated in such a body, man's only hope is to avert these characteristics through the use of the powerful influences of ritual and ceremony. Every household has one or more shrines devoted to this purpose. The more powerful individuals in the society have several shrines in their houses and, in fact, the opulence of a house is often referred to in terms of the number of such ritual centers it possesses. Most houses are of wattle and daub construction, but the shrine rooms of the more wealthy are walled with stone. Poorer families imitate the rich by applying pottery plaques to their shrine walls.

While each family has at least one such shrine, the rituals associated with it are not family ceremonies but are private and secret. The rites are normally only discussed with children, and then only during the period when they are being initiated into these mysteries. I was able, however, to establish sufficient rapport with the natives to examine these shrines and to have the rituals described to me.

The focal point of the shrine is a box or chest which is built into the wall. In this chest are kept the many charms and magical potions without which no native believes he could live. These preparations are secured from a variety of specialized practioners. The most powerful of these are the medicine men, whose assistance must be rewarded with substantial gifts. However, the medicine men do not provide the curative potions for their clients, but decide what the ingredients should be and then write them down in an ancient and secret language. This writing is understood only by the medicine men and by the herbalists who, for another gift, provide the required charm.

The charm is not disposed of after it has served its purpose, but is placed in the charm-box of the household shrine. As these magical materials are specific for certain ills, and the real or imagined maladies of the people are many, the charm-box is usually full to overflowing. The magical packets are so numerous that people forget what their purposes were and fear to use them again. While the natives are very vague on this point, we can only assume that the idea in retaining all the old magical materials is that their presence in the charm-box, before which the body rituals are conducted, will in some way protect the worshipper.

Beneath the charm-box is a small font. Each day every member of the family, in succession, enters the shrine room, bows his head before the charm-box, mingles different sorts of holy water in the font, and proceeds with a brief rite of ablution. The holy waters are secured from the Water Temple of the community, where the priests conduct elaborate ceremonies to make the liquid ritually pure.

In the hierarchy of magical practitioners, and below the medicine men in prestige, are specialists whose designation is best translated "holy-mouth-men." The Nacirema have an almost pathological horror of and fascination with the mouth, the condition of which is believed to have a supernatural influence on all social relationships. Were it not for the rituals of the mouth, they believe that their teeth would fall out, their gums bleed, their jaws shrink, their friends desert them, and their lovers reject them. They also believe that a strong relationship exists between oral and moral characteristics. For example, there is a ritual ablution of the mouth for children which is supposed to improve their moral fiber.

The daily body ritual performed by everyone includes a mouth-rite. Despite the fact that these people are so punctilious about care of the mouth, this rite involves a practice which strikes the uninitiated stranger as revolting. It was reported to me that the ritual consists of inserting a small bundle of hog hairs into the mouth, along with certain magical powders, and then moving the bundle in a highly formalized series of gestures.

In addition to the private mouth-rite, the people seek out a holy-mouth-man once or twice a year. These practitioners have an impressive set of paraphernalia, consisting of a variety of augers, awls, probes, and prods. The use of these objects in the exorcism of the evils of the mouth involves almost unbelievable ritual torture of the client. The holy-mouth-man opens the client's mouth and, using the above mentioned tools, enlarges any holes which decay may have created in the teeth. Magical materials are put into these holes. If there are no naturally occurring holes in the teeth, large sections of one or more teeth are gouged out so that the supernatural substance can be applied. In the client's view, the purpose of these ministrations is to arrest decay and to draw friends. The extremely sacred and traditional character of the rite is evident in the fact that the natives return to the holy-mouth-men year after year, despite the fact that their teeth continue to decay.

It is to be hoped that, when a thorough study of the Nacirema is made, there will be careful inquiry into the personality structure of these people. One has but to watch the gleam in the eye of a holy-mouth-man, as he jabs an awl into an exposed nerve, to suspect that a certain amount of sadism is involved. If this can be established, a very interesting pattern emerges, for most of the population shows definite masochistic tendencies. It was to these that Professor Linton referred in discussing a distinctive part of the daily body ritual which is performed only by men. This part of the rite involves scraping and lacerating the surface of the face with a sharp instrument. Special women's rites are performed only four times during each lunar month, but what they lack in frequency is made up in barbarity. As part of this ceremony, women bake their heads in small ovens for about an hour. The theoretically interesting point is that what seems to be a preponderantly masochistic people have developed sadistic specialists.

The medicine men have an imposing temple, or *latipso*, in every community of any size. The more elaborate ceremonies required to treat very sick patients can only be performed at this temple. These ceremonies involve not only the thaumaturge but a permanent group of vestal maidens who move sedately about the temple chambers in distinctive costume and headdress.

The *latipso* ceremonies are so harsh that it is phenomenal that a fair proportion of the really sick natives who enter the temple ever recover. Small children whose indoctrination is still incomplete have been known to resist attempts to take them to the temple because "that is where you go to die." Despite this fact, sick adults are not only willing but eager to undergo the protracted ritual purification, if they can afford to do so. No matter how ill the supplicant or how grave the emergency, the guardians of many temples will not admit a client if he cannot give a rich gift to the custodian. Even after one has gained admission and survived the ceremonies, the guardians will not permit the neophyte to leave until he makes still another gift.

The supplicant entering the temple is first stripped of all his or her clothes. In everyday life the Nacirema avoids exposure of his body and its natural functions. Bathing and excretory acts are performed only in the secrecy of the household shrine, where they are ritualized as part of the body-rites. Psychological shock results from the fact that body secrecy is suddenly lost upon entry into the *latipso*. A man, whose own wife has never seen him in an excretory act, suddenly finds himself naked and assisted by a vestal maiden while he performs his natural functions into a sacred vessel. This sort of ceremonial treatment is necessitated by the fact that the excreta are used by a diviner to ascertain the course and nature of the client's sickness. Female clients, on the other hand, find their naked bodies are subjected to the scrutiny, manipulation, and prodding of the medicine men.

Few supplicants in the temple are well enough to do anything but lie on their hard beds. The daily ceremonies, like the rites of the holy-mouth-men, involve discomfort and torture. With ritual precision, the vestals awaken their miserable charges each dawn and roll them about on their beds of pain while performing ablutions, in the formal movements of which the maidens are highly trained. At other times they insert magic wands in the supplicant's mouth or force him to eat substances which are supposed to be healing. From time to time the medicine men come to their clients and jab magically treated needles into their flesh. The fact that these temple ceremonies may not cure, and may even kill the neophyte, in no way decreases the people's faith in the medicine men.

There remains one other kind of practitioner, known as a "listener." This witch-doctor has the power to exorcise the devils that lodge in the heads of people who have been bewitched. The Nacirema believe that parents bewitch their own children. Mothers are particularly suspected of putting a curse on children while teaching them the secret body rituals. The counter-magic of the witch-doctor is unusual in its lack of ritual. The patient simply tells the "listener" all his troubles and fears, beginning with the earliest difficulties he can remember. The memory displayed by the Nacirema in these exorcism sessions is truly remarkable. It is not uncommon for the patient to bemoan the rejection he felt upon being weaned as a babe, and a few individuals even see their troubles going back to the traumatic effects of their own birth.

In conclusion, mention must be made of certain practices which have their base in native esthetics but which depend upon the pervasive aversion to the natural body and its functions. There are ritual fasts to make fat people thin and ceremonial feasts to make thin people fat. Still other rites are used to make women's breasts larger if they are small, and smaller if they are large. General dissatisfaction with breast shape is symbolized in the fact that the ideal form is virtually outside the range of human variation. A few women afflicted with almost inhuman hypermammary development are so idolized that they make a handsome living by simply going from village to village and permitting the natives to stare at them for a fee.

Reference has already been made to the fact that excretory functions are ritualized, routinized, and relegated to secrecy. Natural reproductive functions are similarly distorted. Intercourse is taboo as a topic and scheduled as an act. Efforts are made to avoid pregnancy by the use of magical materials or by limiting intercourse to certain phases of the moon. Conception is actually very infrequent. When pregnant, women dress so as to hide their condition. Parturition takes place in secret, without friends or relatives to assist, and the majority of women do not nurse their infants.

Our review of the ritual life of the Nacirema has certainly shown them to be a magic-ridden people. It is hard to understand how they have managed to exist so long under the burdens which they have imposed upon themselves. But even such exotic customs as these take on real meaning when they are viewed with the insight provided by Malinowski when he wrote (1948:70):

> Looking from far and above, from our high places of safety in the developed civilization, it is easy to see all the crudity and irrelevance of magic. But without its power and guidance early man could not have mastered his practical difficulties as he has done, nor could man have advanced to the higher stages of civilization.

REFERENCES

Linton, Ralph. 1936. *The Study of Man.* New York, D. Appleton-Century Co.

Malinowski, Bronislaw. 1948. *Magic, Science, and Religion.* Glencoe, The Free Press.

Murdock, George P. 1949. *Social Structure.* New York, The Macmillan Co.

Now the Ancient Ways Are Less Mysterious

Each June for at least the last four centuries, farmers in 12 mountain villages in Peru and Bolivia follow a ritual that Westerners might think odd, if not crazy. Late each night for about a week, the farmers observe the stars in the Pleiades constellation, which is low on the horizon to the northeast. If they appear big and bright, the farmers know to plant their potato crop at the usual time four months later. But if the stars are dim, the usual planting will be delayed for several weeks.

Now Western researchers have applied the scientific method to this seeming madness. Poring over reams of satellite data on cloud cover and water vapor, Benjamin S. Orlove, an anthropologist at the University of California at Davis, and colleagues have discovered that these star-gazing farmers are accurate long-range weather forecasters. High wisps of cirrus clouds dim the stars in El Niño years, which brings reduced rainfall to that part of the Andes. In such drought conditions, it makes sense to plant potatoes as late as possible.

Professor Orlove's work, which was reported [in January 2000] in the British journal Nature, is just the latest example of indigenous or traditional knowledge that has been found to have a sound scientific basis. In agriculture, nutrition, medicine and other fields, modern research is showing why people maintain their traditions.

Take the Masai of East Africa, who are famous for the kind of high-fat diet, rich in meat and milk, that would make a cardiologist swoon. Timothy Johns, a professor at McGill University in Montreal and director of the Center for Indigenous Peoples' Nutrition and Environment, has long studied the Masai to determine how they stay healthy.

The Masai add the roots and barks of certain plants, including a species of acacia high in antioxidants, Professor Johns said. They also chew a natural gum, related to myrrh, that helps to break down fats.

"It's not a magic bullet protecting the Masai against heart disease," he said. "But there is a benefit from what they are doing."

In a 1998 study, two Cornell University researchers analyzed the spices used in 36 countries and found a correlation between average temperature and cooking with spices like cumin, turmeric, ginger and chili peppers, all of which have antimicrobial properties. The hotter the climate, the hotter the food—in part, at least, to keep it from spoiling.

Sometimes, however, the benefits of traditional knowledge are not so obvious to those outside the culture. In Bali in the 1970's, the Indonesian government, persuaded by international advocates of the "green revolution," forced rice farmers to adopt new growing schemes. Among other things, the farmers were made to stop their centuries-old ritual of meeting in small groups at a series of water temples set at the forks of rivers, to negotiate seasonal schedules for flooding their paddies.

The new techniques resulted in disaster. Farmers were pressured to plant as often as possible. With little coordination of irrigation, water shortages and pest infestation were the norm.

At about this time, J. Stephen Lansing, an American anthropologist, began to study the water temples. What he found, which was supported later by computer modeling, was that the old system was quite sophisticated and efficient, encouraging cooperation among thousands of farmers. Water was shared and controlled through a process involving reciprocal altruism.

"Everybody gets more rice and variation, so there's no reason to be envious of your neighbors," said Professor Lansing, who now teaches at the University of Arizona. "It's a bottom-up system of management that's worked very well." The green revolution, he added, "was very much top down." The traditional system has been re-established.

Professor Orlove has studied similar traditional resource management around Lake Titicaca, on the border between Bolivia and Peru. A distinctive feature of the lake is the reeds growing in its shallows. The people around the lake use them for rafts and livestock feed, among other things.

"They are a major component of the household economy," said Professor Orlove. The residents replant the reeds, which also serve as a spawning ground for some of the 22 species of fish that are unique to the lake.

But indigenous knowledge can be faulty. "Traditional people sometimes get things right, and sometimes get them wrong," said Alan Fiske, a psychological anthropologist at the University of California at Los Angeles. "Some things people do are bad for them." Other anthropologists have challenged the notion that all indigenous groups have somehow developed a blissful oneness with their world.

The problem, Professor Fiske noted, is that verifying traditional knowledge is not easy. The scientific method can be expensive, and data can be difficult to obtain. Professor Orlove's research on the potato farmers would have been impossible even 10 years ago, because the type of satellite data he needed did not exist.

There may be a shortage of data, but there's no shortage of traditional knowledge that awaits possible confirmation by science. James Lynch, an American scientist who has spent the past two decades helping Costa Rican farmers, said he has learned from them the importance of timing. A tree cut down during a new moon, he said, will quickly be ravaged by the insects, while one felled several days before a full moon will stay free of termites for years.

Mr. Lynch now follows the practice. "But I've never seen any scientific study to back it up," he said.

KINSHIP AND MARRIAGE

Each culture provides us with an accepted range of options for human activity. It thus sets limits on human behavior as well as creating its potential. Although the spectrum of accepted or normative behavior in human groups around the world is vast, there are certain patterns that reappear in virtually every society and are validated by almost every culture. These are termed *cultural universals.*

The regulation of sexual behavior and mating is one such cultural universal. Sexual mores vary greatly from one culture to another, but all cultures apparently share one basic value—namely, that sexual intercourse between parents and their children is to be avoided. In addition, most cultures also prohibit sexual contact between siblings. The term for prohibited sex between relatives is *incest*, and because all known cultures attach such strong feelings of revulsion to incest, it is said to be a *taboo.*

The universal presence of the *incest taboo* means that individuals must seek socially acceptable partners and spouses outside their own families. All cultures provide definitions of the categories of persons who are eligible and ineligible to marry or have sex with. These definitions vary in important ways across societies. In our society, for instance, the incest taboo covers relatively few individuals—members of our own nuclear family plus direct lineal relatives and their siblings. However, in societies organized primarily around kinship ties (as most preliterate societies are), the categories of sexually ineligible persons can be very large indeed, including almost all of a given individual's relatives linked through either male (patrilineal) or female (matrilineal) kinship.

The influential French anthropologist Claude Lévi-Strauss (one of the seminal thinkers in the school of thought called Structuralism) argues that the incest taboo created the means for groups to form enduring relationships that promoted survival through alliance building by forcing what amounted to political marriages across group lines. This may well have been true in the past. However, modern society has many other means of organizing enduring relationships among groups; therefore, if Lévi-Strauss's hypothesis is correct, the incest taboo might well become obsolete (that is, if it serves no other purpose but alliance building.) But I suspect that won't happen—for the incest taboo serves many other functions, including the crucial function of protecting members of families from confusing psychological pressures for sex within inherently unequal relationships (such as between parents and children).

In fact, with the erosion of the political function of the incest taboo in modern society, it may become possible to study and understand the profound psychological functions it serves. Nor would we wish to gloss over the biological function of the incest taboo, which by its compelling influence over people's motivations tends to diminish inbreeding within small groups and thereby keeps the human gene pool robustly well mixed—a significant adaptive advantage, as demonstrated by the higher than average presence of genetically carried deformities and illnesses among inbreeding populations.

In Article 36, "Marriage and the Family: For Love, Profit, or Politics," Malcolm McFee and David E. K. Hunter focus on the marriage practices of Vasilika, a Greek village described by anthropologist Ernestine Friedl, to introduce many of the basic concepts used to study marriage and kinship.

Laurel Kendall, in Article 37, "The Marriage of Yongsu's Mother," rounds out Topic 9. It could have fit equally well under the topic on fieldwork, but it was placed here because it gives a graphic description of an arranged marriage that should put to rest once and for all the notion that research subjects' ways of doing things are somehow natural to them. Preindustrial or preliterate people are not simple, and at times what they have to do feels bad to them—even if it is culturally prescribed. In this, they are not different from us. Indeed, suffering some degree of alienation, even within the realm of the culturally normal for one's group, may itself be a cultural universal.

Malcolm McFee and David E. K. Hunter

Marriage and the Family: For Love, Profit, or Politics

Wedding bells! Something old, something new, something borrowed and something blue—along with romance, dating, courtship, love, a honeymoon, and children—that's what marriages are made of. Or so our parents told us.

But there is much they didn't say: that in our society more than half of all marriages end in divorce, that more than one-third of all wives and half of all husbands sooner or later cheat on each other, that family finances will rank way ahead of love and sex as the primary topic of conversation in most marriages. That the stresses of career may undermine personal commitments. That when erotic attraction fades, friendship is the most important trait of successful marriage partners. That in today's economic conditions, prolonged dependence on family and in-laws is the rule rather than the exception. And that single parenthood is the normative family configuration among economically disenfranchised groups.

Simply put, the stories we are told about love, marriage, and family are myths—cultural ideals having much less to do with reality than most of us expect as we enter adulthood.

Anthropologists are well aware of the differences between the "ideal" and the "real"—as well as differences among societies around the world. They study marriage and the family in many societies to learn about ways in which they differ. They also look at common features (so-called cultural universals) across the full spectrum of societies and cultures in order to understand the functions marriage and the family fulfill in human life.

Of course, given the evolutionary thrust of human development toward relying on social groups to meet most of our needs, some form of continuing association between men and women is necessary to care for and educate children. Many possible forms of groupings could serve the purpose, but marriage and the family appear to be ancient, enduring, and almost universal responses to these needs.

Human beings are born relatively undeveloped. The infant has much to learn, the capacity to learn much, and the need for a long period of learning before it can fend for itself. The woman bears the child and provides the initial care and nurture, and she thus fits easily into the role we call *mother*. The mother needs support and protection during the nurturing period. Humans have long divided labor on the basis of sex, and many of the needs of mother and offspring are most conveniently supplied by men. So a man takes the role of provider, the role we call *father*. More mating and more children continue the need of nurture and protection and tend to perpetuate the association.

When women, children, and supporting men live in common residence or proximity, the conditions are present for a *family*. The family is defined by a *social* assignment of rights and privileges and a *social* determination of the roles of spouse, parents, child, and siblings. Public recognition and acceptance of the relationship between men and women constitutes *marriage*. This family may take one of a number of forms that have evolved in response to basic biological needs, although the origins and development in any particular form may remain in doubt.

THE "FOLK" AND "ANALYTICAL" PERSPECTIVES

In studying human institutions, anthropologists distinguish between two different perspectives from which people look at things. The so-called "folk" perspective is the point of view taken by the people whose institutions are being studied: if someone were studying college dating behavior and date rape, for instance, the views of you and your friends would represent the "folk" perspective. However, an outsider may bring an entirely different point of view to bear on an issue; and if that outsider is an anthropologist or other social scientist trying to analyze a culture's institutions, this would be the "analytical" perspective. Neither perspective is more "true" or "correct" than the other—they just have different purposes and, as a result, point to different aspects of the picture.

To illustrate this difference in perspective—and also to shed more light on the institutions of marriage and the family—we turn to the Greek villagers of Vasilika. First, the "folk" perspective.

The traditional Greek farm village wedding represents the ideal that the people of Vasilika hold of a good wedding, but the actual ceremonies vary in the degree to which they approximate this ideal. Many daughters marry townsmen, and many sons move out to city jobs. While their wedding ceremonies might be traditional, the resulting residence and family patterns differ somewhat from those of the young people who remain on the farm.

Vasilika and villages like it house people who farm the neighboring lands. All members of the family participate in some of the farming activities, calling on hired labor only when the demands of the crops exceed the family's resources. Financial success is important to the villagers. Urban ways are considered desirable and are emulated, and people value good houses with some modern amenities.

> The villagers measure prestige and honor by the degree to which a family succeeds in fulfilling its obligations.... The essential obligation is to maintain a ratio between property and children as to enable each child, when the property is divided in equal shares among all the children, to maintain in turn, a decent standard of living.... The ability to transmit wealth is especially important. The villagers consider a man who is rich in lands but has no children an object of pity; the man's wife is considered even more unfortunate. This is because the contemplation of the success of their children gives the life of a married couple a large part of its meaning. (Friedl 1962:18)

Success is not measured solely by achievements in farming. Education is also valued. Not all sons can be farmers, so many are encouraged to get an education and seek urban jobs. Not all girls can marry farmers, so many take jobs in the city and become betrothed to promising urban youths.

The daughter's dowry is very important, for it represents her share in the estate of the parents, paid in advance of their death.

> In short, the bride's father wants to insure, insofar as he is able, the future well-being of his daughter and of her children. He also wants the emotional satisfaction of having been successful at making a good arrangement for her. One village farmer pointed to a field we were passing and explained that he had given it to his daughter as part of her prika (dowry), so that all the cotton from the field was for his grandson. He then went on to say that he had married his daughter well and said of his three-year-old grandson, "Who knows, one day he might become a lawyer or a doctor. He has a brain, the little one." (Friedl 1962:53)

It is in this context that families choose marriage partners for their children, agree on the dowry the daughter will bring, and support the courtship of the couple once the agreement is reached.

In the traditional ceremony between children of farmers, the dowry is carried by young male relatives of the groom from her house to his. The next day, according to Ernestine Friedl's description (which she cautions is incomplete):

> The groom's party, including his marriage sponsor (kumbaros), arrive at the house of the bride. The kumbaros leads the group to the house, only to find the door closed and locked. He begs that the door be opened. The girls inside giggle and demand 1,000 drachmas to open the door. After some bargaining, the kumbaros gives a five-drachma piece and the party comes in. It is the kumbaros who rents the bride's white wedding gown, provides the wedding crowns, the large white candles which are held at the ceremony, and the kufeta, the sugar-covered almonds arranged in small packages of white netting, tied with a white ribbon, which he distributes to each of the guests after the ceremony. After the wedding feast, for which musicians are hired so that the guests can sing and dance, the bride is accompanied to the groom's home by her brothers and sometimes a sister. The women, including the bride, all cry as they leave the girl with her new husband. (Friedl 1962:58)

The difficulty of presenting a description of the situation as the villagers see it is apparent: Even in a more extensive description an observer might miss certain aspects. Here Friedl has mentioned values expressed by the villagers to support her selection.

From the "analytical" perspective, the study of Vasilikan marriage and family begins with the classification of these practices. The evidence shows village exogamy, monogamous marriage, the use of a dowry, and a religious ceremony. For the young couple who will inherit the groom's family land and farm it, residence is patrilocal, and the initial family is an extended family of the vertical type. After the death of the parents, the family will be classed as a nuclear family; the previously dependent son will become the family head. In time, the family might again become extended if an inheriting son marries, and the new couple take their place as dependents of his father.

The Vasilikan practices could be described in a few words by use of these concepts, and comparative analysis might show that these are the categories that identify *Greek* practices in general (Murdock 1967:82). The Greek pattern as a whole could then be compared to patterns of other societies that had been assessed in the same way. For instance, the Basques of Spain, the French-Canadians, the Tigrinya of Africa, the Shantung of China, the Sherpa of Tibet, and the Tamil of India all use the dowry, but their family organization and residence rules vary. The Greeks, French-Canadians, and the Tigrinya all use the dowry and form monogamous nuclear families, but their residence preferences differ. What do these similarities and differences mean? How do the various practices relate to each other and to other aspects of culture? Such questions are not easily answered, but they do call for hypotheses and attempts at explanation. The treatment of these problems often depends, however, on the analytical viewpoint of the investigator.

One frequent generalization offered by anthropologists is that marriages are more often established between groups for economic reasons than between individuals for love. The Greek marriage and family forms can be seen from this perspective as responses to economic pressures. Land is scarce and cannot be continually subdivided to provide cultivatable plots for all offspring. Yet a man needs sufficient children to help with the farm work if he is to avoid excessive costs for hired labor. The dilemma is resolved by educating children and encouraging surplus offspring to seek wage jobs or professions in the city, while keeping one son at home to inherit the farm and marry a bride who will bring a good dowry. Conversely, a man is anxious to provide a dowry for his daughters so that they will make good marriages, provide for his grandchildren, and enhance or maintain his prestige.

In this model, then, the marriages become economic moves to preserve and incorporate land holdings, to work the holdings efficiently to provide cash shares for children who leave, and to build capital for the next generation of farmers. By focusing on the social values and practices related to the tenure, use, and transmission of land, we can develop a comprehensive picture in which marriage and family are two of several strategies serving these goals.

Another common analytical perspective focuses on the functions performed by marriage and family forms. Some of the functions, called *manifest functions*, might be recognized by the villagers themselves. Others, *latent functions*, are recognized by the observer but are unintended and unnoticed by the participants. The marriage, for instance, establishes ties of affinity between families, but it may also channel affection, sociability, economic rights and responsibilities, and loyalties beyond the range of the families concerned. The ceremony symbolizes the unity of Greeks and the unity of the village in the shared religion, awakens the sense of family, and celebrates the values of children, enterprise, and success. The rules of exogamy and the prohibition of marriage within the range of third cousins maintain open ties with many families. The residence pattern for successive farming sons keeps them on their fathers' land and provides continuity in a community of people who know each other well, familiar people whom one can befriend or quarrel with. Marriage and family function with other aspects of the society to reassert Greek values, to maintain the community, and to satisfy felt needs of the people.

SUMMARY

By now you will understand that anthropologists analyze marriage with many different questions in mind: Is there a brideprice, dowry, or gift exchange? Is the system monogamous or polygamous? Where do marital partners live after the wedding? Is the family nuclear or extended? Are people required to marry within or outside their own group? (Or a combination: perhaps inside their ethnic or religious group, but outside their extended family.) Are specified individuals or categories of persons, such as cross-cousins, regarded as preferred marital partners?

The precise definitions of marriage and the family remain a matter of controversy and debate in anthropology, although most scholars would accept the basic ideas we have put forth here. Controversy also arises over how best to view marriage functionally: "alliance theorists" see it as a means of creating alliances among groups (as when royal families from two countries intermarry to cement political loyalties); "descent theorists" see it as a means for preserving the structure of the society by stabilizing the processes of reproduction and childrearing, and the legitimizing of children in society. Here again, neither of these analytical perspectives is more right or wrong than the other—each is concerned with different social functions and therefore emphasizes a particular aspect of the truth.

The truth that we hope you will gather from reading this article is that regardless of the specific forms they take, marriage and the family are essential institutions in virtually all societies and hence must address basic evolutionary needs of the human species. A society that does not sponsor and sustain these institutions risks tearing apart its own social fabric and may not be able to survive.

The Marriage of Yongsu's Mother

The most nerve-wracking days come early in anthropological fieldwork. My assistant and I went from door to door in Enduring Pine Village, administering a routine questionnaire. How many people live in this house? What are their ages? We asked about childbirth, miscarriages, and abortions; about spirit possession, exorcisms, and divinations. We took great pains to explain the purpose of the survey, which was to compile background information on family life and women's experiences in this Korean community. But our carefully rehearsed and excessively polite introductions did not lull my own discomfort at intruding upon the lives of busy countrywomen. We were still seeking the least offensive way to ask our questions and struggling to make sense of the things that we were told.

In the lingering April dusk, we went to Yongsu's Mother's house because we needed a lift, and this would be an easy interview. I had already spent more than a month in the company of this *mansin*, or "shaman," observing her at divination sessions and rituals. She knew that my work included a barrage of questions, and I knew that she loved to talk. She fielded our queries with an air of amusement, prompting my giggling assistant to conduct the interview as if it were a parody.

"Do you practice birth control?"

"Am I a chicken? Can I lay eggs without a mate?"

The anthropologist and her assistant were an appreciative audience, a sympathetic audience, and the mansin would give us more than the routine answers our tedious questions solicited. She told us about the little sister who had contracted smallpox. To entertain and propitiate the smallpox spirit, the family held a *kut*, an elaborate ritual in which all of the family's gods and ancestors appear and speak in the person of the costumed, possessed shamans. The shamans jumped up and down on the porch with such enthusiasm that the floorboards caved in. When the smallpox spirit visits the house, nails should not be driven into wood. But her father ignored the prohibition and repaired the broken porch, and the sick child went blind. They searched for the nails, found one, pulled it out, washed it, and

the little girl regained sight in one eye. Still, she remained sickly and soon died, cradled in her elder sister's arms.

Yongsu's Mother keeps the little girl's spirit with the gods and ancestors in her shrine. When she performs a kut to feast and entertain her own gods, she ties a child's brightly colored skirt and jacket to the belt of the costume she wears to summon the Special Messenger, the smallpox spirit. Her dead sister comes to the kut in the god's entourage; I would meet her at a kut later that spring. Speaking through the lips of a possessed mansin, she would announce

Photo courtesy of Homer Williams.

herself as a princess and claim that she had come to play.

From the loose threads of the survey questions, Yongsu's Mother began to spin bits of tales, constrained and abbreviated by the structure of our interview and the list of questions yet to be posed. When we asked about marriage, the dam burst and the words poured out, rising and falling until the tale was told:

It was market day, I can never forget it. We'd been boiling beans to make soy sauce. I was dressed up in a yellow jacket and a pink skirt, silky stuff, the best you could get back then. I had on my best Korean dress and fresh white stockings. I thought I'd go down and see what the Willow Market was like, and I was on my way out of the gate when a man and a woman arrived. The man asked me, "Is your elder sister home?" I just bawled back, "Sister, someone's here!" She came bustling out to greet them and took them straight to our mother's room. I told Mom I was going out, but she sent me to stoke the fire under the beans.

I kept tossing twigs into the flames while my sister, behind the paper door, kept saying, "Yes, yes, yes." I stuck my head in and asked, "What's going on?" She told me to get them some noodle soup from the Chinese restaurant. I asked, "What about me?" "You can do as you like." So I went and ordered their noodle soup, and when the restaurant boy delivered it, I set it on a tray with some kimchee and shouted in, "Here's the noodles!" My sister told me to come in and sit down. I just plopped the tray down and trudged back outside. I didn't think anything of it, didn't realize they'd come to look me over. I thought that they had come to see my sister and I'd just brought them some noodles for lunch. The man sat by the desk with a handkerchief on his lap and he looked very old. I remembered that afterward. I'd just walked in and out when I brought the noodles.

My sister called for me to take away the tray, so I went back in. That guy hadn't eaten more than three mouthfuls. I took his noodles out to the kitchen to save for later. When my mother came out, I asked her if I could go to the market. She said, "What's all this about going to the market? Where's the money?" I told her I had money, and she asked me where I'd kept it hidden. There wasn't anything to buy out in the country anyway. I just wanted to have a look around.

The man was ready to leave, and everyone stood around saying their goodbyes. I stayed in the kitchen, but as soon as the man left, the matchmaker came looking for me. She said she wanted to have a talk. I told her I was going to the market. She said, "You come right over here and tell me what you think of that guy."

"What do you mean?"

"He's looked you over and you please him. Just say the word and it's settled."

I was flabbergasted. "What nonsense is this? Who says I want to get married? Anyway, I wouldn't marry an old guy like that. Don't even say such things!"

The matchmaker went right back into my sister's room. I wasn't in the mood for the market anymore. I waited for the matchmaker to come out and she started in again, "Tell me what you thought of that guy, just say the word. He's all right, isn't he?"

I howled that I couldn't go through with it. I told them, "Do you think I can't find a husband anywhere? Do you think I have to settle for an old guy like that? I'm going back to Seoul."

Then my sister raised a fuss. "You're so stubborn. With your wretched horoscope, you should marry an older man, someone who's already been married once. I'm your sister. Do you think I'd arrange something that was bad for you?"

When she said that, I was so furious I couldn't hold it in, I ran to the chimney behind the house and sobbed. "She brought us down here because she was lonely. She's made us sell our house. Why is she doing this to me? When the right time comes, I'll gladly get married. Why do they have to marry me off to an old guy?" I raged and cried, and raged some more....

We passed into the twelfth month, the empty time that we don't consider part of the old year. About five days before the wedding, the man gave my sister some money for my permanent and bride's makeup. I took the money and threw it on the ground. "What does this have to do with anything? Does he think I haven't gotten married because I can't afford to permanent my hair?" My sister tried to coax me, but this threw me into a deeper rage. "If I'm set against him, why are you all so anxious to throw me out like this? If our ages were similar it would be all right, but he's old. If you're so keen on this marriage, why not go and investigate him? Do you expect me to marry someone who lives so far away on just the strength of the matchmaker's words?"

"The matchmaker knows the whole story. How come you're so suspicious?"

After the wedding, I left Willow Market with him and cried all the way on the bus. My eyes were swollen. It must have been embarrassing for him.

We got to the Imjin River. That was as far as the bus would go. We needed passes to board the boat, but I said I didn't have one. We had a huge fight right there on the dock. Here I was, all done up in a Korean dress made of silk from Hong Kong, and the angrier I got, the more I wanted to throw myself into the river. By the time my husband had cleared things with the guards and dragged me away to the boat, my feet were frozen stiff. On the other side there was another checkpoint. The guard asked me, "Auntie, do you have a citizen's identification card?" This time I just slipped out my Seoul registration card, showed it to the guard, and walked on through.

As we reached the far side of the river, someone rode up on a bicycle, parked it on the sand, and pulled in the boat. I thought it was just another passenger going to cross the river, but when I looked I saw that he resembled my husband. I'd heard that he had six brothers so I just assumed that this was one of them, but when I asked my husband, he denied it, said it was a distant relation. Even on the way to his home he lied to me.

We walked and walked. My feet swelled up like balloons. I wasn't used to walking. Finally, we came to the village. A girl emerged from one of the houses and threw out a basin of dishwater. She gave me the strangest look. In some odd way she seemed to resemble my husband. She was standing in front of a straw-roofed house, a tumbledown house. It was falling apart at the seams. I hoped with all my might that we would not turn into that house. I followed behind my husband with my eyes cast down to the backs of his shoes. His feet turned into that very gateway. Could he just be stopping by? No such luck. As soon as we were inside the gate, I heard, "Daddy's home, Daddy's home!" Despair!

I stood there in the gateway, stunned. I heard them ask me, over and over again, to come in. There was a three-year-old boy, a little frog baby looking mischievous, and a nine-year-old daughter, the one who works in Seoul now. There was also a twenty-one-year-old daughter; I was barely five years older than her. I thought she was my husband's niece. I thought that she had just come over to help with the housework.

They kept asking me to come inside, so I went in and looked things over. It was laughable. The house was bare. The cupboard held one battered little dish for shrimp sauce. Oh, I was disappointed! I just stood there in the empty kitchen until my husband took me by the hand and led me to the inner room. It was a sorry show there too, only a wooden chest and some quilts piled up. I cursed my sister! Why did I deserve this? That bitch! I had told her to check everything before she married me off. I cried and cried. I couldn't stop. My husband said, "What's done is done. You won't get anywhere by crying about it." But I was fuming. If my sister had lived nearby, I'd

have gone right over and grabbed her. I'd have dragged her there and said, "Feast your eyes on this!" But I didn't know the way back; I had never been in this village before.

The older girl brought in a tray of food. All of the relatives came over. The elder brothers' wives and the elder cousins' wives served the food—rice, toasted seaweed, and kimchee. Since it was the twelfth month, we ate winter kimchee. They kept asking me to eat and I kept saying that I didn't want any. They asked and I refused, again and again. That person, my husband, couldn't eat either. When the elder brother's wife came in and begged me to eat, I had a few mouthfuls just to make them happy.

Then I had to bow to them all. The room was full of people; they swarmed around like maggots. I had no idea who they were. There were relatives to the

Photo courtesy of Homer Williams.

third degree and relatives to the fourth degree. I was dropping down to the floor and bobbing up all night. Finally, the third brother's wife said, "She's had a long journey. She must be tired. Those who haven't received her bows can come back tomorrow." My husband told them that my feet were swollen.

After everyone left, that man, my husband, went outside too. The brothers' wives were fixing a late-night snack. The girl came into the room to get something. She looked at my hand and said, "What a lovely hand!" She asked how old I was. My husband had told me to say that I was thirty-six but I told the truth, "I'm twenty-six."

The girl started. "Twenty-six?"

The elder brother's wife said, "Your skin is still soft like a baby's. With such a lovely face and hands, how can you do a countrywoman's work?" They said, "Your ages are too far apart." They chattered on about how young I was and how old he was while I just sat there. The girl came back into the room. I asked, "How old are you?"

She said, "One."

I said, "You mean twenty-one?"

She nodded.

The brother's wife explained, "My husband's brother is forty-one." Now it dawned on me that this girl was my husband's daughter. I thought, "it will be difficult enough to raise my own children, but how am I ever going to raise these?"

It was already one o'clock in the morning. They rolled out the quilts and told me to rest. My husband came in and sent them all home so I could sleep. He went out to see them off and came back. I couldn't even cry. I just sat there without a word. He came over and tried to take off my jacket. When he reached for the ribbon, I slapped his hand away. I said, "You should have told me the truth. You should have told me that you're forty-one years old and have a twenty-one-year-old daughter. After lying like this, how dare you put your hand to my body!"

Now he was angry. "Who told you that?" But then he said, "Don't worry about my daughter. I'll just marry her off. If I said I had so many daughters, they wouldn't have given you to me. I lied about that, but I really am thirty-seven."

I said, "All right, tomorrow we'll go to the district office and just see how you're registered. I've come all this way. If you turn out to be thirty-seven, I'll stay, but if that's not so, I'm leaving."

I didn't sleep. I held my ground all night. Whenever he reached out to touch me, I slapped his hand away. What could he do? He sat there smoking. He offered to help me take off my padded socks because my feet were sore. I said, "if my feet hurt, that's my business. You leave me alone."

In the morning, the older daughter fixed breakfast and the elder brother's wife came over to help. I stayed in the inner room. When the nine-year-old girl brought water for me to wash my face, she said, "How can this person be my mother?" My husband hit her. He scolded her in a loud voice that all the relatives could hear. It did not bode well for a daughter to be disrespectful to her new stepmother.

They brought in the breakfast tray and again I said that I wasn't going to eat. I hadn't eaten anything for so long that my eyes were turning back inside my head. My husband went out and spoke to his brother's wife. She came in and coaxed, "Since you're here, you might as well eat something. Here, let's eat together." I could have eaten everything on that tray, but I just had a couple of spoonfuls. When she took out the tray, I heard my husband ask how I was. I sat in the room all day without saying a word. He fretted and paced back and forth, back and forth. I can still hear the sound of his feet. He was worried that I might run away.

Hours had passed as Yongsu's Mother narrated the tale of her wedding, a saga well polished by countless retellings for audiences of village women and clients. We were summoned to a late dinner while she hastened to cook up the evening rice for herself and Yongsu. We returned again in the evening and listened into the night. She told us how her elder step-daughter ran away in rebellion and how, as a consequence, her husband began to drink himself to death in shame; how "that man" left her a widow when her own son, Yongsu, was barely a year old; and how she had been forced to survive on slim resources until, a few years later, the gods made her a shaman. Later, when we had translated all that we had heard and recorded, we knew that we were hooked, avid to hear more. Not only did Yongsu's Mother provide a rich ethnographic narrative, she was also a skilled storyteller, rendering her images with delicious turns of phrase. Her feet swelled up like balloons. She kept stoking the fire while her sister kept saying, "Yes, yes, yes." She modestly lowered her gaze to the backs of her husband's feet and saw them turn into the doorway of the hovel that would be her new home. She remembered details: the handkerchief on her future husband's lap, the pot of boiling beans, the half-eaten bowl of noodles, the basin of water in her stepdaughter's hands.

I toyed with the idea of recording a full biography, but was soon preoccupied by my research on shaman rituals. My assistant, who had relished the task of translating Yongsu's Mother's vivid language, left the field when she landed a promising job in Seoul. But Yongsu's Mother took the initiative, announcing that she would tell me the full story of her life. She had already mapped out the narrative: "The story of my childhood and of my father's taking a concubine, the story of my capture and escape during the war and my meeting with the Mountain God, the story of my lover and the birth of my daughter, the story of my marriage, and the story of my becoming a mansin." She told me that when I knew it all my tears would flow. The recurrent themes of her life had already been sounded in the initial interview: betrayal by kin, disappointment in human relationships, the bother and ingratitude of stepchildren, and the power of gods and ancestors to alter human destiny for good or ill.

I suspect that Yongsu's Mother often exaggerates, both to vindicate herself and also to heighten the drama of her performance. Hers is a melodramatic account, told among people who appreciate the purgative value of a good cry. This is not to say that she consciously deceives her audience, but rather that she plays her material for all it's worth. When she told us the story of her marriage, she recreated the innocent maiden of a fairy tale, oblivious to the machinations of a greedy sister who was sealing her fate behind closed doors. But how naïve could she have been? Not only was she twenty-six years old when she married the widower, she had already given birth to an illegitimate child. By the bitter standards of her own society, the bride was past marrying age and damaged goods besides. The scheming sister might rather have tried to make the best of her younger sibling's limited options. And although Yongsu's Mother protested every inch of the way to her husband's house, once there she recognized her lack of alternatives, cut her losses, made a life, and spun out her anger in a tale. Her art was to make old disappointment a good story.

I first heard Yongsu's Mother's account of her marriage in the spring of 1977. I returned in 1985 to tell her that I had finally translated the story of her life, to see if she was still willing to have me publish it, and to ask her help in completing the manuscript. I brought her a copy of my first book, inscribed "to my *mansin* honorable teacher," and heard her cap a discussion with "I've even come out in a book in America." But days passed before I could explain to Yongsu's Mother the real purpose of my visit. I wanted to be certain that she understood what I was about, and I wanted to discuss this project in privacy. This last condition was difficult to achieve in her sociable inner room, but one afternoon, when the last guest had departed and just before her son, Yongsu, returned home from another date, I brought out one of the old tapes and slipped it into my machine.

"You still have those old things?" I tell her about the translations and about the book I plan to publish.

"But in America, what if Koreans read it? They'll think it's shameful." Her world has broadened. When I first knew her, America was on the other side of the earth, the home of the odd-complexioned soldiers who ran in formation on the road by her house, a land she had seen in movies. In 1985, America is where her brother and the kin of her neighbors live, a place where Koreans live. Appreciating her concern, I take a deep breath. I want to protect her and perhaps it is safest to abandon the project, but I also want her to know the worth of her storytelling.

"Americans won't find it shameful; they'll think it's interesting, as interesting as a novel." "As interesting as a novel," she repeats the phrase to herself. "It has social and historical significance," I continue, using a Korean vocabulary that I read rather than speak, the words that do not ordinarily enter village conversation. "Of course, there are people who are incapable of understanding. I know this. I don't want any harm to come to you or Yongsu. As I have done in the past, I will try to keep your name a secret. In the book I've called you 'Yongsu's Mother.' When my friends from Seoul came here for the kut the other day, they kept asking, 'Where's Yongsu's Mother?'" She laughs, and agrees to help me.

I was leaving again. About to depart for a kut with her closest friend and colleague, Songjuk Mansin, Yongsu's Mother presented me with some Korean accouterments for my American kitchen. She gave me a pair of covered rice bowls—a high *chubal*, such as men use, and a woman's short, broad *hap*—and a large rice pot, and then a smaller one, "so that your husband can cook rice when you are away." She saw the very un-Korean premise of my married life and was amused.

"What's her husband like?" Sonjuk Mansin asked Yongsu's Mother.

"Nice, steady-going," she said, and told a story from our visit in the summer of 1983. "It was the middle of the day, no one was around. I heard a faint splashing sound in the bath...I tiptoed in.... And there was the husband doing the laundry!" The prospect of my husband quietly doing laundry to surprise his absent wife was an image so droll as to provoke extended gales of laughter.

"And this," she said, returning to her bag of gifts and drawing out the gourd dipper that I had requested to replicate a birth charm for the American Museum, "this has historical significance. Why, people used to eat their rice out of these. We did that when we visited my grandfather in the country."

"Historical significance." She had taken my words because they intrigued and pleased her. She has observed my life and now tells stories about my household as I tell stories about her telling stories.

POLITICAL AND ECONOMIC ORGANIZATION

All societies have means of molding their members' behavior to conform to group values (general orientations toward good and bad) and group norms (specific expectations of behavior depending on who the actor is and on the social context in which the behavior is taking place). Anthropologists call such means the *mechanisms of social control*, and they distinguish between internal means and external means.

Internal means of control rely on the individual's personal acceptance—through enculturation and socialization—of his or her culture's values and norms. In other words, the individual will feel uncomfortable when the moral order of the society is violated and therefore will be motivated not to transgress the culture's moral code or expectations.

External means of control are the responses of the society or its representatives to specific actions by the individual—either to reinforce (reward) such actions or to diminish the likelihood of their repetition. The former, reinforcing responses, are termed *positive sanctions*. The latter, punishments, are referred to as *negative sanctions*.

Internalized values and norms, together with (external) positive and negative sanctions, operate in all societies. However there is enormous cross-cultural variation in the behaviors that are valued and reinforced (or rejected and punished) and in the specific forms that the means of social control take.

Social organization consists of the web of patterned relationships among people in a society. These relationships must be to some degree predictable; otherwise the fabric of social life would unravel. Hence social control is crucial for every society, and studying the specific means employed to implement them and the particular forms they take tell us a great deal about a society and its culture.

In Article 38, "Life without Chiefs," Marvin Harris looks at a specific turning point in the story of cultural evolution: the invention of agriculture. In this article, he shows how agriculture brought with it the means and even the motivation for hierarchical political structures to emerge. He is far from happy with the result. In fact, he believes it has taken us to the brink of global annihilation.

"In Search of the Affluent Society," Article 39, by Allen Johnson, focuses on consumption rather than production. It argues that the narrow view of economists is inadequate for assessing economic systems and that a critical variable is the quality of life an economic system permits its participants. In comparing Amazonian society to French society, this article emphasizes a point made by Harris: that simple society provides its members with more time for visiting, play, conversation, and rest than does complex (agricultural, industrial and postindustrial) society. He also shares with us some personal questions this raises for him.

It would not be appropriate, however, to leave the somewhat romantic views of Harris and Johnson unchallenged. Recent research has shown that many societies that were thought to be "pristinely" unaffected by agriculture, in fact had centuries of trading relationships with their more sedentary neighbors, and relied on them for many products. Also, the hunting and gathering way of life seems to have supported a lifespan of only thirty years or so, featured high infant mortality, and left many groups close to starvation during summer droughts or seasonal floods.

So although it is undeniable that a society's economic system and political organization are tightly interconnected (as the recent collapse of communist political systems built on centralized socialist economies attests to)—it is a mistake to draw overly generalized conclusions from particular studies. There remains much to be learned about political and economic organization in human societies.

Life without Chiefs

Can humans exist without some people ruling and others being ruled? To look at the modern world, you wouldn't think so. Democratic states may have done away with emperors and kings, but they have hardly dispensed with gross inequalities in wealth, rank, and power.

However, humanity hasn't always lived this way. For about 98 percent of our existence as a species (and for four million years before then), our ancestors lived in small, largely nomadic hunting-and-gathering bands containing about 30 to 50 people apiece. It was in this social context that human nature evolved. It has been only about ten thousand years since people began to settle down into villages, some of which eventually grew into cities. And it has been only in the last two thousand years that the majority of people in the world have not lived in hunting-and-gathering societies. This brief period of time is not nearly sufficient for noticeable evolution to have taken place. Thus, the few remaining foraging societies are the closest analogues we have to the "natural" state of humanity.

To judge from surviving examples of hunting-and-gathering bands and villages, our kind got along quite well for the greater part of prehistory without so much as a paramount chief. In fact, for tens of thousands of years, life went on without kings, queens, prime ministers, presidents, parliaments, congresses, cabinets, governors, and mayors—not to mention the police officers, sheriffs, marshals, generals, lawyers, bailiffs, judges, district attorneys, court clerks, patrol cars, paddy wagons, jails, and penitentiaries that help keep them in power. How in the world did our ancestors ever manage to leave home without them?

Small populations provide part of the answer. With 50 people per band or 150 people per village, everybody knew everybody else intimately. People gave with the expectation of taking and took with the expectation of giving. Because chance played a great role in the capture of animals, collection of wild foodstuffs, and success of rudimentary forms of agriculture, the individuals who had the luck of the catch on one day needed a handout on the next. So the best way for them to provide for their inevitable rainy day was to be generous. As expressed by anthropologist Richard Gould, "The greater the amount of risk, the greater the extent of sharing." Reciprocity is a small society's bank.

In reciprocal exchange, people do not specify how much or exactly what they expect to get back or when they expect to get it. That would besmirch the quality of that transaction and make it similar to mere barter or to buying and selling. The distinction lingers on in societies dominated by other forms of exchange, even capitalist ones. For we do carry out a give-and-take among close kin and friends that is informal, uncalculating, and imbued with a spirit of generosity. Teenagers do not pay cash for their meals at home or for the use of the family car, wives do not bill their husbands for cooking a meal, and friends give each other birthday gifts and Christmas presents. But much of this is marred by the expectation that our generosity will be acknowledged with expression of thanks.

Where reciprocity really prevails in daily life, etiquette requires that generosity be taken for granted. As Robert Dentan discovered during his fieldwork among the Semai of Central Malaysia, no one ever says "thank you" for the meat received from another hunter. Having struggled all day to lug the carcass of a pig home through the jungle heat, the hunter allows his prize to be cut up into exactly equal portions, which he then gives away to the entire group. Dentan explains that to express gratitude for the portion received indicates that you are the kind of ungenerous person who calculates how much you give and take: "In this context, saying 'thank you' is very rude, for it suggests, first, that one has calculated the amount of a gift and, second, that one did not expect the donor to be so generous." To call attention to one's generosity is to indicate that others are in debt to you and that you expect them to repay you. It is repugnant to egalitarian peoples even to suggest that they have been treated generously.

Canadian anthropologist Richard Lee tells how, through a revealing incident, he learned about this aspect of reciprocity. To please the !Kung, the "bushmen" of the Kalahari desert, he decided to buy a large ox and have it slaughtered as a present. After days of searching Bantu agricultural villages for the largest and fattest ox in the region, he acquired what appeared a perfect specimen. But his friends took him aside and assured him that he had been duped into buying an absolutely worthless animal. "Of course, we will eat it," they said, "but it won't fill us up—we will eat and go home to bed with stomachs rumbling." Yet, when Lee's ox was slaughtered, it turned out to be covered with a thick layer of fat. Later, his friends explained why they had said his gift was valueless, even though they knew better than he what lay under the animal's skin:

"Yes, when a young man kills much meat he comes to think of himself as a chief or a big man, and he thinks of the rest of us as his servants or inferiors. We can't accept this, we refuse one who boasts, for someday his pride will make him kill somebody. So we always speak of his meat as worthless. This way we cool his heart and make him gentle."

Lee watched small groups of men and women returning, home every evening with the animals and wild fruits and plants that they had killed or collected. They shared everything equally, even with campmates who had stayed behind and spent the day sleeping or taking care of their tools and weapons.

"Not only do families pool that day's production, but the entire camp—residents and visitors alike—shares equally in the total quantity of food available," Lee observed. "The evening meal of any one family is made up of portions of food from each of the other families resident. There is a constant flow of nuts, berries, roots, and melons from one family fireplace to another, until each person has received an equitable portion. The following morning a different combination of foragers moves out of camp, and when they return late in the day, the distribution of foodstuffs is repeated."

In small, prestate societies, it was in everybody's best interest to maintain each other's freedom of access to the natural habitat. Suppose a !Kung with a lust for power were to get up and tell his campmates, "From now on, all this land and everything on it belongs to me. I'll let you use it but only with my permission and on the condition that I get first choice of anything you capture, collect, or grow." His campmates, thinking that he had certainly gone crazy, would pack up their few belongings, take a long walk, make a new camp, and resume their usual life of egalitarian reciprocity. The man who would be king would be left by himself to exercise a useless sovereignty.

THE HEADMAN: LEADERSHIP, NOT POWER

To the extent that political leadership exists at all among band-and-village societies, it is exercised by individuals called headmen. These headmen, how-

ever, lack the power to compel others to obey their orders. How can a leader be powerless and still lead?

The political power of genuine rulers depends on their ability to expel or exterminate disobedient individuals and groups. When a headman gives a command, however, he has no certain physical means of punishing those who disobey. So, if he wants to stay in "office," he gives few commands. Among the Eskimo, for instance, a group will follow an outstanding hunter and defer to his opinion with respect to choice of hunting spots. But in all other matters, the leader's opinion carries no more weight than any other man's. Similarly, among the !Kung, each band has its recognized leaders, most of whom are males. These men speak out more than others and are listened to with a bit more deference. But they have no formal authority and can only persuade, never command. When Lee asked the !Kung whether they had headmen—meaning powerful chiefs—they told him, "Of course we have headmen! In fact, we are all headmen. Each one of us is headman over himself."

Headmanship can be a frustrating, and irksome job. Among Indian groups such as the Mehinacu of Brazil's Xingu National Park, headmen behave something like zealous scoutmasters on overnight cookouts. The first one up in the morning, the headman tries to rouse his companions by standing in the middle of the village plaza and shouting to them. If something needs to be done, it is the headman who starts doing it, and it is the headman who works harder than anyone else. He sets an example not only for hard work but also for generosity: After a fishing or hunting expedition, he gives away more of his catch than anyone else does. In trading with other groups, he must be careful not to keep the best items for himself.

In the evening, the headman stands in the center of the plaza and exhorts his people to be good. He calls upon them to control their sexual appetites, work hard in their gardens, and take frequent baths in the river. He tells them not to sleep during the day or bear grudges against each other.

COPING WITH FREELOADERS

During the reign of reciprocal exchange and egalitarian headmen, no individual, family, or group smaller than the band or village itself could control access to natural resources. Rivers, lakes, beaches, oceans, plants and animals, the soil and subsoil were all communal property.

Among the !Kung, a core of people born in a particular territory say that they "own" the water holes and hunting rights, but this has no effect on the people who happen to be visiting and living with them at any given time. Since !Kung from neighboring bands are related through marriage, they often visit each other for months at a time and have free use of whatever resources they need without having to ask permission. Though people from distant bands must make a request to use another band's territory, the "owners" seldom refuse them.

The absence of private possession in land and other vital resources means that a form of communism probably existed among prehistoric hunting and collecting bands and small villages. Perhaps I should emphasize that this did not rule out the existence of private property. People in simple band-and-village societies own personal effects such as weapons, clothing, containers, ornaments, and tools. But why should anyone want to steal such objects? People who have a bush camp and move about a lot have no use for extra possessions. And since the group is small enough that everybody knows everybody else, stolen items cannot be used anonymously. If you want something, better to ask for it openly, since by the rules of reciprocity such requests cannot be denied.

I don't want to create the impression that life within egalitarian band-and-village societies unfolded entirely without disputes over possessions. As in every social group, nonconformists and malcontents tried to use the system for their own advantage. Inevitably there were freeloaders, individuals who consistently took more than they gave and lay back in their hammocks while others did the work. Despite the absence of a criminal justice system, such behavior eventually was punished. A widespread belief among band-and-village peoples attributes death and misfortune to the malevolent conspiracy of sorcerers. The task of identifying these evildoers falls to a group's shamans, who remain responsive to public opinion during their divinatory trances. Well-liked individuals who enjoy strong support from their families need not fear the shaman. But quarrelsome, stingy people who do not give as well as take had better watch out.

FROM HEADMAN TO BIG MAN

Reciprocity was not the only form of exchange practiced by egalitarian band-and-village peoples. Our kind long ago found other ways to give and take. Among them the form of exchange known as redistribution played a crucial role in creating distinctions of rank during the evolution of chiefdoms and states.

Redistribution occurs when people turn over food and other valuables to a prestigious figure such as a headman, to be pooled, divided into separate portions, and given out again. The primordial form of redistribution was probably keyed to seasonal hunts and harvests, when more food than usual became available.

True to their calling, headmen-redistributors not only work harder than their followers but also give more generously and reserve smaller and less desirable portions for themselves than for anyone else. Initially, therefore, redistribution strictly reinforced the political and economic equality associated with reciprocal exchange. The redistributors were compensated purely with admiration and in proportion to their success in giving bigger feasts, in personally contributing more than anybody else, and in asking little or nothing for their effort—all of which initially seemed an innocent extension of the basic principle of reciprocity.

But how little our ancestors understood what they were getting themselves into! For if it is a good thing to have a headman give feasts, why not have several headmen give feasts? Or, better yet, why not let success in organizing and giving feasts be the measure of one's legitimacy as headman? Soon, where conditions permit, there are several would-be headmen vying with each other to hold the most lavish feasts and redistribute the most food and other valuables. In this fashion there evolved the nemesis that Richard Lee's !Kung informants had warned about: the youth who wants to be a "big man."

A classic anthropological study of big men was carried out by Douglas Oliver among the Siuai, a village people who live on the South Pacific island of Bougainville, in the Solomon Islands. In the Siuai language, big men were known as *mumis*. Every Siuai boy's highest ambition was to become a mumi. He began by getting married, working hard, and restricting his own consumption of meat and coconuts. His wife and parents, impressed with the seriousness of his intentions, vowed to help him prepare for his first feast. Soon his circle of supporters widened and he began to construct a clubhouse in which his male followers could lounge about and guests could be entertained and fed. He gave a feast at the consecration of the clubhouse; if this was a success, the circle of people willing to work for him grew larger still, and he began to hear himself spoken of as a mumi. Larger and larger feasts meant that the mumi's demands on his supporters became more irksome. Although they grumbled about how hard they had to work, they remained loyal as long as their mumi continued to maintain and increase his renown as a "great provider."

Finally the time came for the new mumi to challenge the older ones. He did this at a *muminai* feast, where both sides kept a tally of all the pigs, coconut pies, and sago-almond puddings given away by the host mumi and his followers to the guest mumi and his followers. If the guests could not reciprocate with a feast as lavish as that of the challengers, their mumi suffered a great social humiliation, and his fall from mumihood was immediate.

At the end of a successful feast, the greatest of mumis still faced a lifetime of personal toil and dependence on the moods and inclinations of his followers. Mumihood did not confer the power to coerce others into doing one's bidding, nor did it elevate one's standard of living above anyone else's. In fact, because giving things away was the essence of mumihood, great mumis consumed less meat and other delicacies than ordinary men. Among the Kaoka, another Solomon Islands group, there is the saying, "The giver of the feast takes the bones and the stale cakes; the meat and the fat go to the others." At one great feast attended by 1,100 people, the host mumi, whose name was Soni, gave away thirty-two pigs and a large quantity of sago-almond puddings. Soni himself and some of his closest followers went hungry. "We shall eat Soni's renown," they said.

FROM BIG MAN TO CHIEF

The slide (or ascent?) toward social stratification gained momentum wherever extra food produced by the inspired diligence of redistributors could be stored while awaiting muminai feasts, potlatches, and other occasions of redistribution. The more concentrated and abundant the harvest and the less perishable the crop, the greater its potential for endowing the big man with power. Though others would possess some stored-up foods of their own, the redistributor's stores would be the largest. In times of scarcity, people would come to him, expecting to be fed; in return, he could call upon those who had special skills to make cloth, pots, canoes, or a fine house for his own use. Eventually, the redistributor no longer needed to work in the fields to gain and surpass big-man status. Management of the harvest surpluses, a portion of which continued to be given to him for use in communal feasts and other communal projects (such as trading expeditions and warfare), was sufficient to validate his status. And, increasingly, people viewed this status as an office, a sacred trust, passed on from one generation to the next according to rules of hereditary succession. His dominion was no longer a small, autonomous village but a large political community. The big man had become a chief.

Returning to the South Pacific and the Trobriand Islands, one can catch a glimpse of how these pieces of encroaching stratification fell into place. The Trobrianders had hereditary chiefs who held sway over more than a dozen villages containing several thousand people. Only chiefs could wear certain shell ornaments as the insignia of high rank, and it was forbidden for commoners to stand or sit in a position that put a chief's head at a lower elevation. British anthropologist Bronislaw Malinowski tells of seeing all the people present in the village of Bwoytalu drop from their verandas "as if blown down by a hurricane" at the sound of a drawn-out cry warning that an important chief was approaching.

Yams were the Trobrianders' staff of life; the chiefs validated their status by storing and redistributing copious quantities of them acquired through donations from their brothers-in-law at harvest time. Similar "gifts" were received by husbands who were commoners, but chiefs were polygynous and, having as many as a dozen wives, received many more yams than anyone else. Chiefs placed their yam supply on display racks specifically built for this purpose next to their houses. Commoners did the same, but a chief's yam racks towered over all others.

This same pattern recurs, with minor variations, on several continents. Striking parallels were seen, for example, twelve thousand miles away from the Trobrianders, among chiefdoms that flourished throughout the southeastern region of the United States—specifically among the Cherokee, former inhabitants of Tennessee, as described by the eighteenth-century naturalist William Bartram.

At the center of the principal Cherokee settlements stood a large circular house where a council of chiefs discussed issues involving their villages and where redistributive feasts were held. The council of chiefs had a paramount who was the principal figure in the Cherokee redistributive network. At the harvest time a large crib, identified as the "chief's granary," was erected in each field. "To this," explained Bartram, "each family carries and deposits a certain quantity according to his ability or inclination, or none at all if he so chooses." The chief's granaries functioned as a public treasury in case of crop failure, a source of food for strangers or travelers, and as military store. Although every citizen enjoyed free access to the store, commoners had to acknowledge that it really belonged to the supreme chief, who had "an exclusive right and ability...to distribute comfort and blessings to the necessitous."

Supported by voluntary donations, chiefs could now enjoy lifestyles that set them increasingly apart from their followers. They could build bigger and finer houses for themselves, eat and dress more sumptuously, and enjoy the sexual favors and personal services of several wives. Despite these harbingers, people in chiefdoms voluntarily invested unprecedented amounts of labor on behalf of communal projects. They dug moats, threw up defensive earthen embankments, and erected great log palisades around their villages. They heaped up small mountains of rubble and soil to form platforms and mounds on top of which they built temples and big houses for their chief. Working in teams and using nothing but levers and rollers, they moved rocks weighing fifty tons or more and set them in precise lines and perfect circles, forming sacred precincts for communal rituals marking the change of seasons.

If this seems remarkable, remember that donated labor created the megalithic alignments of Stonehenge and Carnac, put up the great statues on Easter Island, shaped the huge stone heads of the Olmec in Vera Cruz, dotted Polynesia with ritual precincts set on great stone platforms, and filled the Ohio, Tennessee, and Mississippi valleys with hundreds of large mounds. Not until it was too late did people realize that their beautiful chiefs were about to keep the meat and fat for themselves while giving nothing but bones and stale cakes to their followers.

IN THE END

As we know, chiefdoms would eventually evolve into states, states into empires. From peaceful origins, humans created and mounted a wild beast that ate continents. Now that beast has taken us to the brink of global annihilation.

Will nature's experiment with mind and culture end in nuclear war? No one knows the answer. But I believe it is essential that we understand our past before we can create the best possible future. Once we are clear about the roots of human nature, for example, we can refute, once and for all, the notion that it is a biological imperative for our kind to form hierarchical groups. An observer viewing human life shortly after cultural takeoff would easily have concluded that our species was destined to be irredeemably egalitarian except for distinctions of sex and age. That someday the world would be divided into aristocrats and commoners, masters and slaves, billionaires and homeless beggars would have seemed wholly contrary to human nature as evidenced in the affairs of every human society then on Earth.

Of course, we can no more reverse the course of thousands of years of cultural evolution than our egalitarian ancestors could have designed and built the space shuttle. Yet, in striving for the preservation of mind and culture on Earth, it is vital that we recognize the significance of cultural takeoff and the great difference between biological and cultural evolution. We must rid ourselves of the notion that we are an innately aggressive species for whom war is inevitable. We must reject as unscientific claims that there are superior and inferior races and that the hierarchical divisions within and between societies are the consequences of natural selection rather than of a long process of cultural evolution. We must struggle to gain control over cultural selection through objective studies of the human condition and the recurrent process of history. Not only a more just society, but our very survival as a species may depend on it.

In Search of the Affluent Society

One of the paradoxes of modern life is the persistence of suffering and deep dissatisfaction among people who enjoy an unparalleled abundance of material goods. The paradox is at least as old as our modern age. Ever since the benefits and costs of industrial technology became apparent, opinion has been divided over whether we are progressing or declining.

The debate grows particularly heated when we compare our civilization with the cultures of "primitive" or "simpler" peoples. At the optimistic extreme, we are seen as the beneficiaries of an upward development that has brought us from an era in which life was said to be "nasty, brutish, and short," into one of ease, affluence, and marvelous prospects for the future. At the other extreme, primitives are seen as enjoying idyllic lives of simplicity and serenity, from which we have descended dangerously through an excess of greed. The truth is a complex mix of these two positions, but it is striking how difficult it is to take a balanced view. We are attracted irresistibly to either the optimistic or the pessimistic position.

The issue is of more than academic interest. The modern world is trying to come to grips with the idea of "limits to growth" and the need to redistribute wealth. Pressures are mounting from the environment on which we depend and from the people with whom we share it. Scientists, planners, and policy makers are now talking about "alternative futures," trying to marshal limited resources for the greater good of humanity. In this context it is useful to know whether people living in much simpler economies than our own really do enjoy advantages we have lost.

In his book *The Affluent Society*, economist John Kenneth Galbraith accepts the optimistic view, with some reservations. According to him, the modern trend has been toward an increase in the efficiency of production; working time has decreased while the standard of living has risen through a growth in purchasing power. One of Galbraith's reservations is that he does not see this growth as an unmitigated good. He sees our emphasis on acquiring goods as

left over from times when the experience of poverty was still real and thinks we are ready to acknowledge our wealth and reduce our rates of consumption. The trend over the last 100 years toward a shorter work week, he argues, demonstrates that we are relinquishing some of our purchasing power in exchange for greater leisure.

Galbraith's view that modern affluence both brings us greater leisure and fills our basic needs than any previous economic system is widespread. Yet the first part of this view is almost certainly wrong, and the second is debatable. Anthropologist Marshall Sahlins has shown that hunting-and-gathering economies, such as those found among the Australian aborigines and the San of southern Africa, require little work (three to four hours per adult each day) to provide ample and varied diets. Although they lack our abundance of goods, material needs are satisfied in a leisurely way, and in their own view, people are quite well off.

Sahlins points out that there are two roads to affluence: our own, which is to produce more, and what he calls the Buddhist path, which is to be satisfied with less. Posing the problem of affluence in this way makes it clear that affluence depends not only on material wealth but also on subjective satisfaction. There is apparently plenty of room for choice in designing a life of affluence.

Recent studies of how people in different societies spend their time allow us to make a fairly objective comparison of primitive and modern societies. In one analysis, Alexander Szalai studied middle-class French couples residing in six cities in France—Arras, Besançon, Chalon-sur-Saône, Dunkerque, Épinal, and Metz. Orna Johnson and I, both of us anthropologists, collected similar data when we lived among the Machiguenga Indians of Peru for some 18 months, which were spread over one long and two shorter visits.

The Machiguenga live in extended family groups scattered throughout the Amazon rain forest. They spend approximately equal amounts of time growing food in gardens carved out of the surrounding forest and in hunting, fishing, and collecting wild foods. They are self-sufficient; almost everything they consume is produced by their own labors using materials that are found close at hand. Despite some similarities in how the French and the Machiguenga spend their time (for instance, in the way work is apportioned between the sexes), the differences between the societies are applicable to our purposes.

For reasons that will become clear, we divide ways of spending time into three categories: production time, consumption time, and free time. Production time refers to what we normally think of as work, in which goods and services are produced either for further production (capital goods) or for direct consumption (consumption goods). Consumption time refers to time spent using consumption goods. Eating, and what we think of as leisure time—watching television, visiting amusement parks, playing tennis—is spent this way. Free time is spent in neither production nor consumption; it includes sheer idleness, rest, sleep, and chatting.

Of course, these three categories of time are arbitrary. We could eliminate the difference between consumption time and free time, for example, by pointing out that the French consume beds and the Machiguenga consume mats during sleep. But we want to distinguish time spent at the movies or driving a car from time spent doing nothing—sitting idly by the door or casually visiting neighbors. This supports a main contention of our research: that little agreement now exists on exactly how to measure the differences between dissimilar societies.

For comparative purposes, we broke down our data into five categories of people, two for the Machiguenga and three for the French. For the relatively simple Machiguenga society, a division by gender was sufficient for studying patterns in time use. But for the more complex French society, a male–female breakdown was insufficient because such a division does not allow for working women. We divided the French data into three categories: men, working women, and housewives.

In production time French workers, both men and women, spend more time working outside the home than the Machiguenga do. French men work one and a half hours more per day away from home than do Machiguenga men; employed French women work four hours more per day than do Machiguenga women. French housewives work less outside the home than Machiguenga women do, but they make up for this difference by exceeding their Machiguenga counterparts in work inside the home. French men spend more time working inside the home than do Machiguenga men. All told, French men spend more time engaged in production than do Machiguenga men, and French women (both working and housewives) spend more time in production activities than do Machiguenga women.

The French score equal to or higher than the Machiguenga on all measures of consumption. French men spend more than three times as many hours in consumption as do Machiguenga men; French women consume goods at four or five times the rate of Machiguenga women, depending on whether they are employed or are housewives.

It is in the category of free time that the Machiguenga clearly surpass the French. Machiguenga men spend more than 14 hours per day engaged in free time, compared with nearly 10 hours for their French counterparts, and Machiguenga women have much more free time than French women do—whether or not the French women work.

The immediate question concerns differences in the overall pattern. It seems undeniable, as Sahlins has argued, that modern technological progress has not resulted in more free time for most people. The shrinking of the work week in the last century is probably nothing more than a short-term wrinkle in the historical trend toward longer work weeks. If our modern economy provides us with more goods, it is not simply because technical efficiency has increased. Indeed, the trend toward a shorter work week ended with World War II; since then, the length of the work week has remained about the same.

The increase of consumption time at the expense of free time is both a loss and again. Here we encounter a subtle, complex problem. Increased consumption may add excitement and pleasure to what would otherwise be considered boring time. On the other hand, this increase has the effect of crowding time with consumption activities so that people begin to feel that "time is short"—which may detract from the enjoyment of consumption.

Economist Staffan Burenstam Linder has looked at the effects of higher production and consumption of goods on our sense of time. To follow his argument we must move from the level of clock time to that of subjective time, as measured by our inner sense of the tempo of our lives. According to Linder, as a result of producing and consuming more, we are experiencing an increasing scarcity of time. This works in the following way. Increasing efficiency in production means that each individual must produce more goods per hour; increased productivity means, though it is not often mentioned in this context, that to keep the system going we must consume more goods. Free time gets converted into consumption time because time spent neither producing nor consuming comes increasingly to be viewed as wasted. Linder's theory may account for the differences between the ways the Machiguenga and the French use their time.

The increase in the value of time (its increasing scarcity) is felt subjectively as an increase in tempo or pace. We are always in danger of being slow on the production line or late to work; and in our leisure we are always in danger of wasting time. I have been forcefully impressed with this aspect of time during several field visits to the Machiguenga. It happens each time I return to their communities that, after a period of two or three days, I sense a definite decrease in time pressure; this is a physiological as well as a psychological sensation.

This feeling of a leisurely pace of life reflects the fact that among the Machiguenga daily activities are never hurried or desperate. Each task is allotted its full measure of time, and free time is not felt to be boring or lost but is accepted as entirely natural. These feelings last throughout the field visit, but when I return home I am conscious of the pressure and sense of hurry building up to its former level. Something similar, though fleeting, happens on vacation trips—but here the pressure to consume, to see more sights while traveling, or to get one's money's worth in entertainment constantly asserts itself, and the tempo is usually kept up.

Linder sees a kind of evolutionary progression from "time surplus" societies through "time affluence" societies, ending with the "time famine" society of developed countries. The famine is expressed not only in a hectic pace, but also in a decline of activities in which goods are not consumed rapidly enough, such as spending time with the elderly and providing other social services. As Galbraith has pointed out, we neglect basic social needs because they are seen as economically unproductive.

Not only do we use our time for almost frantic consumption, but more of our time is also devoted to caring for the increasing number of goods we possess. The Machiguenga devote three to four times more of their production time at home to manufacturing (cloth and baskets, for example) than they do to maintenance activities, such as cleaning and doing the laundry; the French pattern is the reverse. This may help account for the failure of modern housewives to acquire more leisure time from their appliances, a situation that has prompted anthropologist Marvin Harris to refer to appliances as "labor-saving devices that don't save work."

On both objective and subjective grounds, then, it appears that economic growth has not given us more leisure time. If anything, the increasingly hectic pace of leisure activities detracts from our enjoyment of play, even when the increased stimulation they bring is taken into account. When we consider the abundance of goods, however, the situation is obviously different. The superiority of modern industrial technology in producing material goods is clear. The Machiguenga, and other people at a similar technological level, have no doubts on this score either. Despite their caution, which outsiders are apt to label "traditionalism," they really do undertake far-reaching changes in their ways of life in order to obtain even small quantities of industrial output.

One area in which the Machiguenga clearly need (and warmly welcome) Western goods is medicine. Despite hopeful speculations in popular writings that Amazon Indians have secret herbal remedies that are effective against infections, cancer, and other conditions, the curative powers of Machiguenga medicine are circumscribed. Antibiotics, even the lowly sulfa pill, are highly effective and much in demand for skin sores, eye infections, and other painful endemic health problems. Medicines to control such parasites as amoebae and intestinal worms bring immediate relief to a community, although people are eventually reinfected. In terms of human well-being, then, even the most romantic defender of the simple life must grant that modern medicines improve the lives of primitive people.

I am much less certain about what other Western goods to offer as evidence of the comparative lack of affluence among the Machiguenga. They have a great abundance of food, for example; they produce at least twice as many calories of food energy as they consume. (The excess production is not surplus so much as a security margin in case someone should fall ill or relatives unexpectedly come to stay for a time.) The Machiguenga diet is highly varied and at times very tasty. The people are attractive and healthy, with no apparent signs of malnutrition. Although they are somewhat underweight by modern standards, these standards may reflect average weights of modern populations that the Machiguenga would regard as overweight.

The highly productive food economy of the Machiguenga depends on metal tools obtained from Peruvian traders. Without an outside source of axes, the Machiguenga would have to give up their semisedentary existence and roam the forest as nomads. Should this happen, they could support fewer people in the same territory—but, if other hunter-collector groups can be used as evidence, nomadic life would result in even shorter workdays. Once again, in quantities of food as well as in quantities of time, the Machiguenga fit Sahlin's model of primitive affluence.

Our affluence exceeds Machiguenga affluence, but as in the case of time, there is the quality of life to take into account. My personal experiences in the field illustrate this aspect of the contrast. In preparing to leave for our first year-long visit to the Machiguenga, Orna and I decided to limit ourselves to the clothing and supplies that would fit into two trunks. This decision led to much agonizing over what to take and what to leave behind. Although we had both been in the field before, we had never gone anywhere quite so remote and we could not imagine how we would get along with so few goods.

The truth, however, was that we were absurdly oversupplied. As our field work progressed we used less and less of our store of goods. It even became a burden to us, since our possessions had to be dried in the sun periodically to prevent rot. As we grew close to the people we were living among, we began to be embarrassed by having so many things we did not really need.

Once, after a long rainy period, I laid my various footgear side by side in the sun to dry. There were a pair of hiking boots, a pair of canvas-topped jungle boots, and two pairs of sneakers. Some men came to visit and began inspecting the shoes, fingering the materials, commenting on the cleats, and trying them on for size. Then the discussion turned to how numerous my shoes were, and one man remarked that I had still another pair. There were protests of disbelief and I was asked if that was true. I said, "No, that's all I have." The man then said, "Wait," and went inside the house, returning with an "extra pair" of sneakers that I had left forgotten and unused in a corner of the room for months. This was not the only occasion on which I could not keep track of my possessions, a deficiency unknown to the Machiguenga.

My feelings about this incident were compounded when I discovered that, no matter which pair of shoes I wore, I could never keep up with these men, whose bare feet seemed magically to grip the slipperiest rocks or to find toe holds in the muddy trails. At about this time I was reading Alfred Russel Wallace's narrative of his years in the Amazon, in which he relates that his boots soon wore out and he spent his remaining time there barefoot—an achievement that continues to fill me with awe. My original pride in being well shod was diminished to something closely resembling embarrassment.

This experience brings up the question of whether goods are needed in themselves or because demand for them has been created by the producers. Galbraith stresses that we cannot simply assume that goods are produced to meet people's real needs. The billions of dollars spent each year on advertising indicate that not all consumer wants arise from basic needs of the individual, but that some are created in consumers by the producers themselves. This turns things around. Instead of arguing, as economists usually do, that our economic system serves us well, we are forced to consider that it may be we who serve the system by somehow agreeing to want the things it seems bent on producing, like dozens of kinds of shoes.

To most economists there is no justification for criticizing the purchasing habits of modern consumers. Purchases simply reflect personal preference, and it smacks of arrogance and authoritarianism to judge the individual decisions of free men and women. Economist Kenneth Boulding has referred sarcastically to such attempts as "theonomics." Economists assume that if there were more satisfying pathways of consumption, people would choose them. But the role of advertising in creating wants leaves open the question of the relationship between the consumption of goods and the fulfillment of needs.

When the task is to consume more, there are three ways of complying. One is to increase the amount of time spent consuming; this is one way the French differ from the Machiguenga. Another way is to increase the total number of goods we possess and to devote less time to each one individually. In a sense, this is what I was doing with the five pairs of shoes. The third way is to increase the elaborateness (and hence the cost of production) of the items we consume. The following instance, which took place at a Machiguenga beer feast, demonstrates that even those manufactured items we consider most practical are both elaborate and costly.

At Machiguenga beer feasts, which last for two or three days until the beer is gone, men often make recreational items like drums and toys. At one beer feast that had been going on for a day and a half, I watched a drum being made. The monkey-skin drumheads were being readied, and I noticed that the man next to me was about to make holes in the edge of the skin for the gut that would be used to tighten the drumhead. I had in my pocket an elaborate knife of fine steel, which had among its dozen separate functions (scissors, file, tweezers, etc.) a leather punch. By the time I had pulled the knife out and opened the punch, my neighbor had already made a perfect hole with a scrap of broken kitchen knife he had kept close at hand.

Then he noticed my knife and wanted to see it. He noted its fine workmanship and passed it around to others, who tested its sharpness and opened all its parts, asking me to explain each one. They wanted to know how much it cost and how they could obtain one.

I interpret this experience in two ways. First, the knife was overelaborate. The Machiguenga met all their own needs for clothing, shelter, and containers with much simpler tools. Second, the elaborateness of the knife was itself an attraction, and its remarkable design and quality of materials could not help but draw the men's attention. They wanted the knife—not craving it, but willing to make serious efforts to get it or something similar if the opportunity arose. It is characteristic of a developed culture's contact with small, isolated societies that the developed culture is not met as a whole, but rather in highly selective ways that emphasize manufactured goods and the aura of the great, mysterious power that made them.

Our examples do not prove that the Machiguenga enjoy a higher quality of life than people who live in an industrial society, but they are not intended to. They do show that the quantitative abundance of consumption goods does not automatically guarantee an advantage to the consumer. And although our experiences among the Machiguenga make it easy to argue for the high quality of their lives—as reflected in their warm family ties, peaceable manners, good humor, intimacy with nature, and impressive integrity—it is also true that we would have regarded a permanent life there as a great personal sacrifice. Orna and I came home partly because it is home, where our lives have meaning, and partly because we did not want to go without some creature comforts that we, for better or worse, regard as highly desirable.

It seems likely, however, that an increasing supply of creature comforts and stimulation will bring us into a dangerous relationship with our environment. Such a confrontation might lead us to think about the costs involved in producing and consuming less. In traditional terms this is almost unthinkable, because the relative affluence of communities has been restricted to quantitative measures such as per capita income or gross national product, which can only increase (good), stay the same (bad), or decline (worse). But these numerical measures, which always discover the highest standard of living in the developed nations of the West, do not necessarily touch on all the factors that contribute to a good quality of life. The concept of quality of life suggests something more complex: a balancing-out of diverse satisfactions and dissatisfactions, not all of which are bought and sold in the marketplace.

Social scientists are trying to develop a broad range of indexes, such as those called "social indicators," that attempt to measure the quality of individual well-being. It has not been the theoreticians but the planners directly involved in applying economic thought to directed social changes, like urban renewal and rural development, who have insisted on such measures. Instead of relying on a single measure, like per capita income, they have added unemployment rates, housing, mental health, cultural and educational resources, air quality, government efficiency, and social participation. Communities, or nations, may rank low on one measure but high on another, and this makes comparisons both fairer and more realistic.

Even here problems remain. For one thing, the social indicators themselves sometimes sacrifice understanding of quality for measures of quantity. For example, the measure of "mental health" has been the suicide rate per 100,000 population—surely a restricted interpretation of the concept. Despite its obvious shortcomings, the measure has the advantage of specifying exactly what we mean by the term "mental health." In comparing communities or cultures we need standard measures, even though quality and quantity are ultimately incompatible.

When we discuss non-Western societies, the existing social indicators do not work very well. Unemployment, housing, and mental health all become hard to define. Economists, for example, often label free time in other cultures as "hidden unemployment"; by clever use of this negative term, they have transformed what might be a good thing into something that sounds definitely bad. In our case, Machiguenga housing, made of palm fronds, palm wood, and various tropical hardwoods, would never qualify as good housing in terms of a housing code, but it is cool, well ventilated, comfortable, and secure. Thus we are still far from developing criteria that allow us to compare the quality of life, or affluence, in diverse societies.

The economy of the United States is changing rapidly. Yet when we try to construct models of the alternative futures open to us, we falter because we lack the means to evaluate them. To turn this process over to the marketplace is not the same as turning it over to the "people" in some absolute democratic sense. People's behavior in the marketplace is strongly influenced, often by subterfuge, by producers who try to convince them that their interests coincide.

To accept the influence of the producers of goods without criticism, while labeling all other efforts to influence constaner patterns as "interference" or "theonomics," amounts to simple bias. Certainly a degree of open-mindedness about what a good quality of life is, and more efforts at learning about the quality of life in other communities, are invaluable as we chart our uncertain future.

FOR FURTHER INFORMATION

Andrews, Frank M. and Stephen B. Withey. *Social Indicators of Well-Being: Americans' Perception of Life Quality.* Plenum, 1976.

Galbraith, John Kenneth. *The Affluent Society.* Houghton Mifflin, 1958.

Linder, Staffan Burenstam. *The Harried Leisure Class.* Columbia University Press, 1970.

Sahlins, Marshall. *Stone Age Economics.* Aldine-Atherton, 1972.

CULTURAL ECOLOGY

Cultural ecology is the study of the ways in which patterns of culture serve to adapt human groups to the difficulties posed by their environment. This specialization grew out of a school of thought from a century ago, called *environmental determinism*—a misuse of evolutionary theory which argued that all facets of culture could be traced to the ways in which they helped adapt the group(s) in which they were found to the environment(s) in which they lived.

Modern cultural ecologists avoid such simplistic, A-leads-to-B kind of thinking—that is, a *deterministic* position—by acknowledging that there are many alternative patterns of thought and behavior that can adapt a group to a given environment. Therefore, when cultural ecologists explain a pattern of behavior in terms of its adaptive significance, they do not claim to be able to say why one particular pattern is adopted in preference to another. Instead, they merely contend that, given the facts of the environment, it is possible to make sense out of culturally normative patterns of behavior that at first glance seem to be curious or even foolish or destructive.

In the first article in Topic 11, Marvin Harris, perhaps the best-known exponent of cultural ecology, seeks to explain the cultural ecology of "India's Sacred Cow"—that is, why in India starving people will refuse to eat beef. By the end of his argument you will find that *not* eating beef can, in the right context, result in having more food! Critics of cultural ecology say that this kind of analysis is reminiscent of the good Doctor Pangloss in Voltaire's *Candide*—whose philosophy in the face of disaster after disaster remained that everything that happens is for the best, in this, the best of all possible worlds. Perhaps, but research and analysis such as Harris's force us to rethink almost everything we think we know about why we do what we do.

John B. Calhoun's "Plight of the Ik and Kaiadilt Is Seen as a Chilling Possible End for Humankind," Article 41, takes the horrifying testimony that came out of the research by Colin Turnbull among the Ik of Uganda and Geoffrey Bianchi among the Kaiadilt of Australia, and shows that the decay of virtually all sustaining aspects of a society is predictable in certain extreme contexts. This was dramatically demonstrated by the butchery that took place in the late 1990s in Rwanda and the Balkans.

Calhoun has investigated these contexts experimentally among populations of mice, and sees alarming parallels there to the fate of the two peoples discussed in his essay. One cannot read this article without becoming deeply concerned over the directions being taken by our own society.

India's Sacred Cow

News photographs that came out of India during the famine of the late 1960s showed starving people stretching out bony hands to beg for food while sacred cattle strolled behind them undisturbed. The Hindu, it seems, would rather starve to death than eat his cow or even deprive it of food. The cattle appear to browse unhindered through urban markets eating an orange here, a mango there, competing with people for meager supplies of food.

By Western standards, spiritual values seem more important to Indians than life itself. Specialists in food habits around the world like Fred Simoons at the University of California at Davis consider Hinduism an irrational ideology that compels people to overlook abundant, nutritious foods for scarcer, less healthful foods.

What seems to be an absurd devotion to the mother cow pervades Indian life. Indian wall calendars portray beautiful young women with bodies of fat white cows, often with milk jetting from their teats into sacred shrines.

Cow worship even carries over into politics. In 1966 a crowd of 120,000 people, led by holy men, demonstrated in front of the Indian House of Parliament in support of the All-Party Cow Protection Campaign Committee. In Nepal, the only contemporary Hindu kingdom, cow slaughter is severely punished. As one story goes, the car driven by an official of a United States agency struck and killed a cow. In order to avoid the international incident that would have occurred when the official was arrested for murder, the Nepalese magistrate concluded that the cow had committed suicide.

Many Indians agree with Western assessments of the Hindu reverence for their cattle, the zebu, or *Bos indicus,* a large-humped species prevalent in Asia and Africa. M. N. Srinivas, an Indian anthropologist, states: "Orthodox Hindu opinion regards the killing of cattle with abhorrence, even though the refusal to kill the vast number of useless cattle which exists in India today is detrimental to the nation." Even the Indian Ministry of Information formerly maintained that "the large animal population is more a liability than an asset in view of our land resources." Accounts from many different sources point to the same conclusion: India, one of the world's great civilizations, is being strangled by its love for the cow.

The easy explanation for India's devotion to the cow, the one most Westerners and Indians would offer, is that cow worship is an integral part of Hinduism. Religion is somehow good for the soul, even if it sometimes fails the body. Religion orders the cosmos and explains our place in the universe. Religious beliefs, many would claim, have existed for thousands of years and have a life of their own. They are not understandable in scientific terms.

But all this ignores history. There is more to be said for cow worship than is immediately apparent. The earliest Vedas, the Hindu sacred texts from the Second Millennium B.C., do not prohibit the slaughter of cattle. Instead, they ordain it as a part of sacrificial rites. The early Hindus did not avoid the flesh of cows and bulls; they ate it at ceremonial feasts presided over by Brahman priests. Cow worship is a relatively recent development in India; it evolved as the Hindu religion developed and changed.

This evolution is recorded in royal edicts and religious texts written during the last 3,000 years of Indian history. The Vedas from the First Millennium B.C. contain contradictory passages, some referring to ritual slaughter and others to a strict taboo on beef consumption. A. N. Bose, in *Social and Rural Economy of Northern India, 600 B.C.–200 A.D.,* concludes that many of the sacred-cow passages were incorporated into the texts by priests of a later period.

By 200 A.D. the status of Indian cattle had undergone a spiritual transformation. The Brahman priesthood exhorted the population to venerate the cow and forbade them to abuse it or to feed on it. Religious feasts involving the ritual slaughter and consumption of livestock were eliminated and meat eating was restricted to the nobility.

By 1000 A.D., all Hindus were forbidden to eat beef. Ahimsa, the Hindu belief in the unity of all life, was the spiritual justification for this restriction. But it is difficult to ascertain exactly when this change occurred. An important event that helped to shape

229

the modern complex was the Islamic invasion, which took place in the Eighth Century A.D. Hindus may have found it politically expedient to set themselves off from the invaders, who were beefeaters, by emphasizing the need to prevent the slaughter of their sacred animals. Thereafter, the cow taboo assumed its modern form and began to function much as it does today.

The place of the cow in modern India is everyplace—on posters, in the movies, in brass figures, in stone and wood carvings, on the streets, in the fields. The cow is a symbol of health and abundance. It provides the milk that Indians consume in the form of yogurt and ghee (clarified butter), which contribute subtle flavors to much spicy Indian food.

This, perhaps, is the practical role of the cow, but cows provide less than half the milk produced in India. Most cows in India are not dairy breeds. In most regions, when an Indian farmer wants a steady, high-quality source of milk he usually invests in a female water buffalo. In India the water buffalo is the specialized dairy breed because its milk has a higher butterfat content than zebu milk. Although the farmer milks his zebu cows, the milk is merely a by-product.

More vital than zebu milk to South Asian farmers are zebu calves. Male calves are especially valued because from bulls come oxen, which are the mainstay of the Indian agricultural system.

Small, fast oxen drag wooden plows through late-spring fields when monsoons have dampened the dry, cracked earth. After harvest, the oxen break the grain from the stalk by stomping through mounds of cut wheat and rice. For rice cultivation in irrigated fields, the male water buffalo is preferred (it pulls better in deep mud), but for most other crops, including rainfall rice, wheat, sorghum, and millet, and for transporting goods and people to and from town, a team of oxen is preferred. The ox is the Indian peasant's tractor, thresher, and family car combined; the cow is the factory that produces the ox.

If draft animals instead of cows are counted, India appears to have too few domesticated ruminants, not too many. Since each of the 70 million farms in India requires a draft team, it follows that Indian peasants should use 140 million animals in the fields. But there are only 83 million oxen and male water buffalo on the subcontinent, a shortage of 30 million draft teams.

In other regions of the world, joint ownership of draft animals might overcome a shortage, but Indian agriculture is closely tied to the monsoon rains of late spring and summer, Field preparation and planting must coincide with the rain, and a farmer must have his animals ready to plow when the

weather is right. When the farmer without a draft team needs bullocks most, his neighbors are all using theirs. Any delay in turning the soil drastically lowers production.

Because of this dependence on draft animals, loss of the family oxen is devastating. If a beast dies, the farmer must borrow money to buy or rent an ox at interest rates so high that he ultimately loses his land. Every year foreclosures force thousands of poverty-stricken peasants to abandon the countryside for the overcrowded cities.

If a family is fortunate enough to own a fertile cow, it will be able to rear replacements for a lost team and thus survive until life returns to normal. If, as sometimes happens, famine leads a family to sell its cow and ox team, all ties to agriculture are cut. Even if the family survives, it has no way to farm the land, no oxen to work the land, and no cows to produce oxen.

The prohibition against eating meat applies to the flesh of cows, bulls, and oxen, but the cow is the most sacred because it can produce the other two. The peasant whose cow dies is not only crying over a spiritual loss but over the loss of his farm as well.

Religious laws that forbid the slaughter of cattle promote the recovery of the agricultural system from the dry Indian winter and from periods of drought. The monsoon, on which all agriculture depends, is erratic. Sometimes it arrives early, sometimes late, sometimes not at all. Drought has struck large portions of India time and again in this century, and Indian farmers and the zebus are accustomed to these natural disasters. Zebus can pass weeks on end with little or no food and water. Like camels they store both in their humps and recuperate quickly with only a little nourishment.

During droughts the cows often stop lactating and become barren. In some cases the condition is permanent but often it is only temporary. If barren animals were summarily eliminated, as Western experts in animal husbandry have suggested, cows capable of recovery would be lost along with those entirely debilitated. By keeping alive the cows that can later produce oxen, religious laws against cow slaughter assure the recovery of the agricultural system from the greatest challenge it faces—the failure of the monsoon.

The local Indian governments aid the process of recovery by maintaining homes for barren cows. Farmers reclaim any animal that calves or begins to lactate. One police station in Madras collects strays and pastures them in a field adjacent to the station. After a small fine is paid, a cow is returned to its rightful owner when the owner thinks the cow shows signs of being able to reproduce.

During the hot, dry spring months most of India is like a desert. Indian farmers often complain they cannot feed their livestock during this period. They maintain the cattle by letting them scavenge on the sparse grass along the roads. In the cities cattle are encouraged to scavenge near food stalls to supplement their scant diet. These are the wandering cattle tourists report seeing throughout India.

Westerners expect shopkeepers to respond to these intrusions with the deference due a sacred animal; instead, their response is a string of curses and the crack of a long bamboo pole across the beast's back or a poke at its genitals. Mahatma Gandhi was well aware of the treatment sacred cows (and bulls and oxen) received in India. "How we bleed her to take the last drop of milk from her. How we starve her to emaciation, how we ill-treat the calves, how we deprive them of their portion of milk, how cruelly we treat the oxen, how we castrate them, how we beat them, how we overload them."

Oxen generally receive better treatment than cows. When food is in short supply, thrifty Indian peasants feed their working bullocks and ignore their cows, but rarely do they abandon the cows to die. When cows are sick, farmers worry over them as they would over members of the family and nurse them as if they were children. When the rains return and when the fields are harvested, the farmers again feed their cows regularly and reclaim their abandoned animals. The prohibition against beef consumption is a form of disaster insurance for all India.

Western agronomists and economists are quick to protest that all the functions of the zebu cattle can be improved with organized breeding programs, cultivated pastures, and silage. Because stronger oxen would pull the plow faster, they could work multiple plots of land, allowing farmers to share their animals. Fewer healthy, well-fed cows could provide Indians with more milk. But pastures and silage require arable land, land needed to produce wheat and rice.

A look at Western cattle farming makes plain the cost of adopting advanced technology in Indian agriculture. In a study of livestock production in the United States, David Pimentel of the College of Agriculture and Life Sciences at Cornell University found that 91 percent of the cereal, legume, and vegetable protein suitable for human consumption is consumed by livestock. Approximately three quarters of the arable land in the United States is devoted to growing food for livestock. In the production of meat and milk, American ranchers use enough fossil fuel to equal more than 82 million barrels of oil annually.

Indian cattle do not drain the system in the same way. In a 1971 study of livestock in West Bengal, Stewart Odend'hal of the University of Missouri found that Bengalese cattle ate only the inedible remains of subsistence crops—rice straw, rice hulls, the tops of sugar cane, and mustard-oil cake. Cattle graze in the fields after harvest and eat the remains of crops left on the ground; they forage for grass and weeds on the roadsides. The food for zebu cattle costs the human population virtually nothing. "Basically," Odend'hal says, "the cattle convert items of little direct human value into products of immediate utility."

In addition to plowing the fields and producing milk, the zebus produce dung, which fires the hearths and fertilizes the fields of India. Much of the estimated 800 million tons of manure produced annually is collected by the farmers' children as they follow the family cows and bullocks from place to place. And when the children see the droppings of another farmer's cattle along the road, they pick those up also. Odend'hal reports that the system operates with such high efficiency that the children of West Bengal recover nearly 100 percent of the dung produced by their livestock.

From 40 to 70 percent of all manure produced by Indian cattle is used as fuel for cooking; the rest is returned to the fields as fertilizer. Dried dung burns slowly, cleanly, and with low heat—characteristics that satisfy the household needs of Indian women. Staples like curry and rice can simmer for hours. While the meal slowly cooks over an unattended fire, the women of the household can do other chores. Cow chips, unlike firewood, do not scorch as they burn.

It is estimated that the dung used for cooking fuel provides the energy-equivalent of 43 million tons of coal. At current prices, it would cost India an extra 1.5 billion dollars in foreign exchange to replace the dung with coal. And if the 350 million tons of manure that are being used as fertilizer were replaced with commercial fertilizers, the expense would be even greater. Roger Revelle of the University of California at San Diego has calculated that 89 percent of the energy used in Indian agriculture (the equivalent of about 140 million tons of coal) is provided by local sources. Even if foreign loans were to provide the money, the capital outlay necessary to replace the Indian cow with tractors and fertilizers for the fields, coal for the fires, and transportation for the family would probably warp international financial institutions for years.

Instead of asking the Indians to learn from the American model of industrial agriculture, American farmers might learn energy conservation from the Indians. Every step in an energy cycle results in a loss of energy to the system. Like a pendulum that slows a bit with each swing, each transfer of energy from sun to plants, plants to animals, and animals to human beings involves energy losses. Some systems are more efficient than others; they provide a higher percentage of the energy inputs in a final, useful form. Seventeen percent of all energy zebus consume is returned in the form of milk, traction, and dung. American cattle raised on Western range land return only 4 percent of the energy they consume.

But the American system is improving. Based on techniques pioneered by Indian scientists, at least one commercial firm in the United States is reported to be building plants that will turn manure from cattle feedlots into combustible gas. When organic matter is broken down by anaerobic bacteria, methane gas and carbon dioxide are produced. After the methane is cleansed of the carbon dioxide, it is available for the same purposes as natural gas—cooking, heating, electricity generation. The company constructing the biogasification plant plans to sell its product to a gas-supply company, to be piped through the existing distribution system. Schemes similar to this one could make cattle ranches almost independent of utility and gasoline companies, for methane can be used to run trucks, tractors, and cars as well as to supply heat and electricity. The relative energy self-sufficiency that the Indian peasant has achieved is a goal American farmers and industry are now striving for.

Studies like Odend'hal's understate the efficiency of the Indian cow, because dead cows are used for purposes that Hindus prefer not to acknowledge. When a cow dies, an Untouchable, a member of one of the lowest ranking castes in India, is summoned to haul away the carcass. Higher castes consider the body of the dead cow polluting; if they do handle it, they must go through a rite of purification.

Untouchables first skin the dead animal and either tan the skin themselves or sell it to a leather factory. In the privacy of their homes, contrary to the teachings of Hinduism, untouchable castes cook the meat and eat it. Indians of all castes rarely acknowledge the existence of these practices to non-Hindus, but most are aware that beefeating takes place. The prohibition against beefeating restricts consumption by the higher castes and helps distribute animal protein to the poorest sectors of the population that otherwise would have no source of these vital nutrients.

Untouchables are not the only Indians who consume beef. Indian Muslims and Christians are under no restriction that forbids them beef, and its consumption is legal in many places. The Indian ban on cow slaughter is state, not national, law and not all states restrict it. In many cities, such as New Delhi, Calcutta, and Bombay, legal slaughterhouses sell beef to retail customers and to the restaurants that serve steak.

If the caloric value of beef and the energy costs involved in the manufacture of synthetic leather were included in the estimates of energy, the calculated efficiency of Indian livestock would rise considerably.

As well as the system works, experts often claim that its efficiency can be further improved. Alan Heston, an economist at the University of Pennsylvania, believes that Indians suffer from an overabundance of cows simply because they refuse to slaughter the excess cattle. India could produce at least the same number of oxen and the same quantities of milk and manure with 30 million fewer cows. Heston calculates that only 40 cows are necessary to maintain a population of 100 bulls and oxen. Since India averages 70 cows for every 100 bullocks, the difference, 30 million cows, is expendable.

What Heston fails to note is that sex ratios among cattle in different regions of India vary tremendously, indicating that adjustments in the cow population do take place. Along the Ganges River, one of the holiest shrines of Hinduism, the ratio drops to 47 cows for every 100 male animals. This ratio reflects the preference for dairy buffalo in the irrigated sectors of the Gangetic Plains. In nearby Pakistan, in contrast, where cow slaughter is permitted, the sex ratio is 60 cows to 100 oxen.

Since the sex ratios among cattle differ greatly from region to region and do not even approximate the balance that would be expected if no females were killed, we can assume that some culling of herds does take place; Indians do adjust their religious restrictions to accommodate ecological realities.

They cannot kill a cow but they can tether an old or unhealthy animal until it has starved to death. They cannot slaughter a calf but they can yoke it with a large wooden triangle so that when it nurses it irritates the mother's udder and gets kicked to death. They cannot ship their animals to the slaughterhouse but they can sell them to Muslims, closing their eyes to the fact that the Muslims will take the cattle to the slaughterhouse.

These violations of the prohibition against cattle slaughter strengthen the premise that cow worship is a vital part of Indian culture. The practice arose to prevent the population from consuming the animal on which Indian agriculture depends. During the First Millennium B.C., the Ganges Valley became one of the most densely populated regions of the world.

Where previously there had been only scattered villages, many towns and cities arose and peasants farmed every available acre of land. Kingsley Davis, a population expert at the University of California at Berkeley, estimates that by 300 B.C. between 50 million and 100 million people were living in India. The forested Ganges Valley became a windswept semi-desert and signs of ecological collapse appeared; droughts and floods became commonplace, erosion took away the rich topsoil, farms shrank as population increased, and domesticated animals became harder and harder to maintain.

It is probable that the elimination of meat eating came about in a slow, practical manner. The farmers who decided not to eat their cows, who saved them for procreation to produce oxen, were the ones who survived the natural disasters. Those who ate beef lost the tools with which to farm. Over a period of centuries, more and more farmers probably avoided beef until an unwritten taboo came into existence.

Only later was the practice codified by the priesthood. While Indian peasants were probably aware of the role of cattle in their society, strong sanctions were necessary to protect zebus from a population faced with starvation. To remove temptation, the flesh of cattle became taboo and the cow became sacred.

The sacredness of the cow is not just an ignorant belief that stands in the way of progress. Like all concepts of the sacred and the profane, this one affects the physical world; it defines the relationships that are important for the maintenance of Indian society.

Indians have the sacred cow; we have the "sacred" car and the "sacred" dog. It would not occur to us to propose the elimination of automobiles and dogs from our society without carefully considering the consequences, and we should not propose the elimination of zebu cattle without first understanding their place in the social order of India.

Human society is neither random nor capricious. The regularities of thought and behavior called culture are the principal mechanisms by which we human beings adapt to the world around us. Practices and beliefs can be rational or irrational, but a society that fails to adapt to its environment is doomed to extinction. Only those societies that draw the necessities of life from their surroundings without destroying those surroundings, inherit the earth. The West has much to learn from the great antiquity of Indian civilization, and the sacred cow is an important part of that lesson.

FOR FURTHER INFORMATION

Gandhi, Mohandas K. *How to Serve the Cow:* Navajivan Publishing House, 1954.

Harris, Marvin. *Cows, Pigs, Wars and Witches: The Riddles of Culture.* Random House, 1974.

Heston, Alan, et al. "An Approach to the Sacred Cow of India." *Current Anthropology,* Vol. 12, 1971, pp. 191–209.

Odend'hal, Stewart. "Gross Energetic Efficiency of Indian Cattle in Their Environment." *Journal of Human Ecology,* Vol. 1, 1972, pp. 1–27.

Raj, K. N. "Investment in Livestock in Agrarian Economies: An Analysis of Some Issues Concerning 'Sacred Cows' and 'Surplus Cattle.'" *Indian Economic Review,* Vol. 4. 1969, pp. 1–33.

John B. Calhoun

Plight of the Ik and Kaiadilt Is Seen as a Chilling Possible End for Humankind

The Mountain—how pervasive in the history of man. A still small voice on Horeb, mount of God, guided Elijah. There, earlier, Moses standing before God received the Word. And Zion: "I am the Lord your God dwelling in Zion, my holy mountain."

Then there was Atum, mountain, God and first man, one and all together. The mountain rose out of a primordial sea of nothingness—Nun. Atum, the spirit of life, existed within Nun. In creating himself, Atum became the evolving ancestor of the human race. So goes the Egyptian mythology of creation, in which the Judaic Adam has his roots.

And there is a last Atum, united in his youth with another mountain of God, Mt. Morungole in northeasternmost Uganda. His people are the Ik, pronounced *eek*. They are the subject of an important new book, *The Mountain People*, by Colin M. Turnbull (Simon and Schuster, $6.95). They still speak Middle-Kingdom Egyptian, a language thought to be dead. But perhaps their persistence is not so strange. Egyptian mythology held that the waters of the life-giving Nile had their origin in Nun. Could this Nun have been the much more extensive Lake Victoria of 40 to 50 millennia ago when, near its borders, man groped upward to cloak his biological self with culture?

Well might the Ik have preserved the essence of this ancient tradition that affirms human beginnings. Isolated as they have been in their jagged mountain fastness, near the upper tributaries of the White Nile, the Ik have been protected from cultural evolution.

What a Shangri-la, this land of the Ik. In its center, the Kidepo valley, 35 miles across, home of abundant game; to the south, mist-topped Mt. Morungole; to the west the Niangea range; to the north, bordering the Sudan, the Didinga range; to the east on the Kenya border, a sheer drop of 2,000 feet into the Turkanaland of cattle herdsmen. Through ages of dawning history few people must have been interested in encroaching on this rugged land. Until 1964 anthropologists knew little of the Ik's existence. Their very

name, much less there language, remained a mystery until, quite by chance, anthropologist Colin M. Turnbull found himself among them. What an opportunity to study pristine man! Here one should encounter the basic qualities of humanity unmarred by war, technology, pollution, over-population.

Turnbull rested in his bright red Land Rover at an 8,000-foot-high pass. A bit beyond this only "navigable" pass into the Kidepo Valley, lay Pirre, a police outpost watching over a cluster of Ik villages. There to welcome him came Atum of the warm, open smile and gentle voice. Gray-haired at 40, appearing 65, he was the senior elder of the Ik, senior in authority if not quite so in age. Nattily attired in shorts and woolen sweater—in contrast to his mostly naked colleagues—Atum bounced forward with his ebony walking stick, greeted Turnbull in Swahili, and from that moment on took command as best he could of Turnbull's life. At Atum's village a plaintive woman's voice called out. Atum remarked that that was his wife—sick, too weak to work in the fields. Turnbull offered to bring her food and medicine. Atum suggested he handle Turnbull's gifts. As the weeks wore on Atum picked up the parcels that Turnbull was supplying for Atum's wife.

One day Atum's brother-in-law, Lomongin, laughingly asked Turnbull if he didn't know that Atum's wife had been dead for weeks. She had received no food or medicine. Atum had sold it. So she just died. All of this was revealed with no embarrassment. Atum joined the laughter over the joke played on Turnbull.

Another time Atum and Lojieri were guiding Turnbull over the mountains, and at one point induced him to push ahead through high grass until he broke through into a clearing. The clearing was a sheer 1,500-foot drop. The two Iks rolled on the ground, nearly bursting with laughter because Turnbull just managed to catch himself. What a lovable cherub this Atum! His laughter never ended.

NEW MEANING OF LAUGHTER

Laughter, hallmark of mankind, not shared with any other animal, not even primates, was an outstanding trait of the Ik. A whole village rushed to the edge of a low cliff and joined in communal laughter at blind old Lo'ono who lay thrashing on her back, near death after stumbling over. One evening Iks around a fire watched a child as it crawled toward the flames, then writhed back screaming after it grasped a gleaming coal. Laughter erupted. Quiet came to the child as its mother cuddled it in a kind of respect for the merriment it had caused. Then there was the laughter of innocent childhood as boys and girls gathered around a grandfather, too weak to walk, and drummed upon his head with sticks or pelted him with stones until he cried. There was the laughter that binds families together: Kimat, shrieking for joy as she dashed off with the mug of tea she had snatched from her dying brother Lomeja's hand an instant after Turnbull had given it to him as a last token of their friendship.

Laughter there had always been. A few old people remembered times, 25 to 30 years ago, when laughter mirrored love and joy and fullness of life, times when beliefs and rituals and traditions kept a bond with the "millions of years" ago when time began for the Ik. That was when their god, Didigwari, let the Ik down from heaven on a vine, one at a time. He gave them the digging stick with the instruction that they could not kill one another. He let down other people. To the Dodos and Turkana he gave cattle and spears to kill with. But the Ik remained true to their instruction and did not kill one another or neighboring tribesmen.

For them the bow, the net and the pitfall were for capturing game. For them the greatest sin was to overhunt. Mobility and cooperation ever were part of them. Often the netting of game required the collaboration of a whole band of 100 or more, some to hold the net and some to drive game into it. Between the big hunts, bands broke up into smaller groups to spread over their domain, then to gather again. The several bands would each settle for the best part of the year along the edge of the Kidepo Valley in the foothills of Mt. Morungole. There they were once again fully one with the mountain. "The Ik, without their mountains, would no longer be the Ik and similarly, they say, the mountains without the Ik would no longer be the same mountains, if indeed they continued to exist at all."

In this unity of people and place, rituals, traditions, beliefs and values molded and preserved a continuity of life. All rites of passage were marked by ceremony. Of these, the rituals surrounding death gave greatest meaning to life. Folded in a fetal position, the body was buried with favorite possessions, facing the rising sun to mark celestial rebirth. All accompanying rituals of fasting and feasting, of libations of beer sprinkled over the grave, of seeds of favorite foods planted on the grave to draw life from the dust of the dead, showed that death is merely another form of life, and reminded the living of the good things of life and of the good way to live. In so honoring the dead by creating goodness the Ik helped speed the soul, content, on its journey.

Such were the Ik until wildlife conservation intruded into their homeland. Uganda decided to make a national park out of the Kidepo Valley, the main hunting ground of the Ik. What then happened stands as an indictment of the myopia that science can generate. No one looked to the Ik to note that their hunter-gatherer way of life marked the epitome of conservation, that the continuance of their way of life would have added to the success of the park. Instead they were forbidden to hunt any longer in the Kidepo Valley. They were herded to the periphery of the park and encouraged to become farmers on dry mountain slopes so steep as to test the poise of a goat. As an example to the more remote villages, a number of villages were brought together in a tight little cluster below the southwest pass into the valley. Here the police post, which formed this settlement of Pirre, could watch over the Ik to see that they didn't revert to hunting.

These events contained two of the three strikes that knocked out the spirit of the Ik. *Strike No. 1:* The shift from a mobile hunter-gatherer way of life to a sedentary farming way of life made irrelevant the Ik's entire repertoire of beliefs, habits and traditions. Their guidelines for life were inappropriate to farming. They seemed to adapt, but at heart they remained hunters and gatherers. Their cultural templates fitted them for that one way of life.

Strike No. 2: They were suddenly crowded together at a density, intimacy and frequency of contact far greater than they had ever before been required to experience. Throughout their long past each band of 100 or so individuals only temporarily coalesced into a whole. The intervening breaking up into smaller groups permitted realignment of relationships that tempered conflicts from earlier associations. But at the resettlement, more than 450 individuals were forced to form a permanent cluster of villages within shouting distance of each other. Suppose the seven million or so inhabitants of Los Angeles County were forced to move and join the more than one million inhabitants of the more arid San Diego County. Then after they arrived all water, land and air communication to the rest of the world was cut off abruptly and completely. These eight million people would then have to seek survival completely on local resources without any communication with others. It would be a test of the ability of human beings to remain human.

Such a test is what Dr. Turnbull's book on the Mountain People is all about. The Ik failed to remain human. I have put mice to the same test and they failed to remain mice. Those of you who have been following *Smithsonian* may recall from the April 1970 and the January 1971 issues something about the projected demise of a mouse population experiencing the same two strikes against it as did the Ik.

FATE OF A MOUSE POPULATION

Last summer I spoke in London behind the lectern where Charles Darwin and Alfred Wallace had presented their papers on evolution—which during the next century caused a complete revision of our insight into what life is all about and what man is and may become. In summing up that session of 1858 the president remarked that nothing of importance had been presented before the Linnean Society at that year's meeting! I spoke behind this same lectern to a session of the Royal Society of Medicine during its symposium on "Man in His Place." At the end of my paper, "Death Squared: The Explosive Growth and Demise of a Mouse Population," the chairman admonished me to stick to my mice; the insights I had presented could have no implication for man. Wonderful if the chairman could be correct—but now I have read about the Mountain People, and I have a hollow feeling that perhaps we, too, are close to losing our "mountain."

Turnbull lived for 18 months as a member of the Ik tribe. His identity transfer became so strong that he acquired the Ik laughter. He laughed at seeing Atum suffer as they were completing an extremely arduous journey on foot back across the mountains and the Kidepo Valley from the Sudan. He felt pleasure at seeing Lokwam, local "Lord of the Flies," cry in agony from the beating given him by his two beautiful sisters.

Well, for five years I have identified with my mice, as they lived in their own "Kidepo Valley"— their contrived Utopia where resources are always abundant and all mortality factors except aging eliminated. I watched their population grow rapidly from the first few colonizers. I watched them fill their metal "universe" with organized social groups. I watched them bring up a host of young with loving maternal care and paternal territorial protection—all of these young well educated for mouse society. But then there were too many of these young mice, ready to become involved in all that mice can become, with nowhere to go, no physical escape from

their closed environment, no opportunity to gain a niche where they could play a meaningful role. They tried, but being younger and less experienced they were nearly always rejected.

Rejecting so many of these probing youngsters overtaxed the territorial males. So defense then fell to lactating females. They became aggressive. They turned against their own young and ejected them before normal weaning and before adequate social bonds between mother and young had developed. During this time of social tension, rate of growth of the population was only one third of that during the earlier, more favorable phase.

Strike No. 1 against these mice: They lost the opportunity to express the capacities developed by older mice born during the rapid population growth. After a while they became so rejected that they were treated as so many sticks and stones by their still relatively well-adjusted elders. These rejected mice withdrew, physically and psychologically, to live packed tightly together in large pools. Amongst themselves they became vicious, lashing out and biting each other now and then with hardly any provocation.

Strike No. 2 against the mice: They reached great numbers despite reduced conceptions and increased deaths of newborn young resulting from the dissolution of maternal care. Many had early been rejected

Unwanted by Ik society, an old man, who remembered times of human caring, lies among the rocks of the mountain, quietly awaiting a lonely death.

Photo courtesy of Colin Turnbull.

by their mothers and knew little about social bonds. Often their later attempts at interaction were interrupted by some other mouse intervening unintentionally as it passed between two potential actors.

I came to call such mice the "Beautiful Ones." They never learned such effective social interactions as courtship, mating and aggressive defense of territory. Never copulating, never fighting, they were unstressed and essentially unaware of their associates. They spent their time grooming themselves, eating and sleeping, totally individualistic, totally isolated socially except for a peculiar acquired need for simple proximity to others. This produced what I have called the "behavioral sink," the continual accentuation of aggregations to the point that much available space was unused despite a population increase to nearly 15 times the optimum.

All true "mousity" was lost. Though physically they still appeared to be mice, they had no essential capacities for survival and continuation of mouse society. Suddenly, population growth ceased. In what seemed an instant they passed over a threshold beyond which there was no likelihood of their ever recouping the capacity to become real mice again. No more young were born. From a peak population of 2,200 mice nearly three years ago, aging has gradually taken its toll until now there are only 46 sluggish near-cadavers comparable to people more than 100 years old.

It was just such a fading universe Colin Turnbull found in 1964. Just before he arrived, *Strike No. 3* had set in: starvation. Any such crisis could have added the coup de grace after the other two strikes. Normally the Ik could count on only making three crops every four years. At this time a two-year drought set in and destroyed almost all crops. Neighboring tribes survived with their cultures intact. Turkana herdsmen, facing starvation and death, kept their societies in contact with each other and continued to sing songs of praise to God for the goodness of life.

By the beginning of the long drought, "goodness" to the Ik simply meant to have food—to have food for one's self alone. Collaborative hunts were a thing of the past, long since stopped by the police and probably no longer possible as a social effort, anyway. Solitary hunting, now designated as poaching, became a necessity for sheer survival. But the solitary hunter took every precaution not to let others know of his success. He would gorge himself far off in the bush and bring the surplus back to sell to the police, who were not above profiting from this traffic. Withholding food from wife, children and aging parents became an accomplishment to brag and laugh about. It became a way of life, continuing after

Rains temporarily turned the Ik's mountain green just before Turnbull returned for a visit.

Photo courtesy of Colin Turnbull.

the government began providing famine relief. Those strong enough to go to the police station to get rations for themselves and their families would stop halfway home and gorge all the food, even though it caused them to vomit.

VILLAGE OF MUTUAL HATRED

The village reflected this reversal of humanity. Instead of open courtyards around each group of huts within the large compound, there was a maze of walls and tunnels booby trapped with spears to ward off intrusion by neighbors.

In Atum's village a whole band of more than 100 individuals was crowded together in mutual hostility and aloneness. They would gather at their sitting place and sit for hours in a kind of suspended animation, not looking directly at each other, yet scanning slowly all others who might be engaged in some solitary task, watching for someone to make a mistake that would elicit the symbolic violence of laughter and derision. They resembled my pools of rejected withdrawn mice. Homemaking deteriorated, feces littered doorsteps and courtyard. Universal adultery and incest replaced the old taboo. The beaded virgins' aprons of eight-to-twelve-year-old girls became symbols that these were proficient whores accustomed to selling their wares to passing herdsmen.

One ray of humanity left in this cesspool was 12-year-old, retarded Adupa. Because she believed that food was for sharing and savoring, her playmates beat her. She still believed that parents were for loving and to be loved by. They cured her madness by locking her in her hut until she died and decayed.

The six other villages were smaller and their people could retain a few glimmers of the goodness and fullness of life. There was Kuaur, devoted to Turnbull, hiking four days to deliver mail, taunted for bringing food home to share with his wife and child. There was Losiké, the potter, regarded as a witch. She offered water to visitors and made pots for others. When the famine got so bad that there was no need for pots to cook in, her husband left her. She was no longer bringing in any income. And then there was old Nangoli, still capable of mourning when her husband died. She went with her family and village across Kidepo and into the Sudan where their village life turned for a while back to normality. But it was not normal enough to keep them. Back to Pirre, to death, they returned.

All goodness was gone from the Ik, leaving merely emptiness, valuelessness, nothingness, the chaos of Nun. They reentered the womb of beginning time from which there is no return. Urination

beside the partial graves of the dead marked the death of God, the final fading of Mount Morungole.

My poor words give only a shadowy image of the cold coffin of Ik humanity that Turnbull describes. His two years with the Ik left him in a slough of despondency from which he only extricated himself with difficulty, never wanting to see them again. Time and distance brought him comfort. He did return for a brief visit some months later. Rain had come in abundance. Gardens had sprung up untended from hidden seeds in the earth. Each Ik gleaned only for his immediate needs. Granaries stood empty, not refilled for inevitable scarcities ahead. The future had ceased to exist. Individual and social decay continued on its downward spiral. Sadly Turnbull departed again from this land of lost hope and faith.

Last summer in London I knew nothing about the Ik when I was so publicly and thoroughly chastised for having the temerity to suspect that the behavioral and spiritual death my mice had exhibited might also befall man. But a psychiatrist in the audience arose in defense of my suspicion. Dr. Geoffrey N. Bianchi remarked that an isolated tribe of Australian Aborigines mirrored the changes and kinds of pathology I had seen among mice. I did not know that Dr. Bianchi was a member of the team that had studied these people, the Kaiadilt, and that a book about them was in preparation, *Cruel, Poor and Brutal Nations* by John Cawte (The University Press of Hawaii). In galley proof I have read about the Kaiadilt and find it so shattering to my faith in humanity that I now sometimes wish I had never heard of it. Yet there is some glimmer of hope that the Kaiadilt may recover—not what they were but possibly some new life.

A frail, tenacious people, the Kaiadilt never numbered more than 150 souls where they lived on Bentinck Island in the Gulf of Carpentaria. So isolated were they that not even their nearest Aboriginal neighbors, 20 miles away, had any knowledge of their existence until in this century; so isolated were the Kaiadilt from their nearest neighbors that they differ from them in such heredity markers as blood type and fingerprints. Not until the early years of this century did an occasional visitor from the Queensland Government even note their existence.

For all practical purposes the first real contact the Kaiadilt had with Western "culture" came in 1916 when a man by the name of McKenzie came to Bentinck with a group of male mainland Aborigines to try to establish a lime kiln. McKenzie's favorite sport was to ride about shooting Kaiadilt. His helpers' sport was to commandeer as many women as they could, and take them to their headquarter on a neighboring island. In 1948 a tidal wave poisoned most of the freshwater sources. Small groups of Kaiadilt were rounded up and transported to larger Mornington Island where they were placed under the supervision of a Presbyterian mission. They were crowded into a dense cluster settlement just as the Ik had been at Pirre.

Here they still existed when the psychiatric field team came into their midst 15 years later. They were much like the Ik: dissolution of family life, total valuelessness, apathy. I could find no mention of laughter, normal or pathological. Perhaps the Kaiadilt didn't laugh. They had essentially ceased the singing that had been so much a part of their traditional way.

The spiritual decay of the Kaiadilt was marked by withdrawal, depression, suicide and tendency to engage in such self-mutilation as ripping out one's testes or chopping off one's nose. In their passive-

ness some of the anxiety ridden children are accepting the new mold of life forced upon them by a benevolent culture they do not understand. Survival with a new mold totally obliterating all past seems their only hope.

So the lesson comes clear, and Colin Turnbull sums it up in the final paragraph of his book: "The Ik teach us that our much vaunted human values are not inherent in humanity at all, but are associated only with a particular form of survival called society, and that all, even society itself, are luxuries that can be dispensed with. That does not make them any the less wonderful or desirable, and if man has any greatness, it is surely in his ability to maintain these values, clinging to them to an often very bitter end, even shortening an already pitifully short life rather than sacrifice his humanity. But that too involves choice, and the Ik teach us that man can lose the will to make it."

SOCIETY AND GENDER ROLES

In the first part of the twentieth century, sociopolitical events, such as the Russian revolution and the rise of socialism, and academic schools of thought, such as behaviorism in psychology, underlined the view that human beings are extraordinarily malleable and that social, historical, and cultural factors are preeminent over biological causes in shaping human behavior. The noted anthropologist Franz Boas and his students led the intellectual movement that, among other things, attacked the viability of the concept of "race" and took an activist stance in combating racism.

In this context, the subject of differences between the human sexes became critical. One feature of the organization of social life that is present in all known societies is the cultural attribution of significance to differences between males and females. Notions of maleness and femaleness vary enormously across cultures, but the distinction between the sexes is made universally, and sex-role attributions and expectations are important organizers of social existence everywhere. Do innate biological differences between the sexes account for these distinctions?

In the early 1930s, Margaret Mead studied and lived with three societies in New Guinea. As she reported in her book, *Sex and Temperament,* she found that in these societies the attribution of qualities of character to the two sexes differed remarkably—both among those societies and in contrast with our own. In her book, which quickly achieved notoriety, Mead argued for the point of view that human nature is "not rigid and unyielding" and that "cultural rhythms are stronger and more compelling than the physiological rhythms which they overlay and distort."

The public was more enthusiastic over *Sex and Temperament* than were most anthropologists, who noted that her research was limited to a matter of months, that she relied on data provided by only one or two informants, that data and hypothesis were poorly separated, and that a subjective bias in the interpretation of the data was all too evident. Even Mead's husband, Reo Fortune, who had collaborated with her in this research, rejected her view that the Arapesh did not distinguish between male and female temperaments.

With the reemergence of feminism in the United States during the late 1960s and 1970s, *Sex and Temperament* was enshrined as a "classic," and its obvious shortcomings were overlooked because its contents could be used to validate feminist critiques of contemporary social life. Mead, herself, participated in the feminist movement, but at the same time she expressed unease about the overinterpretation of her New Guinea materials by the writers of feminist tracts.

Despite the wide range of definitions of "male" and "female" behaviors around the world, there clearly are central tendencies. One such tendency is the power men have over women in most societies. The question many anthropologists have put is: *Why* is this the case? Ernestine Friedl's studies of societies at differing levels of complexity show a broad range of male dominance—from the extreme dominance of the Inuit (Eskimo) men to the relative social equality of the Hazda men and women of Tanzania. Friedl finds a positive correlation between the degree to which men control the production of food and the degree of sexual stratification of social life. If Friedl is right, we should expect a diminishing degree of male dominance in our modern, postindustrial society.

Helen Fisher takes Friedl's point one giant step further in Article 42, "An Immodest Proposal," an excerpt from her book, *The First Sex* (1999). She explores and celebrates the differences between male and female talents and between the male and female minds. These difference, she contends, were built into the wiring of our brains during the course of millions of years of evolution. Without being biologically deterministic, Fisher explains that women tend to have superior linguistic skills; a greater capacity to read nonverbal cues; superior senses of touch, taste, smell, and hearing; a gift for networking and negotiating; an impulse to nurture; and a preference for cooperation, reaching consensus, and leading via egalitarian teams. Men have a superb sense of spatial relations; a talent for solving complex mechanical problems; an ability to focus their attention; and a gift for controlling their emotions.

Noting, as does Friedl, that women lost status and power during the long march from the beginnings of agriculture through the industrial revolution, Fisher argues that the postindustrial, twenty-first century world has created new opportunities for women's talents, which should result in their regaining genuine equality with men.

In Article 43, "Daughters of the Forest," Agnes Estioko-Griffin provides an example of a society in which men control neither the production of food nor the sexual stratification of social life. Among the Agta people of the Philippines, the women hunt large game animals and also have the primary responsibility for raising children.

Finally, in "Life behind the Veil," Article 44, Cherry Lindholm and Charles Lindholm explore the secret world of Muslim women. In recent years, the lot of women has improved in the most progressive Islamic societies: they have won the right to initiate divorce in Egypt and may soon win the right to vote in Kuwait. On the other hand, in fundamentalist Islamic societies, such as Afghanistan under the Taliban, women have been deprived of even the most fundamental of human rights—the right to walk in public unescorted by a husband, father, or brother; the right to an education; the right to work; or the right to receive medical treatment.

Though it may appear to Westerners that Muslim women are the personifications of powerlessness, in fact, the Lindholms report, they are viewed in traditional Islamic society as powerful and dangerous beings.

An Immodest Proposal

There is only one way of seeing things, and that is seeing the whole of them.

—John Ruskin

"What is a woman?" Simone de Beauvoir asked this question in her celebrated 1949 book, *The Second Sex*. She believed that a woman is solely the product of economic and social forces. As she said, "One is not born, but rather becomes, a woman."

Times have changed since Beauvoir wrote these words. A great deal of scientific evidence now demonstrates that all human beings emerge from the womb with circuits in the brain that enable them to act in human ways. Moreover, in some fundamental respects the sexes are not alike. For millions of years, men and women did different jobs, tasks that required different skills. As days turned into centuries and natural selection weeded out less able workers, time carved subtle differences in the male and female brain. A woman is born a woman.

I am a clone; I am an identical twin. My twin sister and I are alike in many ways and different in many others. We laugh alike and our gestures are uncannily similar, but I am an anthropologist and she is a hot air balloon pilot and a painter. Because of this lifelong personal experience, I am acutely aware that parents, teachers, friends, jobs, and myriad other cultural forces dramatically influence how one thinks and acts. Environment and heredity are eternally intertwined, locked in a pas de deux. No two human beings are alike.

Yet men and women emerge from the womb with some innate tendencies and proclivities bred on the grasslands of Africa millennia ago. The sexes are not the same. Each has some natural talents. Each is a living archive of its distinctive past.

Beauvoir's central tenet was correct, however. She endorsed the nineteenth-century view that social traditions emerging during our farming ancestry had forced women into a secondary place in society.

Since the 1970s scholars have established that before humankind adopted a settled farming lifeway, women were powerful economically and socially. On the savannas of ancient Africa women "commuted" to work to gather fruits and vegetables. They left their children in day care with relatives and they returned to camp with much, often most, of the evening meal. In "deep history," as Edward O. Wilson calls humanity's primordial beginnings, the double-income family was the rule. Anthropologists believe that women were regarded as roughly equal with men.

As the agricultural revolution took hold, however, men assumed the primary economic tasks: clearing land, plowing fields, and harvesting crops. Soon they also became the traders, warriors, heads of household, and heads of state. Women in many farming cultures were and still are treated, in many, respects, as what Beauvoir called the "second sex."

With the Industrial Revolution in the West, powerful economic forces began to draw women into the paid workforce. It is no exaggeration to say that this has led to one of the most extraordinary developments in the long journey of *Homo sapiens:* the return of economically powerful women. Women around the world are gradually reacquiring the economic clout they enjoyed hundreds of thousands, even millions of years ago.

They bring to the marketplace many natural talents.

So here is my immodest proposal: As women continue to pour into the paid workforce in cultures around the world, they will apply their natural aptitudes in many sectors of society and dramatically influence twenty-first-century business, sex, and family life. In some important parts of the economy, they will even predominate, becoming the first sex. Why? Because current trends in business, communications, education, law, medicine, government, and the nonprofit sector, known as civil society, all suggest that tomorrow's world will need the female mind.

How do men and women vary? Why did these gender differences evolve? How will women's uniquely feminine attributes change the world?

Winston Churchill once said that in an author's mind a book begins as a toy, turns into a lover, and becomes a tyrant. I don't know about the toy part, but when I began this book, these questions immediately became lovers. I couldn't get them out of my mind. I pored over reams of data on subjects as diverse as brain anatomy, animal behavior, psychology, gender studies, world business, and demography. In no time, I found hundreds of scientific studies documenting biological and psychological differences between women and men.

Women have many exceptional faculties bred in deep history: a talent with words; a capacity to read postures, gestures, facial expressions, and other non-verbal cues; emotional sensitivity; empathy; excellent senses of touch, taste, smell, and hearing; patience; an ability to do and think several things simultaneously; a broad contextual view of any issue; a penchant for long-term planning; a gift for networking and negotiating; an impulse to nurture; and a preference for cooperating, reaching consensus, and leading via egalitarian teams.

Men have many natural talents, too. Among them are superb understanding of spatial relations, a talent for solving complex mechanical problems, an ability to focus their attention, and a gift for controlling many of their emotions. All, I will contend, were built into the architecture of the gendered brain millennia ago.

This is not to say that women and men are puppets dangling from strings of DNA. With the emergence of humanity came the evolution of the cerebral cortex. We think. We weigh a vast array of possibilities. We make choices. We learn new skills. We regularly rise above our inherited nature to make decisions about our lives.

Nevertheless, we do have luggage from the past. These gender differences appear in cultures around the world. They reemerge decade after decade in the same society, despite changing attitudes about women. Many appear in infancy. Many are associated with male or female sex hormones, the androgens and estrogens. Some have been traced to specific genes. Some emerge long before a baby leaves the womb.

Scientists have even discovered how some of these gendered proclivities become installed in the male and female brain. At conception the embryo is neither male nor female. Around the eighth week of fetal life, however, a genetic switch flips. If the embryo is to be a boy, a gene on the Y chromosome directs the gonadal buds to become testes. These developing sex organs then produce male hormones that further build the male genitals. Later they also mold the male brain.

If the embryo is genetically destined to be female, no male hormones act on it and female gonads appear by the thirteenth week of fetal life—followed later by the female brain. Recently scientists have begun to think that a gene on the X chromosome and fetal estrogens also play active roles in constructing the full composition of "woman." But all agree that if male hormones do not kick in to sculpt the growing embryo, it will become a girl.

As a result of these findings, scientists regularly refer to woman as the default plan.

I read these data differently. "Woman" is the primary sex—the first sex. You have to add chemicals to get a man. Hence the first sex from the biological perspective is emerging as the first sex in many spheres of economic and social life.

The distinction between "man" and "woman" is far from simple, however. Each of us is a complex mix of feminine and masculine traits. As Susan Sontag has written, "What is most beautiful in virile men is something feminine; what is most beautiful in feminine women is something masculine." Nobody is wholly male or wholly female.

Even this intriguing amalgam of male and female in each of us is shaped by biology. The fetal brain grows slowly and unevenly, so different parts of the brain become susceptible to sex hormones at different times. Levels of these fetal hormones also change continuously. So tides of powerful sex hormones can masculinize one part of the brain while they leave another region untouched. As a result, every human being lies somewhere along a continuum that ranges from superfeminine to hypermasculine, depending on the amount and timing of hormones the individual was doused with in the womb.

Then environmental forces take up the job of shaping who you are. "It's a girl!" "It's a boy!" As you emerge from the womb, someone announces your gender. In this instant, you are assigned to a category that pigeonholes you all your years. Blue for boys, pink for girls; trucks for one, dolls for the other: many, many social forces direct youngsters, adults, and seniors to behave as one sex or the other. Environmental forces also alter the secretion of neurotransmitters in the brain, the ebb and flow of the sex hormones, even the activities of genes, subtly changing biology and behavior throughout our lives.

Albert Einstein once said of the intellect, "It has powerful muscles, but no personality." Upon the intricate scaffolding of our unique brains, culture builds our unique personalities. Yet the scaffolding remains. Women as a general group do carry within them a host of specific aptitudes—innate talents they will use to make tremendous changes in our modern world.

Two oddly correlated phenomena, the international baby boom and the biology of menopause, will accelerate women's impact on tomorrow.

The huge baby boom generation is reaching middle age. As anthropologists have documented, middle-aged women around the world tend to become much more assertive. This is partially due to cultural forces.

But middle-aged women also get a dividend from nature. With menopause, levels of the estrogens decline, unmasking natural levels of testosterone and other androgens in the female body. Androgens, male sex hormones, are potent chemicals regularly associated with assertiveness and rank in many mammalian species, including people. As this tidal wave of baby boomer women reaches middle age, they will be equipped—not only economically and mentally but also hormonally—to make substantial changes in the world.

"Such a critical mass of older women with a tradition of rebellion and independence and a way of making a living has not occurred before in history," writes historian Gerda Lerner. We stand at the doorway of what may become an age of women.

Each of the first six chapters [of my] book examines specific male/female differences—using data on the brain, information from many cultures, and evidence from anthropology, psychology, sociology, ethology, and other behavioral and biological sciences. Each chapter explores why these biological variations evolved and shows how women's specific gifts are beginning to affect some sectors of society. I give examples of women's impact on the media, education, the service professions, law, medicine, corporations, government, and civil organizations.

In [one] chapter [of my book, *The First Sex*], I discuss menopause, show how women around the world become more influential in middle age, and propose that as women of the international baby boom generation move into their fifties their force will increase—not only in the workplace but in the voting booth. [Three chapters] explore the effect that economically powerful women will have on patterns of sex, romance, and marriage. [Another chap-ter] expresses my hope that men and women will begin to acknowledge their differences, employ women's natural talents in the workforce, and use these data to build rapport with one another. It concludes that men and women are regaining a relationship of equality that is natural to humanity and was common in deep history.

I am optimistic about the future—not only for women but for men. Women's propensity to think contextually and their intense curiosity about people will add variety and texture to what we watch on television. Their faculty for language and appetite for diversity and complexity mill enrich what we read in newspapers, magazines and books—and influence our feelings and beliefs. With their people skills, women will continue to invigorate the service professions, adding comfort and novelty to our work and leisure hours.

Women already bring compassion and patience to hands-on healing. They offer imagination in the classroom. They are broadening our perspective of justice. Their facility for networking and reaching consensus will become more and more important as companies dismantle hierarchical management structures and emphasize egalitarian team playing. With their long-term and contextual view, their need to nurture, and their prominent role in civil society, women will also make major contributions toward solving our worldwide social and environmental ills.

More and more, women are expressing their sexuality, adding zest to life in the bedroom. They are changing the meaning of intimacy and romance. And as society's "kin keepers," they are transforming family life in extraordinary ways.

Women are better educated, more capable, and more interesting than ever before. If there ever was a time in human evolution when both sexes had the opportunity to make satisfying careers and happy marriages, that time is now.

ARTICLE 43

Daughters of the Forest

In the textbook-case foraging society, hunting is a man's job. Anthropologists argue that a sexual division of labor makes sense. Women seem less suited physically for such strenuous activity, and in any case, hunting entails many risks that might endanger their children. The woman's role is to bear and raise babies, dig roots, pick berries, and maybe catch the occasional rabbit. Discussing "The Evolution of Hunting," Sherwood L. Washburn and C. S. Lancaster wrote that "when males hunt and females gather, the results are shared and given to the young, and the habitual sharing between a male, a female, and their offspring becomes the basis for the human family" (in *Man the Hunter*, edited by Richard B. Lee and Irven DeVore).

Taytayan Taginod and other Agta women in the Philippines have not heard this anthropological wisdom and would laugh if they did. Taytayan, now a young grandmother, has long hunted wild "bearded pigs," deer, monkeys, and a variety of smaller forest animals and has spearfished in dangerous rivers.

The Agta live in the Sierra Madre, a heavily forested mountain range that parallels the rugged Pacific coast of northeastern Luzon. The Agta do exploit some ocean resources, but it is the humid rain forest and its streams and rivers that dominate their lives. Traditionally, the forest provided not only food but also bark for clothing, palm fronds and saplings for houses, leaves for bedding, and wood for tools. Today, the Agta obtain metal tools, manufactured cloth, cooking pots, tobacco, and rice in trade for forest products—meat and fish, rattan, orchids, and Manila copal, a tree resin.

Extended family groups—clusters of two or three brothers and sisters, the old folks, and the children—are the living and working units of Agta society. All men hunt, except those living where the encroachment of agricultural groups has decimated the forest and game. Where only Agta live, game is plentiful. Wild pig and deer are abundant, although they fluctuate in numbers through various cycles. Plant foods are less readily available. Wild roots are scattered, difficult to dig, and give low returns for the effort expended. Today, Agta dig wild roots only in times of real hardship or when they feel a desire for traditional foods. They grow upland (dry) rice, corn, cassava, and sweet potatoes, but the yield from these crops is low. Given this situation, the Agta say it makes sense for women to be hunters. Women vary in their patterns of living, but many hunt and nearly all join the men in driving game.

Agta women differ from men in hunting tactics. Men love to enter the forest alone, where they stalk with bow and arrow, wait in ambush for hours by fallen fruit, or spot game at night with flashlights tied to their heads. Women are team hunters. They work with other women or with their men. They almost always prefer to drive with dogs and favor killing with long knives instead of bows and arrows (arrows are apt to endanger the dogs). They are seldom the fanatics that men are, but for some women, love of the hunt dominates all their work.

Taytayan is one of the enthusiasts, as my husband, P. Bion Griffin, and I learned as anthropological guests of her family. Taytayan learned to hunt from her husband, Galpong, whose second wife she had become at age sixteen. Taytayan's older sister, Littawan, was Galpong's first wife. Littawan had been unable to conceive; rather than divorce her, Galpong had taken the younger sister as well. Taytayan soon loved hunting with Galpong or Littawan or both. By the time we became acquainted, all three were mature adults and very successful hunters. Taytayan hunts several times a week, choosing, as the more active women hunters often do, to carry the bow and arrow and to nurture a pack of hunting dogs.

I recall the time she ran a deer for two days, until its feet were raw and bloody and exhaustion had slowed it to the point it could be shot. She had given up the hunt the first day, but the next day, she took her dogs, found the deer, and chased it until it collapsed. Other times she and Littawan hunted, Taytayan leaping ahead to shoot and kill, then asking Littawan to carry the carcass home. The kill, she felt, was fun, but lugging a pig home was no joy at all.

Taytayan takes pleasure in the Agta pastime of telling the story of a hunt. The presence of a tape recorder spurs her and others on, and gives the anthropologists (who can seldom keep up during the actual chase) a better insight into the activity. While Taytayan readily tells the stories of both successful and unsuccessful hunts, the following excerpt reveals much of the character and action of a good hunt.

Littawan and I took off and walked way upstream....
"Say, here are some deer tracks," I said. We went up the side of Tagemuyo Mountain. No tracks there. We walked up the stream bed and crossed. We saw more deer tracks. The dogs were all over the hillside. We kept on but saw nothing. We crossed the stream again and went farther upstream. Those deer were really hiding. "Hala, ha, ha, ha," a monkey cried. "Huu, huu," I called to the dogs. Upstream there were more tracks. We continued, and I said, "There are too many tracks! Where are the dogs?" "Aah, aah," I called to the dogs. I grouped the dogs together where the tracks were clustered. The dogs wouldn't stay together, and one, Tighe, was off on his own.

"Listen! That's a pig!" I said; "Quick, after it!" Littawan urged the dogs on by calling "Arah, arah, arah, arah!" "Hurry up to the next stream!" she yelled. I ran around a pile of fallen rocks and earth and into a swarm of bees. They started stinging me all over my body. My hands became swollen; I was so upset I almost threw away my bow. I ran through the bushes and saw the pig, a large boar. The dogs, Littawan, and I ran after it downstream. I nocked my arrow; Tighe really bit the pig, but it broke loose. I couldn't shoot for fear of hitting the dogs. I finally got an arrow into it but didn't kill it. I then stabbed it several times.

Littawan arrived and tied the pig for carrying. "Are we going to butcher it here or carry it home?" she asked. "Let's butcher it over there," I said, "or we'll starve to death." We roasted the liver and some sweet potatoes I was carrying, and then I said, "Let's go downriver and spearfish." On the way, we gathered grass for broom making to sell to the lowlanders. I spearfished but only got three fish.

When we got home, I hollered, "Bion, come and take our picture, as we are carrying meat." I was carrying the grass and my bow and arrows over my shoulder. That would make a good picture.

While Taytayan learned to hunt after she married, most girls learn before they reach puberty. Later they develop into hunters or give it up, as it suits them. In our camp, which contained twenty-five people, girls of age ten and up accompanied fathers, mothers, aunts, and grandmothers on hunts. The girls carried knives or no weapons at all, but ran as game was taken, helped hold and control the dogs, and aided in butchering and carrying home

Just like boys, Agta girls play with bows and arrows. This photo shows a father teaching his six-year-old daughter how to nock an arrow properly.

Photo courtsey of P. Bion Griffin.

the kills. They learned to recognize the signs of game animals, the fruit and leaves they eat, and how they behave under different conditions. Abey, Taytayan's elderly sister-in-law, recalls learning to hunt as a prepubescent girl.

My mother and I left for the forest. We took the hunting dogs along. We walked upriver. "The dogs are chasing a young wild pig!" called Mother. "Hurry up before they chew it up." "I can't walk because of the thorns," I answered. My mother got angry. "I am going to leave you behind," she threatened. I started to cry; I didn't want to be left in the forest. My mother hit me on the head with a stick. She ran off through the undergrowth and I grudgingly followed.

We reached the place where the dogs had cornered the wild pig. My mother stabbed it with a knife until it died. She also hit the dogs because they kept attempting to drag the pig away. Still angry at me, she told me to carry the pig on my back. I took it down to the river to soak. I wanted to head home since I was already hungry. My mother, however, called the dogs and we proceeded upriver.

The dogs jumped a deer, chased it, and bit its legs. It got away and ran into the river. Mother ran to it, held one of its legs, and stabbed it. "Oh!" she screamed, "It will gore me!" "Take it into the deeper water!" I called. She grabbed and held the deer's head. It finally collapsed. "Drag it to where the pig is," she said. She butchered the deer. I gathered firewood, built a fire, and burned the hair off the pig. After Mother finished the deer, she butchered the pig. I roasted the liver and we both ate.

Mother sent me to cut vines for making a pack to carry the meat. She gave me three legs to carry and we proceeded downriver. My pack was so heavy I was really staggering."

Now a grandmother, Abey is again the weak one, as she hunts with her older daughter, Iring. On one trip, she and Iring killed a pig; Iring carried her one-year-old son on her back. We photographed the dead pig and recorded Iring's tale.

"Let's keep on walking, Mother," I said. She answered, "Wait there for me, because my thighs hurt from climb-ing up the mountainside." I walked along with my baby on my back. I was annoyed at Talengteng [the baby] be-cause he was noisy while I was running. We climbed up the steep trail, I on my hands and knees....

Mother asked, "What is that howling?" "Ho, ho, ho," howled [the dog] Baklayan. I thought, this old woman has weak hearing. That's just a young pig, judging from the pitch of the howling. I had to go faster because my mother couldn't run fast enough. As soon as the old woman ar-rived, she clubbed the pig on the head, but it wouldn't die. She clubbed it again, but it still would not die. I cut vines for tying the pig. She finished tying it, and I took the bow and arrows. The pig was still breathing hard tied to Mother's back. We walked and walked, rested, and chewed betel. While we descended the hill, Mother com-plained, "That old dog is useless. It would have been bet-ter if I had reached the pig and stabbed it."

Just how effective are women hunters? My hus-band and I collected quantitative data and kept daily logs of activities. Of the 296 hunting trips we logged, men made 180, either singly or in groups that in-cluded no women. Another 61 trips were male–female team efforts. Trips involving only women numbered 55. Men, then, are more frequent hunters, but women also participate actively.

An Agta woman hunter returns from a hunting-fishing trip. She is carrying her bow and arrows, a pack of butchered wild pig, and a string of river fish. One of her hunting dogs follows behind.

Photo courtesy of P. Bion Griffin.

The greater frequency of hunting by men is reflected in the percentage of carcass weight they bring home. In our sample, men provided 43 percent of the animals by body weight. Hunting by women accounted for 22 percent, while mixed teams got 35 percent. These figures are also the outcome of differences in hunting techniques.

Men use various tactics and often hunt alone. They lie in wait by fallen fruit to ambush the pigs and deer drawn to feed, or they stalk their prey under cover of jungle thickets. The average pig or deer killed by men using these tactics is larger than that brought down by women, although the better women hunters do kill large, adult game. The power of arrows shot from bows with sixty-pound pull also contributes to men's success in killing large animals. Women's bows seldom pull more than forty-five pounds. Of course, only the best hunters, male and female, regularly get the heaviest game.

While women's contribution by carcass weight is smaller, their hunting success rate is high. In the course of the 296 hunts we tabulated, 73 kills were made. The 180 "men only" trips brought in 31 kills, achieving a 17 percent rate of return. In comparison, women totaled 31 percent, and mixed teams of both men and women totaled 41 percent. These figures show that the use of teamwork and dogs yields the highest kill ratios.

Most of the trips by women involved dogs. Dog teams are expensive to maintain, perform poorly in rainy weather, and frequently die from game attacks, illness, or malnutrition. Well-trained, mature, healthy dogs, however, can be of critical importance to the hunt. Two different tactics may be used. In the first, hunters proceed into the forest and station themselves at ambush points where game is likely to pass. Then, one or more hunters with dogs enter the forest, hoping to surprise game and drive it to the ambushers. The second tactic is for a small team, say a husband and wife or two women, to travel with their dogs until an animal is located. Then, as Taytayan recounted, the chase is on, and the hunters expend huge amounts of energy covering rugged terrain. Very often the animal escapes, but good dogs help insure success.

Just as there is overlap, as well as a difference, in how men and women hunt in Agta society, so too the division of labor in other areas is a matter of emphasis. Everybody spearfishes, for example. Although women in foraging societies worldwide have usually been excluded from hunting, they have often been fishers in coastal and riverine environments.

Among the Agta, spearfishing is done under water, by swimmers wearing primitive goggles and using a large rubber band to propel a wire projectile.

Some fishing is in deep, fast, cold rivers; some in slow and shallow streams. Children start learning to fish when little more than toddlers, eventually turning play into a skill. Boys and girls make forays to streams for safe, shallow-water fishing, their catches becoming picnic snacks. Teen-agers join adults in fishing the larger rivers where large fish abound. Women truly excel in this often daily activity. Nearly all females, from twelve years old to the very old, spearfish.

One of the most important of the Agta's food-getting pursuits, fishing may, in the dry season, provide nearly all their animal protein for days at a time. Even people who are not strong enough for the most rigorous fishing occasionally participate in the special fish drives. Women in advanced pregnancy, the elderly, and the lame may drag the rattan lines, tied with fronds, that span the river and chase fish to the swimmers.

Another large part of women's work among the Agta consists of gathering plant foods, shellfish, honey, and the multitude of items needed for medicines and camp maintenance. Even here, however, men are hardly excluded. Everybody collects honey, with women ably climbing the trees to cut down combs, except when young men can be talked into the task. (Women do not like to climb if they are wearing skirts; modest jogging shorts are the favored attire for work in the forest.) Frequently, all the adults and children in a camp take off for an outing along the beaches of rock and coral, where mollusks and crustaceans are to be had. Men limit their beach activities to spear and line fishing, however.

Women and children are the primary gatherers of wild roots and other plant foods. Men seldom join the women in digging up roots, whether cultivated or wild, and although they work at clearing and planting the family's small plot of dry rice, they are less likely to help harvest the crop. Whole families may work together in cutting the caryota palm tree, extracting the starch-laden pith, and packing the food home. More often, however, parties of women and girls do this arduous work, with lots of joking and horseplay throughout the long day.

As we examine all the work done by women, hunting and its supposed limitations on child rearing come into better perspective. Taytayan and her family exemplify efforts to harmonize food getting and general work with the bearing and raising of children.

Taytayan bore four children, two girls and two boys: only the two daughters survived. In this experience she was typical. We found that one-third to one-half of Agta children die before puberty. Tom Headland, a missionary-anthropologist working many miles to our south, found that about half the children die. In his area, the Agta have been more exposed to the destructive effects of newcomers—disease, alcohol, and depletion of game.

Children are a part of nearly all Agta activities. While older children may be left with baby sitters, nursing infants are carried on their mothers' backs not only on occasional hunting trips but also on forest excursions to secure building materials and food. This day in, day out exposure, which sometimes subjects them to wet and cold conditions, certainly contributes to the illnesses that kill many. Mothers shelter their children from bad weather whenever possible, however, and avoid hunting under such conditions. So although hunting is rigorous, it does not pose any special danger to infants.

Taytayan's two daughters are now rearing families. The elder has four surviving children, while the younger, married only in 1978, has two. Both women learned to hunt with their mother, but now hunt primarily with their husbands. They neglect bows and arrows, preferring to carry only knives. During pregnancy they hunted less, and not until the babies were about six months old did they begin to carry them on short hunts.

Taytayan continues to go after wild pigs, deer, and monkeys, while also tending her grandchildren, even adopting the eldest. Now her companions include nieces, nephews, and, of course, Littawan. Her daughters find her difficult to keep up with because of her vigor and enthusiasm. Taytayan once expressed her interest in rumored "fertility drugs" to me. I asked how in the world she would hunt if she had another baby. "No problem," she said, "Littawan can carry it while we hunt."

Mothers and females in general are most decidedly the major child tenders in Agta society. Mothers do the greatest share, followed by elder sisters and grandmothers. Fathers are fourth, but still spend a significant amount of time caring for their children. Young fathers of two or three children assist their wives in child care every day. These fathers often carry older children, aged about three to eight, on foraging trips outside of camp, tending the children while mothers spearfish or gather. My husband and I have often joined these family expeditions. One of my husband's favorite activities was to accompany a father or grandfather and children on some forest task; the anthropologist had no trouble keeping up with the smaller children!

We even know one little girl of about seven, an only child, who was taken by her devoted father on short hunts. Of course, she did not hunt, and she had to be carried for part of the trip. She did, however, begin to take in the whole world of hunting—the sights, sounds, feelings, and spirit of moving through the jungle in hopes of killing prey. As she grows older, she will learn that women and men are not identical in hunting or in any other aspect of their lives. A division of labor by sex does exist in Agta society. But it is flexible, subject to individual needs and preferences. Women adjust hunting and child rearing to each other and to their other subsistence efforts. If they choose, they too can "bring home the bacon."

Cherry Lindholm and Charles Lindholm

Life behind the Veil

The bazaar teems with activity. Pedestrians throng the narrow streets, wending past donkey carts, cyclists and overloaded vehicles. Vendors haggle in the dark doorways of their shops. Pitiful beggars shuffle among the crowds, while bearded religious mendicants wander about, their eyes fixed on a distant world.

Drifting among the mobs of men are, here and there, anonymous figures hidden beneath voluminous folds of material, who float along like ships in full sail, graceful, mysterious, faceless, instilling in the observer a sense both of awe and of curiosity. These are the Moslem women of the Middle East. Their dress is the customary *chador,* which they wear when obliged to leave the privacy of their homes. The *chador* is but one means by which women maintain their *purdah,* the institution of female seclusion, which requires that women should remain unseen by men who are not close relatives and strikes Westerners as so totally foreign and incomprehensible.

Sometimes the alien aspect is tempered with a touch of Western familiarity. A pair of plastic sunglasses may gleam from behind the lace that covers the eyes, or a platform shoe might peep forth from beneath the hem of the flowing *chador.* Nevertheless, the overall presence remains one of inscrutability and is perhaps the most striking image of Middle Eastern societies.

We spent nine months in one of the most strict of all the *purdah* societies, the Yusufzai Pakhtun of the Swat Valley in the North-West Frontier Province of Pakistan. ("Pakhtun" is the designation preferred by the tribesmen, who were generally called Pathans in the days of the British *raj.*)

We had come to the Swat Valley after a hair-raising ride on a rickety bus from Peshawar over the 10,280-foot Malakand Pass. Winston Churchill came this way as a young war correspondent attached to the Malakand Field Force in 1897. As we came into the valley, about half the size of Connecticut, we passed a sign that said WELCOME TO SWAT. We were fortunate to have entrée into the community through a Swati friend we had made eight years before. In Swat, women are secluded inside the domestic compound except for family rituals, such as marriage, circumcision and funerals, or visits to saints' tombs. A woman must always be in the protective company of other women and is never allowed out alone. It tells a great deal about the community that the word for husband in Pakhto, the language of the Pakhtun, is *khawund,* which also means God.

However, as everywhere, rules are sometimes broken or, more frequently, cleverly manipulated. Our Pakhtun host's stepmother, Bibi, an intelligent and forceful woman, was renowned for her tactics. Once, when all the females of the household had been forbidden to leave the compound to receive cholera inoculations at the temporary clinic next door, Bibi respectfully bowed her head and assured the men they could visit the mosque with easy minds. Once the men had gone, she promptly climbed the ladder to the flat roof and summoned the doctor to the door of her compound. One by one, the women extended their bare arms through the doorway and received their shots. Later, Bibi could honestly swear that no woman had set foot outside the compound walls.

Despite such circumventions, *purdah* is of paramount importance in Swat. As one Pakhtun proverb succinctly states: "The woman's place is in the home or the grave." Years ago in Swat, if a woman broke her *purdah,* her husband might kill her or cut off her nose as punishment and as a means of cleansing his honor. If a woman is caught alone with an unrelated man, it will always be assumed that the liaison is sexual, and public opinion will oblige her husband to shoot her, even if he does not desire her death; to go unavenged is to be known henceforth as *begherata,* or man without honor. As such, he would no longer have the right to call himself Pakhtun.

A shameless woman is a threat to the whole society. Our host remembered witnessing, 30 years ago when he was a child, the entire village stoning an

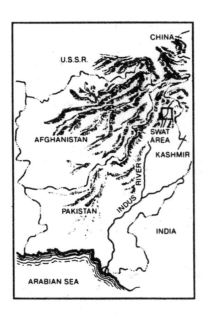

Swat is reached by a 10,280-foot deep pass in the mountains of the Hindu Kush.

Walken Graphics, Inc.

adulteress. This punishment is prescribed by Islamic law, though the law requires there be four witnesses to the sexual act itself to establish guilt. Nowadays, punishments for wifely misdemeanors have become less harsh, though adulterous wives are still killed.

SEDUCTION

In the rural areas, poorer families generally cannot maintain *purdah* as rigorously as their wealthier neighbors, for often the wife must help her husband in the fields or become a servant. Nevertheless, she is required to keep her hair covered at all times and interaction with men to a minimum. Here again, the rules are sometimes flouted, and a poor woman might entice a man with her eyes or even, according to village men who claimed personal experiences, become more aggressive in her seductive attempts and actually seize a man in a deserted alleyway and lure him into her house. Often, the man is persuaded. Such a woman will accept money from her lover, who is usually a man from a wealthy family. Her husband is then a *begherata*, but some men acquiesce to the situation because of the money the wife is earning or because of fear of the wife's socially superior and more powerful lover. But most poor men, and certainly all of the elite, keep their women under strict control.

In the Islamic Middle East, women are viewed as powerful and dangerous beings, highly sexual

and lacking in personal discipline and discrimination. In Middle Eastern thought, sexual intercourse itself, though polluting, lacks the same negative connotations it has in the West. It has always been believed that women have sexual climaxes, and there is no notion of female frigidity. Male impotence, however, is well-documented, and some middle-aged and even young men admitted to us that they had lost their interest in women. Sometimes, though rarely, a young bridegroom will find himself incapable of consummating his marriage, either because he finds his bride unattractive or because he has been previously enchanted by a male lover and has become impotent in a heterosexual relationship. Homosexuality has never been seen as aberrant in the Middle East. As a famous Afghan saying humorously declares: "A woman is for bearing children, a boy is for pleasure, but ecstasy is a ripe watermelon!" However, with Western influence, homosexuality in the Middle East is now less overt. But even when it was common and open, the man was still expected to marry and produce children.

Men must marry, though women are regarded as a chaotic and anarchic force. They are believed to possess many times the sexual desire of men and constitute a potential threat to the family and the family's honor, which is based in large measure on the possession and control of women and their excessive and dangerous sexuality.

Among the Pakhtun of Swat, where the male–female relation is one of the most hostile in the Middle East, the man avoids showing affection to his wife, for fear she will become too self-confident and will begin to assert herself in ways that insult his position and honor. She may start by leaving the compound without his permission and, if unchecked, may end by bringing outside men into the house for sexual encounters, secure in the knowledge that her husband, weakened by his affection for her, will not take action. This course of events is considered inevitable by men and women alike and was illustrated by a few actual cases in the village where we lived.

Women are therefore much feared, despite the pronouncements of male supremacy. They must be controlled, in order to prevent their alarming basic natures from coming to the fore and causing dishonor to their own lineages. *Purdah* is generally described as a system that serves to protect the woman, but implicitly it protects the men and society in general from the potentially disruptive actions of the powerful female sex.

Changes are occurring, however, particularly in the modern urban centers. The educated urban woman often dispenses with the *chador*, replacing it with a simple length of veiling draped over the head or across the shoulders; she may even decide to adopt modest Western dress. The extent of this transformation will depend partly upon the attitude of the community in which she lives.

In the urban centers of the stricter *purdah* regions the public display of *purdah* is scrupulous, sometimes even more striking than that of the tribal village. Behind the scenes, though, the city-dwelling woman does have more freedom than she would have in the village. She will be able to visit not only relatives but friends without specific permission from her husband, who is out at work all day. She may, suitably veiled, go shopping in the bazaar, a chore her husband would have undertaken in the village. On the whole, the city woman will have a great deal more independence, and city men sometimes lament this weakening of traditional male domination.

The urbanized male may speak of the custombound tribesmen (such as the Swat Pakhtun, the Bedouin nomads of Saudi Arabia or the Qashqai herdsmen of Iran) as country bumpkins, yet he still considers their central values, their sense of personal pride, honor and autonomy, as cultural ideals and views the tribesmen, in a very real way, as exemplars of the proper mode of life. Elite families in the cities proudly emphasize their tribal heritage and sometimes send their sons to live for a year or so with distant tribal cousins, in order to expose them to the tribesman's integrity and moral code. The tribesman, on the other hand, views his urbanized relatives as weak and womanly, especially with reference to the slackening of *purdah* in the cities. Though the *purdah* female, both in the cities and in the tribal areas, rarely personifies the ideal virtues of silence, submission and obedience, the concept of *purdah* and male supremacy remains central to the male identity and to the ideology of the culture as a whole.

The dynamic beneath the notion of male supremacy, the institution of *purdah* and the ideology of women's sexual power becomes apparent when one takes an overall view of the social structure. The family in the Middle East, particularly in the tribal regions, is not an isolated element; kinship and marriage are the underlying principles that structure action and thought. Individuals interact not so much according to personal preference as according to kinship.

The Middle Eastern kinship system is known to anthropologists as a segmentary-lineage organization; the basic idea is that kinship is traced through one line only. In the Middle East, the system is patrilineal, which means that the male line is followed,

and all the links through women are ignored. An individual can therefore trace his relationship to any other individual in the society and know the exact genealogical distance between them; i.e., the distance that must be traced to reach a common male ancestor. The system obliges men to defend their patrilineal relatives if they are attacked, but if there is no external force threatening the lineage, then men struggle against one another according to the principle of genealogical distance. This principle is nicely stated in a famous Middle Eastern proverb: "I against my brothers; my brothers and I against my cousins; my cousins, my brothers and I against the world." The cousins in question are of course patrilineal.

PROMISCUITY PHOBIA

Within this system, women appear to have no role, though they are the units of reproduction, the mothers of the sons who will carry on the patriline. Strange as it may seem, this is the core contradiction of the society: The "pure" patriline itself is actually descended from a woman. This helps explain the exaggerated fear of women's promiscuity and supposedly voracious sexuality. In order to protect the patriline, women must be isolated and guarded. Their sexuality, which threatens the integrity of the patriline, must be made the exclusive property of their husbands. Women, while being absolutely necessary for the perpetuation of the social order, are simultaneously the greatest threat to it.

The persistent denigration of women is explained by this core contradiction. Moslem society considers women naturally inferior in intelligence and ability—childlike, incapable of discernment, incompetent to testify in court, prey to whims and fancies. In tribal areas, women are prohibited from inheritance, despite a Koranic injunction, and in marriage they are purchased from their fathers like a commodity. Were women not feared, these denials of her personhood would be unnecessary.

Another unique element of Middle Eastern culture is the prevalence of marriage with the father's brother's daughter. In many areas, in fact, this marriage is so favored that a boy must give explicit permission to allow his patrilineal female cousin to marry elsewhere. This peculiar marriage form, which is found nowhere else in the world, also serves to negate the woman by merging her lineage with that of her husband, since both are members of the same patriline (indeed, are the offspring of brothers). No new blood enters, and the sanctity of the patriline is steadily maintained.

However, this ploy gives rise to other problems: Cousin marriage often divides the brothers rather than uniting them. Although the bride-price is usually reduced in such marriages, it is always demanded, thus turning the brothers into opponents in a business negotiations. Furthermore, giving a woman in Swat carries an implication of inferiority; historically, victors in war took women from the vanquished. Cousin marriage thus renders the brothers' equality questionable. Finally, the young couple's fights will further alienate the brothers, especially since such marriages are notoriously contentious. This is because patrilineal male cousins are rivals for the common grandfather's inheritance (in fact, the Swati term for father's brother's son is *tarbur*, which also means enemy), and a man who marries his patrilineal cousin is marrying the sister of his lifelong opponent. Her loyalty is with her brother, and this is bound to cause frequent disputes.

Though the girl is treated like goods, she does not see herself as such. The fundamental premise of tribal life is the equality of the various landed families. There are very few hierarchies in these societies, and even the leaders are often no more than first among equals. Within this system, which has been described as a nearly perfect democracy, each *khan* (which means landowner and literally translates as king) family sees itself as superior to all others. The girls of the household feel the same pride in their lineage as their brothers and cannot help but regard their husbands' families through jaundiced eyes. The new bride is prepared to defend the honor of her family, even though they have partially repudiated her by negotiating the marriage. Her identity, like that of a man, rests on her lineage pride, which she will fight to uphold. The husband, meanwhile, is determined to demonstrate his domination and mastery, since control of women is the nexus of a man's sense of self-respect.

Hostility is thus built into marriage by the very structure of the society, which pits every lineage against every other in a never-ending contest to maintain an equilibrium of power within this markedly egalitarian culture. The hostility of the marriage bond is evident from its beginnings. The reluctant bride is torn from her cot in her family's house and ensconced on a palanquin that strongly resembles a bier. The war drums that announce the marriage procession indicate the nature of the tie, as does the stoning of the palanquin by the small boys of the village as it is carried through the dusty streets. When the bride arrives at her new husband's house, his family triumphantly fires their rifles into the air. They have taken a woman! The young wife cowers in her veils as she is prodded and poked curiously by the females of the husband's house who try to persuade her to show her face. The groom himself is nowhere to be seen, having retreated to the men's house in shame. In three days, he will creep to her room and consummate the marriage. Taking the virginity of the bride is a highly charged symbolic act, and in some areas of the Middle East the display of the bloody nuptial sheet to the public is a vital part of the wedding rite. Breaking the hymen demonstrates the husband's possession of his wife's sexuality. She then becomes the most junior adult in the household, subordinate to everyone, but, most especially, under the heavy thumb of her mother-in-law.

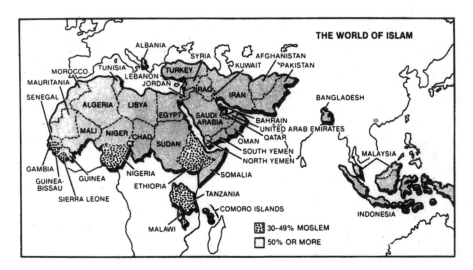

The world of Islam began when Mohammed preached in Saudi Arabia in the seventh century. It fanned out, carrying purdah with it, into Asia and into Africa south of the Sahara.

Walken Graphics, Inc.

The household the bride enters will be that of her husband's father, since the system, as well as being patrilineal, is also patrilocal. She will be surrounded by his relatives and will be alone with her husband only at night. During the day he will pay no attention to her, for it is considered shameful for a man to take note of his wife in front of others, particularly his father and mother. Within the compound walls, which shield the household from the rest of the world, she is at the mercy of her new family.

DOMESTIC BATTLES

Life within the compound is hardly peaceful. Wives squabble among themselves, and wives who have built a power base by having sons even quarrel with the old matriarch, their mother-in law. This is usually a prelude to a couple moving out of the house into their own compound, and husbands always blame their wives for the breakup of the extended family, even though they, too, will be glad to become the masters of their own homes and households.

But the worst fights among women are the fights between women married to the same man. Islam permits polygamous marriage, and legally a man may have four wives. Not all men are financially able to take more than one wife, but most men dream of marrying again, despite the Swati proverb that says, "I may be a fool, but not so much of a fool as the man with two wives." Men who can afford it often do take a second wife. The reason is not sexual desire, for wives do not mind if their husbands have liaisons with prostitutes or promiscuous poor women. Rather, the second wife is brought in to humiliate an overly assertive first wife. Bringing in a second wife is a terrible insult; it is an expression of contempt for the first wife and her entire lineage. The insult is especially cutting in Swat, where divorce is prohibited (though it is permitted in the Koran) and where a disliked wife must either endure her lot or retreat to her family's house and a life of celibacy. Small wonder then that households with two wives are pits of intrigue, vituperation and magical incantation, as each wife seeks to expel the other. The Koran says a man should only practice polygamy if he is sure he can treat each wife equally; the only man we met who was able to approximate this ideal was a man who never went home. He spent his time in the men's house, talking with his cronies and having his meals sent to him.

The men's house is the best-built structure in any village, along with the mosque, which is also prohibited to women. It is a meeting place for the clan, the center for hospitality and refuge and the arena for political manipulation. This is where the visitor will be received, surrounded by men who gossip, doze or clean their rifles. Here, the guest might well imagine that women do not even exist. Only the tea and food that is sent over from the compound nearby tell him of the women working behind the walls.

Formerly, in Swat, most men slept in the men's house, visiting their wives secretly late at night and returning before daybreak. But now only a few elders and some ne'er-do-well youths live permanently in the elegant, aging buildings. Sometimes, however, a man may be obliged to move to the men's house for a few days if his wife makes his home too uncomfortable, for women too have their own weapons in the household battles. Arguments may flare up over almost anything: the husband buying a rotten piece of meat or forgetting to bring home a length of material, the wife ruining some curd or gossiping too much with a neighbor. The wife may then angrily refuse to cook, obliging the husband to retreat to the men's house for food. The man's weapon in fights is violence, while the woman can withdraw domestic services at will.

In the early days of a marriage, when the bride is new to the household and surrounded by her husband's people, she may be fairly meek. But when her status has improved as a result of producing sons, she will become more aggressive. Her lacerating tongue is renowned, and she will also begin to fight back physically as well as verbally. Finally, her exasperated husband may silence her with a blow from a heavy stick he keeps for that purpose. No shame is attached to beating one's wife, and men laugh about beatings they have administered. The women themselves, though they decry their men's brutality, proudly display their scars and bruises, characterizing a neighbor who is relatively gentle to his wife as "a man with no penis."

The older a woman gets the more powerful and fearless she becomes. She is aided by her sons who, though respecting their father, regard him as an obstacle to their gaining rights in land. The old man, who gains his stature from his landholding, is always reluctant to allot shares to his grown sons. Furthermore, the sons' ties of affection are much stronger with the mother. The elderly father, who is generally 10 or 15 years older than his wife, is thus surrounded by animosity in his own house. The situation of the earlier years has reversed itself, and the wife, who began alone and friendless, gains allies in her old age, while the husband becomes isolated. Ghani Khan, a modern Pakhtun writer, has described the situation well: "The Pakhtun thinks he is as good as anyone else and his father rolled into one and is fool enough to try this even with his wife. She pays for it in her youth, and he in his old age."

But many women do not live to see their triumph. In northern Swat, for every 100 women over the age of 60 there are 149 men, compared to the more equal 100 to 108 ratio below 60. The women are worn out by continual childbearing, breast-feeding and a lack of protein. Though fertile in places, the Swat valley is heavily overpopulated with an estimated one million people, and survival is always difficult. The diet consists chiefly of bread, rice, seasonal vegetables and some dairy products. Meat is a rarity and goes to the men and boys as a matter of course. They perpetuate the patrilineal clan and must survive, while women can always be replaced. The lives of men are hard, but the lives of women are harder, as witnessed by their early deaths.

In this environment, people must learn to be tough, just as they must learn to fit the structure of the patrilineal system. Child-rearing serves both functions.

The birth of a boy in Swat is greeted by rejoicing, while the birth of a girl is an occasion for gloom. But the first few years for both sexes are virtually identical. Like most Middle Easterners, the Swatis practice swaddling, binding the baby tightly so that it is immobilized. Ostensibly, this is to help the baby sleep and prevent it from blinding itself with its flailing hands, but anthropologists have hypothesized that swaddling actually serves to develop a certain character type: a type which can withstand great restraint but which also tends to uncontrolled bursts of temper. This hypothesis fits Swat, where privation and the exigencies of the social structure demand stoicism, but where violent temper is also useful. We often saw Swati children of all ages lose themselves in tantrums to coerce their parents, and such coercion was usually successful. Grown men and women as well are prone to fits of temper, and this dangerous aspect makes their enemies leery of pressing them too hard.

Both sexes are indoctrinated in the virtues of their family and its lineage. In marital fights this training is obvious, as both partners heatedly assert, "Your ancestor was nothing, and mine was great!" At a man's death his sister, not his wife, is his chief mourner. And if a woman is killed it is her brother, not her husband, who avenges her.

Child training in Swat produces strong characters. When they give affection, they give it wholeheartedy, and when they hate, they hate bitterly. The conditions under which they live are cruel and cramped, and they respond with cruelty and rigidity in order to survive. But at the same time, the people are able to bear their hard lives with pride and dignity.

BELIEF AND RITUAL

"As members of society, most of us see only what we expect to see, and what we expect to see is what we are conditioned to see when we have learned the definitions and classifications of our culture," anthropologist Victor Turner has observed. But the statement is incomplete: it omits any mention of *beliefs*—bodies of assumptions about the nature of things bolstered by selected facts—which are embedded in every culture and, along with the categories Turner mentions, powerfully organize our experiences of the world around us.

Belief systems deal with everything human beings can perceive and can imagine. Instrumental, or rational–technical, belief systems are concerned primarily with concrete phenomena and tasks. What kind of person makes a good spouse? Which stocks are likely to yield bushels of money to investors? What training methods and dietary regimens should Olympic swimmers undergo? Instrumental beliefs provide answers to these and countless other questions concerning day-to-day existence.

Other beliefs take us beyond daily concerns and address more profound issues, such as the purpose of human existence, the phenomenon of death, and the existence of entities that inherently cannot be verified by the human senses. Such transcendental beliefs always invoke the larger picture when they address concrete tasks or specific issues, as in the case of the Bolivian tin miners described by June Nash in her classic article, "Devils, Witches, and Sudden Death" (Article 45). Without their instrumental and transcendental beliefs, these miners could hardly be expected to cope with the extreme stresses of their extraordinarily dangerous work.

In "The Secrets of Haiti's Living Dead," Article 46, Gino Del Guercio describes the fascinating world of voodoo. Legend has it that zombies are the living dead, raised from their graves by voodoo priests. When Harvard ethnobotanist Wade Davis went to Haiti in 1982, he definitely did not believe in zombies. He learned that voodoo is an integral aspect of a coherent Haitian culture and social structure. What he discovered about zombies lies at the intersection of religious belief and modern science. Davis's book about his experiences, *The Serpent and the Rainbow*, was released as a motion picture in 1988.

Devils, Witches, and Sudden Death

Tin miners in the high Andean plateau of Bolivia earn less than a dollar a day when, to use their phrase, they "bury themselves alive in the bowels of the earth." The mine shafts—as much as two miles long and half a mile deep—penetrate hills that have been exploited for more than 450 years. The miners descend to the work areas in open hauls; some stand on the roof and cling to the swaying cable as the winch lowers them deep into the mine.

Once they reach their working level, there is always the fear of rockslides as they drill the face of the mine, of landslides when they set off the dynamite, of gas when they enter unfrequented areas. And added to their fear of the accidents that have killed or maimed so many of their workmates is their economic insecurity. Like Wall Street brokers they watch international price quotations on tin, because a difference of a few cents can mean layoffs, loss of bonuses, a cut in contract prices—even a change of government.

Working in the narrow chimneys and corridors of the mine, breathing the dust- and silicate-filled air, their bodies numbed by the vibration of the drilling machines and the din of dynamite blasts, the tin miners have found an ally in the devil, or Tio (uncle), as he is affectionately known. Myths relate the devil to his pre-Christian counterpart Huari, the powerful ogre who owns the treasures of the hills. In Oruro, a 13,800-foot-high mining center in the western Andes of Bolivia, all the miners know the legend of Huari, who persuaded the simple farmers of the Uru Uru tribe to leave their work in the fields and enter the caves to find the riches he had in store. The farmers, supported by their ill-gained wealth from the mines, turned from a virtuous life of tilling the soil and praying to the sun god Inti to a life of drinking and midnight revels. The community would have died, the legend relates, if an Inca maiden, Nusta, had not descended from the sky and taught the people to live in harmony and industry.

Despite four centuries of proselytizing, Catholic priests have failed to wipe out belief in the legend, but the principal characters have merged with Catholic deities. Nusta is identified with the Virgin of the Mineshaft, and is represented as the vision that appeared miraculously to an unemployed miner.

The miners believe that Huari lives on in the hills where the mines are located, and they venerate him in the form of the devil, or Tio. They believe he controls the rich veins of ore, revealing them only to those who give him offerings. If they offend the Tio or slight him by failing to give him offerings, he will withhold the rich veins or cause an accident.

Miners make images of the Tio and set them up in the main corridors of each mine level, in niches cut into the walls for the workers to rest. The image of the Tio varies in appearance according to the fancy of the miner who makes him, but his body is always shaped from ore. The hands, face, horns, and legs are sculptured with clay from the mine. Bright pieces of metal or burned-out bulbs from the miners' electric torches are stuck in the eye sockets. Teeth are made of glass or crystal sharpened "like nails," and the mouth is open, gluttonous, and ready to receive offerings. Sometimes the plaster of Paris masks worn by the devil dancers at Carnival are used for the head. Some Tios wear embroidered vests, flamboyant capes, and miners' boots. The figure of a bull, which helps miners in contract with the devil by digging out the ore with its horns, occasionally accompanies the image, or there may be *chinas*, female temptresses who are the devil's consorts.

The Tio is a figure of power: he has what everyone wants, in excess. Coca remains lie in his greedy mouth. His hands are stretched out, grasping the bottles of alcohol he is offered. His nose is burned black by the cigarettes he smokes down to the nub. If a Tio is knocked out of his niche by an extra charge of dynamite and survives, the miners consider him to be more powerful than others.

Another spirit present in the mines but rarely represented in images is the Awiche, or old woman. Although some miners deny she is the Pachamama, the earth goddess worshiped by farmers, they relate to her in the same way. Many of the miners greet her when they enter the mine, saying, "Good-day, old woman. Don't let anything happen to me today!" They ask her to intercede with the Tio when they feel

257

in danger; when they leave the mine safely, they thank her for their life.

Quite the opposite kind of feminine image, the Viuda, or widow, appears to miners who have been drinking *chicha*, a fermented corn liquor. Miners who have seen the Viuda describe her as a young and beautiful *chola*, or urbanized Indian, who makes men lose their minds—and sometimes their paychecks. She, too, is a consort of the devil and recruits men to make contracts with him, deluding them with promises of wealth.

When I started working in Oruro during the summer of 1969, the men told me about the *ch'alla*, a ceremonial offering of cigarettes, coca, and alcohol to the Tio. One man described it as follows:

> We make the *ch'alla* in the working areas within the mine. My partner and I do it together every Friday, but on the first Friday of the month we do it with the other workers on our level. We bring in banners, confetti, and paper streamers. First we put a cigarette in the mouth of the Tio and light it. After this we scatter alcohol on the ground for the Pachamama, then give some to the Tio. Next we take out our coca and begin to chew, and we also smoke. We serve liquor from the bottles each of us brings in. We light the Tio's cigarette, saying "Tio, help us in our work. Don't let any accidents happen." We do not kneel before him as we would before a saint, because that would be sacrilegious.
>
> Then everyone begins to get drunk. We begin to talk about our work, about the sacrifices that we make. When this is finished, we wind the streamers around the neck of the Tio. We prepare our *mesas* [tables of offerings that include sugar cakes, llama embryos, colored wool, rice, and candy balls].
>
> After some time we say, "Let's go." Some have to carry out those who are drunk. We go to where we change our clothes, and when we come out we again make the offering of liquor, banners, and we wrap the streamers around each others' necks. From there on, each one does what he pleases.

I thought I would never be able to participate in a *ch'alla* because the mine managers told me the men didn't like to have women inside the mine, let alone join them in their most sacred rites. Finally a friend high in the governmental bureaucracy gave me permission to go into the mine. Once down on the lowest level of San José mine, 340 meters below the ground, I asked my guide if I could stay with one of the work crews rather than tour the galleries as most visitors did. He was relieved to leave me and get back to work. The men let me try their machines so that I could get a sense of what it was like to hold a 160-pound machine vibrating in a yard-wide tunnel,

or to use a mechanical shovel in a gallery where the temperature was 100° F.

They told me of some of their frustrations—not getting enough air pumped in to make the machines work at more than 20 percent efficiency and constant breakdowns of machinery, which slowed them up on their contract.

At noon I refused the superintendent's invitation to eat lunch at level 0. Each of the men gave me a bit of his soup or some "seconds," solid food consisting of noodles, potatoes, rice, and spicy meat, which their wives prepare and send down in the elevators.

At the end of the shift all the men in the work group gathered at the Tio's niche in the large corridor. It was the first Friday of the month and the gang leader, Lino Pino, pulled out a bottle of fruit juice and liquor, which his wife had prepared, and each of the men brought out his plastic bag with coca. Lino led the men in offering a cigarette to the Tio, lighting it, and then shaking the liquor on the ground and calling for life, "Hallalla! Hallalla!"

We sat on lumps of ore along the rail lines and Lino's helper served us, in order of seating, from a little tin cup. I was not given any priority, nor was I forgotten in the rounds. One of the men gave me coca from his supply and I received it with two hands, as I had been taught in the rituals aboveground. I chewed enough to make my cheek feel numb, as though I had had an injection of novocaine for dental work. The men told me that coca was their gift from the Pachamama, who took pity on them in their work.

As Lino offered liquor to the Tio, he asked him to "produce" more mineral and make it "ripen," as though it were a crop. These rituals are a continuation of agricultural ceremonies still practiced by the farmers in the area. The miners themselves are the sons or grandsons of the landless farmers who were recruited when the gold and silver mines were reopened for tin production after the turn of the century.

A month after I visited level 340, three miners died in an explosion there when a charge of dynamite fell down a shoot to their work site and exploded. Two of the men died in the mine; the third died a few days later in the hospital. When the accident occurred, all the men rushed to the elevators to help or to stare in fascinated horror as the dead and injured were brought up to level 0. They carried the bodies of their dead comrades to the social center where they washed the charred faces, trying to lessen the horror for the women who were coming. When the women came into the social center where the bodies were laid out, they screamed and stamped their feet, the horror of seeing their husbands or neighbors sweeping through their bodies.

The entire community came to sit in at the wake, eating and drinking in the feasting that took place before the coffins of their dead comrades. The meal seemed to confirm the need to go on living as well as the right to live.

Although the accident had not occurred in the same corridor I had been in, it was at the same level. Shortly after that, when a student who worked with me requested permission to visit the mine, the manager told her that the men were hinting that the accident had happened because the gringa (any foreign-born, fair-haired person, in this case myself) had been inside. She was refused permission. I was disturbed by what might happen to my relations with the people of the community, but even more concerned that I had added to their sense of living in a hostile world where anything new was a threat.

The miners were in a state of uneasiness and tension the rest of that month, July. They said the Tio was "eating them" because he hadn't had an offering of food. The dead men were all young, and the Tio prefers the juicy flesh and blood of the young, not the tired blood of the sick older workers. He wanted a *k'araku*, a ceremonial banquet of sacrificed animals.

There had not been any scheduled *k'arakus* since the army put the mines under military control in 1965. During the first half of the century, when the "tin barons"—Patiño, Hochschild, and Arayamao—owned the mines, the administrators and even some of the owners, especially Patiño, who had risen from the ranks, would join with the men in sacrificing animals to the Tio and in the drinking and dancing that followed. After nationalization of the mines in 1952, the rituals continued. In fact, some of the miners complained that they were done in excess of the Tio's needs. One said that going into the mine after the revolution was like walking into a saloon.

Following military control, however, the miners had held the ritual only once in San José, after two men had died while working their shift. Now the Tio had again shown he was hungry by eating the three miners who had died in the accident. The miners were determined to offer him food in a *k'araku*.

At 10:30 P.M. on the eve of the devil's month, I went to the mine with Doris Widerkehr, a student, and Eduardo Ibañez, a Bolivian artist. I was somewhat concerned about how we would be received after what the manager of the mine had said, but all the men seemed glad we had come. As we sat at the entry to the main shaft waiting for the *yatiris*, shamans who had been contracted for the ceremony, the miners offered us *chicha* and cocktails of fruit juice and alcohol.

When I asked one of the men why they had prepared the ritual and what it meant, his answer was:

We are having the k'araku *because a man can't die just like that. We invited the administrators, but none of them have come. This is because only the workers feel the death of their comrades.*

We invite the Pachamama, the Tio, and God to eat the llamas that we will sacrifice. With faith we give coca and alcohol to the Tio. We are more believers in God here than in Germany or the United States because there the workers have lost their soul. We do not have earthquakes because of our faith before God. We hold the crucifix to our breast. We have more confidence before God.

Most miners reject the claim that belief in the Tio is pagan sacrilege. They feel that no contradiction exists, since time and place for offerings to the devil are clearly defined and separated from Christian ritual.

At 11:00 P.M. two white llamas contributed by the administration were brought into level 0 in a company truck. The miners had already adorned the pair, a male and a female, with colored paper streamers and the bright wool earrings with which farmers decorate their flocks.

The four *yatiris* contracted for did not appear, but two others who happened to be staying at the house of a miner were brought in to perform the ceremony. As soon as they arrived, the miners took the llamas into the elevator. The male was on the right and the female to his left, "just the same as a marriage ceremony," one miner commented. Looking at the couple adorned with bright streamers and confetti, there was the feeling of a wedding.

Two men entered the elevator with the llamas and eight more climbed on top to go down to level 340. They were commissioned to take charge of the ritual. All the workers of 340 entered to participate in the ceremony below and about 50 men gathered at level 0 to drink.

At level 340 the workers guided the *yatiris* to the spot where the accident had occurred. There they cast liquor from a bottle and called upon the Tio, the Awiche, and God to protect the men from further accidents—naming all the levels in the mine, the various work sites, the different veins of ore, the elevator shaft, and the winch, repeating each name three times and asking the Tio not to eat any more workers and to give them more veins to work. The miners removed their helmets during this ritual. It ended with the plea for life. "Hallalla, hallalla, hallalla." Two bottles of liquor were sprinkled on the face of the rock and in the various work places.

The *yatiris* then instructed the men to approach the llamas with their arms behind their backs so that the animals would not know who held the knife that would kill them. They were also told to beg pardon for the sacrifice and to kiss the llamas farewell. One miner, noting what appeared to be a tear falling from the female's eye, cried and tried to comfort her. As the men moved around the llamas in a circle, the *yatiris* called on the Malkus (eagle gods), the Awiche, the Pachamama, and finally the Tiyulas (Tios of the mines), asking for their care.

The female llama was the first to be sacrificed. She struggled and had to be held down by two men as they cut her jugular vein. When they disemboweled her, the men discovered that she was pregnant, to which they attributed the strength of her resistance. Her blood was caught in a white basin.

When the heart of the dying llama had pumped out its blood, the *yatiri* made an incision and removed it, using both his hands, a sign of respect when receiving an offering. He put the still palpitating heart in the basin with the blood and covered it with a white cloth on which the miners placed *k'oa*—an offering made up of herbs, coca, wool, and sweets—and small bottles of alcohol and wine.

The man in charge of the ceremony went with five aides to the site of the principal Tio in the main corridor. There they removed a piece of ore from the image's left side, creating a hole into which they put the heart, the blood, and the other offerings. They stood in a circle, their heads bent, and asked for safety and that there be no more accidents. In low voices, they prayed in Quechua.

When this commission returned, the *yatiris* proceeded to sacrifice the male llama. Again they asked the Tio for life and good ore in all the levels of the mine, and that there be no accidents. They took the heart, blood, *k'oa*, and bottles of alcohol and wine to another isolated gallery and buried it for the Tio in a place that would not be disturbed. There they prayed, "filled with faith," as one commented; then returned to the place of the sacrifice. The *yatiris* sprinkled the remaining blood on the veins of ore.

By their absorption and fervid murmuring of prayers, both young and old miners revealed the same faith and devotion. Many of them wept, thinking of the accident and their dead companions. During the ritual drinking was forbidden.

On the following day those men charged with responsibility for the ritual came to prepare the meat. They brought the two carcasses to the baker, who seasoned them and cooked them in large ovens. The men returned at about 1:15 P.M. to distribute the meat. With the meat, they served *chicha*. Some sprinkled *chicha* on the ground for the Pachamama, saying "Hallalla," before drinking.

The bones were burned to ashes, which were then offered to the Tio. The mine entrance was locked shut and left undisturbed for 24 hours. Some remarked that it should be closed for three days, but the company did not want to lose that much time.

During the *k'araku* the miners recognize the Tio as the true owner of the mine. "All the mineral that comes out from the interior of the mine is the 'crop' of the devil and whether one likes it or not, we have to invite the Tio to drink and eat so that the flow of metal will continue," said a young miner who studied evenings at the University of Oruro.

All the workers felt that the failure of the administrators to come to the *k'araku* indicated not only their lack of concern with the lives of the men but also their disregard of the need to raise productivity in the mine.

When the Tio appears uninvited, the miners fear that they have only a short time to live. Miners who have seen apparitions say the Tio looks like a gringo—tall, red-faced, with fair hair and beard, and wearing a cowboy hat. This description hardly resembles the images sculptured by the miners, but it does fit the foreign technicians and administrators who administered the mines in the time of the tin barons. To the Indian workers, drawn from the highland and Cochabamba farming areas, the Tio is a strange and exotic figure, ruthless, gluttonous, powerful, and arbitrary in his use of that power, but nonetheless attractive, someone to get close to in order to share that power. I was beginning to wonder if the reason I was accepted with such good humor by the miners, despite their rule against women in the mines, was because they thought I shared some of these characteristics and was a match for the devil.

Sickness or death in the family can force a man in desperation to make a contract with the devil. If his companions become aware of it, the contract is destroyed and with it his life.

The miners feel that they need the protection of a group when they confront the Tio. In the *ch'alla* and the *k'araku* they convert the power of the Tio into socially useful production. In effect, the rituals are ways of getting the genie back into the bottle after he has done his miracles. Security of the group then depends upon respect toward the sacrificial offering, as shown by the following incident told to me by the head of a work gang after the *k'araku*:

I know of a man who had a vein of ore near where the bones of the sacrificial llama were buried. Without advising me, he made a hole with his drill and put the dyna-

mite in. He knew very well that the bones were there. On the following day, it cost him his life. While he was drilling, a stone fell and cut his head off.

We had to change the bones with a ceremony. We brought in a good shaman who charged us B$500 [about $40], we hired the best orchestra, and we sang and danced in the new location where we laid the bones. We did not work in that corridor for three days, and we spent all the time in the ch'alla.

Often the miners are frightened nearly to death in the mine. A rock falls on the spot they have just left, a man falls in a shaft and is saved by hitting soft clay at the bottom, a tunnel caves in the moment after a man leaves it—these are incidents in a day's work that I have heard men say can start a *haperk'a*, or fear, that can take their lives.

A shaman may have to be called in to bring back the spirit that the Tio has seized. In one curing, a frightened miner was told to wear the clothing he had on when the Tio seized his spirit and to enter and give a service to the Tio at the same spot where he was frightened. The shaman himself asked the Tio to cure his patient, flattering him, "Now you have shown your power, give back his spirit."

The fear may result in sexual impotency. At one of the mines, Siglo XX, when there is full production, a dynamite blast goes off every five minutes in a section called Block Haven. The air is filled with smoke and the miners describe it as an inferno. Working under such tension, a shattering blast may unnerve them. Some react with an erection, followed by sexual debilitation. Mad with rage and fear, some miners have been known to seize a knife, the same knife they use to cut the dynamite leads, and castrate themselves. When I visited Block Haven, I noticed that the Tio on this level had a huge erection, about a foot long on a man-sized figure. The workers said that when they find themselves in a state of impotency they go to the Tio for help. By exemplifying

what they want in the Tio, they seek to repair the psychic damage caused by fear.

After feasting on the meat of the llamas and listening to stories of the Tio, I left the mine. The men thanked me for coming. I could not express the gratitude I felt for restoring my confidence in continuing the study.

Shortly thereafter I met Lino Pino returning from a fiesta for a miraculous saint in a nearby village. He asked me if I would be *madrina* at his daughter's forthcoming confirmation, and when I agreed, his wife offered me a tin cup with the delicious cocktail she always prepares for her husband on the days of the *ch'alla,* and we all had a round of drinks.

Later, when I knelt at the altar rail with Lino and his daughter as we received the wafer and the wine, flesh and blood of another sacrifice victim, I sensed the unity in the miners' beliefs. The miraculous Virgin looked down on us from her marbelized, neon-lit niche, her jewelled finger held out in benediction. She was adequate for that scene, but in the mine they needed someone who could respond to their needs on the job.

In the rituals of the *ch'alla* and the *k'araku,* the power of the Tio to destroy is transformed into the socially useful functions of increasing mineral yield and giving peace of mind to the workers. Confronted alone, the Tio, like Banquo's ghost, makes a man unable to produce or even to go on living. Properly controlled by the group, the Tio promises fertility, potency, and productivity to the miners. Robbed of this faith, they often lose the faith to continue drilling after repeated failure to find a vein, or to continue living when the rewards of work are so meager. Knowing that the devil is on your side makes it possible to continue working in the hell that is the mines.

Gino Del Guercio

The Secrets of Haiti's Living Dead

Five years ago, a man walked into l'Estère, a village in central Haiti, approached a peasant woman named Angelina Narcisse, and identified himself as her brother Clairvius. If he had not introduced himself using a boyhood nickname and mentioned facts only intimate family members knew, she would not have believed him. Because, eighteen years earlier, Angelina had stood in a small cemetery north of her village and watched as her brother Clairvius was buried.

The man told Angelina he remembered that night well. He knew when he was lowered into his grave, because he was fully conscious, although he could not speak or move. As the earth was thrown over his coffin, he felt as if he were floating over the grave. The scar on his right cheek, he said, was caused by a nail driven through his casket.

The night he was buried, he told Angelina, a voodoo priest raised him from the grave. He was beaten with a sisal whip and carried off to a sugar plantation in northern Haiti where, with other zombies, he was forced to work as a slave. Only with the death of the zombie master were they able to escape, and Narcisse eventually returned home.

Legend has it that zombies are the living dead, raised from their graves and animated by malevolent voodoo sorcerers, usually for some evil purpose. Most Haitians believe in zombies, and Narcisse's claim is not unique. At about the time he reappeared, in 1980, two women turned up in other villages saying they were zombies. In the same year, in northern Haiti, the local peasants claimed to have found a group of zombies wandering aimlessly in the fields.

But Narcisse's case was different in one crucial respect; it was documented. His death had been recorded by doctors at the American-directed Schweitzer Hospital in Deschapelles. On April 30, 1962, hospital records show, Narcisse walked into the hospital's emergency room spitting up blood. He was feverish and full of aches. His doctors could not diagnose his illness, and his symptoms grew steadily worse. Three days after he entered the hospital, according to the records, he died. The attending physi-

cians, an American among them, signed his death certificate. His body was placed in cold storage for twenty hours, and then he was buried. He said he remembered hearing his doctors pronounce him dead while his sister wept at his bedside.

At the Centre de Psychiatrie et Neurologie in Port-au-Prince, Dr. Lamarque Douyon, a Haitian-born, Canadian-trained psychiatrist, has been systematically investigating all reports of zombies since 1961. Though convinced zombies were real, he had been unable to find a scientific explanation for the phenomenon. He did not believe zombies were people raised from the dead, but that did not make them any less interesting. He speculated that victims were only made to *look* dead, probably by means of a drug that dramatically slowed metabolism. The victim was buried, dug up within a few hours, and somehow reawakened.

The Narcisse case provided Douyon with evidence strong enough to warrant a request for assistance from colleagues in New York. Douyon wanted to find an ethnobotanist, a traditional-medicines expert, who could track down the zombie potion he was sure existed. Aware of the medical potential of a drug that could dramatically lower metabolism, a group organized by the late Dr. Nathan Kline—a New York psychiatrist and pioneer in the field of psychopharmacology—raised the funds necessary to send someone to investigate.

The search for that someone led to the Harvard Botanical Museum, one of the world's foremost institutes of ethnobiology. Its director, Richard Evans Schultes, Jeffrey professor of biology, had spent thirteen years in the tropics studying native medicines. Some of his best-known work is the investigation of curare, the substance used by the nomadic people of the Amazon to poison their darts. Refined into a powerful muscle relaxant called D-tubocurarine, it is now an essential component of the anesthesia used during almost all surgery.

Schultes would have been a natural for the Haitian investigation, but he was too busy. He recommended another Harvard ethnobotanist for the assignment, Wade Davis, a 28-year-old Canadian pursuing a doctorate in biology.

Davis grew up in the tall pine forests of British Columbia and entered Harvard in 1971, influenced by a *Life* magazine story on the student strike of 1969. Before Harvard, the only Americans he had known were draft dodgers, who seemed very exotic. "I used to fight forest fires with them," Davis says. "Like everybody else, I thought America was where it was at. And I wanted to go to Harvard because of that *Life* article. When I got there, I realized it wasn't quite what I had in mind."

Davis took a course from Schultes, and when he decided to go to South America to study plants, he approached his professor for guidance. "He was an extraordinary figure," Davis remembers. "He was a man who had done it all. He had lived alone for years in the Amazon." Schultes sent Davis to the rain forest with two letters of introduction and two pieces of advice: wear a pith helmet and try ayahuasca, a powerful hallucinogenic vine. During that expedition and others, Davis proved himself an "outstanding field man," says his mentor. Now, in early 1982, Schultes called him into his office and asked if he had plans for spring break.

"I always took to Schultes's assignments like a plant takes to water," says Davis, tall and blond, with inquisitive blue eyes. "Whatever Schultes told me to do, I did. His letters of introduction opened up a whole world." This time the world was Haiti.

Davis knew nothing about the Caribbean island—and nothing about African traditions, which serve as Haiti's cultural basis. He certainly did not believe in zombies. "I thought it was a lark," he says now.

Davis landed in Haiti a week after his conversation with Schultes, armed with a hypothesis about how the zombie drug—if it existed—might be made. Setting out to explore, he discovered a country materially impoverished, but rich in culture and mystery. He was impressed by the cohesion of Haitian society; he found none of the crime, social disorder, and rampant drug and alcohol abuse so common in many of the other Caribbean islands. The cultural wealth and cohesion, he believes, spring from the country's turbulent history.

During the French occupation of the late eighteenth century, 370,000 African-born slaves were imported to Haiti between 1780 and 1790. In 1791, the black population launched one of the few successful slave revolts in history, forming secret societies and overcoming first the French plantation owners and then a detachment of troops from Napoleon's army,

sent to quell the revolt. For the next hundred years Haiti was the only independent black republic in the Caribbean, populated by people who did not forget their African heritage. "You can almost argue that Haiti is more African than Africa," Davis says. "When the west coast of Africa was being disrupted by colonialism and the slave trade, Haiti was essentially left alone. The amalgam of beliefs in Haiti is unique, but it's very, very African."

Davis discovered that the vast majority of Haitian peasants practice voodoo, a sophisticated religion with African roots. Says Davis, "It was immediately obvious that the stereotypes of voodoo weren't true. Going around the countryside, I found clues to a whole complex social world." Vodounists believe they communicate directly with, indeed are often possessed by, the many spirits who populate the everyday world. Vodoun society is a system of education, law, and medicine; it embodies a code of ethics that regulates social behavior. In rural areas, secret vodoun societies, much like those found on the west coast of Africa, are as much or more in control of everyday life as the Haitian government.

Although most outsiders dismissed the zombie phenomenon as folklore, some early investigators, convinced of its reality, tried to find a scientific explanation. The few who sought a zombie drug failed. Nathan Kline, who helped finance Davis's expedition, had searched unsuccessfully, as had Lamarque Douyon, the Haitian psychiatrist. Zora Neale Hurston, an American black woman, may have come closest. An anthropological pioneer, she went to Haiti in the Thirties, studied vodoun society, and wrote a book on the subject, *Tell My Horse*, first published in 1938. She knew about the secret societies and was convinced zombies were real, but if a powder existed, she too failed to obtain it.

Davis obtained a sample in a few weeks.

He arrived in Haiti with the names of several contacts. A BBC reporter familiar with the Narcisse case had suggested he talk with Marcel Pierre. Pierre owned the Eagle Bar, a bordello in the city of Saint Marc. He was also a voodoo sorcerer and had supplied the BBC with a physiologically active powder of unknown ingredients. Davis found him willing to negotiate. He told Pierre he was a representative of "powerful but anonymous interests in New York," willing to pay generously for the priest's services, provided no questions were asked. Pierre agreed to be helpful for what Davis will only say was a "sizable sum." Davis spent a day watching Pierre gather the ingredients—including human bones—and grind them together with mortar and pestle. However, from his knowledge of poison, Davis knew immediately that nothing in the formula could produce the powerful effects of zombification.

Three weeks later, Davis went back to the Eagle Bar, where he found Pierre sitting with three associates. Davis challenged him. He called him a charlatan. Enraged, the priest gave him a second vial, claiming that this was the real poison. Davis pretended to pour the powder into his palm and rub it into his skin. "You're a dead man," Pierre told him, and he might have been, because this powder proved to be genuine. But, as the substance had not actually touched him, Davis was able to maintain his bravado, and Pierre was impressed. He agreed to make the poison and show Davis how it was done.

The powder, which Davis keeps in a small vial, looks like dry black dirt. It contains parts of toads, sea worms, lizards, tarantulas, and human bones. (To obtain the last ingredient, he and Pierre unearthed a child's grave on a nocturnal trip to the cemetery.) The poison is rubbed into the victim's skin. Within hours he begins to feel nauseated and has difficulty breathing. A pins-and-needles sensation afflicts his arms and legs, then progresses to the whole body. The subject becomes paralyzed; his lips turn blue for lack of oxygen. Quickly—sometimes within six hours—his metabolism is lowered to a level almost indistinguishable from death.

As Davis discovered, making the poison is an inexact science. Ingredients varied in the five samples he eventually acquired, although the active agents were always the same. And the poison came with no guarantee. Davis speculates that sometimes instead of merely paralyzing the victim, the compound kills him. Sometimes the victim suffocates in the coffin before he can be resurrected. But clearly the potion works well enough often enough to make zombies more than a figment of Haitian imagination.

Analysis of the powder produced another surprise. "When I went down to Haiti originally," says Davis, "my hypothesis was that the formula would contain *concombre zombi*, the 'zombie's cucumber,' which is a *Datura* plant. I thought somehow *Datura* was used in putting people down." *Datura* is a powerful psychoactive plant, found in West Africa as well as other tropical areas and used there in ritual as well as criminal activities. Davis had found *Datura* growing in Haiti. Its popular name suggested the plant was used in creating zombies.

But, says Davis, "there were a lot of problems with the *Datura* hypothesis. Partly it was a question of how the drug was administered. *Datura* could create a stupor in huge doses, but it just wouldn't produce the kind of immobility that was key. These people had to appear dead, and there aren't many drugs that will do that."

One of the ingredients Pierre included in the second formula was a dried fish, a species of puffer or blowfish, common to most parts of the world. It gets its name from its ability to fill itself with water and swell to several times its normal size when threatened by predators. Many of these fish contain a powerful poison known as tetrodotoxin. One of the most powerful nonprotein poisons known to man, tetrodotoxin turned up in every sample of zombie powder that Davis acquired.

Numerous well-documented accounts of puffer fish poisoning exist, but the most famous accounts come from the Orient, where *fugu* fish, a species of puffer, is considered a delicacy. In Japan, special chefs are licensed to prepare *fugu*. The chef removes enough poison to make the fish nonlethal, yet enough remains to create exhilarating physiological effects—tingles up and down the spine, mild prickling of the tongue and lips, euphoria. Several dozen Japanese die each year, having bitten off more than they should have.

"When I got hold of the formula and saw it was the *fugu* fish, that suddenly threw open the whole Japanese literature," says Davis. Case histories of *fugu* poisoning read like accounts of zombification. Victims remain conscious but unable to speak or move. A man who had "died" after eating *fugu* recovered seven days later in the morgue. Several summers ago, another Japanese poisoned by *fugu* revived after he was nailed into his coffin. "Almost all of Narcisse's symptoms correlated. Even strange things such as the fact that he said he was conscious and could hear himself pronounced dead. Stuff that I thought had to be magic, that seemed crazy. But, in fact, that is what people who get *fugu*-fish poisoning experience."

Davis was certain he had solved the mystery. But far from being the end of his investigation, identifying the poison was, in fact, its starting point. "The drug alone didn't make zombies," he explains. "Japanese victims of puffer-fish poisoning don't become zombies, they become poison victims. All the drug could do was set someone up for a whole series of psychological pressures that would be rooted in the culture. I wanted to know why zombification was going on," he says.

He sought a cultural answer, an explanation rooted in the structure and beliefs of Haitian society. Was zombification simply a random criminal activity? He thought not. He had discovered that Clairvius Narcisse and "Ti Femme," a second victim he interviewed, were village pariahs. Ti Femme was regarded as a thief. Narcisse had abandoned his children and deprived his brother of land that was rightfully his. Equally suggestive, Narcisse claimed that his aggrieved brother had sold him to a *bokor,* a voodoo priest who dealt in black magic: he made cryptic reference to having been tried and found guilty by the "masters of the land."

Gathering poisons from various parts of the country, Davis had come into direct contact with the vodoun secret societies. Returning to the anthropological literature on Haiti and pursuing his contacts with informants, Davis came to understand the social matrix within which zombies were created.

Davis's investigations uncovered the importance of the secret societies. These groups trace their origins to the bands of escaped slaves that organized the revolt against the French in the late eighteenth century. Open to both men and women, the societies control specific territories of the country. Their meetings take place at night, and in many rural parts of Haiti the drums and wild celebrations that characterize the gatherings can be heard for miles.

Davis believes the secret societies are responsible for policing their communities, and the threat of zombification is one way they maintain order. Says Davis, "Zombification has a material basis, but it also has a societal logic." To the uninitiated, the practice may appear a random criminal activity, but in rural vodoun society, it is exactly the opposite—a sanction imposed by recognized authorities, a form of capital punishment. For rural Haitians, zombification is an even more severe punishment than death, because it deprives the subject of his most valued possessions: his free will and independence.

The vodounists believe that when a person dies, his spirit splits into several different parts. If a priest is powerful enough, the spiritual aspect that controls a person's character and individuality, known as *ti bon ange,* the "good little angel," can be captured and the corporeal aspect, deprived of its will, held as a slave.

From studying the medical literature on tetrodotoxin poisoning, Davis discovered that if a victim survives the first few hours of the poisoning, he is likely to recover fully from the ordeal. The subject simply revives spontaneously. But zombies remain without will, in a trance-like state, a condition vodounists attribute to the power of the priest. Davis thinks it is possible that the psychological trauma of zombification may be augmented by

Datura or some other drug; he thinks zombies may be fed a *Datura* paste that accentuates their disorientation. Still, he puts the material basis of zombification in perspective: "Tetrodotoxin and *Datura* are only templates on which cultural forces and beliefs may be amplified a thousand times."

Davis has not been able to discover how prevalent zombification is in Haiti. "How many zombies there are is not the question," he says. He compares it to capital punishment in the United States: "it doesn't really matter how many people are electrocuted, as long as it's a possibility." As a sanction in Haiti, the fear is not of zombies, it's of becoming one.

Davis attributes his success in solving the zombie mystery to his approach. He went to Haiti with an open mind and immersed himself in the culture. "My intuition, unhindered by biases, served me well," he says. "I didn't make any judgments." He combined this attitude with what he had learned earlier from his experiences in the Amazon. "Schultes's lesson is to go and live with the Indians as an Indian." Davis was able to participate in the vodoun society to a surprising degree, eventually even penetrating one of the Bizango societies and dancing in their nocturnal rituals. His appreciation of Haitian culture is apparent. "Everybody asks me how did a white person get this information? To ask the question means you don't understand Haitians—they don't judge you by the color of your skin."

As a result of the exotic nature of his discoveries, Davis has gained a certain notoriety. He plans to complete his dissertation soon, but he has already finished writing a popular account of his adventures. Published in 1987 by Simon and Schuster, it is called *The Serpent and the Rainbow,* after the serpent that vodounists believe created the earth and the rainbow spirit it married. Film rights have already been optioned; in October Davis went back to Haiti with a screenwriter. But Davis takes the notoriety in stride. "All this attention is funny," he says. "For years, not just me, but all Schultes's students have had extraordinary adventures in the line of work. The adventure is not the end point, it's just along the way of getting the data. At the Botanical Museum, Schultes created a world unto itself. We didn't think we were doing anything above the ordinary. I still don't think we do. And you know," he adds, "the Haiti episode does not begin to compare to what others have accomplished—particularly Schultes himself."

THE IMPACT OF MODERNIZATION

Modernization refers to the global transformation of society, a transformation that has its roots in the emergence of the industrial revolution. Although its particular manifestations vary widely due to local social, historical, cultural, political, and economic conditions (and also environmental riches and limitations), students of modernization have noted that certain elements characterize this phenomenon everywhere. As summarized by anthropologist Helen Henderson, these include the following:

1. Subsistence farming gives way to cultivation of agricultural products for the market, and new jobs are created in trade, manufacturing, and administration.
2. New sources of energy are exploited, and individual wage earners operate machines within the industrial system.
3. Specialized educational institutions are created to bring literacy to the masses and impart new skills and knowledge.
4. Urban areas develop rapidly as rural immigrants flow into cities in search of economic opportunities. Urbanites cut their ties with their extended kin, are freed from many traditional restraints, and step into new social roles.
5. The functions of the family (and sometimes the form) change. The family is no longer a unit of production but instead specializes in the socialization of offspring and the organization of consumption.
6. Some scholars would add that modernization also introduces new forms of alienation into the lives of industrial workers, who lose control over the product of their labor and whose work tends to be repetitive and dull.

Modernization, therefore, means far more than a series of adjustments in indigenous economic systems. Rather, it refers to qualitative changes in the organization of society, in culture, and even in individual personalities.

Modernization is a European invention. It was exported from Europe (and America, its descendant) to the so-called Third World through the politics of colonialism and the sociopolitical economy of imperialism. Although its benefits to indigenous societies have been tabulated in terms of increased life spans, better health conditions, rising literacy, and broadened opportunities, the social costs of modernization have been high.

Imperialist nations systematically destroyed indigenous societies' subsistence economies, converting them to specialized cash-crop (rubber, tobacco) or mineral (metal ores, diamonds) economies. Whereas before modernization the native populations could easily provide for their own subsistence needs, they were suddenly forced to participate in an economic system that was controlled from afar, kept down the prices of what they had to offer, made them dependent on high-priced imported goods, and kept their wages low. Thus, modernization created poverty in many areas of the world where, before, the concept simply had no meaning.

In "Requiem for a Lost People," Article 47, William W. Howells documents the horrifying story of the complete annihilation of the aboriginal population of Tasmania (an island south of mainland Australia) by land-hungry European settlers in the nineteenth century. In Article 48, "Societies on the Brink," David Maybury-Lewis lays out current rationales for the continuing destruction of small, semi-isolated societies and also presents anthropologically based arguments against this ongoing trend. He advocates social pluralism and suggests that the alternatives are grim.

What Howells and Maybury-Lewis describe is terrible—and deliberate. Yet it is a mistake to believe, as some people do, that all the awful consequences of contact with Western imperialists that befell indigenous preliterate groups resulted from express plans to exterminate and exploit them. As Geoffrey Cowley points out in "The Great Disease

Migration," Article 49, the European conquerors did not primarily use swords or guns to devastate Native American peoples. Rather, it was the germs they carried with them that accounted for many of the deaths.

In these first years of the twenty-first century, modernization is reaching into the previously inaccessible nooks and crannies of the globe. I recall, more than ten years ago, traveling by boat to reach a remote Fijian island, then hiking through thick vegetation, crossing flooded "roads" knee-deep in water, and finally arriving at a small village. Youngsters ran to greet me and take me to the village...where I found a grocery store, a video rental store, and other children engrossed in playing video games. For better or worse, modern industrial society is reaching into almost every corner of our rapidly shrinking world.

But not yet *everywhere*. In the remote regions of the Amazon, there still are isolated groups of Indians, living their lives as they have for thousands of years, untouched by modern society. In a poignant yet unromantic article, "The Last Tribal Battle," Diana Jean Schemo examines the lives of some of these peoples—often nasty, brutish and short—and asks: should they be fenced off from the modern world?

Clearly, the expansion of industrial society around the globe raises many issues: social, political, ecological, ethical. I hope these articles evoke your concerned attention and provoke you to think deeply about these issues.

Requiem for a Lost People

No segment of humankind can have been rushed into oblivion as speedily as the aboriginals of Tasmania. Dark-skinned and woolly-haired, superficially they looked like Africans, though this is only skin-deep. Anthropologists regret their rapid passing; there is a great deal they would have liked to ask the Tasmanians, but in the early nineteenth century anthropology was a science unborn. There are other things to regret.

Tasmania is the shield-shaped island lying south of Australia's southeast corner. Its towns today give off a staid provincial air, and its countryside is rich in apples and flowers, but a hundred and fifty years ago the keynotes were kangaroos and violence. The island is a little like New England—north for south of course, since it lies in the other hemisphere. Its northern coast, nearest Australia, has the same latitude in the south as has New York in the north, and its southern end, with the city of Hobart, has about the latitude of Portland, Maine. But Tasmania lacks New England's antic weather. Deep snow may fall in the high interior, which is colder than the coast, and there are glaciers in the mountains. Still, while there was some risk from exposure if they were separated from companions and fire, the native Tasmanians essentially wore no clothes. On the shore, winters are mild and summers are cool. Over the year, the average temperature for the day changes only about eighteen degrees, from 46° to 64° Fahrenheit, compared with a swing of well over forty degrees in coastal New England. In fact, the thermometer may go up and down more during a single Tasmanian day than does the day's average during the whole year. Tell that in Boston.

During the late ice age it was colder, with larger glaciers in the center. Almost 25,000 years ago, while it was still a peninsula of Australia, aboriginal hunters are known to have entered Tasmania, to be marooned about twelve thousand years later, when the world's major ice sheets melted and the seas rose.

They were a culturally simple people, like their surviving cousins in Australia, and as time went on they became simpler still, their recent equipment being the most modest on record. When seen by Europeans, they lacked boomerangs, dogs, and hafted stone tools, all of which were invented or acquired in Australia after the original Tasmanians had left. And for some mysterious reason they gave up the catching of fish, although they continued to appreciate shellfish. Evidently the land was good to them, with kangaroos and other marsupials to hunt, and the climate temperate enough so that an occasional cape of animal skin was all they ever wore. Two centuries ago about four thousand natives lived all over the island, except in the rugged mountains. Then, in thirty years, settlers from Australia and England wiped them out.

In the last crisis two men tried to stave off the extermination but only facilitated it, each in his own way. They were Governor George Arthur, with his printed proclamations and "picture boards," and G. A. Robinson, who went out to talk to the natives directly, in their own language. The Tasmanians themselves were neither ferocious nor hostile at first, as much testimony made clear too late. They were dangerous enough when provoked, and they fought to a limited extent among themselves over such things as trespass on hunting grounds or abduction of women, two offenses that the whites at once carried to intolerable excess. As for the "settlers," there could hardly have been a better team to carry out the annihilation. They were convicts, mostly hard cases from Australia. The first lot was accompanied by a handful of freemen given very small land grants to work with convict labor. Since a person might in those days be transported for what now pass as minor crimes (like stealing cars in Massachusetts?), some convicts were fairly decent men, but many, along with the soldiers sent to guard them, were capable of vicious brutality and in fact took pleasure in it. For a hundred years now, the fate of the Tasmanians has been a source of shame and lamentation, in today's high-minded Hobart as in the world at large. But in that time and place, it seems clear now, no other outcome was likely, as the repellent tragedy ran its course.

It started early, with the Risdon Massacre. The first arrivals from Sydney set up camp in 1803 along the mouth of the Derwent River in the vicinity of Hobart, founded a little later. They had already been officially enjoined to treat the natives with kindness, and threatened with punishment for violence to them. But there seems to have been little contact with Tasmanians as the first small farms were set up. Then, on a day in May 1804, about three hundred aboriginals—men, women, and children—appeared out of the woods forming a half-circle to surround kangaroos driven ahead of them. They had no spears, only clubs, and the fact that women and children joined in shows that they were not a war party. But a farmer a short distance away appears to have been frightened, and the semicircle seemed to be surrounding the camp. The officer in command of the soldiers (drunk, by accounts) was persuaded by the camp surgeon to fire on them with cannon loaded with grapeshot, killing a number. How many was not known, since the natives carried off some badly wounded members. The surgeon entertained the chaplain with a dissection of one corpse, and sent some pickled bones to Australia. Children were captured as well.

A few days later, the aboriginals retaliated with an attack on sailors gathering oysters, though no one was killed. In the next couple of years inexpert farming (the settlers were largely townspeople originally) and inept government supply led to a serious food shortage in the colony, which the governor met by setting a good price on kangaroo meat and encouraging hunting. Off into the bush went all who could be given a gun—not homesteaders, but their convict bond servants. Many of these saw at once how much better a free bush life was than harsh treatment and forced labor in the colony. Bushrangers increased in number as time went on, becoming dangerous men skilled in bushcraft, desperadoes of the worst sort who preyed on and murdered settlers, costing successive governors much effort in capturing and hanging them.

They also figured prominently in the long erosion of the native Tasmanians. But hostilities grew up gradually, and developed into the Black War only twenty years later. In spite of the Risdon Massacre, the local natives seemed not to be vindictive, only careful, and of course for some years aboriginals elsewhere in the large island knew little about the whites. Witnesses say they were friendly and helpful at the very start. Later, even when most settlers considered the Tasmanians enemies, other settlers could wander safely in the bush, and their young people joined aboriginal groups in hunting.

Nevertheless, new colonists were pressing up the whole fertile eastern side of the island, and from about 1818 people with more money and importance were taking out large grants of land. Beyond them roamed the bushrangers, capturing native women and often killing off a husband in the process— Tasmanian men were very jealous of their wives. Wifeless settlers often did the same; Robinson, for example, was told of cases in which "stockkeepers had chained the females to their huts with bullock chains for the purpose of fornication." Partners in all this were seal hunters along the north coast, who had established themselves even before the colony in the south, and who remained effectively out of its control. They were American, British, New Zealander, or Polynesian, and as free of restraint or scruple as the bushrangers. Such a man usually supplied himself with two to five aboriginal women for sex and slavery, to help in sealing, hunting kangaroos, and skinning birds, and to be shot out of hand if they failed to get the work done or tried to escape. This glib description covers many specific accounts of atrocities, which we will do without. The point is that, whether or not a Tasmanian husband was actually dispatched for every woman taken, the women were removed as aboriginal mothers, with devastating effects on the next generation. When they gave birth to half-caste children, the women regarded them as despicable and usually killed them.

Bear in mind that the testimony, nauseating as it is, comes from our side, the European. If all the things Tasmanians saw and suffered could be known, the effect would be even more appalling. Settlers were outraged at interference with their land-clearing, and the occasional spearing of cattle by natives: it did not occur to them that Tasmanians, not using the land for farming, might likewise have a sense of outrage— apart from their feelings at being shot up by any white man who took it into his mind. Of course, the Tasmanians were not passive, although reprisal on their part was long in becoming common. Their weapons were simple: carefully chosen stones, and long wooden javelins with fire-hardened points, both thrown with extraordinary marksmanship even at a distance. In later years they used ruses to draw a farmer away front his house, spearing the family in his absence. They were always skilled stalkers and ambushers. They developed the trick of walking while dragging a javelin, between the big toe and the next, through the grass where it could not be seen. Stark naked, such a man seemed to be unarmed— certainly with nothing up his sleeve—until he could approach a settler within easy spearing distance. (Tit for tat, one farmer taught himself to do the same thing with a shotgun.) Some such things they invented on their own, and others they picked up from

The Conciliation, oil painting by Benjamin Duterrau, 1840
George Augustus Robinson, protector of aboriginals, is shown with native
Tasmanians on Bruny Island. The woman beside him is thought to be Truganini.

Photo courtesy of the Tasmanian Museum and Art Gallery.

white bushrangers. They even made up bush-ranging groups themselves in a few instances. An Australian aboriginal convict named Mosquito was sent to Hobart to be a police scout. Bored, he ended by forming a gang of shantytown Tasmanians and taking to the bush, where he enjoyed a long outburst of crime before he was apprehended and suspended.

Back at the center, officialdom tried to control things, with ever smaller success, until at last its hand was forced against the natives willy-nilly, as a result of the cumulative acts of its own unruly subjects. Governor after governor tried in good conscience to carry out the early admonition not to harm the aboriginals, at least as far as words would serve. David Collins in 1810 ordered that violence against the natives be dealt with in the same manner as violence against a "civilized person." Thomas Davey in 1814 proclaimed that recent hostility of the natives was traceable to ill-treatment, especially the kidnapping of children. William Sorrell in 1817–1819 said the same, at great length, sternly forbidding such abductions. Governor Arthur arrived in 1824 and promptly issued a proclamation that he would punish ill-treatment of natives. And he did so, handing out 25 lashes to some colonists who had brutalized native women. (Such brutalities, which usually escaped punishment, were chaining a woman to a log, burning another with firebrands, and making another wear the head of her fresh-killed husband around her neck, and do not include outright murders by shooting, pushing onto a fire, and so on.)

In 1828, Arthur posted another proclamation, again admitting the depredations of the whites, but now trying to calm things by ordering the Tasmanians to stay out of the settled areas unless they procured official passports to gather shellfish on the coast. Of course the natives could not read this document even if they should see it; and the governor had no hot line to the interior—in fact one problem all along was that chiefs who one would expect could be negotiated with did not exist. So in early 1830, Arthur made one more try at proclaiming even-handed treatment for the natives, in a way they might grasp, with his famous picture boards.

They were the 1830 equivalent of propaganda leaflets dropped behind enemy lines. The message is clear enough, to us; its intentional simplicity read something like this: "Natives and whites can mingle in amity; natives should come meet Governor (recognize him by cocked hat); black spear white, black hang; white shoot black, white hang." Citizens who saw them thought them hilarious. But the idea was ingenious, and at least better than printed officialese in its promise of getting across. (It seems to have been suggested by a colonist who had seen a charcoal drawing on a tree done by aboriginals, which showed a settler cart train they had been watching from hiding.) The boards were hung in trees where it was thought aboriginals would see them.

The picture boards had no effect. And the message was false, as earlier proclamations had been. Blacks had indeed been hanged in plenty, some for killing settlers and some who were falsely accused of murders committed by whites. But in the whole story no white was ever hanged for killing a black, in spite of cases of solid testimony to the killing. And little other punishment was handed out for all the murders, kidnappings, maimings, and other crimes against the blacks. This was not, however, squeamishness about using the gallows; on one occasion a single sitting of judges sentenced 37 whites to hang for offenses against whites.

The picture boards were a watershed—the last attempt at asserting native rights to justice. Actually, the wind had been blowing the other way ever more strongly, and the end came rather quickly. Although the governors wanted to protect the Tasmanians, or said they did, nobody else cared; and anyhow, a governor's constituency was the colonists, not the Tasmanians. Nor was a sense of moral responsibility the same as moral conviction. The government, whether local or back home in Britain, was nonplussed by the seemingly homeless, wandering naked savages, and compassion for these uncivilized folk did not extend to letting them interfere with the civilized spreading of farms and towns in a supposedly new and open land. As to spreading the gospel, for once the clergy sat on its hands and did nothing worth mentioning in behalf of the aboriginals. And the ordinary colonist's sense of humanity is epitomized by one of them. This jolly specimen amused a perfectly friendly black by holding an empty pistol to his own head and clicking the trigger. Then he suggested it was the native's turn at the same silly game, handed him a loaded pistol, and watched with satisfaction as the poor man blew his own brains out.

In any case, there was no road back. From about 1825 the Black War was on in earnest. After a generation of their special education by the whites, the Tasmanians were waging total war, with their own cruelties and killings of personally innocent (not always, of course) settlers and their families. The Tasmanians were so successful, in spite of their primitive weapons and their dwindling numbers, that they were actually driving homesteaders back into the towns. The settlers demanded protection, and the government decided that the only solution to the aboriginal problem was extermination (certainly the settlers' choice) or holing them up somewhere out of the way. Governor Arthur's attempt to apply the second expedient was his most bizarre scheme of all, the Black Line.

This came in 1830, just after the picture boards, which were a last despairing cry and far too late. The Line was supposed to operate like a vast kangaroo surround, as used by the natives, starting at the perimeter of the whole settled southeastern third of the

Truganini, the last full-blooded Tasmanian aboriginal to live in Tasmania, died May 8, 1876, and was buried near Hobart. She reportedly had feared a fate similar to the last aboriginal male, William Lanne, who had died seven years before. On the eve of his funeral, a surgeon acting for a scientific society allegedly removed Lanne's skull and substituted another, and competitors made off with his hands and feet. The night after the burial, what remained of the corpse was removed from the grave and was never recovered.

Two years after Truganini's burial, she was exhumed and her skeleton put on display in the Tasmanian Museum and Art Gallery. There it remained for nearly a hundred years. Last April, in response to pressure from people of Tasmanian-aboriginal descent, Truganini's skeleton was cremated and the ashes scattered in Tasmania's D'Entrecasteaux Channel.

This photograph of Truganini was taken in 1866 by Charles A. Wooley and is reprinted courtesy of the Tasmanian Museum and Art Gallery.

island and driving the Tasmanians before it into a cul-de-sac in the Tasman Peninsula at the island's corner. Such a drive had actually been used on the Australian mainland, with a degree of success. But the plains of Victoria were not the rugged and forested terrain of Tasmania. And the Black Line was not black, or thin red, but white, being composed partly of soldiers and partly of convicts but mostly of civilians, taking leave from whatever they were doing in farm or town to become instant woodsmen. It was a major effort for the still modest colony, although it was like executing the Schlieffen Plan with something over three thousand men having little or no training. The government doubtless had no idea how far aboriginal numbers had already ebbed, but there were still significant tribes in the area.

Governor Arthur organized the whole thing on paper in detail. D-day was October 7 and the Line, 120 miles long, started off with a man supposedly at every sixty yards. The story of the operation is a novel in itself. It would be superhuman, in that country, to maintain such a line in order. There were a few actual encounters with natives, and a few fancied ones. Some of these "Down Under Deerslayers" were wounded by their own comrades. One Tasmanian man was caught, as well as a boy about fifteen. Two more were shot dead. After seven weeks, the Line arrived at the neck of the Tasman Peninsula in great excitement and anticipation of the bag of aboriginals hemmed in there by the human net. The peninsula was scoured; it was empty. Newspapers poured scorn on the campaign for having spent £30,000 of His Majesty's money to catch one black man. But the £30,000 had, after all, gone into colonial pockets, and the participants agreed they had had a very good time.

The operation was perhaps the least harmful thing that was ever visited on the Tasmanians, who must have been amazed as they slipped through the Line or watched it pass them by. More effective measures against them were already afoot. One was "roving parties."

With the Black War heating up and with settlers and natives shooting on sight, Governor Arthur in 1826 had proclaimed the need to capture certain natives who had become adept in directing attacks (by learning from the whites), and the next year he divided the country into military districts and then proclaimed martial law—all this, remember, before the picture boards and the Black Line. In 1829 Arthur authorized six parties, staffed by convicts but headed by relatively responsible men, to hunt for natives, and in 1830—but still before the ambitious Line—he offered rewards of £5 a head (£2 for a child) for natives taken alive. This is just the system that has brought the orang-utan to the verge of extinction because, as a newspaper predicted correctly at the time, several would be killed for one captured. The methods of such parties, official or informal, varied from attempts to capture with limited loss of life to outright search-and-destroy missions. In 1827 an informal posse to avenge the death of a settler reported killing or wounding about sixty Tasmanians; and in another case, a party of police that had come under a stone-throwing attack caught the attackers in a defile and killed seventy of them, dashing the brains of the children. The formal roving parties had by the end of 1832 captured 236 aboriginals, obviously at great cost to tribal life.

The other arm of the pincers was George Augustus Robinson, who earned the title of Conciliator. He was raised in the building trades in London, had come to Tasmania to improve himself, and would retire at last to England, living in affluence and mingling with the gentry in Bath, where he died. He was goodhearted though jealous of his prerogatives. He was a devout Wesleyan; he missionized and preached to the Tasmanians as opportunity afforded, but did not let it interfere with his main object of communication. He had great fortitude, self-possession, and persistence. He became convinced by everything he heard, and by his own contacts, that the aboriginals were essentially mild and inoffensive, that their rights had been trampled on, and that they could be conciliated by decent treatment, if it were honest and official. His method was to go out among them everywhere; he had a few helpers, black and white, all unarmed, but he put himself at the head of his party and usually kept the other whites out of sight.

He had arrived in Tasmania in 1824, the same year as Governor Arthur. He soon formed his opinions but had no way of acting on them. Then in March 1829, the governor, in one of his deeds of good intention, published an advertisement in the Hobart *Town Gazette* seeking a man of good character who would try to effect friendly connections with the Tasmanians by taking charge of those on Bruny Island, across the bay from Hobart. The island was already partly settled by whites of the bad sort, and the surviving blacks needed protection and provisions, having little of either.

Robinson at once applied for and got the job, insisting on the salary being raised from £50 to £100 a year. He started his work in a week and carried it on for some months, but it does not seem to have been much of a success in helping the natives, who were a little too close to white civilization. However, it was an experience for Robinson. He observed a surprising mortality rate among the natives, from afflictions of unclear nature. In less than two months he had accumulated a vocabulary of 115 words of the local language and was also preaching in it to the aboriginals. With little formal education and no training he went on recording names and some words on his travels, noting where the languages were different; in spite of his crude renderings this has been an important source of information on these lost tongues. Finally, on Bruny he had met Truganini, an extraordinary girl of sixteen or seventeen, small of build, obviously intelligent, lively, resourceful, brave, and attractive. During his stay she was married (rather against her will) to Wooraddy, who had been mooning after her as the story opened. These two, and a few more Tas-

Tasmanian Aboriginals at Oyster Cove
Taken in 1858 by Francis Russell (Bishop) Nixon, the photograh shows nearly all of the members of the race then living.

manians from Bruny Island and elsewhere, were to accompany Robinson in all his travels, with Truganini as a constant source of intelligence he could not otherwise get, even when she did not know the language of an area.

At the beginning of 1830, Robinson started on his mission to conciliate outlying natives, a mission that would last some five years. He set out from Hobart westward along the coast, with his aboriginals and a few whites, including convicts. He was supported by a whaleboat and a schooner, but he himself went on foot—a trek sometimes extremely arduous—all around the shore, with inland excursions, until he reached Launceston in the northeast, just as the Black Line was kicking off to the south. He spent the next twelve months ranging through the northern interior and visiting the sealers, actually getting many of them to part with their Tasmanian women by threatening government action. The governor was impressed with the apparent success of Robinson in conciliating and bringing in natives, and promised him full support, giving him as his next objective the rounding up of the feared Big River tribe. On the last day of 1831, Robinson made friendly contact with two "sanguinary tribes," the Big River and Oyster Bay, and found that they came to a total of 26 persons: sixteen men, nine women, and one child, who put themselves under his protection. These figures alone reveal a people without a future.

Robinson made three more expeditions between 1832 and 1834, to remnant peoples in the still-wild west. In September 1832, a group of blacks he met in the northwest decided to spear him and his own natives, and he barely escaped by crossing a river on pieces of floating wood—he could not swim— pushed by Truganini. This was his closest call, as recorded in his long, immensely detailed journal. It is full of action, showing that his mission was no triumphal parade, but a long tussle of making contact in unmapped places through unknown languages, persuading aboriginals of his good intentions, and seeing many of those he persuaded change their minds and run off again. It contains his enumeration and naming of natives as he tried to learn facts; and it is larded with stories, some quite fresh, of horrors perpetrated by blacks and whites—though mostly by the latter and sometimes more sickening than any already mentioned. All this time he was bringing in parties of submitted aboriginals. The presumed last lot of Tasmanians was found at the end of 1834 (by Robinson's sons after he had gone back to Hobart in August): it was made up of four women, one man, and three boys, who had wanted to turn themselves in but had been shot at by every white who saw them. One family or small group, however, is known to have remained at large until 1842.

The Conciliator had succeeded: he had rounded up Tasmania's aboriginals in a way everyone official, humanitarian, or extirpationist—could approve. He was given public praise and reward, though he felt it was not prompt enough nor in a measure he was entitled to (he was recompensed for his captures at a kind of wholesale rate, less than the £5 a head previously offered). At his request he was made commandant of the new aboriginal settlement on Flinders Island, off the northeast corner of Tasmania, where all the natives were placed, after some smaller and less hospitable islands had been tried out.

In this windy place, now wearing clothing, which was probably often damp, the captives declined rapidly. There were not many, anyhow. Robinson's listing of natives he met is less than 300, showing how the population beyond the settlement zone had already shrunk, and he brought in less than 200—the roving parties rather more. Many Tasmanians never reached the settlement: of the tribe that had tried to kill him in September 1832, he and his people obtained the submission of eleven in July 1833; nine of these died inside three weeks. When he took up residence on Flinders in 1835, there were only 106 on the island, not counting some he brought with him. Tuberculosis, influenza, and pneumonia continued the execution: in 1837 alone there were 29 deaths. There were a few births, but all infants died in a matter of weeks. Robinson left Tasmania in 1839, to become Protector of the Aborigines in Victoria. Australia. It is possible he took a few Tasmanians with him.

So aboriginal life was extinguished in Tasmania thirty years after the Risdon Massacre. Aboriginal bodies, it is true, went on breathing a while longer, like the mythical dead snake wriggling until sundown. Forty-four survivors (including some half-castes) were taken off Flinders in 1847 and brought down to Oyster Cove near Hobart. By 1854 sixteen were left. By 1870 there was one: hardy little Truganini herself.

She died in 1876, and so they ended. Actually, Robinson had been forced, some time earlier, to return a dozen or so aboriginal women to their sealer consorts on Cape Barren Island, and for all we know one or more of these may have outlived her. At any rate, from such unions there has grown up a present-day population of perhaps two thousand part-aboriginals. But with Truganini's death there went out the last known spark of native speech and ideas and memories. After twenty thousand years.

David Maybury-Lewis

Societies on the Brink

Small societies around the world are currently threatened with extinction. The threat, either implicit or explicit, that they must die so that we may live is something we normally conceal from ourselves under comfortable phrases like "the social costs of development," or "the price of progress." The assumptions behind this sort of thinking need to be examined.

We need first to try to develop some perspective on a problem that is often debated with considerable passion. If we consider the whole span of human history, then it is clear that the majority of the peoples of the world lived until quite recent times in relatively small and relatively isolated societies. The emergence, of powerful tribes, nations, or empires threatened the physical existence and certainly the cultural continuity of smaller, weaker peoples. This is a process that is as old as humankind itself. What has rendered it more dramatic in recent centuries is the development of what we are pleased to call "Western technology." This placed the nations of Western Europe and, later, North America at an enormous advantage and hastened the process of physical and cultural extinction of weaker peoples. Even China, an ancient and powerful civilization which hardly qualifies as a small-scale society, was shaken to its very foundations by the impact of the West. It was able to recover because of its vast reserves, demographic and otherwise. Small societies cannot recover. Instead, they face destruction, either by physical extinction or by absorption into the larger ones that press in on them.

The process has long been recognized; scholars have tried to grapple with its implications since the earliest days of the European expansion. For a while it was a matter for serious debate whether humanoid creatures encountered in other lands were really humans at all. The people in the other lands were equally puzzled. A British party was at first kept in cages by the Singhalese, who tried to determine whether or not they were actually human. We have similar reports from other parts of the world. In fact, even when the conventional attributes of humanity

were granted to alien peoples, debate still raged as to whether they were fully human and therefore entitled to fully human treatment (whatever that might be by the standards of the time and place). Thus it became a matter of grave consequence whether they were or were not considered to be endowed with souls. Similarly, arguments raged as to whether peoples who apparently possessed the basic physical and mental equipment of human beings could nevertheless put themselves beyond the pale by practicing "inhuman" customs.

Cannibalism was usually regarded as one such practice. One can imagine with what *frisson* the Europeans of the sixteenth century read Hans Staden's *True History and Description of the Land of the Savage, Naked and Ugly Maneating Peoples of the New World of America* (1557). The Tupinamba Indians, who once held Staden captive, regularly and ritually killed and ate their prisoners. It was considered a heroic death. A captive warrior, who in some cases might have been living with his captors for years and might even have raised a family there, was led out and clubbed to death in a ceremonial duel, after which the entire community ate him to partake of his heroic essence. Staden also pointed out that the same Tupinamba were horrified by the cruelty of the Europeans with whom they came in contact. They considered the Europeans to be in some sense beyond the pale because of their inhuman customs, such as the routine use of torture in trials and punishments, and the practice of slavery.

The relativistic implications of the Tupinamba view were not, unfortunately, taken seriously by European scholars. The debates concerning the essential humanity of alien peoples and the rights to which they were entitled were conducted in strictly European terms. Even when the arguments were genuine—as in the case of the famous series of debates before the Spanish crown between Las Casas and Sepúlveda—the results were self-serving. When the debate went against the Indians, the local authorities considered that they had learned opinion on their side. When it came out favorably to the Indians, the local authorities refused to abide by its outcome. In the last analysis, the principal argument was power. The stronger tended to find justifications for using the weaker, or at the very least for making the weaker over in the image of the conqueror.

I have referred to these centuries-old arguments because modern versions of them still persist in our own thinking, both in our conventional wisdom and in the assumptions made by our theorists. On the one hand we have what may be called the liberal, neo-Darwinian view that small, weak societies are fated for extinction and that there is not much that can be done about it. Perhaps indeed, according to this view, there is not much that should be done about it, for why expend energy and resources in trying to interfere with irreversible processes that are part of the order of things? On the other hand, there is an orthodox Marxist position that holds that such societies are backward and out of step historically. They must therefore be assisted in getting in phase with history as rapidly as possible or they will be crushed by the relentless and irreversible force of historical process. But the results, in practical terms of these two views are monotonously similar. Small societies are extinguished, culturally, or physically, or both.

These arguments are unsatisfactory. There is no natural or historical law that militates against small societies. There are only political choices. In fact the rhetoric of both the United States and the Soviet Union, to take the two strongest powers in the world today, stresses cultural pluralism as a goal for their own societies and indeed for the world at large. The fact that this rhetoric is not often put into practice is not a matter of natural or historical necessity but of political convenience.

A small society is of course a relative concept. Many nations are small compared with the superpowers but overwhelmingly large compared with some peoples in remote jungle regions who have just come into contact with the outside world. It is the societies at the lower end of this continuum with which I am primarily concerned, although the fact that it is a continuum and that the problem transcends the fate of isolated, tribal populations has certain implications, which I shall also discuss.

Anthropologists have often come to the defense of these tiny, tribal peoples. When they do, these anthropologists are normally attacked with a battery of arguments that need to be explicitly stated and examined.

First it is contended that anthropologists want tribal peoples left alone simply to preserve a traditional way of life. They therefore want to halt the push to explore and exploit the resources of the earth. They are sentimentalists who stand up for the right of

a few to live their own lives in backwardness and ignorance as against the right of the many to use the resources available. Anthropologists are therefore the enemies of development.

This is a serious misrepresentation, which makes the defenders of the rights of small-scale societies seem like the nineteenth-century Luddites, who went around smashing machines in a futile effort to halt the Industrial Revolution. Whether isolated, tribal societies would be better off if the world left them alone is an academic matter. They are not going to be permitted to live in isolation. The people who speak up for them do not argue that they should be left alone or that all exploration and development should be halted. On the contrary, we assume that isolated societies will not be left alone and are therefore concerned with how to soften the impact of inevitable contact so that it will not destroy them in the name of progress. To return to the Luddite analogy for a moment, we do

In the northern Kalahari of Botswana, a San boy squeezes water from a grass sponge into his sister's mouth. The scene reflects the traditional San hunting-and-gathering way of life; the water comes from a depression in the trunk of a monongo tree, whose protein-rich nuts are a vital food source. In the years since this picture was taken, however, cultural change among the San has increased dramatically as a neighboring cattle-keeping people, the Herero, have encroached on their territories.

not try to stem the Industrial Revolution by breaking the machines. We accept its inevitability but question the necessity of chaining children to the machines (as was done in nineteenth-century England) as a means of capital formation.

A second argument is a malicious variation on the first one. According to that, it is claimed that anthropologists would like to keep tribal peoples isolated in what amount to human zoos for their own research purposes.

Again this is a misrepresentation. Anthropologists and others who take an interest in such small societies argue that these peoples' contacts with the outside world should be regulated if they are not to prove destructive. A small society must therefore have a guaranteed territory that it can call its own. This should not be a reservation in the sense that its inhabitants are confined to and imprisoned on it, but rather a home base, which the members of the society can use as a springboard in their efforts to come to terms with the outside world.

Another variation on these arguments stresses the immorality of preventing "backward" peoples from enjoying the benefits of civilization. Who, it is asked, has the right to insist that a relatively isolated society be left alone, to manage without modern medicine and modern consumer goods? Some ardent proponents of this theme wax so eloquent that they make the anxious anthropologist seem like a puritan who is determined to deny color TV to the natives. But the argument, once again, is a distortion of a position that gets little hearing.

Those people who are concerned about the effects of contact are merely urging caution, based on an understanding of the possible harmful effects of such contact. One would have thought that the grim historical record of death, disease, and despair that also accompany the arrival of civilization in remote areas would be sufficient grounds for advocating a cautious approach. We now know a good deal about the diseases that are introduced and we know too that they tend to be unremitting, while the provision of modern medicine is often fitful or inadequate. At a later stage in the process, we know too that the introduction of new industries in remote and not-so-remote areas can lead to cultural breakdown and personal despair within the local population *as well as* providing jobs, increasing income, and so on. This is a familiar dilemma even in advanced societies, which is why people are so anxious to have a say in what happens to their own communities. There is an uneasy suspicion that the arrival of, say, an oil refinery may on balance produce costs for the people of the community where it is located and benefits for people elsewhere. We understand this element of

trade-off keenly enough in advanced societies and yet we often seek to impose oil refineries or their equivalents on societies much less able to cope with them. When the results are not cottages and TV sets but disruption and even death, we tend to shrug our shoulders and reassure ourselves that such costs are unavoidable. I am arguing here that this is not so, and that such costs can be minimized even if not avoided altogether.

But the most insidious argument used against those who speak up for small societies is insidious precisely because it seems so reasonable. Why, it is asked, should such societies be protected anyway? What are the advantages of protecting their way of life? There are in fact many that have been claimed. We can learn from their life styles, since we are clearly so desperately unhappy with our own. We can learn from their views of the world, particularly as concerns the general interrelatedness of things on earth. Many Americans are, for example, discovering a harmony in American Indian views of the world which they find conducive not only to inner peace but also to a more effective use of the environment. There are other arguments that are frequently advanced as reasons for protecting the life style of small societies in different parts of the world. We need to do so in order to further our understanding of human cultural variation. We know too little about how societies work and about how they can be made to work *for* people rather than against them. Besides, it is claimed, the members of the small society will be more useful citizens in the larger one if they come into it with something of their own heritage intact. Then again, there may be genetic advantages in seeing that such groups are not physically extinguished, and so on.

But these are the wrong questions. Supposing we decided that we had nothing more to learn from small societies; that there was no particular genetic advantage in seeing them survive physically and no particular social or philosophical advantage in seeing them survive culturally. Would that then give us the right to eliminate these cultures? Would we be willing to apply a similar reasoning to the sick, the weak, or the aged in our own culture? The question, put that way, is horrifying, which is precisely why I called the original question insidious. If we accept it as a legitimate question, then we find ourselves debating the question of whether it is *useful* to permit another culture to survive. But useful to whom? Presumably the usefulness of their physical and social existence is not in doubt for the members of that culture. What we are in fact debating is whether their existence is useful to *us*. Such thinking can lead to the gas chambers and has done so in our own time. That is why the original question is the wrong one.

The fundamental reason why we must help other cultures to survive is because in all conscience we have no alternative. It is a moral imperative of the sort that insists that the strong ought not to trample on the rights of the weak.

Some writers have referred to the process by which a powerful society extinguishes a weaker culture as *ethnocide,* and have argued that this is (and should be recognized as) a crime analogous to genocide. I understand and sympathize with the passion that informs this view, but I find the formulation of it unhelpful. Homicide is hard enough to define and the arguments concerning the circumstances under which it may or may not be justified are complex. Genocide is even more difficult and its use as a term of opprobrium all too often depends on the point of view of the user. I find the concept of ethnocide more difficult still, and much too vague to be helpful. The moment of a culture's death, even more so than that of a person, is difficult to perceive. The manner of its passing, save in the most obvious cases, is hard to evaluate.

Take some hypothetical cases. A society may occupy the territory of another so that the members of the latter are deprived of their livelihood. Or it may send missionaries into a territory, who then seek to undermine the culture they find. Alternatively, a timber company may move into an area and pay the local people for cutting down the forests off which they have traditionally lived. Again, a new industry may move into an area and effect profound changes in its way of life. Now, all of these changes have some disruptive effect on the local culture. At the same time all of them, save presumably the first instance, bring some benefits. How is one to decide on the precise ratio of costs to benefits that constitutes ethnocide? Indeed, how does one deal with the paradox of a society that may collaborate in its own ethnocide, permitting its culture to be extinguished in exchange for the benefits obtained from another society? In my view, the concept of *ethnocide* is too much of an either/or, life-or-death concept, and does little to help us understand situations where often it is not clear how to knock the gun out of the murderer's hand, or even who the murderer is or which is the gun.

I would insist instead that we are dealing with processes of contact and rapidly induced change that have in the past been known to have serious and even fatal consequences. The problem then is how to soften the contact and how to regulate the change so that its consequences for the small societies are minimally harmful. We are seeking to minimize the costs and to maximize the benefits for the people contacted.

This is not easy to do, however, since the benefits usually accrue to the wider society while the costs are borne largely by the contacted culture. We are thus dealing with a problem as old as humankind itself, namely that of protecting the weak against the strong. It is a problem that is unlikely to disappear and for which there are no easy solutions. Yet there are some things that can be done.

In the first place it is important to insist, as I have done here, on the right of other societies to their own ways of life. Such an insistence is not banal. This right is neither generally accepted nor generally understood. That is why it must be established that small-scale societies are not condemned to disappear by the workings of some abstract historical process. On the contrary, small societies may be shattered and their members annihilated, but this happens as a result of political choices made by the societies that impinge upon them, and for which the powerful must take responsibility. It is not, in any case, inevitable. The smaller societies can be assisted to deal with the impact of the outside world at comparatively little cost to those who bear down upon them. We have now come to recognize the principle that it is reasonable to set aside some part of the profits from the extraction of resources from the earth to be used to offset the ecological damage that may have been done in the process of extracting them. A similar understanding of the human costs of development and a willingness to deal with them is all that is necessary.

Such understanding and willingness cannot be taken for granted. It has to be cultivated and the attempt to cultivate it will not always be successful. It is unlikely, for example, that anybody, however eloquent or theoretically brilliant, could have convinced Hitler of the right of German Jews to their own cultural integrity. In such cases there may be no redress other than warfare or revolution. In many instances, however, the ways of persuasion have hardly been tried, and it is largely out of ignorance that planners make decisions that have such fatal costs for the small societies caught up in their plans. It is therefore vital that anthropologists and others concerned about the problem make people aware of its dimensions and point out that the cost of assisting small societies to become successful ethnic minorities is a comparatively small one, which may well be offset in the long run by the benefits the wider society will reap as a result.

Of course, attempts to protect threatened small-scale societies will not always be successful. The politics of some situations indicate that the minorities are doomed, if not physically, then at least as distinct cultures or subcultures. Yet this is no reason to abandon the effort in despair, any more than we abandon the efforts to avoid war or to construct just societies because these efforts are so often frustrated. I consider the effort to protect the cultural integrity of small-scale societies an issue of equal importance. We are talking not merely about the fate of tiny enclaves of people, buried in the last jungle refuges of this earth. What we are really talking about is the ability of human beings to discover ways to live together in plural societies. It seems to me that this is the critical issue of our times. Our success or failure in this endeavor may well decide whether people anywhere will be able to live in societies based on a minimum of mutual tolerance and respect. The alternatives are unpleasant to contemplate.

Geoffrey Cowley with Mary Talbot

The Great Disease Migration

It wasn't swords or guns that devastated the native Americans.
It was the germs the Europeans carried.

Only weeks before the great conquistador Hernán Cortés seized control of Tenochtitlán (Mexico City) in 1521, his forces were on the verge of defeat. The Aztecs had repeatedly repelled the invaders and were preparing a final offensive. But the attack never came, and the beleaguered Spaniards got an unlikely chance to regroup. On Aug. 21 they stormed the city, only to find that some greater force had already pillaged it. "I solemnly swear that all the houses and stockades in the lake were full of heads and corpses," Cortés's chronicler Bernal Díaz wrote of the scene. "It was the same in the streets and

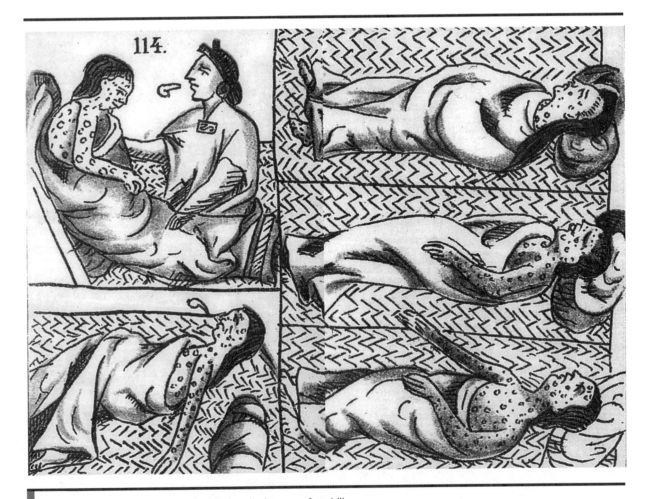

FIGURE 49.1 An Aztec codex depicts the horrors of syphilis.

FIGURE 49.2 Plagues ravaged London and the rest of Europe.

courts…We could not walk without treading on the bodies and heads of dead Indians. I have read about the destruction of Jerusalem, but I do not think the mortality was greater there than here in Mexico …Indeed, the stench was so bad that no one could endure it…and even Cortés was ill from the odors which assailed his nostrils."

The same scent followed the Spaniards throughout the Americas. Many experts now believe that the New World was home to 40 million to 50 million people before Columbus arrived and that most of them died within decades. In Mexico alone, the native population fell from roughly 30 million in 1519 to 3 million in 1568. There was similar devastation throughout the Caribbean islands, Central America and Peru. The eminent Yale historian David Brion Davis says this was "the greatest genocide in the history of man." Yet it's increasingly clear that most of the carnage had nothing to do with European barbarism. The worst of the suffering was caused not by swords or guns but by germs.

Contrary to popular belief, viruses, bacteria and other invisible parasites aren't designed to cause harm; they fare best in the struggle to survive and reproduce when they *don't* destroy their hosts. But when a new germ invades a previously unexposed population, it often causes devastating epidemics, killing all but the most resistant individuals. Gradually, as natural selection weeds out the most susceptible hosts and the deadliest strains of the parasite, a sort of mutual tolerance emerges. The survivors repopulate, and a killer plague becomes a routine childhood illness. As University of Chicago historian William McNeill observes in his book *Plagues*

and Peoples, "The more diseased a community, the less destructive its epidemics become."

By the time Columbus set sail, the people of the Old World held the distinction of being thoroughly diseased. By domesticating pigs, horses, sheep and cattle, they had infected themselves with a wide array of pathogens. And through centuries of war, exploration and city-building, they had kept those agents in constant circulation. Virtually any European who crossed the Atlantic during the 16th century had battled such illnesses as smallpox and measles during childhood and emerged fully immune.

By contrast, the people of the Americas had spent thousands of years in biological isolation. Their own distant ancestors had migrated from the Old World, crossing the Bering Strait from Siberia into Alaska. But they traveled in bands of several hundred at most. The microbes that cause measles, smallpox and other "crowd type" diseases require pools of several million people to sustain themselves. By the time Columbus arrived, groups like the Aztecs and Maya of Central America and Peru's Incas had built cities large enough to sustain major epidemics. Archeological evidence suggests they suffered from syphilis, tuberculosis, a few intestinal parasites and some types of influenza (probably those carried by waterfowl). Yet they remained untouched by diseases that had raged for centuries in the Old World. When the newcomers arrived carrying mumps, measles, whooping cough, smallpox, cholera, gonorrhea and yellow fever, the Indians were immunologically defenseless.

The disaster began almost as soon as Columbus arrived, fueled mainly by smallpox and measles.

Smallpox—the disease that so ravaged Tenochtitlán on the eve of Cortés's final siege—was a particularly efficient killer. Alfred Crosby, author of *The Columbian Exchange,* likens its effect on American history to "that of the Black Death on the history of the Old World." Smallpox made its American debut in 1519, when it struck the Caribbean island of Santo Domingo, killing up to half of the indigenous population. From there outbreaks spread across the Antilles islands, onto the Mexican mainland, through the Isthmus of Panama and into South America. The Spaniards were moving in the same direction, but their diseases often outpaced them. "Such is the communicability of smallpox and the other eruptive fevers," Crosby notes, "that any Indian who received news of the Spaniards could also have easily received the infection."

By the time the conquistadors reached Peru in the 1520s, smallpox was already decimating the local Incan civilization and undermining its political structure. The empire's beloved ruler, Huayna Cápaj, had died. So had most of his family, including the son he had designated as his heir. The ensuing succession struggle had split the empire into two factions that were easily conquered by Francisco Pizarro and his troops. "Had the land not been divided," one Spanish soldier recalled, "we would not have been able to enter or win."

Smallpox was just one of many afflictions parading through defenseless communities, leaving people too weak and demoralized to harvest food or tend their young. Some native populations died out

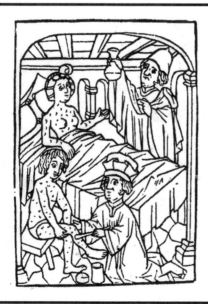

FIGURE 49.3 A 15th-century European woodcut depicts the horrors of syphilis.

altogether; others continued to wither for 100 to 150 years after surviving particularly harsh epidemics. The experience wrought irrevocable changes in the way people lived.

Persuaded that their ancestral gods had abandoned them, some Indians became more susceptible to the Christianity of their conquerors. Others united to form intestinal healing societies and Pan-Indian sects. Marriage patterns changed, too. In North America most pre-Columbian Indians lived in communities of several hundred relatives. Tradition required that they marry outside their own clans and observe other restrictions. As populations died off and appropriate marriage partners became scarce, such customs became unsustainable. People had two choices, says University of Washington anthropologist Tsianina Lomawaima. They could "break the rules or become extinct." Occasionally, whole new tribes arose as the survivors of dying groups banded together. The epidemics even fueled the African slave trade. "The fact that Africans shared immunities with Europeans meant that they made better slaves," says anthropologist Charles Merbs of Arizona State University. "That, in part, determined their fate."

The great germ migration was largely a one-way affair; syphilis is the only disease suspected of traveling from the Americas to the Old World aboard Spanish ships (box, p. 283). But that does not diminish the epochal consequences of the exchange. Columbus's voyage forever changed the world's epidemiological landscape. "Biologically," says Crosby, "this was the most spectacular thing that has ever happened to humans."

That isn't to say it was unique. Changes in human activity are still creating rich new opportunities for disease-causing organisms. The story of AIDS—an affliction that has emerged on a large scale only during the past decade and that now threatens the stability and survival of entire nations—is a case in point. No one knows exactly where or how the AIDS virus (HIV) was born. Many experts suspect it originated in central Africa, decades or even centuries ago, when a related virus crossed from monkeys into people and adapted itself to human cells.

Like venereal syphilis, AIDS presumably haunted isolated communities for hundreds of years before going global. And just as sailing ships brought syphilis out of isolation during the 16th century, jet planes and worldwide social changes have unleashed AIDS in the 20th. War, commercial trucking and the growth of cities helped propel HIV through equatorial Africa during the 1960s. And when the virus reached the developed world during the 1970s, everything from changing sexual mores to

WHO STARTED SYPHILIS?

Experts have long suspected Columbus and his sailors of infecting the Old World with syphilis. It's a reasonable suspicion. The disease, unknown east of the Atlantic until 1493, suddenly raced through Europe and Asia in the decades following Columbus's crossing. Yet skeptics dismiss the seeming connection as a coincidence. Treponemas, the bacteria responsible for syphilis, also causes three milder, nonvenereal diseases (yaws, pinta and bejel). Since those conditions were already common in the Old World, the skeptics reason, venereal syphilis must have been present too, just unrecognized.

Today many experts favor a third explanation midway between the other two. According to this theory 15th-century Europe was no stranger to the syphilis bacterium (*Treponema pallidum*) but local strains had never mastered the art of venereal transmission. What Columbus brought home was an American strain of *T. pallidum* that made syphilis a sexually transmitted disease.

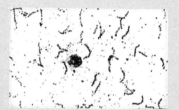

Treponema pallidum

the rise of new medical technologies (such as blood transfusion) helped it take root and thrive.

AIDS won't be the last pandemic to afflict humankind. As the Columbian Exchange makes clear, social changes that spawn one epidemic tend to spawn others as well. Researchers have documented outbreaks of more than a dozen previously unknown diseases since the 1960s. Like smallpox or syphilis or AIDS, most seem to result from old bugs exploiting new opportunities. "What's happening today is just what we've been doing for thousands of years," Crosby says. "Bit by bit by bit, we're getting more homogenized. In the Middle Ages the population got big enough and technologically sophisticated enough to send out a boat and bring back the Black Death. Columbus brought together two worlds that were a huge distance apart. People were living side by side, then elbow to elbow. Soon we'll be living cheek to jowl. Everybody's diseases will be everybody else's diseases."

The Last Tribal Battle

In the remote reaches of the Brazilian rain forest, isolated Indians carry on as they have for thousands of years. Should they be fenced off from the modern world?

For Domingo Neves de Souza, it was only a half-hour's walk to the edge of the unknown. Two years ago in September, he ventured out from the Brazilian rubber plantation where he lived to go fishing. With his two daughters and three of their friends, he pushed deep into the western Amazon, following a winding tributary of the Igarapé River. Hidden in the thick surrounding forest, de Souza had long been told, were naked Indians who still set their lives to the forest's rhythms, just as they had for thousands of years: eating what the forest grew, hunting by bow and arrow. But for the 33-year-old rubber tapper, these Indians were an invisible presence, felt more than seen. Until that day, when they stepped out from the trees.

"Papa, there are people coming," yelled de Souza's 14-year-old daughter, Francisca. According to Francisca's later account, five Indians ran toward them, one dressed in shorts, the others naked. They carried bows and arrows, and were already reaching for them.

"Run, my girl, they'll kill you," de Souza cried as the arrows flew. One hit his left side. Another pierced his back. Turning around, Francisca saw the Indians closing in on her father. As she later reported, she knew right then she would never see him alive again.

An hour later, a posse of rubber tappers headed out to the spot. They found de Souza's body and saw that arrows were only part of the ordeal that had ended his life. Gashes covered his legs, chest and head; all that remained of his eyes were the dark, bloody pools of their sockets. His scalp had been sliced from the skull. The Indians that Francisca and the other children described had vanished, as if soaked back into the forest. But who could they be? Were the killers really *indios bravos*—"wild Indians"—

as the locals called isolated tribesmen? Or had the children's imaginations spun out of control? The rain forest grows rumors along with species, and stories multiplied.

These stories eventually reached the ears of Sydney Possuelo, the Brazilian Government's leading authority on isolated Indians. Possuelo soon traveled to the area where the murder occurred, in the far western state of Acre—but not to solve the crime. For one thing, he was no police detective. What's more, Possuelo had little sympathy for ambushed pioneers; he knew that from Brazil's first days white settlers had ruthlessly slaughtered Indians, burning their villages and abducting their children to work as slaves. The reason he went to Acre was this: a murder by unclothed Indians has often been the first sign of a previously uncontacted Amazon tribe. If isolated people were indeed hiding nearby in the forest, Possuelo wanted to find them—but not to punish them. He wanted to offer the tribe protection, for as long as possible, from the modern world.

Anthropologists believe the Amazon shelters the world's largest number of still-isolated Indians. (The Pacific island of New Guinea is a distant second.) Since the 1970's, Brazil's Government has counted 50 sites that reveal signs of indigenous settlement—many spotted by canvassing the rain forest from the air—though no known tribes are thought to inhabit those particular areas. Possuelo says that these traces were left by approximately 15 tribes of the rain forest that have never been studied or, in some instances, even named by scholars.

By definition, little is known about isolated Indians. Their relics surface in the most remote stretches of the Amazon, hundreds of miles from the nearest roads. It is not known whether the tribes fled to these regions as Brazilians claimed more of the countryside or whether they were always there. Some tribes, like the Igarapé Umeré, in the state of Rondônia, have turned up like the straggling survivors of a shipwreck, with only a handful of members left. By contrast, the Korubu of the Javari Valley reach into the hundreds.

Standing between these tribes and the rest of the world is Possuelo, 59, who has pinpointed seven new tribes in his 40 years as a *sertanista*, the peculiarly Brazilian occupation of Indian tracker. He can look at a footprint in the forest and tell instantly whether it belongs to a forest Indian or a Brazilian settler by the gap between the first two toes: Indians always walk barefoot, so the big and middle toes splay from repeatedly gripping the earth. Over the years, his own foot has come to resemble those of the Indians. But if Possuelo is the world's link to the mysterious tribes of the rain forest, he is also the most formidable obstacle to the rest of the planet's ever knowing them.

As director of the Indian protection agency's department of isolated Indians, Possuelo has almost singlehandedly redefined his agency's traditional role. In the past, the agency, known as Funai, aggressively paved the way for white development of regions occupied by indigenous peoples. But Possuelo argues that virtually every tribe touched by Brazilian society has been destroyed as a result. Rather than flourishing from the medical and technological advances civilization could offer, they have withered from disease, slavery, alcohol consumption and the greed of Brazilians. The numbers bear Possuelo out: the anthropologist Darcy Ribeiro's landmark book, *Indians and Civilization,* concluded that 100 Indian nations disappeared in Brazil between 1900 and 1970, the year his book was published. When Europeans first reached Brazil about 500 years ago, estimates of the Indian population ran from one to six million. It is now 300,000.

An irascible idealist, Possuelo clashes frequently with Brazil's entrenched economic and political interests. Sometimes, the *sertanista*'s outrage at corruption within his own agency is so frank that it seems as if he parachuted into Brazil from another galaxy and will soon be blasted back. Possuelo's last boss tried to fire him in 1996, calling him insubordinate. But Possuelo's standing was so high—particularly among foreign environmentalists and Indian rights advocates—that his boss backed down. As President of Funai in the early 1990's, it was Possuelo who demarcated the largest Indian reservation in the world, 20.5 million square acres, for 23,000 Yanomami Indians, at least temporarily stemming an onslaught by

gold miners against the world's largest surviving Stone Age tribe.

Possuelo argues that much as endangered turtles and jaguars deserve Government protection, Brazil's Indians also need sanctuaries where they can rebuild their numbers and protect their cultures. Ranged against him is a chorus of powerful voices coming from those coveting Indian lands and resources, and their allies in the Brazilian Government. "It won't do to have Indians in the 21st century," a former Government Minister, Helio Jaguaribe, has said. "The idea of freezing man in the first stage of his evolution is, in truth, cruel and hypocritical."

Others claim that Funai hypes the numbers of hidden tribes to prevent Brazilians from exploiting the country's wealth of natural resources. Critics also note that Brazil's Indians represent less than 0.25 percent of the population and yet claim 11 percent of the national territory. Then there are the missionaries, who covet the primitive soul. Don Pederson, who is in charge of research and planning for New Tribes Mission, a Florida-based group, argues that uncontacted tribes are plagued by malaria and dental problems, troubles for which the non-Indian world has ready solutions. "Would you say that you should leave people in dire straits in the ghetto because that's their area, and to go in and provide economic or health assistance is wrong because it would change their lifestyle?" asked Pederson, who has lived with the Yanomami and other tribes.

Still others are knocking on the Amazon's door. The state petroleum company, Petrobras, has made tentative explorations for oil in the Javari Valley. Pharmaceutical companies are hankering to patent genetic materials and forest-based cures. And linguists and other scholars want to track the languages of these unknown peoples.

But it's not only academics and industrialists who are interested in the tribes of the Amazon. At his apartment in Brasilia, Possuelo recently got a letter from a Swedish child, Karin Bark. The girl revealed that she had learned in school about the Korubu tribe, whom Possuelo first contacted in October 1996, and had grown curious about these newly discovered members of the human family.

"Do they eat insects?" she asked. "How many are they? How old can they become? Please answer my questions and tell me other things about the Korubu Indians.

"I want to know."

I, too, wanted to know. And so this past July, I joined Possuelo on a journey into the depths of western Brazil's rain forest. Once there, we would fly over the canopy in search of the tribe that may have violently announced its existence in Acre. Then Possuelo would lead us by boat into the jungle, where he would establish contact once again with the elusive Korubu.

Getting to the Amazon was complicated. We first found ourselves in the outpost town of Jordão, a listless place of high unemployment 120 miles by river from the Peruvian border. Jordão is so remote that it takes eight days by boat to reach the nearest Brazilian city, Rio Branco. The night we arrived, I visited the home of Otavio da Rocha Mello—the owner of the plantation where Domingo de Souza had worked. Like most of the houses near the riverbanks, Mello's tiny house was built on stilts. Inside, candles provided weak light.

Mello described de Souza's murder as part of a silent war by Indians to push whites out. After the killing, he claimed, naked Indians showed up at the local schoolhouse, terrifying the children. People stopped going to the river to bathe in the evening. The tappers, whose work involves trekking through the forest each day, began staying close to home. After 23 years as the local master of the forest, Mello found his jungle fiefdom collapsing.

"It didn't used to be like this," Mello complained. "If the Indians killed a white person, there used to be people who would *go after them!*"

The next morning, I headed with Possuelo to Jordão's airport, a ribbon of dirt running through the center of town, to make our flight over the treetops. It seemed as if everybody in town had come out to watch us wait for the skies to clear. Possuelo sat on the wheel of a single-engine plane and listened as jobless locals complained about being driven out of the forest by *indios bravos*.

Luis Pinheiro de Lima, a 78-year-old Kaxinawa Indian reared by rubber tappers, spoke even more brutally than the whites. He said the Government should go back to its old policy of dominating Indians, casualties be damned. De Lima called isolated Indians *bichos,* or "beasts," and recalled how tappers used to be able to send out mercenaries to hunt down Indians with dogs. But now, he said darkly, Funai "says you mustn't kill them."

Possuelo did not interrupt as de Lima mocked the forest Indians for eating only what they find in the forest, "everything roasted." But then he looked at de Lima and spoke in a voice that sounded almost sad. The practice of "civilizing" Indians killed a lot of your cousins, Possuelo told the old man. "There are still women with the names of the rubber plantations that enslaved them tattooed on their arms. *You know them.*"

In June 1998, from the same crumbling airstrip at Jordão, Possuelo hired a single-engine plane to fly him over the rain forest surrounding the rubber plantation in Acre. He was looking for a sign, however small, of human life.

As far as Possuelo could see from his plane, there was only forest, thick and impenetrable. Finally, after 20 hours scouring just this piece of the Amazon, he saw something. Barely visible through the forest canopy, he spied a clearing in the jungle, with long, narrow Indian huts covered with leaves. A few miles away, he saw another group of huts, similarly built, and a clearing for crops. As his plane flew over, he glimpsed unclothed Indians running into the forest.

With the power of Funai behind him, Possuelo quickly set about cordoning off the area, demarcating a 580-square-mile zone settlers could not legally enter. On a later trip, he found yet a third group of dwellings nearby, less than six feet tall, which suggested a tribe that did not sleep in hammocks. During the ensuing year, he told me, he heard through deputies that one tribe had built more houses and planted more crops. He wondered if relatives had migrated, creating yet more clearings in the canopy.

That's what he was looking for the day we flew together over the forests of Acre. With the sky half-clear, our small plane trundled in and out of the clouds like a growling, airborne dinosaur, passing over miles of uninterrupted treetops. Flying low because of the weather, we could survey only a small area at a time. Normally, Possuelo's work is painstaking, like combing the ocean floor for buried treasure. Indeed, to my eyes the rain forest seemed like an ocean of trees, stretching green as far as we could see in every direction. This time out, however, Possuelo knew where to look.

About 15 minutes after taking off from Jordão, I glimpsed the sight that so thrilled the *sertanista* last June. Through an opening that was little more than a keyhole in the forest canopy, I saw a group of long huts, with pitched brown rooftops like upturned canoes. They appeared to be about 50 feet long, 20 feet wide and 10 feet tall—big enough for several families. We saw no crops planted nearby. The clouds were maddening, like a camera shutter allowing us only brief glimpses of the panorama below. Suddenly, my eyes were drawn to a young naked girl running out of a hut. I wondered if she was fleeing her home because of the sound of our plane. The girl did not look up or behind her, but disappeared quickly into the forest, as if it were a blanket she could pull over herself.

Though I burned to pass over again for another look, Possuelo would not hear of it. He does not even like to fly over hidden tribes once, suspecting that airplanes frighten the tribespeople and sometimes cause them to pack up and move. Indeed, Possuelo has never actually looked into the eyes of these Indians he risks his life to protect. He has never heard their voices or shaken their hands—and probably never will.

Back in Jordão, José Carlos Mireilles, the grizzled chief of Funai for the state of Acre, told me that he sometimes questioned his boss's efforts to protect Indians. Isn't conquest a natural part of human history? Quite apart from the whites, aren't the tribes perennially raiding and killing one another?

Mireilles lived for eight years with Acre's recently assimilated Jaminawa tribe, believed to be closely related to the unnamed tribe Possuelo and I had just flown over. He is not blind to the harsh edges of Indian cultures. Jaminawa youth experiment with sex even before puberty, and girls who become pregnant before marriage undergo painful abortions performed by kneading the abdomen. Sometimes, Mireilles said, the abortion does not work, and the baby is born. In those cases, the unwanted babies are buried alive.

Thirteen years ago, the Jaminawa summoned Mireilles's wife, a medic name Teresa, to deliver the baby of an unmarried teen-ager. She trekked through the rain, working until morning. But upon the baby's birth, the tribe lay the newborn in a small grave that had already been dug. Teresa Mireilles was horrified. "No way," she said. She took the boy from his grave, wiping the dirt from his nose. Mireilles and his wife consider the boy their son.

But if Mireilles does not hold a romantic vision of Stone Age life, neither does he bear illusions about the wonders Brazilian society has to offer. Throughout the century, even well-meaning whites have destroyed tribe after tribe, usually by introducing germs and disease against which the Indians have no defenses: chickenpox, malaria, tuberculosis, the common cold. Other times, Funai has either connived, or unwittingly aided, in the systematic plunder of Indian lands and resources.

"If I could give them 10 or 20 years more without anybody bothering them, I think it's worth it," Mireilles said. "The day the Indians would come out of the forest, I'd tell them: 'Go back to the forest. There's nothing for you here.'"

From Jordão we flew north to Tabatinga, a ramshackle town located at the point where Peru, Colombia and Brazil converge. There, we began our boat journey to visit the Korubu. For Possuelo, this was a homecoming of sorts. He had been away from the Amazon for nearly a year, following a near-fatal car crash that split open his skull, broke his legs and knocked out an eye. Throughout the trip, as he ran into friends he hadn't seen, Possuelo doffed his cap and dropped his head, to show stitches running like expressways over his shiny crown, as if he still could not get over having survived.

After floating southwest for nine hours down the Javari River, we reached the sullen frontier town of Atalaia do Norte. Possuelo's boat pulled in to dock, but he did not stretch his legs on dry ground. Instead, he stayed on board the Waika, the boat that is his home for most of the year. With the area's 13 sawmills silent these days. Possuelo had become the enemy—and he knew it.

The Indian lands upriver brim with timber and freshwater turtles and fish. It would all be there for the taking, were it not for Possuelo. When Funai first planted its flag at the Javari Valley reservation, roughly the size of Florida, it was the Mayor of Atalaia himself who yanked it from the ground in protest. In the streets of the town, residents glared at us. Motor scooters came threateningly close, then made another pass so there was no mistaking their enmity. At the suggestion of the local police, the Waika pulled out in a hurry.

It was three years ago that Possuelo established the first peaceful contact with a fragment of Korubu Indians living in the Javari Valley. Having somehow separated from their tribe about 60 miles north, these Korubu were being ambushed and hunted down by local settlers. A fierce people, the Korubu were nicknamed the *caceteiros,* or "head bashers," for the way they killed enemies. They had already clashed with local Brazilians, once murdering two workers from the Petrobras oil company as hundreds of colleagues watched in astonishment. They had no history of peaceful contact.

On our trip, Possuelo had with him six Indians from tribes whose languages he guessed the Korubu might understand, headed by Bina, a Matis Indian whose face was tattooed to resemble a leopard's, with 10 black lines running like whiskers over his cheeks. Bina's mother was Korubu, abducted as a child during a Matis massacre of the Korubu more than 40 years before. Bina's own tribe had only made contact with Brazilian society when he was a boy.

Possuelo made four forays into the jungle in 1996, each lasting about 10 days, before a small group of Korubu emerged from the leaves to meet him. They were naked and painted with rust-colored patterns on their faces and chests. Short and sturdy, the Korubu walked with their legs wide apart, as if to frighten off animals, and they appeared robust and confident, masters of their small universe. "How beautiful," Possuelo had whispered to himself.

We floated toward the Javari Valley frontier all day. Possuelo reveled in sudden problems, like broken searchlight and engine trouble, that only his expertise could fix. There was a malaria epidemic sweeping the region, and Possuelo, who had already had malaria 36 times, was headed for bout 37—yet he was cheerful. Along the way blue-and-silver dolphins turned cartwheels alongside the boat. Possuelo smiled. "Nature seems to want me back," he said.

The Waika chugged up to a Government outpost, our final destination, an hour after midnight, 19 hours after we began. With lights finally out and the motor silent, I caught the first movements of the local symphony. Bats fluttered overhead, locusts rattled like maracas and owls sang a haunting chorus. From far away came calls I could not identify. Yet they sounded as if they were being repeated and perhaps answered, in the morse code of the jungle.

Could that be the Korubu?

At daybreak, sounds came from across the river. Emerging from our hammocks into the sunlight, we saw six Korubu, square shouldered and tan, with babies resting on mothers' hips. One man wore a polo shirt, but the rest were naked. "*Bina! Bina!*" a man's voice called over the water, steady and insistent. Our translator had returned to the Government outpost since the initial contact and the Korubu remembered him.

The Korubu called to Bina: "We're hungry. Go hunting for us."

A group of Korubu, many of them suffering from malaria, had been camped across the river for days, far from their crops, and had had little to eat. Bina decided to help. He hopped into a speedboat docked next to the outpost and disappeared into the Indian areas with a hunting party. He returned a few hours later with wild boars and crocodiles, blood splattered on the seats.

With two of the animals lying on the speedboat floor, Possuelo crossed over to the Korubu, who swarmed to the boat and surrounded him in bursts of sound. Their voices were loud; to my ears, their languaged sounded bold, even harsh. I watched from a few feet away, in a separate speedboat. The Korubu men wore only a string that was fastened around their hips and looped around their penises; they stood with their chests out and shoulders thrown back. Two Korubu women slid down the riverbank, splashing water over their children to cool down. As the group took us in, they seemed almost angry. "*Pawa! Pawa!*" some declared. Suddenly, one member of our group unzipped a fanny pack and produced a soup spoon. The anger dissolved into wide smiles.

The following day, we returned to the outpost. There we found Xikxu, the patriarch, who looked about 35. He called for the women, who emerged from the forest. One carried a child over one shoulder and a monkey over the other. "*Pawa, pawa,*" two of the Korubu women said, checking my pockets for spoons.

The women carried empty pots and bowls, showing them to me in a wordless version of a shopping list. This time, I understood: the Korubu lived in a pre-metal age, and 8,000 years is long enough to wait for a damned spoon. Through Bina, I promised not to show up again empty-handed.

A young mother, baby perched on her hip and nursing, approached me slowly and touched my curly brown hair. Her own straight black hair was elaborately cut, shaved short in a band across the top of her head and trimmed one length across her temple and at the nape. Tugging the front of my shirt, she gestured for me to open it. She took out my breasts, showing the others that I was built like them. Then she looked down my pants, just to make sure. As direct as she was in her actions, the young mother, who appeared to be no more than 18, smiled gently.

"Maya Washeman," she said, pointing to herself. She pointed to another Korubu woman with a scar across her cheek. "Maya Mona," she said. She gestured at the sad-eyed woman sitting away from us, whose face I recognized from pictures taken of Possuelo's first contact back in 1996. "Maya Doni," she said. Then she pointed at me.

"Maya Diana," I told her.

I wasn't quite sure what "Maya" meant, but it seemed appropriate. But then I was introduced to Washeman's mother. Her name was Maya. Perhaps daughters identified themselves through their mothers' names. Bina couldn't say for certain.

With Bina's help, Washeman asked if I have children of my own. I said no. Then she handed me her own infant son to hold. This remarkable ambassador, I discovered, was the *casus belli* of her entire tribe.

Sitting on the ground, the Indians, through Bina, told a long story. They said they fled from their home tribe when Washeman reached puberty and a Korubu boy wanted to marry her. Maya, however, did not want the boy for her daughter and so fled with her clan. The boy ran after Washeman, kidnapping her. Undaunted, the family turned around and kidnapped her back. They said they ran for months, eventually carving a small canoe to cross the Ituí River. They ran until reaching Ladario, the closest white settlement, where they found bananas growing and stole some for the tribe. By way of introduction, they said, the townsfolk of Ladario chased the Indians and killed two of them.

Since then, the rest of the tribe had secretly been watching Ladario, and—incredible as it seemed, given the gulf in languages and the fear they must have had to overcome—they could identify the killers by name. "Otavio," Xikxu told Bina. Hearing the name chilled me; visiting Ladario the day before, I met the head of the settlement, Otavio Oliveira. He said he was a great friend to the Indians.

On the third day, Possuelo and I paid the Korubu one last visit, this time with some medicine for those suffering through malaria. It was cool under the trees, and quiet. Washeman touched the nape of her son's neck, putting my hand there so I could feel his fever. A few feet away, Maya, the matriarch of the clan, whimpered quietly. She, too, was burning up.

Xikxu scraped a rope-thick vine back and forth over a grater. A liquid the color of worn leaves trickled down. The grater was a wooden club like a miniature baseball bat, flattened on one side, with the chewing end of monkeys' teeth sticking out of the wood.

"Sometimes they drink hallucinogens before they kill somebody or go to war," Possuelo told me quietly in Portuguese, passing the drink. I took a sip, not knowing whether we were drinking the aperitif for war or death. It had the sour, very green taste of something unripe, something that had not found its natural flavor yet. After a few minutes, Possuelo quietly asked Bina about the juice. Bina revealed that the drink was just a social one. In the back of Possuelo's mind, and mine, was the story of the last station chief. Sobral, who angered the Korubu by taking back a tarpaulin one of of Sobral's workers had given them. Two Korubu clubbed the Government agent to death as his colleagues looked in horror from across the river.

Talking to Possuelo, the Korubu laughed over their first meeting with him and remembered hiding when his small plane flew overhead looking for them. Xikxu asked Possuelo why he smoked cigarettes, and Possuelo said it was something Brazilians do socially. As they listened, the Korubu said "mmm," in the same way Americans say "uh-huh." Seemingly apropos of nothing, Washeman asked

Bina a startlingly frank question: "How do you have sex?" The question took us all aback.

"We do it at night," Bina responded.

Sitting there in the jungle, I began to wonder if the Korubu could truly fathom the difference between our world and theirs. And if history proved any guide, I thought, that knowledge, when it came, would shatter them.

In Darcy Ribeiro's book, the son of a *sertanista* describes the first exposure of Kaingáng Indians to São Paulo, which he witnessed as a child. The tribe had encountered Brazilians only two years earlier, when Funai began offering the Kaingáng gifts, like pots and machetes. The Indians saw the gifts as a tribute, and reckoned that they must be far more powerful than this small tribe of Brazilians visiting them in the forest. "Don't worry—we'll protect you," the Kaingáng chief told the Government agents. But then one day the *sertanista* wanted officials in São Paulo to see the isolated Indians for themselves, so he took two of them to the big city.

"They entered the car and took their seats, and appeared talkative and happy as they crossed the forest," Ribeiro writes. "At the first station, as they watched the comings and goings of passengers boarding and disembarking, the Indians exchanged remarks. The stations went by, each one more full of people, because they were already crossing more densely populated regions. A sadness and a humiliation set in among the Indians; they stopped chatting and no longer even answered the Government agent's questions. Astonished, they got off in São Paulo." After being shuttled around the city, the chiefs returned to the jungle, disillusioned. They explained to their people how insignificant they were compared with the modern world. As Ribeiro notes, "Afterward, the prestige they attributed to the whites was of such an order that no tribal value could survive."

At the riverbank, the Korubu showed us a reed they call *nypuk*. The Indians peel the *nypuk*'s sides until it looks like a blade of grass; its long, sharp edge functions as a razor. Wetting her toddler's hair with water. Washeman scraped a precise line across the boy's temple. "Maya is really good at this," she said, looking over at her mother.

"How many thousands of years," Possuelo asked, holding up the reed, "do you think it took them to develop this?"

By the water's edge, Maya whimpered from the malaria. We gave her quinine-based pills in water to drink each day. Next to her, Doni was sad-eyed and quiet. Recently, her baby died minutes after its birth.

A month after I left, Possuelo reported in a phone call, the Korubus watched an anaconda pull one of their children, a 3-year-old girl, underwater. Though they searched frantically, she never surfaced. The 17 remaining tribespeople wept for her in the place she died, day after day.

And so lingering in my mind after my trip to the Javari rain forest was a question: Why preserve a life of hardship? But like gears in a machine, one question triggers the next. What kind of life would the modern world give them?

Possuelo, loving a good debate, argued that he was not defying destiny at all by trying to preserve the Indian way of life. There is nothing inevitable about Brazilian society swallowing up these hidden tribes, just as there was nothing preordained about humans landing on the moon, he said. Staking a nation's flag on a new frontier—whether on another planet or in the wilderness within your own borders—happens through deliberate policies that governments and people pursue.

But Possuelo could not have got this far on idealism alone. He is not naïve. As our journey neared its end, Possuelo acknowledged that however contact comes, the time that isolated tribes have left can probably be measured in decades. And time was precious, he said: not so much to prepare the Indians for contact, as to prepare the whites.

"Right now, the only door to our society that's open to the Indians is through the cellar," Possuelo said. Listen to the language of the settlers, he said, who call Indian lands "uninhabited," as if the natives did not exist. In nearly every case in which whites entered their lands, the Indians were reduced to scrounging for crumbs, as stores of fish, game and timber vanished. Now, drug traffickers are trying to make inroads by building airstrips on their land. Funai's demarcation lines are designed not so much to keep the Indians confined to their ancient lands as to place a limit on white expansion, Possuelo said.

On the deck of the Waika, Possuelo traced the shape of the Javari Valley with his finger, much as the evening before he conjured figures as he gazed up at the clouds. It is true, he said, that the Javari is a rich, unspoiled area that could be developed.

"But why shouldn't the Indians be the ones to exploit it for themselves?" he asked. "Why shouldn't *they* be the ones selling their fish and game commercially?" It is a revolutionary thought in Brazil, where Indians have been virtually trained into dependence from their first moments of contact.

"I want to send Indians from here to school, have them steer our boats along the rivers," Possuelo said excitedly. Up and down the waterways, settlers are suffering through the malaria epidemic. He wanted to set up floating health stations for the river dwellers, run by the Indians. "Let the Indians be the ones drawing their blood, looking at it under the microscope, giving out the medications. Let the whites get used to seeing the Indians in positions of respect."

And that is the heart of Possuelo's dream, which more and more is coming to look like a plan: to turn the dark ecosystem of contact upside down, so that Indians may finally join Brazilian society standing tall. It is a vision he has peddled diligently, inviting small groups of reporters along on his expeditions to win public support, particularly overseas. Recently, the European Parliament awarded $1 million for a project Possuelo drew up to build health posts and provide education to Javari Valley tribes that had already been contacted by Funai officials. Idealist or not, Possuelo was sophisticated enough to apply for the grant through a private foundation—to prevent the money from getting siphoned into the Government's general coffers, or winding up in some politician's pocket. And his last expedition, for the Discovery Channel, carried a price: a 40-foot radio tower for the remote Javari Valley outpost.

But for all his savvy, Possuelo stands practically alone, in his own way isolated as much as the Indians he tracks. He, too, belongs to a vanishing breed. There are fewer than a dozen *sertanistas* in all of Brazil worthy of the name, he said, who did not get their titles as political rewards. And many of them would just as soon see his project disappear.

Indeed, it is impossible to imagine Possuelo's vision without Possuelo. What would have happened to the Government policy on isolated tribes if that car accident had ended his life or if his last boss had succeeded in firing him? Possuelo knows that his critics include not only industrialists, politicians, generals and academics but also fellow *sertanistas*. Like that of the anthropologists, their glory has always grown from presenting new cultures to the rest of the world, as if they had given birth to them. Yet as impossible as his quest may seem, Possuelo is determined to change people's minds. "I'm proposing the exact opposite," Possuelo said. "I say your glory is in *not* discovering them."

PART VI

ANTHROPOLOGY IN THE MODERN WORLD

In this final part of *Anthropology: Contemporary Perspectives,* we look at some of the ways in which anthropologists work in the modern world. I don't mean this to be a manual for deciding whether you want to be a professional anthropologist. Rather, I have included these articles as an attempt to build a bridge between the work of professional anthropologists and the kinds of things you think about—that are important to all of us as individuals and as citizens of this world. Certainly, I hope that this book will stimulate you to apply anthropological knowledge and theory when you think about yourself and the world around you.

CONTEMPORARY APPLICATIONS

In 1928, the "father" of modern anthropology, Franz Boas, wrote a classic text, *Anthropology and Modern Life*. In it he argued that anthropology should not be mistaken for what it sometimes appears to be—the collection of curiosities. Rather, if anthropology is to be a viable scholarly discipline, it should shed light on our own society and, if we are willing to learn its lessons, teach us as a society what to do and what to avoid.

In compiling the articles for this reader I have often felt like a collector—searching and sifting the literature, hoping to find those gems of anthropological scholarship that would stimulate and entertain you while teaching you useful things. In doing so, I have tried not to lose sight of my view that in almost every anthropological undertaking, no matter how remote its concerns seem from modern living, there is a message for the contemporary world.

For this reason, I debated whether it made any sense to include this final topic. After all, virtually all of anthropology has its contemporary implications, if not direct applications. Would not adding a topic on contemporary applications undermine that message?

I finally decided to go ahead and add this topic, but to do it in a way that underlines my view of the vitality and relevance of all facets of anthropology to contemporary life. Thus I have included an article on contemporary medical practice; a discussion of our evolutionary ancestors' diet and its significance for us as individuals and as a species; a look at the human dramas that can be pieced together from bone fragments; the vast knowledge preliterate peoples have gained about their environment—and how the loss of this knowledge may be a loss for us all; and, finally, and more prosaically, how anthropology can illuminate (and help manipulate) patterns of consumption.

Article 51, Lynn Payer's "Borderline Cases," opens this final topic with a description of how medical practice—which, on the surface, appears to be "objective" and rooted firmly in scientific knowledge and advanced technology—really is, itself, a cultural artifact and shows the diversity and unconscious patterning of thought and actions that all expressions of culture exhibit.

In Article 52, "The Stone-Age Diet: Cuisine Sauvage," Melvin Konner discusses our birth as a species—specifically, what our pre-human and early human ancestors ate. He argues that we may be doing ourselves in by shifting our diet away from that of hunter-gatherers, and he provides anthropological evidence to support health educators who advocate a return to a simpler, high-fiber, low-fat diet.

Patrick Huyghe, in Article 53, "No Bone Unturned," reveals the hidden meanings that forensic anthropologists and archaeologists can glean from bones—of recent murder victims and long-dead groups.

Daniel Goleman is interested in what we all may lose when "Shamans and Their Lore May Vanish with the Forests," Article 54. It is more than you may think—including some powerful medicines and other applications of rain-forest plant life.

The final two articles in the book, "Coming of Age in Palo Alto," and "Why Buy Kazoos You Can't Use?" examine how the anthropological perspective can be used to design products as well as study and manipulate people's consumption.

Perhaps your exposure to anthropological knowledge and the perspectives through which anthropologists look at the world and themselves will help you make better, broader, and more thoughtful choices.

I certainly hope so, for this has been the basis for my professional involvement in anthropology as teacher, researcher, writer, and editor.

As I said in the beginning of this book: Welcome to controversy and to the study of anthropology!

Lynn Payer

Borderline Cases: Medical Practice and National Culture

Marie R., a young woman from Madagascar, was perplexed. Hyperventilating and acutely anxious, tired and afflicted with muscle spasms, she visited a French physician who told her she suffered from spasmophilia, a uniquely French disease thought to be caused by magnesium deficiency. The physician prescribed magnesium and acupuncture and advised her that, because of the danger associated with the disease, she should return home to the care of her parents.

Yet when Marie R. ultimately moved to the United States, American physicians diagnosed her symptoms quite differently. As she soon learned, spasmophilia, a diagnosis that increased sevenfold in France between 1970 and 1980, is not recognized as a disease by American physicians. Instead Marie R. was told she suffered from an anxiety disorder; only after taking tranquilizers and undergoing psychotherapy did her condition improve. Now she seems cured, though she still wonders what she has been cured *of*.

Western medicine has traditionally been viewed as an international science, with clear norms applied consistently throughout western Europe and North America. But as Marie R.'s experience illustrates, the disparity among the diagnostic traditions of England, France, the United States and West Germany belies the supposed universality of the profession. In 1967 a study by the World Health Organization found that physicians from several countries diagnosed different causes of death even when presented with identical information from the same death certificates. Diagnoses of psychiatric patients vary significantly as well: until a few years ago a patient labeled schizophrenic in the U.S. would likely have been called manic-depressive or neurotic in England and delusional psychotic in France.

Medical treatments can vary as widely as the diagnoses themselves. Myriad homeopathic remedies that might be dismissed by most U.S. physicians as outside the realm of scientific medicine are actively prescribed in France and West Germany. Visits to the many spas in those countries are paid for by national health insurance plans; similar coverage by insurance agencies in the U.S. would be unthinkable. Even for specific classes of prescription drugs there are disparities of consumption. West Germans, for instance, consume roughly six times as much cardiac glycoside, or heart stimulant, per capita as do the French and the English, yet only about half as much antibiotic.

In one recent study an attempt was made to understand why certain coronary procedures, such as angiography—a computer-aided method of observing the heart—and bypass surgery, are done about six times as frequently in the U.S. as they are in England. Physicians from each country were asked to examine the case histories of a group of patients and then determine which patients would benefit from treatment. Once cost considerations were set aside, the English physicians were still two to three times as likely as their American counterparts to regard the procedures as inappropriate for certain patients. This result suggests that a major reason for the frequent use of the procedures here has less to do with cost than with the basic climate of medical opinion.

The diversity of diagnoses and treatments takes on added importance with the approach of 1992, the year in which the nations of the European economic community plan to dissolve all barriers to trade. Deciding which prescription drugs to allow for sale universally has proved particularly vexing. Intravenous nutrition solutions marketed in West Germany must contain a minimum level of nitrogen, to promote proper muscle development; in England, however, the same level is considered toxic to the kidneys. French regulators, following their country's historic preoccupation with the liver, tend to insist with vigor that new drugs be proved nontoxic to that organ.

Ultimately the fundamental differences in the practice of medicine from country to country reflect divergent cultural outlooks on the world. Successful European economic unification will require a concerted attempt to understand the differences. At the same time, we Americans, whose medicine originated in Europe, might gain insight into our own traditions by asking the same question: Where does science end and culture begin?

West German medicine is perhaps best characterized by its preoccupation with the heart. When examining a patient's electrocardiogram, for example, a West German physician is more likely than an American internist to find something wrong. In one study physicians following West German criteria found that 40 percent of patients had abnormal EKGs; in contrast, according to American criteria, only 5 percent had abnormal EKGs. In West Germany, patients who complain of fatigue are often diagnosed with *Herzinsuffizienz,* a label meaning roughly weak heart, but it has no true English equivalent; indeed, the condition would not be considered a disease in England, France or the United States. Herzinsuffizienz is currently the single most common ailment treated by West German general practitioners and one major reason cardiac glycosides are prescribed so frequently in that country.

In fact, for older patients, taking heart medicine is something of a status symbol—in much the same way that not taking medicine is a source of pride among the elderly in the U.S. Some West German physicians suggest that such excessive concern for the heart is a vestige of the romanticism espoused by the many great German literary figures who grappled with ailments of the heart. "It is the source of all things," wrote Johann Wolfgang von Goethe in *The Sorrows of Young Werther,* "all strength, all bliss, all misery." Even in modern-day West Germany, the heart is viewed as more than a mere mechanical device: it is a complex repository of the emotions. Perhaps this cultural entanglement helps explain why, when the country's first artificial heart was implanted, the recipient was not told for two days—allegedly so as not to disturb him.

The obsession with the heart—and the consequent widespread prescription of cardiac glycosides—makes the restrained use of antibiotics by West German physicians all the more striking. They decline to prescribe antibiotics not only for colds but also for ailments as severe as bronchitis. A list of the five drug groups most commonly prescribed for patients with bronchitis does not include a single class of antibiotics. Even if bacteria are discovered in inflamed tissue, antibiotics are not prescribed until the bacteria are judged to be causing the infection. As one West German specialist explained, "If a patient needs an antibiotic, he generally needs to be in the hospital."

At least a partial explanation for this tendency can be found in the work of the nineteenth-century medical scientist Rudolph Virchow, best known for his proposal that new cells arise only from the division of existing cells. Virchow was reluctant to accept the view of Louis Pasteur that germs cause disease, emphasizing instead the protective role of good circulation. In Virchow's view numerous diseases, ranging from dyspepsia to muscle spasms, could be attributed to insufficient blood flow to the tissues. In general, his legacy remains strong: if one is ill, it is a reflection of internal imbalances, not external invaders.

In French medicine the intellectual tradition has often been described as rationalist, dominated by the methodology of its greatest philosopher, René Descartes. With a single phrase, *cogito ergo sum,* Descartes managed logically to conjure forth the entire universe from the confines of his room. His endeavor is looked on with pride in France: every French schoolchild is exhorted to "think like Descartes."

Abroad, however, Cartesian thinking is not viewed so favorably, as it often manifests itself as elegant theory backed by scanty evidence. When investigators at the Pasteur Institute in Paris introduced a flu vaccine that had the supposed ability to anticipate future mutations of the flu virus, they did so without conducting any clinical trials. More recently, French medical workers held a press conference to announce their use of cyclosporin to treat AIDS—even though their findings were based on a mere week's use of the drug by just six patients. American journalists and investigators might have been less puzzled by the announcement had they understood that, in France, the evidence or outcome is not nearly as important as the intellectual sophistication of the approach.

Disease in France, as in West Germany, is typically regarded as a failure of the internal defenses rather than as an invasion from without. For the French, however, the internal entity of supreme importance is not the heart or the circulation but the *terrain*—roughly translated as constitution, or, more modernly, a kind of nonspecific immunity. Consequently, much of French medicine is an attempt to shore up the *terrain* with tonics, vitamins, drugs and spa treatments. One out of 200 medical visits in France results in the prescription of a three-week cure at one of the country's specialized spas. Even Pasteur, the father of modern microbiology, considered the *terrain* vital: "How many times does the constitution of the injured, his weakening, his morale…set up a barrier to the invasion of the infinitely tiny organisms that is insufficient."

The focus on the *terrain* explains in part why the French seem less concerned about germs than do Americans. They tolerate higher levels of bacteria in foods such as foie gras and do not think twice about kissing someone with a minor infection: such encounters are viewed as a kind of natural immunization. Attention to the *terrain* also accounts for the diagnostic popularity of spasmophilia, which now rivals problems with hearing in diagnostic frequency. One is labeled a spasmophile not necessarily because of specific symptoms but because one is judged to have some innate tendency toward those symptoms.

Although French medicine often attempts to treat the *terrain* as a whole, the liver is often singled out as the source of all ills. Just as West Germans tend to fixate on herzinsuffizienz, many French blame a "fragile liver" for their ailments, whether headache, cough, impotence, acne or dandruff. Ever since French hepatologists held a press conference fourteen years ago to absolve the liver of its responsibility for most diseases, the *crise de foie* has largely gone out of style as a diagnosis—though one still hears of the influence of bile ducts.

Unlike their French and West German counterparts, physicians in England tend to focus on the external causes of disease and not at all on improving circulation or shoring up the *terrain*. Prescriptions for tonics, vitamins, spa treatments and the like are almost absent, and antibiotics play a proportionally greater role. The English list of the twenty most frequent prescriptions includes three classes of antibiotics; in West Germany, in contrast, the top-twenty list includes none.

English physicians are also known for their parsimony, and for that reason they are called (by the French) "the accountants of the medical world." They do less of virtually everything: They prescribe about half as many drugs as their French and West German counterparts; and, compared with U.S. physicians, they perform surgery half as often, take only half as many X rays and with each X ray use only half as much film. They recommend a daily allowance of vitamin C that is half the amount recommended elsewhere. Overall in England, one has to be sicker to be defined ill, let alone to receive treatment.

Even when blood pressure or cholesterol readings are taken, the thresholds for disease are higher. Whereas some physicians in the U.S. believe that a diastolic pressure higher than ninety should be treated, an English physician is unlikely to suggest treatment unless the reading is more than a hundred. And whereas some U.S. physicians prescribe drugs to reduce cholesterol when the level is as low as 225 milligrams per decaliter, in England similar treatment would not be considered unless the blood cholesterol level was higher than 300.

To a great extent, such parsimony is a result of the economics of English medicine. French, U.S. and West German physicians are paid on a fee-for-service basis and thus stand to gain financially by prescribing certain treatments or referring the patient to a specialist. English physicians, on the other hand, are paid either a flat salary or on a per-patient basis, an arrangement that discourages over-treatment. In fact, the ideal patient in England is the one who only rarely sees a physician—and thus reduces the physician's workload without reducing his salary.

But that arrangement only partly accounts for English parsimony. Following the empirical tradition of such philosophers as Francis Bacon, David Hume and John Locke, English medical investigators have always emphasized the careful gathering of data from randomized and controlled clinical trials. They are more likely than their colleagues elsewhere to include a placebo in a clinical trial, for example. When the U.S. trial for the Hypertension Detection and Follow-up Program was devised, American physicians were so certain mild hypertension should be treated, they considered it unethical not to treat some patients. A study of mild hypertension conducted by the Medical Research Council in England, however, included a placebo group, and the final results painted a less favorable picture of the treatment than did the American trial.

Almost across the board, the English tend to be more cautious before pronouncing a treatment effective. Most recently experts in England examined data regarding the use of the drug AZT by people testing positive for HIV (the virus associated with AIDS). These experts concluded that the clinical trials were too brief to justify administration of the drug, at least for the time being. Americans, faced with the same data, now call for treatment.

American medicine can be summed up in one word: aggressive. That tradition dates back at least to Benjamin Rush, an eighteenth-century physician and a signer of the Declaration of Independence. In Rush's view one of the main obstacles to the development of medicine was the "undue reliance upon the powers of nature in curing disease," a view he blamed on Hippocrates. Rush believed that the body held about twenty-five pints of blood—roughly double the actual quantity—and urged his disciples to bleed patients until four-fifths of the blood had been removed.

In essence, not much has changed. Surgery is more common and more extensive in the U.S. than it is elsewhere: the number of hysterectomies and of cesarean sections for every 100,000 women in the population is at least two times as high as are such rates in most European countries. The ratio of the rates for cardiac bypasses is even higher. Indeed,

American physicians like the word *aggressive* so much that they apply it even to what amounts to a policy of retrenchment. In 1984, when blood pressure experts backed off an earlier recommendation for aggressive drug treatment of mild hypertension, they urged that nondrug therapies such as diet, exercise and behavior modification be "pursued aggressively."

To do something, anything, is regarded as imperative, even if studies have yet to show conclusively that a specific remedy will help the patient. As a result, Americans are quick to jump on the bandwagon, particularly with regard to new diagnostic tests and surgical techniques. (Novel drugs reach the market more slowly, since they must first be approved by the Food and Drug Administration.) Naturally, an aggressive course of action can sometimes save lives. But in many instances the cure is worse than the disease. Until recently, American cardiologists prescribed antiarrhythmia drugs to patients who exhibited certain signs of arrhythmia after suffering heart attacks. They were afraid that not to do so might be considered unethical and would leave them vulnerable to malpractice suits. But when the treatment was finally studied, patients who received two of the three drugs administered were dying at a higher rate than patients who received no treatment at all. Likewise, the electronic monitoring of fetal heart rates has never been shown to produce healthier babies; in fact, some critics charge that incorrect diagnosis of fetal distress, made more likely by the monitors, often leads to unnecessary cesarean sections.

Even when the benefits of a treatment are shown to exceed the risks within a particular group of patients, American physicians are more likely to extrapolate the favorable results to groups for which the benefit-to-risk ratio has not been defined. American physicians now administer AZT to people who are HIV-positive. But some physicians have taken the treatment a step further and are giving the drug to women who have been raped by assailants whose HIV status is unknown—to patients, in other words, whose risk of infection may be low. Whether the pressure for treatment originates with the patient or with the physician, the unspoken reasoning is the same: it is better to do something than it is to do nothing.

Unlike the French and the West Germans, Americans do not have a particular organ upon which they focus their ills—perhaps because they prefer to view themselves as naturally healthy. In reading the obituary column, for instance, one notices that no one ever dies of "natural" causes; death is always ascribed to some external force. Disease, likewise, is always caused by a foreign invader of some sort. As one French physician put it, "The only things Americans fear are germs and Communists." The germ

mentality helps explain why antibiotic use in the U.S. is so high: one study found that American physicians prescribe about twice as much antibiotic as do Scottish physicians, and Americans regularly give antibiotics for ailments such as a child's earache for which Europeans would deem such treatment inappropriate. The obsession with germs also accounts for our puritanical attitudes toward cleanliness: our daily washing rituals, the great lengths to which we go to avoid people with minor infections, and our attempts to quarantine people with diseases known to be nontransmissible by casual contact alone.

Nor do Americans exhibit much patience for the continental notion of balance. Substances such as salt, fat and cholesterol are often viewed by U.S. physicians as unmitigated evils, even though they are essential to good health. Several studies, including a recent one by the National Heart, Blood and Lung Institute in Bethesda, Maryland, have shown that if death rates in men are plotted against cholesterol levels, the lowest death rates are associated with levels of 180; cholesterol levels higher or lower are associated with higher death rates. Low cholesterol levels have been linked to increased rates of cancer and even suicide—yet Americans tend to be proud when their levels are low.

The array of viable medical traditions certainly suggests that medicine is not the international science many think it is. Indeed, it may never be. Medical research can indicate the likely consequences of a given course of action, but any decision about whether those consequences are desirable must first pass through the filter of cultural values. Such a circumstance is not necessarily bad. Many of the participants at a recent symposium in Stuttgart, West Germany, felt strongly that the diverse medical cultures of Europe should not be allowed to merge into a single one. Most medical professionals, however, ignore the role cultural values play in their decisions, with unfortunate consequences.

One result is that the medical literature is confusing. The lead paper in a 1988 issue of *The Lancet*, for example, superficially appeared to satisfy international standards of medical science. Its authors were German and Austrian; the journal was English; and the paper itself, which addressed the treatment of chronic heart failure, made reference to the functional classification of this disorder by the New York Heart Association. But on a closer look an American cardiologist found that many of the patients referred to in the paper would not, according to U.S. standards, be classified as having heart failure at all. Fewer than half of the patients' chest X rays showed enlargement of the heart, an almost universal finding in people with heart failure as diagnosed in the U.S. It would take a careful reader—or one attuned to German diagnostic traditions—to ferret out such misleading results.

The diverse ways different countries practice medicine present a kind of natural experiment. Yet because few people are aware of the experiment, no one is collecting the rich data the experiment could supply. What is the effect, for example, of the widespread prescription of magnesium for spasmophilia in France and for heart disease in West Germany? Likewise, soon after the hypertension drug Selacryn was introduced to U.S. markets, two dozen people died of liver complications attributed to the drug. Yet Selacryn had already been used for several years in France. Had similar cases gone unnoticed there and been attributed to the fragility of the French liver? Lacking an awareness of their differing values, medical experts of different nations may be missing out on an opportunity to advance their common science.

Finally, recognizing American biases may help us head off medical mistakes made when our own instincts lead us astray. As English medicine frequently illustrates, it is *not* always better to do something than it is to do nothing. And as the continental outlook reveals, a more balanced view of the relation between the individual and the disease might make us less fearful of our surroundings. If we put our own values in perspective, future decisions might be made less according to tradition and more according to what can benefit us most as physicians and patients.

Melvin Konner

The Stone-Age Diet: Cuisine Sauvage

In 1972, when I left the Kalahari Desert, and the !Kung San bands that reside there, I had a vastly enriched comprehension of hunter-gatherer cultures, enough data for a doctoral dissertation, and a very enlightening sense of embarrassment. I had gone to Africa to pursue not only specific scientific goals but also some personal philosophic ones, among them the confirmation of a naïve, almost Rousseauian vision of a rather noble savage. On the plains of Botswana, I expected to find the beauty of the human spirit in "pure" form, unadulterated by the corrupting influences of civilization. The not-so-noble savages I in fact encountered—and came to know so well and, in some instances, to love—proved capable of selfishness, greed, jealousy, envy, adultery, wife abuse, and frequent conflict ranging from petty squabbles to homicidal violence. Not that they were any worse than we are; they just weren't evidently better. Thus I learned a lesson that sooner or later impresses itself on almost every anthropologist: it is a risky business, at best, to project human ideals onto our evolutionary past. The noble savage does not exist—and never did.

It was with a sense of irony, then, that I read an editorial in *The New York Times* this past June suggesting that a paper I had recently written with a colleague perpetuated "the myth of the Noble Savage." Perhaps my surprise was unjustified; by then I should have been inured to odd and unflattering characterizations of the paper. The preceding months had seen a flurry of publicity about it. It had been billed in the popular press as espousing a "caveman diet," and *The Washington Post* had ventured the tongue-in-cheek prediction that my co-author and I would soon publish a best-selling book with such a title. Meanwhile, *The New England Journal of Medicine,* which published the paper, had received letters of more serious intent, questioning on scientific grounds the merit of our argument.

The episode had begun innocently enough. During the summer of 1983, I got a call from S. Boyd Eaton, an Atlanta radiologist and advocate of preventive medicine who wanted to collaborate on a study of hunter-gatherer societies. Eaton, I soon discovered,

believed that in the study of such societies were to be found critical insights into the human condition as well as, perhaps, the key to a comprehensive theory of human biology and behavior. That is not to say that he believed the myth of the noble savage. Rather, he simply subscribed to what anthropologists call the hunter-gatherer party line: regardless of whether ancient hunter-gatherer societies were in any sense noble, their genetic endowment was very similar to ours. This belief rests on the considerable body of evidence suggesting that 95 or 98 or 99 percent of human evolution—depending on what you want to call human—took place in societies sustained by hunting and gathering. Inasmuch as genetic change in the mere ten thousand years since the advent of agriculture has probably been trivial, the argument goes, we are in essence hunter-gatherers transplanted out of skins and huts into three-piece suits and high-rise condominiums.

My once faithful adherence to that party line had been shaken in an oblique way by my experience in Africa. The trip to the Kalahari, after all, had been motivated by both my belief in the existence of the noble savage and my commitment to the hunter-gatherer hypothesis; the ensuing disillusionment had somewhat indiscriminately diluted both. But as I talked with Eaton, I regained some respect for the party line—enough, certainly, to proceed with our collaboration.

We set out to study the diet of ancient hunter-gatherer societies against the backdrop of recent research on nutrition. Using anthropological data on the few extant groups (including the !Kung San) as well as paleontological and archaeological findings about various hunter-gatherer societies that flourished between two million and ten thousand years ago, we proposed a model of what human beings ate during the better part of their evolution. Broadly similar studies had been conducted before, but we enjoyed the benefit of quite good numbers—credible data amassed over decades of modern research. Moreover, we added what proved to be a provocative comparison between our hypothesized paleolithic diet and two other diets: that of the average American today, on the one hand, and that recommended by physicians and scientists, on the other.

The results were mostly predictable but no less impressive for it. The paleolithic diet consistently met or exceeded the standards being proposed for shifting the American diet toward a more healthful pattern. For example, the ratio of polyunsaturated to saturated fat consumed by the typical American is 0.44. It is now recommended that this ratio be moved closer to 1.00 to protect against atherosclerosis—the epidemic illness underlying most heart disease and strokes. In the paleolithic age, we estimated, this ratio was even higher—around 1.41. Sodium, a suspected cause of high blood pressure, is consumed by the average American at the rate of 2,300 to 6,900 milligrams per day, despite recommendations that the rate be cut to between 1,100 and 3,300. Our hunter-gatherer ancestors, it appears, consumed only about 690 milligrams of sodium per day. For fiber, which may protect against several diseases of the bowel, including cancer, the figures were 19.7 grams per day for Americans, 30 to 60 grams recommended, and 45.7 grams estimated for paleolithic man. The high level of fiber intake among hunter-gatherers also implies a low intake of sugars and other simple carbohydrates widely considered too common in the American diet. Once complex carbohydrates, such as those found in fruits and vegetables, are added, the percentage of daily calories derived from carbohydrates in the late Paleolithic period amounts to about the same as it does today. But the percentage of protein was much higher and the percentage of fat markedly lower. (Large quantities of fat are thought to contribute to cancer of the colon, breast, uterus, and prostate.)

The paleolithic estimate corresponds to the typical American diet rather than to the nutritional ideal in one respect: cholesterol intake. Like the high paleolithic protein level, this is due to heavy reliance on meat; cholesterol, being the major constituent of animal cell membranes, is abundant even in lean meats. Nonetheless, contemporary hunter-gatherers have extremely low levels of serum cholesterol, which reinforces the recent finding that the major dietary determinant of serum cholesterol is not, paradoxically, cholesterol, but saturated fat.

Our paper concluded that there was an impressive convergence between the paleolithic diet—the diet that evolution designed us to eat—and the generally healthful diet prescribed by modern nutritional science. "The diet of our remote ancestors," we wrote, "may be a reference standard for modern human nutrition and a model for defense against certain 'diseases of civilization.'"

In a burst of optimism, we sent the paper to *The New England Journal of Medicine*, arguably the most prestigious medical periodical in the world. To our pleasant surprise, the journal accepted the paper and published it on January 31 of this year, under the title "Paleolithic Nutrition: A Consideration of Its Nature and Current Implications." I knew that the health and medicine sections of many newspapers regularly report the journal's more arresting findings. Still, I was not prepared for the reaction that our rather offbeat paper (offbeat, at least, by the journal's standards) generated.

Days before we even saw the published paper, Eaton and I began to receive telephone calls from an array of newspaper and broadcast journalists ranging from science reporters to food editors. Several reporters adopted the phrase "caveman diet" and went on to use it despite our insistence that it was not only misleading but it was also insulting to contemporary hunting-and-gathering peoples. A few representative headlines: "Cavemen Cooked Up a Healthy Diet" (*USA Today*); "Cave Man Takes a Healthy Bite Out of Today's 'Civilized' Diet" (*The Atlanta Journal*); "Check Ads for Specials on Sabertoothed Tigers" (*The Atlanta Constitution*). There were many amusing cartoons and drawings, but the graphics award surely must go to *The Fort Lauderdale News/Sun-Sentinel*, which ran a series of "paleolithic" recipes accompanied by a color photograph of an actor grotesquely made up as a caveman—skins, club, tooth necklace, and all. Even distinguished journalistic institutions were not above this sort of humor. *The Washington Post*, after predicting the appearance of our book-to-be on the best-sellers' list, added, "Some day in the near future you'll look out at daybreak and see people all up and down your street come loping out of their homes wearing designer skins and wielding L. L. Bean stoneaxes while every dog, cat and squirrel in the neighborhood runs for cover."

Ellen Goodman, the much-loved syndicated columnist based at *The Boston Globe*, ridiculed us in an uncharacteristically harsh tone. Her piece was accompanied by an etching of savages dancing, captioned "Make mine mastodon." The column seemed marred by resentment—the resentment of a noncompliant patient sermonized yet again by highminded, pesky physicians. "But I am convinced," she concluded, "that the average Paleolithic person was the very role model of good health when he died at the ripe old age of 32."

By and large, though, I got a good laugh out of the copy. I am enough of a writer to realize what a superb target our article made. Most of the jokes and cartoons were presented side by side with fairly serious summaries of the paper, and the pieces generally got the message across—and to a much larger audience than we could have reached without such help. (Fellow physicians and scientists had sent us scores of letters, the majority of them positive.) As Eaton pointed out after we had stopped laughing and finished licking our wounds, the attention to our ideas was what counted, and we had now become one more small force for preventive medicine in a sea of cultural forces aligned against it.

Needless to say, the critiques that appeared in the journal itself were more serious in intent than was the popular commentary. One reader pointed out that paleolithic hunter-gatherers would likely have eaten a lot of honey—a challenge to our contention that their consumption of simple carbohydrates was meager. (In fact, the Pygmies of Zaire have recently been found to gorge themselves on caches of honey.) But we countered that there was no way our ancient ancestors could have consumed anywhere near the 108 pounds of sugar a year now eaten by the average American child, and that the archaeological record shows a massive increase in tooth decay accompanying the rising consumption of refined carbohydrates. Another critic questioned one of our basic premises—that there has been little genetic change since the hunting-gathering era. This is an important issue and it calls for further research; but all studies of modern hunter-gatherers suggest an overwhelming genetic continuity between them and us.

For the present, then, our model of paleolithic nutrition seems to have some claim on the truth. Still, the criticisms published by the journal were serious enough to lend weight to the barb thrown by *The New York Times*: "Did people of the early Stone Age eat more healthily than their urban successors? The issue is being vigorously chewed in the New England Journal of Medicine, and it tastes like the myth of the Noble Savage."

Had we indeed projected today's medical ideals onto our evolutionary past? I won't speak for Eaton, but I know myself well enough to concede that possibility; I don't purport to be conscious of all my motivations, and it may well be that I was inspired to accept Eaton's invitation to collaborate by the same naïveté that drew me to the Kalahari as a graduate student. But whatever the inspiration for our study, we took pains to conduct it by the rules. We spent months examining and reexamining our premises and our data, and we were very hard on any interpretation that even hinted at romanticism. But a solid core of good data survived our harshest scrutiny, and the burden of proof now rests with those who doubt that the diet of hunter-gatherers, whether recent or ancient, was qualitatively better than the average American's.

A scientific hypothesis, after all, should be evaluated not on the basis of its authors' motives but on the basis of its merits. It does not find its way into a respectable journal because it was nobly conceived or because it is guaranteed to be right, but because it is sufficiently interesting and sufficiently supported by facts to warrant admission, at least temporarily, into the stream of scientific discourse. Scientists' motivations must come from somewhere, and the realities of research are such that the pure pursuit of truth is often asked to coexist with a certain amount of advocacy. The best we can hope is that the resulting discourse resembles the contending thoughts in a single, rather superior mind—contradiction progressing toward synthesis.

No Bone Unturned

Clyde Snow is never in a hurry. He knows he's late. He's always late. For Snow, being late is part of the job. In fact, he doesn't usually begin to work until death has stripped some poor individual to the bone, and no one—neither the local homicide detectives nor the pathologists—can figure out who once gave identity to the skeletonized remains. No one, that is, except a shrewd, laconic, 60-year-old forensic anthropologist.

Snow strolls into the Cook County Medical Examiner's Office in Chicago on this brisk October morning wearing a pair of Lucchese cowboy boots and a three-piece pin-striped suit. Waiting for him in autopsy room 160 are a bunch of naked skeletons found in Illinois, Wisconsin, and Minnesota since his last visit. Snow, a native Texan who now lives in rural Oklahoma, makes the trip up to Chicago some six times a year. The first case on his agenda is a pale brown skull found in the garbage of an abandoned building once occupied by a Chicago cosmetics company.

Snow turns the skull over slowly in his hands, a cigarette dangling from his fingers. One often does. Snow does not seem overly concerned about mortality, though its tragedy surrounds him daily.

"There's some trauma here," he says, examining a rough edge at the lower back of the skull. He points out the area to Jim Elliott, a homicide detective with the Chicago police. "This looks like a chopping blow by a heavy bladed instrument. Almost like a decapitation." In a place where the whining of bone saws drifts through hallways and the sweet-sour smell of death hangs in the air, the word surprises no one.

Snow begins thinking aloud. "I think what we're looking at here is a female, or maybe a small male, about thirty to forty years old. Probably Asian." He turns the skull upside down, pointing out the degree of wear on the teeth. "This was somebody who lived on a really rough diet. We don't normally find this kind of dental wear in a modern Western population."

"How long has it been around?" Elliott asks.

Snow raises the skull up to his nose. "It doesn't have any decompositional odors," he says. He pokes a finger in the skull's nooks and crannies. "There's no soft tissue left. It's good and dry. And it doesn't show signs of having been buried. I would say that this has been lying around in an attic or a box for years. It feels like a souvenir skull," says Snow.

Souvenir skulls, usually those of Japanese soldiers, were popular with U.S. troops serving in the Pacific during World War II; there was also a trade in skulls during the Vietnam War years. On closer inspection, though, Snow begins to wonder about the skull's Asian origins—the broad nasal aperture and the jutting forth of the upper-tooth-bearing part of the face suggest Melanesian features. Sifting through the objects found in the abandoned building with the skull, he finds several loose-leaf albums of 35-millimeter transparencies documenting life among the highland tribes of New Guinea. The slides, shot by an anthropologist, include graphic scenes of ritual warfare. The skull, Snow concludes, is more likely to be a trophy from one of these tribal battles than the result of a local Chicago homicide.

"So you'd treat it like found property?" Elliott asks finally. "Like somebody's garage-sale property?"

"Exactly," says Snow.

Clyde Snow is perhaps the world's most sought-after forensic anthropologist. People have been calling upon him to identify skeletons for more than a quarter of a century. Every year he's involved in some 75 cases of identification, most of them without fanfare. "He's an old scudder who doesn't have to blow his own whistle," says Walter Birkby, a forensic anthropologist at the University of Arizona. "He knows he's good."

Yet over the years Snow's work has turned him into something of an unlikely celebrity. He has been called upon to identify the remains of the Nazi war criminal Josef Mengele, reconstruct the face of the Egyptian boy-king Tutankhamen, confirm the authenticity of the body autopsied as that of President John F. Kennedy, and examine the skeletal remains of General Custer's men at the battlefield of the

Little Bighorn. He has also been involved in the grim task of identifying the bodies in some of the United States' worst airline accidents.

Such is his legend that cases are sometimes attributed to him in which he played no part. He did not, as *The New York Times* reported, identify the remains of the crew in the *Challenger* disaster. But the man is often the equal of his myth. For the past four years, setting his personal safety aside, Snow has spent much of his time in Argentina, searching for the graves and identities of some of the thousands who "disappeared" between 1976 and 1983, during Argentina's military regime.

Snow did not set out to rescue the dead from oblivion. For almost two decades, until 1979, he was a physical anthropologist at the Civil Aeromedical Institute, part of the Federal Aviation Administration in Oklahoma City. Snow's job was to help engineers improve aircraft design and safety features by providing them with data on the human frame.

One study, he recalls, was initiated in response to complaints from a flight attendants' organization. An analysis of accident patterns had revealed that inadequate restraints on flight attendants' jump seats were leading to deaths and injuries and that aircraft doors weighing several hundred pounds were impeding evacuation efforts. Snow points out that ensuring the survival of passengers in emergencies is largely the flight attendants' responsibility. "If they are injured or killed in a crash, you're going to find a lot of dead passengers."

Reasoning that equipment might be improved if engineers had more data on the size and strength of those who use it, Snow undertook a study that required the meticulous measurement of some of the most admired fleshbearing skeletons in the world. When Snow's report was issued in 1975, Senator William Proxmire was outraged that $57,800 of the taxpayers' money had been spent to caliper 423 young airline stewardesses from head to toe. Yet the study, which received one of the senator's dubious Golden Fleece Awards, was firmly supported by both the FAA and the Association of Flight Attendants. "I can't imagine," says Snow with obvious delight, "how much coffee Proxmire got spilled on him in the next few months."

It was during his tenure at the FAA that he developed an interest in forensic work. Over the years the Oklahoma police frequently consulted the physical anthropologist for help in identifying crime victims. "The FAA figured it was a kind of community service to let me work on these cases," he says.

The experience also helped to prepare him for the grim task of identifying the victims of air disasters. In December 1972, when a United Airlines plane crashed outside Chicago, killing 43 of the 61 people aboard (including the wife of Watergate conspirator Howard Hunt, who was found with $10,000 in her purse), Snow was brought in to help examine the bodies. That same year, with Snow's help, forensic anthropology was recognized as a specialty by the American Academy of Forensic Sciences. "It got a lot of anthropologists interested in forensics," he says, "and it made a lot of pathologists out there aware that there were anthropologists who could help them."

Each nameless skeleton poses a unique mystery for Snow. But some, like the second case awaiting him back in the autopsy room at the Cook County morgue, are more challenging than others. This one is a real chiller. In a large cardboard box lies a jumble of bones along with a tattered leg from a pair of blue jeans, a sock shrunk tightly around the bones of a foot, a pair of Nike running shoes without shoelaces, and, inside the hood of a blue wind breaker, a mass of stringy, blood-caked hair. The remains were discovered frozen in ice about 20 miles outside Milwaukee. A rusted bicycle was found lying close by. Paul Hibbard, chief deputy medical examiner for Waukesha County, who brought the skeleton to Chicago, says no one has been reported missing.

Snow lifts the bones out of the box and begins reconstructing the skeleton on an autopsy table. "There are two hundred six bones and thirty-two teeth in the human body," he says, "and each has a story to tell." Because bone is dynamic, living tissue, many of life's significant events—injuries, illness, childbearing—leave their mark on the body's internal framework. Put together the stories told by these bones, he says, and what you have is a person's "osteobiography."

Snow begins by determining the sex of the skeleton, which is not always obvious. He tells the story of a skeleton that was brought to his FAA office in the late 1970s. It had been found along with some women's clothes and a purse in a local back lot, and the police had assumed that it was female. But when Snow examined the bones, he realized that "at six foot three, she would probably have been the tallest female in Oklahoma."

Then Snow recalled that six months earlier the custodian in his building had suddenly not shown up for work. The man's supervisor later mentioned to Snow, "You know, one of these days when they find Ronnie, he's going to be dressed as a woman." Ronnie, it turned out, was a weekend transvestite. A copy of his dental records later confirmed that the skeleton in women's clothing was indeed Snow's janitor.

The Wisconsin bike rider is also male. Snow picks out two large bones that look something like twisted oysters—the innominates, or hipbones, which along with the sacrum, or lower backbone, form the pelvis. This pelvis is narrow and steep-walled like a male's, not broad and shallow like a female's. And the sciatic notch (the V-shaped space where the sciatic nerve passes through the hipbone) is narrow, as is normal in a male. Snow can also determine a skeleton's sex by checking the size of the mastoid processes (the bony knobs at the base of the skull) and the prominence of the brow ridge, or by measuring the head of an available limb bone, which is typically broader in males.

From an examination of the skull he concludes that the bike rider is "predominantly Caucasoid." A score of bony traits help the forensic anthropologist assign a skeleton to one of three major racial groups: Negroid, Caucasoid, or Mongoloid. Snow notes that the ridge of the boy's nose is high and salient, as it is in whites. In Negroids and Mongoloids (which include American Indians as well as most Asians) the nose tends to be broad in relation to its height. However, the boy's nasal margins are somewhat smoothed down, usually a Mongoloid feature. "Possibly a bit of American Indian admixture," says Snow. "Do you have Indians in your area?" Hibbard nods.

Age is next. Snow takes the skull and turns it upside down, pointing out the basilar joint, the junction between the two major bones that form the underside of the skull. In a child the joint would still be open to allow room for growth, but here the joint has fused—something that usually happens in the late teen years. On the other hand, he says, pointing to the zigzagging lines on the dome of the skull, the cranial sutures are open. The cranial sutures, which join the bones of the braincase, begin to fuse and disappear in the mid-twenties.

Next Snow picks up a femur and looks for signs of growth at the point where the shaft meets the knobbed end. The thin plates of cartilage—areas of incomplete calcification—that are visible at this point suggest that the boy hadn't yet attained his full height. Snow doublechecks with an examination of the pubic symphysis, the joint where the two hipbones meet. The ridges in this area, which fill in and smooth over in adulthood, are still clearly marked. He concludes that the skeleton is that of a boy between 15 and 20 years old.

"One of the things you learn is to be pretty conservative," says Snow. "It's very impressive when you tell the police, 'This person is eighteen years old,' and he turns out to be eighteen. The problem is, if the person is fifteen you've blown it—you probably won't find him. Looking for a missing person is like trying to catch fish. Better get a big net and do your own sorting."

Snow then picks up a leg bone, measures it with a set of calipers, and enters the data into a portable computer. Using the known correlation between the height and length of the long limb bones, he quickly estimates the boy's height. "He's five foot six and a half to five foot eleven," says Snow. "Medium build, not excessively muscular, judging from the muscle attachments that we see." He points to the grainy ridges that appear where muscle attaches itself to the bone. The most prominent attachments show up on the teenager's right arm bone, indicating right-handedness.

Then Snow examines the ribs one by one for signs of injury. He finds no stab wounds, cuts, or bullet holes, here or elsewhere on the skeleton. He picks up the hyoid bone from the boy's throat and looks for the telltale fracture signs that would suggest the boy was strangled. But, to Snow's frustration, he can find no obvious cause of death. In hopes of identifying the missing teenager, he suggests sending the skull, hair, and the boy's description to Betty Pat Gatliff, a medical illustrator and sculptor in Oklahoma who does facial reconstructions.

Six weeks later photographs of the boy's likeness appear in the *Milwaukee Sentinel*. "If you persist long enough," says Snow, "eighty-five to ninety percent of the cases eventually get positively identified, but it can take anywhere from a few weeks to a few years."

Snow and Gatliff have collaborated many times, but never with more glitz than in 1983, when Snow was commissioned by Patrick Barry, a Miami orthopedic surgeon and amateur Egyptologist, to reconstruct the face of the Egyptian boy-king Tutankhamen. Normally a facial reconstruction begins with a skull, but since Tutankhamen's 3,000-year-old remains were in Egypt, Snow had to make do with the skull measurements from a 1925 postmortem and X-rays taken in 1975. A plaster model of the skull was made, and on the basis of Snow's report—"his skull is Caucasoid with some Negroid admixtures"—Gatliff put a face on it. What did Tutankhamen look like? Very much like the gold mask on his sarcophagus, says Snow, confirming that it was, indeed, his portrait.

Many cite Snow's use of facial reconstructions as one of his most important contributions to the field. Snow, typically self-effacing, says that Gatliff "does all the work." The identification of skeletal remains, he stresses, is often a collaboration between pathologists, odontologists, radiologists, and medical artists using a variety of forensic techniques.

One of Snow's last tasks at the FAA was to help identify the dead from the worst airline accident in U.S. history. On May 25, 1979, a DC-10 crashed shortly after takeoff from Chicago's O'Hare Airport, killing 273 people. The task facing Snow and more than a dozen forensic specialists was horrific. "No one ever sat down and counted," says Snow, "but we estimated ten thousand to twelve thousand pieces or parts of bodies." Nearly 80 percent of the victims were identified on the basis of dental evidence and fingerprints. Snow and forensic radiologist John Fitzpatrick later managed to identify two dozen others by comparing postmortem X-rays with X-rays taken during the victim's lifetime.

Next to dental records, such X-ray comparisons are the most common way of obtaining positive identifications. In 1978, when a congressional committee reviewed the evidence on John F. Kennedy's assassination, Snow used X-rays to show that the body autopsied at Bethesda Naval Hospital was indeed that of the late president and had not—as some conspiracy theorists believed—been switched.

The issue was resolved on the evidence of Kennedy's "sinus print," the scalloplike pattern on the upper margins of the sinuses that are visible in X-rays of the forehead. So characteristic is a person's sinus print that courts throughout the world accept the matching of antemortem and postmortem X-rays of the sinuses as positive identification.

Yet another technique in the forensic specialist's repertoire is photo superposition. Snow used it in 1977 to help identify the mummy of a famous Oklahoma outlaw named Elmer J. McCurdy, who was killed by a posse after holding up a train in 1911. For years the mummy had been exhibited as a "dummy" in a California funhouse—until it was found to have a real human skeleton inside it. Ownership of the mummy was eventually traced back to a funeral parlor in Oklahoma, where McCurdy had been embalmed and exhibited as "the bandit who wouldn't give up."

Using two video cameras and an image processor, Snow superposed the mummy's profile on a photograph of McCurdy that was taken shortly after his death. When displayed on a single monitor, the two coincided to a remarkable degree. Convinced by the evidence, Thomas Noguchi, then Los Angeles County coroner, signed McCurdy's death certificate ("Last known occupation: Train robber") and allowed the outlaw's bones to be returned to Oklahoma for a decent burial.

It was this technique that also allowed forensic scientists to identify the remains of the Nazi "Angel of Death," Josef Mengele, in the summer of 1985. A team of investigators, including Snow and West German forensic anthropologist Richard Helmer, flew to Brazil after an Austrian couple claimed that Mengele lay buried in a grave on a São Paulo hillside. Tests revealed that the stature, age, and hair color of the un-

earthed skeleton were consistent with information in Mengele's SS files; yet without X-rays or dental records, the scientists still lacked conclusive evidence. When an image of the reconstructed skull was superposed on 1930s photographs of Mengele, however, the match was eerily compelling. All doubts were removed a few months later when Mengele's dental X-rays were tracked down.

In 1979 Snow retired from the FAA to the rolling hills of Norman, Oklahoma, where he and his wife, Jerry, live in a sprawling, early-1960s ranch house. Unlike his 50 or so fellow forensic anthropologists, most of whom are tied to academic positions, Snow is free to pursue his consultancy work full-time. Judging from the number of miles he logs in the average month, Snow is clearly not ready to retire for good.

His recent projects include a reexamination of the skeletal remains found at the site of the Battle of the Little Bighorn, where more than a century ago Custer and his 210 men were killed by Sioux and Cheyenne warriors. Although most of the enlisted men's remains were moved to a mass grave in 1881, an excavation of the battlefield in the past few years uncovered an additional 375 bones and 36 teeth. Snow, teaming up again with Fitzpatrick, determined that these remains belonged to 34 individuals.

The historical accounts of Custer's desperate last stand are vividly confirmed by their findings. Snow identified one skeleton as that of a soldier between the ages of 19 and 23 who weighed around 150 pounds and stood about five foot eight. He'd sustained gunshot wounds to his chest and left forearm. Heavy blows to his head had fractured his skull and sheared off his teeth. Gashed thigh bones indicated that his body was later dismembered with an ax or hatchet.

Given the condition and number of the bodies, Snow seriously questions the accuracy of the identifications made by the original nineteenth-century burial crews. He doubts, for example, that the skeleton buried at West Point is General Custer's.

For the last four years Snow has devoted much of his time to helping two countries come to terms with the horrors of a much more recent past. As part of a group sponsored by the American Association for the Advancement of Science, he has been helping the Argentinian National Commission on Disappeared Persons to determine the fate of some of those who vanished during their country's harsh military rule: between 1976 and 1983 at least 10,000 people were systematically swept off the streets by roving death squads to be tortured, killed, and buried in unmarked graves. In December 1986, at the invitation of the Aquino government's Human Rights

Commission, Snow also spent several weeks training Philippine scientists to investigate the disappearances that occurred under the Marcos regime.

But it is in Argentina where Snow has done the bulk of his human-rights work. He has spent more than 27 months in and around Buenos Aires, first training a small group of local medical and anthropology students in the techniques of forensic investigation, and later helping them carefully exhume and examine scores of the *desaparecidos,* or disappeared ones.

Only 25 victims have so far been positively identified. But the evidence has helped convict seven junta members and other high-ranking military and police officers. The idea is not necessarily to identify all 10,000 of the missing, says Snow. "If you have a colonel who ran a detention center where maybe five hundred people were killed, you don't have to nail him with five hundred deaths. Just one or two should be sufficient to get him convicted." Forensic evidence from Snow's team may be used to prosecute several other military officers, including General Suarez Mason. Mason is the former commander of the I Army Corps in Buenos Aires and is believed to be responsible for thousands of disappearances. He was recently extradited from San Francisco back to Argentina, where he is expected to stand trial this winter.

The investigations have been hampered by a frustrating lack of antemortem information. In 1984, when commission lawyers took depositions from relatives and friends of the disappeared, they often failed to obtain such basic information as the victim's height, weight, or hair color. Nor did they ask for the missing person's X-rays (which in Argentina are given to the patient) or the address of the victim's dentist. The problem was compounded by the inexperience of those who carried out the first mass exhumations prior to Snow's arrival. Many of the skeletons were inadvertently destroyed by bulldozers as they were brought up.

Every unearthed skeleton that shows signs of gunfire, however, helps to erode the claim once made by many in the Argentinian military that most of the *desaparecidos* are alive and well and living in Mexico City, Madrid, or Paris. Snow recalls the case of a 17-year-old boy named Gabriel Dunayavich, who disappeared in the summer of 1976. He was walking home from a movie with his girlfriend when a Ford Falcon with no license plates snatched him off the street. The police later found his body and that of another boy and girl dumped by the roadside on the outskirts of Buenos Aires. The police went through the motions of an investigation, taking photographs and doing an autopsy, then buried the three teenagers in an unmarked grave.

A decade later Snow, with the help of the boy's family, traced the autopsy reports, the police photographs, and the grave of the three youngsters. Each of them had four or five closely spaced bullet wounds in the upper chest—the signature, says Snow, of an automatic weapon. Two also had wounds on their arms from bullets that had entered behind the elbow and exited from the forearm.

"That means they were conscious when they were shot," says Snow. "When a gun was pointed at them, they naturally raised their arm." It's details like these that help to authenticate the last moments of the victims and bring a dimension of reality to the judges and jury.

Each time Snow returns from Argentina he says that this will be the last time. A few months later he is back in Buenos Aires. "There's always more work to do," he says. It is, he admits quietly, "terrible work."

"These were such brutal, coldblooded crimes," he says. "The people who committed them not only murdered; they had a system to eliminate all trace that their victims even existed."

Snow will not let them obliterate their crimes so conveniently. "There are human-rights violations going on all around the world," he says. "But to me murder is murder, regardless of the motive. I hope that we are sending a message to governments who murder in the name of politics that they can be held to account."

Shamans and Their Lore May Vanish with the Forests

The symptoms indicated tetanus: fever, stiffness and lockjaw so severe that the victim could barely drink through a straw. His illness upset his entire village of 500 or so on the coast of an Indonesian island.

The distressed villagers called in a local shaman, or native healer, who had the man take a compound of pressed plants. Within 24 hours the symptoms of tetanus had faded.

"I was never able to identify the plants he used," said Dr. Paul Taylor, curator of Asian Ethnology at the Smithsonian Institution, who witnessed the apparent cure during field work in Indonesia. "By local custom, he could only reveal that to an apprentice."

Dr. Taylor is an ethnobotanist, combining the study of anthropology and botany to learn the ways native peoples use plants. He is one of a growing band of ethnobotanists who are racing to discover as much as possible about native pharmacopeias before the shamans who use them die out. Some have even become understudies to shamans to discover new medicines and other innovative uses of plants.

While skeptics may argue that the lore of native healers is mere superstition, the ethnobotanists see shamanic knowledge as the result of a trial-and-error process refined over thousands of years. Ethnobotanists hope to take a scientific short cut to discovering new uses for the tens of thousands of plants with which native peoples are intimately familiar.

But the shamans are a dying breed. Like a bellwether species whose decline signals that an entire ecosystem is in peril, the dwindling number of shamans is a sign of the demise of their cultures.

Today most shamans are elderly, members of the last generation to have fully learned native lore. Ethnobotanists report that, around the world, younger generations are rapidly losing interest in learning what the local shaman knows, lured away by the pulls of the modern world. In more and more native groups, there is no one to whom shamans can pass on their knowledge.

"Each time a medicine man dies, it is as if a library has burned down," said Dr. Mark Plotkin, an ethnobotanist at Conservation International, a Washington-based foundation seeking to save endangered ecosystems.

"We often talk about disappearing species, but the knowledge of how to use these species is disappearing much faster than the species themselves," Dr. Plotkin said. "The knowledge that's being lost most rapidly is information on healing plants."

In an effort to preserve the wisdom of shamans, Dr. Plotkin is initiating what he calls a "sorcerer's apprentice" program that will encourage young tribal members to take up the mantle of elderly shamans.

For example, the Tirio people, a tribe on the Brazil-Surinam border, use about 300 plants for medicine, Dr. Plotkin has discovered. "The six or so shamans among the Tirio are all between 55 and 65," Dr. Plotkin said. "But the young people don't respect them. Not one shaman has an apprentice." Furthermore, younger people often disdain local remedies in favor of newly available modern medicine.

Dr. Plotkin has been trying to persuade the elders of the tribe to have a younger Tirio record what the shamans know before they die. In Costa Rica, Conservation International, as part of the same program, convened a meeting of the medicine men of the Bibri tribe toward the same end; similar efforts are planned for tribal communities in Colombia, Ecuador, Guyana and Surinam.

IN VOGUE IN AMERICA

The efforts of outsiders to collect the knowledge of the shamans is in itself a boost. "When we go into the community and show the outside world values this information highly, it enhances the shaman's status," said Dr. Michael Balick, director of the Institute of Economic Botany at the New York Botanical Garden.

With Dr. Rosita Arvigo of the Ix Chel Tropical Research Center in Belize, Dr. Balick is writing a book on the local plants people in Belize could use for healing—a lore fast disappearing among them.

The lack of interest in shamans and their lore among young people in native cultures is ironic:

shamanism is in vogue in America. Workshops in shamanistic practices like rhythmic drumming that induces a trance, and herbal remedies are offered in many cities; tour packages promise vacationers the chance to meet shamans on trips abroad.

Faddish interest aside, the notion that the lore of medicine men is a valuable resource about to be lost forever is more than romantic sentiment: ethnobotanists point to the potential harvest for modern medicine.

"Of more than 265,000 known plant species, less than 1 percent have been tested for medical applications, or even for the chemical compounds they contain," said Dr. Balick. "Yet out of this tiny portion have come 25 percent of medicines."

Plants are such a potentially rich source of medicines because nature economizes in the chemical compounds it uses, distributing them throughout the forms of life on the planet. Substances that are building blocks of plants often have effects on the chemistry of the human body, or on the viruses and bacteria that attack it. The most recent example is taxol, found in the bark of the Pacific Yew tree, which has been found to be effective in treating ovarian and other cancers.

NOT MANY YEARS LEFT

Ethnobotanists point to an earlier discovery, vinca alkaloids from the rosy periwinkle, which were among the first drugs found effective in chemotherapy, and are still in wide use. Known among natives of the Caribbean as a treatment for diabetes, the periwinkle failed follow-up tests for treating diabetes by drug companies in the 1950's, as well as a later test by the National Cancer Institute for use with cancer. But more extensive testing by scientists at the Eli Lilly & Company established the medical value of the rosy periwinkle abstracts.

"There are apt to be great medications to be discovered in the other plant species," said Dr. Balick. "But because the species—and the people who know their uses—are disappearing so quickly, we have just 10 to 15 years to do this work."

The renewed scientific interest in the lore of shamans comes after a lull of two decades. During that time phamaceutical companies largely ignored ethnobotany as a route to discovering new medicines, preferring instead to pursue methods for artificially synthesizing medications. But ethnobotanists say that new techniques, such as those for storing and transporting plant specimens, are improving the chances for scientific success.

Typical of the renewed efforts is Dr. Plotkin's recent expedition to the Tirio tribe. He collected specimens that included a fungus used to treat earaches, a sap for the relief of burns and leaves that are made into a powder for treating skin fungi.

The potential harvest is not limited to medicines. "To the peoples of the rain forest, plants are the source of myriad products, including latexes, essential oils and foods," said Dr. Plotkin. "Most every major commodity in the international marketplace was first discovered by native peoples. An American breakfast, from cornflakes and bananas, to coffee, sugar, and orange juice, and even hash brown potatoes, is all based on foods that originated in the tropics."

With the intensifying of efforts to save vanishing species in the world's rain forests and other imperiled ecosystems has come the realization that the opportunity to discover new medicines or other valuable products in these areas is fast disappearing. In the last four decades, nearly half the world's tropical rain forests have been lost. Two-thirds of the world's plant species are in the tropics.

One sign of the quickened scientific interest in ethnobotany is a $2.5 million contract from the National Cancer Institute to Dr. Balick, along with scientists at the Missouri Botanical Garden and at the University of Illinois, to collect plants that may contain compounds useful in the treatment of cancer or AIDS. He has found shamans' lore an efficient tool.

In a field study in the rain forest in Belize, Dr. Balick compared using random collection of plant species with an ethnobotanical approach, in which only the plants that local people say have medical uses are collected. The plants were then sent to a cancer research facility in Maryland. There they were made into extracts that were put in test tubes containing human blood T cells infected with the AIDS virus.

Of the 20 plants collected on the shaman's advice, five killed the AIDS virus but spared the T cells. But of 18 plant species gathered randomly, just one did so. The findings do not mean that the plants necessarily are a cure for AIDS; many substances that kill the virus in the test tube are ineffective or unusable in the body. But all the plants that showed promise in this test will go through further testing.

"The 1990's may be the last chance to preserve what native healers know about the rain forest," said Dr. Balick. "We're in danger of losing this knowledge in the next generation. There's already been a tremendous loss."

Ethnobotanists say much of the loss is due to the larger forces that threaten the cultures of native peoples, including values passed on through television and radio.

STRATEGY TO SAVE FORESTS

Even so, up to 80 percent of primary health care in third world countries is provided by native healers. "We still find in many countries a very strong network of traditional healers, but as the rain forest dies, so do their supplies—and so does their ability to use their knowledge," Dr. Balick said. Some ethnobotanists see in their work a strategy for saving the rain forests by making them more valuable intact than if they were lumbered or leveled for farming. "Many tropical products can be harvested without destroying a single plant, much less a whole ecosystem," he said.

For example, the nut of the tagua plant, found in the Amazon rain forest, is now being marketed as an ivory substitute. Patagonia, a California sportswear company, has agreed to use tagua buttons on its clothes, and other clothing companies have expressed interest.

Some scientists worry that fortunes may be made from discoveries among native remedies without benefiting the native peoples themselves. That has largely been the case since the early 1800's, when the British explorer Charles Waterton was guided through the jungles of Guyana by Makushi Indians to the plant from which they extracted curare for their arrowheads. Curare is still used today as a muscle relaxant during surgery.

"The Makushis never received any compensation for the discovery of a product worth millions," said Dr. Plotkin. "Today their entire culture is on the verge of disappearing."

Dr. Jason Gray, an anthropologist who directs Cultural Survival, a foundation in Cambridge, Mass., said: "It's a question of intellectual property rights. People whose medical lore leads to a useful product should have a stake in the profits. Unless we return some profits to them, it's a kind of theft. We have to figure out ways to make the rain forests pay for themselves, so these peoples can continue to exist."

Katie Hafner

Coming of Age in Palo Alto

Anthropologists find a niche studying consumers for companies in Silicon Valley.

In 1981, while doing postdoctoral field work in cultural anthropology, Bonnie A. Nardi lived with villagers in Western Samoa, trying to understand the cultural reasons that people there have an average of eight children.

Today Dr. Nardi works at AT&T Labs West in Menlo Park, Calif., and has no regrets. She left academia in 1984 and is considered a pioneer among anthropologists who are employed by high-tech companies to examine consumers' behavior in their homes and offices.

"Usually people say, 'What is an anthropologist doing here?'" Dr. Nardi said. "But when I explain that I study how people use technology in order to get new ideas for products and services, it instantly makes sense."

No longer do companies study consumers' psyches only by asking people what they think about technology and how they use it. Now they conduct observational research, dispatching anthropologists to employ their ethnographic skills by interviewing, watching and videotaping consumers in their natural habitats. In the past several years, companies like Apple, Motorola, Xerox and Intel, as well as telecommunications and cable companies, have brought anthropologists into the corporate fold. The goal is to apply what the anthropologists learn to new product concepts. "It's the extreme form of understanding the customer," Dr. Nardi said.

Half of all anthropologists with doctorates are going to work outside universities, said Susan Squires, president-elect of the National Association for the Practice of Anthropology, which represents anthropologists outside academia. High competitive pressure and short product cycles mean that corporate field work is usually much briefer than academic research and fewer people are studied. While the work might not be considered reliable enough to be published in a traditional anthropology journal, companies can use the results to help them make marketing and product-design decisions.

Observational research isn't new for American industry. It can be traced to the 1930's and 1940's, when social scientists began examining productivity during the Depression and World War II, said Marietta Baba, chairwoman of the anthropology department at Wayne State University in Detroit. "They left industry completely in the 60's and 70's," Dr. Baba said. "They came back in the 80's and there has been a slow, steady increase since then." The rise in corporate employment for anthropologists has roughly paralleled a drop in academic opportunities. Hallmark Cards has an anthropologist. The automotive industry employs at least a dozen, and so does Andersen Consulting.

But it is in the high-tech arena, with intense pressure and high rate of product failures, that studying consumers' habits at very close range is currently most popular, Dr. Squires said.

"We go out into the consumer space, into people's homes—we go to where the people are," said Tony Salvador, an experimental psychologist at Intel, where he is called a design ethnographer. "If we're interested in their homes, we go there. If we're interested in what they do on vacation, we go on vacation with them."

Sometimes an ethnographic inquiry will lead to new ways to use an existing technology or will generate new technologies. It was a 1996 study of pager use in rural China, where there is a scarcity of phones, that prompted Motorola to start thinking seriously about two-way paging outside urban markets, said Jean Canavan, an anthropologist who is the manager of culture and technology initiatives at Motorola.

"The context is really critical," Ms. Canavan said. "If we want to develop technologies that really fit into the way people live their day-to-day lives, then we have to understand how people really live."

Many anthropologists work with a concept called embodied knowledge—tacit, nonscientific knowledge—and look for ways to incorporate such information into product design. Embodied knowledge is "basically the intelligence in your muscles," Dr. Nardi said.

"You aren't born knowing how to ride a bicycle," Dr. Baba said. "You don't learn by reading a book. With experience, your body comes to 'know' how to ride a bike."

Paying attention to embodied knowledge helped Matsushita build a better bread maker in 1987. The company sent a team of engineers to be apprenticed for several months to a master bread chef at the Osaka International Hotel in Japan. The magic ingredient turned out to be a special maneuver the chef executed with his hand while kneading the dough, so the engineers figured out how to mimic the movement with the machine.

"Anthropologists are trained in those patient, detailed ways of watching for hundreds of hours and taking everything down in minute detail, which is where the knowledge is—in the tiny details," Dr. Baba said. An understanding of movement skills has helped in the design of things like the computer mouse, joystick and touch screen. The mouse, for instance, lets the hand mimic the way the eyes scan a computer screen.

The social aspects of technology particularly interest anthropologists like the ones in Dr. Salvador's group at Intel. Three and a half years ago, the group was set up when the company began considering other consumer products after releasing its Pentium processor. "It was selling really well into homes, and people were saying we have to build more things for the home," he said. "We thought maybe we should understand more about the home."

The group members embarked on a study of 10 families with young children. They visited each family for an evening, eating dinner with the family and analyzing the organization of the home and the family's daily routine.

Dr. Salvador's group found that the kitchen and family room were the most important rooms in the house. "Very rarely are people alone in those spaces," he said. "Social relationships are very important." Dr. Salvador's findings may not seem like much of an epiphany, but his work has helped lead Intel to look beyond the notion of a PC as a device generally used by someone seated at a desk alone in a room and to understand the importance of whole families using and sharing computing devices.

Anne McClard and Ken Anderson, anthropologists who are married to each other, do similar observational research at Media One, a cable provider that AT&T recently agreed to purchase. Ms. McClard and Mr. Anderson are part of Media One's Broadband Innovation Group. Their charge is to find new users and

new uses for the company's services and, as Ms. McClard put it, "to make broadband living a reality."

To study Internet usage patterns, companies also install tracking systems on subjects' computers. But those kinds of studies are a poor substitute for the serendipitous twists and turns of actual interviews, anthropologists say.

Dr. Nardi said it was also important to couple interviews with observations to pick up on the knowledge and behavior people exhibit but do not think to mention. In her book *Information Ecologies: Using Technology with Heart* (M.I.T. Press, 1999), Dr. Nardi describes a study she did of a broadcast video and audio system in a hospital. She noticed that the surgical staff told jokes during routine parts of an operation. "This became an issue when the multimedia system began to broadcast audio to remote parts of the hospital," she said in an interview. The jokes and banter, she said, relieved tension during lengthy operations. "But no one would ever have said in an interview, 'We tell jokes during surgery,'" she noted. Dr. Nardi and her colleagues recommended that the hospital add a feature to the system so the surgeons would know whether the audio component was turned on.

Ms. McClard and Mr. Anderson of Media One have had similar experiences. Last summer, they conducted a study called Always On, in which they observed families with cable modem connections, which allow computers to have a constant connection to the Internet at very high speeds, in an effort to understand what it is like to have such a link to the Internet in one's home.

The two anthropologists found that people with constant connections were often unaware of changes in their behavior. For instance, the people would often walk over to the computer to perform tasks like retrieving E-mail even if they were busy with tasks somewhere else. But they hardly notice that they are doing it, Mr. Anderson said.

Such observations by anthropologists can be important for sales later on. When Canon first introduced its color printers for the home market in 1995, said Dr. Squires, who works for GVO, a consumer product consulting company in Palo Alto, Calif., consumers did not know what to do with them. So a team of researchers from GVO went into homes to examine refrigerator doors and bedroom walls for the types of printed material families create and exchange. The result was Canon Creative, the greeting card, T-shirt and poster software that comes bundled with the printers. Sales of the printers took off, Dr. Squires said.

But corporate anthropologists operate under constraints that make their jobs harder. Ms. McClard said the year and a half she took for an academic project seemed like "a real luxury" from the standpoint of the corporate world. A project for, say, Media One lasts just a few months.

So many of those anthropologists find it hard to present their findings, often from limited field samples, in a way that interests the people in the company who plan and design products. "Part of the challenge is telling the story in a way that makes it compelling to people who have the power to develop products," Ms. McClard said.

Ms. McClard and Mr. Anderson videotape most of their interviews. "When engineers see the people talking, they are more convinced than if we told them stuff," she said. "We have to bring the experience alive for people. We don't have the numbers. The only thing we have is the experience of the people we go out to see."

Larry Prusak, executive director of I.B.M.'s Institute for Knowledge Management, a research organization, in Cambridge, Mass., said he believed that the number of anthropologists in industry would continue to grow.

"There's going to be a huge flourishing of industrial anthropologists in the next 20 years," he said, adding that this was especially true in the technology sector because companies were continuing to study technology's potential for mimicking human behavior. "We're in the infancy in this area, and I don't think anyone would tell you differently."

ARTICLE 56

Why Buy Kazoos You Can't Use?

Because stores are smarter than you are. A retail anthropologist tells all.

For nearly 20 years, clients like Burger King, Blockbuster, and Revlon have been calling on Paco Underhill, a retail anthropologist, and his colleagues at Envirosell to help them sell you more. In his new book *Why We Buy: The Science of Shopping* (Simon and Schuster, [1999]), Underhill shares secrets he has gleaned through in-store trackers and video cameras. *U.S. News* Senior Editor Linda Kulman spoke with Underhill to learn what makes you flash your cash.

In a booming economy, why do retailers need to know how shoppers behave?
When my grandfather went to buy a car, he knew he was a Mercury man. When my mother went into the grocery store, she wouldn't have thought of buying anything other than Scott Tissue. When I walk into a grocery store, I may have some brand predispositions, but I assume a lot of things work. And I'm always happy to buy a deal. The consumer-product-marketing world has gone from a polite little battle where Sears competes with JCPenney or Coke competes with Pepsi to a good old-fashioned bar fight where everyone is scrambling for America's discretionary dollars.

How does gender affect shopping patterns?
Women are especially sensitive to what we call the butt-brush factor. We are a posteriorly sensitive species. The more we're bumped from behind in a busy aisle, the less likely we are to turn from browsers into buyers. Men and women differ when they try things on. If a man takes clothing into a dressing room and it fits, there's a pretty good chance he'll buy it. If a woman takes clothing into a dressing room, she may buy it, or it may go into her imaginary closet.

When stores advertise a sale, does that actually mean anything?
A sale is sort of like collecting coupons. It's almost lost its meaning. The problem is that the American consumer, particularly for apparel, often refuses to buy anything that isn't on sale. But I wonder about the number of people who think they're getting a deal because they're buying in bulk. Buying in bulk either leads to consuming in bulk or to waste. How many households have a three-year supply of toilet paper waiting for Hurricane Anna to strike?

When does buying become irresistible?
The key to selling you shoes, for instance, is getting you comfortably seated to try the shoes on. I've always noticed that at Nordstrom's, the chairs are pretty low. Once you're down, its a lot harder to get up. And they not only get you the shoes you ask for, but they also bring you out a couple more. It's hard to resist someone who's down on his knees at your feet.

A good retailer understands that perceptions are just as important as reality, and occasionally, even more important. Restoration Hardware is a wonderful store where you can get lost and where that act is a pleasurable experience. Almost everything that you buy there you probably can buy somewhere else cheaper. They have a chest of drawers that sells for more than $1,000 being used to sell a kazoo that might cost $3. At the local five-and-dime, you can find [a kazoo] for $1.50, but it never looks so good as it does on that chest.

What is the most immediate turnoff?
Waiting. Our research has found that people will have an accurate perception of how long they've waited up to 2½ to 3 minutes. If someone stands around for five minutes, often they'll say, "Oh, I was here for 10 minutes." But people's perception of waiting time can be affected if you give them something to do. There are Scandinavian banks where you get a number like at a bakery. You sit down and read. You're not nearly as irritated as if you were standing in line waiting for a woman to empty her piggy bank at the teller window.

Will online retail kill stores?

Internet geeks are a little like vegans. They think their diet is going to save the world, but the world really doesn't need saving. If I look at where the Internet succeeds—books, music, prerecorded videos, porn, stock trades—it's all things that don't have a smell or a touch. My fervent contention is that online is not a replacement for retail but a tool. So the idea that retail is going to wither away is bogus. And I think, while the Web is going to be a pivotal part of our lives, it's going to be integrated. And I welcome that integration.

GLOSSARY

Abbevillean (or Chellean) culture The earlier of two stages in the hand ax (bifacial core tool) tradition, lasting approximately 1,000,000 to 400,000 B.P.; found across southerly and medium latitudes of the Old World, radiating out from Africa to southwest Europe and as far east as India; associated with *Homo erectus*.

absolute dating Physical-chemical dating methods that tie archaeologically retrieved artifacts into clearly specified time ranges calculated in terms of an abstract standard, such as the calendar.

acclimatization The process by which an organism's sweat glands, metabolism, and associated mechanisms adjust to a new and different climate.

acculturation Those adaptive cultural changes that come about in a minority culture when its adherents come under the influence of a more dominant society and take up many of the dominant culture's traits.

Acheulian culture The second stage of the hand ax bifacial core tool tradition; associated primarily with *Homo erectus*; found in southern and middle latitudes all across the Old World from India to Africa and West Europe, lasting in toto from about 400,000 to 60,000 B.P.

adaptation The processes by which groups become fitted, physically and culturally, to particular environments over several generations. This comes about through natural selection on the biological level and the modification and selective passing on of cultural traits and practices on the cultural level.

adaptational approach A theoretical approach to cultural change with the underlying assumption that, in order to survive, human beings must organize themselves into social, economic, and political groups that somehow fit in with the resources and challenges of a particular environment.

adultery Sexual intercourse by a married person with a person other than the legal spouse.

Aegyptopithecus An especially important Oligocene ape form, dated to 28 million years ago, and found in the Fayum area of Egypt. It represents a probable evolutionary link between the prosimian primates of the Paleocene and Eocene, and the apes of the Miocene and Paleocene. *Aegyptopithecus* probably was ancestral to *Dryopithecus*, and thus possibly to modern apes and humans.

affinal kin A kin relationship involving one marriage link (for example, a husband is related by affinity to his wife and her consanguineals).

age grades Specialized hierarchical associations based on age that cut across entire societies.

agnatic kin Kin related to one through males.

agonistic interactions A term used mostly to refer to animal behavior that is aggressive or unfriendly, including the behavior of both the initiator and the recipient of aggression.

agriculture Domesticated food production involving minimally the cultivation of plants but usually also the raising of domesticated animals; more narrowly, plant domestication making use of the plow (versus horticulture).

alleles Alternative forms of a single gene.

alliance theory A theoretical approach to the study of descent that emphasizes reciprocal exchanges among descent groups as the basic mechanism of social integration.

allomorph In language, one of the different-sounding versions of the same morpheme (unit of meaning).

allophone In language, one of the different sounds (phones) that represent a single phoneme.

altruistic act In evolutionary psychology, an act that benefits another organism at a cost to the actor, where cost and benefit are defined in terms of reproductive success.

alveolar ridge Thickened portions of the upper and lower interior jaws in which the teeth are set.

ambilineal descent The reckoning of descent group membership by an individual through either the mother's or the father's line—at the individual's option. See also *cognatic descent*.

androgens The hormones, present in relatively large quantities in the testes, that are responsible for the development of the male secondary sex characteristics.

angular gyrus An area of the brain crucial to human linguistic ability that serves as a link between the parts of the brain that receive stimuli from the sense organs of sight, hearing, and touch.

animatism The attribution of life to inanimate objects.

animism The belief that objects (including people) in the concretely perceivable world have a nonconcrete, spiritual element. For human beings, this element is the soul.

anomie The state of normlessness, usually found in societies undergoing crises, that renders social control over individual behavior ineffective.

Anthropoidea Suborder of the order of Primates that includes monkeys, apes, and humans.

anthropology The systematic study of the nature of human beings and their works, past and present.

anthropometry A subdivision of physical anthropology concerned with measuring and statistically analyzing the dimensions of the human body.

anthropomorphism The ascription of human characteristics to objects not human—often deities or animals.

antigens Proteins with specific molecular properties located on the surface of red blood cells.

ape A large, tailless, semi-erect primate of the family *Pongidae*. Living species include the orangutan, gorilla, chimpanzee, bonobo, gibbon, and siamang.

applied anthropology The use of anthropological concepts, methods, theories, and findings to achieve a desired social goal.

archaeological site See *site*.

archaeology The systematic retrieval, identification, and study of the physical and cultural remains that human beings and their ancestors have left behind them deposited in the earth.

aristocracy The privileged, usually land-owning, class of a society (for example, the ruling nobility of prerevolutionary France).

articulatory features Speech events described in terms of the speech organs employed in their utterance rather than from the nature of the sounds themselves.

artifact Any object manufactured, modified, or used by human beings to achieve a culturally defined goal.

ascribed status The social position a person comes to occupy on the basis of such uncontrollable characteristics as sex, age, or circumstances of birth.

assemblage The artifacts of one component of a site.

assimilation The disappearance of a minority group through the loss of particular identifying physical or sociocultural characteristics.

associated regions Broad regions surrounding the three geographical centers where agriculture was invented. Here different plants and animals were domesticated, and then spread individually throughout the whole area.

Aurignacian culture Upper Paleolithic culture that some scholars claim may represent a separate Middle Eastern migration into Europe; flourished in western Europe from 33,000 to 25,000 B.P. The Aurignacians began the European tradition of bone carving. The skeletal remains associated with this culture are the famous Cro-Magnon fossils.

australopithecine An extinct grade in hominid evolution found principally in early to mid-Pleistocene in eastern and southern Africa, usually accorded subfamily status (*Australopithecinae*, within *Hominidae*).

Australopithecus afarensis Early australopithecine form, dating to about 5.5 million years ago, found in the Afar region of Ethiopia and other parts of East Africa. Current debate centers on whether or not this form was directly ancestral to human beings.

Australopithecus africanus The original type specimen of australopithecines discovered in 1924 at Taung, South Africa, and dating from approximately 3.5 million years ago to approximately 1.6 million years ago. Belongs to the gracile line of the australopithecines.

Australopithecus boisei One of two species of robust australopithecines, appearing approximately 1.6 million years ago in sub-Saharan Africa.

Australopithecus habilis See *Homo habilis*.

Australopithecus robustus One of two species of robust australopithecines, found in both eastern and southern Africa, and dating from about 3.5 million years ago to about 1 million years ago.

avunculocal residence The practice by which a newlywed couple establishes residence with, or in the locale of, the groom's maternal uncle. A feature of some matrilineal societies that facilitates the men's maintaining their political power.

Aztec civlilization Final postclassic Mesoamerican civilization, dated from about A.D. 1300 to 1521, when Cortes conquered and destroyed the empire. The Aztec capital at Tenochtitlán (now Mexico City) housed some 300,000 people. Aztec society was highly stratified, dominated by a military elite.

balanced reciprocity The straightforward exchange of goods or services that both parties regard as equivalent at the time of the exchange.

baboon Large, terrestrial Old World monkey. Baboons have long, doglike muzzles, short tails, and are highly organized into troops.

band The simplest level of social organization; marked by very little political organization and consisting of small groups (50 to 300 persons) of families.

bartering The exchange of goods whose equivalent value is established by negotiation, usually in a market setting.

behavioral ecology See *evolutionary psychology.*

bifaces Stone artifacts that have been flaked on two opposite sides, most typically the hand axes produced by *Homo erectus.*

bifurcation Contrast among kin types based on the distinction between the mother's and father's kinfolk.

bilateral descent The reckoning of descent through both male and female lines. Typically found in Europe, the United States, and Southeast Asia.

bilateral kin A kin relationship in which an individual is linked equally to relatives of both sexes on both sides of the family.

bilocal residence The practice by which a newly-wed couple has a choice of residence, but must establish residence with, or in the locale of, one or the other set of parents.

bipedalism The predominant use of the hind (two) legs for locomotion.

blade tool A long and narrow flake tool that has been knocked off a specially prepared core.

bound morpheme In language, a unit of meaning (represented by a sound sequence) that can only occur when linked to another morpheme (for example, suffixes and prefixes).

B.P. An abbreviation used in archaeology, meaning before the present.

brachiation A method of locomotion, characteristic of the pongids, in which the animal swings hand over hand through the trees, while its body is suspended by the arms.

breeding population In population genetics, all individuals in a given population who potentially, or actually, mate with one another.

brideprice A gift from the groom and his family to the bride and her family prior to their marriage. The custom legitimizes children born to the wife as members of her husband's descent group.

Broca's area An area of the brain located toward the front of the dominant side of the brain that activates, among other things, the muscles of the lips, jaw, tongue, and larynx. A crucial biological substratum of speech.

brow ridge A continuous ridge of bone in the skull, curving over the eyes and connected across the bridge of the nose.

burins Chisel-like Upper Paleolithic stone tools produced by knocking small chips off the end(s) of a blade, and used for carving wood, bone, and antlers to fashion spear and harpoon points. Unlike end scrapers, burins were used for fine engraving and delicate carving.

call systems Systems of communication of nonhuman primates, consisting of a limited number of specific sounds (calls) conveying specific meanings to members of the group, largely restricted to emotional or motivational states.

capitalism Economic system featuring private ownership of the means of production and distribution.

cargo cults Revitalization movements (also designated as revivalist, nativistic, or millenarian) that received their name from movements in Melanesia early in the twentieth century. Characterized by the belief that the millenium will be ushered in by the arrival of great ships or planes loaded with European trade goods (cargo).

carotene A yellowish pigment in the skin.

carpal tunnel syndrome An ailment in which the tissues of the wrist and hand become inflamed and press on the nerves that run through the carpal tunnel, causing pain, numbness and weakness.

caste A hereditary, endogamous group of people bearing a common name and often having the same traditional occupation.

caste system A stratification system within which the social strata are hereditary and endogamous. The entire system is sanctioned by the mores, laws, and usually the religion of the society in question.

Catarrhini Old World anthropoids; one of two infraorders of the suborder of *Anthropoidea*, order of

Primates. Includes Old World monkeys, apes, and humans.

catastrophism   A school of thought, popular in the late eighteenth and early nineteenth centuries, proposing that old life forms became extinct through natural catastrophes, of which Noah's flood was the latest.

cephalic index   A formula for computing long-headedness and narrow-headedness:

$$\frac{\text{head breadth}}{\text{head length}} \times 100$$

A low cephalic index indicates a narrow head.

Cercopithecoidea   One of two superfamilies of the infraorder *Catarrhini,* consisting of the Old World monkeys.

cerebral cortex   The "grey matter" of the brain, associated primarily with thinking and language use. The expansion of the cortex is the most recent evolutionary development of the brain.

ceremonial center   Large permanent site that reveals no evidence of occupation on a day-to-day basis. Ceremonial centers are composed almost exclusively of structures used for religious purposes.

chador   Customary dress in traditional Moslem societies in which women are completely covered in a long, shapeless gown with only their eyes visible to others.

Chatelperronian culture   A western European Neanderthal culture that co-existed with Cro-Magnon culture. It featured a mixture of typical Neanderthal and Cro-Magnon tools but did not have any of the typical Cro-Magnon art and bone tools.

Chavin culture   Highland Peruvian culture dating from about 1000 to 200 B.C. It was the dominant culture in the central Andes for some 700 years.

Chellean handax   A bifacial core tool from which much (but not all) of the surface has been chipped away, characteristic of the Abbevillean (or Chellean) culture. Produced by *Homo erectus.*

chiefdom   Estate, place, or dominion of a chief. Currently the term is used also to refer to a society at a level of social integration a stage above that of tribal society, characterized by a redistributive economy and centralized political authority.

chimpanzee (*Pan troglodytes*)   Along with the gorilla and the orangutan, one of the great apes; found exclusively in Africa; one of *Homo sapiens*'s closest relatives.

choppers   Unifacial core tools, sometimes called pebble tools, found associated with *Homo habilis* in

Olduvai sequence, and also with *Homo erectus* in East Asia.

chromosomal sex   The sex identity of a person determined by the coded message in the sex chromosome contributed by each parent.

chromosome   Helical strands of complex protein molecules found in the nuclei of all animal cells, along which the genes are located. Normal human somatic cells have forty-six chromosomes.

circumcision   The removal of the foreskin of a male or the clitoral sheath of a female.

circumscription theory   Theory of the origins of the state advanced by Robert Carneiro and others that emphasizes natural and social barriers to population expansion as major factors in producing the state.

civilization   Consists of all those lifestyles incorporating at least four of the following five elements: (1) agriculture; (2) urban living; (3) a high degree of occupational specialization and differentiation; (4) social stratification; and (5) literacy.

cladistics   A taxonomic system that uses only the branching order of lineages on evolutionary trees, rather than similarity in form or function, to classify the relatedness of life forms.

clan   An exogamous unilineal kin group consisting of two or more lineages tracing descent from an unknown, perhaps legendary, founder.

class   A stratum in a hierarchically organized social system; unlike a caste, endogamy is not a requirement (though it is often favored), and individuals do have the possibility (though not the probability) of moving to a neighboring stratum.

class consciousness   An awareness by members of a social stratum of their common interests.

Classical archaeology   A field within archaeology that concerns itself with the reconstruction of the Classical civilizations, such as Greece, Rome, and Egypt.

Classic period   Spectacular and sophisticated Mesoamerican cultural period dated from A.D. 300 to 900; marked by the rise of great civilizations and the building of huge religious complexes and cities. By A.D. 500, the Classical city of Teotihuacán housed some 120,000 people.

class system   A stratification system in which the individual's position is usually determined by the economic status of the family head, but the individual may potentially rise or fall from one class to another through his or her own efforts or failings.

coevolutionary circuit   In evolutionary psychology, the central tenet of gene–culture coevolutionary theory. Here genes dictate patterns of neural structures and hormonal systems. These impose epigenetic rules, which, in turn, find expression in the form of cultural institutions of traditions. See also *epigenetic rules* and *gene–culture coevolutionary theory*.

cognatic descent   A form of descent by which the individual may choose to affiliate with either the mother's or father's kinship group. See also *ambilineal descent*.

cognatic kin   Those relatives of all generations on both sides of the family, out to some culturally defined limit.

collateral kin   Those nonlinear relatives in one's own generation on both sides of the family, out to some culturally defined limit.

colonialism   The process by which a foreign power holds political, economic, and social control over another people and establishes outposts of its own citizens among that people.

comparative linguistics (historical linguistics)   A field of linguistics that attempts to formally describe the basic elements of languages and the rules by which they are ordered into intelligible speech.

communication   The exchange of information between two or more organisms.

communist society   A society marked by public or state ownership of the means of production and distribution.

composite family   The situation in which multiple marriages are practiced or in which the residence rule requires a couple to reside with parents. See also *extended family* and *polygamy*.

consanguineal kin   A kin relationship based on biological connections only.

continental drift   Hypothesis introduced by Alfred Wegener, in the early twentieth century, of the breakup of a supercontinent, Pangaea, beginning around 225 million years ago and resulting in the present positions of the continents.

cooperative act   In evolutionary psychology, an act that benefits another organism while giving a benefit to the actor, where benefit is defined as an increase in reproductive success.

core tool   A rough, unfinished stone tool shaped by knocking off flakes, used to crush the heads of small game, to skin them, and to dissect the carcasses.

couvade   The custom, in many societies, for fathers to participate in the period of recuperation, after their wives give birth, by remaining inactive for a long period of time—often much longer than the women.

cranial index   Anatomical measure computed on skeletal material, otherwise similar to the cephalic index.

cranium   The skull, excluding the jaw.

creation myth   A religiously validated tale, unique to each culture, in which ancestors become separated from the rest of the animal kingdom, accounting for the society's biological and social development.

Cro-Magnon   A term broadly referring to the first modern humans, from 40,000 to 10,000 B.P. Specifically refers to humans living in southwestern France during the same period.

cross-cousins   Cousins related through ascending generation linking kin (often parental siblings) of the opposite sex (for example, mother's brother's children or father's sister's children).

cultural anthropology   The study of the cultural diversity of contemporary societies. It can be divided into two aspects: ethnography and ethnology.

cultural area   A part of the world in which the inhabitants share many of the elements of culture, such as related languages, similar economic systems, social systems, and ideological systems; an outmoded concept that is seldom used.

cultural assemblage   See *assemblage*.

cultural components (of a site)   All the different divisions that can be found in a site.

cultural ecology (of a group)   The ways in which a group copes with and exploits the potentials of its environment.

cultural evolution   The process of invention, diffusion, and elaboration of the behavior that is learned and taught in groups and is transmitted from generation to generation; often used to refer to the development of social complexity.

cultural relativism   A methodological orientation in anthropology, the basis of which is the idea that every culture is unique and therefore each cultural item must be understood in its own terms.

culture   The patterned behavior and mental constructs that individuals learn, are taught, and share within the context of the groups to which they belong.

cuneiform   Wedged-shaped writing developed by the Sumerian civilization.

cytoplasm   The living matter in a cell, except the nucleus.

Darwinism   The theoretical approach to biological evolution first presented by Charles Darwin and Alfred Russel Wallace in 1858. The central concept of the theory is natural selection, referring to the greater probability of survival and reproduction of those individuals of a species having adaptive characteristics for a given environment.

demographic study   Population study, primarily concerned with such aspects of population as analyses of fertility, mortality, and migration.

dental formula   The number of incisors, canines, premolars, and molars found in one upper and one lower quadrant of a jaw. The human formula, which we share with the apes and Old World monkeys, is shown below:

$$\frac{\begin{array}{cccc} I & C & P & M \\ 2 & 1 & 2 & 3 \end{array}}{\begin{array}{cccc} 2 & 1 & 2 & 3 \end{array}}$$

deoxyribonucleic acid (DNA)   The hereditary material of the cell, capable of self-replication and of coding the production of proteins carrying on metabolic functions.

descent   The practice of bestowing a specific social identity on a person as a consequence of his or her being born to a specific mother and/or father.

descent group   A corporate entity whose membership is acquired automatically as a consequence of the genealogical connections between members and their offspring.

descent rule   The principle used to trace lineal kin links from generation to generation. A child is filiated to both of its parents, but the descent rule stresses one parent's line and sex as links with others, over the other parent's line and sex.

descriptive kinship terminology   The classification of kinspeople in ego's (the individual's) own generation, with a separate kin term for each kin type.

descriptive linguistics   The careful recording, description, and structural analysis of existing languages.

diachronics   The comparative study of culture and society as they change through time in a specified geographical area.

differential fertility   A major emphasis in the modern (or synthetic) theory of evolution, which stresses the importance of an organism actually reproducing and transmitting its genes to the next generation.

diffusion   The spread of cultural traits from one people to another.

diffusionism   The belief held by some European cultural anthropologists of the nineteenth and early twentieth century that all culture began in one or a few areas of the world and then spread outward.

diluvialism   A school of thought, popular in the late eighteenth and early nineteenth centuries, claiming that Noah's flood accounted for the existence of extinct fossil forms.

diploid number   The number of chromosomes normally found in the nucleus of somatic cells. In humans, the number is forty-six.

displacement   The process by which sexual, aggressive, or other energies are diverted into other outlets. When these outlets are socially approved, the process is called sublimation.

divination   The use of magic to predict the behavior of another person or persons, or even the course of natural events.

division of labor   The universally practiced allotment of different work tasks to subgroupings of a society. Even the least complex societies allot different tasks to the two sexes and also distinguish different age groups for work purposes.

DNA   See *deoxyribonucleic acid.*

domesticants   Domesticated plants and/or animals.

dominance hierarchy   The social ranking order supposed to be present in most or all primate species.

dominant allele   The version of a gene that masks out other versions' ability to affect the phenotype of an organism when both alleles co-occur heterozygotically.

double descent   A form of descent by which an individual belongs both to a patriline and a separate matriline, but usually exercises the rights of membership in each group separately and situationally.

dowry   The wealth bestowed on a bride or a new couple by her parents.

Dryopithecus   The most common Miocene ape genus, known from Africa, Europe, and Asia, and dated from 20 to 10 million years ago. A forest-dwelling ape with about six or seven species, *Dryopithecus* was most probably ancestral to modern apes and may have been ancestral to humans.

duality of patterning   A feature of human language, it consists of sequences of sounds that are themselves meaningless (phonemes) and also of units of meaning (morphemes).

ecological niche   Features of the environment(s) that an organism inhabits, that pose problems and create opportunities for the organism's survival.

ecology   The science of the interrelationships between living organisms and their natural environments.

ecosystem A system containing both the physical environment and the organisms that inhabit it.

egalitarian society A society that makes all achieved statuses equally accessible to all its adult members.

electron spin resonance (ESR) A high-tech dating technique in which a sample of organic fossil material is ground up and exposed to a strong magnetic field. The magnetic field reacts in direct proportion to the number of trapped electrons that a sample contains: The older the fossil, the more upset the magnetic field becomes.

emics The culturally organized cognitive constructs of a people being investigated (the "folk perspective"). See *etics*.

enculturation The lifelong process of learning one's culture and its values and learning how to act within the acceptable limits of behavior in culturally defined contexts.

endogamy The custom by which members of a group marry exclusively within the group.

enthnographic analogy A method of archaeological interpretation in which the behavior of the ancient inhabitants of an archaeological site is inferred from the similarity of their artifacts to those used by living peoples.

environment All aspects of the surroundings in which an individual or group finds itself, from the geology, topography, and climate of the area to its vegetational cover and insect, bird, and animal life.

epigenetic rules According to evolutionary psychologists, biologically determined regularities in human thinking and behavior. The incest taboo and xenophobia are examples. See also *coevolutionary circuit* and *gene–culture coevolutionary theory*.

estrogens The hormones, produced in relatively large quantities by the ovaries, that are responsible for the development of female secondary sex characteristics.

estrous cycle The approximately four-week reproductive cycle of female mammals.

estrus The phase of the approximately four-week cycle in female mammals during which the female is receptive to males and encourages copulation.

ethnic group A group of people within a larger social and cultural unit who identify themselves as a culturally and historically distinct entity, separate from the rest of that society.

ethnicity The characteristic cultural, linguistic, and religious traditions that a given group of people use to establish their distinct social identity—usually within a larger social unit.

ethnobotany A scientific discipline combining anthropology and botany that studies the ways native peoples use plants, particularly as medicines.

ethnocentrism The tendency of all human groups to consider their own way of life superior to all others and to judge the lifestyles of other groups (usually negatively) in terms of their own value system.

ethnography The intensive description of individual societies, usually small, isolated, and relatively homogeneous.

ethnology The systematic comparison and analysis of ethnographic materials, usually with the specification of evolutionary stages of development of legal, political, economic, technological, kinship, religious, and other systems.

etics The perspective of Western social science in general and anthropology in particular, as applied to the study of different cultures. See *emics*.

evolution The progress of life forms and social forms from the simple to the complex. In Herbert Spencer's terms, evolution is "change from an indefinite, incoherent homogeneity to a definite, coherent heterogeneity; through continuous differentiations and integrations." In narrow biological terms, evolution is the change in gene and aliele frequencies within a breeding population over generations.

evolutionary progress The process by which a social or biological form can respond to the demands of the environment by becoming more adaptable and flexible. In order to achieve this, the form must develop to a new stage of organization that makes it more versatile in coping with problems of survival posed by the environment.

evolutionary psychology The discipline that studies the effects of genetic inheritance and biological structures on behavior. In humans, the study of how the diversity of human behavior and societies reflects the adaptation of individuals to their social and ecological environments. Behavior is seen as adaptive if it results in an individual's reproductive success compared with others. Also known as behavioral ecology and sociobiology.

excessive fertility The notion that organisms tend to reproduce more offspring than actually survive; one of the principal points in Darwin's theory of organic evolution.

exchange marriage Usually describes the situation in which two men marry each other's sister. The term is sometimes used for more complicated patterns in which groups exchange women to provide wives for the men.

exogamy   The custom by which members of a group regularly marry outside the group.

extended family   A linking together of two or more nuclear families: horizontally, through a sibling link; or vertically, through the parent–child link.

family   A married couple or other group of adult kinsfolk and their immature offspring, all or most of whom share a common dwelling and who cooperate economically.

family of orientation (family of origin)   Nuclear or elementary family (consisting of husband, wife, and offspring) into which an individual is born and is reared and in which he or she is considered a child in relation to the parents.

family of procreation   Nuclear or elementary family (consisting of husband, wife, and offspring) formed by the marriage of an individual, in which he or she is a parent.

feudalism   The sociopolitical system characterizing medieval Europe, in which all land was owned by a ruling aristocracy that extracted money, goods, and labor (often forced) from the peasant class in return for letting the peasants till the soil.

fictive kin   Extensions of the affect and social behavior usually shown toward genealogically related kin to particular persons with whom one has special relationships—godparents, blood brothers, and so on.

field study   The principal methods by which anthropologists gather information, using either the participant-observation technique to investigate social behavior, excavation techniques to retrieve archaeological data, or recording techniques to study languages.

fitness   See *reproductive success.*

flake tool   A tool made by preparing a flint core, then striking it to knock off a flake, which then can be worked further to produce the particular tool needed.

folklore   Refers to a series of genres or types of culturally standardized stories transmitted from person to person (usually orally or by example).

folk taxonomy   The cognitive categories and their hierarchical relations characteristic of a particular culture by which a specific group classifies all the objects of the universe it recognizes.

foraging society   A society with an economy based solely on the collection of wild plant foods, the hunting of animals, and/or fishing.

Foramen magnum   The "large opening" in the cranium of vertebrates through which the spinal cord passes.

formal negative sanction   Deliberately organized, social response to individuals' behavior that usually takes the form of legal punishment.

formal positive sanction   Deliberately organized, social response to individuals' behavior that takes the form of a ceremony sponsored by a central authority conveying social approval.

formal sanction   Socially organized (positive or negative) response to individuals' behavior that is applied in a very visible, patterned manner under the direct or indirect leadership of authority figures.

fossils   Remains of plant and animal forms that lived in the past and that have been preserved through a process by which they either leave impressions in stone or become stonelike themselves.

free morpheme   In language, a unit of meaning (represented by a sound sequence) that can stand alone.

functionalism   A mode of analysis, used particularly in the social sciences, that attempts to explain social and cultural phenomena in terms of the contributions they make to the maintenance of sociocultural systems.

functionalist anthropology   A perspective of anthropology associated with Bronislaw Malinowski and A. R. Radcliffe-Brown. The former emphasized the meeting of biological and psychological "needs," the latter social "needs."

gametes   The sex cells that, as sperm in males and eggs in females, combine to form a new human being as a fetus in a mother's womb.

gender identity   The attachment of significance to a self-identification as a member of a sexually defined group and the adopting of behavior culturally appropriate to that group.

gender roles   Socially learned behaviors that are typically manifested by persons of one sex and rarely by persons of the opposite sex in a particular culture.

gene   The unit of biological heredity; a segment of DNA that codes for the synthesis of a single protein.

gene–culture coevolutionary theory   An evolutionary psychological concept involving the evolutionary interactions between genes and human culture. See also *coevolutionary circuit* and *epigenetic rules.*

gene flow (admixture)   The movement of genes from one population into another as a result of interbreeding in cases where previous intergroup contact had been impossible or avoided because of geographical, social, cultural, or political barriers.

gene frequency   The relative presence of one allele in relation to another in a population's gene pool.

gene pool   The sum total of all individuals' genotypes included within a given breeding population.

generalized exchange (reciprocity)   The giving of gifts without expecting a direct return but in expectation of an "evening out" of gifts in the long run.

generative grammar (transformational grammar)   A theory about a specific language that accounts in a formal manner for all the possible (permitted) strings of elements of that language and also for the structural relationships among the elements constituting such strings.

genetic drift   The shift of gene frequencies as a consequence of genetic sampling errors that come from the migration of small subpopulations away from the parent group, or natural disasters that wipe out a large part of a population.

genetic load   The number of deleterious or maladaptive genes that exist in the gene pool of a population or entire species.

genetic plasticity   A characteristic of the human species that allows humans to develop a variety of limited physiological and anatomical responses or adjustments to a given environment.

genome   The total genetic make-up of an individual; all the genes within a typical cell.

genotype   See *genome*.

geographic center   One of three regions in the world—the Middle East, East Asia, and the Americas—in which agriculture probably was invented independently.

gift exchange   The giving of a gift from one group or individual to another with the expectation that the gift will be returned in similar form and quantity at that time or at a later date.

glottochronology   A mathematical technique for dating language change.

group selection   The differential reproduction of groups, often imagined to favor traits that are individually disadvantageous but evolve because they benefit the larger group.

gonadal sex   Refers to the form, structure, and position of the hormone-producing gonads (ovaries, located within the pelvic cavity in females, and testes, located in the scrotum in males).

gorilla (*Gorilla gorilla*)   The largest of the anthropoid (great) apes and of the living primates; found exclusively in Africa.

government   The administrative apparatus of the political organization in a society.

gracile australopithecines   One of the two lines of australopithecine development, first appearing about 5.5 million years ago; usually refers to the fossil forms *Australopithecus africanus* and *Australopithecus afarensis*.

grammar   According to Leonard Bloomfield, "the meaningful arrangements of forms in a language."

grid system   A method of retrieving and recording the positions of remains from an archaeological dig.

Habilis   See *Homo habilis*.

habitation site   A place where whole groups of people spent some time engaged in the generalized activities of day-to-day living.

hand ax   An unspecialized flint bifacial core tool, primarily characteristic of the Lower and Middle Paleolithic, made by chipping flakes off a flint nodule and using the remaining core as the tool; produced by *Homo erectus*, later by *Homo sapiens neanderthalensis*.

hand ax tradition   A technological tradition developed out of the pebble tool tradition, occurring from about 600,000 to about 60,000 years ago during the Lower and Middle Paleolithic; primarily associated with *Homo erectus*.

haploid number   The number of chromosomes normally occurring in the nucleus of a gamete (sex cell). For humans, the number is twenty-three (one-half the diploid number).

Harappan civilization   Civilization in the northwest corner of the Indian subcontinent (roughly, in present-day Pakistan), which reached its peak about 2000 B.C. Its major cities were Mohenjo-Daro and Harappa.

Hardy-Weinberg law   The principle that in large breeding populations, under conditions of random mating and where natural selection is not operating, the frequencies of genes or alleles will remain constant from one generation to the next.

hemoglobin   Complex protein molecule that carries oxygen through the bloodstream, giving blood its red color.

heredity (genetics)   The innate capacity of an individual to develop characteristics possessed by its parents and other lineal ancestors.

heritability   The proportion of the measurable variation in a given trait in a specified population estimated to result from hereditary rather than environmental factors.

heterozygote The new cell formed when the sperm and egg contain different alleles of the same gene.

heterozygous A condition in which two different alleles occur at a given locus (place) on a pair of homologous (matched pair of) chromosomes.

histomorphic metric analysis A technique for dating the maturity of fossil bones.

historical archaeology The investigation of all literate societies through archaeological means.

historical linguistics The study of the evolutionary tree of language. Historical linguistics reconstructs extinct "proto" forms by systematically comparing surviving language branches.

holism The viewing of the whole context of human behavior—a fundamental theme of anthropology.

Holocene The most recent geologic epoch; it began about 10,000 years ago.

homeostasis The process by which a system maintains its equilibrium using feedback mechanisms to accommodate inputs from its environment.

home range (of a primate group) An area through which a primate group habitually moves in the course of its daily activities.

hominid The common name for those primates referred to in the taxonomic family *Hominidae* (modern humans and their nearest evolutionary predecessors).

Hominidae Human beings, one of *Hominoidea*. See also *hominid.*

Hominoidea One of two superfamilies of *Catarrhini*, consisting of apes and human beings.

Homo erectus Middle Pleistocene hominid form that is the direct ancestor of *Homo sapiens*. It appeared about 1.9 million years ago and flourished until about 200,000 to 250,000 years ago. *H. erectus* was at least five feet tall, with a body and limbs that were within the range of variation of modern humans, and had a cranial capacity ranging from 900 to 1200 cubic centimeters.

Homo habilis ("handy man") A fossil form, dating from more than 2 million years ago, whose evolutionary status is disputed. Some physical anthropologists regard it as early *Homo*—the first members of our own genus. Others regard it as an advanced form of gracile australopithecine. This is the earliest hominid with which stone tools have been found in unambiguous relationship.

Homo sapiens neanderthalensis The first subspecies of *Homo sapiens*, appearing about 300,000 years ago and becoming extinct about 35,000 B.P. Commonly known as Neanderthals.

Homo sapiens sapiens The second subspecies of *Homo sapiens*, including all contemporary humans, appearing about 60,000 years ago. The first human subspecies was the now extinct *Homo sapiens neanderthalensis.*

homologous A matched pair; usually refers to chromosomes, one from each parent, having the same genes in the same order.

homozygote The new cell formed when the sperm and egg contain the same allele of a particular gene.

homozygous A condition in which identical genes occur at a certain locus on homologous (matched pair) chromosomes.

horizontal extended family A household and cooperating unit of two siblings and their respective spouses and children.

hormonal sex The type of hormone mix (estrogens or androgens) produced by the gonads.

horticulture The preparation of land for planting and the tending of crops using only the hoe or digging stick; characterized especially by the absence of use of the plow.

hunting and gathering society A society that subsists on the collection of plants and animals existing in the natural environment. See *foraging society.*

hybrid vigor The phenomenon that occurs when a new generation, whose parent groups were from previously separated breeding populations, is generally healthier and larger than either of the parent populations.

hydraulic theory A theory of the origins of the state advanced by Karl Wittfogel that traces the rise of the state to the organization, construction, and maintenance of vast dam and irrigation projects.

hypoplasia A dental condition caused by malnutrition in which the teeth do not develop fully. Many Neanderthals suffered from this health problem.

hypothesis A tentative assumption, which must be tested, about the relationship(s) between specific events or phenomena.

ideology A belief system linked to and legitimating the political and economic interests of the group that subscribes to it.

imperialism The expansionist policy of nation-states by which one state assumes political and economic control over another.

Inca Empire Empire of the Late Horizon period of Peruvian prehistory, dated about A.D. 1438 to 1540. The ninth and tenth Incas (kings) seized control of a

3,000-mile-long empire stretching from Quito to central Chile. The Incas had a highly sophisticated political organization.

incest Usually refers to sexual relations between father and daughter, mother and son, or brother and sister. In some societies the definition is extended to include larger numbers of consanguineal relatives, especially if the society is organized along the principle of lineages and clans.

incest taboo The nearly universal prohibition against sexual intercourse between family members, with the limits of incest varying from culture to culture on the basis of the society's kinship system and forms of social organization.

independent invention The process in which two or more cultures develop similar elements without the benefit of cultural exchange or even contact.

independent assortment See *Law of Independent Assortment.*

Indus Valley civilization See *Harappan civilization.*

industrialism The form of production characterizing post-agricultural societies, in which goods are produced by mechanical means using machines and labor organized into narrowly defined task groups that engage in repetitive, physically simplified, and highly segmented work.

industrialization The process involving the growth of manufacturing industries in hitherto predominantly agrarian, pastoral, or foraging societies.

industrial society A society with a high degree of economic development that largely utilizes mechanization and highly segmented labor specialization for the production of its goods and services.

infanticide The killing of a baby soon after birth.

informal sanction A social response to an individual's behavior that is enacted individually by group members, with minimal organization by social authority.

informant A member of a society who establishes a working relationship with a fieldworker, providing him or her with information regarding that society.

instrumental belief system An organized set of ideas about phenomena necessary for survival and for performing day-to-day (functional) tasks.

integration, cultural The condition of harmonious pattern maintenance potentially characterizing cultural systems.

interglacial Refers to periods during which glaciers retreat and a general warning trend occurs in the climate.

internalized controls An individual's beliefs and values that mirror the beliefs and values of the group culture and that induce the individual to behave in ways appropriate to that culture.

invention The development of new ideas, techniques, resources, aptitudes, or applications that are adopted by a society and become part of its cultural repertoire.

involution Evolution through which a biological or social form adapts to its environment by becoming more and more specialized and efficient in exploiting the resources of that environment. Sometimes called specific evolution.

irrigation The artificial use of water for agriculture by means of human technology when naturally available water (rainfall or seasonal flooding) is insufficient or potentially too destructive to sustain desired crop production.

ischial callosities Bare, calloused areas of skin on the hindquarters, frequently found in terrestrial or semiterrestrial Old World monkeys.

kill site A place where prehistoric people killed and butchered animals.

kibbutz A collective settlement in Israel with strong emphasis on communal life and values; one of the forms of cooperative agricultural villages in Israel that is collective (to a greater or less degree) in the organization of work, ownership of all resources, child rearing and living arrangements.

kin category A terminologically distinguished aggregate of persons with whom one might or might not have frequent interaction, but who are conceived to stand in a clearly understood genealogical relationship to the user of the term.

kindred The network of relatives linked genealogically to a person in a culturally specified manner. Each such network is different for each person, with the exception of siblings.

kinesics The study of body movement as a mode of communication.

kin group A terminologically distinguished aggregate of persons with whom one stands in specified genealogical relationships and with whom one interacts frequently in terms of these relationships.

kin selection An evolutionary pychological theory that states that it is in an individual's genetic interests to behave altruistically when the recipient of the altruistic act is closely related. Specifically, an altruistic gene enjoys a net benefit when the benefit to the recipient, (B), multiplied by the degree of relatedness to the recipient, (r), is greater than the cost suffered by the altruist, (C); $Br > C$.

kinship The social phenomenon in which people establish connections with each other on the basis of genealogical linkages in culturally specified ways.

kinship terminology The set of contrasting terms that designate the culturally significant genealogical linkages between people and the social networks these perceived relationships generate.

knuckle walking The characteristic mode of terrestrial locomotion of orangutans, chimpanzees, and gorillas. These apes walk with a partially erect body posture, with the forward weight of the body supported by the arms and the hands touching the ground, fingers curled into the palm so that the back of the fingers bear the weight.

language The characteristic mode of communication practiced by all human beings, consisting of sounds (phonemes) that are strung together into a virtually limitless number of meaningful sequences.

Law of Independent Assortment Gregor Mendel's second principle. It refers to the fact that the particular assortment of alleles found in a given gamete is independently determined.

Law of Segregation Gregor Mendel's first principle. It states that, in reproduction, a set of paired alleles separate (segregate) in a process called *meiosis* into different sex cells (gametes); thus, either allele can be passed on to offspring.

legal sanction A formal, socially enacted negative response to an individual's or group's noncompliance with the law, or a legal decision meant to compel that compliance.

lemur A diurnal, semiterrestrial prosimian having stereoscopic vision. Lemurs are found only on the island of Madagascar.

levirate The practice by which a man is expected to marry the wife or wives of a deceased brother.

lineage A unilineal, consanguineal kin group tracing descent from a known ancestor and found in two forms: patrilineage, in which the relationship is traced through males; and matrilineage, in which the relationship is traced through females.

linguistic anthropology A subfield of anthropology entailing the study of language forms across space and time and their relation to culture and social behavior.

linguistics The study of language, consisting of two large subcategories: (1) historical linguistics, which is concerned with the evolution of languages and language groups through time, and with reconstructing extinct proto-languages from which historically known languages differentiate; and (2) descriptive linguistics, which focuses on recording, transcribing, and analyzing the structures of languages distributed across the world today.

little tradition The localized cultures of rural villagers living in the broader cultural and social contexts of mass industrial society, with its "great tradition." The term is rarely used because it is very ethnocentric.

locus The position of a gene on a chromosome.

"Lucy" See *Australopithecus afarensis.*

Magdalenian culture The most advanced of the Upper Paleolithic cultures, dating from 17,000 to 10,000 B.P. Confined to France and northern Spain, the Magdalenian culture marks the climax of the Upper Paleolithic in Europe. The Magdalenians produced a highly diversified tool kit but are most famous for their spectacular cave art.

magic The usually ritualized behavior that is intended to control, or at least to influence significantly, the basic processes of the universe without recourse to perceptibly instrumental acts.

mana A diffuse force or energy-like entity that suffuses through various objects, places, and even people; recognized in various parts of the world but especially well known in Polynesia and Melanesia.

market economy A system in which goods and services are exchanged, and their relative values established, in marketplaces, generally via the use of money as a standard of value.

market exchange The process of distributing goods and services and establishing their relative value (frequently in terms of money) at centers of trade known as markets.

marriage A difficult term to define, given enormous cross-cultural variety. However, all societies recognize (publicly) connections between two or more persons that confer social legitimacy to their children—which is the basic minimum of marriage.

matriarchy A form of family organization characterized by the domination of domestic life or society as a whole by women.

matricentric family A family that is headed by a woman, often serially married to a number of men.

matrifocal family A family form in which the mother, sometimes assisted by other women of the household, is the most influential socializing agent and is central in terms of cultural values, family finances, patterns of decision-making and affective ties.

matrilateral prescriptive cross-cousin marriage The rule by which a man must choose his spouse from among his mother's brother's daughters or their social equivalents.

matrilineage   A kinship group made up of people all of whom trace relationships to one another through female links and are descended from a known female ancestor.

matrilineal descent   The principle by which lineal kin links are traced exclusively through females—that is, a child is descended from his or her mother, mother's mother, and so on.

matrilocal residence   The practice by which a newlywed couple moves into residence with, or in the locale of, the bride's mother's kin group.

Maya civilization   The best-known Classic Mesoamerican civilization, located on the Yucatan peninsula and dated from before A.D. 300 to 900. Less intensely urban than Teotihuacán, it is marked by the building of huge ceremonial centers, such as Tikal in Guatemala.

melanin   The brown, granular sustance found in the skin, hair, and some internal organs that gives a brownish tint or color to the areas in which it is found.

Mesolithic (Middle Stone Age)   A term of convenience used by archaeologists to designate immediately preagricultural societies in the Old World—13,000 to 6000 B.P. A frequently used diagnostic characteristic is the presence of microliths, small blades often set into bone or wood handles to make sickles for the harvesting of wild grains. In Europe, this period also featured the invention of the bow and arrow as a response to the emergence of forests with the shift from Pleistocene to Holocene climate.

messianic movement   A revitalization movement based on the belief that a person or god will arrive to cure the evils of the world.

metallurgy   The techniques of separating metals from their ores and working them into finished products.

microlith   A small stone tool made from bladettes, or fragments of blades, associated with the Mesolithic period, approximately 13,000 to 6000 B.P.

migration   A permanent or semipermanent change of residence by a group, usually involving movement over large distances.

millenarianism   A revivalistic movement reacting to the perceived disparity between ideal and real social conditions, with the belief that this gap is about to close, usually with disastrous consequences for nonbelievers.

minority   A group that is distinguished from the larger society of which it is a part by particular traits, such as language, national origin, religion, values, or customs. The term may also be used to refer to groups that, though a plurality in numbers, are nevertheless discriminated against socially, politically, and/or economically by the society's dominant patterns (for example, women in the United States).

mitochondrial genes   Genes used to calculate the genetic distance between populations; unlike genes in the cell nucleus, mitochondrial genes are passed to offspring almost exclusively by the mother.

modernization   The process in which traditional social units (such as tribes or villages) are integrated into larger, over-arching units (such as nation–states), while at the same time being split into units of production (such as factories) and consumption (such as nuclear families) that are characteristic of industrial societies.

moiety   The name used to refer to a group that is one of two units of a larger group (for example, each clan of a society composed of two clans is a moiety). Both groups are usually, but not always, based on unilineal descent and are exogamous.

money   A medium of exchange characteristic of market economies that is easily replaceable and/or exchangeable for another of like kind, portable, divisible into combinable units, and accepted by all participants in the market system in which it is used.

monkey   A small or medium-sized quadrupedal primate. There are two groups of monkeys: Old World and New World. Only New World monkeys have prehensile tails. Most monkeys are arboreal, have long tails, and are vegetarians.

monogamy   The marriage rule that permits both the man and the woman only one spouse at a time.

monogenesis   The theory that the human species had only one origin.

mores   The important norms of a society. They have compelling social and emotional commitment and are rationalized by the society's belief system.

morpheme   The smallest unit of meaning in a language.

morphological sex   The physical appearance of a person's genitals and secondary sex characteristics.

multilinear evolution   The study of cultural evolution recognizing regional variation and divergent evolutionary sequences.

mutation   A rapid and permanent change in genetic material.

myths   Sacred tales or narratives that usually deal with the issue of origins (of nature, society, humans) and/or transformations.

nasal index   The ratio calculated from the width and height measurements of the nose; it was used by early physical anthropoligists to classify human "races."

national character   Personality characteristics shared by the inhabitants of a nation—no longer a scientifically valued concept.

nativism   A revitalization movement initiated by members of a society to eliminate foreign persons, customs, and objects in order to improve their own way of life.

natural selection   The process through which certain environmentally adaptive biological features are perpetuated at the expense of less adaptive features.

Neanderthal (*Homo sapiens neanderthalensis*)   A subspecies of *Homo sapiens* living from approximately 300,000 years ago to about 35,000 years ago and thought to have been descended from *Homo erectus*. See also *Homo sapiens neanderthalensis*.

negative reciprocity   A form of gift exchange in which the giver attempts to get the better of the exchange.

negative sanction   A punitive social response to an individual's behavior that does not meet with group approval.

neoclassicism   A new school of geneticists who propose that most of the molecular variations in natural populations are selectively neutral.

Neolithic (New Stone Age)   A stage in cultural evolution marked by the appearance of ground stone tools and frequently by the domestication of plants and animals, starting about 10,000 years ago.

neolocal residence   The practice by which a newly-wed couple is expected to establish its own independent residence, living with neither the husband's nor the wife's parents or relatives.

neontology   A division of physical anthropology that deals with the comparative study of living primates, with special emphasis on the biological features of human beings.

network study   An analysis of interpersonal relations, usually focused on a particular individual (ego), that examines the character of interactions between ego and other individuals.

New Archaeology   Primarily an American development, the New Archaeology attempts to develop archaeological theory by using rigorous, statistical analysis of archaeological data within a deductive, logical framework.

nomadism   A characteristic trait associated with a number of ecologically adaptive systems, in which continuing residential mobility is necessary for the subsistence of the group, with a resulting lack of permanent abode.

nonverbal communication   The transmission of communication between organisms without the use of speech. Modes of communication include gesturing (with voice and body) and manipulating space between the communicating organisms.

norm   A standard shared by members of a social group to which members are expected to conform.

nuclear family   A small social unit consisting of a husband and wife and their children, typical of a monogamous marriage with neolocal residence; also forms a functioning subunit of extended and otherwise composite families.

oasis hypothesis   A theory of plant and animal domestication advanced by V. Gordon Childe, in which he suggests that in the arid Pleistocene environment, humans and animals congregated around water resources, where they developed patterns of mutual dependence.

Oldowan culture   The oldest recognized Lower Paleolithic assemblage, whose type site is Olduvai Gorge (Tanzania), dating from about 2.2 to 1 million years ago and comprising unifacial core (pebble) tools and crude flakes

Olmec culture   The first civilization in Mesoamerica and the base from which all subsequent Mesoamerican civilizations evolved. Located in the Yucatan peninsula, it is dated from 1500 to 400 B.C. Olmec art first appeared in 1250 B.C., and the civilization flourished at its height from 1150 to 900 B.C.

order   A taxonomic rank. *Homo sapiens* belongs to the order of *Primates*.

orangutan (*Pongo pygmaeus*)   A tree-dwelling great ape found only in Borneo and Sumatra. It has four prehensile limbs capable of seizing and grasping, and very long arms. The orangutan is almost completely arboreal.

ovaries   The female gonads, located within the pelvic cavity.

Paleolithic (Old Stone Age)   A stage in cultural evolution, dated from about 2.5 million to 10,000 years ago, during which chipped stone tools, but not ground stone tools, were made.

paleontology, human   A subdivision of physical anthropology that deals with the study of human and hominid fossil remains.

paradigm, scientific   A concept introduced by Thomas Kuhn (1962): the orthodox doctrine of a science, its training exercises, and a set of beliefs with which new scientists are enculturated.

paralinguistics The study of the nonphonemic phonetic overlays onto the phonological system used to convey special (connotative) meanings.

parallel cousins Cousins linked by ascending generation relatives (often parental siblings) of the same generation and sex (for example, mother's sister's or father's brother's children).

participant observation A major anthropological field research method formally conceptualized by Bronislaw Malinowski, in which the ethnographer is immersed in the day-to-day activities of the community being studied.

pastoralism A type of ecological adaptation found in geographically marginal areas of Europe, Asia, and Africa where natural resources cannot support agriculture, and hence the people are partially or entirely devoted to the care and herding of animals.

patriarchy A form of family organization in which power and authority are vested in the males and in which descent is usually in the male line, with the children being members of the father's lineage, clan, or tribe.

patrilateral parallel cousin marriage A marriage between brothers' children.

patrilineage An exogamous descent group based on genealogical links between males that are traceable back to a known male ancestor.

patrilineal descent The principle by which lineal kin links are traced through males (that is, a child is descended from his or her father, father's father, and so forth).

patrilocal residence A postmarital residence rule by which a newlywed couple takes up permanent residence with or near the groom's father's extended kin group.

peasants Rural, agricultural members of civilizations who maintain a very traditional lifestyle (often rejecting urban values) while tied into the wider economic system of the whole society through markets, where they sell their produce and purchase goods.

pebble tool The first manufactured stone tools consisting of somewhat larger than fist-sized pieces of flint that have had some six or seven flakes knocked off them, unifacial core tools; associated with *Homo habilis* in Africa and also *Homo erectus* in East Asia.

persistence hunting A unique hunting ability of humans in which prey is hunted over vast distances, often for days at a time.

pharynx The throat above the larynx.

phenotype The total structure, physiology, and behavior of an individual.

phoneme In language, the basic unit of recognized but meaningless sound.

phylogeny The tracing of the history of the evolutionary development of a life form.

phonetic laws Patterns of change in the sounds used by languages as they evolved, expressed as rules or principles of change.

phonological system The articulatory phonetics and the phonemic system of a language.

phonology The combined study of phonetics and phonemics.

phratry A unilineal descent group composed of at least two clans claiming to be related by kinship. When there are only two such clans, each is called a moiety.

physical anthropology The study of human beings as biological organisms across space and time. Physical anthropology is divided into two areas: (1) paleontology, which is the study of the fossil evidence of primate evolution, and (2) neontology, which is the comparative biology of living primates.

pigmentation Skin color.

Piltdown man A human skull and ape jaw "discovered" in England in 1911 and thought by some to be a "missing link" in human evolution. It was exposed as a fraud in 1953.

Pithecanthropus erectus See *Homo erectus*.

plate tectonics The branch of geology that studies the movement of the continental plates over time; popularly known as "continental drift."

Platyrrhini One of two infraorders of the primate suborder *Anthropoidea*, consisting of all the New World monkeys; characterized by vertical nostrils and, often, prehensile tails.

plow An agricultural tool generally requiring animal power, used to loosen, aerate, and invert the soil so as to cover weeds, expose a large area of soil to weathering and prepare a seed bed. Its presence differentiates agriculture from horticulture (limited to the use of digging sticks and hoes).

pluralism A characteristic of many complex societies, marked by the presence of several or numerous subgroups that coexist within a common political and economic system.

political anthropology The field of cultural anthropology that deals with that aspect of social behavior known as political organization and that concerns itself specifically with the organization and management of the public affairs of a society, especially pertaining to the sources and uses of power.

political economy The interpretation of the economy and the system of power and authority in a society, most frequently studied from a conflict theory perspective.

political organization That subsystem of social organization that specifically relates to the individuals or groups who are responsible for managing affairs of public policy or who control the appointment or action of those individuals or groups.

polyandrous family A family in which a woman has more than one husband at the same time.

polyandry A relatively rare form of multiple marriage in which a woman has more than one husband at the same time.

polygamy Any form of marriage in which more than two persons are married to one another.

polygenesis The theory that the human species had more than one origin.

polygynous family A family in which a man has more than one wife at the same time.

polygyny The most common form of multiple marriage, allowing a man to have more than one wife at the same time.

pongid A common term for the members of the *Pongidae* family, including the six modern apes: the orangutan, gorilla, chimpanzee, bonobo, gibbon, and siamang.

positive sanctions A social response to an individual's behavior that takes the form of a reward.

positivism An approach to knowledge embodying empiricism and the scientific method, with its built-in tests for truth.

possession A trance state based on the culturally supported belief that curative or malevolent spirits may displace people's personalities and use their bodies as vehicles for temporary residence.

potassium-argon (KAr) dating An absolute dating technique that uses the rate of decay of radioactive potassium (K^{40}) into argon (Ar^{40}) as its basis. The half-life of K^{40} is 1.3 billion ± 40 million years.

potlatch Ceremonial feasting accompanied by the giving of gifts to guests according to rank; practiced by the Native Americans of the Northwest Coast of the United States and Canada; a form of economic redistribution.

power, political The ability of leaders to compel compliance with their orders.

prehistoric archaeology The use of archaeology to reconstruct prehistoric times.

Primates The order of mammals that includes humans, apes, Old and New World monkeys, and prosimians.

primatologist One who studies primates.

profane All that which is ordinary, or not sacred.

prosimii (prosimian) The most primitive suborder of *Primates*, including lemurs, lorises, tarsiers, and similar creatures.

Protestant ethic A set of values, originally associated with the rise and spread of Protestantism in Europe, that celebrates the virtues of self-discipline, hard work, initiative, acquisitiveness, and thrift.

proxemics The study of the manipulation and meaning of space.

psychological sex The self-image that a person holds about his or her own sexual identity.

purdah Custom in traditional Moslem societies in which women are secluded and remain unseen to all males except close relatives.

quadrupedalism Locomotion by the use of four feet.

quarry site In archaeology, a place where prehistoric people dug for flint, tin, copper, and other materials.

race A folk category of the English language that refers to discrete groups of human beings who are uniformly separated from one another on the basis of arbitrarily selected phenotypic traits.

racial minorities Groups that are categorically separated from the majority members of the larger society on the basis of arbitrarily selected phenotypic traits.

radiocarbon (C^{14}) dating An absolute physical-chemical dating technique that uses the rate of decay of radioactive carbon (C^{14}) which is present in all plants, to stable carbon (C^{12}) as its basis. The half-life of C^{14} is 5568 ± 30 years. The technique is useful for dating remains from 5,000 to 50,000 years old, although a new technique may extend its range to about 100,000 years while reducing the margin of error.

Ramapithecus A late Miocene hominoid, found in India, Kenya, and Europe, that lived from 14 to 9 million years ago. Until recently, *Ramapithecus* was accepted by some scholars as the first true hominid, though recent discoveries have placed this form in the evolutionary lineage of the orangutan.

random (genetic) drift A shift in gene and allele frequencies in a population due to sampling "error." When a small breeding population splits off from a larger one, its collection of genes may not adequately represent the allele frequencies of the larger population. These differences compound over succeeding generations, until the two populations are quite distinct. Along with mutation, gene flow, and natural selection, random drift is one of the mechanisms of organic evolution.

range (of a primate)   See *home range.*

rank society   A society in which there is equal access to land and other economic resources but unequal access to positions of prestige.

recessive allele   A version of a gene that is not able to influence an organisms phenotype when it is homologous with another version of the gene. See also *dominant allele.*

reciprocal altruism   In evolutionary psychology, the exchange of altruistic acts between two individuals to the advantage of both.

reciprocity   The giving and receiving of gifts, usually consisting of material items, favors, or specific forms of labor.

redistribution   The enforced giving of surplus goods to a centralized authority, who then distributes them back to members of the society according to social conventions and the authority's own predilections.

reference group   The aggregate of people that an individual uses for comparison when assessing or evaluating his or her own and others' behavior.

reformulation   The modification of a new cultural trait, or cluster of traits, by a group to fit its own traditions and circumstances; part of the process of culture trait diffusion.

relative dating   In archaeology, the determination of the sequence of events; a relative date specifies that one thing is older or younger than another.

religious beliefs   The sets of convictions held by members of a society with regard to the supernatural, transcendental, and fundamental issues, such as life's meaning.

reproductive success   In evolutionary biology, the total number of offspring of an individual surviving to a given age; also called *fitness.*

revitalization movements   Religious movements of a reformative nature that arise among exploited or disorganized groups (often after socioeconomic or political traumas) and that attempt to reinject culturally salient meaning into people's lives—often through a radical assault on existing conditions and/or institutions.

revivalistic movement   A revitalization movement espousing the reintroduction of previous religious (or political) forms.

ribonucleic add (RNA)   Any of the nucleic acids containing ribose. One type—messenger RNA—carries the information encoded in the DNA to the site of protein synthesis located outside the nucleus.

rifting   The sliding of the continental masses against one another's edges.

rites of passage   Rituals marking changes in status or social position undergone as a person passes through the culturally recognized life phases of his or her society.

rites of solidarity   Various rituals, usually but not necessarily religious, which in addition to their intended purposes also develop and maintain feelings of group cohesiveness among participants.

rituals   Culturally prescribed, consistently repeated, patterned sequences of (group) behavior.

RNA   See *ribonucleic acid.*

robust australopithecines   One of two lines of australopithecines, appearing some 3.5 million years ago and surviving until approximately 1 million years ago or even later; thought to have embodied two successive species, *Australopithecus robustus* and *Australopithecus boisei.*

role conflict   The emotional stress experienced by a person whose socially expected behaviors are irreconcilable. This happens when a person occupies diverse social positions (statuses) yet in a given situation must act in terms of two or more of them (for instance, a U.S. senator who is also a stockholder asked to vote on legislation that would affect the corporation in which he or she owns shares).

roles   The expected (normative) behaviors that every society associates with each of its statuses.

Rosetta stone   A tablet containing three parallel texts written in Egyptian hieroglyphics, demotic script, and Greek. In 1822, Jean François Champollion used the stone to decode the hieroglyphics.

sacred   A category of things, actions, and so on set apart as holy and entitled to reverence.

salvage archaeology   The attempt to preserve archaeological remains from destruction by large-scale projects of industrial society (such as a dam or highway construction).

sanctions, social   The responses a social group makes as a consequence of an individual's behavior.

savanna   Tropical or subtropical grasslands.

scapulimancy   The use of charred cracks in the burned scapula (shoulder bone) of an animal to divine the future.

scientific racism   Research strategies based on the assumption that groups' biological features underlie significant social and cultural differences. Not surprisingly, this kind of research always manages to find "significant" differences between "races."

scraper   An Upper Paleolithic stone tool made from blades with a retouched end; used for carving wood, bone, and antlers to make spear points.

secondary sex characteristics   Physiological changes developing at and after puberty, such as body hair, breasts, and voice changes.

Segregation, Law of   See *Law of Segregation.*

self-concept   A person's perceptions and evaluative feelings about his or her continuity, boundaries, and qualities.

semantics   The relationship between signs and what they represent; the study of semantics is essentially the study of meaning.

semiotic   The study of signs and sign-using behavior in general.

serial marriage   The process by which a man or woman marries and divorces a series of partners in succession.

seriation   A technique of relative dating in which the relative dates of artifacts may be reconstructed by arranging them so that variations in form or style can be inferred to represent a developmental sequence and, hence, chronological order.

sexual dimorphism   A difference between the males and females of a species that is not related directly to reproductive functions.

sexual identity   The expectations about male and female behavior that affect the individual's learning ability, choice of work, and feelings about herself or himself.

shamanism   The process by which certain gifted persons establish (usually with the aid of a trance or an ecstatic state of excitement) direct communication with the supernatural for the benefit of their social group.

sickle cell   A red blood cell that has lost its normal circular shape and has collapsed into a half-moon shape.

sickle-cell anemia   An often fatal disease caused by a chemical mutation that changes one of the amino adds in normal hemoglobin. The mutant sickle-cell gene occurs in unusually high frequency in parts of Africa and the Arabian peninsula. Individuals heterozygotic for the sickle-cell gene have a special resistance to malaria; homozygots suffer severe anemia.

sign   An object, gesture, or sound that represents something else.

silent trade   A form of exchange with no face-to-face interaction between the parties involved, often practiced where potential for conflict between groups exists. Traded items are simply left at agreed-upon places by, both parties.

site   A concentration of the remains of (human) activities or artifacts.

Sivapithecus   A late Miocene hominoid found in India and Kenya, closely related to *Ramapithecus,* and thought by some scholars to be the first true hominid.

slash-and-burn agriculture   A shifting form of cultivation with recurrent, alternate clearing and burning of vegetation and planting in the burnt fields; also called swidden (or shifting) cultivation.

slavery   An extreme form of coerced work organization wherein the rights to people and their labor are owned by others, and in which both subordinate and superordinate positions are inherited.

social class   A stratum in a social hierarchy based on differential group access to means of production and control over distribution; usually but not necessarily endogamous, with little—but some—openness.

social control   Practices that induce members of a society to conform to the expected behavior patterns of their culture; also, mechanisms through which a society's rulers ensure the masses' conformity with the rules of the social order.

Social Darwinism   The doctrine that makes use, or misuse, of Charles Darwin's biological evolutionary principles to explain or justify existing forms of social organization. The theory was actually formulated by Herbert Spencer.

social identity   The socially recognized characteristics of a person that indicate his or her social position(s).

socialism   A socioeconomic form characterized by public ownership of all strategic resources and major distribution mechanisms. It features centralized economic and social planning and it is conceived by some Marxists to be a transitional stage to communism, in which centralized bureaucracies will "wither away."

social mobility   The upward or downward movement of individuals or groups of individuals in a society consisting of social hierarchies and unequal distribution of such social resources as occupations, education, power, and wealth.

social organization   The ordering of social relations within social groups in which individuals' choices and decisions are visibly patterned.

social stratification An arrangement of statuses or groups within a society into a pattern of socially superior and inferior ranks (or groups) that are open to a greater or lesser degree.

social structure The total pattern of eco-centered relationships (such as kinship systems and friendship networks) that occur within a society.

societal structure The total aggregate of discrete, bounded subgroups that compose a society.

society A socially bounded, spacially contiguous aggregation of people who participate in a number of overarching institutions and share to some degree an identifiable culture, and that contains within its boundaries some means of production and units of consumption—with relative stability across generations.

Sociobiology See *evolutionary psychology.*

sociogram The full description, in the form of a catalog, of all the social behaviors of a species.

sociolinguistics The study of the societal correlates to variations in the patterning of linguistic behavior.

somatic cells The cells that make up all the bodily parts and that are constantly dying and being replaced; does not include central nervous system cells or sex cells.

sorcery A negatively connotative term to refer to magic—the use of supernatural agencies—to further the practitioner's goals.

sororal polygyny A marriage involving two or more sisters as wives of the same man at one time.

sororate The practice by which women are expected to marry the husband of a deceased sister.

spacing mechanisms The behaviors between neighboring groups of animals that help to maintain them at some distance from each other.

speciation The process of gradual separation of one interbreeding population into two or more separate, noninterbreeding populations.

species The largest naturally occurring population that interbreeds (or is capable of interbreeding) and produces fully fertile offspring.

speech community An aggregate of persons who share a set of conventions about how verbal communication is to take place.

state A set of institutions in a stratified society that operates to maintain the status quo by: (1) organizing the provision of needed services; (2) planning the production and use of needed resources; (3) quelling internal discontent by buying off or subduing rebellious minorities or subordinate classes; and (4) organizing, administering, and financing the protection of the society against hostile external forces.

statuses The interrelated positions in a society, with each position carrying certain expectations of behavior (roles) with respect to those persons occupying the same and/or interrelated positions.

stereoscopic vision Overlapping fields of vision resulting when the eyes are located toward the front of the skull, improving depth perception.

stereotype The attribution of certain presumed, invariable personality or behavioral characteristics to all members of a particular group, most notably those groups defined by religion, sex, nationality, or ethnicity.

stimulus diffusion The transfer of a basic idea from one culture to another, in which the idea is reinterpreted and modified to the extent that it becomes unique to the receiving group.

strategic resources The category of resources vital to a group's survival.

stratified society A society in which there is a structured inequality of access among groups not only to power and prestige, but also to the strategic resources that sustain life.

stratigraphy The arrangement of archaeological deposits in superimposed layers, or strata.

structural-functionalism An anthropological school of thought emphasizing the mutual interdependence of all parts and subgroups of a society, interpreting relationships between such groupings as contributing to the ongoing pattern maintenance of the society.

structuralism An analytical approach based on the assumption that observed phenomena are specific instances of the underlying, generalized principles of relationship or structure.

structural linguistics The study of the internal structures of the world's languages.

subculture The culture of a subgroup of a society that shares its fundamental values, but that also has its own distinctive folkways, mores, values, and world view.

subsistence strategies Technological skills, tools, and behaviors that a society uses to meet its subsistence needs.

substantivists A group of economic anthropologists who deny that economic models derived from developed market economies can be applied universally to all economic systems.

supernatural   Refers to all things that are believed to exist but are beyond verifiability through the human senses.

supernatural beliefs   Organized systems of thoughts, ideas, and concerns regarding entities whose existence is not verifiable through the human senses.

superposition   In archaeology, the perception that, under normal circumstances, a stratum found lying under another stratum is relatively older than the stratum under which it is lying.

supraorbital ridge   The torus, or bony bar, surmounting orbital (eyeball) cavities; it is large and continuous in apes and quite small and divided in *Homo sapiens.*

swidden farming   Shifting cultivation, with recurrent, alternate clearing and burning of vegetation and planting in the burnt fields. Fallow periods for each plot last many times longer than the periods of cultivation. See also *slash-and-burn agriculture.*

symbol   A sign that represents some other (complex) thing with which it has no intrinsic connection.

synchronics   The comparison of biological, linguistic, archaeological, and ethnographic data across a wide geographical area at one arbitrarily selected point in time.

syntax   The relationships between signs. The study of syntax is the study of the rules of sequence and combination of signs.

synthetic theory (of evolution)   A modern theory of evolution based on the Darwinian theory but emphasizing differential fertility (as opposed to differential mortality).

systematics   The study of the kinds and diversity of objects and of the types of relationships existing among them.

taboo (tabu)   The belief in negative supernatural consequences that attach to the performance of certain acts or the violation of certain objects or places.

tabula rasa   The concept proposed by John Locke (1690) that people are born with blank minds and that they learn everything they come to know through their life experiences, socialization, and enculturation into groups.

taxonomy   The science of constructing classifications of organisms.

technology   A society's use of knowledge, skills, implements, and sources of power in order (1) to exploit and partially control the natural environment and (2) to engage in production and reproduction of its goods and services.

tell   A stratified mound created entirely through long periods of successive occupation by a series of groups.

tenancy   A form of forced agricultural labor under which farmers plant their crops in the land owner's fields but owe the land owner a certain proportion of the crops they harvest.

territoriality   Defense by an animal of a geographically delimited area.

testes   The male gonads, suspended outside the body cavity in the scrotum.

test pit   In archaeology, a pit that is dug at carefully selected positions in a site to reveal information about buried artifacts and stratigraphy.

thalassemia   Like sickle-cell anemia, a blood anemia carried by populations that are or have been in malaria-infested areas of the world—especially around the Mediterranean, Asia Minor, and southern Asia. Like sickle-cell anemia, it also represents an example of balanced polymorphism.

Third World   Originally referred to non-Western peoples of the colonized societies of Asia, Africa, and Latin America. More recently, the term has also been associated with national minorities within the United States and Canada, such as Chicanos, African Americans, Native Americans, Puerto Ricans, and Asian Americans.

Three-Age System   The concept delineated by Christian Thomsen (1836) in which he identified three successive stages in cultural evolution: the Stone Age, the Bronze Age, and the Iron Age.

Toltec civilization   Postclassic Mesoamerican civilization, dated from A.D. 900 to about 1300. The Toltecs perpetuated many of the themes of Classic culture. Their capital of Tula was sacked around 1160, and they were eventually replaced by the Aztecs.

totemism   The symbolic association of plants, animals, and objects with groups of people, especially the association of exogamous clans with animal species as their emblems and/or mythological ancestors.

trade   The exchange of goods between people.

traditionalism   The organizing of behavior in terms of standards derived from the past.

tradition (archaeological)   The similarity in cultural elements and forms over a considerable span of time at a given site or group of sites in a geographically delimited area.

transcendental belief system   A belief system providing people with organized ideas regarding states of existence inherently beyond the capacities of their senses to register and about things that are impossible for them to learn from their personal experience.

transhumance   The seasonal migration of domesticated livestock and their herders for the purpose of grazing different pastures at different times of the year; usually rotation between highlands and lowlands.

tribalism   The orientation toward tribal membership—rather than toward citizenship in nation–states—as the criterion of political allegiance and behavior.

tribe   A relatively small group of people (small society) who share a culture, speak a common language or dialect, and share a perception of their common history and uniqueness. Often refers to unstratified social groups with a minimum of (or no) centralized political authority at all, organized around kinship lines.

type site   In archaeology, a site used to represent the characteristic features of a culture.

typology   A method of classifying objects according to hierarchically arranged sets of diagnostic criteria.

underdevelopment   The condition of state-level societies that have been exploited by the industrialization of the European, American, and Japanese nations and that have themselves failed to benefit from industrialization.

underwater archaeology   The retrieval and study of ships, dwellings, and other human remains that have been covered over by water in the course of time.

undifferentiated (social) system   A social system in which the ascriptive qualities of sex, age, or kinship determine social relations in most domains of society.

uniformitarianism   The theory, developed by Charles Lyell, that the geological processes shaping the earth are uniform and continuous in character.

unilineal descent   The reckoning of kinship connections through either exclusively female (matrilineal descent) or male (patrilineal descent) links.

unilineal evolution   The theory that all human societies evolve through specific stages that are usually defined in terms of the occurrence of increasingly complex social and cultural elements.

unit of deposition   All the contents of each stratum in an archaeological site that are conceived to have been deposited at the same point in time (as measured by archaeologists).

unit of excavation   Subdivision of an archaeological site made by an archaeologist to record the context in which each remain is found.

Upper Paleolithic culture   The culture produced by modern *Homo sapiens sapiens*, beginning about 35,000 years ago. It is characterized by pervasive blade tool production, an "explosion" of artistic endeavors (cave painting), highly organized large-game hunting, and the efficient exploitation of previously uninhabited ecological niches—including the population of the New World, perhaps beginning as early as 40,000 years ago.

urban anthropology   The application of anthropological research techniques and methods of analysis to the study of people living in cities.

urbanism   An ill-defined term designating those qualities of life that presumably characterize all city lifestyles.

urbanization   The worldwide process of the growth of cities at the expense of rural populations.

uterine kin   Kin related to one through female links.

uxorilocal residence   The practice by which a newlywed couple takes up residence near the bride's mother's family but does not become a subordinate group contained within a larger extended family.

Valdivian culture   A coastal Ecuadorian culture, dated from 3200 B.C., in which the earliest pottery found in the Americas has been unearthed. Some archaeologists believe the pottery was introduced to the New World by Japanese visitors from the Jomon culture—a view hotly disputed by others.

values   The ideals of a culture that are concerned with appropriate goals and behavior.

verbal communication   The uniquely human use of language to communicate.

vertical extended family   A family in which parents, their married children, and their grandchildren share a residence and constitute a functioning social unit.

virilocal residence   The practice by which a newlywed couple moves near the residence of the groom's father but does not become a subordinate group contained within a larger extended family.

voluntary association   A group of persons who join together for a common objective or on the basis of a mutual interest.

Wernicke's area   The brain site where verbal comprehension takes place, located in the temporal lobe of the dominant hemisphere.

Westernization The transplanting of industrial European-American institutions to developing countries.

witchcraft The use of magic to control the behavior of another person or persons.

worldview (*Weltanschauiing*) The corpus of beliefs about the world shared by members of a society, and represented in their myths, lore, ceremonies, social conduct, general values, and so on.

yeomanry In feudal societies, those who were granted special privileges in land and produce in exchange for military service in the militia of the lord.

Zinjanthropus A 1.75-million-year-old australopithecine fossil found in Kenya by Mary Leakey and thought to be a form of *Australopithecus robustus*.

CREDITS

1. "Finding Anthropology" by Phillip Whitten and David E. K. Hunter is reprinted by permission of the authors.
2. "Darwinism Defined: The Difference between Fact and Theory" by Stephen Jay Gould is copyright © 1987. Reprinted with permission of *Discover* Magazine.
3. "The Great Leap Forward" by Jared Diamond is copyright © 1989. Reprinted with permission of *Discover* Magazine.
4. "The Secret Life of the Neanderthal" by Sharie Rudavksy is copyright © 1986. Reprinted by permission of OMNI, copyright © 1986 Omni Publications International, Ltd.
5. "The Search for Early Man" by Robert A. Foley is reprinted with the permission of *Archaeology Magazine*, Vol. 42, No. 1. Copyright the Archaeological Institute of America 1989.
6. "Designed for Another Time: Modern Problems for an Ancient Species" by Lee Cronk is reprinted by permission of *The Sciences* and is from the January/February 1992 issue. Individual subscriptions are $28 per year. Write to: The Sciences, 2 East 63rd Street, New York, NY 10021.
7. "What Are Friends For?" by Barbara Smuts is reprinted with permission from *Natural History* (February, 1987). Copyright © 1987 The American Museum of Natural History.
8. "Games Primates Play" by Marc D. Hauser is copyright © 1989. Reprinted with permission of *Discover* Magazine.
9. "On Becoming Human" by Boyce Rensberger is copyright © 1983 *Science*. Reprinted by permission.
10. "What Do Women Want?" by Elizabeth Cashdan is from *Evolutionary Anthropology* (5:4), copyright © 1996. Reprinted by permission of Wiley-Liss, Inc., a subsidiary of John Wiley & Sons, Inc.
11. "Isn't She Lovely?" by Brad Lemley is copyright © 2000. Reprinted with permission of *Discover* Magazine.
12. "Racial Odyssey" by Boyce Rensberger is reprinted by permission of *Science Digest*.
13. "'Race': Myths under the Microscope" by Albert Jacquard is from the UNESCO Courier, November 1988.
14. "The Tall *and* the Short of It" by Barry Bogin is copyright © 1998. Reprinted with permission of *Discover* Magazine.
15. "Fingerprints in the Sand" by Richard Monastersky is reprinted with permission from *Science News*, the weekly newsmagazine of science. Copyright © 1990 by Science Service, Inc.
16. "Garbage Demographics" by William Rathje and Cullen Murphy is reprinted by permission of the authors.
17. "Temples of Doom" by Heather Pringle is copyright © 1999. Reprinted with permission of *Discover* Magazine.
18. "The First Americans" by Sharon Begley and Andrew Murr is from *Newsweek*, April 26, copyright © 1999 Newsweek, Inc. All rights reserved. Reprinted by permission.
19. "Images of the Ice Age" by Alexander Marshack is reprinted with the permission of *Archaeology Magazine*, Vol. 48, No. 4. Copyright © 1995 The Archaeological Institute of America.
20. "New Clues Show Where People Made the Great Leap to Agriculture" by John Noble Wilford. Copyright © 1997 by the New York Times Co. Reprinted by permission.
21. "Brewing an Ancient Beer" by Solomon H. Katz and Fritz Maytag. Reprinted with the permission of *Archaeology Magazine*, Vol. 44, No. 4. Copyright © 1991 The Archaeological Institute of America.
22. "The World's First City" by Orrin C. Shane III and Mine Küçük is reprinted with the permission of *Archaeology Magazine*, Vol. 51, No. 2. Copyright © 1998 The Archaeological Institute of America.
23. "The Cradle of Cash" by Heather Pringle is copyright © 1998. Reprinted with permission of *Discover* Magazine.
24. "Rise of Civilization: Mesopotamia to Mesoamerica" by Henry T. Wright. Reprinted with permission of *Archeology Magazine*, Vol. 42, No. 1. Copyright © 1989 The Archaeological Institute of America.
25. "Empires of Dust" by Karen Wright is copyright © 1998. Reprinted with permission of *Discover* Magazine.
26. "The Gift of Gab" by Matt Cartmill is copyright © 1998. Reprinted with permission of *Discover* Magazine.
27. "Koko: 'Fine Animal Gorilla'" by Michael J. Frisbie is reprinted by permission of the author.
28. "Women's Talk" by Ellen Rudolph is copyright © 1991 by the New York Times Co. Reprinted by permission.
29. "The Power of Talk" by Deborah Tannen is reprinted by permission of *Harvard Business Review*. From "The Power of Talk" by Deborah Tannen, September–October 1995. Copyright © 1995 by the President and Fellows of Harvard College, all rights reserved.